edited by
peter jarvis

The age of LEARNING

education and the knowledge society

First published in 2001

Kogan Page Limited
120 Pentonville Road
London N1 9JN
UK

Stylus Publishing Inc
22883 Quicksilver Drive
Sterling VA 20166–2012
USA

British Library Cataloguing in Publication Data

A CIP record for this book is available from the British Library.

ISBN 0 7494 3412 0 (paperback)
ISBN 0 7494 3411 2 (hardback)

Typeset by Saxon Graphics Ltd, Derby
Printed and bound by Creative Print and Design (Wales), Ebbw Vale

Contents

Contributors

Dr Tom Black has taught secondary school sciences in Nigeria and the UK, and been a lecturer in Education in Zambia, Northern Ireland and Surrey. His current research and development interests are in educational measurement, educational technology and quantitative research design.

Dr Bob Brownhill is a senior lecturer in the School of Educational Studies, University of Surrey. His current interests are in the philosophy of ethics of teaching and learning.

Dr Colin Griffin is an Associate Lecturer in the School of Educational Studies, University of Surrey. He has published books and articles on curriculum and policy, and is particularly interested in policy analysis of lifelong learning. His latest book is *Training to Teach in Further and Adult Education,* with David Gray and Tony Nasta.

Dr John Holford is Senior Lecturer at the University of Surrey, a founder member of the Centre for Research in Lifelong Learning, and Director of the School of Education's postgraduate teaching programme. His recent research has been into the social and historical analysis of lifelong learning and the learning society, and he is currently leading a European study into adult learning of citizenship and governance. He is author or editor of several books, and is Reviews Editor of the *International Journal of Lifelong Education.*

Professor Peter Jarvis is Professor of Continuing Education and currently convenor of the Centre for Research in Lifelong Learning, University of Surrey. He is a former Head of Department of Educational Studies. He is the founding editor of the *International Journal of Lifelong Education* and widely published. He has recently written *The Practitioner-Researcher* (published by Jossey-Bass), Kogan Page published his latest book *Learning in Later Life* in 2000, and he is currently writing *Universities, Corporate Universities and the Higher Learning Industry,* which will be published by Kogan Page in 2001.

Professor Stephen McNair is Professor of Education and Head of the School of Educational Studies at the University of Surrey. He was formerly

Director of Research at the National Institute of Adult Continuing Education and a Higher Education Adviser to the Department for Education and Employment.

Dr Linda Merricks is a lecturer in the School and Director of Studies of the Centre for Continuing Education. Her research interests include progression, credit and other curricula matters in continuing education, policy and practice in lifelong learning and learning partnerships.

Professor Gill Nicholls is Professor of Education at the School of Educational Studies, University of Surrey. She is the convenor for the Centre of Professional and Work-related Learning. Her research areas are science education and professional development. She has significant publications in the area of teaching and learning and science education. Her most recent book is *Professional Development in Higher Education: New perspectives and directions* (Kogan Page, 2000).

Dr Julia Preece has been a lecturer at the University of Surrey since 1998. Prior to this she was at Lancaster University, where she was responsible for an action research project exploring exclusion and educational participation issues amongst social and cultural minority groups. Her current research interests are citizenship, lifelong learning, adult education and social exclusion.

Dr Paul Tosey is a senior lecturer in the School of Educational Studies, and Director of the Human Potential Research Group. He joined the School at the University of Surrey in 1991, and was responsible for validating and coordinating for five years the highly successful MSc in Change Agent Skills and Strategies, an advanced training for organizational development consultants. He has published on topics such as the learning organization and experiential learning processes. His current research is into the experience and unintended learning of participants in organizational change.

Preface

Learning has come to the forefront of the educational agenda in many countries of the world – the knowledge society, the learning society, the learning organization and so forth are now all common terms. The terms appear in policy and strategy papers of the Euopean Union and of many countries in and beyond the European community. Traditional views about education appear to be threatened as it becomes a commodity in the learning market. Learning has itself become a contested concept and the discourse about it is being captured by the world of work.

The learning society is one of the products of globalization and knowledge, learning and education are inextricably intertwined with global capitalism. Education is regarded as a servant to global capitalism, enabling transnational companies to function more effectively in the knowledge society. Learning has become a central plank in governmental education policy in many countries and it is being treated as an investment, adding value to human and social capital, resulting in employability and then in work, which makes an even greater contribution to the economy, rather than being treated as a natural human process that results in the development of people as human beings.

The title of the UK government's *The Learning Age* (DfEE, 1998) captures something of this ethos and we have adapted the title for this book, but our adaptation also illustrates that our agenda is different. In this book we have tried to step back a little and to analyse some of the key features of this age in relation to education and learning, such as its social and political processes, and also to question its ethics. We have done so from a variety of different academic positions and from a variety of interests and concerns. In it we present different and even critical perspectives on this era, recognizing, however, that profound changes are taking place as a result of the processes of globalization that are affecting the whole of the educational institution.

The book provides a multi-disciplinary analysis of lifelong learning and the learning society in its broadest sense. It contains five main sections and:

- examines the way that these phenomena have emerged;
- analyses the concepts themselves;
- discusses some of the ways in which the learning society actually functions;

- assesses the implications of the learning society for other sectors of the educational institution;
- reflects on the age of learning.

The issues that we examine are relevant to most societies in the world and this book is written for an international audience, although many of the illustrations we use are taken from the UK, since in many ways it has been at the forefront of these changes. The book has been written for practitioners and students of lifelong learning and the learning society and it is relevant to:

- students of lifelong learning, whether they are teachers or post-graduates, in all branches of education;
- educators in the professions and human resource developers;
- managers and administrators;
- policy makers at both local and national level;
- social scientists interested in the learning society.

The authors are members of the Centre for Research in Lifelong Learning in the School of Educational Studies at the University of Surrey. The School is a comparatively large one and has a wide range of interests in post-compulsory education and training. The Centre was established within it as the Lifelong Learning Group in 1996, but was subsequently reconstituted as the Centre in 1998. Its aims are:

- to focus on scholarly research, both theoretical and empirical, national and international in the field of lifelong learning;
- to provide a strong foundation for advanced studies of lifelong learning in the University of Surrey;
- to analyse and advise on developments in policy and practice in lifelong learning in the UK and overseas, and their impact.

Members of the Centre are actively involved in teaching, research and consultancy in the UK and abroad. They also hold positions in professional and other associations involved in lifelong education in the UK, Europe and the United States.

Among the Centre's previous publications are *Towards the Learning City* (Jarvis *et al*, 1997), *Theory and Practice of Learning* (Jarvis, Holford and Griffin, 1998) and *International Perspectives of Lifelong Learning* (Holford, Jarvis and Griffin, 1998). Centre members are also working on a further book on the learning society which will also be published by Kogan Page. The first of these publications emerged from a research project that the Centre undertook in the City of London and currently the Centre is leading a Framework 5 research project of learning governance and citizenship in Europe, under the leadership of John Holford, with partners from the universities of Barcelona, Helsinki, Leuven and Nijmegen and from the Andragogical Centre in Ljubljana.

Members of the Centre also constitute the main teaching team for the distance learning MSc course offered by the School which has three strands:

- Lifelong Learning;
- Applied Professional Studies in Education and Training;
- Information Technology.

They also supervise doctorate students, both face-to-face and at a distance, in all aspects of lifelong learning.

References

DfEE (1998) *The Learning Age – A renaissance for a new Britain*, DfEE, London

Holford, J, Jarvis, P and Griffin, C (eds) (1998) *International Perspectives on Lifelong Learning*, Kogan Page, London

Jarvis, P, Holford, J and Griffin, C (1998) *Theory and Practice of Learning*, Kogan Page, London

Jarvis, P, Holford, J, Griffin, C and Dubelaar, J (1997) *Towards the Learning City*, Corporation of London Education Department, London

THE EMERGENCE OF THE LEARNING SOCIETY

Chapter 1

The emerging idea

Linda Merricks

This chapter aims to describe the main developments of adult and vocational education in the 20th century and how, in conjunction with this, the linked concepts of the learning society, lifelong learning and the learning age have developed.

During the 20th century there has been growing interest in adult education. A number of different bodies have been involved in the provision of this education and various policy decisions have affected funding and the development of classes. However, throughout the period there have also been constants, one of which has been the tension between vocational and non-vocational education. For example, the 1902 Education Act gave responsibility for adult education to the newly created LEAs, but this was seen very clearly as scientific and technical, or largely vocational education. A year later, the Workers Educational Association (WEA) was founded, aiming to make university education, that is non-vocational education, available to the working classes.

This distinction also underlay many of the conclusions of the *Final Report of the Adult Education Committee,* produced by the Ministry of Reconstruction in 1919, which dominated thinking on adult education provision in Britain for decades. Its overall assumption was that 'adult education' was non-vocational and this was clearly spelt out in the terms of reference, which were 'To consider the provision for, and possibilities of, Adult Education (other than technical and vocational) in Great Britain, and to make recommendations' (Ministry of Reconstruction, 1919, Letter from the Chairman to the Prime Minister: 1). Its conclusions were, not surprisingly, therefore, that adult education should be based on non-vocational subjects. 'The scope of adult education' was, for instance to include, 'citizenship', seen as one of the most popular aspects of adult courses, but more importantly 'music and languages', 'literature and drama' and 'natural science' (Ministry of Reconstruction, 1919: 169). Technical and vocational subjects, although briefly considered, were excluded.

Technical education, though it must be an integral part of our educational system, is not an alternative to non-vocational education. The latter is a universal need, but whether the former is necessary or not depends upon the character of the employment. Even where technical education was available:

> it should be liberalised as far as possible by the inclusion in the curriculum of pure science and of studies which will enable the student to relate his own occupation to the industry of which he is a part, to appreciate the place of that industry in the economic life of the nation and the world, and to interpret the economic life of the community in terms of social values. (Ministry of Reconstruction, 1919: 174–75)

Even the chapter on 'Technical Education and Humane Studies' called for 'the development of opportunities for personal development and for the realisation of a higher standard of citizenship' through the broadening of vocational training to incorporate 'the intellectual and spiritual treasures of the race' (Ministry of Reconstruction, 1919: 153).

Against this 'liberal and humane' ideal of learning for learning's sake stood an equally well-established tradition of working-class self-education for vocational reasons. The four London polytechnics founded in the late 19th century drew heavily on working men and women who sought to improve their position in life through a lifelong commitment to improving their working skills. At the moment Albert Mansbridge founded the WEA, Battersea Polytechnic had 2,513 students at evening classes largely drawn from the poorest areas of South London – and nearly a third of them were women. Nor was it only the polys. By the 1900s both the City & Guilds and the Royal Society of Arts offered nationally recognized qualifications in technical and vocational skills. By 1914 upwards of 22,000 students took City & Guilds examinations. These examinations provided a ladder at different levels through which a working man or women could 'rise' through their trade or profession (see Merricks, 2000).

The extent to which adult education can be split in two illustrates one of the fundamental questions about adult education, and its history. Simply and crudely: what is its purpose? There are many different answers, which are not always mutually exclusive and which tend to reflect changes in the wider economic and cultural society. Two of them reflect the differences described here. Liberal adult education is related to education for citizenship. It is seen primarily as a way of learning how society works and how the individual fits that society. Its benefits tend not, at least immediately, to be economic and are to both the individual and to the society. In contrast, vocational education, or training as it is usually described, is directly related to economic improvement, seen by the student as primarily for individual gain, although companies and the wider society can see more general benefits. These differences explain the divergent student bodies attracted to the kinds of course offered. Throughout the 20th century, the appeal of vocational education has been great to a large number of students, the majority of whom have been young working people (Merricks, 2000. On the other hand, with some notable exceptions, liberal adult education has appealed generally only to the middle class, to women, and to the elderly (Merricks, 2001).

The differences also explain, if rather crudely, the issues that have dictated the direction in which adult education has been pushed by policy makers. The 1919 Report was written against a background of social unrest, both military and civilian. In this situation 'citizenship' was seen as a moral and civic virtue, but also as a means of social control. This is clear in the lecture notes prepared by the Army Education Service in 1918 and distributed to regimental officers. These stressed the 'duties' (sic) of citizenship, the need for education to enable the citizen to make up 'his' mind about the facts of an argument and, significantly, lectures on the evils of Bolshevism (MacKenzie, 1992: 21–24). In this perspective the 1919 Report, with its emphasis on similar ideas of citizenship, can be seen as one tool in the processes of constructing a peaceful society.

However, from the early 1920s growing unemployment began to reveal that the problems of reconstruction were primarily economic. As a result, adult education policy shifted rapidly to training for employment, first for those finding themselves out of work through their war-time activities, like women and ex-servicemen, but then for those hit by shifts in manufacturing (Field, 1996). However, the extent to which the only training offered to women, many of whom had spent the war working in factories, was in domestic work shows that the economic and cultural can never be clearly split.

Mass unemployment from the late 1920s to the outbreak of war in 1939 quickened and widened the demand for a politically informed, and usually left-wing, adult education. This was particularly obvious in areas like South Wales and parts of the North where there were strong existing traditions of working-class education. The central point for much of this education was the National Council of Labour Colleges, which organized classes at local level until the 1960s as well as having a 'permanent' residential base, first in Oxford then in London (Craik, 1964). There were also other 'residential' adult education colleges, especially Ruskin College, founded in 1898 and closely associated with the trade union movement. These democratic and non-vocational aspects of education were strengthened during the war by the classes run in the army by the Army Bureau of Current Affairs (ABCA). ABCA's classes were aimed centrally at 'current affairs and citizenship education' (MacKenzie, 1992: 190).

Since World War II, different theories of adult education and learning have developed, which attempt to bridge this divide and to make adult learning a worthwhile experience for students and a sensible investment for funding bodies. Although these developments are in part educational, additional impetus has been given by the economic downturn, or series of downturns since the 1970s, in the USA, Europe and Britain. As in the interwar period, the recession led to a consideration of what has been seen as the failure of education and training that has allowed our competitors, especially along the Pacific Rim, to overtake the Western world in manufacturing production. Much has been made of the excellence of the education systems in these countries, which is seen as the most significant factor in their success. None the less, the possibility of a lessening of their growth might lead to a reconsideration of the theory.

Until or unless this takes place, the link between learning and economic success is seen to be firmly made and so the intention has clearly been to improve the learning of the less successful countries by attempting to instil the ideal of lifelong learning. This notion has a long history, probably beginning in the USA in 1916 when Dewey wrote: 'the inclination to learn from life itself and to make the condition of life such that all will learn in the process of living in the finest product of schooling' (quoted in Jarvis, 1983: 32). In Britain, similar sentiments were expressed in the 'Introductory Letter' to the 1919 Report, where A L Smith wrote in his letter to the Prime Minister, 'adult education is a permanent national necessity, an inseparable aspect of citizenship, and therefore should be universal and lifelong' (Ministry of Reconstruction, 1919: 5). However, the idea of lifelong learning has been influential only since it was adopted by the United Nations Educational, Scientific and Cultural Organization in Faure's report (Faure et al, 1972). This Report made important claims for the possible effects of lifelong learning. Echoing the 1919 Report, it was argued that education should be universal and lifelong, but it also went further, not just claiming that education precedes economic development but suggesting that it also prepares an individual for a society of the future.

While lifelong learning was being proposed for individuals, the need for preparation for a society of the future was seen to point to changes in the education of society as a whole. These changes were encapsulated in the idea of the 'Learning Society' theorized by Schon (1971). Ranson (1998: 2) defined the learning society as a society:

- which learns about itself and how it is changing;
- which needs to change the way it learns;

- in which all its members are learning;
- which learns to democratically change the conditions of learning.

The two notions of lifelong learning and the learning society had a broad appeal. In Scandinavia, especially Sweden, the ideas of Husén (1974) helped to reform the whole theory of schooling and to develop very successful mechanisms for lifelong learning. Husén argued: 'the task of reforming education to meet the needs of a changing society required a critical review of the institutionalized nature of schools, without moving to the excess of "de-schooling"' (Ranson, 1998: 4). In the US a 'Lifelong Learning Act', the Mondale Act, was passed in 1976, promising $40 million a year between 1977 and 1982, but lifelong learning never gained the support in the US that it has enjoyed elsewhere.

It is ironic that while these theories about the learning society were being developed, in Britain 'the great tradition' of university adult education was losing its sense of direction. The immediate post-war expansion in adult education had included the appointment of a number of young, politically committed tutors like Raymond Williams and E P Thompson. Despite this, in 1956 Harold Wiltshire, Head of the Nottingham Extra-Mural Department, argued that 'the "great tradition" of university adult education had lost its old dynamic, principles, purpose and relevance'. He continued that this tradition had been committed to humane, non-vocational liberal studies 'as a means of understanding the great issues of life'. He concluded that this tradition was opposed to examinations and awards (quoted in Fieldhouse and Associates, 1996: 217). By the 1950s this approach was under attack by a more technical, vocational and, above all, award-oriented tradition. A sign of this change was a very great reduction in the proportion of courses run jointly with the WEA. While the number of university courses rose from 2,635 in 1947/8 to 7,957 in 1968/9, the number of joint courses grew only from 1,570 to 2,169.

What these figures conceal is a subtle shift. While the WEA continued to follow the tradition of liberal non-vocational courses, university departments were beginning to change, offering shorter and even vocational courses. In 1954 the Ashby Report recommended that the restrictions on both length of courses and the provision of vocational and technical courses should be lifted. These conclusions contributed to an expansion in the number of extra-mural departments and to wider curricula. Some of these new departments were delighted by this freedom to construct programmes, but it was regretted by many. For example, the vice-chancellor of Leeds University pointed out in 1963 that 'the contemporary world has no belief in, and no use for, education at all', meaning by this adult education for social purpose (quoted in Fieldhouse and Associates, 1996: 218).

However, the foundation of the Open University (OU) in 1969, after a long period of debate, at least suggests that a section of adult educationalists and a large number of students thought otherwise. Initially at least the OU was determinedly 'non-vocational', reflecting perhaps its founders', especially Jennie Lee's, origins within, and respect for, the 'great tradition' of working-class adult education. From the start there were real tensions between the OU and older forms of adult education, not least because many felt the OU received the lion's share of financial support going to the non-compulsory sector. This view was confirmed when the new Conservative government's White Paper, *Education: A framework for expansion* (DES, 1971) paid little attention to adult education. The reason for this was, as William Van Straubenzee, an involved minister later said 'Adult education [was] already receiving substantial and increasing sums through the Open University' (Sargant, 1996: 295).

Equally important was the view that what the OU was doing was in some ways against the spirit of adult education. Distance learning broke the personal face-to-face contact which many saw as a vital part of the adult education tradition. Further, the OU offered accredited courses which, even if they were not directly vocational, had a vocational element – an element that has certainly got stronger over the years – and is clearly represented in the OU Business School.

To an extent these debates were already going on as the OU was being created. In 1969 the Labour government set up the Russell Committee to assess the need for the provision of non-vocational education in England and Wales. However the Committee did not report until 1972, and it reported to a much less sympathetic Conservative government (Sargant, 1996: 295) The Russell Report made few new recommendations, and in many ways had little impact. However, in arguing that university adult education should be seen as part of the overall provision of adult education, not as an intrinsic part of higher education, the Report, while apparently reinforcing 'traditional' ideas actually spoke clearly for a new generation in adult education. These were the radical, socially committed and left-wing tutors associated with organizations like 'History Workshop' or ' Centreprise'. Often ex-adult students themselves, they wanted to keep adult education separate from the 'degree machine' of the universities and move it 'into the community', setting up permanent centres within that community. Central to this move 'back to the roots' were new classes and programmes based not within a tradition of liberal education but on community 'needs', like basic literacy and numeracy programmes for adults. Many of these programmes targeted, for the first time, groups that had previously been difficult to recruit, for example the unemployed, working-class women at home, the disabled or ethnic minorities. These initiatives also sought to provide wider access to higher education for these groups.

By the mid-1980s, the extra-mural departments had been through decades of change and emerged in a confused state. Their name had changed to 'continuing education', they were encouraged to help economic regeneration through vocational and accredited courses, and they were encouraged to fill any shortfall in recruitment in the 'mainstream' university. These changes finally removed any sense of a specific purpose in providing liberal adult education as the main responsibility of university continuing education. In 1987, the Government announced the end of Responsible Body status, through which specific funding for liberal adult education had been allocated to university departments of continuing education. This was a prelude to greater changes still, which came about as a result of the abolition of the binary divide between polytechnics and universities in 1992. Traditionally there had been no separate provisions for extra-mural work in the polytechnics; rather it was seen as part of their mainstream, regional provision. As a result of their change to university status, pressure grew on the 'old' universities to bring lifelong learning into their mission statements. In 1994 HEFCE changed the funding for adult education. From 1995/6 only award-bearing courses were eligible for HEFCE-directed funding. Since that date all funded students have become 'part' of the main student body and departments have been 'mainstreamed'. For many this seemed to mark the end of traditional liberal education within the university sector.

Despite this the tensions between learning for learning's sake and vocational learning have not disappeared. I have argued in detail elsewhere (Merricks, 2001) that many students express a strong preference for non-accredited courses for a variety of reasons, many of them derived from the ideas of the 'great tradition'. More strikingly, the discussions on the practicalities of lifelong learning and the learning society have revived the arguments about the 'purpose' of adult education.

The origin of government interest in lifelong learning lies in the economic recession which characterized most Western economies from the mid-1980s. In the US, as early as 1983, the dangers of falling behind the skills revolution were connected to the necessity for educational reform. The National Commission on Excellence in Education argued in their report that 'educational reform should focus on the goal of creating a Learning Society', specifying that to achieve this, education should be universal and lifelong – just as had been argued throughout the 20th century. In Sweden, participation in learning has been encouraged to the point where almost half the adult population is involved in some organized learning activity. The importance of these ideas can be seen in the description of 1996 as 'European Year of Lifelong Learning'. This had its origin in a 1993 European Union paper entitled, significantly, *Growth, Competitiveness, Employment* (see Tuckett, 1997: 6). The background to the paper is familiar:

> The rapidly changing technology and economic structure of Western societies, the consequent need for a more highly trained and flexible workforce, and the

demographic projections of an ageing workforce and society into the twenty-first century. These and related influences constitute a strong case for a radical revision and extensions of post-compulsory education which should be characterized by a recognition that education throughout and beyond 'working life' is essential. (Watson and Taylor, 1998: 21)

In 1995 the European Commission published a 'white paper', *Teaching and Learning: Towards the learning society*, whose objective was to help Europe move towards the knowledge-based society as a necessary step in economic and social progress. The paper catalogued three 'factors of upheaval' that were destabilizing society: the impact of the information society; the impact of industrialization; and the impact of the scientific and technical world. The proposed solution to these was twofold: reintroducing the merits of building 'active citizenship' and building up employability. The problem with these views is that, as Tuckett (1997) and Watson and Taylor (1998) point out, there is a potential tension between the two elements. The 'vocational' aspect could be justified in terms of pragmatic economic need, but notions of knowledge designed to create a more democratic or informed society are rather more difficult to justify, especially since even ideas about 'citizenship' have historically embraced very different views. In practice this problem was dealt with within the EU by concentrating on vocational training initiatives.

In fact in the UK this view had already been articulated by adult education's traditional friend, the Labour Party. The Labour Party policy statement of 1996, 'Opening Doors to a Learning Society', is dominated by an emphasis on the importance of education and training. The document says:

> Labour's vision is of an educated democracy in which good education ceases to be restricted as a competitive prize at arbitrary points throughout life but becomes the very basis for economic, political and cultural success.

However, the most powerful theme throughout the document is one of economic success. For instance:

> everyone has an entitlement to a high-quality lifelong education... without this entitlement individuals will be unable to be part of the multi-skilled, creative and adaptable workforce we will need in the twenty-first century.

The only kind of learning for personal fulfilment or citizenship is to occur in later life when 'changes in life expectancy increase learning in retirement' (Ranson, 1998: 134–36).

Interestingly, many of these views were shared by the then Conservative government in *Lifetime Learning: A policy framework* (DfEE, 1996). Its view of the importance of lifetime learning is very similar to that of the Labour Party, although there is no mention even of democracy. For them, 'Lifetime learning matters to the economy, to businesses, to communities and to individuals. It is important socially, culturally and economically.' However, when this sentence is elaborated into ten points, eight of them refer to the advantages of learning which will lead to increased mobility in the workforce and so to increased employment opportunities. Learning will sustain the country's and individual businesses' competitiveness and it will help to build productive communities. Otherwise, again the retired will benefit from learning, but even here there is an economic advantage: 'older people with a background of continuing learning are likely to remain active in the economy and community for longer'. Beyond this there is a vague promise: 'Learning offers individuals personal fulfilment' (Ranson, 1998: 143–44).

All these reports – EU, Labour Party and Conservative Party – have common elements. All stress that education is a 'lifelong' process continuing long into the post-compulsory period. However, all equally appear to regard 'learning' in terms of the economic advance of the individual and then of society (although this relationship remains untested). Strikingly, all three use the phrase 'learning society' without any real thought of what that means beyond some vague notion of 'everyone learning'. However, as Coffield and Williamson (1997: 2–3) put it:

> the modern *economic imperative*... tells only half the story; it needs to be matched by a *democratic imperative*, which argues that a learning society worthy of the name ought to deliver social cohesion and social justice as well as economic prosperity to all its citizens.

However, ideas of the 'economic imperative' are not hegemonic, even within educational policy discussions. For example, *Scotland as a Learning Society*, published by the Scottish Community Education Council, starts from a very different standpoint. Their initial definition of a learning society is much closer to Coffield and Williamson's and to the radical movements of the 1960s and 1970s – 'a society whose citizens value, support and engage in learning, as a matter of course, in all areas of activity'. When this is developed into seven more detailed points, only one of them, the last, refers to purely economic factors. The others range widely to include social, political and cultural factors which would effect democratic processes, critical awareness, environmental protection and reform of schooling (Ranson, 1998: 157).

It could, of course, be argued that this vision can afford to be idealistic as its programme is the least likely to be implemented. However, the Kennedy Report, published by the Further Education Funding Council in 1997 and hailed as an important new vision of the learning society, echoes this general thrust. Again, a very brief quotation illustrates this:

> Our work over the last two years has confirmed our conviction that learning is central to both economic prosperity and the health of society. We believe that the achievement of economic goals and social cohesion are intertwined.

Although there is no simple listing of main points here, this intertwining of learning leading to success in personal, social and community terms with economic development is a constant theme: 'We found that while recent policy acknowledges both the economic and social benefits of learning, it does not recognize sufficiently their interdependence.'

One more example must suffice. The Kennedy Report's discussion of the technological innovations that have accelerated changes in the world of work is accompanied by a discussion of new and changing skills that will be needed to keep up with the challenge of these changes. However, this section ends with a discussion of how the technologies that will fuel these changes in the workplace will impact on domestic and community life. Finally, like the majority of the theorists of the learning society examined here, the report argues for universal learning:

> developing the capacity of everyone to contribute to and benefit from the economic, personal, social and cultural dimensions of their lives is central to achieving the whole range of goals we set ourselves as a nation. (Ranson, 1998: 163–67)

Centrally important to universities in the last years of the 20th century has been the Dearing Report, published in 1997. The extent to which Dearing attempts to combine the two streams identified above suggests some shifts towards a more balanced view. Although concentrating on higher education and so from a different perspective than either the Scottish Community Council or Kennedy, Dearing recognizes that:

> the purpose of education is life enhancing: it contributes to the whole quality of life. This recognition of the purpose of higher education in the devel- opment of our people, our society, and our economy is central to our vision… UK higher education must be part of the conscience of a democratic society, founded on respect for the rights of the individual and the responsibilities of the individual to society as a whole. (Quoted in Ranson, 1998: 170–71)

It seems, though, that the Kennedy and Dearing agendas, in so far as they develop a notion of a learning society which goes beyond economic progress, were too radical for the Labour Government. In *The Learning Age:*

A renaissance for a new Britain, the Green Paper published in February 1998, only months after Dearing, the rhetoric returns straight to the 1994 statement. David Blunkett opens his foreword by saying:

> Learning is the key to prosperity – for each of us as individuals, as well as for the nation as a whole. Investment in human capital will be the foundation of success in the knowledge-based global economy of the twenty-first century. This is why the Government has put learning at the heart of its ambition. (DfEE, 1998: 7).

Tony Blair, the Prime Minister, conveys the same message more succinctly: 'Education is the best economic policy we have' (DfEE, 1998: 9).

This emphasis is continued through the paper. Within its 82 pages, only one paragraph directly addresses broad questions about the social and cultural aspects of the learning age which, significantly, has now replaced the 'learning society'. In the learning age:

> Community, adult and family learning will be essential... It will help improve skills, encourage economic regeneration and individual prosperity, build active citizenship, and inspire self-help and local development. We propose to draw on the considerable experience of community development projects to help us see how leadership and involvement in the neighbourhood can be part of the learning process and how community education can support such self-help. (DfEE, 1998: 48)

In this view of the world, not even the retired will in future have the opportunity of learning for self-fulfilment and citizenship. The only reference to the retired is a negative one: 'We do not think it would be appropriate to make income-contingent loans available to students who do not plan to re-enter the labour market following their studies and so would not be in a position to repay' (DfEE, 1998: 30). Against this kind of economy-led policy, the enormous growth in numbers joining the University of the Third Age, where fees are very low or non-existent, is hardly surprising. In addition, the appeal of an organization where topics for courses are suggested by the members and there is no formal assessment or accreditation to those who feel no need for 'more qualifications', is great.

But perhaps it goes deeper than that. As Watson and Taylor eloquently argue, any discussion of the 'purpose' of adult education must of necessity, even in a 'postmodern' age, engage with questions of value. They propose three possible value systems: one in which education has a purely vocational purpose; one in which personal development is the central purpose of education; and a third in which the purpose of education is to develop a critical, even radical view of the world. Watson and Taylor argue that for much of its history adult education has been dominated by the 'personal development' or liberal model but that this model has been consistently under attack from first the left and then the right since the 1970s (Watson and Taylor, 1998: 138–40).

At present it appears that vocationalism has won, yet as Dearing writes, 'As the world becomes ever more complex and fast-changing, the role of higher education as a guardian or transmitter of culture and citizenship needs to be protected' (NCIHE, 1997, Summary Report: 12). This seems to point at least to a model of lifelong learning that is more than simply constant work-based learning updating of work skills. Yet current government policy seems unwilling to take this on board – the division between economics and citizenship seems as sharp as at any point in the 20th century.

References

Coffield, F and Williamson, B (1997) *Repositioning Higher Education*, SRHE/OU Press, Buckingham

Craik, W W (1964) *Central Labour College*, Lawrence and Wishart, London

Department of Education and Science (1971) *Education: A framework for expansion*, DES, London

DfEE (1996) *Lifetime Learning: A policy framework*, HMSO, London

DfEE (1998) *The Learning Age: A renaissance for a new Britain*, HMSO, London

European Commission (1995) *Teaching and Learning: Towards the learning society*, EC, Luxembourg

Faure *et al* (1972) *Learning To Be: The world of education today and tomorrow*, UNESCO, Paris

Field (1996) in eds R Fieldhouse and Associates, *A History of Modern British Adult Education*, pp 333–53, NIACE, Leicester

Fieldhouse, R and Associates (eds) (1996) *A History of Modern British Adult Education*, NIACE, Leicester

Husén, T (1974) *The Learning Society*, Methuen, London

Jarvis, P (1983) *Adult and Continuing Education. Theory and practice*, Croom Helm, Beckenham

Labour Party (1996) *Opening Doors to a Learning Society: A policy statement on education*, Labour Party, London

MacKenzie, S P (1992) *Politics and Military Morale: Current affairs and citizenship education in the British Army, 1914–1950*, Oxford University Press, Oxford

Merricks, L (2000) 'Technical and vocational – a challenge to the hegemony of adult liberal education', in eds Anthony Cooke and Ann MacSween, *The Rise and Fall of Adult Education Institutions and Social Movement*, Peter Lang, Frankfurt and Main.

Merricks, L (2001) 'Managing change in a postmodern system – an "extreme" case study', *Journal of Access and Credit Studies*, to be published in Spring 2001

Ministry of Reconstruction (1919) *Adult Education Committee. Final Report*, HMSO, London

NCIHE (1997) *Higher Education in the Learning Society*, The Stationery Office, Norwich

Ranson, S (ed) (1998) *Inside the Learning Society*, Cassell, London

Sargant, N (1996) 'The Open University', in eds Fieldhouse and Associates, *A History of Modern British Adult Education*, NIACE, Leicester

Schon, D (1971) *Beyond the Stable State: Public and private learning in a changing society,* Norton, New York

Tuckett, A (1997) *Lifelong Learning in England and Wales: An overview and guide to issues arising from the European Year of Lifelong Learning,* NIACE, Leicester

Watson, D and Taylor, R (1998) *Lifelong Learning and the University: A post-Dearing agenda,* Falmer Press, London

Chapter 2

Social, economic and political contexts

Stephen McNair

This chapter is concerned with the social, economic and political contexts in which the idea of lifelong learning has emerged. It looks at globalization, which has intensified economic competition and brought greater cultural interchange and conflict; the rise of the knowledge economy – a social and economic change perhaps as profound as the transition from agrarian to industrial economies; the emergence of information and communication technologies as driving forces of economic and social change; and demographic changes. Finally, it touches on one of the major shifts of developed economies at the end of the 20th century: the revision of conceptions of the role of the state and the market.

Globalization

Globalization is the process whereby worldwide economic and social forces supplant those of nation and locality. It changes the relative economic position of particular countries and economies; it changes the nature of social interactions and structures; it changes what is a required of an education and training system; and it changes the competitive position of particular education and training providers.

Global economic competition comes about as the ease of communication and the spread of skills increase the proportion of economic activity that can operate beyond national borders. As work is able to move to wherever it is cheapest to hire labour, so individual firms and countries have to identify and fight to sustain their particular niches. As the UK Government commented:

> A UK publisher prepares text in India and publishes in China. Even the smallest local company is operating in a global market... either directly, or as a supplier to a larger company... Many of the changes are beyond the control of governments. In the increasingly global market place there is no hiding place, no comfortable backwater. Change will not stop and others will not rest. (DTI, 1994: para.1.18)

In this world, countries have to choose between low-value-added, low-skilled and low-paid production, and high-value-added, highly skilled and highly paid work, and while most developed countries face significant weaknesses in the skills base required to pursue the latter, they see the alternative as economically and socially suicidal. In the UK this concern is reflected in a succession of white papers on competitiveness, while at international level it is reflected in the development of annual comparative education indicators by the Organization for Economic Cooperation and Development (OECD *Education at a Glance,* annual).

Globalization is also a social force. Education has always been one of the primary ways in which nations and communities establish and maintain identity and values, but as travel becomes easier and more common, and telecommunications universal in the developed world, there is increasing contact between people of very different cultures. For Europe, the 1950s and 1960s saw a series of waves of global immigration in the wake of decolonization, followed by the beginning of the emergence of notions of European, as distinct from national, identity. The end of the Cold War, the reunification of Germany and the collapse of Yugoslavia started new movements of population and ideas.

If social and political tensions are to be minimized, some form of learning is needed to enable people (both incomers and hosts) to understand and work with people with unfamiliar backgrounds and value systems, and to establish common notions of citizenship. While some migrant populations participate strongly in education and training as a means of integration and economic success, others remain apart, either because of cultural resistance or because their previous experience (sometimes in illiterate rural communities) provides little preparation for participation in their new countries. The diversity of national qualifications systems aggravates this, since immigrants are often handicapped by lack of recognition of their previous qualifications (Dadzie,1993), and the harmonizing of qualifications systems through initiatives like the European Credit Transfer System (ECTS) has proved a difficult task, even within Europe.

Globalization is also an issue for the market in education and training. International activity in education is not new: a few countries have a long tradition of providing education to other countries (particularly their former colonies). Countries like the UK have had a large education trading industry for many years – both importing students from overseas and exporting programmes for delivery abroad. The spread of English as the de facto international language has increased this penetration, and brought other English-speaking nations into the market. However, in the 1990s the opportunities offered by integrated information and communication technologies led a growing number of education and training agencies, particularly in the USA and the UK, to seek ways of operating more actively across national boundaries. The late 1990s saw the beginnings of a genuinely global delivery of education, both online and face to face, and although such initiatives are in their infancy, there is no doubt that the scope for global competition in education is substantial. This is particularly true in the private sector, led by multinational agencies and products, which need consistent support regardless of location, and have developed their own qualifications systems. (Microsoft Corporation, for example, accredits qualifications in the use of its software, which are delivered by commercial organizations worldwide.)

Global competition faces education (and HE institutions in particular) with the same pressures as any other industry. Since distance and online learning have high start-up and infrastructure costs, economies of scale are critical. Large English-speaking institutions start with a major advantage, through their size and ownership of the language of the mass market, while some smaller institutions may have real difficulty in surviving. The urgency of the issue was recognized in 1999 by the UK Government (Thorne, 2000), and by the UK Committee of Vice Chancellors and Principals, who commissioned a study of the emerging global market (Middlehurst *et al*, 2000).

Technology and the knowledge economy

The notion that a knowledge-based economy is replacing the industrial economy, in the same way as the latter replaced the agrarian one, is now widely accepted among policymakers. The central notion is that most economic value is now generated by trade in knowledge, rather than in manufactured goods. This happens in two ways: through a growth of highly skilled and individualized service industries (advice, consultancy, research, publishing, etc) and by a shift in what makes manufactured goods valuable. In the 'old' economy, for example, a designer played a critical role in producing a product, but most of the costs lay in raw materials and labour. In the 'new' economy, the typical product is the computer. The physical resources and direct labour required to build a computer are trivial compared to the millions of human hours devoted to designing cumulative generations of hardware and software, and to providing the consultancy and servicing required to enable people to use it.

A key element in the growth of the knowledge economy has been technological change, which has accelerated through the 20th century (DTI, 1997). It has frequently been predicted that this will reduce employment, leading to large-scale social disruption. However, in the UK, the period of rapid technological change in the 1990s coincided with a period of growth in the number of people employed, and there is little evidence of an overall long-term reduction in employment as a result of technological change. In education, despite politicians' expectations of savings, the arrival of new technologies (especially ICT) has generally led to more work being done by the same number of people, rather than the same work by fewer.

The technologies with the most profound effects, socially, economically and in education, are ICT, which have dramatically increased the speed and volume of communication. To this, the Internet has added access to, and creation of, information on an unprecedented scale, and information abundance is a defining feature of the new economy. In the industrial economy information was scarce, and access to it was a source of power. Managers, teachers and politicians could mediate it, controlling the behaviour and choices of others. Now information is constantly being generated and is widely, if not universally, available. Where the key skills of the old economy were specialization and obedience to managers with superior knowledge, those of the new economy include knowing how to select and manage information and add value to it, for oneself or for a potential customer. These require intellectual skills rather than manual ones, and a combination of intellectual flexibility, transferable skills and sound underpinning knowledge (Harvey et al, 1997; Rajan, 1997; Stewart, 1997).

The primary effect of technological change has been to reduce the number of low-skilled jobs and increase the number of high-skilled ones, since it is in the elimination of routine and repetitive tasks that technology brings the most immediate economic benefits to firms, making those in work more productive, and creating opportunities for the enterprising to use their talents in new and more demanding areas. Reich (1993) has described the consequent changes in the labour market as the rise of the 'symbolic analysts', a new dominant social class whose business is the exchange and management of knowledge. His warning of the potential dangers of a society divided into three classes – the symbolic analysts who create and manipulate knowledge, the service class who support them, and a large force of people with no stable economic role at all – has been influential in stimulating the English-speaking world to consider the issue of social exclusion. He argues that it is not merely unethical for a society to exclude a proportion of its population from the social and personal benefits that come from employment, but it is also wasteful (since potential talent is being unused) and politically unsustainable (because the rich will be unwilling to pay to support the unemployed, who will in turn revolt against social and economic exclusion).

Similar arguments have emerged in management debates. Handy (1994) and Peters (1988) have both argued that the manufacturing economy used only the intellectual effort of a small minority of managers, leaving the majority as 'hands' (to use the Victorian term) without brains. The knowledge economy has no role for hands alone, and those excluded from the knowledge processes represent both a waste and a threat to the firm. The implication for both the economy and the individual is that more and better education is required by all, to bring the least educated into the knowledge economy and to move the educated constantly higher. These are the forces that led, in many developed countries in the late 1990s, to the emergence of the notion of a 'third way' in economics and politics, based on inclusion rather than division (Giddens, 1998).

Employment and the new labour market

The mid-20th century was the heyday of the large corporation, especially in the US and UK. The basis of industrial growth was large manufacturing organizations, expanding from local bases to operate at national and global levels, through economies of scale and by the integration of products and services. However, competition at the higher skilled end from the rapidly developing economies of Asia, and at the lower end from a range of countries that could offer much lower labour costs, began to squeeze the economies of Europe and the US, and the inherent rigidities of such large organizations began to be apparent. The last quarter of the century saw the revival, especially in the US and UK, of small- and medium-size enterprises (SMEs), defined by the EU as having fewer than 250 employees. Such firms were seen as capable of greater flexibility and as engines for innovation, and Government saw their development as a priority. In Britain a succession of competitiveness white papers from governments at both ends of the political spectrum focused heavily on this (DTI, 1994, 1998) and it led to the creation of employer-led Training and Enterprise Councils (TECs) to manage and coordinate much work-related training, and a range of government-funded and commercial support services for small firms.

By the late 1990s small firms (with fewer than 50 employees) constituted 99 per cent of all firms in the UK economy, and employed 45 per cent of the workforce (DfEE, 2000). However, they were not a homogenous group: some grow from an individual with an idea; others from people made redundant by large firms or by the conscious splitting of large firms into smaller, more focused units. For the firm, such changes can bring greater flexibility and responsiveness, but they call for more sophisticated skills of negotiation, partnership and self-management on the part of individuals and firms, since a growing number of projects call for the linking of the skills of a number of small specialist organizations (Rajan, 1997).

A further dimension of industrial change arises from the power of new technologies to shift industrial production from the creation of large volumes of identical products to mass production of individually tailored ones. The rise of the electronic newspaper demonstrates this. Where once the physical production of a newspaper depended on massive economies of scale in the operation of machinery and distribution, it is now possible to produce individualized electronic newspapers, with each reader specifying the topics to include, the sources to draw from, and how and when the information is to be transmitted to his or her computer. Where the first generation of technological change in newspapers eliminated skilled manual tasks like typesetting, the next wave eliminates the physical factory that prints paper, and the hierarchies of managers who supervised this. Employment growth is in creating systems for harvesting and managing the information, and a growing proportion of the workforce are journalists, analysts, writers, programmers and designers.

Technology also changes the dynamics of the relationships between firms. It makes individualized production possible, and by speeding up communication, makes 'just in time' production easier. Firms increasingly concentrate on their core business, outsourcing to others work that they do not believe adds value to their particular business, and expecting these subcontractors to deliver tailored products to tight timescales. At the same time, technologies are providing customers with more sophisticated information about rival products. The result is an increasing pressure to raise quality, to manufacture and deliver rapidly (eliminating warehousing – another area of low-skill employment). Above all, the skills of managing information, and of negotiating and partnership become essential between firms, with higher expectations of quality control and flexibility of production (National Skills Task Force, 1998).

The impact of all these industrial changes for learning is twofold. On the one hand, individuals need more sophisticated technical skills, and those skills are rapidly changing, often in unpredictable ways. On the other, the generic skills of negotiating, gathering and managing information become critical. The traditional skills of higher-level academic education become more valuable, as can be seen in the rise of graduate employment, not primarily for technical expertise, but for the generic analytical and personal skills which higher education provides (AGR, 1995).

Changing life patterns

A further set of trends affects individuals and their life patterns. Over a quarter of a century we have seen major change in the typical life career, with the dramatic extension of life expectancy, the rise of the age at which people enter the labour market, the growth of women's employment and educational levels, international mobility and the decline of the 'job for life'.

The rapid extension of the lifespan, resulting from improved health and living conditions and greater affluence is a feature of all developed countries in the 21st century. Average life expectancy for men and women in the UK has risen. Most people will now spend more of their lives outside the workforce than in it: a dramatic reversal of the picture a generation earlier. This poses social and economic challenges to societies organized on the basis that the bulk of an individual's lifespan is spent in economically productive activity, generating wealth to support an economically inactive minority of children and retired people. The question of what 'retirement' means, and how to manage public and private resources across the lifespan, becomes more pressing when most retired people are physically fit and intellectually capable. However, public policy has tended to be dominated, for understandable reasons, by health and income issues. Although retired people do not tend to make heavy demands on the service, the bulk of health expenditure is concentrated in the last few years of life. Consequently, relatively little attention has been paid to the educational issues which arise.

Although it represents a declining proportion of the total lifespan, paid employment continues to dominate public perceptions of 'adultness'. For most people it provides identity, meaning and social frameworks as well as money. However, for individuals, the workplace has become a less stable environment. In 1950 it was conceivable that school-leavers could enter employment in a firm and remain there until retirement, many doing the same job throughout that period and the 'high flyers' progressing in a planned and orderly way up a career ladder managed by a hierarchy of senior colleagues. This form of career was a defining characteristic of the middle classes in the industrial age (Watts, 1999).

The accelerating speed of technological change and the dismantling of the large corporations undermines this. Few employing organizations are likely to continue to exist, at any rate in the same form, for 40 years. Few industries are likely to remain stable for that time. In 1993, the OECD's *Jobs Study* (1994) estimated that the average individual leaving school in the developed world would have five separate jobs in a working life, for each of which major retraining would be needed. The result is that individuals are being forced to live with much higher levels of uncertainty in the workplace, developing the skills of managing their own working lives, and selling their talents, in new ways.

A further notable shift was the arrival in the second half of the 20th century of women in the workforce, to the point where they now constitute a majority, although their earnings remain below those of men. Furthermore, their educational levels are progressively exceeding those of men, and they are more frequently employed in growth occupations and industries. Their arrival in the labour market is gradually exerting pressure to change working practices and hours. Whether the shift towards part-time employment that is associated with their participation is a good thing is less clear.

The decline of employment in traditional manufacturing and extractive industries has led to the disappearance in some communities of what were traditionally seen as 'men's jobs', and there is a growing policy concern that in some communities boys and young men opt out of education early, being overtaken in education and in the labour market by women. This population of low-skilled, and potentially disaffected, men is potentially a serious social as well as economic problem (McGivney, 1998).

There are two common factors to these changes. The first is a blurring of boundaries between employment and non-employment. Young people enter the workplace on work experience and in part-time jobs, an increasing proportion of workers work 'part-time', and a growing number retire on a part-time basis, or undertake major voluntary 'work'. The second factor is that the structures that supported individuals in managing their lifetime careers in the past are weakening. To cope in this world, individuals will need increasing skills in self-management, to be good at anticipating and responding to change, and perhaps above all to be good learners.

Public, private and voluntary

The years following World War II were dominated in Europe by steady economic growth and a broad social democratic consensus. There was a wide agreement among all political parties that the state could and should play a major part in shaping the lives of individuals and in economic management, and the public sector took much greater responsibility than before the war for education, health, pensions, creating a legal framework for employment and economic activity.

In the 1970s, for a variety of reasons, it became clear that this model would not deliver all the benefits hoped for, and global economic and social pressures began to challenge its underlying assumptions. As a result, a major feature of the 1980s and 1990s was a shift in the boundaries and relationships between public, private and voluntary sectors. Work like provision of public transport, which had previously been seen as the exclusive preserve of the public sector was transferred, wholly or in part, to the private, and new kinds of partnership developed between the sectors.

An example of this in the education and training field is the creation of the employer-led TECs, which devolved to local bodies functions that had previously rested with government departments. The rationale was that 84 local bodies would be closer to the real needs, and that a diversity of responses to needs would be more creative. Government also hoped that TECs would increase the efficiency of local education and training by stimulating competition from the private sector. Furthermore, as the labour market and economy become more unpredictable, the risks involved in single national decisions on training issues become greater. Since a misjudgement of the market by national government will inevitably cause greater damage than even half the TECs making the same mistake, devolution of decision making makes economic sense, as well as reducing the political risks to ministers.

Apart from economic concerns, central government sought to reduce the power of local government, and its progressive constraint of local authority finances fell disproportionately on adult education provision. In due course the governance and funding of FE colleges and the polytechnics were removed from local authority control by the Education Acts of 1988 and 1992. In this climate the private sector grew, providing in some cases more flexible and high-profile services, especially in the more lucrative areas like work-based training for managers and technical staff, and in the development of distance and open learning approaches. However, sometimes what were apparent changes, like the rise of 'corporate universities' represented merely a rebadging of existing training services, or remained heavily dependent on public sector institutions (Middlehurst et al, 2000). Despite much change, at the end of the 20th century the relative roles of the private and public sector remained fairly clearly divided, with the private sector dominating much of the training provided directly for employers, especially for managers and in the IT-related areas, while the public sector remained heavily concentrated on initial education and programmes leading to formal qualifications.

Another dimension of the shift to a private sector model of education has been increasing competition between institutions and the privatization of knowledge. Traditional academic and educational values in the public sector encouraged the sharing of ideas and good practice, but some of the moves to stimulate efficiency through competition in the 1980s and early 1990s led to increased defensiveness, with institutions reluctant to share ideas, and HE institutions increasingly concerned to protect their intellectual property as a source of financial gain

Conclusion

The educational implications of the developments described in this chapter are profound. Within a generation we have moved from a world where most people could still expect to undertake little or no education or training after adolescence, to one where such education is a condition of economic survival for most if not all. They have overturned the notion that education and training are solely a preparation for, and separate from, life and work, with students in work experience, part-time workers and part-time retired people blurring the boundaries of entry and exit from the workforce. They are also gradually changing notions of when learning is needed, who should pay for it and what needs to be learnt. Increasingly it is happening in the workplace, home and community, with the assistance of, amongst others, public and private education and training agencies, libraries, publishers, broadcasters, and Internet service providers.

This challenges education and training providers (in the public and private sectors) to develop radically new ways of supporting learning. In a rapidly changing economic and social context, lifelong learning cannot be a matter of delivering the same courses in different modes and locations (though that is itself a challenge for many providers). Educators need to find ways of integrating learning into the workplace and community settings, using the potential of a knowledge-rich society to develop learning in life, rather than seeing it as 'courses' undertaken separately as a preparation for them. Furthermore, we are likely to see new and more complex mixes of public and private support for learning, with the state increasingly acting as a regulator of a mixed public/private market, rather than as a planner or provider.

The qualities that people need to develop through learning are also changing. Education is critical to ensuring that no one is excluded from participation in a knowledge-based economy and society, but for everyone the level of skill requirements is rising, with a growing focus on qualities such as learning to learn, self-management and self-confidence, negotiation, and critical thinking. Above all, perhaps, the skills of gathering and interpreting information and using knowledge in all its forms are a priority in a society that is, for the first time in human history, information rich (AGR, 1993). While these have been traditional strengths of some kinds of higher and adult education, they have not been the central focus of much previous public sector education. The challenge of the learning age is to develop systems and strategies in the public and private sectors, to enable people to develop these.

References

AGR (1993) *Roles for Graduates in the Twenty First Century: Getting the balance right*, Association of Graduate Recruiters, Cambridge

AGR (1995) *Skills for Graduates in the 21st Century*, Association of Graduate Recruiters, Cambridge

Dadzie, S (1993) *Working with Black Adult Learners: A practical guide*, NIACE, Leicester

DfEE (2000) *Labour Market and Skill Trends*, DfEE, Sheffield

DTI (1994) *Competitiveness: Helping business to win*, HMSO, London

DTI (1997) *Moving into the Information Society: An international benchmarking study*, Department of Trade and Industry, Communications and Information Industries Directorate, London:

DTI (1998) *Building the Knowledge Driven Economy*, Cmd 2563, The Stationery Office, Norwich

Giddens, A (1998) *The Third Way*, Polity Press, Cambridge

Handy, C (1994) *The Empty Raincoat*, Hutchinson, London

Harvey, L, Moon, S and Geall, G (1997) *Graduates Work: Organizational change and students' attributes*, Centre for Research into Quality, University of Central England, Birmingham

McGivney, V (1998) *Excluded Men: Men who are missing from education and training*, NIACE, Leicester

Middlehurst, R *et al* (2000) *The Business of Borderless Higher Education*, CVCP, London

National Skills Task Force (1998) *Towards a National Skills Agenda: First Report of the National Skills Task Force*, Department for Education and Employment, Sheffield

OECD Centre for Educational Innovation and Research (annual) *Education at a Glance: OECD indicators*, OECD, Paris

OECD (1994) *The OECD Jobs Study*, OECD, Paris

Peters, T (1988) *Thriving on Chaos: Handbook for a management revolution*, Macmillan, Basingstoke

Rajan, A (1997) *Britain's Flexible Labour Market: Is it working?*, DfEE, London

Reich, R B (1993) *The Work of Nations: Preparing ourselves for 21st century capitalism*, Simon & Schuster, London

Stewart, T A (1997) *Intellectual Capital: The new wealth of organizations*, Doubleday, New York

Thorne, M (ed) (2000) *Foresight: Universities in the future*, Office of Science and Technology, London

Watts, A C (1999) 'Reshaping career development for the 21st century', inaugural professorial lecture, University of Derby Centre for Guidance Studies

Chapter 3

The changing educational scene

Peter Jarvis

Education, in the West, received a significant boost to the rationale for its existence with the dawn of the Reformation. Early education was devoted to teaching children and adults literacy so that they could read the Bible and achieve individual salvation. Since the Bible was regarded as divinely inspired people were expected to learn unquestionably its truths – but once people learn, their learning cannot be controlled, so that there is another sense in which the Reformation was the first stage in the process of secularization that has resulted in the world that we know today. The Protestant churches, especially the more Calvinistic ones, led the way in generating the changes that were to lead to further major changes in society. It could be argued that without the Reformation there would have been no Enlightenment.

While there have been many changes in society since that time, we shall focus upon just two – the Enlightenment (the birth of modernity) and the period since the 1970s when some scholars have claimed that we have entered a postmodern world. The chapter contains a brief section on education in the post-Enlightenment period; it then examines the social changes that have occurred since the 1970s and, finally, looks at the effects of these changes on the educational scene.

Modernity

The Enlightenment was both an historical era and a period of rapid intellectual change. Hamilton (1992: 21–22) has suggested 10 different features that characterize this period, although some of them had their beginnings in the Reformation:

1. the primacy of reason;
2. all knowledge and thought about the natural and social world are based on empirical facts;
3. scientific knowledge is based upon experimental method;
4. reason and science can be applied to every situation;
5. natural and social conditions can be improved as a result of reason and science;
6. the individual is the starting point for all knowledge;
7. all individuals are essentially the same despite different beliefs;
8. people are free to believe, trade, communicate, etc without external constraint;
9. the characteristics of human nature are universal;
10. traditional religious authority should be opposed.

Many of these characteristics have become embedded in contemporary Western culture, giving it a sense that it was the apex of civilization, but, as suggested below, there are fundamental errors in these characteristics that have become problems as society continues to change. However, they were believed to be truths at that early time, and the truth discovered by science and reason had to be taught to the masses of the people. Gradually mass education emerged for children, in the UK culminating in the 1870 Education Act. There was also a wide variety of adult education movements, such as the Mechanics Institutes, all dedicated to the transmission of those discoveries that one generation thought its members should know and that the next generation should be building upon (see Chapter 1).

Teaching was a matter of transmitting a truth and learning was merely internalizing it or copying it. Education became reproductive and early learning theory, behaviourism, was a result of the same processes – based upon measurable 'scientific' data and reproduction of what was taught. Learning became identified with rote learning and training with copying the established skills and procedures.

However, as the period progressed, gradual changes occurred. The work of Piaget (1929 *inter alia*) in the West and Vygotsky (1978, 1986) in Russia focused on the way that children learnt and Dewey (1938) emphasized experience, so that education took on more of a child-centred approach and discovery learning became increasingly important. In adult education, there was a greater emphasis on the adult's experience (Lindeman, 1926) as a basis of learning, and from 1929 (Yeaxlee) the idea that education is a lifelong process grew in importance.

At the same time, new scientific discoveries were making people aware that there was a great deal of new knowledge in existence and that they might have to continue their education and training beyond school and university.

Further training, in-service training, continuing education and similar concepts were emerging. In addition, it was becoming recognized that adults were actually self-directed learners (Houle, 1961). By the 1970s, knowledge was changing so fast that it became inevitable that education in all its forms also had to change. Education was obviously a recipient of the dominant social pressures for change, rather than being a major force for change in itself. Kerr *et al* (1973) were already suggesting that education was the hand-maiden of industry.

Reason and science had been promulgating change throughout the whole of the post-Enlightenment period and new discoveries were making the speed of change faster than ever before. These changes were to alter education but more at the adult end of the educational lifespan.

Capitalism flourished in the world of modernity, but, by its very nature, it was bound to generate change and expand its market. However, the changes were not merely a matter of corporations competing within state boundaries and then reaching beyond them to purchase raw materials and sell finished commodities. Now the corporations spanned the globe, at first as multinationals and later as transnational companies. The world was becoming a global village that was also to be a highly competitive global market.

By the beginning of the 1970s Western business was threatened by the oil crisis and the growing superiority of the commodities of Japan and the other Pacific Rim countries. Businesses in the West tried a number of different strategies in order to retain their control and profitability. Manufacturing industries began locating some of their production in third-world countries; forms of protectionism were tried, but GATT operated against it. They attempted to cut costs in order to become more productive, but this was not always successful. They then embarked on company mergers and takeovers in order to reduce administrative costs and enhance their profitability. This, then, was the period when monetarist economics gained ascendancy in theory as well as in practice.

With the introduction of information technology, this was also the period when the process of globalization speeded up (see Chapter 2) and the world became a smaller place. Positive and technological knowledge were changing increasingly rapidly. The fundamentals of the Enlightenment were being questioned, if not eroded, and some scholars began to ask whether the Enlightenment project was over: late or postmodernity had appeared. But this new society was a global market with a capitalist sub-structure driven by information technology. It was a knowledge society; knowledge workers needed to keep abreast of developments and, even more significantly, they became creators of a great deal of them – for new knowledge was now being generated in the workplace and away from the laboratory. New award-bearing courses were being introduced at all levels, new ways of recognizing non-classroom learning were being introduced, and accreditation of prior experiential learning became acceptable. Indeed, learning theory itself is changing and becoming experiential, although behaviourism, like some of the other ideas of modernity, still has its disciples.

With the rapid developments in and spread of information technology, it is hardly surprising that institutions began to deliver education and training in the same manner. Otto Peters (1983: 95–113) argued, for instance, that distance education was a form of industrial production and as the means of production have changed so have distance education techniques By the 1990s many educational institutions were using electronic means for the delivery of some, if not all, of their courses.

The educational scene has undergone tremendous change as we approach 'the learning society'; the next section of this chapter outlines some of them.

Changes in educational theory and practice

From childhood and adult to lifelong education

From both the Reformation and the birth of the Enlightenment, all age groups were encouraged to learn the truths that were being discovered. After 1870, school education grew by virtue of its compulsory nature and education was seen by many as preparing children for adulthood; 'education' was generally assumed to refer to 'schooling'; anything else was 'adult education'. Perhaps the popular distinction introduced in the US by Malcolm Knowles (1980) between pedagogy and andragogy reflects this divide.

During the 20th century considerable efforts were made in Britain to emphasize the place of adult education (see the 1919 Report preface as an example; University of Nottingham, 1980). Adult education really became accepted in the UK as a result of the 1944 Education Act, which placed certain responsibilities on local education authorities to ensure the provision of further education within their areas. As early as 1929, however, Yeaxlee began writing about lifelong education. 'Adult education' was developing strongly when it was overtaken by 'lifelong education', the latter spurred on by the adoption of the idea by the OECD and UNESCO (Lengrand, 1975).

This actually led to two different approaches to lifelong education, one favoured by OECD and adult educators generally, and the other by UNESCO. In the former, there was a popular idea that people should have an adult educational entitlement after they left school – this became known as 'recurrent education', a term used in some of its publications (see OECD, 1973, for example). In the latter, the term that gained popularity was 'continuing education', ie education might continue after schooling. This concept carried no implications of educational entitlements and, not surprisingly, it became widely accepted in the UK in the 1980s. Continuing education has no end point and so the transition to lifelong education, in the late 1980s/early 1990s, was a simple one. However, the two different philosophies of lifelong education are still apparent in the European Union.

With the ageing of society, we are now beginning to see an increase in education for older people, through the growth of Universities of the Third Age, Elderhostel and other such organizations. However, the discourse about lifelong education, especially lifelong learning, is beginning to be controlled by the discourse about work, so that its meaning is becoming limited to work-life learning, and schooling hardly enters the discourse at all.

From teacher-centred to student-centred education

Education was traditionally about teaching the truths that one generation considered valuable enough to be preserved and passed on to the next, but there are at least four reasons why there has been a greater emphasis placed on student-centred learning of late:

1. While behaviourism was the generally accepted theory of learning, education was naturally teacher-oriented. But as other theories began to emerge, such as the cognitive theories of Piaget emphasizing the developmental stages of growth and its relation to the child's learning, education became more student-centred.
2. In the 1960s some of the more progressive ideas of the American philosopher John Dewey (1916, 1938), emphasizing the children's experience, were incorporated into school education.
3. It was during the same period that Malcolm Knowles (1980, *inter alia*) in the USA popularized andragogy, which was a student-centred approach to adult education. Some adult educators rightly claimed that this was no new discovery, since adult education had always been student-centred. Be that as it may, Knowles' ideas became extremely popular; his own intellectual pedigree can be traced back to John Dewey through Lindeman – Knowles' first educational employer and a person who had a great influence on his work.
4. As the modernity era was drawing to a close, the speed of change of knowledge was such that it became much more difficult to equate knowledge with truth. The debate about the relativity of all knowledge began to emerge and educators could no longer specify 'correct' knowledge or truth, so that they had to place greater emphasis on the learners' own beliefs about the content of their learning.

After the expressive period ended in the mid-1970s, the values of student-centred learning became much more widely recognized. Nevertheless, the extent to which it was practised, rather than being merely rhetoric, is open to question. There is no doubt that the rhetoric of learner-centred education is still very strong, not only in adult education, but in human resource development. However, there are conservative forces, especially in school education, which would seek to return to more traditional teaching methods.

From classical curriculum to romantic curriculum to programme

The curriculum is a selection from culture and the classical curriculum implied that there was only one truth, or interpretation, of the material to be taught; there was only one possible way of presenting that curriculum knowledge. However, it was accepted in England in the 1960s that in a multicultural society there is more than one possible interpretation of cultural knowledge, that is there is more than one type of history, religion etc. The 1960s saw the development of curricula that recognized this; they were called 'romantic curricula', reflecting the 1960s 'romantic' period (Lawton, 1973; Griffin, 1983).

This pluralistic society led to the recognition that it was becoming increasingly difficult to prescribe precisely what should be taught in the school week, despite many efforts by the government to do just this. But by the 1990s, it was widely recognized that there is just too much knowledge to get into every curriculum, so options have been built in to the system. This recognition was even truer in higher education, where modules have been developed on a wide range of topics, resulting in students being presented with a programme of courses from which to choose. Modular programmes also form the basis a great deal of school education in the US.

The changing status of knowledge

Knowledge was regarded as the fruit of reason and scientific method and must, therefore, be true. However, as early as 1926, the German sociologist, Max Scheler (Stikkers, 1980) began to chronicle the way that different types of knowledge were changing at different speeds, with positive and technological knowledge changing much more rapidly than religious knowledge. He suggested that knowledge seemed to be changing 'hour by hour'; now it is changing minute by minute and second by second. With this rapid change, it is almost impossible to regard knowledge as a truth any more – we are now talking about something that is relative and can be changed again as soon as some new discovery is made. The way that knowledge is changing has been analysed by Lyotard (1984), who regards a great deal of it as narrative, and in this sense he has tried to retain something of the value-free nature of the concept. Foucault (1972), on the other hand, has treated knowledge as discourse which is ideological and that which becomes accepted as truth is usually the discourse of the powerful. Consequently, the knowledge taught has to be understood more critically than ever before, so that critical theory has also entered the educational vocabulary.

The world is awash with new discoveries – but this means that there is a greater need for the knowledge-based occupations to keep up with the new developments. Indeed, Lyotard (1984) argued that performativity has become the basis for knowledge to be regarded as legitimate and so knowledge is now only true for the time being. This has resulted in education having to become much more flexible in what it offers and much less authoritarian.

From rote learning to learning as experiential and reflection

When knowledge was regarded as something true, something that had been verified either by the force of rational logic or by scientific research, then it was to be learnt, that is, it had to be memorized. However, it is now recognized that learning stems from experience and that learners develop their own narratives.

Since most knowledge is either narrative or discourse, it all has to be considered, criticized and reflected upon in order to ascertain the extent to which it contains any truth. Hence rote learning has become less significant and learners are expected to reflect upon their learning experiences (Kolb, 1984; Jarvis, 1987, 1992), although authoritarianism in some forms of management and teaching still enforces rote-learning procedures.

From face-to-face to distance

Education has traditionally been conducted face-to-face. Only in extremely large and sparsely populated countries, like the Australian outback, Russia, etc, were alternatives used. With the advent of new information technology, all of this was to change.

In 1970, the birth of the British Open University was to be a catalyst in the new information society in education. It proved that educational courses could be delivered successfully at a distance, through print, radio and television. With the rapid development of information technology, distance education has been transformed yet again. Even the Open University, with its Fordist methods of production (Rumble, 1995) is having to find new markets and new modes of production – and other universities with post-Fordist techniques of production have already been exploiting a global market for education.

Educational courses are now being delivered through the World Wide Web, and adults can study when and where it is convenient for them. Time and space have been transformed in education.

With the development of distance education and the recognition of the significance of practical knowledge, it is now possible to understand how learning workstations might be introduced into the work place by corporate universities and by the University for Industry.

From the few to the many

The British system of education has always been rather elitist, training the few to assume responsible positions in government, the professions and the church. Hence, the school curriculum was narrow and selective, with a great proportion of children being condemned to blue-collar occupations early in their education. Comprehensive reforms tried to overcome this, but they were not regarded as being very successful.

By the 1980s, there was still only a small percentage of young people going on to higher education. This was regarded as a waste of people's talents and it was certainly not enough to provide new workers to fill all the knowledge-based jobs. Consequently, the education reforms of the late 1980s and early 1990s in the UK – in line with a general democratic feeling in society – expanded higher education to a mass system, with more than 30 per cent of young people being able to attend university. This reflected the form of higher education to be found in the US, but it has not yet been introduced in many other countries in the world.

However, the expansion of higher education to mass education has not really overcome the problem of widening access to those who come from the marginalized or excluded groups, so that there is still considerable concern about universities expanding their student entry to cater for the socially excluded.

From emphasis on the liberal to the vocational

While there is a sense in which the educational institution has always acted as a filter preparing the elite of the land for their work, there has been a general rhetoric that education has had a humanistic basis preparing the whole person for adulthood. Naturally these two do not have to be in opposition but the rhetoric has distracted attention for the selective and divisive functions of education. Even so the Open University began as a 'liberal arts university' since it was easy to offer these courses at a distance. This actually reflected a great deal of the debate that had gone on in school education in the 1960s and early 1970s. R Peters (1977) had argued that the aims of education were to produce a rounded person (an educated man) rather than one who was oriented just to work.

However, as society, and consequently education, became less welfare-oriented and society developed a more knowledge-based workforce, so it became more incumbent on people to learn the knowledge necessary to keep abreast of the demands of their work. Continuing education, which had subsumed adult education, almost became synonymous with continuing professional, or vocational, education. New degree courses mushroomed in universities and colleges of higher education, nearly all of which were vocational.

Employers now became the clients of educational institutions, since it was often they who were paying for their employees' continuing vocational education – the students ceased to be the clients. But employers have specific demands for their own industry and educational institutions are relatively slow to change. Many employers already had large training institutions, which became even more technical and knowledge based, and they have become much more academically acceptable. This has led to some employers seeking to establish their own universities (Eurich, 1985; Meister, 1998) – British Aerospace set up its own university in the UK in 1997. The new Labour government has also granted finance for the establishment of the University for Industry.

For a while liberal adult education was almost completely sidelined, although it is currently in receipt of some government funding. At the same time, a whole new area of non-vocational education is emerging with third-age education. Throughout the developed world, this non-formal education is expanding rapidly, as Universities of the Third Age in the UK, Europe and Australasia and as Institutes of Learning in Retirement and Elderhostel in the US.

From theoretical to practical

Until very recently, education in one form or another has had a monopoly in teaching all forms of theory, and it has been generally felt that theory had to be taught before new recruits to a profession could go into practice. The idea that practitioners applied theory to practice was widely accepted and research was conducted in order to build up the body of knowledge that could be taught to the next generation of recruits. By the 1970s, this view was being questioned in a number of ways. Stenhouse (1975), for instance, suggested that teachers should research their own practice; after all they were implementing their curriculum. At the same time, Lyotard (1984) was suggesting that the legitimation of all knowledge in the future would be through its performativity (he later modified the 'all').

Practice became more central to teaching and learning, and with the development of experiential learning theories it is hardly surprising that problem-based education, and then work-based learning, became more significant. Naturally, this was also in accord with the corporate world's own aims to educate its own workforce. Increasingly, we have seen continuing education courses, at Masters level, being totally work-based. Now, we are beginning to see practitioner doctorates emerge – and with this, there is an increasing emphasis on practical knowledge (see Jarvis, 1999).

From single discipline to multi-disciplinary to integrated knowledge

As a result of the Industrial Revolution and Enlightenment, the individual disciplines of study emerged and knowledge about society began to be categorized by discipline – philosophy, sociology, psychology, etc. Each of the disciplines developed its own array of sub-disciplines and even overlapping sub-disciplines such as social psychology.

By the 1960s this discipline division was beginning to be recognized as somewhat artificial and there emerged ideas of multi-disciplinary study. Consequently, it was possible to study the social sciences – and look at each of the social sciences and even at their different interpretations of the same phenomenon, so that we could have a philosophy of education, a sociology of education and even a social-philosophy of education. The new universities, especially Keele in the 1960s and the Open University in 1970, introduced multi-disciplinary foundation courses of study. The Open University has still retained them, even as compulsory until the mid-1990s, although pressure to drop multi-disciplinary foundation courses has been fairly strong in some quarters.

As the orientation to research and study became more practice-based, it was recognized that practice is not multi-disciplinary but demands integrated knowledge. Knowledge has become widely recognized as a seamless robe. Practical knowledge is integrated and it is knowledge about doing things, eg nursing knowledge, teaching knowledge, so that it is impossible to divide it into its separate elements. It might be suggested that this makes nursing, for instance, a discipline. However, it is possible to have a sociology of nursing but not a nursing of sociology. The same is true for education. Hence, there is something profoundly different about practical knowledge – it is integrated and subjective. The growth of continuing education vocational courses is to be found in this area of integrated practical knowledge.

From welfare needs to market demands (wants)

As the modular approach to the curriculum becomes more acceptable, the idea that education is part of the welfare provision of society becomes less dominant. Now the idea that we have needs-meeting curricula has become less important and the idea of needs has changed its connotations (Jarvis, 1985;

Griffin, 1987). Need no longer refers to a generalized need of potential students; it refers to those special needs, perhaps those which are residual in society and even ones which can be eradicated through good governance.

Once education ceases to be welfare provision, it can only become market provision – and this is precisely what Bacon and Eltis (1976) argued – Britain had to transform its welfare provision into wealth producers. This is the economics of monetarism, introduced by the American economist Milton Freidman. Education had to be seen to be a money earner, which was much simpler after the success of the Open University and the realization that the wide choice of modules that it offered constituted a market for 'off-the-shelf' courses. Educational needs had turned into a matter of supply and demand – a market.

This process has been exacerbated since funding for higher education has been restricted and higher education institutions are having to compete with each other in order to attract students – the educative society has become a learning market.

From education and training to learning

It will be seen from this chapter that there has been a gradual move away from the traditional view of education as the means by which the older generation passes on to the next generations that knowledge it regards as worthwhile and valuable. Now, formal education is not the only way to pass on worthwhile knowledge to the next generation and, as one among many, its status has diminished.

In addition, the traditional distinction between education and training has disappeared with the need of all workers to have practical knowledge at the different levels at which they work, including postgraduate degree level. Learning is a status-free term, unlike education or training, and as training (or vocational education) became more crucial to the knowledge society, it also became status-free. Unfortunately, there is a sense in which vocational education is now taking over the educational discourse.

Conclusion

In the preceding sections we have been able to see how the amount of knowledge is growing at an exponential rate, demanding some form of continuing learning from all who work with it. At the same time the number of people needing to learn has grown immensely and the spread of the World Wide Web means it is now possible to transmit learning materials to people throughout the world. They can learn at their own pace, in their own time and in their own environment. This is clearly the start of an age of learning.

References

Bacon, R and Eltis, W (1976) *Britain's Economic Problem: Too few producers,* Macmillan, Basingstoke

Dewey, J (1916) *Democracy and Education,* Free Press, New York

Dewey, J (1938) *Experience and Education,* Macmillan, New York

Eurich, N (1985) *Corporate Classrooms,* Carnegie Foundation for the Advancement of Teaching, Princeton, NJ

Foucault, M (1972) *Archaeology of Knowledge,* Routledge, London

Griffin, C (1983) *Curriculum Theory in Adult and Lifelong Education,* Croom Helm, Beckenham

Griffin, C (1987) *Adult Education as Social Policy,* Croom Helm, Beckenham

Hamilton, P (1992) 'The enlightenment and the birth of social science', in ed S Hall and B Gieban, *Formations of Modernity,* Polity Press, Cambridge

Houle, C O (1961) *The Inquiring Mind,* University of Wisconsin Press, Madison, WI

Jarvis, P (1985) *The Sociology of Adult and Continuing Education,* Croom Helm, Beckenham

Jarvis, P (1987) *Adult Learning in the Social Context,* Croom Helm, Beckenham

Jarvis, P (1992) *Paradoxes of Learning,* Jossey-Bass, San Francisco, CA

Jarvis, P (1999) *From Practice to Theory,* Jossey-Bass, San Francisco, CA

Kerr, C, Dunlop, J T, Harbison, F and Myers, C A (1973) *Industrialism and Industrial Man,* 2nd edn, Penguin, Harmondsworth

Knowles, M (1980) *The Modern Practice of Adult Education,* 2nd edn, Association Press, Chicago, IL

Kolb, D (1984) *Experiential Learning,* Prentice-Hall, Englewood Cliffs, NJ

Lawton, D (1973) *Social Change, Educational Theory and Curriculum Planning,* Hodder and Stoughton, London

Lengrand, P (1975) *An Introduction to Lifelong Education,* Croom Helm, Beckenham

Lindeman, E C (1926) *The Meaning of Adult Education,* New Republic, New York

Lyotard, J-F (1984) *The Postmodern Condition,* Manchester University Press, Manchester

Meister, J (1998) *Corporate Universities,* revised edn, McGraw-Hill, New York

OECD (1973) *Recurrent Education: A strategy for lifelong learning,* OECD, Paris

Peters, O (1983) 'Distance teaching and industrial production', in eds D Stewart, D Keegan and B Holmberg, *Distance Teaching: International perspectives,* Croom Helm, Beckenham

Peters, R (1977) *Education and the Education of Teachers,* Routledge and Kegan Paul, London

Piaget, J (1929) *The Child's Conception of the World,* Routledge and Kegan Paul, London

Rumble, G (1995) 'Labour market theories and distance education', *Open Learning,* **10,** 1–3

Stenhouse, L (1975) *An Introduction to Curriculum Research and Development,* Heinemann, Oxford

Stikkers, K (1980) *Problems of a Sociology of Knowledge – Max Scheler,* Routledge and Kegan Paul, London

University of Nottingham (1980) *The 1919 Report,* Department of Adult Education, University of Nottingham

Vygotsky, L (1978) *Mind in Society,* Harvard University Press, Cambridge, MA

Vygotsky, L (1986) *Thought and Language,* revised and edited by A Kozulin, MIT, Cambridge, MA

Yeaxlee, B (1929) *Lifelong Education,* Cassell, London

PART TWO

LEARNING AND THE LEARNING SOCIETY

Chapter 4

From education policy to lifelong learning strategies

Colin Griffin

Strategies for lifelong learning or the learning society are beginning to supersede traditional forms of education policy making, both at the national and the international level. This chapter considers the implications of lifelong learning in terms of policy analysis, locating it in the broader context of social, economic and political policy.

First, the background to current education, training and lifelong learning policies is described in terms of the global trends that are affecting the role of the state, and which have been introduced in earlier chapters. Some examples of policy issues and debates are introduced. Aspects of lifelong learning that reflect traditional education policy objectives, such as knowledge and skills, socialization, and the formation of the workforce, are then outlined. It is suggested that new kinds of analytic categories are needed in order to understand the changes currently underway: we need to distinguish, for example, between education and learning, and between policy analysis and policy theory. It is also necessary to distinguish between public, social and welfare policy, and especially between policy and strategy. Strategies for lifelong learning are analysed in relation to culture, leisure and lifestyle, and related to the neo-liberal reform of the welfare state. Finally, it is argued that education policy making is being superseded by lifelong learning strategy-formation.

The background to issues and debates

The UK Government White Paper *Learning to Succeed* (DfEE, 1999) sets out the reasons why change is necessary in the provision of post-16 learning opportunities. These include the shortcomings of the existing system, such as low participation rates, persistent social exclusion, poor levels of basic skills, poor support and guidance, and inappropriate forms of provision. However, the primary focus is upon the need to develop the kinds of skills required by a competitive workforce:

> The skill needs of the future will be different from those of today and it is clear that we will not keep pace with the modern economies of our competitors, if we are unable to match today's skills with the challenge of the developing information and communication age of tomorrow. As labour markets change, we must develop a new approach to skills, and to enabling people, and businesses, to succeed. (DfEE, 1999: 3)

Accordingly, policy will be formulated in response to the existing provision of education and training, and directed towards improving it, by raising participation levels and removing barriers to learning.

These kinds of lifelong learning policies for the UK reflect global forces acting upon education and training, and can be discovered in a whole range of national and international policy documents which emerged as a result of initiatives such as the European Year of Lifelong Learning in 1996 (EC, 1996; OECD, 1996; UNESCO, 1996).

However, in policy terms, the debate goes far beyond the global need to respond to the new conditions of employment, competition and the technological revolution in production. Policies for education and training need to be located in a wider context of social order and citizenship, both of which feature in the policy literature of national and international governments and organizations. For example, there is a focus on social exclusion as well as on the need to foster a European citizenship in the European Commission's *White Paper on Teaching and Learning* (EC, 1996).

So policies for lifelong learning, and their reflection of a learning society, are not merely policies for teaching and learning, or even for education and training, but form an integral part of wider social and economic policy. This represents a considerable break with the past, when policies for education could be fairly clearly distinguished from policies for other things such as citizenship, social order and global economic competition.

There are, however, tensions between what might be described as the *human* capital element of lifelong learning and its potential for *social* capital. Thus, in Britain, for example, the Secretary of State's introduction to the Green Paper on the learning age included elements of both. While suggesting that learning throughout life 'can build human capital by encouraging creativity, skill and imagination', it is argued on the same page that:

> Learning enables people to play a full part in their community and strengthens the family, the neighbourhood and consequently the nation. It helps us fulfil

our potential and opens doors to a love of music, art and literature. That is why we value learning for its own sake and are encouraging adults to enter and re-enter learning at every point of their lives as parents, at work and as citizens. (DfEE, 1998: 1)

However, in the White Paper (DfEE, 1999) that followed, it is clear that human capital for employment, rather than social capital for individual and social fulfilment, is what lifelong learning entails, and there is little reference to the value of learning for its own sake in the later document.

This section concludes with some examples of contested policy issues in lifelong learning. But first, here is a typical statement of the policy context:

> The policy challenge for governments is to provide for economic advance at the same time as ensuring that all its citizens are able both to participate in that process and to take benefit from it; for without contributions from all its citizens – from all its potential pool of talent – the chances of a country's achieving economic stability and social cohesion are likely to be significantly impaired. As we approach the twenty-first century many governments are addressing this challenge through policies associated with the realization of lifelong learning for all. (Chapman and Aspin, 1997: 64)

The authors go on to elaborate the policy context in terms of the knowledge economy, unemployment, population trends, labour-force participation rates, technological change, wages, globalization, social changes in family structures, social exclusion, life-chances, and so on.

The policy context of lifelong learning is therefore extremely broad, and it could be argued that it is now *so* broad that conventional policy analysis is incapable of grasping it and new policy categories are required. In particular, it has been argued that we need to think in terms of global learning strategies, rather than educational policy as such (Griffin, 1999a,b). To illustrate this argument, here are three examples of ways in which policy is more prob-lematic than would appear from the typical policy context example quoted above.

Lifelong learning and the rhetoric of democracy

One of the most important functions of policy analysis is to sustain a critical analysis of its discourse, and in the case of lifelong learning this has generally been the rhetoric of liberal democracy. The association of lifelong learning or the learning society with democracy has long been established. Critical views of the onset of the global neo-liberal economic order tend to view lifelong learning policies as a likely counterweight to the increasing tendencies towards social exclusion and social inequality:

> The challenge for the time is to create a new moral and political order that
> responds to the needs of a society undergoing a historic transition. The limita-
> tions and contradictions of the post-war polity, together with the flawed
> conception implied in the present neo-liberal restructuring, begin to suggest
> the presuppositions for any new order that is to gain the consent of the public
> as a whole… The creation of a moral and political order that expresses and
> enables an active citizenship within the public domain is the challenge of the
> modern era. (Ranson, 1994: 105)

There is a widely held view that lifelong learning policies are intimately
concerned with social democratic government, which is often linked to a
view of the fundamentally democratic process of learning itself:

> the development of new knowledge is a process intimately connected with the
> conditions of open communication which are the hallmark of democratic,
> open societies. (Williamson, 1998: 206)

These views have been a fundamental assumption of adult educators
throughout the 20th century, but with the onset of lifelong learning
strategies it cannot be denied that the rhetoric of democracy or citizenship
has surfaced much more strongly in the discourse of policy. For some, it has
become too strident, and the rhetoric of learning as a universal panacea for
social exclusion and inequality has become too far removed from the social
and economic realities. Thus, for some, there remain considerable obstacles
in the way of Britain, for example, becoming a learning society (Coffield,
1997a).

In fact, it has been suggested that the rhetoric surrounding lifelong
learning, with its promises of universal citizenship and social democracy,
has, since the European Year of Lifelong Learning in 1996, created an
entirely new profession of 'learning philosophers'. Elsewhere Coffield
(1997b) has identified what he calls nine 'learning fallacies' that have become
the bedrock of lifelong learning policy, but which according to him are
without empirical or research evidence. These will be familiar to anyone
who has studied the policy context of lifelong learning or the learning society
since 1996. They are, according to Coffield (1997b: 4–7): Read.

1. 'The most important form of capital in the global market is human
   capital.' In some formulations this becomes: 'The *only* form of capital
   which is important now is human capital.'
2. 'Lifelong learning will transform the educational curriculum from one
   based on knowledge to one based on individual skills.'
3. 'There's no such thing as a non-learner. We're all learning all the time.'

4. 'A strategy for lifelong learning can be created by combining together all existing initiatives for the various phases of education from pre-school to adult education.'
5. 'Learning is individual. It is often pursued in groups, but the experience is uniquely personal. Learning theory examines how learning takes place within individuals.'
6. 'A Learning Society can be created by passing the main responsibility to individuals.'
7. 'All children can succeed at school provided the leadership of the head is effective.'
8. 'We can now safely forget about teaching. The focus of attention must now be on learning.'
9. 'Learning is fun or always should be.'

If these statements are, as Coffield suggests, merely 'learning fallacies', then the research base of lifelong learning policy is inadequate or even non-existent. It is certainly true that arguments about whether or not learning is essentially individual or social remain rhetorical, and no research could prove either proposition to be empirically true except in a rather empty way. Interestingly, Coffield has pursued his argument about learning with another figure in lifelong learning policy, Sir Christopher Ball, in a debate about different visions of the learning society: individual responsibility versus social structure (RSA, 1999: 83–90) There is, in fact, a view that lifelong learning, with its emphasis on individual learning and responsibility, is part of a policy of withdrawal on the part of the state from the public provision of education, along with other public services of a welfare nature; this is our second example of the fundamentally problematic nature of lifelong learning policy.

Lifelong learning policy and social reform

Apart from the significance of globalization and information technology, together with their consequences for competition and the nature of employment and work, we need to locate lifelong learning policy in another global trend, namely the flight from public provision towards a liberal market economy. A cornerstone of this process is individual responsibility and the reform of welfare and other social services. This has been accompanied by the growth of the private provision of services, and by the government's retreat to a strategic role in the face of globalization and market economics. The so-called crisis of welfare has been identified in every country with a welfare state, from Sweden to New Zealand. In Britain, there is clear evidence that lifelong learning policy is closely associated with wider policies for the reform of the welfare state: 'learning... will be at the heart of the government's welfare reform programme' (DfEE, 1998: 6)

The arguments about whether learning is an individual or a social phenomenon can usually be aligned with arguments about whether lifelong learning policies are progressive or not, in the old social democratic sense of 'progressive': the argument between Coffield and Ball is, in fact, as much about individual and social *responsibility* for learning as about learning as such. And this raises the issue of state or public provision. Elliott (1999) has suggested that lifelong learning policy, according to which responsibility for learning will rest with the individual, is little short of a rationale for the systematic starvation of education provision of public funding, and the encouragement of a market economy in learning in every sector of the system. Certainly, policy initiatives such as Individual Lifelong Learning Accounts (Smith and Spurling, 1997) would seem to confirm the view that lifelong learning is intended to reflect markets, tax breaks and voucher schemes (Jarvis *et al*, 1997) as ways of inducing individuals to undertake their own learning rather than depend on the state for education provision. The government's strategic role is one of 'steering' through selective intervention, by way of measures such as target setting, league tables and performance indicators, rather than by way of mandating and sanctioning the objectives of policy.

Policy must be much more broadly conceived than as merely a response to the conditions of global capitalism and information technology. It must be broadened to include the threats posed to social security by increasing social inequality and social exclusion that are the consequences of the new global conditions.

If we look at the policy literature of lifelong learning, the stress upon citizenship, inclusion, participation and forms of governance are not hard to find. Hitherto these were only *implicit* in education policy, except that adult educators often tended to stress the significance of access to learning for social cohesion and solidarity.

Now, the citizenship element of lifelong learning policy is as important as the content of learning in terms of knowledge and skills themselves. It has, in short, become an *explicit* feature of such policy. For example, the European Commission is concerned with European citizenship as much as with Europe's capacity to compete in the world markets (EC, 1996). This was a point developed at the First European Conference on Lifelong Learning (Sussmuth, 1998) At the same conference, however, Michael Young posed the question 'Can lifelong learning prevent the breakdown of society?' (Young, 1998) As with Coffield's question 'Can the UK become a learning society?' (Coffield, 1997a), we can see that rhetoric and rhetorical questions continue to characterize the policy discourse of lifelong learning. In fact, Young took broadly the same view as Coffield, that the inherent individualism in much of the concept of lifelong learning would not contribute much to inclusive citizenship and the struggle against social exclusion:

In my argument the overemphasis on the individual has been the villain of the piece. Individual development, individual choice, individual destiny, and all this while the scale of the world economy to which all of us belong willy-nilly is getting more vast and more impersonal by the day. A frightening paradox in itself. The conclusion, which in my view follows is that the future may well be on the side of lifelong learning which needs to become less individualist and more collectivist. (Young, 1998: 29)

The policy debate therefore still reflects issues of collectivism and individualism, markets and provision, and human and social capital. But it is a debate conducted often at the level of rhetoric and, as Coffield implies, there is little research evidence underpinning lifelong learning policy.

Lifelong learning and postmodern society

The policy discourse of lifelong learning reflects, according to some, the fact that we are leaving behind the kind of modern society of which public education systems were a characteristic feature. A society of risk (Beck, 1992) and ambiguity or ambivalence (Bauman, 1991) has generated a body of theory which in turn is finding expression in the kind of research needed to inform policy, such as the government's Social Exclusion Unit set up in 1998, or the Centre for the Analysis of Risk and Regulation now being established at the London School of Economics. The latter exists 'to explore the development of the concept of risk and its management' (LSE, 1999).

Institutions such as these should, in theory, be capable of producing a more research-informed lifelong learning policy. Nevertheless, concepts such as citizenship and governance are themselves being redefined in ways reflecting the lifelong learning discourses. The model of citizenship is now much more entrepreneurial and inclusive, in ways that are being studied in the forms of risk and social exclusion, and a model of the citizen is increasingly of one who is *both* self-employed *and* self-educated. And although such models are challenged by writers such as Coffield and Young from empirical and ideological positions, nevertheless, some lifelong learning policies could be said to reflect more of a privatized than a publicly provided education system. Taking Elliott's point about lifelong learning, namely that it may actually be anti-educational in that it diverts funds and resources away from the public education system, it is possible to conceive of lifelong education policy as the first step in the dismantling of the state education system.

Usher has analysed lifelong learning in relation to identity and risk, arguing that:

changing conceptions of knowledge and the need to understand knowledge in terms of its location in different social practices means that lifelong learning cannot be seen simply as a structure of provision but as a signifier with many different significations. (Usher, 1999: 65)

Usher's approach, however, is not simply that of a postmodernist analysis, but is also taken from an adult education provision perspective. He is concerned with the problem of identifying adult education as a form of provision in the risk society. The analysis, however, entails that *all* such forms of provision become problematic in the new postmodern order of things:

> the very notion of 'lifelong learning' implies that education can no longer claim a monopoly over learning simply because it is a formally constituted field since a multiplicity of activities in many contexts involve learning and hence can be deemed 'educational'. Lifelong learning foregrounds the simultaneous boundlessness of learning, ie that it is not confined by pre-determined outcomes or formal institutions, and its postmodern quality, ie its inherent discursive and socio-cultural contextuality. (Usher, 1999: 80)

As we shall see, this view of lifelong learning as having none of the recognizable characteristics of formal systems of provision effectively removes it from the sphere of conventional policy analysis.

We have now reviewed some salient policy issues in lifelong learning, such as its relation to democracy, citizenship and inclusion, individualism and collectivism, welfare reform and the market economy, and identity and risk in postmodern discourse. Out of all this has emerged the paradoxical view that lifelong learning is a rhetorical concept with little or no research base, and that in any case it could not be conceptualized as a form of public provision. If this is, indeed the case, then lifelong learning is effectively removed from the scope of policy analysis, as this has traditionally been applied to education and training systems. For many, of course, this is far from the case, and we need now to consider lifelong learning as a reconceptualization of the education system itself, rather than as something so rhetorical or abstract that it cannot be grasped in the same way.

Lifelong learning as education policy

The view that lifelong learning is just another name for a more integrated ('joined up'), more accessible, more relevant, more accountable education system is projected by many policy documents. As far as policy is concerned, lifelong learning is simply the new name for education and training to be given in these post-industrial, postmodern, post-welfare times. Its background and context have, of course, changed as a result of global capitalism and the revolution in knowledge, technology and communications, but essentially lifelong learning is concerned with the same *content* as that of traditional education and training systems. This content consists of knowledge, attitudes and skills appropriate to the new conditions.

If this is, indeed all that lifelong learning amounts to, then it can be analysed as a form of policy in the same way as education itself. Here is a definition of lifelong learning that lends itself both to recognizably *educational* criteria and also to educational policy analysis as this has so far been developed:

> Lifelong learning is the development of human potential through a continuously supportive process which stimulates and empowers individuals to acquire all the knowledge, values, skills and understanding they will require throughout their lifetimes and to apply them with confidence, creativity and enjoyment in all roles, circumstances, and environments. (Longworth and Davies, 1996: 22)

The authors proceed to develop the meanings of all the constituent terms in their definition. The result is recognizably a definition of the education and training process over an individual's lifetime, from a developmental perspective. It focuses on the acquisition of knowledge, values, skills and understanding which should be made possible over the whole of a lifetime, together with the total range of contexts of human experience in which these may be developed. The rest of the book describes the *system* through which such lifelong learning might be delivered, and looks at the role of the school, the workplace, learning organizations, higher education and learning communities.

It is an individualistic view of lifelong learning, precisely the one we have seen criticized by writers such as Coffield and Young. Indeed, the authors quote with approval the 'learning beatitudes' of Ball (1992) that the former challenged so strongly, together with their individualistic basis.

We are concerned, however, with the role of the government and the significance for policy in all this. The first point to make is that most of the criteria of lifelong learning contained in the definition are measurable in terms of outcomes or performance. At least, they are as measurable as those traditionally associated with education and training, not all of which were quantifiable in any case. In this sense, it is a view of lifelong learning *as* education, which could, in principle, be subject to conventional policy analysis.

However, what is said here about the role of government in all this is very significantly different from what it was in relation to traditional education and training provision. In short, it is not a very proactive role:

> Through its economic and political power, government is the enabler of lifelong learning programmes, values and attitudes. It has the ability to define

targets, support worthwhile initiatives, change systems, influence developments and turn ideas into action. Where national government can provide
encouragement and establish the means of disseminating good practice, local
government can initiate new projects to make lifelong learning work in the
regions. Radical measures would include tax incentives, investment grants for
new technologies and ministerial committees with the remit to produce plans
and to implement them. (Longworth and Davies, 1996: 18)

The key word here is government as *enabler*. This envisages a very different
role from that traditionally associated with education policy, where governments *mandated* and *sanctioned* policy. It is, in fact, a role for government
consistent with the neo-liberal or minimalist stance, and it is also significant
that tax incentives and investment grants are seen as radical departures. In
short, this is a view of lifelong learning as a form of education policy for neo-
liberal, welfare reform conditions.

At this point, we need to consider the consequences of these differing
concepts of lifelong learning from the perspective of policy analysis.

The need for new analytic categories

We have seen that there are visions of lifelong learning that do not easily lend
themselves to conventional education policy analysis, as well as some that
do. The reasons why some do not are that they are too vague, too unquan-
tifiable, with insufficient possibilities for measurement and control. For
example, there is often a mention of the need to 'change the culture' of
society in favour of learning, whereas in fact it would never be possible to
know whether or not this had happened without resorting to circular arguments about the meaning of 'culture'.

Nevertheless, there *are* important implications for how we should analyse
lifelong learning in policy terms. For example, there are certain important
categorical distinctions that become necessary in trying to grasp *all* these
various concepts of lifelong learning within a single framework of analysis.
Here are some examples, from Griffin (1999b):

- The distinction between *education* and *learning*: whereas education
  suggests some kind of provision, not necessarily formal, learning is not
  something that could be *reduced* to education or training. Consequently,
  some models of lifelong learning policy are *reductionist*.
- An example of a reductionist model would be to *equate* the learning
  society with a society in which everyone learns. Some models reduce the
  concept of lifelong learning, or that of the learning society itself, to measurements of *participation* in provision, or qualifications and credentialism,
  for example.

- The distinction between *function* and *provision*: education is an object of some form of provision, whereas learning is a *function* of individual, social or corporate life, and therefore integral to its survival and growth.
- The distinction between *policy* and *strategy*: the role of government is strategic, or *enabling*, as we saw in the case of Longworth and Davies' definition quoted above. In other words, the government no longer *determines* the outcomes of policy but makes it possible for others to do so (by providing incentives) and restricts itself to setting targets and establishing performance and outcomes indicators.
- The distinction between *markets* and *quasi-markets*: this is a distinction established by policy analysts in the provision of welfare services such as health and housing. The market in education, or learning, should not be confused with an *economic* market. Voucher schemes and tax breaks are strategic *interferences* in the marketplace to enable certain outcomes to be preferable to others.

It is suggested that we need to make these kinds of analytic distinctions in considering a range of lifelong learning policies. They represent categories that are often confused, leading to reductionist models in practice, and contributing to the oft-remarked vagueness of the whole idea of lifelong learning.

An example of the above confusion is the introduction of terms such as 'learning revolution' or 'learning culture' into the policy debate, as though these could be established with the same degree of certainty as more conventional objects of policy. As has been observed, it is highly questionable whether changes in 'culture', as opposed to habit, expectation or practice, could be engineered by policy alone.

Culture, leisure and lifestyle

The association of lifelong learning with the concept of a 'learning culture' or a 'cultural revolution in learning' is by now quite familiar. A recent report provides a typical example:

> At the heart of our advice and underpinning all of our recommendations is a conviction that successful implementation of the government's strategy for lifelong learning will depend upon promoting widespread and systematic changes of culture in our society, creating opportunities for lifelong learning for all. (NAGCELL, 1999: 8)

Although the meaning and intention of such points as these are perfectly clear and justifiable, they do make conventional policy analysis problematic when it comes to lifelong learning. As the authors of this report go on to say: 'Cultures are usually especially resistant to attempts to change them from the outside or to impose unwanted modifications upon them' (ibid). It also has to be said that there is no reason to think that 'culture' is something universally shared by all members of society alike. Indeed, the concept of culture is one long associated with social division and inequalities of power and status in society. The imposition of external sanctions is part of what is normally understood by the policy process, however, so the use of the word 'strategy' is more appropriate than that of 'policy', as was suggested above, in the case of lifelong learning.

This example points up a whole area in the conceptualization of lifelong learning that removes it from the conventional policy analysis framework and from the ways in which educational policy has been traditionally approached. There are a variety of 'post-education' ways of conceiving lifelong learning, such as:

- The consumer credit model, which puts control over learning provision in the hands of individual consumers by way of voucher schemes or tax breaks and other incentives (Smith and Spurling, 1997).
- The cultural/lifestyle model, according to which learning is linked to culture, class and other social divisions through everyday practices and habituation (Usher et al, 1997).
- The leisure/consumption model. Field (1996) has described ways in which education and training might be thought of as representing forms of consumption, and the policy literature of lifelong learning generally reinforces a view of learning as a form of consumption in market conditions.
- The social or cultural capital model, which is concerned with idea of learning in non-educational settings such as family and community, and the extent to which such learning may be contrasted with the more individualistic human capital model which is often associated with the economics of education (Schuller and Field, 1998).

These are examples of ways in which we might think of lifelong learning in 'cultural' terms, that is, integrated into everyday practices and values, rather than imposed from without in the form of traditional educational provision.

Conclusion

All of these approaches are associated with 'postmodern' perspectives on education and society. They are also consistent with the reform of the welfare system of which lifelong learning policy may be an integral element. They stress markets, individual choice and responsibility, and reflect the perceived failure of traditional educational provision to adapt to post-industrial, post-welfare or postmodern times. Indeed, it has long been suggested that lifelong learning is a sign that we are approaching the post-education society itself (Evans, 1985).

These directions in which the discourse of lifelong learning is turning are very significant for policy analysis. We have seen that in some conceptualizations, there is little to choose between what is called lifelong learning and what was called the education and training system. For purposes of policy analysis, however, other concepts of lifelong learning remain too incoherent and ambiguous to make much sense of.

However, if we regard the role of the government as *strategic* in relation to lifelong learning, rather than as *policy forming* in relation to education, then it becomes possible to locate lifelong learning in the wider social, economic, political and cultural trends that are the subject of this book.

References

Ball, C (1992) *Profitable Learning,* Royal Society of Arts, London

Bauman, Z (1991) *Modernity and Ambivalence,* Polity Press, Cambridge

Beck, U (1992) *Risk Society: Towards a new modernity,* Sage, London

Chapman, J D and Aspin, D N (1997) *The School, the Community and Lifelong Learning,* Cassell, London

Coffield, F (1997a) 'Can the UK become a learning society?' The Fourth Annual Education Lecture, King's College School of Education, London

Coffield, F (ed) (1997b) *A National Strategy for Lifelong Learning,* University of Newcastle Department of Education, Newcastle upon Tyne

Department for Education and Employment (DfEE) (1998) *The Learning Age: A renaissance for a new Britain,* The Stationery Office, Norwich

(DfEE) (1999) *Learning to Succeed: A new framework for post-16 learning,* The Stationery Office, Norwich

Elliott, G (1999) *Lifelong Learning: The politics of the new learning environment,* Jessica Kingsley, London

European Commission (EC) (1996) *Teaching and Learning: Towards the learning society,* White Paper on Education and Training, European Commission, Brussels

Evans, N (1985) *Post-Education Society: Recognizing adults as learners,* Croom Helm, Beckenham

Field, J (1996) 'Open learning and consumer culture', in eds P Raggatt, R Edwards and N Small, *The Learning Society: Challenges and trends,* Routledge in association with the Open University, London

Griffin, C M (1999a) 'Lifelong learning and social democracy', *International Journal of Lifelong Education,* **18** (5), 329–42

Griffin, C M (1999b) 'Lifelong learning and welfare reform', *International Journal of Lifelong Education,* **18** (6), 431–52

Jarvis, P, Holford, J, Griffin, C and Dubelaar, J (1997) *Towards the Learning City: An evaluation of the Corporation of London's adult education voucher schemes,* Corporation of London, London

London School of Economics (LSE) (1999) *Risk and Regulation: The launch,* LSE, London

Longworth, N and Davies, W K (1996) *Lifelong Learning,* Kogan Page, London

National Advisory Group for Continuing Education and Lifelong Learning (NAGCELL) (1999) *Creating Learning Cultures: Second report* (Fryer Report) NAGCELL, London

Organization for Economic Cooperation and Development (OECD) (1996) *Lifelong Learning For All,* OECD, Paris

Ranson, S (1994) *Towards the Learning Society,* Cassell, London

Royal Society of Arts (RSA) (1999) *RSA Journal,* 4/4

Schuller, T and Field, J (1998) 'Social capital, human capital and the learning society', *International Journal of Lifelong Education,* **17** (4), 226–35.

Smith, J and Spurling, A (1997) *Individual Lifelong Learning Accounts: Towards a learning revolution,* National Institute of Adult Continuing Education, Leicester

Sussmuth, R (1998) 'Adult education, European citizenship and the role of the regions', in eds P Alheit and E Kammler, *Lifelong Learning and its Impact on Social and Regional Development: Contributions to the first European conference on lifelong learning,* Bremen, 3–5 October 1996, Donat Verlag, Bremen

United Nations Educational, Scientific and Cultural Organization (UNESCO) (1996) *Learning: The treasure within* (Delors Report), UNESCO, Paris

Usher, R (1999) 'Identity, risk and lifelong learning', in ed P Oliver, *Lifelong and Continuing Education: What is a learning society?,* Ashgate Publishing, Aldershot

Usher, R, Bryant, I and Johnston, R (1997) *Adult Education and the Postmodern Challenge: Learning beyond the limits,* Routledge, London

Williamson, B (1998) *Lifeworlds and Learning: Essays in the theory, philosophy and practice of lifelong learning,* National Institute of Adult Continuing Education, Leicester

Young, M (1998) 'Can lifelong learning prevent the breakdown of society?', in eds P Alheit and E Kammler, *Lifelong Learning and its Impact on Social and Regional Development: Contributions to the first European conference on lifelong learning,* Bremen, 3–5 October 1996, Donat Verlag, Bremen

Chapter 5

The learning society

Colin Griffin and Bob Brownhill

The first half of this chapter traces the emergence of the idea of the learning society, and identifies a range of models and definitions, and the threads of continuity which link all together into an identifiable concept. However, it also emerges that the philosophical perspectives underpinning them can themselves be very diverse. The second half of the chapter therefore explores the philosophical issues raised by the various definitions and models of the learning society which have been put forward during the last decades of the 20th century.

One of the most significant characteristics of the age of learning is the way in which learning itself has ceased to be attributed solely to individuals, and has taken on a range of corporate identities. Although learning theory has focused mainly on the learning that takes place in the lives of individuals, increasingly learning is attributed to communities, organizations and society itself. We have become familiar, for example, with the idea of the learning organization as a way of thinking about corporate identity (Easterby-Smith *et al*, 1999). The idea of the family, the community and the workplace as sites of learning are also familiar aspects of the current focus on lifelong learning and the learning society (Oliver, 1999). Lifelong learning itself often means not only that individuals continue to learn over the whole of their lives, but that every aspect of their lives presents opportunities for learning.

There are various ways of defining the learning society, as we shall see, but what they all have in common is a broad concept of learning, one that cannot always be contained in traditional educational settings. The first half of this chapter will review the history of the concept of the learning society, concluding with some models reflecting current research.

The emerging concept

Although the idea of lifelong learning or lifelong education is not new, that of the learning society has had to wait for the kinds of global and techno-logical change we associate with the second half of the 20th century. In particular, the dawning realization that educational systems could no longer be thought of as either *sufficient* sources of learning or the *only* source of learning meant that learning had to be more broadly conceived than simply as a process of education. This is a distinction that has to be established at the outset, because, as we shall see, it is possible to define a learning society as simply one with a highly developed education and training system. This distinction between learning and education was therefore developed amongst the earliest statements of the idea. We will now consider three early formulations of the learning society, those of Robert M Hutchins, Torsten Husén and Roger Boshier, before looking at the way in which educational and policy research is producing models for the society of today.

All of these, in their different ways, represent models of society, and not just of learning and education, which is why the distinction between learning and education is an important one to establish at the outset.

Robert M Hutchins

Hutchins produced one of the earliest statements in his book, *The Learning Society* in 1968, and saw the need to distinguish between what he called education and the educational systems. For him (1968: 125), the origins of the learning society lay in the inadequacy of educational systems to cope with the demands being put on them:

> In the closing decades of the 20th century, the aims of educational institutions seemed obviously archaic. In a world that was beginning to be plagued with surplus manpower, they were furiously grinding out more. In a world that was towards an international community, they were building up manpower in the name of national power, prosperity and prestige. In a world thirsty for wisdom, they were giving little thought to this need and redoubling their efforts to meet needs that were becoming obsolete.

Faced by the rapidity of change, and the impossibility of educational institutions being able to adapt because they were so tied to the politics and the culture of society, Hutchins reviewed possibilities of greater flexibility, such as paid educational leave. But, he asked, 'Is it possible to go further and foresee the learning society?'

> This would be one that, in addition to offering part-time adult education to every man and woman at every stage of grown-up life, had succeeded in

transforming its values in such a way that learning fulfilment, becoming human, had become its aim and all its institutions were directed to this end. (Hutchins, 1968: 134)

This early account of the learning society , therefore, went beyond the idea of universal access to educational institutions towards a view of learning at the heart of society's culture and values.

Torsten Husen

Six years after Hutchins' book, Torsten Husén (1974) published one with the same name. This was a collection of essays, many concerned with education in his native Sweden, but also containing some more futurological studies on educational themes. Like Hutchins, Husén doubted the capacity of educational institutions to cope with the demands of a rapidly changing world, but was less utopian than, for example, the recently published Faure Report on lifelong education (UNESCO, 1972), at least according to the English editor of his book.

Husén's is a much more technological vision of the learning society than Hutchins', which, as we have seen, described it in terms of culture and values. Hutchins anticipated the role of communication and technology in relation to knowledge and information:

> Among all the 'explosions' that have come into use as labels to describe rapidly changing Western society, the term 'knowledge explosion' is one of the most appropriate. Reference is often made to the 'knowledge industry', meaning both the producers of knowledge, such as research institutes, and its distributors, eg schools, mass media, book publishers, libraries and so on. What we have been witnessing since the mid-1960s in the field of distribution technology may well have begun to revolutionize the communication of knowledge within another ten years or so. (Husén,1974: 239)

Husén predicted that the learning society would be a knowledge and information society, and he also made predictions that have become commonplace assumptions about society since, such as the movement towards equal opportunities, and the shift from manufacturing to service industry as the basis of production. Twelve years later Husén revisited the learning society in another collection of essays on futurological themes (Husén, 1986). By this time, the consequences of the 'knowledge explosion' were fully apparent:

> It should suffice to point out that much of what we learned when we went to school is becoming obsolete. The ravages are wreaked not only by time alone

but also by the headlong surge of science and technology as it affects our daily lives. (Husén, 1986: 139)

Husén's vision of the learning society is futurological in the sense that it is based upon projections from current trends in communications technology, and the likely consequences of these for knowledge, information and production. They have largely come true.

We have now seen in the concepts of the learning society of Hutchins and Husén two highly contrasted views, one based on classical humanism, the other on educational futurology. These two studies came from the US and Sweden respectively, but other approaches are possible, and we now turn to one from New Zealand that is based upon democratic participation as the basis of the learning society.

Roger Boshier

Boshier's book *Towards a Learning Society* was published in 1980, and is written from the perspective of adult and continuing education. It reflects the central part played by adult education in the development of many of the themes associated with the learning society, but especially that of the significance of participation on the part of adults:

> A full functioning lifelong education system will result in the creation of a learning society where adult education and learning are normal and common place, not the exclusive preserve of childhood or adolescence but an inherent right of all citizens, as inalienable as clean water and good shelter. In a learning society, the educational institutions will no longer have a monopoly on education but will be linked with informal systems to provide continuous learning for all. (Boshier, 1980: 1)

This is a view of the learning society which shares with others a sense of the inadequacy of educational institutions, but which emanates from a radical democratic position as much as from a humanist vision or futurological and technological projections:

> The notion of a learning society stems from third force psychology, widespread disenchantment with traditional education, the writings of educational radicals such as Illich, Goodman and Freire, and the unprecedented transformation wrought by economic and social changes associated with evolving technology. (Boshier, 1980: 2–3)

This is a view of the learning society based on *integrated provision* of education accessible to all over the whole of the lifetime.

In the three visions of the learning society that have now been briefly reviewed, there are both similarities and differences. They are all conscious of the capacity of education systems to deal with it. But they are based upon quite different perspectives: humanism, futurology and democracy. All of these perspectives continue to be represented, in degrees, in current accounts of the learning society. If we take a more recent account, for example, it is possible to trace all of the elements of the earlier versions, with just some differences of emphasis:

> There is a need for the creation of a learning society as the constitutive condition of a new moral and political order. It is only when the values and processes of learning are placed at the centre of the polity that the conditions can be established for all individuals to develop their capacities, and that institutions can respond openly and imaginatively to a period of change. Two organizing principles provide the framework for the learning society: that the essential structure of *citizenship* should be developed through the process of *practical reason*. (Ranson, 1994: 106)

So there is an essential continuity between the earlier accounts of the learning society and more current ones. Three models have emerged, which seem to reflect the basic principles upon which the idea is founded:

- The *cultural* model, which sees the learning society as one characterized by particular *values* around learning, either humanistic or other.
- The *technological* model, which sees the learning society as made possible by developments in communications technology, but which also sees it as *integral* to evolving patterns of life in work, family, community or whatever.
- The *democratic* model, which sees the learning society as fundamentally an expression of citizenship or democracy, and which stresses the *participative* nature of provision for learning.

These models can all be discerned in the policy literature and discourse of lifelong learning, which more often than not is directed towards the establishment of a learning society. Whether emanating from national or international sources, all such documents lay stress upon citizenship, cultural change, equal opportunities, access for all, technological development, the 'knowledge revolution', broadening participation and so on.

This section of the chapter will end with a review of some contemporary research-based models of the learning society, which are not, however, necessarily seen as mutually compatible. In other words, whatever the humanistic, technological or democratic origins of these models, they remain the subject of political and ideological debate.

Contemporary models of the learning society

In the UK, the ESRC's Learning Society Programme has generated a range of alternative models in the course of research projects into knowledge and skills for employment (Coffield, 1997).

In the first place, there is the issue of whether or not the whole debate about the learning society is a *normative* one or not. In other words, it is possible to take a view of the learning society as something that either exists or not, through participation studies and quantifiable accounts of *how much* learning people are actually doing. This approach has a pedigree as long as adult education research itself, and makes the learning society a purely *descriptive* concept. So there are *normative* and *descriptive* models to begin with; of the ones introduced so far, Husén seems to be the most descriptive.

Another research group in the ESRC programme has distinguished four models of the learning society, which Coffield summarizes as follows:

- the *schooling* model is defined by the goal of achieving high levels of participation in full-time post-compulsory education;
- the *credentialist* model prioritizes increasing the proportion of the population with qualifications;
- the *access* model stresses the need to improve online access to education and training throughout people's lives;
- the *reflexive* model stresses the importance of an expanded view of learning as a wide distribution of the capacity to learn, and prioritizes learning as a major feature of all social relationships, personal, organizational and societal. (Young *et al*, 1997).

These four models, on which current research into the learning society is based in the ESRC programme, all find reflection in the models generated by the literature of the learning society over the last 30 or 40 years. Indeed, in some respects, the stress upon participation and credentialism in times of such rapid change as ours seems rather outdated. Nevertheless, as Coffield (1997: 2) points out, 'Enough has been said already to make clear that, even within The Learning Society Programme itself, The Learning Society is a contested and multi-dimensional concept.'

Coffield himself offers two contrasting models of the learning society, which he calls the *technocratic* model and the *social polarization* model. The technocratic model, which the author claims to find represented in most of the government's policy for lifelong learning, reflects the need for workforce skills in conditions of global competition. It is used to justify the expansion of the education system itself to provide an appropriately skilled and flexible workforce of lifelong learners.

The social polarization model, on the other hand, reflects what the author sees as the growing polarization of contemporary Britain, whereby the combination of participation rates and the qualifications system is producing an employment system that increases the gap between those with and those without qualifications and employment.

The conclusion of this analysis is that many definitions of the learning society acknowledge a conflict between the *economic* and the *democratic* imperatives. As we saw in the case of the earlier accounts, this has been inherent since the idea of the learning society first began to be developed. However, the conflict goes deeper than that between economics and politics. The learning society raises issues of a philosophical kind, especially about the nature of learning and knowledge, as well as about the identity and autonomy of learners. The issues traditionally associated with liberal, vocational and other forms of education do not disappear with the advent of lifelong learning and the learning society. The remainder of this chapter will consider some of these philosophical issues.

Philosophies of the learning society

In this section we look at and develop the three models put forward by Hutchins, Husén and Boshier from a philosophical perspective. The models are:

- cultural values/humanistic;
- futurological/technological;
- democracy/participation/citizenship.

Cultural values/humanistic model

Hutchins raised an important question about the nature of the person who could be the archetype for inclusion in the learning society. This person had in fact been foreshadowed in the work of the 18th century moral philosopher Immanuel Kant (Paton, 1961) and the writings of a liberal school of educationalists led by the 20th century philosopher of education R S Peters (Peters, 1972). Kant had developed the notion of a rational, autonomous individual. This individual acted independently of any authority and made his or her own choices and decisions, and because of that was both responsible and accountable for them. He or she was essentially a moral creature who acted for the sake of the moral law, but, as Kant argued, it was his or her responsibility to legislate this moral law into effect with universal intent. It was a notion of a rational individual, who could act impersonally and impartially, ruling out emotions, self-interest, and the interests of the groups to which he or she belonged, for the sake of acting rightly and in an unbiased way. It was virtually a picture of a demi-god. It was very much an individualistic concept, but if all acted rationally for the sake of the moral law it was thought a 'kingdom of ends' (Paton, 1961) could come about.

The theory also had political and educational connotations, for it meant that all human beings, as potential autonomous individuals, were equal and should be shown respect. The notion of respect was important for it meant that all individuals should be treated as 'ends in themselves' and not used for some other purpose and treated as 'a means to an end'; for instance, not used for the good of the economy, or the glorification of the state. Peters developed the notion in the educational sphere with his concept of an 'educated person' who was able to understand things by recognizing the principles that lay behind them. He or she was to be a fully rounded person steeped in culture and able to make rational choices and decisions based on evidence and argument.

The model of teaching these neo-Kantian ideas expressed was called the 'rule model' of education by Israel Scheffler (1967). The emphasis was on reason, and reason is a matter of abiding by rules and principles. In the cognitive realm reason is justice to the evidence, a careful weighing up of evidence and arguments for and against, in the interests of arriving as close to the truth as possible. In the moral realm reason is action on principle freely chosen by the moral agent. It is impartial and without prejudice. It includes the moral notion of respect for other people as like oneself, autonomous self-lawmakers. A rational person is one who is consistent in thought and in action, abiding by impartial and generalizable principles, which are freely chosen and also binding on oneself. The aim of education is to build up individuals who have an autonomous and rational character that underlies science, morality and culture. The notion leads to the concept of the self-directed learner, which we will look at in the next section.

Some obvious criticisms can be made of this model. It appears too individualistic, although not a selfish individualism, and also puts a great emphasis on cognitive ability, while seemingly downgrading the affective side of personality. Peters (1972) nevertheless argued that the aim of education was to produce this sort of educated person, and that it could be seen that education therefore had intrinsic value with no need of further justification. He used the argument to denigrate commercial and industrial training, which was merely concerned with using people for the immediate good of the economy. In the long run this glorious amateur was more likely to serve society better than one trained in specific skills.

Another side to this liberal tradition was expressed by the educational and political philosopher Michael Oakeshott (Oakeshott, 1933). He argued that finding it too difficult to understand the world as a whole, we looked at the world through different 'modes of experience', and that these modes actually had become the cultural achievements of humankind. For instance, in science we considered the world under the category of quantity and were concerned with measurement; we had also chosen to look at the world from the poetic point of view, the historical, etc. These modes of experience, or 'conversations of mankind' as he sometimes called them, had developed their own language, concepts and methodology, and we had the opportunity to immerse ourselves in them and, perhaps, with sufficient application, even to become a connoisseur within a certain realm. The theory was one of lifelong learning within one's culture, for he recognized that at school we could only scratch the surface and maybe just learn the language of a particular mode. It was also a theory of authority and control, where practice within the modes had to be learnt from the master practitioners until gradually one may become an adept oneself. The excesses of individualism were controlled through the framework of the culture.

In some respects, the notion was repeated again in the 1960s by the post-Wittgenstein philosopher of education Paul Hirst (Hirst, 1974). He changed the modes of experience into 'forms of knowledge' and also called them 'linguistic inter-subjectivity'. The intention was to give greater stability to our knowledge base, as Plato had done in classical times with his theory of forms, but, of course, for Hirst Platonic metaphysics was no longer available, so hence his linguistic inter-subjectivity as substitutes for the Platonic forms. Hirst had a number of forms and each had its own language, concepts and methodology. He argued that they were separate and could not be mixed, and that indeed they should become the basis for the curriculum in academic schools. To become educated a student had to be conversant with a fair number of the forms. The new individual was now completely bound within the parameters of the favoured disciplines and the received culture.

Futurological/technological model

In spite of the strong conservative element within liberal educational thinking (Brownhill and Smart, 1989), the idea of the autonomous individual continued to develop with an emphasis on the idea of the self-directed learner. The notion is an essential component of lifelong learning: if a person is to succeed as a lifelong learner then it is incumbent on that person to become a self-directed learner and to know not only how to learn but how to put it into practice as well. To achieve such a skill and become a self-directed learner, the first ability to be acquired is to learn how to learn. An emphasis is put on a student's independence, and on his or her own responsibility for developing his or her learning. The aim is to develop students who have the ability to stand on their own feet and make decisions in the educational and other spheres. Ideally they should move from autarchy, the normal ability to make decisions, to autonomy, which in this sense is a much heightened ability to make independent choices and decisions (Benn, 1976). Self-directed learning also fosters the ability to make a clearer rational decision for oneself or for the group one may represent. There is also a notion of being positive, of taking active steps to achieve one's goals, rather than being passive and waiting in the hope that something may turn up or be provided by a benefactor.

In the educational sphere the notion of self-directed learning also has a tendency to de-institutionalize the educational process, for, as self-directed learners, students will not need traditional educational institutions, which offered in return for submission to their authority the possibility of knowledge. This tendency was further strengthened by the development of information technology and the World Wide Web. The development of self-directed learning not only encourages a person-centred approach to learning, where the action of the teacher is to stimulate independence, but also gives the teacher a new role as a resource for the student amongst many other resources.

It can be seen that a full-blooded autonomous self-directed learner can become frightening to the teacher. A teacher is no longer seen as an authority but as a resource to be used, a purveyor of either useful or useless information and skills, a competent or incompetent technician.

The idea of the self-directed learner is also very attractive for business, industry and the professions. A person who is able to plan his or her own career may be able to develop some idea about the prospects for a company or see how it might be improved. A person who can see what skills are needed to keep up the momentum of a career can also benefit a company by keeping them up to date. A person who wants to learn and knows how to learn by keeping abreast of developments in modern information technology and by keeping up with expanding knowledge in his or her own and related fields is a good acquisition for any company.

The liberal notion of the autonomous individual working within a learning framework became attractive to vocational and professional educators. Indeed, traditional aims of liberal education have been synthesized with arguments concerning the aims and needs of vocational and professional education, and modern business practice. Of particular interest is the use made of the liberal concept of autonomy and its relationship to the idea of the self-directed learner within a learning organization.

The professional notion of competency has been attached to both. In order to be competent a person must be able to carry out his or her role adequately and/or effectively. It incorporates the notion of the practitioner being educated so that he or she can achieve a level of practical excellence acceptable to colleagues who make the assessment. It therefore provides a concept of a standard of performance below which one would be deemed incompetent. At one level it might be the ability of a craftsman to wire a house successfully – a purely practical skill, but at a higher level it might include the ability to understand the theory that lies behind the wiring. The standard of competence is not stable but depends on the judgement of other professionals. It also has a moral dimension, for competent practitioners are seen as having responsibility for their work and they can be considered accountable for their work. This enables them to be praised for good work or blamed for bad work. It therefore can be associated with quality assurance and the use of standards and assessment against standards.

It implies something more than reaching a standard and then forgetting about it, for it embraces an idea of professional ideology that includes the idea of lifelong competency to maintain levels of excellence in one's practice. A professional then has a duty to maintain his or her own competence at a high level by careful practice and by keeping up to date with developments in the profession. It is sometimes thought that the notion of competence should be related to technicians rather than autonomous professionals, and that teachers are also being looked at in this way rather than as autonomous professionals (Johnson, 1983).

The idea of capability has become associated with the concept of the autonomous professional. It is often considered the goal that students in higher education should be encouraged or led to achieve. It makes use of the liberal notion of autonomy and therefore of the development of the self-directed learner, but it remains very much a notion of a highly competent professional manager, who can eventually and at a very high level make important decisions in the interests of his or her employer.

It includes the notion of being able to stand on one's own feet and make decisions, being self-starting, being a self-directed learner, having commitment to what one is doing, being prepared to take responsibility, being able to work at an excellent standard, and setting very high standards for oneself. The notion takes on board the Kantian idea of being a self-legis-lator, and therefore of having a duty to the moral law but under a commercial guise – business ethics unlike pure ethics is concerned with reciprocation or mutual self-interest.

A contrast is often made between the capable independent person and the incapable dependent person (Burgess, 1986). For instance, in the sphere of knowledge and skills, the independent capable person is self-motivated, the skills and knowledge needed are negotiated with the teacher, and are integrated together so that they become coherent, and as they have been properly understood they can be adapted to new situations and the knowledge and skills can be extended. The incapable dependent person acquires received opinion determined by others, the knowledge and skills are fragmented and therefore cannot be adapted, and he or she is told how to do things. They also have contrasting attitudes. The capable independent person is committed, self-updating and exhibits professional integrity, honesty and an ability to innovate. The incapable dependent person has no commitment, does not update unless told to, and will not accept responsibility for his or her actions.

We can wonder that if a capable independent person is produced within the professional context, how far should he or she be autonomous professionally? Does the notion include overriding the firm's interests for the common good? Or having the impartiality to blow the whistle on transgressors of the legal and moral code? The questions raise the possibility of a conflict of interests between one's duty as a citizen to society and one's duty to one's firm or profession. It can only be overcome if the culture of the employing organization includes the value of the public good within its own culture and where it is an important component of the learning framework within that organization.

The discussion has indicated that the traditional distinction between training and education (Peters, 1972) is now out of date. The reason for this is that modern industry and commerce now need an adaptable intelligent workforce, and motivated independent managers who can lead firms and professions in a highly competitive environment. It also has another aspect, for it wants people who are motivated and committed. The commitment, in part, may be to an economic lifestyle, but in order to be really successful it needs to be a way of life that gives self-fulfilment, and a self-fulfilment that is gained through work. The moral dimension of capitalism has come full circle. In the 19th century Karl Marx criticized capitalism for alienating men and women from their labour, for preventing self-fulfilment through work. Marx's future Utopia would get rid of the alienation and return humankind to its true relationship with work. The capitalism of the millennium now proposes to do the same.

The learning society of future commerce and industry also has a political aspect. The new workforce demands respect and some say in the development of work. It is a potential democratic force that expects to be taken into account and listened to. The learning organizations of commerce and industry have the potential for improving efficiency and motivating the organizations to greater economic progress for the sake of themselves and society.

Democracy/participation/citizenship model

The notion of the autonomous individual and of the self-directed learner has important political connotations, for it is part of the ideology of liberal democracies. It postulates a person who can and is willing to participate in political action and decision making. Indeed, education for citizenship is very much part of the concept of lifelong learning and therefore of the learning society. It can be seen as a development of liberal ideology with the notion of autonomous individuals who are moral agents, and should be respected as such. It is also anti-paternalistic, as people have the ability to plan and make decisions about their own lives, and therefore need not be treated as children. It has another feature: it provides principles to limit the authority and power of the state. As far as possible the state should not interfere in the lives of individuals; as J S Mill argued, it should not be paternalistic or enforce public morals. It is interesting to note that Mill's democratic society (Mill, 1954) was based on a picture of the academic community searching after the truth (Brownhill and Smart, 1989), and also postulated that participation in the political process had an educational function in that it showed people how to be politically active and thereby learn from their activity. Mill also argued that a free society would bring about greater utilitarian benefits not only for the individual but for society as well – a position later taken up and recently expressed in the pragmatic liberalism of von Hayek (1960).

In the previous section we saw how the development of learning organizations in commerce and industry led to their democratization, and therefore an internal structural force within the economy. This raises the question of how they are to be brought into the wider political arena. Traditionally workers and employer organizations were seen as interest groups that could put pressure on governments to take into account their interests. But there were other proposals, for instance, the corporatism of Moseley and the fascists, with similar proposals from Macmillan on the Conservative side and, indeed, even the Fabian Society represented in the writings of Sir Julian Huxley. Of course, because of the corporatism of the Nazis and fascists, these suggestions appear to be non-starters, but, nevertheless, a new solution seems to be required to meet the political pretensions of the newly democratic forces expressed in the learning organizations of commerce and industry.

This analysis has shown how all the three models are related to neo-liberal ideas. Hutchins' model is in the liberal education tradition, putting stress on the aim of education and its relationship to the development of a certain type of person achieving self-fulfilment within the traditional parameters of cultural values. The idea simply extends the values of liberal education to lifelong learning and the learning society. The futurological/technological model, developed by Husén, can be seen as denying the distinction between education and training developed by liberal educationalists, but more importantly, it takes over, into the world of commerce and industry, notions about individual autonomy, decision making and self-fulfilment through work in the process of lifelong learning. The democratic/participation/citizenship model of Boshier returns to the basis of liberal ideas, and their belief in respect for persons, who should be listened to and taken into account in any policy decisions. The learning society becomes very much like J S Mill's idea of a liberal society.

References

Benn, S I (1976) 'Freedom, autonomy and the concept of a person', *Proceedings of the Aristotelian Society*, 11 Jan, pp 109–30.

Boshier, R (ed) (1980) *Towards a Learning Society: New Zealand adult education in transition,* Learning Press, Vancouver

Brownhill, R J and Smart, P B (1989) *Political Education,* Routledge, London

Burgess, T (ed) (1986) *Education for Capability,* NFER-Nelson, Windsor

Coffield, F (1997) 'Can the UK become a learning society?', The Fourth Annual Education Lecture, Kings College School of Education, London

Easterby-Smith, M, Araujo, L and Burgoyne, I (eds) (1999) *Organizational Learning and the Learning Organization: Developments in theory and practice,* Sage, London

Hayek, F A von (1960) *The Constitution of Liberty,* Macmillan, Basingstoke

Hirst, P (1974) *Knowledge and the Curriculum,* Routledge and Kegan Paul, London

Husén, T (1974) *The Learning Society,* Methuen, London

Husén, T (1986) *The Learning Society Revisited,* Pergamon Press, Oxford

Hutchins, R M (1968) *The Learning Society,* Penguin, Harmondsworth

Johnson, R (1983) 'The Manpower Service model of education', *Cambridge Journal of Education*, **13**, 2

Mill, J S (1954) *Utilitarianism, Liberty, Representative Government,* Dent, London

Oakeshott, M (1933) *Experience and its Modes,* Cambridge University Press, Cambridge

Oliver, P (ed) (1999) *Lifelong and Continuing Education: What is a learning society?,* Ashgate Publications, Aldershot

Paton, H (1961) *The Moral Law,* Hutchinson, London

Peters, R S (1972) 'Education and the educated man', in R F Dearden, P H Hirst and R S Peters, *Education and the Development of Reason,* Routledge and Kegan Paul, London

Ranson, S (1994) *Towards the Learning Society,* Cassell, London

Scheffler, I (1967) 'Philosophical models of teaching', in ed R S Peters, *The Concept of Education,* Routledge and Kegan Paul, London

United Nations Educational, Scientific and Cultural Organization (1972) *Learning to Be: The world of education today and tomorrow,* the Faure Report, UNESCO, Paris

Young, M, Spours, K, Howieson, C and Raffe, D (1997) 'Unifying academic and vocational learning and the idea of a learning society', *The Journal of Education Policy,* **12** (6), 527–37

Chapter 6

Lifelong Learning

Bob Brownhill

In this chapter lifelong learning is examined from a philosophical perspective. The first part looks at the distinction between lifelong learning and education, arguing that although the distinction is not completely clearcut, it does help in an understanding of governmental policy. The second part examines the aim of lifelong learning, and a distinction between the authentic and inauthentic person. The third part looks at how relativism challenges the very basis of the normative concepts that lie at the heart of different versions of the learning society, and therefore of the process of lifelong learning. The fourth part looks at the 'knowledge explosion' and the development of the consumer society, and its influence on lifelong learning. The final part raises the question of whether the University of the Third Age is a radical departure in the development of the learning society or whether it can be considered in a more traditional way.

Lifelong learning and education

It is often the case that 'lifelong learning' and 'lifelong education' are used interchangeably. This can be confusing, for we are really bound to practise lifelong learning as we go through the experiences of life. Education on the other hand can be associated with our experience of institutional formal education at school and beyond. Langford (1985) actually associates the concept of education with the process that goes on at institutions until we leave school. He has the notion that we can complete our education and then, of course, learn other things, but he does not see the things we do after school as part of the process of education. Jarvis (1998) follows this line of

thought and extends it, pointing out that the state can provide further institutionalized opportunities for learning beyond the school, and in the
modern world opportunities for learning can be provided on a formal basis
by commercial and industrial institutions, which are keen to develop the
specific skills of their employees for the workplace. He states, 'Education is a
public phenomenon and provides public recognition for the learning that it
provides'(Jarvis, 1998: 60).

This notion of public recognition is important, for it is now possible to
bring learning that was previously considered informal within the educational framework. Currently, relevant but informal learning of knowledge
and skills can be used as a basis for claiming credits both for entering educational institutions and for gaining their nationally recognized qualifications.
This development provides a challenge to the distinction between education
and learning, since both job-specific and leisure-time learning can be used as
a basis for accreditation. Of course, the reason for this development is a
governmental desire to extend educational opportunities by getting people
to reflect on the knowledge and skills they have acquired in order to gain
greater recognition for them in their workplace, a recognition which should
not only benefit themselves but also their employer and society. Generally,
however, it can be argued that this is related to the reflective society (Jarvis,
1998) and the emphasis education now has on vocationalism, but the process
can also be made use of for personal self-fulfilment, which also carries the
political dimension of fulfilled, happy citizens.

Self-education can also be lifelong, but it has connotations of consciously
setting out goals to be achieved rather than a post hoc recognition of the
educational potential of one's previous random learning. There does seem to
be a distinction between learning and education, but it is now possible to
bring most learning within the educational framework with appropriate
advice and instruction from the institutions that provide for the accreditation of prior (experiential) learning. The learning goes through an
institutional process and is transformed into educational qualifications. It
can also be argued that whereas learning by its very nature is essentially
private and individualistic, education has a public dimension, and by getting
learning recognized by a public institution a person moves into the public
world. Importantly a challenge is also made to the distinction between
leisure learning, learning for one's own pleasure, and 'real' learning, which is
seen to be related to learning that is useful for one's job. This is important as
government funding tends to go to that which is seen as useful to the
economy.

This in itself brings out certain features of the learning society, some of
which were mentioned in the last chapter. The concept of the learning
society also has a futuristic, utopian dimension, in one sense, related to the

private sphere of self-reflection, which can provide a consideration of one's fundamental values and therefore of one's very identity. It is therefore concerned with change, with changing one's perception of oneself, and thereby altering one's situation in society. In this sense it might have a positive dimension because it is concerned with action – to reflect on oneself and to move beyond a superficial examination of what one says are one's values to an examination of what one actually does and, subsequently, to a consideration of one's fundamental values. It can reveal one's 'real' self and provide the necessary basis for actual autonomy, as one recognizes why one makes certain choices rather than others and on what basis they are made. It also gives an opportunity to plan for self-fulfilment.

However, it can be argued that it is impossible to reveal one's fundamental values as they are too deeply embedded in the tacit dimension (Polanyi, 1958). Yet if this is the case we can never be said to act completely rationally or autonomously. The idea that we can is in itself a neo-Kantian, liberal utopian dream or illusion. Likewise in the public sphere, we can never achieve the ideal of a completely rational learning society, as this again requires rational autonomous individuals, or the Marxian mirage of self-fulfilment in one's work, or the capitalist one for that matter! Indeed, this hope has a religious or metaphysical dimension as recognized by some educators (Jarvis and Walters, 1993), and is an educational dream. Yet it has another aspect and this is of a developing market aspect of consumer society (Jarvis, 1998). This is related to the non-idealistic selfish individualism mentioned in the section on relativism below.

Learning and becoming a person

Human beings are not born as persons, for they can be seen as being in a process of becoming. The learning experiences they gain and develop can be seen as part of a process that is not only part of the development of their own self-identity, but also incorporates their identity as social beings. It is a process that takes place throughout life. As Aristotle pointed out, becoming implies not only an essential nature but also a potential to realize an essential nature (Ackrill, 1981). We become what we are by experiencing the culture in which we exist by interacting with others, and by reflecting on those experiences and interactions. Without this socio-cultural milieu we could not exist as persons. Yet we know that the social world is fragmented, consisting of differences in wealth, class, race, gender, etc, and that our experiences differ. The self-identity we may develop will be greatly influenced by our circumstances. In some sense then, we have a tendency to reproduce the same sort of people and the same values and social milieu. Our own world has certain features which are particular to our technological development, for instance, mass production and our domination by bureaucracies, in relation not only to the state but to our employers as well. A feature of both modern industry and bureaucracy is its tendency to standardize and reproduce clone-like people. These features are related to the learning process, for in order to become clone-like we have to accept received opinion and be unreflective about our experiences (Jarvis, 1998).

Authenticity

Questions arise then as to how we can be true to our essential nature and what in fact is this essential nature? Cooper (1983), in examining the work of Nietzsche, identifies two possible models for authenticity and calls them the Polonian and the Dadaist models. The Polonian model is based on his remark to his son, 'To thine own self be true.' The Dadaist claims that the only requirement for authenticity is that a person's actions and commitments should arise from spontaneous choices. Cooper suggests that both points of view arise out of a concern for oneself. The first implies that human essence precedes existence, so people should lead their lives in accordance with their essential nature, while the second emphasizes the need for people to be free to lead free lives and therefore make their own decisions, so that they are able to distinguish themselves from others. In both cases, inauthenticity is shown when the self is inhibited in expressing itself either by not acting in accordance with its essence or in not accepting what it has become.

Of course, an individual is not isolated, for he or she comes into relationships with other persons. Buber (1959) calls this the 'I-Thou' relationship, where an individual establishes a living relationship with others. It is within this relationship that the human values of truth, justice, love, etc exist, and without it they cannot exist. Human interaction is a characteristic of living in society, and therefore authenticity can only be gained by acting in the world. However, it is the act of relationship that is important, as a true authenticity recognizes and respects other people's autonomy, and by this respect helps their autonomy to develop. A few philosophers (Rogers, 1961) argue that being and becoming are the most important features in human life (Jarvis, 1992), and that human learning is its vehicle.

As in political philosophy there remains a tension between autonomy and community, but numerous philosophers (Taylor, 1989) attempt to surmount the conflict by arguing that the greatest degree of autonomy can be achieved in the right community: a community that allows individuals to express their essence. In the previous chapter we saw how the liberal philosophers of education saw its aim as developing what R S Peters (1972) called the 'educated person' and, indeed, this seems to be the ultimate aim of lifelong learning as well. The aim of education and learning, in this sense, is transformational, developing an individual's capacity to be a rational autonomous person, who respects others, and, in the main, this is achieved by the process of learning and self-reflection on that learning. It also has an organizational element for it can only be achieved in a learning society, where individual initiative is recognized and likewise one's contribution to the society also becomes part of the general achievement of society. It is therefore a feature of the just society, where everyone's achievements and successes are respected and acknowledged (Lucas, 1980).

In the previous chapter we saw how the notion of the rational autonomous person, working within a learning organization has also become part of the theory of learning in the workplace. A modern theory of learning goes well beyond initial schooling – to learning in the workplace, learning from the cradle to the grave, and also to future generations.

Learning, education and relativism

A feature of extreme moral relativism is that it endangers the whole project of ethical discourse and all our value concepts, which we have seen in theories of both learning and education. It is argued that in contemporary society shared values have broken down, and because of this it is no longer possible to write of society speaking with one voice (McIntyre, 1984). We no longer speak one moral language, but several. Indeed, the primary language we speak and through which we express an understanding of ourselves is now highly individualistic, and because of that it is no longer suited to talk about the public interest or of the common good. Traditional moral language has lost its meaning. We have moved on: the language has remained the same but the context of shared beliefs and values in which it was used has passed. The language that was meaningful to an older generation is no longer meaningful to a younger one. It is simply used to express emotion, disguise intention, manipulate people and support double standards (McIntyre, 1984).

If the argument is accepted, it means that in public life traditional concepts and justifications can be used but will not be followed. The scandals over public sleaze in the last decade are an example of this. For example, during the greater part of the last century there was an accepted principle that a minister in the government was ultimately responsible for what went on in his department, but at present lip-service is paid to the principle and doctrine of ministerial responsibility and accountability but no ministerial resignations follow major mistakes and a scapegoat is found lower down the chain of authority. Yet, this is only a reflection of what is now happening in the private sphere, where the language of moral autonomy is often used to cover the pursuit of self-interest with no attempt at universal application. The decisions made are entirely subjective and are only ostensibly moral. Where there was once a coherent discourse now there is just the assertion of arbitrary wills hidden behind moral language. We can see how such an argument challenges the very basis of the discourse about the aims of education and learning, but also leads to an argument that we just exist as we are and that, therefore, there is no proper distinction between the essence and existence of a person, or the authentic person and the inauthentic. Indeed, it really argues that the very notion of a person is an unobtainable idea and that persons, in the Kantian or Peters' sense, do not exist since their existence depends on a moral base.

McIntyre allows that, in principle, it would be possible to have a rational moral discourse, but the historical situation we are now in prevents it from actually happening. We now speak too many moral languages, share too few common assumptions and goals and become split apart by the widest divides. Since the 1930s many moral philosophers have argued that in spite of the use of moral, other-regarding language (Ayer, 1936), we are, in fact, merely pushing our personal preferences and asserting our own feelings. No wonder there can be no agreement on fundamental moral issues. These arguments are stating that in fact there is no real morality. The language of morality is simply used to cover up the assertion of individual emotions and preferences. McIntyre's argument is really a reiteration of the emotive reaction theories of the 1930s.

This postmodern argument also has an educational dimension. Educational points of view are value-based, often reflecting our own moral goals for society, but if these views have no moral base and reflect our own subjectivity, and a recognition that there is no truth as such, then all education can be classed as a type of indoctrination, where we are not educating students for their own ends but using them to further our own prejudices and desires. Indeed, in the last chapter we saw how the three models of the learning society were based on different normative points of view; relativism would argue that they exhibit the mere prejudices of their authors. Each interpretation is as valid as the next one, so for example Kant's views on freedom and autonomy were just the passing fantasies of an obscure German philosopher, and Richard Peters' 'educated man' merely reflected his own whim. Evidence and reasoning under the doctrine of relativism just become rhetoric, part of the art of persuasion. This doctrine would ultimately destroy all our ideals about religion, morality, politics and education, arguing that they are virtually meaningless with no objectivity.

The argument can be put in a different way – there is morality but not a general coherent morality. In a pluralistic society it is a situation where the competing moral standpoints of different groups meet in conflict. However, this is aggravated by the fact that even these standpoints are breaking down as the differing groups come into conflict with others and begin to realize that their own beliefs do not have universal approval. The recognition of different groups may lead to tolerance, but relativism breaks down the beliefs and destroys the confidence of the competing groups and their former certainty. The collapse of the coherent beliefs of the groups in turn leads to the assertion and pursuit of individual preferences and feelings, and, consequently, so does lifelong learning.

The consumer society as a learning society

Consumerism can be dated back to the late 18th century (Campbell, 1987). Campbell argues that it can be traced back to the Romantic period when pleasure became the means of assessing the truth and beauty that our creative imagination had revealed. A longing to enjoy these creations became the basis for obtaining new phenomena and was the basis for the beginnings of consumerism. Clearly there can be no market in goods without a demand, and demand arises because people desire to obtain something. However, this desire can come from two sources: either a person's own volition or a creation of this volition from the outside. This created the puffer or advertiser whose function was to boost the demand for a product by stimulating personal desires. Learning about new plays and poetry became fun and part of European culture, but the literary magazines where aimed at an elite interested in high culture. It was only as the opportunity to become educated improved during the 19th century, with the development of popular magazines and newspapers, that advertising could really take off and inveigle new consumers into the market place. Many of the advertisements were merely informative, offering consumers a useful service, but gradually the practice and art of puffery was taken over from the theatre and became general practice, and goods of any quality could be sold.

Education had a difficult time. Many people had unfortunate experiences of the strict discipline and punishments of the Victorian teachers, which were often continued with later generations well into the 20th century. The practice and doctrine of 'spare the rod and spoil the child' was only abandoned in state schools in England in the second half of the 20th century. The methods of selection for advanced education meant that the vast majority of children were branded as failures, and the likelihood of any worthwhile career had to be abandoned. All this was in spite of the fact that from early in the 19th century education was seen as the key to social and political advancement for the working class. Paradoxically, the Butler Education Act of 1944 (Sturt, 1967), for unforeseen social reasons, reinforced class divisions and the traditional image of education for the select few. In order to sell education, learning had to be seen as fun. I well remember attending a University of London extra-mural department training course for new tutors in the late 1960s at their Westonbirt Summer School, where a lecturer gave a riveting and theatrical performance; my supervisor stated: 'That's how you should do it, keep 'em happy.' In the extra-mural section at the University of Surrey we also spent much time sorting out titles for courses so they would appear to be fun and attractive to potential students. In fact it was probably the creation of the Open University in the UK that finally separated learning from education, for students could follow their own interests in the comfort of their home, watching television or listening to the radio and learning at their own pace, with the added advantage of being able to get recognized qualifications if they became committed and enthusiastic enough. It also had the advantage of moving adults out of any setting that could remind them of school and into the consumer society (Jarvis, 1998).

The rapid development of information technology has made a vast range of knowledge accessible, so that all aspects of knowledge are available to a person who wishes to learn and there is a great opportunity for the self-directed learner. It is noticeable how new undergraduates give many references to work on the World Wide Web, and now it has become almost mandatory for educational institutions, educational consultants, publishers and related businesses to have their own Website for advertising and offering their online services. At the same time there is a great opportunity for the producers of learning materials, who have become far wider than traditional educational institutions, themselves just another player in a booming educational market. It is also clear that access to information technology is necessary for today's consumers, and a computer and access to the World Wide Web is an essential status symbol for anyone with pretensions to improving their lot. The desire to satisfy one's wants is increasingly pulling people into the worldwide learning market.

Beyond education: the University of the Third Age

At the beginning of this chapter a distinction was made between education and learning, and it was argued that education had an institutional aspect that distinguished it from learning. The case of the University of the Third Age (U3A) is an interesting phenomenon. Is it a form of institutionalized learning and therefore part of education, or is it a self-organized leisure activity that is concerned with learning? It is certainly the case that its appeal is to older people who have in general retired from their occupations and therefore do not fall within the government's vocational orientation.

Education, of course, is also related to power and the control functions of governments, and no conscious attempt has been made to bring this group within this power framework. It could be argued that this is because the discipline of their former education and working life have so much inculcated the virtues of submission to authority and a non-critical stance to government policy that formal control is no longer necessary. In her thesis on the function of learning in later life, Noble (1993) looked at attitudes to learning in a branch of the U3A. She quoted one of her interviewees, who in answering the question 'What is the function of your learning?' said, 'In short – it does you good!' Merriam and Caffarella (1991) argue that this sentiment could be the universal view of the function of learning, since most educators believe in the goodness of continued learning.

Mezirow (1990) has insisted that learning is a basic human right. The Carnegie inquiry into the Third Age reported that when we are older, personal development can once again become a central concern (Schuller and Bostyn, 1992). Noble argues that by taking part in meetings and setting up organizations of the third age, participants are declaring their interest in a future for this age group and the recognition of the value of their continuing learning. Noble (1993: 101) concludes:

> In the past older people may have been marginalized, or segregated within society. We need to encourage groups like the U3A to enable older people to claim learning opportunities for themselves, not to see retirement as the beginning of the end, a final gloomy chapter in their lives.

Another argument is put beyond the desire for self-development. An interviewee from the U3A considered the value of learning when we are older in health and economic terms:

> You are going to get far less illness and cost the state a lot less money, which would probably be far better spent on adult and old age education and facilities... I think it would pay society to put money into it – it keeps older people healthy if they are active. (Noble, 1993: 104)

It does seem that the U3A can be seen as a learning organization clearly separate from government control, but, nevertheless, there does seem a residual desire to gain access to governmental resources and become another branch of the governmental educational provision.

Conclusion

This chapter has provided a wide survey and analysis of issues in lifelong learning. It indicated how lifelong learning is essentially related to a new liberal notion of self-fulfilment. Indeed, it seems to be more neo-Kantian than that, for it is concerned with achieving self-fulfilment through one's own efforts – an ideal to be sought after and achieved rather than being part of one's essential nature. It seems the notion of human essence and one's real authenticity are misnomers, for we do not reveal them like a pair of kidneys when we are cut open. They are not hidden somewhere inside us, but are an ideal of humanity that needs to be sought after, and possibly achieved through our own efforts. In this sense lifelong learning is a process of discovery, and it is also why we need to have some beliefs in the journey, and therefore attempt to refute relativism. The new consumer society, on the whole, seems advantageous for the autonomous self-directed learner, offering many new resources for him or her to complete the task.

The final section on the University of the Third Age is slightly ambivalent, for it recognizes the initiative to carry lifelong learning into old age, but also a vague longing to move from personal autonomy to a notion of state control and direction. Although, probably reflecting the doubts of old age, 'Should one really rely on oneself or look to the certainties of social provision?' Or, perhaps more positively, 'If there are resources available from the government, then, it is sensible and legitimate to put in a claim for them.'

References

Ackrill, J L (1981) *Aristotle the Philosopher,* Oxford University Press, Oxford

Ayer, A J (1936) *Language, Truth and Logic,* Gollancz, London

Buber, M (1959) *I and Thou,* Clarke, Edinburgh

Campbell, C (1987) *The Romantic Ethic and the Spirit of Modern Consumerism*, Blackwell, Oxford

Cooper, D (1983) *Authenticity and Learning: Nietzsche's educational philosophy*, Routledge and Kegan Paul, London

Jarvis, P (1992) *Paradoxes of Learning,* Jossey-Bass, San Francisco, CA

Jarvis, P (1998) 'Paradoxes of the learning society', in eds J Holford, P Jarvis and C Griffin, *International Perspectives on Lifelong Learning,* Kogan Page, London

Jarvis, P and Walters, N (eds) (1993) *Adult Education and Theological Interpretations,* Kreiger, Malabar, FL

Langford, G (1985) *Education, Persons and Society,* Macmillan, Basingstoke

Lucas, J (1980) *On Justice,* Clarendon Press, Oxford

McIntyre, A (1984) *After Virtue,* University of Notre Dame Press, Notre Dame, IN

Merriam, S B and Caffarella, R S (1991) *Learning in Adulthood: A comprehensive guide,* Jossey-Bass, San Francisco

Mezirow, J (1990) *Fostering Critical Reflection in Adulthood,* Jossey-Bass, San Francisco

Noble, L (1993) 'The Function of Learning in Later Life', unpublished MSc, University of Surrey

Peters, R S (1972) 'Education and the educated man', in eds R F Dearden, P H Hirst and R S Peters, *Education and the Development of Reason,* Routledge and Kegan Paul, London

Polanyi, M (1958) *Personal Knowledge,* Routledge and Kegan Paul, London

Rogers, C R (1961) *On Becoming a Person,* Constable, London
Schuller, T and Bostyn, A M (1992) *Learning, Education and Training in the Third Age,* Research Paper, No 3, Carnegie United Kingdom Trust, Dunfermline
Sturt, M (1967) *The Education of the People,* Routledge and Kegan Paul, London
Taylor, C (1989) *Sources of the Self,* Cambridge University Press, Cambridge

PART THREE

THE MECHANICS OF THE LEARNING SOCIETY

Chapter 7

Paying for the age of learning

Stephen McNair

The economics of lifelong learning

Like all good things, learning has to be paid for. Even where the learning is informal and there is no exchange of money, the learner is choosing to invest time and energy that he or she could have spent in other ways. Most learning, however, calls for much more elaborate and complex financial equations.

This chapter is concerned with how lifelong learning (primarily in the post-initial phase) can be paid for. It argues that understanding the problem is difficult, because the field is complex, and recognition that post-initial education and training can and should be seen as a coherent body of activity for policy-making purposes is relatively recent. It outlines what has to be paid for, and the need to balance the financial burden between learners, employers and the state. It also explores the way in which markets have begun to be used to allocate resources, and some of the other proposals for reform that have been considered in recent years. It does not describe in detail the particular funding systems of current institutions, since such systems are in constant change and development.

For any economic good there is a natural price, at which the benefits to the customer are perceived to match the effort required to raise the money. If the price is too high, resources are wasted and the benefits are disappointing. If it is too low, the expected benefits will not be achieved. If a firm or country invests too little in education and training, its skill and knowledge base declines and it becomes uncompetitive in a global marketplace. If it invests too much, or in the wrong things, the resources are wasted. As a result, governments are always reviewing judgements on what is being paid, for what, by whom and with what outcomes. The same principles apply where individuals invest in their learning: will spending this money benefit me, economically or in some other way, and is the price worth the outcomes?

Background – understanding the system

Understanding the funding of lifelong learning is not easy. After the end of compulsory schooling, learners are found in many places, funded in different ways and for different reasons, by themselves, their employers or the state. Furthermore, existing systems for providing programmes have not grown up in response to a coordinated plan: rather they are the result of a series of quite separate historical developments, modified, improved and compromised over for decades.

During the 1970s, reflecting the growing policy interest in lifelong learning, both the Council of Europe (Simpson, 1973) and the Organization for Economic Development and Cooperation attempted to give some shape to the disorganized body of data. However, the OECD (1977) commented that:

> Before national policies for the promotion of adult education can be formu-
> lated with any precision, it is obvious that detailed information is required
> about the present scale of expenditure and the means employed for financing
> programmes. [p 4]
>
> One explanation for the equivocal position of adult education is that the
> public authorities are poorly informed about its real nature and scope and do
> not have the data, whether statistical or not, necessary for the formulation of
> practical policies for expansion. [p 6]

Subsequently, the Advisory Council for Adult and Continuing Education (ACACE, 1982), the Manpower Services Commission (MSC, 1981) and its successor, the Training Agency (DfEE, 1989) tried to understand the shape and size of the overall education and training market in the UK. However, the situation remains complex (see Smith and Spurling, 1999, for one of the clearest accounts of the funding flows in lifelong learning). We have a great range of suppliers, including public and private providers of courses and support systems, organized through the higher, further and adult education sectors, with distinct systems for work-related and community-based learning. Each has its own ways of collecting and publishing (or not publishing), financial information and measuring activity. Furthermore, the question of what is being counted is also problematic, since much learning takes place in informal ways, outside the reach of agencies that identify themselves as 'education' or 'training', where the definition of 'learning' is as unclear as the measurement of spending.

The demand side is also complex. Because, until recently, post-initial learning existed as a marginal activity of organizations and institutions (universities, further education colleges, local education authorities and individual firms) whose main function was elsewhere, there has been a plethora of different systems, many not clearly planned or managed, for channelling money and for accounting for it. Furthermore, there has been a constantly evolving pattern of special initiatives, from government and others, designed to address particular economic or social issues. Thus a major flow of funds may be injected by the DfEE to address a shortage of teachers, or to improve literacy levels by encouraging reading in the family. Other government departments may inject resources for quite different reasons: the DTI to raise skills levels in a particular occupation, or the Department of Health to improve public understanding of how to avoid heart disease. The European Union adds a range of diverse funding programmes with objectives like overcoming social exclusion, encouraging European mobility, or addressing particular regional or sectoral economic problems. Often such initiatives are developed independently, creating overlaps and inconsistencies in funding which make tracing what is spent, on what and on what terms, extremely difficult.

A large proportion of formal learning happens outside public sector institutions, and here it is especially difficult to gather reliable information. We have private companies whose main business is selling education or training; private sector organizations which provide training (on and off the job) to support their main business; voluntary agencies (like the Workers Educational Association) whose main function is education; and others which train their volunteers or members to provide services to clients or members. None of these agencies necessarily feels the need to describe themselves as 'educational', nor do they necessarily see any need to gather and publish data on their expenditure on learning. Indeed, for those whose commercial business is education or training, such information may be commercially sensitive, and thus deliberately kept secret.

It will never be possible, therefore, to have a comprehensive and accurate picture of what is spent on lifelong learning, where and with what results. Nevertheless, government needs to try to understand the whole system, since it can choose to influence what is made available, how and to whom, not only by funding public institutions but by regulating the private sector through legislation, tax incentives, quality standards or formal recognition.

What is to be paid for and who benefits?

In any education or training system money is needed for a variety of purposes. It is necessary to pay for teachers, materials production and distribution, classrooms and workshops, for technology to underpin delivery and, in the case of much work-related learning, for the release and replacement of staff. The scale and balance of the expenditure varies considerably between formal, informal and non-formal modes of learning. Since it is easier to define funding flows for the more formal kinds of learning, the others often tend to be neglected. However, one must remember that the less formal modes of learning are both large in volume and significant in impact. It is also important to recognize the infrastructure costs of supporting development, innovation and new modes of delivery, like the recent growth of independent local learning centres.

The simplest approach to public funding, which one might describe as the integrated model, was the norm in the UK for universities and adult education until the early 1990s. Here, all of the activities were carried out by a single kind of public sector institution, with each university designing its own programmes, teaching them, assessing the learners and awarding qualifications. The state funded this through a simple block grant to the university, based on student numbers, with some adjustment to reflect the fact that some courses have higher costs (for laboratories, workshops, support of students on placements, etc). The state also paid maintenance grants to support living costs for those students who studied full time (but not part time).

This integrated model was never universal across post-school learning in the UK, and has been challenged from two directions. First, a variety of pressures have broken up the integration of functions, leading to the emergence of new specialist agencies for assessment, materials production or provision of infrastructure. Secondly, the rationale for funding provision through institutions rather than learners has also been challenged on ideological and practical grounds.

In further education the functions had always been partially disaggregated, particularly in relation to assessment and awarding, reflecting the role of FE in preparing people for particular kinds of employment. While the FE college is usually responsible for designing and teaching most of its programmes, the assessment requirements are normally set and managed by external bodies like the City & Guilds of London Institute (CGLI). During the 1980s, government intervened to make this system more transparent and more responsive to employers' needs by developing a national system for defining and assessing occupational standards across the whole workforce through National Vocational Qualifications. Increasingly, these qualifications were used as a measure of the performance of educational institutions, and a tool for funding, allocating resources on the basis of NVQs achieved ('outcome-based funding'), rather than courses run.

A second area where the integrated model has come under challenge is from the expansion of open and distance learning forms of education and the rise of ICT-based programmes. New modes of learning distribute costs differently, and some elements are much more expensive. Resource-based and open learning approaches typically spend much more of their costs on initial development (including the design and publication of materials and setting up distribution systems), and less on teaching once they have begun to recruit (since staff are delivering a more standardized package of services). As a result they can benefit from large economies of scale, but the start-up costs are beyond the capacity of most traditional providers. The cost of developing a single online degree programme has been estimated at £1 million (CVCP, 2000) and only the Open University (which has major economies of scale as a very large open learning provider) or a consortium of institutions can seriously contemplate such a level of investment.

One result of this has been the rise of more complex patterns of partnership to develop and deliver programmes. Some FE and HE institutions have chosen to go into partnership with ICT suppliers, who are better equipped to design and manage complex ICT infrastructures. Some universities, for example have contracted out the running of their ICT systems to commercial ICT companies, including in some cases the provision of hardware and software, maintenance, staff and student support and the development of new teaching and administrative systems. This frees academic staff to concentrate on their core functions. Providers are also increasingly using commercially developed resources (authoring systems and interactive learning tools and packages) to support their development activity, where once they would write their own software for such purposes.

Another area where change has happened is in access to libraries and databases. Where traditionally education providers provided library services, with access to journals, books and other materials for their own students, the emergence of online services has changed the balance. Publishers now provide online access to batteries of journals, providing learners in subscribing institutions, or those who wish to subscribe privately, with immediate online access to a vast range of material not previously easy to obtain. Most recently, the Internet has transformed access to information. Its ability to provide direct access to information online, bypassing education and training institutions may, in time, change the economics of the formal providers.

Who should pay?

Because the general public's perception of 'education' is dominated by the universal experience of initial schooling, it is generally thought of as a 'free' service. In reality, of course, a 'free' education service is merely one paid for by the state from taxation. Governments constantly make choices about the relative value of different ways of investing taxpayers' money, and of regulating any private market that may exist. The state must decide how much to pay, and for what, and how to balance its contribution with those of employers and individual learners. As constraints on resources have met growing demand, this issue has been increasingly debated (Ball, 1992; Barr and Falkingham, 1993)

The simplest principle for funding any service is that the beneficiary should pay. At a theoretical level this is simple: each stakeholder – individual, employer and state – should pay for those kinds of education that benefit them directly. However, little, if any, learning is that simple, and the political implications of introducing 'rational' change may be prohibitive. Furthermore, some established kinds of education might actually produce no economic return. In 1992, Bennett demonstrated that some kinds of qualification produce no overall increase in lifetime earnings, and the extent of the gain often depended heavily on the learner's sex and parent's social class (Bennett *et al*, 1992).

During the 1980s government increasingly defined its role in funding post-school learning in terms of return to the economy through explicitly 'vocational' skills. Broadly, the state said, in creating the new FE sector through the Education Acts of 1988 and 1992, courses leading to recognized qualifications (assumed to produce benefits in economic productivity) would be paid for by the state, while others would not, and the 1992 Act applied a similar principle to HE.

However, at the end of the 20th century there were a number of signs that this crude distinction between 'vocational' and 'non-vocational' learning was being eroded in the minds of policy makers. As we move from a manufacturing to a service economy, the skills and knowledge which individuals require become more generic, and the boundaries between job-specific and personal education are eroded. While there is certainly a growing demand for job-specific training, and the development of the NVQ framework was an attempt to support this, the 'soft skills' of self-management, team-working, learning to learn, etc are rising in importance in the labour market. These are qualities that may be as well developed in 'non-vocational' programmes as in vocational ones. For example, the skills of 'learning to learn', which are critical to the individual's ability to remain employable in a rapidly changing labour market, can be acquired through courses in painting or German as well as through formal management education. Furthermore, there are good economic justifications for encouraging individuals to develop the full range of their talents and interests, since firms are constantly finding themselves moving into new and unexpected areas of business. When this happens a workforce of confident learners will be more adaptable than one of narrowly trained individuals.

Arguments of this kind were advanced in the 1980s when Ford pioneered the notion of the Employee Development Advisory Programme (Beattie, 1997), under which funds were made available for employees to study anything not directly related to their current employment. The benefits to the firm were seen as increased flexibility (with a wider skills base), more capable learners (since individuals had been encouraged to recognize and develop their learning skills in areas where they were already motivated), and a greater loyalty, bred from the sense that the firm cared about its employees as more than mere units of production. The result was a dramatic increase in the number of employees undertaking learning, many of whom had not previously engaged in any formal learning since school.

Learning also has social benefits beyond the crudely economic, and in the late 1990s the UK government recognized the importance of the 'non-economic' benefits of learning by creating a national research unit to study how engagement in learning impacts on health, crime, citizenship, family cohesion and parenting, and active ageing. This work, which relates to cohesion of the community and to the creation of cultural and social capital, argues that a healthy society and a healthy economy rest on networks of trust and mutual collaboration that are built on and supported by a range of kinds of education which do not have immediate economic benefit. An example is the extent to which engagement in formal learning in old age improves health outcomes for individuals, and reduces costs for public health and social services. Here education supports the individual but produces both individual and communal benefits.

The last decades of the 20th century saw a marked policy shift towards market-led models of funding in education and training, at least in the English-speaking world. However, in reality, it is extremely difficult for government to allow the market a free rein, for three major reasons. In economic terms, the pure market may not deliver efficient investment in training, with long-term consequences for competitiveness. In social and economic terms, the issue of ensuring that individuals are not excluded from the benefits of society by lack of access to education remains a policy concern, since the uneducated are not economically productive, and are thus an economic burden (and potentially socially disruptive) regardless of moral concerns. Furthermore, government is the customer for many kinds of education – the training of teachers, doctors and police, and cannot leave this to the vagaries of supply and demand. As a result government seeks to use its funding levers, directly by setting up schemes like Family Literacy, or indirectly by requiring Funding Councils to develop targeted programmes and initiatives like the Widening Participation funding initiatives in both FE and HE.

Another emerging need results from expanding life expectancy. Current policies were developed when retirement was a brief period after the completion of a working life, with an expectation of poor health and little educational demand. Life expectancy has now extended dramatically, and the question both of how to prepare people for this long period of physically and mentally active, but economically inactive, life has not yet been adequately addressed by policy makers. Whether education for this active retired population should be funded in the same way as the education of the economically active is an unresolved issue.

Alternative models, and managing change

The clear trend of public policy during the 1980s and 1990s was away from planning and towards market models for the allocation of resources, and this was strongly felt in education and training.

Traditionally, large areas of provision have been funded directly by government through institutions. Government paid the institution to provide a specified number of places, either in general or in specific areas, and the institution then sought to fill those places with willing students. In some cases government also subsidized providers in other ways to ensure that they remained active in the market. In the next largest area, work-related learning, the employer usually played the same role. It was only in a minority of areas that individuals paid their own costs, and therefore acted like consumers would in any other market.

In recent years it has been increasingly argued that this 'supply-led' approach is inefficient. As the labour market becomes more volatile and unpredictable the notion of government planning on a large scale becomes less defensible. Such mechanisms are inevitably slow to change, and liable to fail to recognize emerging trends and needs. This was the rationale for creating, in the late 1980s, the Training and Enterprise Councils. The 84 TECs were designed to be consortia of interests, led by local employers, which would coordinate the development of local education and training markets in response to employer and local economic needs. This development transferred much control of funding for work-related learning from central government to local groupings, but the model remained strongly supplier-led, with TECs developing working relationships with their key suppliers in the public and private sectors.

A much more radical notion extends the same principle of devolution of decision making beyond a local consortium of employers to the learners themselves. Here the state and the employer would make resources available to individuals to buy as consumers in an open education and training market. The same principle of devolving decisions as near as possible to those who have to live with their consequences applies, and the risks are still further spread. This is the basis of the proposals for Individual Learning Accounts (ILAs), described in a theoretical form by Smith and Spurling (1997), building on the experience of a range of pilot projects, including the Ford Employee Development Advisory Programme and the City of London's Learning Voucher scheme (Jarvis *et al*, 1997).

The proposal was that individuals would hold earmarked personal bank accounts that could be used to pay for learning in the open market. Money could be paid in by the individual, the employer and the state, and the state would subsidize this with tax relief on the account (provided the expenditure was on learning). Perhaps in time, most of the resources for education previously channelled through institutions would be placed in ILAs. The approach has a number of evident advantages. It encourages individual personal career planning and ownership of training plans, increasing responsible decision making and motivation to learn. It puts any risk involved in choices of what to study and how more on the individual, who must live with the outcome. It enables the employer or state to invest selectively in particular kinds of need or particular classes of individual (by paying larger sums into the accounts of those with particular needs, like low skills, or people from disadvantaged communities), and it encourages planning over a lifetime.

However, there are a number of evident problems. For individual learners to behave like effective customers there must be a well-developed market in education and training, where people can make informed choices between rival opportunities. However, since existing provision is dominated by public sector institutions, funded through and therefore responsive to central planning mechanisms, there is little experience or inclination to respond to individual demand (which is more complex and confusing than dealing with a few large clients). Furthermore, an effective market depends on informed consumers, and effective systems of guidance are not in place to inform learner choice. Neither are there well-understood ways of describing learning opportunities across public and private sectors, or of comparing qualifications. A further concern, as with student loans, is that those who already benefit most from education and training would take up opportunities disproportionately, with a skewing of public investment away from government's concern with the inclusion of the lowest skilled. This concern is reinforced by the evidence that people in lower socio-economic groups are less likely to value education and training, and are much more reluctant to incur debt in any form to pay for it.

Because of these anxieties, the scheme was introduced on a relatively small scale, managed through the TECs, with the state providing £150 to an individual who invested £25. Nevertheless, the government commitment to creating 1 million such accounts over a five-year period was a substantial investment in an experiment.

The ILA is a classic case of an initiative that is intellectually defensible in principle, and could have very great benefits in terms of creating a learning society, but faces major problems in implementation. It is impossible to test the theory without a major change in the workings of the whole system, moving to individual accounts most of the money that currently flows through national funding bodies to public sector institutions. This would be hugely destabilizing for the institutions, and it is likely that individuals would not, in the short term, actually spend the money. The private sector would take time to expand to meet the new market, while demand for public sector programmes would be likely to drop dramatically, as inexperienced purchasers failed to use their new funds. The market would shrink dramatically, and many good current providers would become bankrupt. However, without such a move, the public sector will continue to respond to the drivers from the national funding agencies, and the private sector will continue to concentrate on the more lucrative niche markets with particular employers. To make the major change requires an act of faith probably beyond the capacity of any government, and the first steps towards such a scheme were very tentative ones, using marginal money.

How to bring about change?

Smith and Spurling's (1999) description of the current funding systems for lifelong learning in the UK as 'chaotic and confusing' is, if anything, an understatement. Systems have grown incrementally, modified repeatedly by different political and administrative interventions, to encourage or discourage particular kinds of activity or kinds of learner, and to reduce public expenditure, but most major change is modified in response to political and public opinion. Rational decisions to produce a tidy, comprehensible and fair system can rarely be implemented, since almost always someone will be vociferously disadvantaged, and concessions to them then create new levels of complexity.

Furthermore, however much all the stakeholders might like a clear, fair and comprehensible system, in practice this is very difficult to achieve. Unless change is phased over a considerable period there is liable to be major disruption to systems. A classic case was the transfer of funding for FE from local education authorities to the Further Education Funding Council in 1992. The 80-plus LEAs had very different experience of managing FE, with some LEAs having a single college and others managing a dozen or more, and their levels of expertise and interest in the sector varied greatly. As a result the FEFC inherited over 80 separate funding systems, with widely varying levels of resourcing for similar provision. The Council was expected to harmonize and modernize this system, introducing a comprehensible and fair formula funding methodology. However, it was also expected to ensure that all the existing colleges continued to function effectively, since it was not politically acceptable to allow some areas of the country, or some occupational sectors to lose their provision altogether. Colleges with high levels of resourcing before reorganization had to be protected from potentially disastrous reductions in staffing, while additional resources for others had to be injected at a pace that was manageable and did not lead to waste. As a result, a decade after reorganization some colleges were still experiencing painful transitions.

Change is also intensely political. An example is the experience of the introduction of student fees in HE in the late 1990s. Following the rapid (and largely unplanned) expansion of HE in the late 1980s, it became clear that the system faced a funding crisis, and both major political parties agreed to refer this to a national inquiry. In 1997 government was faced with the inevitable recommendation that full-time university students should make a financial contribution (eventually set at 25 per cent) towards the costs of their higher education. (Part-time students always had paid fees in HE, but it is an indication of how the general public views lifelong learning that this was generally overlooked in the debates on HE funding.) This was based on the principle that the beneficiary should pay, since graduates in general earn significantly more over the lifespan than non-graduates. The underlying policy is undeniably rational: participation in HE is a selective benefit, taken up overwhelmingly by the more prosperous (participation is very heavily skewed towards higher socio-economic groups), and it results in substantially higher lifetime earnings (especially for students from poorer backgrounds), although Bennett et al (1992) had demonstrated that it is precisely these students who gain most financially over the lifespan from HE. There are good grounds in social equity for expecting these people, who can in the main afford to do so, to pay, especially since there is little evidence that they will be deterred from participating by a modest fee. However, they are also a politically sophisticated group, well able to make their opposition heard, using the government's policy concern for inclusion and a public perception of withdrawing 'free education' to oppose the policy.

Conclusion

A series of studies and reports from national and international bodies have, over the last 30 years, repeatedly called for the introduction of a more coherent and consistent policy framework for the funding of lifelong learning. Current systems are not rational in allocating priorities between different kinds of learner and different kinds of need, nor do they treat individuals fairly or consistently on the basis of payment for benefits. Furthermore, they are complex and confusing for learners, employers and policy makers, and every new initiative to address this adds to the complexity.

The broad shift from a public sector planned model towards something more like a market has been introduced (not without much pain in some sectors), but what is provided, for whom and on what terms is very uneven. It remains true that the main financial and educational benefits from post-school learning go to the young and the better educated. However, the political and practical constraints on action have, to date, frustrated those who would introduce more rational and radical systems.

References

ACACE (1982) *Continuing Education: From policies to practice*, ACACE, Leicester

Ball, C (1992) *Profitable Learning,* Royal Society of Arts, London

Barr, N. and Falkingham, J (1993) *Paying for Learning,* LSE Welfare State Programme, London

Beattie, A (1997) *Working People and Lifelong Learning: A study of the impact of an employee development scheme*, NIACE, Leicester

Bennett, R, Glennester, H and Nevison, D (1992) *Learning Should Pay*, BP Educational Service, London

CVCP (2000) *The Business of Borderless Education,* Committee of Vice Chancellors and Principals, London

DfEE (1989) *Employers' Activities: A study of funding, activity and attitudes,* HMSO, London

Jarvis, P, Holford, J, Griffin, C and Dubelaar, J (1997) *Towards the Learning City,* Corporation of London Education Department, London

MSC (1981) *Towards a New Training Initiative,* Manpower Services Commission, Sheffield

OECD (1977) *Learning Opportunities for Adults, Vol. IV: Participation in adult education,* OECD, Paris

Simpson, J (1973) *Feasibility Study in the Collection of Adult Education Statistics,* Council of Europe, Strasbourg

Smith, J and Spurling, A (1997) *Individual Learning Accounts: Towards a learning revolution,* NIACE, Leicester

Smith, J and Spurling, A (1999) *Lifelong Learning: Riding the tiger,* Cassell, London

Woodhall, M (1980) *The Scope and Costs of Education and Training for Adults in Britain,* ACACE, Leicester

Chapter 8

Work-related learning

Paul Tosey and Stephen McNair

Learning in the arena of work is a theme of particular contemporary significance. The subject is prominent in spheres of policy, academia and
business.

In UK government policy, work-related learning has become a prominent
subset of the 'lifelong learning' movement, yielding proposals for initiatives
such as the University for Industry. Dearing (NCIHE, 1997) drew attention
to a need for part-time modes of continuing professional development, and
for courses of study provided in collaboration with employers. Gray (1999)
notes that work-based learning is seen as a key mechanism for widening
access to higher education, with the University for Industry playing a central
role.

Academic interest in the subject is reflected both in publications (Boud
and Garrick, 1999) and in forms of educational activity. The latter includes
degrees through work-based learning now available in UK universities,
including the School of Educational Studies at Surrey.

The topic is problematic, and influenced by trends that are described
earlier in this book. In particular Boud and Garrick highlight 'the dissolving
of boundaries between learning and work, in both practice and theory'
(1999: 1), and 'a focus on knowledge as a commodity and resource; the
notion of the "knowledge worker"' (1999: 3). Changing notions of work and
career have implications for the focus and purpose of learning. There
appears to be a blurring of boundaries between institutions. While the traditional place of education could be seen as a preparation for work, now
academics are increasingly taking learning into the workplace; there are
more placements and sandwich degrees than ever before; and 70 per cent of
undergraduates are in part-time employment already.

In this chapter we:

- consider terms and definitions;
- identify and summarize forms of work-related learning in industrial and post-industrial society;
- pose a critical view that explores the role of learning in relation to control;
- suggest a synthesis of these views and speculate on future directions.

Definitions and scope

Several closely related terms exist within this field; 'work-based learning', 'work-related learning', and 'workplace learning' are the more prominent. For the purposes of this chapter we do not discriminate sharply between these, and for consistency's sake we will use the term 'work-related learning'; however, we do discuss issues relating to what is meant by these terms.

Boud and Garrick use the term 'workplace learning', and acknowledge that the literature is confusing and diverse. There is no single theory of workplace learning; instead there are various theories covering different facets. Boud and Garrick (1999: 6) identify and summarize three main purposes that may be found:

- Improving performance for the benefit of the organization (of self as worker; of the team or work community; of the enterprise).
- Improving learning for the benefit of the learner (for self; for one's personal growth and lifelong learning).
- Improving learning as a social investment (for citizenship, including the environment; for team or work community, including 'learning organizations'; for future enterprises, 'creating the future').

So, at its widest, the term could denote any learning that occurs through work or in the workplace. More narrowly, it could denote learning that is designed to improve productivity.

Informal and incidental learning

Many sources emphasize informal and incidental, as well as formal, dimensions of work-related learning (for example, Marsick and Watkins, 1989). This widens the scope to learning that is triggered in a workplace setting even if not formalized, sanctioned or even recognized by employers. According to Gray (1999: 1):

Eraut *et al* (1998)... argue that, what they term workplace learning, is a largely hidden element of lifelong learning and one which has not been accorded the eminence it deserves in policy documents. They argue that formal learning in the workplace (the main focus of UK government policy) provides only a small part of what is learned at work. Most learning that arises is not planned and is non-formal, resulting from the challenge of the work itself and from interactions with people in the workplace.

Similarly Marsick (1987: 4) gives a broad definition, saying that workplace learning is:

the way in which individuals or groups acquire, interpret, reorganize, change or assimilate a related cluster of information, skills and feelings. It is also primary to the way in which people construct meaning in their personal and shared organizational lives.

Work-based vs classroom learning

Some literature emphasizes the nature of work-based learning by contrasting it with classroom-based learning. For example:

Raelin (2000) argues that work-based learning can be distinguished from traditional classroom learning in a number of important ways. Firstly, work-based learning is centred around reflection on work practices; it is not merely a question of acquiring a set of technical skills, but a case of reviewing and learning from experience. Secondly, work-based learning views learning as arising from action and problem solving within a working environment, and thus is centred around live projects and challenges to individuals and organizations. Work-based learning also sees the creation of knowledge as a shared and collective activity, one in which people discuss ideas, and share problems and solutions. Finally, work-based learning requires not only the acquisition of new knowledge but the acquisition of meta-competence – learning to learn. (Gray, 1999: 2)

Similarly the Department for Education and Employment in the UK contrasts work-based learning with 'academic' or course-based learning, as shown in Table 8.1.

These sources appear to emphasize the nature of work-based learning as any intended learning that does not use traditional classroom methods of learning. These sources highlight not only the mode of learning but also what is perceived as the typical aims and content – though many educators, especially those in fields such as management education and facilitator development (Tosey and Gregory, 1998) might dispute strongly this rather stereotypical view of academic learning.

Table 8.1   Academic and work-based learning (DfEE, 1996: 5)

'Academic' or course-based learning	Work-based learning
Focuses on knowing about	Focuses on knowing how to
Emphasis often on teaching	Emphasis often on learning and mentoring
Greater emphasis on cognitive skills	Emphasis often on transferable skills and competences
Provides students with the knowledge, theories, and concepts and the tools relevant to understand and conceptualize	Provides students with the experience to carry out routine tasks effectively and to identify non-routine or unpredictable situations
	Requires students to develop reflective skills, to reflect on their actions and to develop and refine their own conceptual models

What Raelin in particular signals is a link with 'action learning' (Pedler, 1997), an important influence on contemporary practice, and a topic we discuss further below.

What is 'work'?

Looking at definitions of work-related learning also raises the question of what one considers 'work' to be. The distinction between 'work' and 'non-work' has long been problematic; arguably it is more so today. Authors like Charles Handy have been emphasizing the shifting nature of work and work organization:

> By 1993, in Britain... only 55 per cent of all those in work or seeking work were in full-time jobs inside organizations. In the US it was 60 per cent. The figure in other countries is higher but coming down. More by accident than by design, Britain leads the way. Before very long, having a proper job inside an organization will be a minority occupation. (Handy, 1994: 171)

One could even see government policy in the UK as seeking to redefine work as 'active citizenship' rather than employment.

The phrase 'workplace' learning, therefore, might appear to imply that work happens collectively in an identifiable location such as an office or a factory. For increasing numbers of people, such as homeworkers or those with portfolio careers, this is no longer true. What is the workplace in the age of the virtual office?

We also need to consider what types of activity count as 'work'. Is this confined to paid employment? If so, what about voluntary work? Family work? Or post-retirement work? In common with other areas of society, traditional boundaries are increasingly fluid.

This also affects what we understand by 'career'. This refers less and less to a planned progression through a recognizable career structure, and more and more it seems to the (post hoc) construction of one's 'work history' as a coherent story.

These are not debates we can pursue here, but we note that a broad remit for work-related learning might include any learning that is pursued as a result of, or which arises from, a work role, whether that role be in an employed, self-employed, voluntary or domestic setting.

Within the full scope of work-related learning we might therefore need to include a wide range of learning opportunities and activities that are related in some identifiable way to the experience of work. These would embrace formally accredited programmes of study that are based in the workplace, methods for learning in workplace settings (such as training or action learning), and incidental personal learning arising from work.

The emergence of work-related learning

Next we consider how contemporary ideas about work-related learning have emerged. It is possible to review the nature and history of work-related learning through different perspectives. One of these would see a story of developments in methods for enhancing productivity, with increasing sophistication of approach, and varying degrees of governmental interest in the workplace for wider economic gains. Alternatively, it might be seen as a story of the regulation of individual learning, experience, behaviour and aspiration through socialization, rewards and sanctions. These two positions represent an inherent tension or dialectic in the notion of work-related learning, concerning the extent to which learning is formalized, regulated or legitimized, whether by employers, institutions or government.

These are not the only perspectives that could be construed, but in the remainder of this chapter we explore this dialectic by giving a flavour of both stories by tracing developments in work-related learning in industrial and post-industrial society.

First we give an account of work-related learning as a progression of forms, showing (and this might be described as a modernist assumption) increasing sophistication. An analogous, not identical, form of story is told by Pedler (1997: 12–14). They trace the emergence of the 'learning company' idea as a succession of emergent solutions to crises in training and development. With time, our knowledge and technology of learning may be seen to have improved steadily. Two prominent concerns have been: (1) methods and mechanisms for the recognition or accreditation of (the outcomes of) learning, and (2) methods for the facilitation and support of (the process of) learning. So, in storyboard form we might characterize the development of this tale as follows.

From craft and apprenticeship to training

We begin with the notion of apprenticeship as learning (a notion that, interestingly, has resurfaced in the 1990s through the work of Lave and Wenger, 1991). Over time, the apprentice acquired the skills and the experience to become identified as a practitioner of a craft. Apprenticeship was a rite of passage as much as a curriculum.

As a broad generalization, the division of labour led to the fragmentation of work and the decline of apprenticeship. With industrialization, 'schooling' became more prominent in the workplace, in the form of training for specific jobs or skill-sets. Workers are hired to perform specified tasks, rather than to practice crafts, and learning becomes the development of competence in specialized tasks. Scientific management ('Taylorism', for example) emphasized an ergonomic approach, teaching employees how to perform tasks so as to be most productive.

Personal and organizational development

Training emerged from the functional emphasis of the era of scientific management and begins to address wider issues of worker satisfaction. This is frequently associated with the human relations movement, although as Huczynski (1993) and Collins (1998) among others point out, it is deceptive to classify early human relations as being humanistic or 'person-centred'. More accurately, they argue, additional (human) factors were taken into account in a continuing pursuit of productivity.

Nevertheless this heralded a trend towards a more developmental flavour to work-related learning, especially for managerial and professional employees. This was reflected in the emergence in the late 1950s and 1960s of organization development (French et al, 1994), T-group training, and an emphasis on personal and interpersonal skills.

This emphasis was accompanied by an increasing awareness of limitations in formalized learning and an interest in experiential learning. While 'experiential learning' is a problematic term (see for example Boud et al, 1993), the work of David Kolb (1984) has been especially influential. Kolb's experiential learning cycle emphasizes action as well as reflection, theory as well as practice, as essential components.

Action learning

One part of this strand, and pre-dating Kolb's work, is the 'action learning' movement, particularly through the work of Reg Revans (for example, Revans, 1983; Pedler, 1997). Concentrating on managers' learning, the essence of an action learning approach is that people will learn more through addressing and solving real problems in their workplaces than through formalized courses where learning is abstracted from the real working context.

Action learning is, significantly, a social process. Revans (1983: 11), for example, states:

> It is recognized ignorance not programmed knowledge that is the key to action learning: men [sic] start to learn with and from each other only when they discover that no one knows the answer but all are obliged to find it.

From this principle comes the idea of the action learning set, a group in which members are 'comrades in adversity' and support each other in their learning. Revans also emphasized the role of systematic research in action learning and saw it as building on, rather than aiming to replace, the academic tradition. However, it is a 'real time' learning process, a means by which managers engage in problem solving in the workplace and test their proposals through implementation. For Revans, therefore, action is almost the sea in which learners swim – it is only through action that we can bridge our subjective worlds with social reality. This seems highly compatible with the more recent views put forward by Eraut, among others.

The rise of the learning organization

The economic crises of the 1980s, especially in the West, gave rise to new 'business imperatives'. Business organizations had now to compete harder to survive, strive for excellence, and unlock the 'cultural' secrets of Japan's conspicuous success. Contemporary interest in the 'learning organization' dates from that era.

The notion of the learning organization has many facets, and is another problematic concept. We discuss it further in the following chapter, but we suggest that the development of the learning organization concept over 10–15 years has been influential on contemporary ideas about work-related learning. Thus it seems that learning became framed – in principle, and in practice in a number of organizations – as core to business, relevant to all employees and to business performance rather than as a general luxury and occasional necessity. This is surely an important rationale for the acceptance of work-related learning.

Two further aspects are worth highlighting. First, formal systems have come to be valued for more than their instrumental or functional nature. Performance appraisal systems, for example, become learning mechanisms. An anecdote about the difference between American and Japanese attitudes towards quality control may illustrate this shift. In the USA, it is suggested, the purpose of quality control is to find mistakes and fire those responsible. In Japan, it is to find variations, exploit their potential as new products, and reward those responsible.

A second facet is the emphasis by those such as Marsick and Watkins (1989) on the significance of informal and incidental learning. Incidental learning is defined as 'a by-product of some other activity, such as task accomplishment, interpersonal interaction, sensing the organizational culture, or trial-and-error experimentation' (1989: 6–7). This does not mean learning can be left to chance, and that no structures, facilitation, resources or so on are needed. However, it draws attention to the vast potential for learning that lies in the workplace, a theme picked up by those who contrast work-related with classroom learning.

Work-related learning as regulation and control

Let us now rehearse a more radical and critical argument: the idea of work-related learning as a kind of 'deregulated regulation'.

We can read the practice of work-related learning as a genuine attempt to pursue the mutual interests of individuals, employers and society. This is a unitarist view that could be contrasted with pluralist or radical views (Collins, 1998), which question the extent to which interests are, or can be, common.

From this alternative perspective, let us suggest that those in positions of power in society – such as employers and politicians – have long recognized (whether explicitly or implicitly) the need for members of the workforce to display contradictory characteristics:

- a level of compliance with managerial, business or societal needs, and an ability to act autonomously, with initiative, entrepreneurial spirit or autonomy;
- being motivated by extrinsic rewards (eg money) and by the intrinsic satisfactions of doing a good job;
- flexibility (ie adaptable when authorities want workers to change functions, jobs or even careers), and loyalty and dependability.

The list could go on. But the point is that learning in the workplace can be seen as representing more a series of dilemmas (for politicians, workers and bosses alike) than a set of relatively technological problems. Developments in work-related learning can therefore be seen as a succession of attempts to accommodate, or perhaps even resolve, some of these dilemmas, rather than as increasingly sophisticated methods for the achievement of non-problematic aims.

This implies that work-related learning can be seen also as a rhetoric or discourse that aims to persuade learners towards particular actions, but which also seeks to conceal inherent contradictions. This view is related, therefore, to the arguments of authors such as Coffield that education appears to have been redefined as an instrument of economy, and that the rhetoric of lifelong and workplace learning needs critique:

> the challenge... is to confront the argument that, behind the benevolent intentions and the high flown rhetoric, lifelong learning, the learning society and the learning organization are all being propounded to induce individuals to become more-or-less willing participants in learning for life and to bear an increasing proportion of the costs of such learning without end. (Coffield, 1999: 11)

There are some characteristics of work-related learning that might be cited in support of this alternative perspective:

- the reliance of the discourse of work-related learning on appeals to the needs of business or society, as if these are either not controversial, or definable authoritatively by those of high status, or both;
- implicit threats of what might happen to those who do not follow the exhortations of the rhetoric (for example, a suggestion that those who do not enthusiastically adopt the ethic of lifelong learning have no excuse and may be regarded as an impediment to the economic welfare of society);
- denials of contradiction in the espoused view (for example, suggestions that learning per se is valued, without condition, coupled with clear differentiation in practice between particular forms of learning that are recognized or rewarded, and other forms that are not).

Consider, for example, the following quote:

> There are few places left for employees at any level who do not continue to learn and improve their effectiveness throughout their working lives. There is no place for managers who do not appreciate their own vital role in fostering learning. (Boud and Garrick, 1999: 1)

Incidentally, Boud and Garrick appear to be reflecting on, rather than advocating, this state of affairs. But this quotation illustrates the way in which employees are now exhorted to learn, because it is taken to be essential to the survival and success of the institutions on which we depend. It is reminiscent of Tom Peters' exhortation in the 1980s that we should all 'love change' (Peters 1988) and so we might be persuaded to consider such assertions as fashion more than truth. This could leave the UK government in a dilemma – while campaigning against social exclusion, what place is there for the person who chooses not to learn?

From this perspective one might ask to what extent the value of learning has become an orthodoxy, if not a dogma. The literature on the learning organization, for example, tends to imply that learning is inherently a good thing, rather than to examine how learning may be valued, influenced and generally related to issues of power. We suggest it is helpful to ask 'learning of value for whom, and in what ways'? This is the approach taken by critical education theory (summarized, for example, in Burgoyne and Reynolds, 1997).

One could generate further examples. Suffice it to say that from this perspective, advocacy of work-related learning could be seen not as a transparent effort to improve individuals, organizations and society, but as an attempt to intervene very profoundly in the personal and vocational lives of citizens. Structures of accreditation, resourcing and access could be interpreted as attempts to constrain and regulate individual and organizational choices about learning into forms that have been prescribed by authorities of various kinds. Several researchers (Coffield, 1999; Marsick and Watkins, 1989) have asserted that the most important learning is not formalized. Yet it appears that time and again regulation of some kind is seen as desirable.

If we revisit our 'storyboard' from this perspective, we might pick out some very different features. For example, the controversies over scientific management are generally well-rehearsed. As a counterpoint to this emphasis on informal learning, moves to formalize and standardize learning are also common. For example, there was a substantial push towards management competencies in the UK in the 1980s and 1990s, linked to the development of schemes of National Vocational Qualifications. Recent policy and practice in the UK also appear characterized by a strong concern with accreditation ('Accreditation is key to work-based learning', DfEE, 1996: 2).

We might dwell more on the way class divisions seemed to become reflected in the differential status and trappings of management training courses (eg in comfortable residential hotels) compared with shop-floor training (eg in rudimentary classrooms). Two traditions may be seen as arising from a common root in the exclusion of manual workers. First, the worker education movement attended to non-vocational learning in a liberal mode, and prefigured liberal adult education (and now, perhaps, mass access to liberal higher education). The second was associated directly with the trade union movement, traditionally more radical (for example in the 1970s) but which, arguably, has become increasingly vocational and regulated.

Finally, we might also dwell further on the way that issues of learning in the workplace are typically framed as technological, non-controversial and non-political (Reynolds, 1997). Recent theorists (such as Lave and Wenger, 1991) emphasize the extent to which work-related learning, in its broadest sense, is to a very significant degree about participation, acquiring membership and identity and so on. Their notion of 'situated learning' expresses the idea that learning is not only, or even primarily, a means to a functional output in organizations: it is a feature of the process of participation in the social or organizational system. The output of learning is not products or services, but legitimization of the person's participation. As Gherardi *et al* (1998: 276) describe it:

> on-the-job learning is no longer equated with the appropriation or acquisition of bits of work-related knowledge, but it is understood as the development of new identity based on participation in the system of situated practices.

The process of socialization, for example, is in this sense a learning process. Marsick and Watkins (1989) refer to the concept of the 'hidden curriculum', which expresses the idea that much learning, perhaps the most potent, may be tacit or unstated – for example, regulation of behaviour according to cultural norms. It is interesting that Lave and Wenger's theory renews interest in the notion of apprenticeship. While it can be criticized for representing little that is genuinely new, it encapsulates a number of important and relevant ideas about the social nature of learning.

Whether or not one is persuaded by this alternative type of perspective, we emphasize how changing forms of work-based learning can be seen as shifting patterns of accommodation to various dilemmas. Not, we hasten to add, evolving forms necessarily, because that might imply progress; but modulations in a dance. In this dance, there is no clear consensus about goals of learning in workplaces, nor is there any agreed morality of workplace participation. This leaves issues of work-related learning rather more at sea, in the sense that it is much more difficult to identify preferred ways forward. But this perspective also helps us to explore the extent to which the packaging in which issues of learning are wrapped may be seen as ideological rather than common sense.

Conclusion

We do not intend to propose a resolution to this dialectic. To see it as an 'either–or' issue is too narrow, though. For example, accreditation sometimes suits employers and sometimes does not (eg when it increases mobility to the detriment of the employing organization). Similarly it suits employees sometimes and not others. It probably does not help employers to be narrowly instrumental in defining learning, nor does it suit individuals to shun the workplace in order to create independence or become emancipated. People can respond to the rhetoric of lifelong and work-related learning by building up a portfolio in order to loosen dependence on employers, rather than succumbing to greater control.

Some of these contradictions are illustrated by Ford's Employee Development Programme (EDP), through which all employees were given an amount of money to spend on their learning and left complete freedom to choose. There was no simplistic or singular outcome, nor could it be said that this was clearly either a benevolent impulse from Ford, or an instrumental approach. Ford was not being entirely altruistic, in that the EDP was a response to a downturn in the market. In this light the EDP could be seen as successful and a skilled way of managing this downturn. Some used the EDP to prepare for life outside Ford; some to enhance their promotion prospects; some to re-skill. Therefore this could be interpreted as either benevolent or manipulative: the latter if one sees it as a skilled way of managing downturn, reducing resistance to change, and maintaining regard of employees for the employer.

There appears to be clear evidence of enthusiasm for the practice of work-related learning, and a healthy level of debate about its meaning and purposes. As a facet of the learning age, an ingredient in the postmodern mix, work-related learning appears to be both vibrant and important. To conclude, we cite three themes that strike us as relevant and potentially important for future developments.

The first is our view that the focus of teaching, learning and accreditation needs to be increasingly on the process rather than the content of learning. In other words, we should be concerned more with the quality (validity and rigour) of the process of learning than with its content or output.

We argue that this would not only attend to what is known about the importance of informal and incidental learning, but also emphasize recognition of individuals' ability to learn (their 'learning to learn') more than their acquisition of content or attendance. This implies, for us, a more prominent role for processes such as action learning. It also implies a need to support and develop educators who can genuinely facilitate such processes; it makes little sense to continue to see educators primarily as skilled deliverers of specialized content.

Second, the notion of 'career' may have weakened, and in the secular sense work has probably become less vocational. But there is evidence of a resurgence in the (original) sense of vocation as a 'calling', and in notions of spirituality in the workplace (Briskin, 1998; Mitroff and Denton, 1998). Among other things, this implies that individuals may be less and less inclined to treat work-related learning as an instrumental activity, or to consent unquestioningly to the agendas of organizations or governments.

Third and finally, we would emphasize learning as ethos more than mechanism. It seems appropriate to us to aim, especially in organizations, to build communities of practice predicated upon learning (for example, as 'peer learning communities' – Tosey and Gregory, 1998) rather than to develop impressive but ultimately unintegrated programmes of learning. This, we would argue, increases the likelihood of ownership by individuals and offsets the risks involved in prescribing learning as a duty.

References

Boud, D and Garrick, J (eds) (1999) *Understanding Learning at Work,* Routledge, London

Boud, D, Cohen, R and Walker, D (eds) (1993) *Using Experience for Learning,* Society for Research into Higher Education and Open University Press, Buckingham

Briskin, A (1998) *The Stirring of Soul in the Workplace,* Berrett-Koehler, San Francisco

Burgoyne, J and Reynolds, M (eds) (1997) *Management Learning: Integrating perspectives in theory and practice,* Sage, London

Coffield, D (ed) (1999) *Why's the Beer Always Stronger up North? Studies of lifelong learning in Europe,* The Policy Press, Bristol

Collins, D (1998) *Organizational Change: Sociological perspectives,* Routledge, London

DfEE (1996) *Work-Based Learning,* (briefing paper), The Stationery Office, Norwich

Eraut, M, Alderton, J, Cole, G and Senker, P (1998) *Development of Knowledge and Skills in Employment,* Final Report of a Research Project funded by 'The Learning Society' Programme of the Economic and Social Research Council, University of Sussex Institute of Education

French, W L, Bell, C H and Zawacki, R A (eds) (1994) *Organization Development and Transformation,* 4th edn, Irwin, Burr Ridge, IL

Gherardi, S, Nicolini, D and Odella, F (1998) 'Towards a social understanding of how people learn in organizations: the notion of the situated curriculum', *Management Learning,* **29** (3), 273–97

Gray, D (1999) 'Work-based learning, action learning and the virtual paradigm', paper presented at the European Conference on Educational Research, Lahti, Finland, 22–25 September

Handy, C (1994) *The Empty Raincoat: Making sense of the future,* Hutchinson, London

Huczynski, A A (1993) *Management Gurus: What makes them and how to become one,* Routledge, London

Kolb, D (1984) *Experiential Learning: Experience as the source of learning and development,* Prentice-Hall, NJ

Lave, J and Wenger, E (1991) *Situated Learning,* Cambridge University Press, Cambridge

Marsick, V J (ed) (1987) *Learning in the Workplace,* Croom Helm, Beckenham

Marsick, V J and Watkins, K E (1989) *Informal and Incidental Learning in the Workplace,* Routledge, London

Mitroff, I and Denton, E (1998) *A Spiritual Audit of Corporate America: A hard look at spirituality, religion, and values in the workplace,* Jossey-Bass, San Francisco

National Committee of Inquiry into Higher Education (1997) *Higher Education in the Learning Society* (The Dearing Report), The Stationery Office, Norwich

Pedler, M (1997) 'Interpreting action learning', in eds J Burgoyne and M Reynolds, *Management Learning: Integrating perspectives in theory and practice*, Sage, London

Peters, T (1988) *Thriving on Chaos,* Macmillan, Basingstoke

Raelin, J A (2000) *Work-Based Learning: The new frontier of management development,* Prentice Hall, New Jersey

Revans, R (1983) 'Action learning: its origins and nature', in ed M Pedler, *Action Learning in Practice,* Gower, Aldershot

Reynolds, M (1997) 'Learning styles: a critique', *Management Learning,* **28** (2), 115–33

Tosey, P and Gregory, J (1998) 'The peer learning community in higher education: reflections on practice', *Innovations in Education and Training International,* **35** (1), 74–81

Chapter 9

Facilitating access to learning: educational and vocational guidance

Julia Preece

> The key to the development of 'the learning society', which we will need if we are to manage the economic and social changes of the next decades, must lie in helping adults to recognize their learning needs and find effective opportunities to meet them, while helping the providers of education and training to recognize and respond to those needs. Thus we see educational guidance for adults not at the periphery of the education service but at its centre. (UDACE, 1985: 22)

This chapter provides a critical overview of the relatively scarce literature on adult guidance. It explores the current context by highlighting some of the influences on guidance policy since 1970 in the UK and Europe and discusses some tensions between ideology and practice. It concludes with a comment on recent government initiatives in England.

The guidance context and its milestones

Formal educational and vocational guidance for adults is a relatively young activity. Although careers guidance services were available in schools from the early 1960s, the first UK educational guidance service for adults did not open until 1967. Guidance has suffered from piecemeal funding and almost no legislative input. Guidance as a resource for adults started to emerge properly in the UK and the rest of Europe in the 1970s, primarily as a consequence of the development of continuing education provision. In 1982 the

National Association of Educational Guidance for Adults was launched and by 1984 there were about 50 independent guidance services for adults (Eagleton, 1991).

While there were a number of UNESCO and European reports between 1977 and 1984 (UNESCO, 1977, 1981; European Bureau of Adult Education, 1981), perhaps the first real UK milestone in terms of policy influence came in 1985 with UDACE's publication, *Helping Adults to Learn*. This advocated the need to increase awareness of educational opportunities for adults through a range of agencies and professions. The publication advocated that guidance should be a staged activity, which could take place at pre-enrolment, enrolment, on-course or end-of-course phases. Guidance activities themselves would involve, to varying degrees, activities of informing, advising, counselling, assessing, enabling, advocating clients and giving feedback to institutions on client needs. UDACE advocated that a network of agencies should be involved in this work, ranging from specialist careers information services to general advisers, libraries, employers, teachers, health services and the media (UDACE, 1985). This report helped give guidance a more visibly central position in subsequent UK adult education and training debates and was followed closely by a second UDACE report, *The Challenge to Change: Developing educational guidance for adults* (1986). This report added to its seven guidance activities four definitions and five values, which would underpin the guidance framework (in Brown, 1991: 277). These are that guidance is:

- a helping process that overlaps with personal and vocational guidance;
- a process of clarifying options for the learner;
- undertaken at all stages of learning;
- informed by five values; that is, guidance should be:
  - client-centred;
  - confidential;
  - open and accessible;
  - independent;
  - freely available.

These principles remained virtually unaltered for the next 10 years, with limited research or theoretical debate about the guidance process. There is still no legislative framework for adult guidance, though recently the political climate for establishing a guidance rationale has strengthened. Watts and Van Esbroeck (1998) and others highlight a new context for guidance, embedded in global economic goals to increase efficiency and reduce student wastage in the context of drives to widen participation in all forms of post-compulsory education. The goals are influenced by an increasing awareness of current trends in world market competition, cross-nation mobility, the volatility of labour markets, the influence of new technologies, lifelong learning needs for labour force upskilling, and closer connections generally across European countries. With the increasing complexity of learning options as courses and credits are acquired in smaller bites at various stages in the learning career, guidance services are becoming a necessary part of ensuring effective use of scarce educational resources.

The guidance world comes from different traditions, however – principally counselling (and to this Watts and Van Esbroeck, 1998, add psychotherapy), careers and education. From these traditions are emerging a number of issues and initiatives:

- a new and broader definition for educational and vocational guidance and its related professions;
- increasing scrutiny of the original guidance principles and values;
- a growing concern with quality assurance and the professionalization and training of guidance workers;
- the evolution of new centralized services – particularly in the UK.

New and broader definitions for education and vocational guidance and its related professions

The problem with defining guidance lies with its broad-based origin in different professions and its need to accommodate the whole range of education and learning, from basic skills to higher education. Guidance facilities also need to cater for the whole range of adult learning needs, from people with learning disabilities to people from different cultures and professionals seeking to update their skills.

Watts and Van Esbroeck (1998) recently documented some cross-Europe trends, structures, categories, roles and tasks for guidance. They identify a number of trends. For example, guidance is now seen as more important across Europe as a continuous process from school and throughout adult life. A more professional model of guidance is evolving with a greater emphasis on looking for ways to develop the client as an active agent in the guidance process, rather than a receiver of information. There is also an increasing interest in the European dimension of guidance provision alongside concerns for quality and standards. The emerging strategy is of careers education and guidance within education and employment, with some access to neutral careers guidance. This trend of course also implies a strong vocational slant to the role of guidance. These trends have been documented by Plant (1990), who traced recent advances in networking amongst professionals across countries. Such activities are still piecemeal and usually linked to national borders where there is particularly fluid migration activity.

Running alongside the tendency for professional networking also appears to be a broadening concept of the range of guidance processes and skills required by staff. Watts and Van Esbroeck (1998), for example, expand considerably on the UDACE model for guidance. They suggest there are 21 tasks for guidance workers. Included in these are the provision of: information, short- and long-term individual or group counselling, advice, facilitating self-help and self-assessment, diagnostic assessment, referral, planned guidance teaching programmes, liaison and partnerships, coaching, advocacy, feedback and follow up. Watts places a stronger emphasis on psychological counselling and personal support needs than much of the earlier European literature (for example, Plant, 1990). He also emphasizes the diverse roles of people who have a guidance or learning support responsibility. These include the 'first-in-line' adviser who acts as a receptionist and first point of initial assessment, then more specialist roles such as study counsellors, social workers, placement officers for work or other field experience and psychiatry-related counselling roles. The guidance worker therefore may be educative, career oriented, tutorial focused or psychological.

The tasks of guidance workers have received some attention over the years and there have been a number of comparative studies of guidance structures and processes (Plant, 1990; Watts, 1994, 1997; Clayton, 1999). They note some disparity between services, but also some common trends, such as guidance being multifaceted and delivered by a range of agencies at various learning stages. The service emphasis is usually on the first stage of guidance where it is free at the point of entry. There is also a tendency to focus on vocational guidance or for guidance to be attached to employment initiatives or education institutions, delimiting the possibility of neutral guidance. However, there is relatively little literature on the qualitative experience of guidance from the provider or client point of view. The literature that does address these issues has revealed some tensions between policy models and the reality of practice, with an implication by some that perhaps the guidance process itself is under-theorized.

Increasing scrutiny of the original guidance principles and practices

Some emerging areas of research interest are the:

- concept of impartiality, particularly at the pre-entry stage;
- notion of a pre-pre-access, proactive aspect of guidance;
- process of guidance as a helping and enabling activity throughout a course;
- gender dimension in guidance.

Impartiality of information and advice

The UDACE five principles were underpinned by a person-centred, confidential, facilitative counselling approach. The goal of this approach is to enable the client to make informed decisions about his or her own learning choice. Along with the raised profile of guidance, two trends have followed, indicating a more centralized interpretation of this provision as economically, rather than socially, driven. The enhanced focus on ensuring adults contribute to labour market needs has meant that guidance and counselling have been attached to employment initiatives. This, coupled with increasing competition between course providers, has raised concerns about how impartial guidance services are in reality. Connelly et al (1998) discuss the tensions between providers who place priority on filling student places on the basis of funding and the more ideological notion of guidance as learner-centred and unprejudiced. They suggest, however, that adults do not expect to get impartial guidance from educational institutions. They cite the paradox that a preferred source of guidance is frequently friends and relatives, based on a need to 'trust' their guidance source. This usually means the preferred source is also likely to be unreliable – in that friends and relatives are least likely to be fully informed about the range of provision available. So, 'These two factors of impartiality, client-centredness and completeness of information may be in tension to some extent' (Connelly et al, 1998: 144). They see these tensions as illustrated by the two guidance roles of information giving and humanistic (enabling the client to understand his or her needs).

There are some emerging concerns, then, about a service that is linked to college marketing strategies and required to operate in collaboration with a range of guidance networks with variable access to different sources of information by guidance givers. Alongside this is the client's own perception of what he or she wants or is entitled to from guidance:

> Guidance which is clinically impartial, objective and free from opinion may not always be perceived by clients as being in their best interests, and indeed, adults may expect a more judicious approach from professional workers. (Connelly et al, 1998: 149)

Similarly there is a danger of oversimplifying the client-guidance relationship in that impartiality will be influenced by different power relations in the interaction, the context of the interview, the needs of the client, etc. This is one of the few attempts to research and analyse the implications of terminology, which has now been embedded in guidance ideology for some time. Clearly there is more room for research in this area.

A pre-pre-access stage of guidance

Another area where research is limited is the issue of who accesses existing systems and how much the guidance model itself militates against reaching the people most in need of guidance. Houghton and Oglesby (1996) reviewed the Higher Education Quality Council document, *A Quality Assurance Framework for Guidance and Learner Support* (HEQC, 1995). The report referred to the four phases of student life identified by UDACE (1985) where institutions should be offering learner support. The authors highlighted the difficulties of developing a guidance structure for higher education that was modelled on a study pattern of full-time undergraduates who would go through the prescribed linear process of student life. A lifelong model of learning may involve multiple exit and re-entry points, requiring differential guidance interventions.

More significantly the HEQC model is advocated to ensure, 'That students should be helped in ways which connect with their purposes and expectations in study' (Houghton and Oglesby, 1996: 146). This approach implies, they felt, a degree of self-directed autonomy that many new learners may not have: 'For this group of students, guidance and details about learner support... need to be taken out to them and actively offered' (ibid). So a system that relies on students seeking information for themselves may fail to reach the very people most in need. There is a stage, for instance, when advice and guidance may be needed for some adults, 'before they might be ready to class themselves as learners'. As argued by Connolly *et al* (1998) they suggest that for such learners the most likely locus for guidance will be amongst informal sources such as community workers and voluntary organizations. Indeed Chapman and Williams (1998) discussed the development of IT-based interactive guidance packages on these lines. It is for these groups of learners that most of the qualitative research has taken place in terms of the on-course guidance experience. And it is here that the now accepted principles, values and tasks are explored in reality contexts. Those reality contexts suggest that guidance in the early stages may require a relationship that emphasizes the nurturing of confidence rather than information giving.

Guidance as an on-course helping process

Two research examples address the experience of on-course guidance. Houghton (1998) takes us through her role as a guidance officer/personal tutor on a year-long university-based course for long-term unemployed adults. Preece (1999) reports on interviews with tutors and students involved in short courses in community settings. In both reports the processes of guiding and supporting are seen as depending upon the skills and interventions of the tutor – anticipating needs, seeking out needs and nurturing self-awareness among students. Their role is one of proactive help and not a reliance on the learner's autonomous, self-directed seeking out of information and support. An emerging model for guidance that forefronts the client as an active agent in the process may well, therefore, delimit initial participation by the adults most in need of support. McGivney (1999) also emphasizes the importance of personal support in helping women returners, bringing us to another underdeveloped feature of guidance awareness.

The gender dimension

While there has been the occasional theoretical exploration of the guidance relationship (Usher and Edwards, 1995), Bailey (1993) introduces the need to theorize the guidance process from a feminist perspective. She questions the lack of a gender (and its concomitant class, race and disability) dimension which recognizes the particular discourse and power relationships for women. She suggests that a feminist approach (in a profession that is probably dominated by women) would explore the emotional and psychological influences on women in relation to education. She suggests that impartiality is a subjective male concept, which can, for women, help to reinforce the status quo. She therefore questions the universal value of such an approach. These comments would support the above concerns for new learners. This aspect of guidance awareness, of course, has implications for guidance training, though a gender dimension is not discussed in the literature on this subject since it is concerned more with the mechanics of a training structure.

The limited amount of research with marginalized groups that has been undertaken suggests much more work needs to go into analysing practice against ideological definitions of the guidance process. Such findings would inform policy and funding and ultimately increase the efficiency and training of people who undertake guidance activities.

The training of guidance staff

Quality concerns have raised awareness of the need to devote attention to the training of guidance staff. There are two dimensions to the training debate. On the one hand there is a need to establish a professional training system that accommodates the diversity of guidance activity; on the other there is also a need to ensure that the training provided meets current demands and trends for the guidance profession. Training, as Watts and Van Esbroeck (1998) identify, is a contested field with stakeholder interests from a range of professions including careers, counsellors, education and psychology. Although there are established training routes for counselling and psychotherapy, there seems to be little generic training for people engaged in educational guidance. Indeed, there is no qualification for the HE dimensions of guidance. Bissell and Southwood (1995) identify a Certificate and Diploma in Adult Guidance organized by the Lead Body for Advice and Guidance in Scotland, and Clayton (1999) notes 11 UK institutions that offer a postgraduate diploma in careers guidance. On the European front there is increasing incorporation of guidance as an aspect of labour market training programmes.

In spite of the piecemeal nature of guidance training there is now a recognized need for training development. This includes an update on the generic approach to the three dimensions of guidance (vocational, educational and psychological). UDACE's skills-based list of informing, interview, advice, counselling, administration, management outreach and IT now need to be supplemented with a broader understanding of the context for guidance. Plant (1990) and Watts and Van Esbroeck (1998) emphasize the need for a European dimension, including understanding of transnational and transfrontier developments (Plant). Alongside this is the more localized context – the role of professional guidance services where varied professional organizations support the interests of guidance and each offers a specialist dimension (teaching, administration, careers, counselling. etc). Plant suggests there are signs of an emerging strategy – careers education and guidance within education, career development in employment, and access to neutral careers guidance. There is now greater emphasis on encouraging the individual to be an active agent in the guidance process, shifting the focus from providing information and placement towards an 'emphasis on fostering students' capacity to manage their own career development' (Plant, 1990: 60). The new skills required to accommodate these broader political trends include a greater concern with student diversity (Watts and Van Esbroeck, 1998) and a more holistic approach to student development (Clayton, 1999), more in keeping with a lifelong learning model. Within this new model is a need for understanding new ways of delivering guidance, building on IT advances and accommodating non-standard lifestyles. So mechanisms such as distance learning study centres and telephone guidance are all seen as having a future role in guidance training.

Diversity of guidance delivery also has implications for how students process information and are enabled to be active in the way they use it. So more sophisticated ways of understanding how to link across services and integrate different forms of guidance become part of the new training model (Watts and Van Esbroeck, 1998). Clayton (1999) provides a timely warning, however, that socially excluded groups need targeted, non-bureaucratic approaches that are locally based, empathic and welcoming. There is yet again a danger that in the drive for standardization and technological enhancement some diverse groups will remain excluded. Quality control mechanisms should, therefore, arguably include monitoring of who is not using guidance services as well as their effectiveness for those who do. So how are the new initiatives in the UK addressing these concerns for quality, diversity, training and holistic approaches?

Current UK initiatives

During 1998 the Labour government launched three interrelated initiatives to supplement its Green Paper, *The Learning Age*, all of which have a direct or indirect bearing on the development of guidance provision for adults in England. These were:

- the New Deal;
- the University for Industry (UfI);
- Learndirect.

More recently, *Local Information Advice and Guidance for Adults in England: Towards a National Framework* (DfEE, 1999) was launched. The equivalent Scottish documents offered a slightly more enhanced focus on guidance and Connolly *et al* (1998) have documented some of the tensions and implications for the Scottish system.

This section therefore focuses on how the National Framework for England is shaping up at the time of writing. The New Deal scheme, established in 1998, is an extension of the government's Welfare to Work project, designed primarily for 18–24-year-olds, with the goal of increasing the employability of the long-term unemployed. The programme offers the unemployed a menu of New Deal pathways: employment, full-time education and training, contributing to the environment task force, or voluntary sector involvement. It entails a partnership between a range of organizations such as local authorities, careers and probation services, employers, training organizations, unions, charities and voluntary organizations. Clients are allocated a New Deal Personal Adviser and will in the first instance be 'invited' to attend for interview, resulting ultimately in compulsory attendance (Donnelly *et al*, 1998).

The UfI (now delivering the organization's objectives through Learndirect) is essentially a brokering service designed to create a national learning network. It will be a technology-based resource which commissions learning programmes and sustains 'an accessible system of support and guidance services' (Hillman, 1996: v). Its goal is to provide 'learning on demand' (p. vi). Its strategy is to consult with existing providers, identify flagship areas, target groups and commission providers to deliver to those target groups in the home, community or workplace. Access would be via local learning centres, primarily serviced by a telephone hotline, 'Learndirect'.

More recently these projects have been supplemented with a local Information, Advice and Guidance (IAG) strategy: 'Local learning information and advice that can complement and support the services that will be available nationally through Learning Direct and the UfI' (www. iag01.1999). The IAG services will be at a local level, contracted to local providers who agree to a set of quality standards to be in place by 2001. The initiative is largely in response to the claim that 'some adults have a need for a more targeted service, which may include an in-depth guidance interview' (iag03). The service will be free at the point of entry, though additional services may be charged for. It is designed to provide 'impartial guidance' on the basis of local partnership arrangements with a lead body in each partnership cohort. Partnerships will link with employment services and Learndirect through the UfI. Quality assurance standards will include staff having an appropriate qualification. IAG services will be delivered in geographically designated lifelong learning partnership areas. The strategic funding goal for this initiative is to ensure successful networking and liaison and avoid duplication of provision, while compensating for the lack of face-to-face contact in the technology-based Learndirect and UfI schemes. IAGs will need to demonstrate how they would deliver services and meet the needs of under-represented and minority groups.

An examination of these services in relation to the earlier parts of this chapter provides a matrix of unplugged as well as filled gaps. For instance, the basis for a standardized qualification is being positioned, though we don't know the required content of such a qualification. Similarly the existing incoherence of a fragmented delivery service is being rationalized and coordinated at apparently local as well as broader levels, using information technology. Direct telephone services are available to those who are already autonomous learners, while specific outreach strategies are implied, if not specified, in the expectations for demonstrable widening participation activities by IAGs. What appears to be missing, however, is the acknowledgement of a need for a European dimension to the provision and, perhaps, a failure to specify the role of guidance itself. Is it an information provider, a counselling service, a personal support service or combination of these? Equally, in view of the research, which emphasizes the importance of on-course learning relationships and the need to understand differential service needs at progression levels, it is difficult to understand how the whole guidance service will be monitored or provided beyond the initial point of delivery. In short, it is a welcome service, but described outside the context of existing literature on what guidance is or should be.

The New Deal, on the other hand is presented as a highly targeted monitoring service where tutors support and monitor the client's progress from beginning to end. The guidance principles of learning choice and developing autonomy are, however, removed.

Conclusion

The educational purpose of guidance is in a state of flux. In the UK the relationship between vocational, psychological and educational guidance and access to learning is evolving. From a service that was incoherent, fragmented and available only to the self-directing learner, designed to give the learner an opportunity to make informed decisions about his or her learning needs, new priorities are emerging. The service is being coordinated and targeted at those least likely to seek it out for themselves. At the same time elements of informed choice are being replaced with directives and close monitoring of learner progress.

Alongside these policy developments emerging trends across Europe indicate the need for broad, cross-national partnerships and cross-cultural dimensions to an increasingly vocationalist approach to learning. These international practice trends are being supplemented independently by some qualitative research into the kind of guidance relationship required by those most on the margins of learning. Those studies show the need for a more holistic, multidimensional and empathic service, which combines strategic targeting with user-friendly, familiar contacts. It remains to be seen whether the IAG evolution is able to pick up some of these missing dimensions in current policy thinking and ultimately the practice of guidance.

References

Bailey, D (1993) 'Gender and educational guidance: questions of feminist practice', *British Journal of Guidance and Counselling*, **21** (2), 161–74

Bissell, B and Southwood, A (1995) 'Report on the work of the Adult Education Guidance Initiative in Scotland', *Scottish Journal of Adult and Continuing Education*, **1** (2), 65–70

Brown, J (1991) 'What is educational guidance?', *Adults Learning*, **2** (10), 277–78

Chapman, I and Williams, S (1998) 'IT-based guidance: reaching the parts that other guidance cannot reach', in ed J Preece, *Beyond the Boundaries: Exploring the potential of widening provision in higher education*, pp. 39–46, NIACE, Leicester

Clayton, P (1999) *Access to Vocational Guidance for People at Risk of Social Exclusion*, University of Glasgow

Connelly, G, Milburn, T, Thomson, S and Edwards, R (1998) 'Guiding adults impartially: a Scottish study', *Studies in the Education of Adults,* **30** (2), 142–55

DfEE (1999) *Local Information Advice and Guidance for Adults in England: Towards a national framework,* http://www.lifelonglearning.co.uk/iag

Donnelly, C, Nimmo, M, Convey, P (1998) *The New Deal Handbook,* Unemployment Unit and Youthaid, London

European Bureau of Adult Education (1981) *The Development of Information, Guidance and Counselling Services,* EBAE, Brussels

Higher Education Quality Council (1995) *A Quality Assurance Framework for Guidance and Learner Support,* HEQC, London

Hillman, J (1996) *University for Industry,* IPPR, London

Houghton, A (1988) 'Extending the guidance boundaries', in ed J Preece, *Beyond the Boundary: Exploring the potential of widening provisions in higher education,* NIACE, Leicester

Houghton, A and Oglesby, K L O (1996) 'Guidance and learner support: developing threshold standards', *Adults Learning,* **9** (7), 15–16

McGivney (1999) *Returning Women,* NIACE, Leicester

Plant, P (1990) *Transnational Vocational Guidance and Training for Young People and Adults,* CEDEFOP, Berlin

Preece, J (1999) 'Higher education courses in the community: issues around guidance and learning support for non traditional students', in ed P Oliver, *Lifelong Learning and Continuing Education: What is a learning society?',* Ashgate, Aldershot

UDACE (1985) *Helping Adults to Learn: Educational guidance for adults,* UDACE, London

UDACE (1986) *The Challenge to Change: Developing educational guidance for adults,* UDACE, London

UNESCO (1977) *Report on the Ways and Means of Strengthening Information and Counselling Services for Adult Learners,* UNESCO, Paris

UNESCO (1981) *The Forms, Methods and Techniques of Vocational and Educational Guidance,* UNESCO, Paris

Usher, R and Edwards, R (1995) 'Confessing all? A postmodern guide to the guidance and counselling of adult learners', *Studies in the Education of Adults,* **21** (1), 9–23

Watts, A G (1994) *Education and Vocational Guidance in the European Community,* European Commission, Brussels

Watts, A G (1997) 'Developing local lifelong learning strategies', *British Journal of Guidance and Counselling,* **25** (2), 217–27

Watts, A G and Van Esbroeck, R (1998) *New Skills and New Futures: Higher education guidance and counselling services in the European Union,* VUB Press, Fedora

PART FOUR

IMPLICATIONS OF THE LEARNING SOCIETY

Chapter 10

Implications of the learning society for education beyond school

Linda Merricks

'Education beyond school' is an enormous topic. Conventionally and popularly, it has been seen to refer to tertiary education: university or college courses taken more or less immediately after leaving school. Beyond this, a rather smaller group might also include in their definition part-time, leisure-based adult education classes offered by the Workers Educational Association (WEA). Others might include skill-based courses, often offered by private, profit-making companies, which lead to qualifications that recognize achievement, like garden design certificates that are not necessarily vocational in intent for all students.

Recently, and increasingly, the definition has shifted, with an emphasis on vocational courses intended to update workplace skills or retrain those with redundant skills. There is also a growing recognition of the place of part-time academic courses that lead to certificates or diplomas of higher education or degrees. This breadth is too much to adequately encompass in one chapter, and work-based learning has been dealt with in Chapter 8. This chapter, therefore, concentrates on the three areas offering mostly non-vocational education to adult students: the higher, further and continuing education sectors.

The implications for 'education beyond school' in the construction of the learning society are wide reaching. The most fundamental is the shift towards lifelong learning, the provision of learning for anyone and everyone at all stages of life and most particularly after the end of compulsory education. The three sectors that have conventionally been the providers of education beyond school are:

- higher education, teaching to degree level and beyond in universities, and the polytechnics;
- further education, which has taken place primarily within the further education colleges and has concentrated on vocational training, especially for school-leavers;
- adult or continuing education, which has been provided by a number of agencies, most importantly the university extra-mural departments, the WEA and the local authorities.

Although their overall aims have been similar, the boundaries between these sectors have been almost impenetrable. However, the development of the learning society will demand the removal of these artificial barriers, and the evolution of a coherent system of borderless education within which the needs of the whole population are recognized. Within this system, the essential differences of the various providers will need recognition to remove the present wasteful competition, and flexibility will be the most crucial element enabling students to move between institutions, constructing the learning experience most suited to each individual. In these changes, the market will play an increasingly important role. Students who are aware of the price they pay for their learning become critical consumers and demand that the service provided meets their needs, not those perceived to reflect some ill-defined 'academic excellence'.

Overall, the changes that are demanded will be facilitated by an increased role for IT within the learning institutions. The encroachment of IT does more than change the mode of provision of learning. The learning society demands that IT is harnessed to the needs of the learner. Flexibility of access is one great shift resulting from this. Learning is not confined to the 'classroom' but can already be accessed in the home, workplace and cafés. Soon it will be available in supermarkets, shopping centres and leisure centres. However, this is not the only change taking place. IT has demanded a radical consideration of how learning occurs and the design of materials to reflect these conclusions. In moves as fundamental as those that took place in the classroom early in the 20th century as outmoded rote learning was replaced by an emphasis on understanding, the university lecture is being replaced by interactive modules demanding conscious participation from the student. Finally, the knowledge society demands new skills for knowledge workers to replace the now-outmoded mechanical and physical skills of the recent industrial past.

Implications for higher education

Higher education in Britain remains dominated by ideals essentially created in the 19th century which, although modified, continue to strongly influence much thinking about university education. In this view university students are a minority, an elite of bright, middle-class school-leavers who are full-time students normally living, at least through term time, at the institution. Their educational needs are centred on the cultural capital signified by a degree whose curriculum is defined and validated by an autonomous institution. The students attending the institution by implication chose that programme of study and can expect little control over what they learn. The late 20th century shift towards mass higher education greatly increased the number of students in the universities, but has not always altered the basic assumptions. Lip service is generally paid to the ideals that should lead to increased student choice and flexibility in the construction of a learning programme and some changes have been made, but they remain limited and are often fiercely resisted, especially in the pre-1992 universities. However, while the universities coped with educating a small elite, they have so far failed to deal with the education of the 30–50 per cent of the population demanded by the knowledge society

Despite this, at present it seems likely that many of the universities will continue to draw the majority of their intake from the full-time 18–22-year-old student grouping. However, there are bound to be changes as a result of the creation of a 'market' in education in which there is real competition for 'well-qualified' students. It seems that a new binary divide is emerging within the university sector that will create two groups of institutions. On the one hand there is a group of mostly pre-1992 universities totalling perhaps some 40 in all which, because of their perceived academic status, will gradually receive both the highest number of undergraduate applications from well-qualified 18–22-year-olds, and research funding from government and industry. This will give them enormous power and ability to resist government pressure to conform to the agenda of the learning age and defend their traditional positions and practices. For example, some of these universities have sought to move out of the inspection framework set up by the Quality Assurance Agency, using 'free market' arguments to justify buying in cheaper and more cost-effective auditors. Similarly, some would argue, any liberalization on the issues of fees could divert considerable extra income into the elite institutions, making them still less willing to accept government direction.

On the other hand, a group of about 60 or 70 institutions, mainly drawn from the post-1992 universities, will find themselves increasingly powerless in this competitive 'market', for both research funding and full-time 18–22-year-old students. A number of these institutions will be increasingly forced to follow the government strategy in relation to a wider and more flexible higher education sector if they are to survive. This will create problems. For example, as we shall see below, the further education sector appears likely to threaten this group by providing degree programmes. As a result of the 'new binary divide', these institutions have a much stronger imperative to change the nature of their teaching and learning provision, and especially to extend their student base outside the 'conventional' recruitment pool. This has fundamental implications for the 'boundaries' of the higher education sector.

These 'new' universities, the ex-polytechnics, have been more flexible than the older universities. The polytechnics always saw a part of their brief to meet regional needs by providing an education for students of all ages, by offering part-time courses, and with flexible timetabling. Their curriculum has also been more open, with interdisciplinary courses and vocational courses playing a large part in their programmes. Most significantly, their courses have been offered in different ways, with an emphasis on part-time and evening and weekend timetabling which has enabled and encouraged students from a far wider range of backgrounds to attend. However, and in part because of this flexibility, the polytechnics were seen as academically second rate, their awards easier to achieve and their students less 'good'.

These problems need to be confronted in a variety of ways, and higher education institutions face a considerable challenge if the demands of the learning society are to be met. Indeed, faced with competition from new degree providers in further education some may literally be fighting for their existence. Flexibility will be essential both in the institutions and their programmes. For example, entrance demands will need to be less rigid so that not only will students come from more varied backgrounds in terms of age, class and ethnicity, they will also have diverse educational histories. More radical than this, students will not necessarily enrol at the beginning of a three-year programme of study, nor stay until the end. They will need to be able to shift between institutions, maximizing the opportunities to construct learning programmes tailored to their individual needs. Modular programmes are the beginning of this process, but they need to be accepted across the sector. Minimally, modular programmes will be required so that parts of courses can be taken at different institutions or times of life and part-time study can be a possibility.

This is a central part of the present shift from the concept of 'education' to the concept of the 'measurement of learning'. Within this AP(E)L, already well advanced in some areas, will need to be universally recognized. Systems for the Accreditation of Prior Learning (APL) and Accreditation of Prior Experiential Learning (APEL) are designed so that learning achieved can be used to replace entry requirements and, more contentiously, to request advanced standing or excusal from courses. The difficulties are myriad. The assessment of discipline-specific applications is relatively straightforward, as the relevance and equivalence of one course on Shakespeare to another is easily seen. However, the relevance of courses on Shakespeare to Archaeology is more difficult to estimate. These problems are magnified when AP(E)L claims are considered. How does the undoubted learning that takes place in bringing up children count if admission to a mathematics degree is requested? Because of cases like this, AP(E)L tends to rely on the presentation of a folio of evidence of learning and to be used most often in general skills courses or in work-based learning. The rather trite examples used above show why the universities, with their strict discipline-based curricula, have ignored such questions. Nonetheless, if a truly flexible post-compulsory system as demanded by lifelong learning in the learning society is to be developed these difficulties will need to be addressed. This is especially the case if students dip in and out of education throughout their lives, changing institution and subject as they will be encouraged to do if the current plans for the University for Industry and Individual Learning Accounts become government policy.

However, it is possible that market forces will push many of these changes. As student finance changes and students are paying more and more of their own costs, they will demand consumer choice. There is already strong anecdotal evidence that this is beginning to happen. Similarly, employers, working in an increasingly competitive global market place, will require relevant skills and learning. Nevertheless, we should beware of seeing these forces as neutral. The demands of the market are not the only factor to be taken into account when looking at a programme of ambitious educational reform, as the power of the elite universities to resist change has shown.

For the future there are even more radical changes in view. Attempts to implement the proposal in *The Learning Age* (DfEE, 1998) for associate degrees, taking two years or equivalent instead of three for a BA/BSc, will re-ignite discussions about the quality of degrees and who should provide them, while the insistence on the acquisition of skills – basic, IT and others – will raise concerns about the discipline content of courses.

The question of IT also raises the question of distance learning, a key part of the learning age strategy:

> In future, learners need not be tied to particular locations. They will be able to study at home, at work, or in a local library or shopping centre, as well as in colleges and universities. People will be able to study at a distance using broadcast media and online access. (DfEE, 1998: 17)

However, although the Open University has shown what can be done in providing quality courses for large numbers of part-time, distant students, obstacles like academic arguments about progression are put in the way of their implementation in taught courses from first degrees through to PhD. IT also opens the door to globalization. To many this is seen as unproblematically positive, but real difficulties do remain especially in a competitive environment in which boundaries between countries as well as between public and private are eroded. Putting it crudely, as a writer in the *THES* did early in 2000, if you can choose between the University of Poppleton 'live' and MIT 'online' for your MBA, there really is little competition. What this means is that where virtual learning is put in place it must be customer-focused. Alongside this it might be suggested that the real advantages of traditional learning and teaching should continue to be investigated.

Finally, and perhaps one of the most difficult questions, will be the role of the HEIs in learning partnership arrangements. Already, local and regional Lifelong Learning Partnerships are being developed, but are most often between local industries, councils and further education providers. Currently, where they play a part, universities are often represented by their continuing education departments. However, in future it could be possible for universities to franchise part or all of their degree programme to the further education sector. But recent experience of overseas franchising suggests this is not as simple and profitable as it sounds.

Despite all this the most important feature of the learning society in higher education will prove to be the lowering of the traditional barriers between sectors and the development of one boundary-less education sector where learning can be accessed by anyone anywhere and courses are provided by institutions in meaningful partnerships with each other so that students are able to complete the learning they need, to progress from level to level regardless of which institution provides the necessary qualification. This is the vision behind the Learning and Skills Councils that are now replacing Training and Enterprise Councils across the country. However, should higher education institutions fail to meet these challenges, the further education sector, long seen as the poor relation of post-school education, is anxious to play a major part in this learning.

Nevertheless, real problems remain. Although the government sees these partnerships as an important feature of the new learning age, and it seems likely that funding will follow these initiatives, yet it will almost certainly lead to a further strengthening of the new 'binary divide' discussed above. In this situation those elite institutions like Oxbridge, which can attract funding from sources other than the government, are likely to remain firmly outside such arrangements, leading to the glorious vision of learning for all being seen by many as yet more second-rate education.

It is too soon to attempt to judge the effects of most of the changes outlined here, or even whether they will actually take place. Government funding can push for change in particular directions, but the needs of society and the learners might change, and the strength of resistance in traditional institutions should not be underestimated.

Implications for further education

Further education, with its emphasis on vocational training has, until recently, and especially the 1990s, been the poor relation of post-compulsory education in terms of both funding and public esteem – the two sides of the same coin. However, the changes in funding resulting from the 1992 Further and Higher Education Act, the importance given to the Kennedy Report as well as the prominence of further education in *The Learning Age* and *Learning to Succeed* (DfEE, 1999) suggest that this is changing.

As discussed above, one of the main shifts associated with the learning age is a new emphasis on learning throughout life. This learning should be neither random nor 'for its own sake', but for the dual purpose of creating 'a strong economy and an inclusive society' (DfEE, 1998: 11). In economic terms the government has argued that the UK has fallen behind its major competitors in the training of the workforce. While at level 4 (first degree or equivalent) or above, the UK performs well against some of its competitors, at the intermediate and technician levels the comparison shows the UK to perform poorly. Although the precise connection between these comparisons and Gross Domestic Product remains open to argument, the government is clear about how to improve economic performance. The vision of the learning age set out in *Learning To Succeed* 'is to build a new culture of learning and aspiration which will underpin national competitiveness and personal prosperity'(para.1.7). The result of this new culture will be a knowledgeable, flexible workforce with skills that will lead to lifelong employment, probably in a series of jobs.

However, if the learning society is to realize its true potential, this emphasis on the economic will need to be balanced by learning to live in the community. This will mean learning about democracy and community values, and learning how those values come to help build a more equitable and just society. Ideally, these values will be seen to apply not just to the human society but also to the constructed and natural environment. The dangers of ignoring this aspect of society are clearly spelt out in the news that bombards us every day. As *The Learning Age* (DfEE, 1998: 11) claims:

> learning contributes to social cohesion and fosters a sense of belonging, responsibility and identity. In communities affected by rapid economic change and industrial restructuring, learning builds local capacity to respond to this change... learning lies at the heart of the Government's welfare reform programme.

However, although there has been an expansion in this sector, the failure to reach the national targets for education and training has so far shown that the expansion has not been sufficient in terms of numbers. More importantly, too few students have successfully achieved a qualification. The target set by the National Advisory Council for Education and Training Targets in 1995 was for at least three out of five of the adult workforce to be qualified to the equivalent of NVQ level 3 by 2000. To reach this target from the 1995 standard of only two in five of the adult population having attained this level, over a million adults were needed to qualify each year. Kennedy (1998: 165) felt that achieving the current targets remained a significant challenge.

Although it will not help in achieving the 2000 target, the government has responded to these and similar figures by firstly setting a more realistic target of increasing the percentage of adults who have achieved level 3 from the current 45 per cent to 50 per cent by 2002 (DfEE, 1999, para.1.10). To reach these targets, the government argues, it has already acted through a programme of investment in further education and training planning to increase substantially the funding available to the FE sector.

As the necessary knowledge will need to be acquired, new opportunities for learning are to be funded. This will be done in a number of ways, but the emphasis throughout is on partnerships. For example, the University for Industry will deliberately push funding towards the FE sector. The UfI is being set up to correct what global competition has revealed as an under-educated and under-trained workforce, which has been blamed, in part, for the increasing gap in productivity between Britain and its competitors. One of its effects will be to bring the FE sector to the fore in funding and public recognition and as a powerful force in the creation of local and national industry and education partnerships.

The continuing education sector

As already discussed in the opening chapters, what was the adult-education and is now the continuing-education (CE) sector went through a number of fundamental changes of direction during the 20th century. In addition to this, many of the changes described above will put pressure for change in the sector if it is to survive. The role of CE in the learning society is the least clear of all post-school provision. The reasons for this probably stem from its ambiguous role throughout the 20th century. It seems strange that as lifelong learning comes to prominence and the image of CE as an academic discipline is growing through research and national and international organizations, the actual practice has an uncertain future.

Non-accredited, liberal adult education taught from university continuing education departments is no longer funded, and so has become the province of the WEA and the University of the Third Age (U3A). The WEA has retained its presence in an increasingly competitive environment, pressed especially by the U3A, which is enormously popular and continuing to grow. The formula of democratic organization of classes so that students control what they choose to learn, low or no fees and no assessment clearly appeals to retired students. Access courses and basic skills teaching, together with vocational courses, are now provided almost entirely through the FE colleges; proposed changes in funding will increase this provision. Community courses, providing introductory or specialized courses for disadvantaged groups, are now committed to a precarious existence, relying on government or European funding, normally short-term, for their existence.

These changes have left CE with a more limited role. Since 1992 CE courses, which are funded through the Higher Education Funding Council (HEFC), are required to be accredited and to lead to an award. The award can be a certificate or diploma of higher education or a degree and is required to be of HE standard. In some places, this requirement has led to pressures on CE departments. While the old extra-mural departments, as the name suggests, often had a rather uncomfortable relationship with their parent institution, at least the differences were clearly defined. The shift to CE and especially to the responsibility for teaching credit-bearing courses has obscured the difference between full-time mainstream and CE departments. In a number of places, the shifts to mainstreaming of CE departments following the 1992 Education Act were taken literally, and the different disciplines within CE departments were absorbed into the full-time university departments. Even when successful, this has resulted in a loss of identity for the previous CE staff and of the specific CE courses.

Elsewhere, the relationships between CE and the parent body have remained difficult or even worsened since 1992. This is primarily because there is now competition within the institutions for students. Part-time study is attractive to a number of mature students who work or have family commitments; the flexibility of AP(E)L and modular programmes will also appeal to these people. Perhaps most importantly, the erosion and then the final ending of student grants plus the 'top-up' fee introduced in 1998/9 now seem to have acted as a massive deterrent to non-standard entry students taking degrees full-time. As a result of these factors the numbers of applications for full-time study has, in some institutions at least, ceased to grow, and some departments have experienced difficulty in filling places. In such a situation envious or predatory glances towards the CE students may be detected, particularly as the profile of CE students is changing. Traditionally, the majority of students in adult education have been elderly, middle-class and female. However, as the accredited programmes are becoming common and the need for and advantages of qualifications become apparent, this is beginning to change. The student body is younger and the balance of sexes more even.

Difficulties between departments may be exacerbated because CE degrees are usually interdisciplinary, in 'Combined Studies' or 'Landscape Studies', which are also seen as inferior to the single-honours programme. This is partly because the departments themselves are normally 'interdisciplinary' in nature, composed of specialists from a number of disciplines, so that there may be only one historian or geographer. However, the lack of single-honours degrees may also be a result of pressure from outside the department as other departments 'protect' their subject areas.

The shift towards award-bearing programmes is having an effect on the students. Those enrolling for degree programmes tend to be younger and to be searching for a qualification, not just learning 'for interest'. In turn, this is, at least in our institution, revitalizing the teachers in the CE department. Despite the exhaustion of constant change during the 1990s, they are now enjoying the challenge of these new, demanding but rewarding students. It is hoped that membership of the local and regional learning partnerships which are currently being established across the country will extend this role. The FE sector will be looking for progression routes for students as it continues its vocational and access roles. The CE departments with a similar commitment to part-time, flexible learning for mature students should provide the way forward.

Meanwhile, certificate and other accredited courses continue to be offered in more traditional adult education classes across the country. Although some of the students have migrated to the WEA and the U3A, a substantial number prefer the challenge of structured university adult education courses. There are already a number of students from these classes working towards certificates and diplomas.

In these ways, the CE departments have found a role for themselves in the developing context of lifelong learning and the associated new funding regimes. It is perhaps ironic that, having reached this point, debate about the constitution of the learning society should begin to question how and where the social and cultural skills loosely contained within 'citizenship' might be taught beyond the classroom. Liberal adult education is one obvious answer. This would lead to an expansion of the role of CE again, if not to a reversal of present policies.

Conclusion

The consequences of the idea of a learning society for post-school education are potentially enormous and far reaching, Many will be matters of detail and the concern of only one part of the sector, However, in conclusion, certain key elements can be isolated:

- Access to courses must be open to all suitably qualified and able students.
- Programmes of study must be constructed to allow students to learn in bite-size chunks throughout the whole of their lives. It may be more administratively convenient for students to remain with one course for three years but this will become less and less normal.
- Curricula must be devised which will allow learning for the whole person.
- Post-school education must become more 'customer-focused' in terms of both delivery and course content. This might involve 'virtual' education or IT, but it also should take advantage of the strength of 'traditional' face-to-face methods.
- Centrally a 'learning age' must be accompanied by the dissolution of boundaries that have traditionally divided private and public, university and college, education and training.
- It must be recognized that these changes have to involve the whole sector. The ability of a minority of 'elite' institutions to remain outside these changes will, as in the past, fundamentally challenge the system's academic credibility.

References

DfEE (1998) *The Learning Age: A renaissance for a new Britain,* DfEE, London
DfEE (1999) *Learning to Succeed: A new framework for post-16 education,* DfEE, London
Kennedy, H (1998) 'A self-perpetuating learning society', in ed S Ranson, *Inside the Learning Society,* Cassell, London

Chapter 11

The school in the age of learning

John Holford and Gill Nicholls

In one very important sense, the age of learning is already a reality. Until the 19th century, only a small elite in any society received a formal education. But by World War I, elementary schooling had become universal in most of the industrialized countries. During the two decades after World War II, secondary education followed suit. In 1960 fewer than one in two of 6–11-year-olds in the developing countries were enrolled in school; by the mid-1980s roughly three-quarters were (Colclough with Lewin, 1993: 18). The 20th century was, more than any other before it, a century of universal schooling. As the historian Eric Hobsbawm (1994: 12) reminds us, it was in the 20th century that – for the first time in human history – it became possible to describe most human beings as literate.

The very ubiquity of schooling today means we often ignore how significant an achievement this was. Widespread literacy is fundamental to political as well as social and economic development. Few of the distinctive features of 20th century industrial economies – let alone 21st century 'knowledge' economies – would be possible without it. Although it is arguable that the economy provided the driving force for mass literacy, there is little question that the school has been the instrument by which it was achieved.

Of course, in this book the phrase 'age of learning' has a rather wider meaning, and it was only in the mid-1990s, for example, that British policy began to refer to 'lifelong learning' (Dearing, 1996). This chapter therefore has two main purposes. It examines what this new 'age of learning' means for the systems of mass schooling that have developed over the past century and a half. And it discusses whether, and in what ways, schooling is, for good or ill, shaping the emerging learning society. These two aims – essentially, how schools shape the age of learning, and vice versa – are examined through discussions of a series of topics.

Compulsory learning

Traditionally, a defining difference between the organization and ethos of schools on the one hand and of other areas of education on the other has been the question of compulsion. From the later 19th century boys and girls in Western societies have, by and large, been obliged by law to go to school. The age ranges to which this applied extended gradually upwards until the 1960s, by which time most children between the ages of roughly 5 and 15 were attending school. Above the school-leaving age, attendance in any form of education has been voluntary. A frequent term for education after the school-leaving age has been 'post-compulsory' education. This has been used to refer to a large array of activities: for instance, all those sectors commonly labelled 'further', 'higher', 'post-secondary', 'tertiary', 'continuing' or 'adult' education, together with (chiefly work-related) training of various kinds.

For some, compulsion makes schooling fundamentally different. This view was implicit in much of the influential educational literature of the 1960s and 1970s. Perhaps most famously, Ivan Illich (1973) saw schooling as oppressive and monopolistic: while appearing to liberate and provide routes to enhanced status, in reality schools make citizens *dependent* on formal education. In his view, schools were servants of the consumer society, designed to shape children early in life for roles as docile and conformist workers and consumers. His critique of schools, it should be said, was of a piece with his critique of modern bureaucratic service societies. Instead of freeing people, formal education only provides them with the competence to learn what is prescribed. A comparable critique emerged from the Marxist left. Schools exist to prepare children for their role in the capitalist economy, argued Bowles and Gintis (1976), and their clear priority is to produce disciplined workers for the capitalist economy. They also serve to sort people for the roles they are allotted by the capitalist economy.

Both these critiques served to emphasize the role of the school as a disciplining agent. Schools, in this view, are disciplined internally in order to generate students who will accept the disciplines within society more broadly. Two comments are perhaps worth making at this point. First, there is a good deal of evidence – not to mention social theory – to support the notion that schools are agents of social discipline. This is not the place to rehearse it, but the Manchester Education Aid Society's argument in 1866, at the height of the debate in Britain about establishing a national system of primary education, is an apposite illustration:

> The first need of society is order. If order is to be produced in men and women, what kind of preparation for it is that which leaves the children as wild as young ostriches in the desert? When for the first ten or twelve years of

life there has been no discipline either in life or in body – when cleanliness has been unknown – when no law of God or man has been considered sacred, and no power recognised but direct physical force – is it to be expected that they will quietly and industriously settle down in mills, workshops, warehouses or at any trade in the orderly routine of any family, to work continuously by day, morning and evening, from Monday to Saturday? The expectation is absurd. Continuous labour and sober thought are alike impossible to them. (Quoted in Simon, 1974: 359)

There is a certain irony that these arguments were strongest during the 1960s and 1970s – precisely the period when, it is commonly said, discipline in schools was weakest.

If schools can be accused of being over-disciplined and even authoritarian, it was common in the 1960s and 1970s to contrast this with the freedom and respect accorded to participants in adult education. In her influential book, *Adults Learning*, Rogers (1971: 19) stated a general view: 'The freedom of adult students to stop coming to a class is one of the things which makes teaching in adult education a very different proposition from teaching in schools.' Others emphasized the democracy of adult education – and often saw the adult class as a particular and even paradigmatic expression of that democracy – or the essential equality between teacher and student. *Teaching on Equal Terms* (Rogers, 1969), the title of one book, is illustrative. Malcolm Knowles took presumptions such as these and fashioned them into a theory. Compulsory schooling demanded 'pedagogy', in which the learner was dependent and organized according to a set curriculum. In contrast, voluntary, free, autonomous adult education required 'andragogy' (Knowles, 1970).

From perspectives such as these, some adult educators were deeply suspicious of lifelong education when the term became relatively common following the Faure Report (1972). Lifelong education would mean labelling people as inadequate – lifelong (Ohliger, 1974). Illich and Verne (1976) foresaw people 'imprisoned in a global classroom'. But is the contrast between the compulsion of schooling and the freedom of adult education really so sharp? The tendency in the last two decades has been to play down the differences.

Several factors have had a part in this. The notion that there are two neatly defined groups who receive education – children and adults – does little justice to the complexity of provision. There are marked differences between the curriculum and organizational regimes of British primary and secondary schools, for instance. Many secondary schools that offer A-levels have rather different rules for their sixth-form students than for their younger classes; school sixth forms are in any case legally 'post-compulsory'. At the same time, education of those aged 16 and above is highly variegated.

To use the British labels (other countries differ in terminology, but not in diversity), the sectors known as further, higher, continuing professional and continuing education are markedly different.

How far is 'post-compulsory' education really non-compulsory? It is true that the legal requirement to attend school on a full-time basis applies only within specific age ranges, but in fact there are increasingly strong requirements on adults to attend various forms of continuing education or training. In recent decades, governments and the public have expected professions to become more accountable. One of the ways professional bodies have responded is to require their members to undertake continuing education if they are to retain their licence to practice. Lawyers, doctors, dentists, nurses, many medical-related professions and accountants have gradually adjusted to this regime. Debate about the desirability of this, strong in the 1980s (Rockhill, 1983; Collins, 1991), has now subsided. Indeed, this is now so much part of an implicit bargain between the state and the professions that it is open to question whether governments would allow professions to do away with these requirements.

At the same time, many employers now require their workers to undertake staff development – more commonly in larger firms, and for higher-status staff, it is true. Sometimes this is highly structured, leading to formal qualifications of some kind, as part of well-organized programmes. More often, perhaps, it involves ad hoc work by consultants, trainers and staff developers, in staff conferences or team meetings. For some employers, commitment to such training is part and parcel of a managerial commitment to an external standard, such as 'Investors in People' in the UK, or a quality standard such as the ISO 9000 series.

In Britain the new 'Curriculum 2000' for 16–19-year-olds is beyond 'formal' compulsory schooling. However, in reality it requires all 16–19-year-olds to complete some form of education. This may be vocational or academic. Some study full-time in schools or colleges; others are in paid employment, but study part-time. In either case, what they study must address 'key skills' defined by the government's curriculum. While there is no legal requirement for young people to take the training or education thus defined, those who choose not to do so are ineligible for state welfare benefits.

So the absence of a legal requirement to attend education by no means implies an absence of compulsion. This is not, of course, to say that attending a company training session is the same as going to school. The differences are evident. But it does suggest that the notion of adult learning as a freely undertaken enterprise, in which all partake as equals, significantly overstates the case. Implicitly, the message may confirm the worst fears of Illich and his contemporaries – to ask whether lifelong learning is compatible with the compulsion of schooling misses the central truth, that so far as the experience of the learner is concerned, lifelong learning is in many respects itself compulsory.

A school curriculum for lifelong learning

Schooling is designed to prepare children for life. One of the assumptions of 'lifelong learning' as a policy, of course, is that we cannot realistically now say what particular skills people will require throughout their life. They will change their jobs, even their careers, quite frequently. Arguably, therefore, it no longer makes much sense for schools to teach specific skills, especially in the vocational area. Thinking along these lines, schools should not prepare people for particular jobs. Rather, they should develop skills and attitudes that will enable children to mature into capable adult learners, providing them with the skills to readjust and reposition themselves throughout their working life.

What should these lifelong learning skills and attitudes be? A prime mover in the international drive towards lifelong learning policies has been the Organization for Economic Cooperation and Development – the association of most of the world's richest nations. In 1993, it convened a conference on 'The Curriculum Redefined'. This raised some key issues:

> What might be the minimum of subject matter to be included in the compulsory school curriculum? How should general skills such as learning to learn and learning to solve problems be built in? What might be the right mix of knowledge and skills that a school can provide? How and by what means can learners acquire this? What learning environments, in and out of school, are best suited...? How might what is learned in a person's younger years be made more relevant to the opportunities and challenges which confront them in early adulthood and beyond? (Quoted in Chapman and Aspin, 1997: 90–91)

Answering these questions is not so straightforward as posing them. The OECD emphasized the importance of 'basic elements of literacy and numeracy'; beyond that is more difficult. School curricula are constrained by strong national political pressures as well as by international policies. Some of these may have little connection with lifelong learning. For example, most countries expect students to have a grounding in their own national history. There is a very good case to be made for the importance of historical understanding as a skill for lifelong learning. But studying Tudor Britain is not obviously more important for this purpose than studying the Philippines under American rule or China under the Ming.

Examples of the approaches taken in major policy documents can, however, be instructive. The Secretary's Commission on Achieving Necessary Skills in the USA (SCANS, 1991) was concerned about the competencies – basic and thinking skills, personal qualities – which students would need for the workplace of the future. It identified five types of competence that would enhance the transition from school to work:

1. Resources: the ability to identify, organize, plan and allocate resources.
2. Interpersonal: the ability to work with others in teams, teach others, serve clients, exercise leadership, negotiate and work with diversity.
3. Information: the ability to acquire, organize, interpret, evaluate and communicate information.
4. Systems: an understanding of complex interrelationships, and the ability to distinguish trends, predict impacts, and monitor and correct performance.
5. Technology: the ability to work with a range of technologies and choose tools appropriate to particular tasks.

Something like a common approach has emerged over the past decade or so, in documents as geographically diverse as the SCANS report, the European Commission's White Paper, *Teaching and Learning: Towards the learning society* (EC, 1995), and the Hong Kong Education Commission's *Framework for Education Reform* (Education Commission, 1999) – though not all are to be found in each. These can be summarized as follows:

- all school students should develop a fundamental grounding in mathematical and literacy skills;
- they should develop skills in the use of information technology;
- they should develop analytical and thinking skills, with an emphasis on 'process' rather than 'content';
- there is a strong emphasis on developing group and interpersonal skills, linked to the notion that in their working lives, individuals will move quite frequently between different working groups, teams and so forth;
- there is an emphasis on establishing forms of teaching and assessment which situate knowledge and skills in the 'real world'.

There is, however, a further consideration that requires emphasis. It derives from the knowledge that, in reality, academic performance in schools is a good predictor of participation in forms of post-school education. For this reason (among others), there has been a widespread emphasis on establishing criterion-based and competence-based assessment schemes. These are seen as providing better motivation, since with criterion-based assessment credit is given for what a child learns, in contrast to normative-based assessment regimes in which credit is only given for what a child learns relative to other children. A competence-based scheme also tends, it is argued, to emphasize the applicability of knowledge in concrete settings.

Schools and the community

Schools form by far the most numerous and widespread of formal educational institutions. The question of their relationship to the community arises from two rather different motives. On the one hand, there is the desire – related to the concern to make the curriculum more relevant to the world of work – to bring real-world perspectives into the activities of the school. Behind this lies the principle that relevance to the real world will enhance the effectiveness of school-based learning, and make it more likely to engender lifelong learning habits. A common feature, though not a necessary one, is the view that children should be exposed at school to perspectives from the world of business and work. The European Commission argues for 'bringing schools and the business sector closer together' as one of its five key objectives in building a learning society. 'Education must be opened up to the world of work'; companies must be involved in the training drive not only as regards workers but also as regards young people and adults'; and 'cooperation must be developed between schools and firms' (EC, 1995: 38–39). In Britain, 'Young Enterprise' – a formal part of the National Curriculum – encourages close school/industry partnerships such as enterprise education and work placements.

On the other hand, there is the sense that the capital of schools – their buildings, their teachers, their expertise – could be more fully utilized for the benefit of the entire community's lifelong learning, rather than just for children. UNESCO, in its *Agenda for the Future,* for example, argued for 'opening schools, colleges and universities to adult learners', and in particular for:

> requiring institutions of formal education from primary level onwards to be prepared to open their doors to adult learners, both women and men, adapting their programmes and learning conditions to meet their needs. (UNESCO, 1997: 14)

This can be seen as reflecting two overlapping concerns. There is a long and influential tradition in educational thought, and particularly in adult education, which argues that schools should be a focus of educational activity among the community at large. In fact, this goes rather deeper than a mere concern to make efficient use of resources. It can be traced back to the pioneering work of community education in the 1960s and 1970s, which itself was attempting to address problems thrown up by research in the first two decades of mass secondary education in Britain ; work such as Jackson and Marsden (1962) and Douglas (1964), which seemed to show that working-class children's relatively poor academic performance in school was linked to their family and community circumstances. For the Educational Priority Areas experiment of the 1960s, the community school was defined as 'one which ventured out into and was welcomed in the community until the visionary time arrived when it was difficult to distinguish school from community' (Midwinter, 1972: 161). In practical terms this meant 'home–school links', which would 'increase the educational understanding of the parent and the social understanding of the teacher' (Halsey et al, 1972: 118). 'Only if education in the schools is relevant to the children's direct experiences will it engage their attention and interest' (Halsey et al, 1972: 117). This view of the community school as the key agent in educational change, especially for the economically and socially deprived, remains important.

At the same time, governments since the 1970s have been seeking ways to make all public sector institutions more cost-effective. Although this tendency has many contradictory features, we can see the concern behind many developments. These include using school buildings for adult as well as for children's education, and encouraging schools to raise income from selling courses to adults in the community. They include the aim of encouraging greater private investment in education: by parents in their children's schools, by individuals in their own lifelong learning, by businesses in various community initiatives. They include financial initiatives such as 'treating capital investment and investment in training on an equal basis' (EC, 1995), and the British government's experimentation with individual learning accounts.

The 'learning school'?

Schools are institutions for teaching and learning, but how far are they, in the jargon of today, 'learning organizations'? If we focus not on the school, but on schooling – formal education at the primary and secondary levels – we find that this question bifurcates. On the one hand, there is a question about the nature of the school as an organization: how far does it encourage learning by its staff? On the other is the related issue of how teachers learn to be teachers: how well their professional education prepares them for a life as a teacher, how well in-service education and training ensures their continued professional development. We turn first to how far the organizational environment of the school encourages learning.

In a learning society characterized by change, organizational flexibility and technological innovation, the school often seems a very traditional institution. With very few exceptions, all children go to school. In most schools, relatively large groups of children – in Britain often over 30 – are taught in classrooms by teachers. The desks or tables may look more modern than those of 50 or 100 years ago; they may be laid out in different ways. There may be a computer or two. But by and large, someone who went to school 50 or 100 years ago would recognize the school classroom as what it is. Contrast this with the change that has taken place in many – though not all – workplaces. In 1911 about three-quarters of the population was employed in manual occupations; 90 years later the proportion is said to be less than one-quarter. Few workers now have experience of the factory 'shop floor'. Those who do, now supervise computer-controlled machines. Today's workers are found in offices, in the 'service economy', and often in small 'flexible' workplaces.

There are exceptions and caveats, of course. Many have pointed to the parallels between the work regimes of the modern telephone call-centre and that of the Victorian factory. But the contrasts between manual labour, chiefly in factories and mills, of the Victorian worker and the service sector working environments which most people experience today are marked.

Schools may be designed as places for children to learn, but they are also, of course, working environments – principally for teachers, though also for clerical workers, cleaners, technicians, and so forth. Teachers teach students in classrooms today as they have for decades. When the bell rings, a timetable directs them to another group of students, another topic, perhaps another room, just as teachers' timetables have done for a century and more. At secondary level, teachers still teach subjects in which they have specialist expertise. On the face of it, this would seem to provide stable rather than changing working environments for staff, and to contrast rather starkly with the flexibility of the working environment in the 'real world'.

Does a system of schooling organized in this way provide a learning environment for its staff? In fact, the nature of the teaching profession has been a matter of concern to educational administrators and planners in many countries. From their point of view, teachers appear resistant to change. This is partly logistical: the sheer number of teaching staff means that significant change in the school curriculum is remarkably difficult to achieve. (Most British children, for instance, are taught French at secondary school. Perhaps they should be taught Spanish or Chinese instead? But logistically, making this happen is so difficult that the issue is never seriously considered.) But apart from the logistics, there is also a question of the outlook, values and attitudes of the profession.

Various approaches to overcoming the teaching profession's perceived 'resistance to change' have been attempted (see, for example, Fullan, 1993; Hargreaves, 1997). Some involve a move towards making the school look more like the 'learning organization' of management literature. Many school management structures have become 'flatter', with fewer tiers of management and staff grouped in teams rather than departments. But for most schools this has taken them only a few steps down the road, and can often seem more a matter of terminology than substance. Another approach is to make the environment in which schools function more like the environment that (it is supposed) nurtures change and learning organizations. Thus we have attempts to make schools compete in a quasi-market, rewarded for how well they meet measurable targets (chiefly student numbers, examination grades and performance in inspections). Along the same lines, the British government is keen to encourage some diversity among schools. To this end it allows – even encourages – different forms of school government. It encourages different missions or 'status' (technology, arts and language, for example). It rewards success in generating financial sponsorship from the private sector.

These are altering the environment within which schools operate, and – at the level of rhetoric at least – the changes in Britain have been quite profound over the past two decades. (Interestingly, changes of government have brought little change in the thrust of policy.) But governments have shied away from creating anything more than a very attenuated market for primary and secondary education. For most schools, the reality is considerable stability in what they teach, in their student and staff numbers, in their income, in their location. The market is illusory. Flexible 'learning organizations' are not created in such environments. Instead, educational administrators have been forced back on the traditional armoury of the manager of a large and internally stable workforce: incentive payment schemes, promotional structures, appraisal systems (see, for example, DfEE, 1998).

Schools, teachers, citizenship and values

There is a widespread view that an age of learning must also be an age in which men and women are able freely to exercise judgement in society. This is commonly expressed in the language of 'citizenship'; it may be no accident that policy concern with education for citizenship has arisen in parallel with the policy shift towards lifelong learning. The relationship between citizenship and the age of learning is discussed further in Chapter 17; this section considers only the implications for education in schools.

In Britain, the Crick Report (Advisory Group on Education for Citizenship and the Teaching of Democracy in Schools, 1998: 7) set citizenship as one of its primary aims: 'For people to think of themselves as active citizens, willing, able and equipped to have an influence in public life and with critical capacities to weight evidence before speaking and acting.' The report further enforced this by suggesting that 'Individuals must be helped and prepared to shape the terms of such engagement by political understanding and action' (p. 10).

These statements imply that a healthy and vibrant democracy requires a public that is not acquiescent, hostile or suspicious, but has a broad understanding of major contemporary ideas. The implication is that teachers and schools will be – if they are not already – at the forefront of delivering such ideals to students. Teachers can cultivate among their students the realization that the judgements they make can influence the public arena. Developing judgement is vital for citizenship. Beiner (1983: 163) suggests that 'judgement is… irreducible to algorithm'. What is required is not a 'decision procedure', but an education in hermeneutic insight, taste and understanding. What does this mean for pedagogy and learning for the teacher?

Teachers need to enable students to understand both the values and biases they hold and how these will be used in making judgements. Schools and local communities provide a good context for pupils to examine issues and events and to become involved in activities and experiences where the emphasis is on learning through action (Advisory Group on Education for Citizenship and the Teaching of Democracy in Schools, 1998: 37). Through this type of involvement pupils can be helped and guided through the issues, political, civic and social, related to information and knowledge. Such engagement can lead to balanced decision making, incorporating some of the requirements and expectations of citizenship and values.

Citizenship is fundamentally concerned with social relationships between people, and relationships between people and institutional arrangements of complex industrial societies. Thus exploring citizenship and values within the school curriculum requires an examination of teachers, pupils and institutions (schools and society as a whole). In Mills' terms (1970), we are concerned with what kinds of person we are able to be and the kinds of person we might be. Understanding the conceptions of citizenship and values in the curriculum requires an understanding of the 'self' and the manner in which institutional arrangements (in this case the school) may provide opportunities for, or place constraints upon, self-development (in this case the pupil).

The teacher is pivotal to learning in this way in school. But to what extent are teachers themselves educated to become citizens in the way described in the Crick Report? In Britain, teachers are increasingly expected to teach citizenship and values both in and through the curriculum. From September 2000 this will be required by law, with each subject area stating specifically how citizenship and values will be represented within the discipline. This presents teachers with a considerable task and responsibility: they must educate for citizenship, when they may themselves have had no formal training in either citizenship or values. This makes it difficult to set the responsibility for education for citizenship solely on the school and the teachers within them. Although active citizenship is clearly a desirable goal, involvement in community groups requires a sense of civic responsibility and political skill. Both can be promoted in school, but for teacher and pupil alike a learning ethos is required.

As schooling has become widespread, so it has become politically more important. Education is one of the largest items of government spending in virtually every country; in Britain, for example, it now far outstrips spending on defence. But although, in the developed countries at least, political debate about education has often been fierce, it is common ground that schools are a good thing (see Husén, 1979, for a summary of the challenges that arose at this time). The issues in dispute have been how they should be organized, whether their curricula could be better, how we can get more children to attend them, how the quality of teaching can be improved, and so forth. As a 'through life' perspective on education and learning permeates policy agendas, the existence of schools has not – yet – been questioned. Radical change is, however, clearly expected.

References

Advisory Group on Education for Citizenship and the Teaching of Democracy in Schools (1998) *Education for Citizenship and the Teaching of Democracy in Schools:* Initial report, Qualifications and Curriculum Authority, London

Beiner, R (1983) *Political Judgement,* Methuen, London

Bowles, S and Gintis, H (1976) *Schooling in Capitalist America. Educational reforms and the contradictions of economic life,* Routledge and Kegan Paul, London

Chapman, J D and Aspin, D N (1997) *The School, the Community and Lifelong Learning,* Cassell, London

Colclough, C with Lewin, K M (1993) *Educating all the Children: Strategies for primary schooling in the South,* Clarendon Press, Oxford

Collins, M (1991) *Adult Education as Vocation. A critical role for the adult educator,* Routledge, London

Dearing, R (1996) *Review of Qualifications for 16–19 year olds. Full report,* School Curriculum and Assessment Authority, London

Department for Education and Employment (DfEE) (1998) *Teachers: Meeting the challenge of change,* The Stationery Office, Norwich

Douglas, J W B (1964) *The Home and the School. A study of ability and attainment in the primary school,* McGibbon and Kee, London

Education Commission (Hong Kong) (1999) *Review of the Education System: Framework for education reform. Learning for life: education blueprint for the 21st century,* Education Commission, Hong Kong

European Commission (1995) *Teaching and Learning: Towards the learning society,* European Commission, Brussels

Faure, E *et al* (1972) *Learning to Be,* UNESCO, Paris

Fullan, M (1993) *Changing Forces,* Falmer Press, London

Halsey, A H *et al* (1972) *Educational Priority. Vol. I: EPA problems and priorities,* HMSO, London

Hargreaves, A (1997) *Beyond Educational Reform,* Open University Press, Buckingham

Hobsbawm, E (1994) *The Age of Extremes: The short twentieth century 1914–1991,* Michael Joseph, London

Husén, T (1979) *The School in Question. A comparative study of the school and its future in Western societies,* Oxford University Press, Oxford

Illich, I (1973) *Deschooling Society,* Penguin Books, Harmondsworth

Illich, I and Verne, E (1976) *Imprisoned in a Global Classroom,* Writers and Readers Publishing, London

Jackson, B and Marsden, D (1962) *Education and the Working Class,* Routledge and Kegan Paul, London

Knowles, M (1970) *The Modern Practice of Adult Education: Andragogy versus pedagogy,* Association Press, New York

Midwinter, E (1972) *Priority Education: An account of the Liverpool project,* Penguin Books, Harmondsworth

Mills, C W (1970) *The Sociological Imagination,* Penguin Books, Harmondsworth

Ohliger, J (1974) 'Is lifelong education a guarantee for permanent inadequacy?', *Convergence,* **7** (2), 47–58

Rockhill, K (1983) 'Mandatory continuing education for professionals: trends and issues', *Adult Education,* **33**, 2

Rogers, J (ed) (1969) *Teaching on Equal Terms,* BBC, London

Rogers, J (1971) *Adults Learning,* Penguin Books, Harmondsworth

Secretary's Commission on Achieving Necessary Skills (SCANS) (1991) *What Work Requires of Schools,* SCANS, US Department of Labor, Washington, DC

Simon, B (1974) *The Two Nations and the Educational Structure 1780–1870,* Lawrence and Wishart, London

UNESCO (1997) *Adult Education: The Hamburg Declaration* [and] *The Agenda for the Future,* Confintea: Fifth International Conference on Adult Education, 14–18 July, UNESCO Institute for Education, Hamburg

Chapter 12

Corporations and professions

Peter Jarvis and Paul Tosey

The world of work has changed almost beyond recognition over the past generation or two. Previously manufacturing, through high-volume Fordist-type production techniques, had been at the heart of work. Many workers were employed in assembly lines undertaking repetitive work, and one of the ways to keep the workers undertaking rather mindless repetitive work was to pay them high wages, as the motor car industry demonstrated. Another was the fear of losing one's job. Workers were organized through bureaucratic organizations; indeed, the State itself was (and remains) a giant bureaucracy. At the top of the hierarchy of the workforce were the professionals – those elite people who worked with knowledge and policy – and some managers. They were the highly trained elite who ran most aspects of society.

By the 1960s and 1970s it was becoming apparent that these high-volume industries were not economically efficient. The large first-world manufacturing companies were already competing, not always successfully, with Japanese manufacturing, and they recognized that the only solution was to transfer their manufacturing to places where employees would undertake the same production work at a fraction of the cost. Some large bureaucracies and the professions remained, as did much of the bureaucratic style of management. The West immediately placed a greater emphasis on leisure and the new service industries emerged.

However, another profound change occurred at the same time: the birth of the Internet. Developed in the USA as a defence mechanism to prevent a Soviet takeover or destruction of the American communication systems, networks of thousands of computers provided the basis of what was to become the informational technology revolution (Castells, 1996). Once IT spread, it became a mechanism that facilitated the globalization process, enabling companies to transfer decisions, capital, etc between countries almost instantaneously. But IT became more than just a mode of communication: it also became the basis of new technologies and new modes of production; it generated new commodities and it facilitated the creation and commodification of knowledge itself. A new generation of knowledge workers emerged to fill the void left by the decline in manufacturing. But technological knowledge changes rapidly, and as it changed so the speed of change throughout the first world increased. A new revolution was occurring. First-world societies assumed a form of advanced capitalism and, as Castells (1996: 91) wrote:

> What is distinctive is the eventual realization of the productivity potential contained in the mature industrial economy because of a shift toward a technological paradigm based on information technologies.

Work became much more complex but also high value, as opposed to high volume. The number of people in the labour force working with knowledge increased. Reich (1991) suggests that three types of worker emerged: the symbolic analyst (knowledge worker), in-person service worker (service workers) and the routine production services worker. He suggested (1991: 179) that in the 1950s there was no more than 8 per cent of the American workforce that could be classified as knowledge workers (professionals), whereas in the 1980s the proportion was 20 per cent and likely to continue to increase.

Reich and Castells both concentrate on the type of work undertaken, and it is certainly true that the unions and associations of many occupations and professions have continued to organize their own vocational education outside the educational framework. There is, however, some evidence, from our own professional experience, that suggests that some of them are considering ways of getting these courses accredited within a more traditional academic framework.

Frankl et al (1999: 14) sought to combine both occupational type and employing organizational type in the research. They note that the organizations in which this changing workforce is employed have also changed. They analysed three forms of workers: service worker, entrepreneurial worker and knowledge worker within the context of their employment situation. They looked at the organizations within which they worked, using two stereotypes as an analytical framework: regimented and empowered. The former is much more hierarchical and bureaucratic, while the latter is based on knowledge and learning and is more collegial. They found that the stereotypes were not entirely accurate: service workers did work in more regimented environments but the picture is overdrawn and, therefore, invalid; knowledge workers did work in empowered conditions but even here the picture is not entirely accurate; sales workers are more autonomous and rely on their social skills.

Organizations, of whatever form, do need to face the challenges of this ever-changing world. Bureaucratic organizations appear to have a great deal more inertia built into their system, so their response to new technologies and the new knowledge is achieved in a more regimented manner, passing new procedures down the hierarchical chain. Other less bureaucratic organizations are more likely to be able to respond to the new demands in more flexible ways.

In all of these changing situations the workforce requires further education and training, and new organizational forms are emerging that enable this to occur. Two responses are discussed here: the learning organization and the corporate university.

The learning organization

In an article published in the UK in 1989, Pedlar *et al* noted that the term 'learning organization' had already begun to enter mainstream thinking. It was soon popularized both by Pedler *et al* (1991) and by Senge (1990). A closely related but not identical term, 'organizational learning', can be traced back to the work of Argyris and Schon (1978). Burgoyne *et al* (1994) affirm the 'multi-directional' nature of the term and its development. Accordingly, there are many proposed definitions of learning organizations. For example, Pedler *et al* (1989: 2) define the learning company as 'an organization which facilitates the learning of all its members and continually transforms itself'.

Being a learning organization includes, but is more than, encouraging the learning of individual employees. The 'learning organization' concept considers the possible links between individual and collective learning. It also gives rise to an emphasis on 'knowledge management' and the idea that knowledge, not monetary capital or other tangible assets, is the organization's most precious resource. Watkins and Marsick (1993: 8–9) incorporate several themes into their depiction of the learning organization:

> The learning organization is one that learns continuously and transforms itself. Learning takes place in individuals, teams, the organization, and even the communities with which the organization interacts. Learning is a continuous, strategically used process – integrated with, and running parallel to, work. Learning results in changes in knowledge, beliefs and behaviours. Learning also enhances organizational capacity for innovation and growth. The learning organization has embedded systems to capture and share learning.

In Senge's view, the essence of the learning organization lies in the presence of five 'disciplines':

1.   personal mastery;
2.   mental models;
3.   shared vision;
4.   team learning;
5.   systems thinking.

Like Pedler *et al*, Senge's perspective on the learning organization also draws on numerous influences. The 'discipline' that receives most attention in the book is systems thinking, which is derived from cybernetics. It is of the same family of ideas as Argyris' learning loops. Senge (1990: 141) emphasizes other disciplines too. It is noteworthy that these include personal mastery, which 'goes beyond competence and skills... [and] goes beyond spiritual unfolding or opening, although it requires spiritual growth'. This emphasizes a link between the personal development of employees and the capacity for organizational learning.

What of the relationship between 'learning organization' and 'organizational learning'? Definitions of the former focus on what this type of the organization appears to be, and how it is characterized. The latter is concerned more with the 'how' of learning – the processes through which learning takes place. Swieringa and Wierdsma (1992: 33) write:

> By the term 'organizational learning' we mean the changing of organizational behaviour. The changing of organizational behaviour is a collective learning process... an organization has not automatically learned when individuals within it have learned something. Individual learning is a necessary but not sufficient condition for organizational learning.

This definition differentiates organizational learning, a collective process, from individual learning, suggesting that thinking about the learning organization might equally be concerned with collective learning processes. But this is not necessarily the case. 'Learning organization' seems to denote a wider category than merely the learning processes and this includes:

•   ideas;
•   analysis and prescription about the nature of organizations;
•   how they can be effective.

Jones and Hendry (1992: iv) say that 'Learning organization theorists concentrate on the "soft" rather than the "hard" measures in looking at organizational development'. Roth and Niemi (1996) identify three prominent themes in the literature of the learning organization:

1. Adaptation, change and environmental alignment of organizations.
2. The multiple levels of learning within organizations.
3. Interpretation, meaning and the worldview of organizations.

An often-cited example of the implementation of learning organization ideas is that of Ford. There, according to some accounts, each employee was given an annual learning budget and was allowed to spend it on any form of learning they chose – there was no requirement to demonstrate that it was vocational, or to obtain permission from a managerial authority. Other examples include Shell, through its approach to strategic planning; Rover Learning Business is another prominent example.

While open to the criticism that the literature is rather idealistic, the learning organization concept has generated excitement, perhaps a renewed optimism that learning is in everybody's interests, employees and employers alike. Policy on the learning age in the UK, and specific developments such as the creation of 'individual learning accounts' could be seen as being strongly influenced by learning organization ideas.

What does not yet appear to have emerged is any significant convergence of ideas or practices. Whether or not such a convergence is desirable or even likely is, of course, debatable. We should ask to what extent the benefits of the learning organization idea have been distributed evenly. Has it fallen mainly to shop-floor workers to be flexible and to re-skill themselves? Clearly, the different types of workforce do require different forms of training and, traditionally, employers have also taken some responsibility for training their workforce, but with the coming of the knowledge-based society this is changing rapidly.

The corporate universities

As the learning society has emerged and corporations have become more involved in the education and training of their staff, there have been many calls for partnership between the corporations and the education system. But Eurich (1985: 15) suggested that in the US this has not always been feasible:

> Differences in mission between the two systems have led, however, to marked contrast in styles that hamper cooperation. Higher education enjoys a more leisurely and wider time frame... To the corporate world, 'time frames' are costly and company controls well understood.

Despite the rhetoric of partnership, and some has occurred in the US, universities and corporations have frequently started from opposite poles, and cooperation between them has proved to be neither feasible nor desirable as far as some of the more established universities have been concerned. It has engendered distrust and discomfort, if not disdain; it has often been abandoned as not worth the effort on either side.

Meister (1998: 62) states quite clearly why these companies need to adapt new ideas quickly and have consequently started corporate universities:

> The goal of these 'knowledge industries' is to learn faster than competitors. [The] CEOs recognize that only as learning spreads widely and deeply throughout the company will the organization be able to successfully compete in the global marketplace.

In terms of Frankl's typology, it would be true to say that many university departments and schools are knowledge-intensive and empowered, so it might be expected that they could react rapidly to the demands of the social system. However, this would not be true for all academics, many of whom are interested only in pursuing their research and who prefer to retain the status quo. Since university administration tends to be of a much more bureaucratic nature, it is also slow to change. Pressure from the schools and departments will induce change eventually, but that pressure may first have to overcome the caution of some of the academics and the administration, so that universities are not always able to respond to these demands for rapid change.

Even so, Meister went on to point out that there have been many areas of cooperation in the US, especially with community colleges (similar to colleges of further education in the UK). At the same time, Carnevale *et al* (1990a: 106) noted that educational institutions provide a great deal of the training and upgrading of the American workforce, although many universities 'have not moved to create special offices that work specifically on customized training programs within industry'. They suggested (1990b: 69) that the two-year colleges were much more aggressive in developing their links with industry and commerce.

It is significant to note here that the area where there has been most response to the corporate demands for more education has been further education, since the universities have partially responded to the continuing education demands from the professions. This is not to defend the universities, since they tend to be extremely conservative, as Eurich claims, but some of them have gradually been forced to expand their postgraduate and research programmes in response to these demands.

Eurich (1985: 48) also recorded the fact that by the time she was writing in the USA, there were approximately 400 companies that had their own learning centres, many of which were called universities. This figure has grown rapidly and by 1995 there were over 1,000 corporate universities, and corporate training budgets totalled $52 billion – an increase of 15 per cent since 1990 (Rowley *et al*, 1998: 34). (The exact amount of money spent on training in America appears to be something of an estimate, since Carnevale *et al* (1990b: xi) suggest that it is $210 billion annually.) The size of this budget demonstrates the investment that business and industry are prepared to put into learning – budgets that often exceed entire nations' expenditure on traditional continuing professional education. Meister (1998: 182) also points out, however, that the corporations which have started their own universities do look for partnerships with universities, although they are spelling out the skills that they require from college graduates.

In UK there have been similar developments: British Aerospace's Virtual University, the University of Lloyds TSB (the bank), and other major companies have their own training centres, academies, and so forth. There has not been any research into the British corporate universities yet, although it is beginning with a project almost completed at the University of Surrey but not published by the time this chapter was written, following some work developed by the University of Queensland (*THES*, 9.7.99). As a result, the following paragraphs concentrate on the research in the US.

Research into corporate training programmes began in the 1980s in the US, not only by Eurich but also by others such as Casner-Lotto (1988). In 1994, Meister published the first research work about the 'corporate universities' (a revised edition appeared in 1998 in which she updated all of this research as a result of having founded Corporate University Xchange Inc – a corporate university consulting firm). In this initial work she examined 30 corporations she regarded as being Corporate Quality Universities, all of which emphasized employee lifelong learning as essential to building a workforce able to compete in the global market. By 1998 she was able to list 50 corporate universities that regard training as lifelong learning rather than something to do and somewhere to go to get trained. The types of organization that started their own corporate university tend to be those that Frankl *et al* characterize as 'empowered'.

Significantly, however, it is not only the workforce to whom training is offered. Motorola, amongst others, also expects its supply and distribution chains to participate in its programmes. Mesiter (1994: 22) suggested that:

> The goal has become to instil the entire chain with an understanding of the company's quality vision as well as a passion to continuously learn, so that learning happens as a part of an individual's job, either at a computer work station, working with a team of suppliers, in customer forums, or alone via a self-paced workbook or audio/videotape. The emphasis on promoting a spirit of continuous lifelong learning is what makes Corporate Quality Universities so different from the traditional corporate classrooms of the past decade.

However, while some of these universities are now only serving their supply and distribution chains, others are much more ambitious:

> The Iama Company, a $300 million privately held company serving the premium pet food market, has developed Iama University specifically to provide training to business channel members, including pet store owners, distributors, veterinarians, and breeders. (Meister, 1998: 45)

Since the universities have learners from outside the company, they are expected to earn fees. Meister (1998: 52–3) shows that Motorola expects 63 per cent of its costs to be recouped by income gained from its own activities, and it has even started its own publishing business – Motorola University Press based at Schaumburg in Illinois. Sun Microsystems expected its university to be self-funded by the year 2000.

Meister (1994: 23) isolated the essence of these universities, which is fourfold:

1. building a competency-based training curriculum for each job;
2. providing all employees with a common vision of the company;
3. extending training to the company's entire customer/supply chain;
4. serving as a learning laboratory for experimenting with new approaches and practices for the design and delivery of learning initiatives.

The workforce of these large companies comprises more than the knowledge workers, so the idea of the elitist university has disappeared. The workers being educated in the corporate universities need to be able to do and to know, so that teaching theory has disappeared to a great extent and practical knowledge lies at the heart of the curricula. Programmes have been designed for their function within the company, concentrating on aspects of education and training that would have traditionally been the preserve of further education but also straddling the divide between it and higher education. Each module is especially designed for a specific job or procedure, based in practice, and involves practical knowledge. It is summed up with the 'three Cs' of the core curriculum:

1. corporate citizenship – know how the company works, and its values and vision (see Chapter 16 for further discussion on this element);
2. contextual framework – know the company's customers, competitors and their best practices;
3. competencies – know and practise both established and new job competencies.

Seven competencies are regarded as core (Meister, 1998: 105–26):

1. learning to learn;
2. communication and collaboration;
3. creative thinking and problem-solving;
4. technological literacy;

5. global business literacy;
6. leadership;
7. career self-management.

Significantly, learning skills top this list because learning and working are now being regarded as the same thing. The skill of learning involves asking the right questions, identifying the components of complex ideas, and assessing the relevant material, utilizing the skills to specific tasks (Meister, 1998: 105). These leading companies need to be learning organizations and so the corporate universities focus on learning. The fact that all workers should be lifelong learners underlines the idea that the corporate quality university should be a learning laboratory; one of the faculties in the British Aerospace Virtual University is the Faculty of Learning.

Research into learning in corporate universities is not really involved in the biology, sociology or psychology of learning, but in the ways that employees may learn more efficiently what they need to know for their work at the time when they need it. Gradually that learning will be under the employees' control and will be provided in 'modular multisensory instructional modules' (Meister, 1994: 121) of between 5 and 10 minutes each. Indeed, much of this learning will be what the Corning Education and Training Center calls the SMART Process – self learning, motivation, awareness, responsibility and technical competence (Meister, 1994: 129). Transnational companies will research learning styles to see, for instance, if the same instructional material can be provided in different countries and cultures, or whether it will be more efficient to prepare different material for different cultures.

Thus it may be seen how the corporations are embracing the lifelong learning discourse and changing the context within which a great deal of it has traditionally been undertaken.

Conclusion

The vast expansion in knowledge has meant that the traditional professions have lost their elite position. Now a great proportion of the labour force works with knowledge – perhaps we are all professionals now! Certainly more of us are. The fact that there is now a much greater proportion of knowledge workers means that the traditional route into the professions through initial education and university has had to change, and universities have had to expand their initial intake of students to respond to these demands. However, completion of a first degree is only to arrive at the door of employment for many. It is the end of initial education.

For other workers who do not have the initial opportunity to study for a first degree, many of the corporate universities are offering modular learning

.ties that can be built up into a first degree; they are entering part-
.ps with traditional universities to enable this to happen. There is now
a .eater participation in learning than ever before – and what was traditionally recognized as higher education is undergoing fundamental change.

Working and learning are becoming synonymous for many people – their
work also becomes their research. They are becoming practitioner
researchers (Jarvis, 1999) because not only is work the site for learning, it is
also the site for research.

References

Argyris, C and Schon, D (1978) *Organizational Learning,* Addison-Wesley, Reading, MA

Burgoyne, J, Pedlar, M and Boydell, T (eds) (1994) *Towards the Learning Company,* McGraw-Hill, Maidenhead

Carnevale, A P, Gainer, L J, and Villet, J (1990a) *Training in America,* Jossey-Bass, San Francisco, CA

Carnevale, A, Gainer, L and Schutis, E (1990b) *Training the Technical Workforce,* Jossey-Bass, San Francisco, CA

Casner-Lotto, J and Associates (1988) *Successful Training Strategies,* Jossey-Bass, San Francisco, CA

Castells, M (1996) *The Rise of the Network Society* (Vol 1 of *The Information Age: Economy, society and culture*), Blackwell, Oxford

Eurich, N (1985) *Corporate Classrooms,* Carnegie Trust for the Advancement of Teaching, Princeton, NJ

Frankl, S, Korcynski, M, Shire, K and Tam, M (1999) *On the Front Line,* Cornell University Press, Ithaca, NY

Jarvis, P (1999) *The Practitioner Researcher,* Jossey-Bass, San Francisco, CA

Jones, A M and Hendry, C (1992) *The Learning Organization: A review of the literature and of practice,* Centre for Corporate Strategy and Change, Business School, University of Warwick, Coventry

Meister, J (1994) *Corporate Quality Universities,* Irwin and ADTD, Burr Ridge, IL

Meister, J (1998) *Corporate Universities,* revised and updated, McGraw-Hill, New York

Pedler, M, Burgoyne, J and Boydell, T (1989) 'Towards the learning company', *Management Education and Development,* **20** (1), 1–18

Pedler, M, Burgoyne, J and Boydell, T (1991) *The Learning Company,* McGraw-Hill, Maidenhead

Reich, R (1991) *The Work of Nations,* Simon and Schuster, London

Roth, G L and Niemi, J (1996) 'Information technology systems and the learning organization', *International Journal of Lifelong Education,* **15** (3), 205–15

Rowley, D, Lujan, H and Dolence, M (1998) *Strategic Choices for the Academy,* Jossey-Bass, San Francisco, CA

Senge, P (1990) *The Fifth Discipline,* Doubleday, New York

Swieringa, J and Wierdsma, A (1992) *Becoming and Learning Organization: Beyond the learning curve,* Addison-Wesley, Wokingham

Times Higher Education Supplement (1999) 'Corporate units muscle in', 9 July, p. 3

Watkins, K and Marsick, V (1993) *Sculpting the Learning Organization,* Jossey-Bass, San Francisco, CA

Chapter 13

Implications for the delivery of learning materials

John Holford and Tom Black

Learning in the information society

The age of the learning society has also been called the age of information. Radical advances in information and communications technology (or 'telematics') over the past two decades have generated an explosion of opportunities for accessing information and person-to-person communication. The technical possibilities that present themselves to the designers of teaching and learning media and materials would have been unimaginable only a relatively few years ago. These possibilities have also presented themselves, at least in outline, to policy makers. The consequence is that policy documents about the learning society often convey the impression that information and communications technologies (ICT) provide the answers to all the problems of creating a learning society.

This message comes in two forms. There is the simplistic assertion that ICT changes the nature of learning relationships, and provides vast new opportunities for learning. For example, 'The information society is going to change teaching methods by replacing the excessively passive teacher/pupil relationship with a new – and seemingly promising – interactive relationship' (CEC, 1995: 7) Secondly, and more subtly, there is the importance of ensuring that skills in the use of ICT are not confined to narrow sections of the population. The first Fryer Report in the UK warned against the risk of 'differential access to, and use of, the new technologies' becoming 'the basis of additional divisions' (NAGCELL, 1997: 88). The warning is valid since only those in society with access to the hardware would benefit.

Behind the warning is the assumption that those without access to new information technologies will be socially excluded from the learning society. This has implications not only for parts of modern Western society, but also for developing countries.

An important question then arises: is the use of new ICT essential to creating a learning society, or is it just another technological aid? It is difficult to argue this on a logical basis, and historically assertions of the importance of a radical extension of educational opportunities pre-date awareness of contemporary ICT and its possibilities. However, the learning society literature has a strongly 'futuristic' dimension, and few authors have been able to resist the attractions of what new technologies may offer. This chapter therefore explores some of the implications of the potential and the limitations of the role of ICT in the provision of learning, and how far it can underpin a learning society.

The promise of new learning technologies

The attractions of the new ICT for the development of learning were stated in the first Fryer Report:

> Harnessing their use will provide additional means to open up access, overcome barriers to learning associated with distance and timing, give new opportunities for both individual and group learning and constitute mechanisms through which to create and disseminate new learning materials. Properly related to arrangements to give students reliable information and guidance and linked to facilities for interaction with other learners and tutorial support, the new technologies can also offer opportunities to widen participation and bring high quality learning schemes to learners at an affordable cost. (NAGCELL, 1997: 86)

We find this line of thinking not only in the UK, but also internationally. New ICT, and how the information society relates to education and learning, have been important issues for international organizations in recent years. The OECD, for example, has studied 'the impact of ICT on educational systems in relation to teaching and learning processes, curricula, the role and function of teachers, and education and learning institutions' (Dimitropoulos, 2000: 34).

Flexibility

A key perception is that new technologies will permit the widespread individualization of learning. Rather than having access to new knowledge or skills only when educational institutions make them available, we should be able to learn what we want or need at our own pace at the time most appropriate to us as individuals. They also mean that we can study wherever is convenient, rather than having to transport ourselves to a college, school or university. Through using ICT, we will be able to purchase units of learning (often called modules) on our own terms, rather than accepting the curricula specified by educational institutions.

ICT therefore permits the 'individual learning revolution' (Cm 3790, 1998: 17) to be carried through on a far more thorough basis. It is a vision of the individuals, suitably guided, purchasing units of learning for themselves, according to their own personal preferences and requirements and, in doing so negotiating their own 'learning contracts' with a range of providers in the learning marketplace. This is a key basis of the claim that the learning age will provide enhanced opportunities for all. The assumption behind this is that all the learning will occur using the technology, which ignores the question, 'What is the best medium for the learning task?' One size rarely fits all.

Cheapness

Lurking behind much of the rhetoric on ICT is the assumption that it will make education cheaper. This is not new: for the past half-century, and perhaps more, educational policy makers and managers have tended to see new technologies as solving the problem of ever-escalating costs. The premises on which this belief is founded seem to be that new technologies will enable institutions to:

- increase their productivity, since individual teachers will be able to teach much larger numbers of students at the same time;
- reduce production costs, for instance through offering information on CD-ROMs and the Web, rather than through traditional printed books and journals;
- take advantage of more distant markets, since they are no longer tied to their own localities;
- form consortia and 'partnerships' more readily, and thus both avoid or reduce development costs and identify and meet new market niches.

Unfortunately, not all of these are true when one looks at the real costs of development and delivery. Taking each of the above in turn, there are limitations to these claims:

- There is the assumption that teachers could teach more students in the same time, but this does not differentiate among subject matter or skills.
- Interactions by e-mail can actually take longer per student than face-to-face conversation.

- Passing the cost on to the learner might seem like a good idea, but not all learners would agree. Combining this with the alternative of reading vast amounts of text onscreen (something very few people like to do), delivery by CD or the Internet could be a marketing disaster, driving learners away.
- Distant markets are desirable, but can require additional development costs to take into account cultural, environmental and societal differences.
- Consortia assume that educational institutions will cooperate rather than compete. While there is no doubt that some costs can be saved, there will be times when the benefits do not appear on the scale promised.

Innovation

In the search for productive uses of new ICT, there is an element of 'technophilia'. The sheer possibilities of ICT produce a sense that there *must* be important opportunities to be gained. This is, no doubt, the educational counterpart of the 'dot.com' hysteria of the world's stock markets – though arguably it has lasted rather longer. We need to be conscious of this, for there is an almost ideological or irrational element to the constant quest for *new* and *innovative* uses of ICT in learning. Organizations look for innovative uses of ICT, almost as though that is more important than good or effective uses of ICT (or of traditional learning technologies, for that matter). And yet it is understandable, for alongside the promise of new technologies, there is a nagging fear: if we do not do it and our competitors do, we will lose out. We know that innovation in ICT is fast; we believe it is getting ever faster. If we do not innovate, others will; we will be left behind, unable to compete effectively in ever-changing markets. For example, how far will the international market for higher education develop – will high-prestige (chiefly US) institutions, marketing their expertise in Europe, bring British higher education to its knees?

Profit

If educational institutions can become more flexible and responsive, and improve their productivity and win new markets, then – perhaps – they can cease to be a burden on the public purse and become profit-making enterprises. This is, by and large, a contemporary vision rather than a reality, but it is a vision that has enough 'success stories' among selected private universities to keep it alive and influential. Outside these, the success stories are rarely at the level of whole institutions, let alone whole educational systems. Selected programmes answer an exceptional public demand (the MBA is an example), while others do not.

Nevertheless, governments have been remarkably successful in encouraging educational organizations, especially in the post-compulsory sector, to find ever-increasing proportions of their running costs from non-public sources. Within colleges and universities, some individual departments and units succeed in 'making money' from the marketing of courses (though many more do not), and these often make use of new learning technologies. Outside the public sector, the market for learning is growing: management consultants, law firms and so forth are increasingly aware of how their 'intellectual property' can be marketed, and do market it – in some cases – to marked effect.

Realities

ICT, outreach and partnership

Without doubt, ICT has the potential to provide a range of opportunities that can enhance the value of the 'learning age'. It can bring learning materials to new audiences. ICT is, for instance, a key feature of the work of the University for Industry (UfI) in Britain – the organization designed to promote and facilitate learning in the workplace. It aims to provide public access 'to UfI learning materials, learning services and ICT facilities', using 'interactive learning, terrestrial, satellite and digital television and the broader opportunities of interactive learning' (Cm 4392, 1999: 40).

Distance learning materials in any form have the potential to carry education into remote geographical areas, or to carry specialized knowledge into areas where no specialist institution would be financially viable. In the UK, the Open University has since the 1960s pioneered the application of ICT in distance learning, and in many ways to very considerable effect. In the past decade or so, other universities have developed 'niche' distance learning programmes. Many of these are in management and business, and virtually all have been designed to exploit a perceived market opportunity.

The opportunities that ICT offers for collaboration or 'partnership' are also substantial, and indeed this is another principal role of the UfI. The government has charged the UfI with establishing a 'network of UfI-endorsed learning centres, based in a wide range of locations, including colleges, libraries, community centres, employers' premises, and shopping malls' (Cm 4392, 1999: 40). Of course, such collaborations can be on a variety of bases, and typically some partners play more equal parts than others. Nonetheless, the development and use of ICT-based learning materials offer opportunities for collaboration.

Variety and choice

Of course, the ability to offer learning programmes at a distance implies significant changes in the relationship between teachers and learners, and major changes to the possibilities available to educational providers.

International opportunities

Among the changes are the opportunity to recruit students from across the world. Until the late 1980s, even distance education organizations were constrained. Few sought to offer programmes outside their own country. The Open University, for instance, with few exceptions, resisted offering courses outside the UK until the mid-1990s. From the late 1980s, however, universities and colleges began to see their students as 'markets' and no longer confined to their own countries. Institutions – and countries – varied, of course, in how quickly and enthusiastically they embraced this change. Australia and Britain were early entrants to the global marketplace, driven by domestic funding regimes, but simultaneously benefiting from the advantages of the English language. Of course, recruiting students from across the world brings challenges as well as opportunities, but there are clearly genuine opportunities for increasing international and cross-cultural understanding.

A larger range of offerings

In principle, at least, there are real opportunities to increase the range of offerings available to learners, and thus to widen choice. This is chiefly because the expertise of one institution can be transmitted to others. Thus one could, in principle, offer a module on Chinese philosophy within a philosophy curriculum, even though the 'home' institution has no expertise in the area. Educational expertise, moreover, can to some degree be 'stored' – an outstanding lecture, a module on an unpopular subject, ready for a later cohort of learners. And such offerings can be made to relatively small numbers of students in one institution, because the costs of development can be shared with others organizations, and spread over a wider range of students. This works when there is a free exchange of 'credit' for learning from one institution to another.

Flexibility in timing

In principle, ICT provides learners with the opportunity to study at their own pace and at a time when the matter is important. No longer does knowledge have to be learnt and then remembered until needed; now we can study the relevant module when it is relevant. And rather than attending every Thursday evening for two hours, we can fit our study into convenient niches in our schedules. There still have to be limitations on how long one can spend on a unit of study, but the flexibility within a unit is to be explored by the learner. This does assume that the learner has the self-regulatory skills to complete a module in isolation, sometimes without any direct contact with tutors.

Problems

However, if there are advantages, there are also potential problems. Many are the opposite face of the very advantages we have mentioned; they tend to be risks of practice rather than ideals of theory. Let us look at these.

Cost of development

The production of learning materials using ICT is a costly exercise – substantially more costly than merely expecting a trainer or teacher to deliver the same material in a classroom setting. These costs are not typically those of direct printing of the materials; they are costs associated with transforming the intellectual expertise into a written (or audio-visual) form, suitable for individual learners to engage with successfully. This is because of the complex nature of learning: it does not always deal with just the acquisition of fact. Higher-level learning demands more effort in planning and delivery. As a rule, these costs are only effectively reduced on a unit-cost basis, that is, by using them with large numbers of students.

This is the basis of the success of the Open University in the UK, which has used a variety of media, tutorials and summer schools to meet the varying cognitive demands of different courses – but even it is being forced to reduce its support services to students. Other institutions, even relatively well-supported institutions such as the Open University of Hong Kong (OUHK) have found that they can function effectively only by negotiating the purchase of many learning packages from other institutions. The OUHK, for instance, makes widespread use of materials originally authored by universities in Europe, the US and Australia. It makes some amendments and additions, to be sure, but the savings associated with not having to 'start from scratch' are vast. (By the same token, of course, the arrangements make substantial additions to the finances of the universities from which it buys the materials.)

Too few students

One result of the high origination costs is that student numbers need to be maintained at a relatively high level. A distance learning course that cannot maintain strong student recruitment has poor prospects, unless, of course, it is subsidized from another source. Without buoyant recruitment and income, the ability to reinvest in the programme – to keep it up to date – is constrained. It also means that while the 'ideal' of being able to offer the course to relatively small numbers of students in scattered locations is not impossible, no programme can function on this basis alone. A programme must have a secure and relatively large core of students (in their capacity as purchasers of the product).

Materials production and revision

The development and revision of learning materials is not merely costly; it is also logistically complex. It requires the involvement not only of people with expertise in the subject of the materials themselves – whether car maintenance or African religions – but also of people with skills in instructional design, and in graphic design, publishing and printing. Of course, sometimes these skills may be combined in one person; but this is unusual. No few organizations, stimulated by the enthusiasm of multi-skilled individuals, have underestimated the challenges of maintaining a system of materials production and revision. Multi-skilled and highly motivated staff depart; but students must continue to be supported and systems maintained.

ICT brings with it additional costs to those of the printed material, depending on the nature of the learning task. Computer-assisted learning (structured learning, simulations) can cost upwards of £50,000 per hour of student learning. Quality video (regardless of how it is delivered, on CD or over the Internet) is an expensive medium. Animations and graphics require the input of skilled personnel, which comes at high cost.

Transience

The problems of materials production and revision are the more pressing because of the increasingly brief shelf life of materials in most disciplines. We know that knowledge is ever more transient and provisional – this is one of the principal planks in the case for lifelong learning. What this means for learning materials is that the ideal of materials being a 'store' of up-to-date knowledge, and the problems of small numbers of interested students being spread out over time (as well as geographically) are only very partially overcome. Few institutions are now prepared to accept that materials more than about five years old can be up-to-date, and their reluctance is matched by that of the learners. And the appearance of materials is now a good guide to their vintage, looking dated after only a relatively brief passage of time.

ICT presents its own problems. For example, the use of Web sites may seem beneficial because the information is current, but these often have a finite life and can disappear without notice. This means that learning materials that refer learners to Web sites must be continually monitored and updated.

Interactive learning and learner support

When we move – as is now increasingly common – from the production of self-access learning packages to maintaining interactive on-line support for learners, the costs escalate again. Interactive support online may vary from a simple e-mail system to a more sophisticated online discussion forum or 'virtual classroom'. Software support from such systems as Learning Space or First Class are beneficial but have a human cost as well as software licensing. Someone has to monitor student–student interactions and be willing to respond to enquiries at short notice.

Other types of interaction place more demands on tutors, including telephone, video or online conferencing or seminars. There may be face-to-face workshops or tutorials at study centres, or student counselling. There are demands of marking and returning student assignments with comments. All these may provide substantial advantages for the learner, but for the educational provider there are significant additional costs in time and in the need for rapid response. Essentially, while the set-up and maintenance costs of materials production are the same regardless of student numbers (so that large student numbers mean low unit costs), the costs of interactive support vary in proportion to the number of students. And many institutions and tutors have found that learners' demands expressed through e-mail can make more calls on staff time and resources than meeting learners face-to-face.

Curriculum and focus

One of the attractions of the availability of a wide range of learning materials is the freedom of choice and flexibility it offers to the learner, but this also presents difficulties. In the 1980s and early 1990s many educational institutions, universities in particular, were overtaken by enthusiasm for 'modularization'. This was seen as a panacea since it broke the learning tasks into smaller units than a whole degree or certificate or sub-discipline. Among its more enthusiastic advocates, some supported it because (potentially) it allowed learners virtually unfettered freedom of choice in the content of what they studied. It was to be an exercise in learner autonomy and daring to be free. The experience of modularization has highlighted some of the pitfalls of unrestrained freedom of choice of learning materials. In practice, there is a balance to be struck between the notion of establishing a curriculum – providing an educational or intellectual logic to the study of a subject – and acknowledging that learners are intelligent and capable of making sensible choices. The coherence of programmes of learning – a coherence that can be provided by a strong core of common study – is also vital to their sense of identity, and to their marketing. Programmes that incorporate virtually unlimited freedom of choice are therefore prone to lose in the market place.

Learner progression and assessment

Linked to the question of curriculum is the issue of learner progression. In any programme of study, learners should advance. They should be aware of what they know, and of how their learning is advancing. How far is this compatible with learner autonomy and free choice?

There are significant difficulties. Progression implies some structured approach, with the learner moving between various identifiable points in some kind of rational sequence. Of course, there can be a wide range of points and sequences, but there is a good case to be made that the random selection of learning opportunities allows neither the identification of these points, nor the organizing of learning opportunities into a sequence which facilitates progression between them. Also, few subjects are so broad and shallow as to have no progression or accumulation of skills. Most subjects build from simple to complex, require a refinement in skill development, and are more than a huge collection of facts that can be acquired in any order.

Within large-scale programmes of study, such as in schools and university degree programmes, there have been some shifts in recent years towards a relatively more structured curriculum with clearly identifiable points that can be 'benchmarked' against comparable programmes, or against learning requirements, and at which individual learners' progress can be assessed. When it comes to the experience of the individual learner in society, how far he or she is capable of making judgments about progression remains unclear. There have been some interesting recent experiments with self-assessment as a mechanism for encouraging learning among the relatively 'excluded', but their success remains unclear (Holford, 1999).

Bureaucracy

A key issue for delivering learning materials in the learning society is the keeping of records. If we could rely on individuals to maintain records of their learning effectively and honestly, this would present no concerns. Unfortunately, neither institutions nor society at large are prepared to accept that men and women can be relied on to keep records efficiently and scrupulously. Not unnaturally, there is more concern about the occasional abuser – the unqualified doctor, plumber or financial adviser – than about the great majority.

In these circumstances, the question of bureaucracy, of the need for effective organization and record-keeping, arises. In any system of learning, the tracking of individuals and their progression is a substantial task. Schools evolved procedures – registers, roll-calls, and the like – which have proved relatively robust within their own walls. Systems for tracking learners in a learning society, where study can be lifelong, nationwide (and even international) presents a considerably greater challenge. Learners will progress from varying starting points, at different rates, through different sets of learning experiences, to different end-points. The problems of maintaining effective records of this are massive.

Policies and schemes such as assessment of prior learning (APL) and progress files (NAGCELL, 1997: 84) are attempts to begin to address this problem. This is particularly true if learners are going to exploit this new freedom and acquire modular credit for a qualification from more than one institution. 'The needs of adults are different', however, as the government acknowledged in Learning to Succeed (Cm 4392, 1999: 48). It is not clear that an effective record-keeping system is feasible beyond the age of about 20 if we are talking about lifelong learning. There still may be a need for individuals to keep their collections of certificates or credits from the various institutions in which they have studied.

Competition

One of the attractions of establishing a learning society for some is that it will be market-oriented and thus more responsive to the demands of learners. Again, this is two-edged. Markets imply competition, and in competitive environments there are losers as well as winners. They can actively discourage cooperation across institutions, reducing the potential benefits of drawing on expertise on a worldwide basis. Educational entrepreneurs are involved in a process of doing 'better' than the competition. In recent years we have seen the risks, as educational bodies, some of them relatively prestigious, have offered programmes of dubious value, especially though not only in overseas markets. This has generated calls for stronger regulation, and indeed the regulatory frameworks that now apply to much of education in Britain can often seem stultifying to the professional educator. They are also costly.

Learner needs

An interesting perspective on what a learning society would mean for the delivery of learning materials is provided by addressing the question: what do learners need? What are the essential or desirable features of any system of learning support?

Communication

It is clear that learners need, or commonly desire, a way of communicating with other students. This is not universal, of course. A few people study quite happily in isolation. But a system of learning should incorporate mechanisms for interaction with other learners who are at roughly comparable points in their studies.

Interaction with teachers

Learners need meaningful interaction with teachers or tutors. They need opportunities for feedback on their work. And they need the opportunity to clarify points that they have only partially understood. They need this partly for the formal feedback; many learners also want personal support. Skill development is particularly challenging. Some skills are easily developed in the presence of a tutor or within a group, or very difficult to do at a distance and may demand considerable interaction with the tutor.

Confidence and regularity

Learners require some degree of confidence, regularity and security in their learning. There is, of course, a sense in which we learn from change and from the unexpected. But much more profoundly we require patterns of regularity to provide us with the confidence that what we are learning is valuable, and will continue to be so. This clearly makes a case for educational institutions to provide boundaries within which relatively secure patterns of study and progress can be established. Within these boundaries, the institutions should be seeking to establish coherence and structure within programmes, perhaps around specified core modules, a prescribed sequence of study, and relatively standard timings. It also means that educational institutions and policy makers should ensure that the currency of qualifications is not debased.

Learning resources

Students require learning resources appropriate to their needs, commensurate with the cognitive emphasis of the learning outcomes, and consistent with their learning situation. This implies a satisfactory level of resourcing, of course, but is also implies a clear definition of learning outcomes and intent, and transparent arrangements for resource allocation.

Administration and records

There will need to be reliable databases (in the broadest sense) to support effective monitoring of student progress. There will be a need for a fair system of assessment of prior learning and credit transfer among institutions. This has implications for maintaining equivalence in quality of learning as well as content.

Learning materials

Effective systems for the development, review and updating of learning materials, and for their quality assurance, are essential. To be competitive an institution has to invest in its courses in order to maintain its advantage.

Staff

Although much of the 'feel' of the arguments about the importance of good learning materials, and the possibility of learning at a distance, suggest a change in the role of the teacher, in practice the importance of educational staff – whether teachers, trainers, instructional designers, educational technologists – is enhanced. Not only this, but they must maintain a common purpose and team spirit. They must do this often in the context of a more fragmented working environment, for they may be working in different parts of an organization, rather than in the same department, or even in different companies. As so often, the human factor is critical.

Summary

The use of ICT in the delivery of learning, particularly with the aim of facilitating the expansion of the learning society, offers many advantages, but it also has its limitations. Like many of the past innovations in teaching and learning, the new technologies can neither solve all the problems nor be used blindly. If anything, new technologies place a greater decision-making burden on the teacher-developer. The choices are numerous, the options can be expensive, and the need to be cost-effective is ever present. There is no justification for using a medium just because it is there and is fashionable. The teacher-developer needs to match the medium with the learning task, taking into account cognitive emphasis, the learner's situation and back-ground, and the availability of the medium itself. ICT is unlikely to solve all the problems, but it should add another tool to the toolbox to make learning more effective – but only if it is used wisely.

References

Cm 3790 (1998) *The Learning Age: A renaissance for a new Britain*, The Stationery Office, Norwich

Cm 4392 (1999) *Learning to Succeed: A new framework for post-16 learning*, The Stationery Office, Norwich

Commission of the European Communities (CEC) (1995) *Teaching and Learning: Towards the learning society*, White Paper on Education and Training, Office of Official Publications of the European Communities, Luxembourg

Dimitropoulos, A (2000) *International Educational Research in the 1990s: A survey*, Office of Official Publications of the European Communities, Luxembourg

Holford, J (1999) *Planning to Learn: Evaluation of a union learning fund project*, Learning Through Life Foundation, London

National Advisory Group on Continuing Education and Lifelong Learning (NAGCELL) (1997) *Learning for the Twenty-First Century*, First report of the National Advisory Group, Chair: Professor R H Fryer, NAGCELL

Chapter 14

Implications for including the socially excluded in the learning age

Julia Preece

> Lifelong education is potentially both enlarging and transformative, and potentially controlling and domesticating. (Mayo, 1997: 77)

This chapter looks at how social exclusion is understood in the European and UK contexts and how perceptions of exclusion influence policies for inclusion in education and training. We briefly explore some policies and theories that affect or demonstrate issues arising from the social inclusion debates. These are:

- adult basic education;
- European social policy and social exclusion;
- social capital and citizenship;
- education for social purpose.

We ask how far strategies and ideologies of the new learning age are meeting the needs of society as a whole, especially among social groups who are outside of the mainstream of learning provision.

It is argued that there are different kinds of educational 'tendencies' that shape the ideologies and therefore outcomes of educational participation. Shanahan (in Mayo, 1997: 58) identifies four: academic, training, professional and community. The predominance of either tendency is linked to social policy and government economic transition needs at any point in time. Shanahan claims that the academic and training tendencies are linked primarily to ideas of individualistic learning and reliance on a market-led approach to education. Similarly, although professionals might be trained as change agents in this process their role is largely determined by the former tendencies. The latter 'community' tendency emphasizes collective development through empowerment and transformation. Mayo (1997: 54) suggests, however, that governments often reinterpret this kind of education for development in terms of its functional rather than human rights value. These trends can be followed across most initiatives for educational inclusion, whether it is in relation to integrating learning for people with disabilities or for people with special language, literacy or other needs. One of the most recently documented examples of how ideologies of inclusion are manifested through language and practice is seen in the way adult basic education has developed in the UK.

Adult basic education

The adult literacy movement is an indicator of how discourses for 'inclusion' and 'social justice' can often be reinterpreted in the political drives for expediency and simplification of marginalization issues. It is estimated that one in five people has difficulty with literacy or numeracy (Moser, 1999). Withnal (1994) and Hamilton (1996) have both traced how the UK adult literacy movement achieved particular impetus through campaigns for social justice during the 1960s, largely through the voluntary sector. In spite of this, government intervention in response to the campaign succeeded in presenting the problem of illiteracy as a social deficit issue (cure or blame the victim). Hamilton (1996: 148–49) discusses the implications of how these different interpretations would be played out in practice. She offers several competing discourses for literacy:

> *Literacy for emancipation* implies a radical critique of elite culture… and existing unequal power relations among existing social groups… *literacy for social control*… is seen as a way of maintaining the status quo, functionally shaping responsible, moral and economically productive citizens.

While the radical critique might have been the informal starting point for new community-based initiatives, the reality would often be presented through policy as something less challenging to the dominant regime. Hamilton states that from the social control discourse emanated the *'deficit model of literacy,'* which emerged in policy terms as 'remedial or special needs education', rather than an initiative to empower individuals or groups. The ensuing process of providing adult basic education (ABE) since the 1960s has increasingly turned into a functional, skills-based approach. Once this ideology was achieved, ABE became a statutory form of provision through the 1992 Further and Higher Education Act. Its potential for active engagement with non-formal learning would then remain dependent on uncoordinated and fragmented (and therefore unthreatening) local initiatives.

Public attention has been drawn to the 'problem' of literacy through increasing media involvement and most recently through the DfEE-commissioned Moser Report (1999). Nevertheless the focus of attention is on addressing the economic consequences of a workforce that cannot read to a certain common standard. The emphasis therefore is on identifying the scale of the problem in terms of economic efficiency and national renewal. The goal of the Moser Report is to stimulate strategies for engendering functional literacy through a national qualifications system and measurable targets.

These kinds of tension between failure/deficit discourses for inclusion and more radical social justice models for empowerment reoccur in most initiatives to address the question of marginalization, whether they relate to education or other social concerns. They are not exclusive to the UK, as Mayo (1997) indicates in her analysis of adult education initiatives throughout the world. The tensions are evident throughout current European policies for social inclusion and the impact those policies have on the agenda of British politics. A recent OECD (1999) report does attempt to broaden this perspective by highlighting the economic connection between adult learning and development of social capital as a means of demonstrating the value of education for social purpose. The concept of social capital will be explored later in this chapter. It will be useful first, however, to look at aspects of the European social action programme for the period 1995–2000, since the trend of Europe is towards a more functional model for inclusion, with consequent effects on education policy.

European social policy and social exclusion

The underlying goal of European policy is to create a united Europe. Employment and the evolution of a single market, which will increase Europe's competitiveness with the wider world, are political priorities. Areas of concern which threaten this goal are identified as:

- low labour mobility across nations;
- increasing skills gaps in a fast-changing world;
- the lack of equal opportunities between men and women.

Social exclusion is seen primarily in terms of poverty derived from uneven employment. For instance the UK government in 1997 identified an increase in the last two decades of:

- workless households from 9 to 20 per cent;
- children living in households with less than half the average income;
- disparity in earnings rates for those who left school at 16 compared with those who did not;
- disparity between top and lower earners, especially for women.

Notwithstanding the focus on poverty and employment, social exclusion is also described as multifaceted. It is suggested by some that society or social processes themselves can exclude people 'from systems which facilitate social integration' (Howarth and Kenway, 1998: 80). The socially excluded therefore cover a multitude of groups. Their common denominator is that they do not seem to comply with normal expectations of systems of 'fitting in'. They may be 'unemployed', 'homeless', 'disabled', 'disaffected youth', 'illiterate' or some such other category. Policy initiatives, however, which are often designed to integrate, also have a tendency to see integration as a normalization process. Integration of excluded sectors of society is often based on a particular notion of 'normal' human behaviour (Preece, 1999). In this context policy may be responding to globalization trends for convergence or sameness but it potentially denies some people's need for a local identity and the opportunity to create a sense of self or community on their own terms (Beck, 1998).

The perceived 'integration' solution for an inclusive society is to increase the mobility capacity of the workforce, along with constant skills updating and the improvement of employability qualities such as a willingness to adapt to changing labour demands (EC, 1998). Integration therefore is construed primarily as a levelling procedure, ensuring everyone operates from the same platform of attitudes, values and qualifications. There are problems with such a notion of integration, as this chapter explains. Indeed, even age differences are not accommodated in an employability model of inclusion. Although there is an acknowledgement of an increasing retired and ageing population, for example, the policy focus is firmly on developing the skills and qualities of those already in work and 'at risk of exclusion from the labour market'. The aim is to 'maintain and develop the capacities of people during their working life cycle' (EC, 1998: 14). The European social action programme conceives the learning society as one where people independently take up their own re-skilling and knowledge updating throughout their working life, not necessarily through paper qualifications but through validated evidence documented on personal skills cards. The 1995 European White Paper *Teaching and Learning* states that one of its primary goals is to tackle social exclusion in education and training. It proposes to address perceived exclusion from educational capabilities amongst certain social groups through:

- second-chance schooling for young people and adults;
- closer links with industry, such as offering work experience;

- increasing multilingual proficiency, so that everyone learns at least three languages.

It is against this backdrop that the UK Social Exclusion Unit formulated its policies for increasing the employability of young people at risk of exclusion (DfEE, 1998). In 1999 the Labour government introduced a Social Exclusion Unit to its portfolio of education and welfare reform. The UK initiatives centre round a welfare to work strategy, to shift the notion that welfare is an alternative to employment. Welfare is to be regarded as a mechanism for getting into work, supplemented by tax credits if wages are not high enough. The goal of these strategies is to stimulate a new discourse – a perception that the benefit system is creating a social exclusion of dependency and that learning should be associated directly with 'earning power' (DfEE, 1997).

Some have argued, however, that a focus on employability alone will not necessarily develop the kind of societal, learning-age cohesion envisaged for a modern, inclusive world. Moreover, a programme of educational regeneration, which relies exclusively on learning for paid employment, will inevitably exclude increasingly large sectors of the population. Giddens (1998) and Beck (1998) argue, for example, for a definition of employment and wealth creation that recognizes active participation in voluntary organizations as an alternative to employment: 'Those who commit themselves to voluntary organizations are no longer available for the labour market and in this sense are no longer "unemployed". They are active citizens' (Beck, 1998: 63).

Political definitions and policies, therefore, have a tendency to influence how society is seen as a whole. It is only when we try to match common definitions against different sections of society that we begin to realize that policies themselves can contribute to exclusion.

The European 1997 Green Paper *Towards a Europe of Knowledge* tries to move beyond this instrumental notion of learning, which just trains people for work, by looking at a broader definition of knowledge. It identifies three dimensions of knowledge under the headings 'citizenship', 'employability' and 'competencies'. Notions of employability and competencies echo those already articulated in the European White Paper (EC, 1995). The concept of citizenship is an attempt to address the statelessness consequences of increasing mobility between nations. Citizenship, however, tends to be seen primarily in terms of demonstrated loyalty to converging transnational civic and state policy and not as a social goal in itself (EC, 1995: 4). It is constructed, for example, through concepts such as 'common values', a 'sense of belonging' and 'active solidarity'. Awareness of cultural or social difference is subsumed under the more liberal phrase 'mutual understanding of diversity'. While the word 'diversity' suggests some recognition of difference between social groups, the general trend is towards encouraging convergence through assimilation of differences.

At the same time UK policies are now seeking a broader understanding of learning value. For instance, the government is trying to establish the non-economic benefits of learning, particularly where learning occurs in local communities (DfEE, 1999). These might be measured in terms of increased citizenship activity or some kind of reduction of demands on welfare agencies as a result of increasing participation in learning. Learning therefore is also potentially a mechanism for generating broad social values, defined as social capital. Social capital is said to complement the human capital of employability skills and is becoming the rationale for developing learning opportunities that may not have immediate functional goals or economic value. Social capital is seen as a means for regenerating citizenship attitudes and behaviours by stimulating a sense of community.

Social capital and citizenship

Social capital can be understood from a radical or more conservative perspective, and depends partly on whether social cohesion or educational achievement is the focus of the argument. Beck (1998) and Giddens (1998) suggest that when we try to define social capital it is the social activity itself that needs to be acknowledged as worthwhile. Community groups often struggle for recognition on this basis. So Beck (1998: 63–64) argues that by giving their grass roots social action a credible visibility within the discourse for inclusion, such activity gains 'economic, organizational and political weight'. Giddens makes the economic connection with this kind of activity by calling it 'social capital'. Capital denotes the exchange value of what has been gained:

> Conventional poverty programmes need to be replaced with community focused programmes that permit more democratic participation as well as being more effective. Community building emphasizes support networks, self help and the cultivation of social capital as a means to generate economic renewal in low income neighbourhoods. (Giddens, 1998: 110)

Coleman (1988, 1994), Putnam (1995) and Schuller and Field (1995) discuss social capital in relation to educational achievement. They define social capital as a public way of supporting society's norms. While their research focuses on different age cohorts, they all identify levels of initial education as predictors of levels of 'civic engagement' (Putnam, 1995: 667). This kind of capital is defined by Coleman as constituting a set of social structures and social relations that are based on three forms of behaviour. These derive from connections with, and activity in, social networks such as clubs, societies and community projects. He stresses, however, that behavioural indications of social capital are not confined to the localized environment. It is their transferability across social groups that gives them capital. These forms of behaviour consist of:

- *Obligations and expectations* developed through mutual activity and a common purpose. This ultimately entails reciprocal arrangements between members and the development of mutual trust.
- A network of communication – *information channels* – an outcome of reciprocal arrangements, which can be called upon by members of that network outside their original social purpose.
- *Norms of collective interest*, which evolve over time, are internalized and act as self-defining sanctions on the behaviours of other members.

If people have high social capital, it is argued, they are more likely to participate in formal learning. Social capital that is defined by behaviours with broad appeal will usually meet the requirements of the dominant social group. This will, of course, marginalize the social behaviours that operate within less dominant social or cultural groups, rendering their values and norms less important – and potentially making them less employable. In a piece of research involving residents of Northern Ireland, Schuller and Field found that people who are members of certain well-established social networks were more likely to have initially high human capital (employability skills), but the relationship between social capital and lifelong learning for adults as a whole was less established. The concept of social capital is therefore complex with regard to lifelong learning. Nevertheless, theorists have argued there is a causal link between indirect economic gains to the state and participation in social capital. Perhaps the link lies in Beck's request that the social action itself must be given 'organizational and political weight' before its real benefits can be measured. In other words, not all social activities seem to count in discourses that try to define social capital (Preece, 1999).

A telling clue to this suggestion lies in feminist literature, which discusses concepts of citizenship (the civic engagement aspect of social capital). Oommen (1997) and Brine (1999) argue, for instance, that the whole definition of citizenship is class dominated and gender blind, often ignoring the absence of women from those activities most highly regarded for active citizenship: 'The young, the lower class and women are not equal citizens in the context of public participation' (Oommen, 1997: 10). Indeed, the title of citizen is not even a right for migrant communities. Ackers (1998) and Lister (1997) argue for a 'feminist citizenship' that gives due accord to women's agency' (Lister, 1997: 5) and acknowledges their private spheres of activity such as 'caring'. They also apply this argument to other minority groups such as black or disabled people. It is these latter points that suggest the complexity of measuring educational achievement and social participation amongst groups that are now frequently described in political terms as 'socially excluded'.

In relation to people with learning difficulties, for instance, Riddell *et al* (1999: 50) suggest that social capital theories tend to blame social exclusion on the excluded themselves: 'Doubts remain... as to whether current policies have succeeded in enhancing the social capital of people with learning difficulties and, more fundamentally, if lack of social capital is a cause or effect of social oppression.' She picks up the problem of describing social inclusion via a normalization model. That is, people can be integrated if they adopt dominant social norms:

> Although functionalist versions of social capital may seek to specify the conditions necessary for the development of warm and inclusive societies, the inability of some people with learning difficulties to contribute to such a society may locate them as social pariahs, excluded to strengthen other people's sense of belonging or to act as a warning of the consequences of social deviance. (Riddell *et al*, 1999: 62)

She makes the point that other excluded groups have been making similar arguments for some time and that social theories 'send out signals about the way things ought to be' (*ibid*). Social capital is therefore defined within its parameters of dominant social values. It is in danger of taking less account of difference as a defining category and more concerned with normalization and assimilation processes of 'integration'.

Alongside these debates about the relationship between social capital and educational participation runs a similar debate about the nature of the learning content itself. This argues for learning provision that has a strong social agenda – one which, it might be claimed, prepares people for a more inclusive form of citizenship and social capital – which in itself can generate interest in lifelong learning but with a less individualistic approach than the employability model.

Education for social purpose

Education for social purpose has its origins in the community education and worker education world of the early 1900s. It started off as an attempt to bridge the gap in learning opportunities between the rich and middle classes, who had access to more liberal academic education provided by universities, and the functional skills training that was made available to the poor or working classes. It was often seen as providing a left of centre political edge to understanding social issues of the time and where the working classes or minority social groups could engage in critical debate on issues that affect their daily lives. The present, strongly vocationalist approach to lifelong learning leaves in some doubt whether the socially excluded will continue to have access to this form of learning. Taylor (1997) offers some thoughts on why this may be the case, as well as some arguments for the retention of social purpose education. He draws his analysis from the continuing education scene, which has a long history of educational provision for marginalized social groups.

Taylor (1997) suggests that the collapse of communism in Eastern Europe has led to a decline in socialism as an ideological reference point for political and social groups. This has had a knock-on effect on the ideological purposes of education. The entrepreneurial, free-market approach of European policies for education and training reflect this position. Hence, he proposes, there is a need to find new ways of constructing an ethic for education and training whose outcomes reach beyond human capital or mutualism.

The UK at least has had a long tradition of continuing education provision for adults that has a largely social and community, rather than vocational or individualist, purpose:

> Social purpose continuing education has been concerned to empower, through educational experience and input, individuals and more particularly collective groups within the working class and disadvantaged sectors of those societies. (Taylor, 1997: 93)

To this end, such education has been primarily about facilitating societal change, but taught from within the social and cultural values of the participants. While much of this education was organized through trade unions, it has also been the cornerstone of much local and informal education, as a partnership between education providers and community groups. The curriculum for such community groups is usually designed around a particular local issue such as housing or welfare, rather than a more recognizable and transferable subject-specific curriculum. This education is justified because, among other reasons, it does not silence the marginalized learner voice. The curriculum includes the marginalized by taking seriously issues that are important to learners from different social groupings and building an educational framework from that base. In other words, different social values are acceptable and included as part of the teaching material. The educational goal is not to normalize, rather to celebrate diversity but raise awareness of issues confronting a diverse and pluralistic society.

This kind of education is far removed from the policies of social exclusion that nurture qualities of employability, mobility and a willingness to adapt to changing labour demands. Even in social capital terms, which are about fostering a sense of cohesion and common values across communities, social purpose education has other goals. Social purpose education recognizes the differences *within* communities and, as such, might be seen as threatening broader goals of social cohesion. Social purpose education, however, aims to give marginalized groups a sense of self-worth that may in itself bring about the kind of mutual understanding of diversity advocated in the European White Paper.

Conclusion

This chapter has looked at models of social inclusion in terms of policy and theory. It has suggested there might be other models of social inclusion that extend the common notion of social capital as a unifying societal backdrop for stimulating learning. It poses the idea that social capital does exist among the socially excluded; however, their norms and values are disregarded by society. This in turn marginalizes people and delimits their chances of participation in the labour market on equal terms.

Including the socially excluded in the learning age is a complex business. It requires a fine balance between fostering inclusion while recognizing difference – and nurturing stability and cohesion while avoiding the continued exclusion of those marginalized social identities that are already disadvantaged by the majority. How far the efforts of evolving policies for social inclusion have succeeded in reaching this balance perhaps depends on whether the concept of inclusion is seen as fostering diversity in preference to cohesion or whether there is a middle way that grounds both values in policy.

References

Ackers, L (1998) *Shifting Spaces: Women, citizenship and migration within the European Union*, Polity Press, Cambridge

Beck, U (1998) *Democracy Without Enemies*, Polity Press, Cambridge

Brine, J (1999) *Undereducating Women: Globalising inequality*, OUP, Oxford

Coleman, J S (1988) 'Social capital in the creation of human capital', *American Journal of Sociology Supplement*, **94**, S95–S120

Coleman, J S (1994) *Foundations of Social Theory*, Belkrup, Cambridge, MA

DfEE (1997) 'Empowering People and Communities for a Better Future', speech on the launch of the Social Exclusion Unit, dfee.gov.uk/empowering/speech.htm

DfEE (1998) *Bringing Britain Together: A national strategy for neighbourhood renewal*, Social Exclusion Unit, London

DfEE (1999) *The Wider Benefits of Learning*, The Moser Report, DfEE, Sheffield

European Commission (1995) *Teaching and Learning: Towards the learning society*, White Paper, DG XXII, EC, Brussels

European Commission (1997) *Towards a Europe of Knowledge*, Green Paper, EC, Brussels

European Commission (1998) *Social Action Programme 1998–2000*, Employment and Social Affairs, EC, Luxembourg

Giddens, A (1998) *The Third Way*, Polity Press, Cambridge

Hamilton, M (1996) 'Literacy and ABE', in R Fieldhouse and Associates, *A History of Modern British Adult Education*, NIACE, Leicester

Howarth, C and Kenway, P (1998) 'A multi-dimensional approach to social exclusion indicators', in ed C Oppenheim, *An Inclusive Society: Strategies for tackling poverty*, IPPR, London

Lister, R (1997) *Citizenship – Feminist Perspectives*, Macmillan, Basingstoke

Mayo, M (1997) *Imaging Tomorrow: Adult education in transformation*, NIACE, Leicester

Moser, C (1999) *Improving Literacy and Numeracy for Adults: A fresh start*, Summary and Recommendations of the working group chaired by Sir Claus Moser, DfEE, London

OECD (1999) *Overcoming Exclusion through Adult Learning*, OECD, Paris

Oommen, T K (1997) *Citizenship and National Identity*, Sage, London

Preece, J (1999) *Combating Social Exclusion in University Adult Education*, Ashgate, Aldershot

Putnam, R D (1995) 'Tuning in and tuning out: the strange disappearance of social capital in America', *Political Science and Politics*, **18** (4), 664–83

Riddell, S, Baron, S and Wilson, A (1999) 'Social capital and people with learning difficulties', *Studies in the Education of Adults*, **31** (1), 49–65

Schuller, T and Field, J (1995) 'Social capital, human capital and the learning society', *International Journal of Lifelong Education*, **17** (4), 226–35

Taylor, R (1997) 'The search for a social purpose ethic in adult continuing education in the new Europe', *Studies in the Education of Adults*, **29** (1), 92–100

Withnal, A (1994) 'Literacy on the agenda: the origins of the adult literacy campaign in the UK', *Studies in the Education of Adults*, **26** (1), 67–85

PART FIVE

REFLECTIONS ON THE AGE OF LEARNING

Chapter 15

The public recognition of learning

Peter Jarvis

The concept of the 'learning society' is, in one sense, quite paradoxical since learning is something that occurs in individuals and is a private process, whereas society is social and public. This paradox can be solved in part by suggesting that in this instance 'learning' is an adjective qualifying 'society' – but how can a private process describe a social phenomenon, except metaphorically? However, there is another way of interpreting this juxtaposition of terms – for learning is a private process but social processes are public, and in a rapidly changing society, where individuals are forced to learn all the time, there needs to be some control or recognition, or both, of the individual process by the wider society. This chapter seeks to explore this public/private relationship.

Habermas (1989) has highlighted the changing nature of the relationship between the private and public spheres in society. From the outset (pp. 1–2), he indicates something of the complex use of these terms – especially 'public'. Public relates to openness, to recognition by the wider society and the public domain is a specific one in relation to the private one. He also argues (p. 6) that from its earliest times in Greek civilization, the public domain was where individuals sought honourable distinction away from the home, where 'the wants of life and the procurement of the necessities of life were shamefully hidden'. The presentation of 'effortless superiority' has emerged under these conditions, or as Goffman (1959) would argue: *The Presentation of Self in Everyday Life*.

Within this framework, it is perhaps easier to understand this paradoxical juxtapositioning of the private learning and public society, and we do so in three distinct sections: the individual and private nature of learning; the public recognition of private learning; the public consumption of learning.

The individual and private nature of learning

One of the obvious strengths of behaviourist theories of learning, which reflect the period in which they evolved, is that exponents of such theories can claim empirical evidence that learning has taken place, since they define learning as a process of permanent behaviour change as a result of experience (Borger and Seaborne, 1966: 14). Therefore, any change in behaviour as a result of experience is learning. But, of course, it is not, although learning may occur in the process of changing behaviour. Ormrod (1995: 5) recognizes that this approach to learning is not sufficient in itself and she adds a second strand to this definition, that learning is 'a relatively permanent change in mental associations due to experience'. Significantly, the cognitivist definition is one that means that learning is something that cannot be observed or measured empirically. It removes learning from the sphere of empirical science.

However, in more recent times a third approach to learning has emerged – the experiential, which is much closer to a social scientific understanding of learning. Kolb (1984: 41) captured the essence of the period when he concentrated on human experience and helped to change the emphasis from the cognitive one. He suggested that learning is a process whereby 'knowledge is created through the transformation of experience'. Now it is not only the person being transformed, it is the experience that the individual has which is changed. But even this definition is still too narrow, since human beings learn a far broader range of phenomena than knowledge, so that learning might now be viewed as a process of constructing and transforming experience into knowledge, skills, attitudes, values, emotions, beliefs and the senses. Learning is the process of internalizing all experiences individuals have in the external world and making them part of the individual.

Despite their differences, all of these approaches to learning share two things: they all focus on the individual and on the individual's experience. Learning is an individual process, it is personal and a part of one's private world, even though many of the experiences that individuals have occur in the social world. There is one other similarity in all the definitions, that is the idea of 'change' or 'transformation', either change in behaviour or in mental associations in the learners, whereas the experiential definitions focus on the transformation of the experience itself and consequently of the individual learner. Learning then is essentially individual and private.

But learning does not always or necessarily occur in private; learning occurs in public places, in work, in education and so on. However, one thing about this global world is that it is always changing, and behaviourists could, and do, see the changing society (or organization) as a learning society or learning organization in precisely this sense. But if learning societies are merely changing societies, the concept carries neither a great deal of meaning nor significance. Nevertheless, as we pointed out earlier, learning does occur in the process of change, but the changing nature of society is not learning in itself. The rapid and fundamental changes that are occurring in global society as a result of information technology and the competitive market are generating the necessity for all individuals to keep on learning merely to remain a member of their society or organization. Since all people's learning is individual, this is necessarily an individuating process and society is consequently fragmenting – unless there are other forms of 'social glue' that hold it together. Postmodern thinkers have been emphasizing the fragmentary nature of contemporary society (Bauman, 1995, *inter alia*).

There is a sense then in which learning is paradoxical – it can be used for the good or the ill of society – and while I do not want to extend this analysis here (see Jarvis, 1992), it can be seen that it might threaten the stability of a society if learners were free to learn what they want and use the results of their learning for their own ends, so that it has traditionally been controlled or managed by the public sphere. Traditionally the educational institution has undertaken this task – it has devised the curriculum, selecting from culture that knowledge which was regarded as worthwhile, transmitted it through controlling didactic modes, and examined and acclaimed 'correct' learning. Sociologists have long been aware of the reproductive nature of education (Bourdieu and Passeron, 1977). The control or management of private learning is still a fundamental need if society is not to break into fragments, or as Mrs Thatcher could famously (but in many ways wrongly) proclaim – there is no such thing as society ! But two questions do emerge: is it going to be state education systems that retain the monopoly of the control and management function of all learning; and is the need for the control and management going to be as great as globalization occurs?

Significantly, the major form of education that is not controlled or managed is that education which is occurring amongst the third age. In the Universities of the Third Age, there are:

- no specified curricula;
- democratic processes of choosing what subjects to study and how they are to be taught and learnt;
- no regulations and inspections;
- no examinations.

It is as if the controlling and managing bodies are not concerned with this form of learning – it provides no means for the learners of playing a major role in the public sphere, neither does it offer a route into any form of employment – unless there is some form of recognition of the learning that occurs by a potential employer. Consequently, it requires no public recognition. Third-age learning is still an essential part of a rapidly changing society, and in this sense it is still a feature of the learning society, but it is far from threatening to the stability of society, and it serves different functions to the learning that requires some form of public recognition. It can remain private learning and continue to be learning in the private domain.

In the global society, the public recognition of learning is for purposes other than retaining the stability of society, and as we examine it we look to the manner in which learning was controlled and managed publicly in more traditional societies when change was not so rapid.

The public recognition of private learning

Throughout its history society has had mechanisms for both the control and public recognition of individuals' learning, for instance, in traditional society, when people grew and developed more quickly than their culture changed. Individuals could not remain in the same role and status in society forever; children became adults, adults parents and parents elders – but during that period society appeared to change little. In other words, they had to pass through the structures and classifications of society relating to their age, and in order to do so they had formally to learn new roles. The process of role change is important to this argument. Van Gennep (1960) distinguished three phases to this process of rites of passage: a process of ritualizing the individual out of one status, a period of liminality and a final process of ritualizing the person into a new status.

For our purposes these latter two stages are important. Liminality is one of those phases in life when individuals, having been removed from the structures of society, no longer fit into the classifications and structures of society. During this period they were excluded from social interaction within the tribe, and regarded as either unclean or dangerous. It is, however, a period of learning during which they learnt the knowledge necessary for them to be able to assume successfully a new status and role in society. Turner (1969: 81) describes it thus:

> Liminal entities, such as neophytes in initiation or puberty rites, may be represented as possessing nothing. They may be disguised as monsters, wear only a strip of clothing, or even go naked, to demonstrate that, as liminal beings, they have no status, property, insignia, secular clothing indicating rank or role, position in the kinship system – in short, nothing that may distinguish them from their fellow neophytes or initiands. Their behaviour is normally passive or humble; they must obey their instructors implicitly, and accept arbitrary punishment without complaint. It is as though they are being reduced or

ground down to uniform conditions to be fashioned anew and endowed with additional powers to enable them to cope with their new station in life.

Naturally, individuals learnt a great deal about how to play their new role before they embarked upon this initiation ritual, but this was private and not articulated. During the period of initiation, they were taught in a most authoritarian manner how to play their new role in society. They learnt in a non-reflective way, and they were certainly not the authors of the experiences from which they learnt. But this was regarded as a dangerous period for society: there was always a chance that the initiands might not learn correctly or that they might not fit perfectly into the social structures, and so they had to be humble, or be humbled, so that they could be remoulded to fit into their new position.

Having undertaken this period of liminality, the initiands were ritualized back into society in their new roles and with their new statuses. Perhaps very primitive people did not have the language of learning and certainly not of qualifications and awards, but in ritualizing individuals back into society they were publicly recognizing the learning that had occurred as a result of the teaching.

In the medieval period, there were clearly similarities with a number of features in later pre-modern society, especially in the West. Examples include apprenticeship rituals when young people had completed their time of learning with the master craftsman and their learning was then publicly recognized in some ritual and membership of an appropriate guild. Public schools are another example; children of the ruling classes were sent to them in order to prepare them for public service and, in a sense, it was the creation of the ruling community that was more important than anything else, so that in leaving the schools their position in society was recognized and they could assume high office, often through ritual induction – such as ordination if they were entering the church.

Later ritual was replaced with examinations and certain organizations were granted the right to set examinations and award certificates to those who could demonstrate that they had learnt sufficient to pass the examination. In each of these, the society as a whole, the guild or the school (representing society) controlled the learning and recognized it publicly either through public ritual or through the award of some form of certificate. The individual learning was recognized both socially and publicly.

However, in the learning society this is no longer possible. Individuals who work in knowledge industries are producing new knowledge as a result of the work that they undertake – they are learning all the time. People are also adapting to the changes that innovations in society create and a great deal of learning occurs in the experiences of daily life. Additionally, individuals are able to purchase learning materials and CD ROMs for use with their personal computers, they are able to access the World Wide Web, and so on. People are able to learn from all types of sources and it is still both individual and private, and in such a market place it is now no longer possible to manage or control the curriculum or programme of private learning. There is no way that a curriculum can be set, but, as may be seen above, there are still mechanisms of control – the recognition of learning.

Accreditation of prior (experiential) learning (APEL or APL – the latter is usually used when all the learning in the portfolio has taken place in already accredited courses) has, therefore, entered the educational vocabulary; now private learning is beginning to be recognized publicly. The mechanisms for this have been made easier since education itself has been forced to adapt to all the changes in late-modern society and to restructure its programmes along modular lines as a result of market-led demands. Courses now comprise a number of modules, each carrying a specific weighting which, it is suggested, should take a specific number of learning hours to complete.

Now individuals can construct their own portfolio of individual learning, which might be private learning, institutionalized learning or a mixture of the two and which may also include learning that occurs in the workplace. With this portfolio, they may seek recognition for their learning from an awarding body, which may specify that the portfolio is worth a certain number of modules (or hours of learning) that can be remitted against another course of study. In this manner private learning receives public recognition.

Different educational institutions, however, may place different values on the learning that is reported in the portfolio and two dangers emerge as a result of this. The first is that learners take their portfolio to a number of different institutions to see which will place the greatest value on it. The second is that educational institutions will compete with each other for students in the educational market and try to be more generous in their award than their rival institutions. In this case APEL becomes discount selling and student recruitment assumes the form of the sales person trying to entice potential students to purchase one of the institution's own educational products.

Nevertheless, unless the learner possesses a certificate, there is no guarantee that the learning has taken place, so most courses run by educational institutions offer a certificate at the end. In a sense, the certificate serves the same purpose as the change in behaviour for the behaviourist. It is a guarantee that the learning has occurred, even though the learners might now have forgotten what they learnt and the behavioural change might be for a reason other than the learning that is claimed to have occurred. The certificate, or the symbol, has now become more important in the public domain that the actual learning that occurred in the private one.

In precisely the same way, that portfolio of learning might be taken to a potential employer; if the employer accepts it, it is another form of public recognition. But the employer may also recruit individuals into the company with relatively low academic qualifications and provide routes to higher positions. Among those routes may be training in the organization's own educational institution. The private learning is recognized within the company, without certification, as individuals work their way up to elite positions, from which they may then proceed to play major roles in the wider society. In this sense, large corporations have become quasi-public spheres recognizing the learning that occurs in everyday work life and enabling status change without the accompanying ritual.

Nevertheless, for many people the ritual has been replaced by the certificate, which in turn has been replaced in part by the public acceptance of a personal history of learning – but in all cases society is recognizing publicly the private and individual learning that has occurred. We will return to the certificate in the following section.

The public consumption of learning

In the learning society a great deal of private and individual learning occurs, but unless that learning receives public recognition, a certificate, there is no guarantee that it has taken place, so that increasingly educational institutions are producing modules and other learning packages that can be awarded certificates. Whole courses are now subdivided and individual modules, or whole sections of the course, might be sold separately and more easily in the new market place of learning.

However, it need not only be the educational institution that produces such courses. Eurich (1985: 97) discovered that:

All 18 corporate institutions [the number she discovered] operate what might be called an 'open admissions' policy. They are, quite literally, open to all qualified persons outside the sponsoring corporation. While this is quite literally true, one exception requires notice: MacDonald's Hamburger University basically only serves its employees, but it admits students from its major supplier companies and has perhaps eight or so a year.

The important point is that these are not typically 'in-house' educational programs for employees. The Rand, Wang and Arthur D Little institutes do not serve the employees of their parent corporations; each admits students who meet their admission requirements from any college or university, any company, or from any country. Their graduates cannot expect employment from the sponsoring firm.

As noted in Chapter 12, Meister (1998) has suggested that many of the corporate universities are now expected to make a financial return on their investment, so they are also offering awards and have entered the market place of learning. No longer does the traditional educational institution have the monopoly on publicly accrediting private learning.

Learning programmes or packages have become commodities to be bought. Indeed, educational courses are products to be purchased, but, as Baudrillard pointed out, the commodities need symbols. He suggests that 'in order to become an object of consumption, the object must become a sign' (Baudrillard, in Poster, 1988: 22) and that consumption is 'a systematic act in the manipulation of signs' (*ibid*). Consequently, the symbol being advertised is the qualification, whether it is NVQ, BSc, MSc, MBA or PhD, and education is now being consumed like any other commodity. Much of the private learning, like university extra-mural classes and adult education, is now more likely to be supported by the state or other funding body if it is accredited – the world of individual learning has now been publicly recognized.

It is not just education that is moving in this direction, Bauman (1992: 17) writes:

> Literature, visual arts, music – indeed, the whole sphere of the humanities – was gradually freed from the burden of carrying the ideological message, and ever more solidly set inside market-led consumption as entertainment. More and more the culture of consumer society was subordinated to the function of producing and reproducing skilful and eager consumers.

However, the eager consumers of learning may be reflecting a significant change in lifestyle. It may not only be the awards of learning that need to be publicly recognized; it may be that the symbols of learning are important for the presentation of the self in a learning society. Consequently, other symbols of learning may also be purchased, as Featherstone (1991: 19) points out:

> knowledge becomes important: knowledge of new goods, their social and cultural value, and how to use them appropriately. This is particularly the case with aspiring groups who adopt a learning mode towards consumption and the cultivation of a lifestyle. It is for groups such as the new middle class, the new working class and the new rich and upper class, that the consumer-culture magazines, newspapers, books, television and radio programmes which stress self-improvement, self-development, personal transformation, how to manage property, relationships and ambition, how to construct a fulfilling lifestyle, are most relevant. Here one may find most frequently the self-conscious autodidact who is concerned to convey the appropriate signals through his/her consumption activities.

Learning and the wider cultural phenomena are changing and being commoditized, so that people do not just have to learn how to fit into a society that has an apparently unchanging culture. Everything is changing and the culture of consumption in which the individual consumes the commodity is the order of the day. In this instance, learning is an individual act of consumption, and the learning market becomes a symbol of the learning society. However, consumption of a market commodity is still private until such time as the process is complete and a certificate is awarded by an institution that has the public legitimation to make the award, or the symbol has been presented and effectively accepted.

The fact that the world of private learning is being publicly recognized is a phenomenon of the learning society. There still remain areas of private learning that seek no public recognition, such as a great deal of private life. The largest private institutionalized form rests with older people. There has been a tremendous growth in learning organizations for older people, such as the Universities of the Third Age – they are private, non-governmental organizations. Their members adopt the slogan that anybody can teach and anybody can learn and their courses carry no public recognition. The elders can still stand outside of society and their learning need not be controlled or recognized by society.

Conclusion

A paradox that emerges as a result of the elders' learning is that they may be undergoing genuine learning experiences, learning new things and growing and developing as human beings. In a sense their learning is real. However, unless it is certificated there is another sense in which it is not recognized as learning – certificated learning becomes 'real' learning and their real learning becomes 'unreal'. The certificate becomes a sign of real learning and there is a danger that learning will become defined by the possession of a certificate and the actual human processes of learning will be regarded as less significant than the certification that has taken place. This is precisely the same as the weakness with the behaviourist approach, where the change of behaviour – the sign that learning had occurred – was defined as the learning itself.

References

Bauman, Z (1992) *Intimations of Postmodernity*, Routledge, London
Bauman, Z (1995) *Life in Fragments*, Blackwell, Oxford
Bourdieu, P and Passeron, J-F (1977) *Reproduction*, Sage, London
Borger, R and Seaborne, A (1966) *The Psychology of Learning*, Penguin Books, Harmondsworth

Eurich, N (1985) *Corporate Classrooms: The learning business,* Carnegie Foundation for the Advancement of Teaching, Princeton, NJ

Featherstone, M (1991) *Consumer Culture and Postmodernism,* Sage, London

Goffman, E (1959) *The Presentation of Self in Everyday Life,* Penguin Books, Harmondsworth

Habermas, J (1989) *The Structural Transformation of the Public Sphere,* Polity Press, Cambridge

Jarvis, P (1992) *Paradoxes of Learning,* Jossey-Bass, San Francisco, CA

Kolb, D (1984) *Experiential Learning,* Prentice-Hall, Englewood Cliffs, NJ

Meister, J (1998) *Corporate Universities,* revised and updated, McGraw-Hill, New York

Ormrod, J (1995) *Human Learning,* 2nd edn, Merrill, Englewood Cliffs, NJ

Poster, M (ed) (1988) *Jean Baudrillard: Selected writings,* Polity Press, Cambridge

Turner, V (1969) *The Ritual Process,* Penguin Books, Harmondsworth

van Gennep, A (1960) *The Rites of Passage,* Routledge and Kegan Paul, London

Chapter 16

Questioning the learning society

Peter Jarvis

The learning society appears to be a vision in nearly all EU and government educational documents; it is almost as if it may be equated with the good society. It is axiomatic that it is a good thing and something to be striven for, primarily so that we can have a highly trained workforce to compete in the global economy, and secondarily – and a long way behind – for the enrichment of the population. Everybody has to be a lifelong learner; here the emphasis is placed upon apparently autonomous individuals to learn, grow and develop and to assume their place in society as workers and, then, as citizens. It is their responsibility. The emphasis on the individual is interesting for a number of reasons, some of which were mentioned in the last chapter, but it is to another that we turn our attention in this chapter.

Lifelong learning has become the accepted terminology in the learning society discourse, rather than lifelong education – this is a learning society rather than an educative one. Perhaps this is the nub of the question: is today's society actually a learning one or is it an educative one? This is not a matter of semantics but a major question about the control of individual's learning and also about how lifelong education is being defined for the next generation. Underlying these question lie others of an ethical and political nature and it is necessary to look briefly at these within the context of this discussion. For this purpose we draw a distinction between education and learning that is extremely broad.

One of the first scholars who emphasized learning but was fearful of the way in which education would grow was Ivan Illich (1971), who wrote *Deschooling Society* (see also Schon, 1971), but he also wrote, with Etienne Verne, another essay about lifelong education, *Imprisoned in a Global Classroom* (1976). In the first part of this chapter we revisit this essay and explore some of those ideas again. Thereafter, we examine lifelong learning and suggest that it is a utopian ideal, but like most utopian ideals it serves the function of pointing us beyond where we are to a better society (Levitas, 1990). In the third part of this chapter we analyse the social pressures that have given rise to the learning society and raise some questions about them; this relates to the discussion in the second chapter of this book about globalization.

Imprisoned in a global classroom – revisited

In order to understand fully their concerns, it is necessary to note that Illich and Verne (1976) distinguished between education and learning, and that for them education was a form of didactic instruction with no other teaching method playing a part. In fact this clear-cut separation of teaching and learning harmed their analysis, inasmuch as they failed to recognize the learning that can and does take place in community and work situations, in everyday life in fact, and they failed to see that a greater emphasis would be placed on learning as the changes about which they were writing developed. Secondly, they were writing before the significance of information technology was widely recognized, so their views about corporations tend to reflect the ideas of industrialization rather than the fact that large proportions of the workforce now work with knowledge and produce new knowledge in the course of their work. In addition, they saw the state as underwriting a new system of factory schools for adults. Clearly some of their fears are allayed by the fact that learning as well as teaching is emphasized in today's learning society and that while there is something of a partnership between the state and the corporations, the state should have some different priorities, such as citizenship and democracy. However, some of their other fears remain to be examined.

When Illich and Verne wrote this text, there were considerable movements in France to institute *education permanente*, with early legislation about taxing corporations' budgets to pay for further education and training of the workforce. They opposed this by suggesting that:

> This is taken as a compulsory contribution from the French worker to provide for training that he does not want, from which he hardly benefits, but which serves to adapt, integrate, tame and dominate him. (1976: 9)

Indeed, their concern is that the existence of lifelong education, which people are expected to attend, is a permanent guarantee of human inadequacy and incompetency, so that individuals become subject to instruction throughout their whole life. However, this view of education is to be contested: education does not in itself always signify inadequacy; it might signify that confident knowledgeable people can be aware that they need to build on their knowledge by attending classes given by other experts in order to keep abreast of all the changes that are occurring..

Nevertheless, on another level, they are correct since education generally reinforces and reproduces the social structures of a society, despite its claims to the contrary (Bourdieu and Passeron, 1977; Giddens, 1998). Many years ago Max Weber illustrated one of the mechanisms by which this occurs:

> When we hear from all sides the demand for the introduction of regular curricula and special examinations, the reason behind it is, of course, not a suddenly awakened 'thirst for education'; but the desire for restricting the supply for those positions and their monopolization by the owners of educational certificates. Today the 'examination' is the universal means of this monopolization, and therefore examinations irresistibly advance. As the education prerequisite to the acquisition of the educational certificate requires considerable expense and a period of waiting for full remuneration, the striving means a setback for talent (charisma) in favour of property. (Gerth and Mills, 1948: 241–42)

Of course, access to examinations (at the appropriate level) is now much easier and smaller bites of learning are examined or accredited – for purposes of marketability rather than equality. Even so, much of this argument still holds good.

At the same time, the promise that anybody can succeed and climb up the social hierarchy as a result of more education is held out to the workers today in precisely they same manner as Illich and Verne suggested. In this society in which individuality is emphasized, anybody can learn and gain accreditation for their learning – it is their fault if they do not – and the possibility of social advancement is held out to them. This is an issue that has to be addressed, and it is not a new one. The Workers Educational Association in the UK, the Folk High Schools in Denmark and many other adult education movements, for instance, have always opposed qualifications for adult educational courses because they recognize that while an individual gaining qualifications might climb up the social hierarchy, the social conditions for the remainder would not be altered. Basically they argue that it is not the incompetence of the individual but the inequality of the system and the accident of birth that results in some people enjoying privilege while others suffer deprivation. It might be argue that in contemporary society the barriers between the different stages in the social hierarchy have become easier to penetrate, society has become more open, so that given the opportunity more people might become socially mobile upwards, but whether this is a result of their lifelong education is more questionable. Nevertheless, it does not obviate the fact that there is still a social hierarchy, a rich and a poor, and that education still serves to reinforce the social differences.

The training is to be provided by a new professional group – adult educators with university status – who will control an 'educational mega-machine'. Human resource developers and consultants have certainly become large and dominant professional groups during this time, influencing society in a multitude of ways – perhaps they are much more influential than even Illich and Verne (1976) feared. In this essay, they were also very concerned about the:

- industrialization of education (p. 13);
- commercialization of knowledge (p. 13);
- ways in which education would be used primarily for the benefit of the 'capitalists of knowledge and the professionals licenses to distribute it' (p. 13);
- fact that a new hidden curriculum would emerge (p. 13);
- fact that many training courses will be about understanding the employing company in order to instil company loyalty (p. 17);
- institutionalization of permanent education that will transform society into a planet-sized classroom watched over by a few satellites (p. 20);
- fact that existence itself becomes the subject of a study course (p. 14);
- growth of the bureaucratic control of humankind (pp. 20–21).

There can be no doubt that education has been industrialized. Much distance education is itself a product of the industrialization process (Peters, 1984) and this has widened the participation in education, though the fees charged by most providers mean that only those who can afford it can benefit from it. The government's idea of learning accounts is designed, in part, to offer something of a solution to this, although it clearly does not overcome the inequalities of the system. Even so, distance education has given more opportunity to people worldwide to enjoy its benefits. It has also tended to weaken the personal contact between teacher and learners and between learners themselves – which has probably resulted in a greater degree of acceptance of the provided text and far less engagement in critical discussion with teachers and peers. However, there are some signs that contemporary electronic systems are allowing some degree of peer inter-action to proceed, although the learners are still individualized and apart, so that combined and collaborative student activities are harder to achieve.

Their fears about the commercialization of knowledge are well founded, for with the development of knowledge societies (Stehr, 1994) knowledge has not only been a driving force for change, it has become a commercial product in its own right. Companies possessing such knowledge try to keep it secret until such times as it can be marketed – industrial espionage is a tool in this commercial competition. Knowledge of all forms can be bought and sold in the market place. In addition, research to produce new knowledge is often driven by the same commercial concerns. Lyotard (1984: 45) wrote that:

> Capitalism solves the scientific problem of research funding in its own way: directly by financing research departments in private companies, in which demands for performativity and commercialization orientate research first and foremost towards technological 'applications'; and indirectly by creating private, state and mixed-sector research foundations that grant program subsidies to university departments, research laboratories, and independent research groups with no expectation of an immediate return on the results of the work.

Government policy in the 1980s was that business and industry would fund a great deal of university research. Clearly this is happening, but the research is now directed much more towards commercialization, whereas there remains a fundamental need for 'blue skies' research. Research itself should not be defined by its immediate usefulness.

Their third concern is also well founded, since most of the government policy statements on lifelong learning place considerable emphasis on the need to develop a competent workforce to compete in the global market place (EU, 1995; DfEE, 1998, 1999). What Illich and Verne did not foresee, however, was the failure of the state educational system to keep abreast of the speed of change that industry demanded. Eulich (1985), for instance, pointed out that the cultures of education and commerce were very different and that as the education system was unable to keep up with the speed of change in the global market, the corporations would start their own educational institutions. Illich and Verne (p. 16) felt that the French law of 1971 on vocational education would result in the return to factory schools – they certainly never foresaw the possibilities of the corporate universities which are springing up throughout the United States and now starting in UK and elsewhere (Meister, 1998).

Education has become industrialized; indeed, Kerr *et al* (1973: 47) claimed that education had become the handmaiden of industrialism. They suggested that:

> The higher education system in industrialized countries stresses the natural sciences, engineering, medicine, managerial training – whether private or public – and administrative law... There is a relatively smaller place for humanities and the arts, while the social sciences are strongly related to the training of managerial groups and technicians for the enterprise and government.

They lay out a clear curriculum that reflects the ethos of modernity but also the curriculum in many education and training institutions. This is a curriculum that omits studies of all forms of civic education and values, and which does not address the fundamental questions of humanity. It is significant, however, that the study of democracy and citizenship is returning to the governmental education agenda.

Perhaps this governmental agenda is needed, since Illich's and Verne's fears about training courses supplied by the employing company have been fully realized as large corporations are now teaching their employees about 'corporate citizenship' (Meister, 1998: 93–98). Meister quotes Judy Schueler of the University of Chicago Hospital:

> Our vision in creating the orientation program for UCH was to develop a program where our employees could learn to be good citizens. To us, a good citizen moves beyond performing just the job tasks. Rather a good citizen acts like he/she is the owner of the business, desires to satisfy customers, understands that customer satisfaction comes from how the job is done, and takes responsibility for continually striving to do a better job. (p. 93)

There is nothing here about democracy, human rights or values – but a lot about how to be responsive to the company and learn how to be a better employee (citizen). In a sense, this is the business world taking over the democratic discourse of civic society. Indeed, the corporate universities have a traditional classical curriculum and there is a considerable danger that other educational institutions will forsake human studies for the sake of vocational ones.

Of the final points that need mentioning, they were fearful of the bureaucratic control over humankind that was emerging when they wrote, and which it might be said has now arrived. Giddens (1985: 312) makes the point that surveillance is quite fundamental to social organization in all forms of state. The possibilities of surveillance have increased enormously as a result of electronic techniques, and if an electronic recognition system is introduced attached to learning accounts or to some form of continuous educational career record, then a new form of surveillance will become possible.

They were concerned that existence itself would become a focus for study – perhaps one would wish that the curriculum of many educational courses might actually include discussion of existential questions. While existence features in the agenda of global capitalism through genetic research, existential questions feature far less prominently.

However, we can see that Illich and Verne raised some valid criticisms about lifelong education and that some of their fears have been realized, and so there are questions about the social pressures that have given rise to the learning society that do need further discussion.

Lifelong learning

The distinction between education and learning is crucial in Illich's writing. While the social structures of privilege and poverty are reproduced by the educational institution, he regarded learning as something that could free the individual. Education is constraining and controlling but learning is liberating. The simple dichotomy appears very plausible at first sight, although it is less so on further examination. Teaching and education can inspire learners; facilitative teaching techniques can free individuals to discover new knowledge; critical pedagogy can help learners become aware of the problems of contemporary society; and even some forms of didactic teaching can produce critical thought amongst learners. In contrast, just being left to learn without guidance might produce feelings of inadequacy, hopelessness, a sense of inability to master complex ideas, and so on. Consequently, education and learning are not dichotomous terms.

Nevertheless, it would be true to say that the rhetoric of much lifelong learning implies that individuals are free to assume responsibility for their own learning, although there is no real emphasis on the outcomes of such learning except in terms of employability. It is almost as if employability has become synonymous with a form of useful citizenship. There is certainly little or no emphasis in much lifelong learning literature on criticality, evaluating the type of society in which we live or freeing the learners to think and do their own thinking. Learning in the learning society is about becoming flexible but not free. Now, individual responsibility means that individuals have to make themselves employable. Learning is not regarded as the polar opposite to education in the manner that Illich and Verne treat it.

Lifelong learning carries connotations of continuing to learn, at least throughout the working life. There are some references to learning throughout the whole of life – but like the study of the humanities being subservient to the study of science, learning throughout the whole life does not appear to be as important as learning throughout the work life – but this is the discourse of capitalism. However, placing learning for work before learning for life is to make at least two mistakes: it is to misunderstand the human function of learning and it is to place more value on work than on life itself. Indeed, the 'person' is frequently omitted from the discourse: people are no more than mechanisms helping to make the system function efficiently – and learning is undertaken for this end.

But learning is as crucial as breathing to the human being. It is the process whereby individuals develop their own minds, sense of self and identity, biography and their own history. Learning is the very basis of our humanity – it is the process of internalizing the external world and being able to locate ourselves within it. It not a matter of learning a skill, but of a person learning a skill: it is the *person* that is crucial. Teachers do not teach subjects or skills, they teach *individuals* subjects and skills. Work should also be regarded in human terms – it does provide meaning and purpose for many people, although it can be alienating for others. It is not the value of humanity that is emphasized in most of the lifelong learning literature, but being able to work so that employers or the country can complete in the global market.

While learning is generally seen as a good thing, it must be recognized that in some situations it may also be regarded as less than good. In *Paradoxes of Learning* (Jarvis, 1992) I demonstrated how some learning which is good in certain situations may produce bad outcomes, how non-reflective learning might reinforce the status quo and the stability of a society, whereas reflective learning might lead to fragmentation in society, how the search after meaning in contemporary society raised more questions than it answered, and so on. Lifelong learning can lead to many good outcomes, but it might have other unforeseen consequences, and it is for this reason that those who have power in society seek to control people's learning. In the last chapter we showed how the certification system exercised control over learning, but in non-governmental organizations, such as Universities of the Third Age, we should expect to see greater freedom to learn whatever the learners wish.

The social forces underlying the learning society

In the earlier chapters of this book we explored the idea that global society is driven by two substructural forces: the control of capital and the control of information technology. Like everything else, education and learning are part of the superstructure. The global world is still a capitalist market thriving on competition and innovation in the market in order to continue to sell more commodities and make more profit. The motor for a great deal of what has occurred in the past 30 years, since globalization took off, has been information technology (Castells, 1996). The speed with which this technology has changed has increased beyond all measure and capitalist competition is exacerbating the speed of change. Knowledge is changing at very rapid rates; people are having to learn new knowledge. New knowledge is producing new commodities to be sold on the market; people are having to learn new lifestyles to adapt to the new commodities they are purchasing. People want to learn new things about the world in which they live; the capitalist market is producing more learning-type commodities. For many people, this is an exciting time of growth and development; there is more space to enjoy the pleasures of living.

But this is still a competitive world and competition produces losers as well as winners. The emphasis in government documents is on the positive aspects of learning and of being successful, although there is always some reference to the socially excluded, those who will not benefit from the type of society in which we live – who cannot purchase the commodities of the advanced capitalist societies and who cannot benefit from all the new opportunities to learn. Neither the socially excluded nor the low-waged who do not earn sufficient to be able to afford health care insurance (over 40 per cent of the American workforce) in the advanced capitalist system constitute a major part of the curriculum of the lifelong learning agenda being advocated by these documents.

Yet the dangers inherent in this situation are apparent for all to witness – this is not a utopian society but a fragmented and divisive one. It is estimated, for instance, that in California as many as half a million comfortably off people live inside walled communities in order to protect themselves and their belongings from the poor who might steal them, and that there are another 50 similar communities under construction (Rifkin, 1995: 212). Rifkin rightly sees this type of situation as a very dangerous one. The rich get richer at the expense of the poor. Bauman (1998: 92) points out that in the past 20 years 'the total income of the 20 per cent poorest Americans fell by 21 per cent, while the total income of the 20 per cent richest Americans rose by 22 per cent'. But this is a global phenomenon – a United Nations report estimates that if the 225 richest men in the world were to give 4 per cent of their wealth to the world's poor, it would give all of them access to elementary education, medical facilities and adequate nutrition (cited in Bauman, 1999: 174). But it is to some of these poorer countries that the producers turn to manufacture the commodities that can be sold on the world markets, and almost the whole of sub-Saharan Africa is excluded from the gains of the global processes. This is not yet on the curriculum of the learning society, although there appears to be a growing concern about these issues.

Conclusion

The social forces that have produced the learning society have also produced a situation of exclusion and instability. This is not just dangerous, it is immoral. (Some politicians are trying to overcome some of these problems, for instance through debt relief for the world's poorest nations.) The lifelong learning agenda is certainly biased in favour of capitalism and open to considerable criticism. But then the educational curriculum has always been socially and culturally reproductive.

The whole social, political and educational scene has changed beyond recognition in the past 30 years. There is a new language in education and many more possibilities exist than ever before, and not everything that Illich and Verne feared has come to pass. Indeed, the agenda of the learning society appears to be expanding and funds are being made available to research such important topics as democracy and citizenship in society and not in the corporation. But the problems that confronted education when Illich and Verne wrote still confront the learning society and neither learning nor education in themselves are going to change the system – they are merely recipients of the social forces of global capitalism. Utopian visions (Ranson, 1994) of a new social and moral order in the learning society may exist and one of their functions is always to show us that there is something better to which we can aspire than that which we currently have.

References

Bauman, Z (1998) *Work, Consumerism and the New Poor,* Open University Press, Buckingham

Bauman, Z (1999) *In Search of Politics,* Polity Press, Cambridge

Bourdieu, P and Passeron, J-C (1977) *Reproduction,* Sage, London

Castells, M (1996) *The Rise of the Network Society* (Vol 1 of *The Information Age: Economy, society and culture*), Blackwell, Oxford

DfEE (1998) *The Learning Age,* DfEE, London

DfEE (1999) *Learning to Succeed,* DfEE, London

Eurich, N (1985) *Corporate Classrooms,* Carnegie Trust for the Advancement of Teaching, Princeton, NJ

European Union (1995) *Teaching and Learning: Towards the learning society,* European Union, Brussels

Gerth, H H and Mills, C W (eds) (1948) *From Max Weber,* Routledge and Kegan Paul, London

Giddens, A (1985) *The National State and Violence,* Polity Press, Cambridge

Giddens, A (1998) *The Third Way,* Polity Press, Cambridge

Illich, I (1971) *Deschooling Society,* Penguin Books, Harmondsworth

Illich, I and Verne, E (1976) *Imprisoned in a Global Classroom,* Writers and Readers Publishing, London

Jarvis, P (1992) *Paradoxes of Learning,* Jossey-Bass, San Francisco, CA

Kerr, C, Dunlop, J T, Harbison, F and Myers, C A (1973) *Industrialism and Industrial Man,* 2nd edn, Penguin Books, Harmondsworth

Levitas, R (1990) *The Concept of Utopia,* Philip Allan, New York

Lyotard, J-F (1984) *The Postmodern Condition,* Manchester University Press, Manchester

Meister, J (1998) *Corporate Universities,* revised and updated, McGraw-Hill, New York

Peters, O (1984) 'Distance teaching and industrial production: a comparative interpretation in outline', in eds D Sewart, D Keegan and B Holmberg, *Distance Education: International perspectives,* Routledge, London

Ranson, S (1994) *Towards a Learning Society,* Cassell, London

Rifkin, J (1995) *The End of Work,* G P Putnam's Sons, New York

Schon, D (1971) *Beyond the Stable State,* Penguin Books, Harmondsworth

Stehr, N (1994) *Knowledge Societies,* Sage, London

Chapter 17

Civil society and citizenship in a learning age

John Holford

Lifelong learning and citizenship

In his Foreword to *The Learning Age* Green Paper, Britain's Secretary of State for Education and Employment argued that people should 'take advantage of new opportunities' for learning in three main ways. These corresponded to key social roles. As parents, 'encouraging, supporting and raising the expectations of our children', we can learn alongside them. As 'members of the workforce', we can learn in and out of work. As citizens, 'we can balance the rights we can expect from the state, with the responsibilities of individuals for their own future, sharing the gains and the investment needed' (Blunkett, 1998: 8).

The rather vacuous phraseology of this statement about citizens – with no reference whatever to learning – reflects the body of government policy. How families can support learning is a recurring feature of policy, driven by the desire to improve learning in schools. Learning at work is a central feature, driven by the needs of the economy. In contrast, what learning as citizens might consist of – apart from better teaching of citizenship in schools – and how it should be supported remain obscure.

However modest the content of policy, the Labour government's rhetoric about citizenship in the learning age is strong. In the same Foreword to *The Learning Age*, David Blunkett was lyrical:

> The Learning Age will be built on a renewed commitment to self-improvement and on a recognition of the enormous contribution learning makes to our society. Learning helps shape the values which we pass on to each succeeding

generation. Learning supports active citizenship and democracy, giving men and women the capacity to provide leadership in their communities. As President John F Kennedy once put it: 'Liberty without learning is always in peril and learning without liberty is always in vain'. (Blunkett, 1998: 8)

When it came to drafting his Secretary of State's Foreword to the White Paper *Learning to Succeed*, Blunkett again stressed this theme. In his first paragraph he wrote:

> Lifelong learning can enable people to play a full part in developing... the capacity of the community in which they live and work... It also contributes to sustaining a civilized and cohesive society, in which people develop as active citizens and in which generational disadvantage can be overcome. (Blunkett, 1998: 3)

The policy outlined in *Learning to Succeed*, however, contained no proposals designed to encourage people to learn to be citizens.

The purpose of this chapter is not to expose inconsistency between policy rhetoric and outcome. All governments are susceptible to such criticism. Rather, we seek to explore the relationship between learning and key concepts such as citizenship, civil society, democracy, social cohesion and community. Prominent they may be, but the Secretary of State's claims boil down to little more than assertions that learning – in unspecified and undifferentiated ways – 'supports active citizenship and democracy', develops 'the capacity of the community' and 'contributes to sustaining a civilized and cohesive society'.

The lack of detail may stem ultimately from a simple fact: the relationship between citizenship and learning is ill-charted territory. We know relatively little about how people learn their attitudes, values and beliefs about being 'citizens'. A number of important educational traditions and movements relate to citizenship: political education in the Workers' Educational Association and the Labour College movement between the world wars, mass education and community development in the British colonies in the 1940s and 1950s (Holford, 1988), inner-city community development in the 1960s and 1970s (eg Halsey, 1972; Lovett, 1975) are a few of many examples. Ethically and ideologically informed theories, chiefly of a prescriptive kind, abound (eg Freire, 1972; Lovett, 1975; Brookfield 1987). But neither theory nor practice has been subjected to rigorous empirical analysis. Beyond this the suspicion remains that social, political and economic change have rendered obsolete any lessons this experience may offer.

An issue that recurs, in varying forms, is the question of causality. Does good education produce good citizens, or is a good civil society the prerequisite for good education? Does a learning society require social cohesion, or is social cohesion the product of a learning society?

Learning, risk and stability

Much of the political and policy rhetoric about lifelong learning implies that it is inevitable, or at least essential. Change is seen as increasingly rapid and unpredictable. 'We are in a new age – the age of information and global competition. Familiar certainties and old ways of doing things are disappearing... We have no choice but to prepare for this new age...' (Cm 3790, 1998: 9). Here – and it is typical – the rhetoric emphasizes change in the economy. It speaks of globalization, flexibility at work, the end of security of employment and traditional careers. The keyword is 'risk'. Risk-taking has always been central to capitalist economies but, as Sennett (1998: 80) remarks, today risk 'is no longer meant to be the province only of venture capitalists or extraordinarily adventurous individuals. Risk is to become a daily necessity shouldered by the masses.' *The Learning Age* makes this contrast with the Industrial Revolution explicit. Then, innovation was the province of a few; now, 'everyone must have the opportunity to innovate' (Cm 3790, 1998: 10).

So far as economic life is concerned, we know well – or are frequently told – what this means. We must constantly learn in order to keep up with changing technologies: new hardware, new software, new production techniques, and so forth. We must also master 'soft skills': new ways of working, new ways of relating to other people. And we must do so not just once, or once in a while, but continually. Today's managers, for instance, celebrate flat organizational structures, networks. Employees of such organizations deal with other employees who themselves have rapidly shifting roles: this morning a manager, this afternoon a fellow team-member. At the same time, more and more people work in organizations that are themselves small and changing. Not many of these organizations expect or seek to grow. They meet market opportunities by collaborating with other small enterprises. But today's partners were yesterday's competitors, and will be again tomorrow. Learning is therefore not just about the techniques of production, but about how to collaborate, how to form teams, how to trust yesterday's competitor – and how to compete with yesterday's partner.

So we must learn because we must compete, and competing successfully means adapting to a new world of flexibility and change. Such is the message. But the more we think about this message, the more it ceases to be a simple one. This world of risk – however flexible and changing – cannot be an arbitrary or haphazard one. If it were, there would be no point in learning. The kernel of the policy message is that we can master skills and develop attitudes and knowledge that will make us more likely to succeed. The assumption is that the new flexible economy, the risk society, the learning society – whatever name we may use – is structured or patterned. When we plan our actions, our calculations of whether we shall succeed may prove mistaken, but they can be rational.

Of course, this is a commonplace. Entrepreneurs – the classical individual risk-takers of economic theory – rely on these structures and patterns. They learn from their experiences. They assume some relationship between how people behaved in the past and how they will behave in future. They develop and use their social networks – their 'social capital' (Coleman 1988). Most important of all, perhaps, they assume that they will be able to enjoy the profits or their enterprise: the money they save will not be lost; their property will not be confiscated. What this means is that learning societies must involve what sociologists call *social institutions*.

There is then a major irony, almost a contradiction, in discussions of the learning age. We need a learning society because today's economy is so unpredictable and rapidly changing. Yet we can only succeed in it by learning to make use of its regular patterns. In fact, we can go rather further than this. People will only choose to invest time and money in their own learning – especially in any formal kinds of learning, such as schooling or training courses – if they have a reasonable expectation that they will benefit by it. Unless society and the economy are relatively well ordered, unless social institutions support both predictable patterns of behaviour and a level of trust between different members of society, no sensible person could have such an expectation.

Civil society

The tension can be expressed simply thus. The economic conditions that require 'lifelong learning' are those of flexibility, uncertainty, change. But a 'learning society' must contain social institutions and patterns or regularity. A tension between the economy and the market on the one hand, and social relationships on the other is a recurring one in social theory. By and large, since the time of Adam Smith economists have examined how goods and services can be produced efficiently within a relatively stable system of social institutions. Sociologists, historians and others have spent more time considering why stable social institutions emerge, how they are sustained, and what happens when they break down.

The tension can also be found in classic works of political philosophy. Thomas Hobbes, writing immediately after the English Civil War, saw the need for an overwhelmingly powerful ruler, his *Leviathan*, to impose and sustain social order. Without such a ruler, men and women would remain in a 'state of nature': this was anarchic, without law, without order, without industry 'because the fruit thereof is uncertain'. People were in constant fierce competition; there was 'no Society; and which is worst of all, continual fear of violent death'. Their lives were 'solitary, poor, nasty, brutish and short'. For later theorists, such as Locke and Rousseau, the 'state of nature' was far more attractive. 'Man is born free', wrote Rousseau, 'and everywhere he is in chains.' They were concerned less with the awfulness of life without a powerful ruler than with how far such rulers were entitled to limit the liberties of the individual.

This philosophical debate paralleled the emergence of what is commonly referred to as 'civil society'. The 'absolutist' system of rule, typical of 17th and 18th century Europe, involved the state moving 'up and away from the larger society, to a level of its own'. From this level, society appeared as many private individuals, who the state saw 'as subjects, taxpayers, potential military draftees, etc' – a 'suitable object of rule' (Poggi, 1978: 78). But members of society 'below' were seeing themselves more as having distinct interests, which could conflict with those of the ruler. They were concerned not to be 'an object of political management by a state operating chiefly in the light of interests exclusive to itself', but rather to see the state 'become an instrumentality of society's autonomous, self-regulating development' (Poggi, 1990: 53).

Another way of putting this is that the members of civil society wanted to be citizens, to play a full part in shaping how they were governed. They formed and expressed this desire in various ways. A common thread was establishing voluntary associations: private clubs, scientific and literary societies, and dissenting religious sects. In most countries, few people could participate in what would today be seen as 'politics' until late in the 19th century at the earliest, partly because the franchise was restricted, but partly also because the number of formally constituted political institutions was very small. Civil society therefore came to refer not only to the people (the citizens), but also to the networks of voluntary associations and institutions that enabled them to express their views.

For much of the 20th century the notion of civil society was seldom used. Western societies mostly thought of themselves as democracies. All or most adults could vote; they could do so quite frequently. A contrast was typically made instead between the democratic or pluralist political institutions of the West, and authoritarian or 'totalitarian' political systems (both Fascist and Communist). But in fact the Italian Marxist Antonio Gramsci had used the concept of 'civil society' to analyse the different ways European societies developed before Communists came to power. He pointed out that in countries such as Tsarist Russia, 'the State was everything, civil society was primordial and gelatinous', while in the West civil society was more developed (Gramsci, 1971: 238). Strong civil societies – networks of institutions and associations – made it difficult for revolutions (in the sense of insurrections) to succeed.

The reason for this is not hard to discern. Voluntary associations perform a number of functions. They provide companionship and enjoyment. In them, men and women form attitudes and opinions about how they should behave towards one another. They provide prestige. They enable people to express views in a collective way, and sometimes to do so in opposition to a powerful government agency, company or individual. By doing so, they convince many people that the way their society is organized works quite well – 'Things may not be perfect, but they're good enough, and we've a lot to lose.' Of course, it's important that *enough* people feel like this. If they don't, voluntary associations can become a threat to the established power, rather than the reverse, by providing a forum for opposition. But this is rare. Even when people do not support a particular regime, participation in voluntary institutions often seems to generate common assumptions that opposition should be expressed in legitimate ways. So another way of looking at civil society is to see it as an arena in which men and women learn to be citizens.

This proposition can be put in different terms: civil society is a site for 'informal' citizenship education. The notion of informal education derives from the work of Coombs (1985) and refers to unorganized, unsystematic or unintended lifelong learning (from home, work, the media, etc). Informal education is, according to Coombs, the source of most of learning over a lifetime, but he suggests that what an individual learns is strongly dependent on his or her own particular learning environment. On this basis, we would suspect that people's informal citizenship education would be shaped by their own particular set of social institutions.

Citizenship

But what is citizenship? It has been described as a 'particular bond' between people making up the population and the state (Poggi, 1990: 28). This is a useful notion that reminds us that other kinds of bonds have existed. In medieval feudal societies, vassals classically bound themselves to their lords by oaths of loyalty and by continuing obligations such as military service, garrisoning the lord's castles and attending his court. In return they typically received a landed estate. Even formally 'free' peasants were bound by the customary law of the estate where they lived (Hilton, 1977: 44–62). They had no say in its government – this was the preserve of the lord and, when the lord wished, his vassals – though some vassals, such as King John's barons at the time of Magna Carta, came to expect a larger say.

Neither king nor barons were 'citizens', however: the king was lord, the barons his vassals. The concept of citizen derives in the West from the self-governing republics of ancient Greece and Rome, and was re-appropriated from the 18th century to assert the desire of civil society for a say in government. At the core of the notion is the idea of membership of a community (a word closely linked to 'common'; Williams, 1976: 65–66). But citizenship has always been a contested concept. In particular, who counts as a citizen has varied. In ancient Greece and Rome, as in the USA, slaves were not citizens. In most countries, women were excluded until the 20th century. In many countries, such as the UK until 1918, only those who owned property could vote. In many countries, from South Africa to the US, the vote has been limited to certain ethnic groups. And, of course, while who can vote is partly a formal matter – what the law says – in practice the political rights of individuals, and even of large groups, can also be severely limited by informal pressure.

There has been another important way in which citizenship has been contested. This stems not so much from who counts as a citizen, but what we include within the notion of 'citizenship'. The 'bottom line' has been the right to participate in government, chiefly represented in the right to vote. But it is often argued that there is more to 'being a citizen' than such narrowly political matters as the right to vote. In a classic discussion, the sociologist T H Marshall argued that citizenship is composed of three elements: political, civil and social. The political element refers to those aspects we have already mentioned: the right to participate in the exercise of political power, as a voter, candidate or legislator in national or local government.

Marshall's civil dimension comprises 'rights necessary for individual freedom – liberty of the person, freedom of speech, thought and faith, the right to own property and to conclude valid contracts, and the right to justice' (Marshall, 1950: 10). By the social element he meant:

> the whole range from the right to a modicum of economic welfare and security to the right to share to the full in the social heritage and to live the life of a civilized being according to the standards prevailing in the society. The institutions most closely connected with it are the educational system and the social services. (p. 11)

This 'three-dimensional' view of citizenship provides a useful way of analysing citizenship, and in particular allows us to chart some of the areas of contestation about the concept. For Marshall, history demonstrated a progressive extension of citizenship:

> it is possible, without doing too much violence to historical accuracy, to assign the formative period in the life of each [element] to a different century – civil rights to the eighteenth, political to the nineteenth, and social to the twentieth (Marshall 1950: 14).

Such optimism is no longer possible. The final decades of the 20th century saw intense dispute in the 'Anglo-Saxon' world about whether social welfare was properly a matter of citizenship. At the same time, a number of East and South-East Asian leaders saw the West as over-emphasizing the political and civil dimensions of citizenship; the social dimension (social welfare, underpinned by strong economic growth) is, they argued, far more important.

Challenges to democracy

In his book *The End of History*, written in the aftermath of the collapse of the Eastern Europe's socialist regimes, Fukuyama (1992) argued that human historical processes had culminated in a universal capitalist and democratic order. One of the less damaging effects of the subsequent history of the former 'Soviet bloc' countries has been to demonstrate the silliness of this claim. In fact, far from enshrining universal democracy, the years since 1989 have brought unprecedented challenges to those who seek to establish or strengthen democratic systems of government. This reality is stark in countries such as Russia. But in rather different ways, democracy has also been subject to unprecedented challenges in the West.

For most of the 20th century, the central feature of Western politics was the polarity of Right and Left. This was defined primarily in terms of attitudes to the economic system: capitalism and free markets on the one hand; central planning and state control on the other. By and large, it determined not only national and international political alignments, but also political allegiances within nations. Socialist or Communist parties shaped the politics of most European countries – though in some cases only because they succeeded in convincing others that whatever their differences, loyalty to the free market was overriding. The collapse of 'real socialism' in Eastern Europe destroyed this polarity. At a stroke, socialism lost its reputation for both progress and power. To the Left, even socialists long critical of the Soviet system were laid low. For the Right, it no longer made sense to suggest that socialism was a real and present danger.

Left and Right were not solely ideological: they also described loyalties underpinned by social class. In origin the loyalties derived from perceptions of interest: the Left, socialists, communists, were on the side of social and economic equality, fair pay, organizing production in the interests of the workers; the Right, conservatives, were on the side of freedom for business, free enterprise, rights of property. But once these associations were formed, quite early in the 20th century, they became embedded through class and institutional loyalties. Until the 1970s, social class was the most important determinant of a person's political allegiances in most European countries.

But a key feature of the last third of the century was patterns of work and employment that broke down many class identities.

Another powerful source of identity in many Western countries throughout the 20th century was religion. It was a key factor in political allegiance, especially – but not only – in countries where Christian Democratic parties were strong. But religion could also be a strong factor in civil society, shaping proper conduct, how people related to one another and what they thought. It was certainly a strong force for stability in many countries. But the decline of church affiliation continued virtually unchecked throughout the 20th century among both Protestants and Catholics. Late in the century there was, of course, something of a surge in support for various sects and cults in the West, but except perhaps in the USA, even this did little to stem the primary fact of the erosion of religious affiliation.

Throughout most of the 20th century the nation-state provided an important focus for loyalty and identity. This can be seen in the patriotism associated with European imperialism in the late 19th century, and in the passions of two world wars. But it was no less central to the break-up of the European empires in the two decades after 1945. The new states of Asia and Africa devoted much of their energies to 'nation-building': attempting to construct national identities from the relatively arbitrary geographical constructs of European exploration, carpetbagging and diplomacy. Following the collapse of the Soviet Union and Yugoslavia, a host of new nation-states was thrust onto the world stage; each too had a project of creating or shaping a national identity.

Yet towards the end of the century, with the pressures of globalization, the future of the nation-state seemed anything but secure. Powerful nations in Western Europe voluntarily submitted to the larger authority of the European Union, abandoning such sacred cows as their own currencies. The most powerful nation-states have been unable to suppress long-standing terrorist movements. The power of global capitalism seems beyond the authority even of the largest nations.

Many nation-states struggled to maintain their unitary nature against the pressures of ethnicity. This was particularly evident in the breakdown of the Soviet Union and of Yugoslavia, although clearly other factors played a major part in both of these. But the final decades of the 20th century also saw the break-up of Czechoslovakia and strong regional tensions, linked to ethnic identities, in countries as diverse as Belgium, Canada, Spain and the UK. And this is to leave aside the tensions and identities linked to ethnicity that have no particular local base. In the US, these identities can be traced back to the slave trade. In Europe, immigration from former colonies is a major factor. But migration is a continuing feature of the international division of labour (Cohen, 1987).

Many concerns have recently arisen about how Western societies should be governed. While there is today little challenge to the democratic order from advocates of authoritarian rule (in the West; this is not so true in Africa or Asia), there is a good deal of anxiety about whether the mechanisms of rule, representation and participation are adequate. Thus Britain has devolved power to legislatures in Wales and Scotland, and restructured local government. At the European level, the relationship between European, national and regional levels of government is questioned. At an international level, the challenge is whether national governments can control transnational corporations and what the possibilities and limits of international authority are.

A number of authors (eg Lyotard, 1984; Benhabib, 1992; Bauman, 1993) have argued that there is a common feature in these developments. As primary affiliations – class, party, nation, religion – have eroded, they have not been replaced by new or different 'primary' or 'ideological' identities, but rather by affiliations that are more subjective or pragmatic. These include identities linked not only to ethnicity and migration, but also to those of gender. But they also, it is argued, include more pragmatic affiliations, some linked to new social movements – pollution, for example. This has implications both for our understanding of civil society and for the nature of citizenship.

Rethinking learning and citizenship

There is, to sum up, a tension between a principal plank in the case for lifelong learning – the pace of social change, the transience of social relationships, the need for flexibility and adaptability – and the need for a learning society to be in important respects structured, regular and predictable. This parallels the tension in social theory between market and social relationships. It is now widely accepted that markets are social as well as economic institutions. Civil society as a concept reflected the need for emergent capitalism in the 17th and 18th centuries to assert itself against absolutist European sovereigns, and the modern notion of citizenship also grew up in this context. It has been a contested concept, as various social groups have struggled to extend or limit its application. In 1950, Marshall saw it as comprising three elements (civic, political and social) that represented a progressive extension of rights in society. Fifty years later such optimism is difficult to sustain: democracy was subject to many challenges in the late 20th century.

In this light, the need to rethink our notions of citizenship and civil society comes into sharper focus. Marshall's notion of citizenship was a liberal one, conceived within the context of the nation-state, and at the high tide of social democracy. In the context of global capitalism, where transnational companies are often beyond the authority of national governments, even the fullest citizenship of a nation-state may offer little in relation to the real challenges of our time. This throws up the question of whether we should seek citizenship of a global society, and if so how this aspiration can be expressed. Some of today's social movements and pressure groups are clearly transnational, powered by the possibilities of travel and electronic communication. But the question of whether international institutions are subject to influence by such pressure remains open.

Even at the national level, our understanding of how learning and citizenship are related remains embryonic. Still more do we remain unclear about how this relationship may be changing under the pressures of rapid social change. The comparative study of how citizenship is learnt remains in its infancy. Key questions remain to be resolved. At their heart is the issue of directions of causality. Is a learning society the product of a strong civil society, or is a strong civil society the outcome of a learning society? Since in reality both probably play a role, how can their relative roles be disentangled? These are the fundamental issues for research. If they can be resolved, we may make progress on more prosaic issues such as how the institutional mechanisms by which learning is delivered can be more effective in delivering appropriate knowledge, skills and attitudes related to citizenship and democracy, and what kind of civil society is necessary for the construction of a learning society.

References

Bauman, Z (1993) *Postmodern Ethics,* Blackwell, Oxford

Benhabib, S (1992) *Situating the Self: Gender community and postmodernism in contemporary ethics,* Polity Press, Cambridge

Blunkett, D (1998) Foreword, in Cm 3790, *The Learning Age: A renaissance for a new Britain,* pp. 7–8, The Stationery Office, Norwich

Brookfield, S (ed) (1987) *Learning Democracy: Eduard Lindeman on adult education and social change,* Croom Helm., Beckenham

Cohen, R (1987) *The New Helots. Migrants in the international division of labour,* Gower, Aldershot

Coleman, J S (1988) 'Social capital in the creation of human capital', *American Journal of Sociology,* **94**, S95–S120

Cm 3790 (1998) *The Learning Age: A renaissance for a new Britain,* The Stationery Office, Norwich

Coombs, P (1985) *The World Crisis in Education,* Oxford University Press, Oxford

Freire, P (1972) *Pedagogy of the Oppressed,* Penguin Books, Harmondsworth

Fukuyama, F (1992) *The End of History and the Last Man,* Free Press, New York

Gramsci, A (1971) *Selections from the Prison Notebooks,* eds Q Hoare and G Nowell Smith, Lawrence and Wishart, London

Halsey, A H (ed) (1972) *Educational Priority. Vol. 1: EPA problems and policies*, HMSO, London

Hilton, R (1977) *Bond Men Made Free. Medieval peasant movements and the English rising of 1381*, Methuen, London

Holford, J (1988) 'Mass education and community development in the British colonies1940–1960', *International Journal of Lifelong Education*, **7** (3), 163–83

Lovett, T (1975) *Adult Education, Community Development and the Working Class*, Ward Lock, London

Lyotard, J-F (1984) *The Postmodern Condition: A report on knowledge*, Manchester University Press, Manchester

Marshall, T H (1950) *Citizenship and Social Class and Other Essays*, Cambridge University Press, Cambridge

Poggi, G (1978) *The Development of the Modern State. A sociological introduction*, Hutchinson, London

Poggi, G (1990) *The State. Its nature, development and prospects*, Polity Press, Cambridge

Sennett, R (1998) *The Corrosion of Character. The personal consequences of work in the new capitalism*, W W Norton, New York

Williams, R (1976) *Keywords: A vocabulary of culture and society*, Fontana, Glasgow

Chapter 18

Future directions for the learning society

Peter Jarvis and Julia Preece

In this book we have examined:

- the processes of change that have led to the emergence of lifelong learning and the learning society;
- the concepts themselves;
- developments within the learning society;
- issues of policy and costing;
- the mechanics of the learning society;
- implications for a number of institutions in society.

We have offered a critical analysis of the age of learning and in this brief final chapter we want to make a number of suggestions about future directions that this rapidly changing society might take. From the outset we have to recognize that despite the implications of a number of policy statements, learning is neither the major cause of change nor should it be assumed that 'poor' education is the reason why there are insufficient highly educated recruits in the workforce. Education as a system has always been a super-structural phenomenon with little autonomous influence of its own. Its purpose and activities change as a result of the forces that are generated by the substructure of society. Consequently it is necessary to examine the substructural processes (see Chapter 2) in order to understand the relationship between learning and change, so we briefly return to the subject of globalization. Thereafter we recognize that the knowledge demands of global capitalism are not necessarily going to satisfy all the people all the time and point to possible new areas of educational development. Finally, we ask the question: what lies beyond the learning society?

The forces of change

Globalization (see Beck, 2000, for an introduction to the debate) has become a buzzword in contemporary society and in so doing it has partially replaced the modern/postmodern debate. Yet the conditions of late or postmodernity have been caused by the processes that operate under the term 'globalization'. From an over-simplistic perspective, this can be understood as thinking of the *world* as having a substructure and a superstructure. The simple Marxist model of society was that each *society* had its own substructure and a superstructure. For Marx, the substructure was the ownership of the means of production, but that concept has since become outdated. Now the substructure is the control of capital. Capital represents the exchange value of societal, global or individual wealth. In this sense capital is more than just financial capital since it also includes intellectual capital, essential for the knowledge society. But now the use of this capital is facilitated by the control of information technology on a global scale. The substructure of large sectors of the world has changed from ownership to control, and from material wealth to economic and intellectual capital. Marx's analysis was from a societal perspective, while globalization is more concerned about the whole world and, consequently, the decline of the state. For Marx, the market became the mechanism of wealth production, but in globalization the competitive market becomes the mechanism for corporate growth and dominance (Korten, 1995).

Indeed, corporations have already grown so large and powerful that even the British government has to go 'cap in hand' to the large corporations (like Ford) with requests and financial inducements to them to keep their manufacturing in Britain. But if the corporations decide otherwise there is little that governments can do to persuade them to change their policies. Indeed, we have seen the legal battle of the super-state (the USA) and the super-corporation (Microsoft) going on for years now, and if the super-state cannot defeat the super-corporation, the implications are considerable for the whole world. Certainly the power of the state is in decline.

The speed of change is increasing as the battle to control the market continues. Large corporations fight with each other to produce new commodities that they can bring to the market. The amount now spent on research and development is tremendous: the proportion of the total cost of many commodities on the market may be more than 80 per cent of the whole. Unlike corporations, universities can rarely recoup the monies spent on research through the sale of their products, although we are gradually seeing major research developments in universities being marketed through the formation of university companies, such as biomedical and drugs research, and management consultancies. But this is not so true for research in the humanities and many of the social sciences.

The corporations are not only producing their own research, as we have already seen, they are also undertaking their own human resource development (Chapter 12). They need many more highly educated recruits and, consequently, this is having its effect on what is expected from higher education (Chapter 10). But the question needs to be asked whether the production of a highly trained workforce is the major purpose of education, or are there not other reasons why an educational service has been established in most societies of the world? Certainly the corporations are influencing education and it is not unusual to find corporate representatives taking their places in government advisory committees on education at every level.

The market mechanism produces winner and losers – but so does every form of competition. To 'leave it to the market' (in Mrs Thatcher's famous phrase) is to generate success and create failure – but not always on merit! Those who succeed in the market-driven education system have to invent a discourse of meritocracy, as they have done in other sectors of society. While education has to some extent served that purpose for certain populations in the past, now the global discourse of competitiveness illustrates the hollowness of this claim.

The plight of the socially excluded is well known – they are often categorized as 'lazy', 'work-shy', unwilling to 'get on their bikes' and go and find a job. But this is hardly true for the population of Ethiopia! The dangers of a totally market- driven competitive global economy are that the rich people and nations get richer and the poor and socially excluded get poorer and are becoming redundant to the global economy. Paradoxically in almost every government document about education and learning, the need to address social exclusion is being argued for economic reasons. While there are consequently some efforts to reach the socially excluded (Chapter 14), it is often far too little and far too late – especially in third-world terms. Writers like Bauman (1998a, 1998b, 1999) are highlighting these social problems and raising ethical concerns for a more equitable distribution of global wealth, at the same time as public demonstrations against global capitalism are occurring on the streets of London, Washington and Seattle. The fact that these demonstrations are occurring is indicative, perhaps, of the need for a transnational civil society – other than the World Bank and International Monetary Fund – in which the people can play a different kind of citizenship role. An example is Greenpeace, which represents learning being used as social rather than simply human (skills) capital. Indeed, the new radical discourse might well be ethical rather than revolutionary.

It is within this type of debate that learning has to find a place and the educational institution has to work out its future.

The future of education

Globalization poses both opportunities and problems for education on a worldwide scale. Some countries are better positioned than others to maximize the benefits from a technologically shrinking world. Institutions within those countries, however, are responding differentially, creating new rivalries and new tensions for the education system as a whole. These new tensions are being played out against an essentially embedded ideology for education.

Education is usually portrayed as a reproductive force (Bourdieu and Passeron, 1977; Giddens, 1998), with Althusser (1972) regarding it as an ideological state apparatus. Freire (1972), on the other hand, thought that education could play a role in overcoming oppression and in most of his writing he illustrates how this might happen. Even so, judging from the changes that have already occurred and which have been documented in this book, we can expect that education will still be a reproductive agency within the context of globalization. Education and learning are both beginning to play a role in the competitive global market. Universities are becoming more like corporations – some more than others – and consequently, they will continue to act that way. The large universities will get larger, irrespective of quality, and the mega-universities will become transnational ones, not only through the use of information technology and distance education but also through the mechanisms of the market. But these same mechanisms will mean that this education business, worth $3.5 billion in the USA alone (and growing at 10 per cent per annum – and far more worldwide) will bring more competitors into the market:

> Colleges and universities are being assaulted from several directions with new competitors, new technologies, and new approaches to education. Many have chosen to ignore the warning signs, hoping it will all just go away. Others have rolled out a few online courses or have encouraged deans to develop new programs. Few institutions have developed a coherent strategy for ensuring success in the new environment. (Blustain *et al*, 1999: 51)

Indeed, Meister (1988) points out that in the US many corporate universities are increasingly targeting students who are not employees of the organization, as a way of meeting the aim of making the corporate universities self-funding (Chapter 12). More significantly, she points out that where partnerships have emerged they have more likely been between business and community colleges (further education and two-year degree colleges) than the four-year degree universities. This could clearly happen in the UK, with further education and the post-1992 universities being more able to change and more flexible than the more traditional universities. However, during this period of rapid growth in corporate universities, there have been closures among the colleges in the American educational system.

Educational institutions are going to have to play a role in the learning market – and in the distance education one – which means that they are going to have to look at even more ways of becoming competitive. They are going to have to become more flexible, introduce new delivery systems and reach out to a larger market through these systems. There are problems here because it takes many years for academics to prepare themselves to play their academic role and they are, quite understandably and rightly, loath to change their academic specialisms. This means that the adaptability of such institutions is inhibited unless the institutions themselves enter into partnership arrangements that enable the differing specialisms of academics to be used with a wider student body. Once education begins to go down the road of mergers, we can also expect takeovers, asset-stripping and all the other mechanisms of the market.

Education is going to be forced to introduce innovative delivery systems, which might mean fewer students attending the campuses (Chapter 13). This is especially true as institutions try to keep costs low, and will have implications for residential higher education, for instance. However, if education follows the route into distance education, then there will be a need for fewer professional educators, since the labour-intensive work of teaching can be reduced by having fewer, but better-known, teachers teaching through video and other media to greater numbers of students, but with more academic assistants to support the students and to mark their assignments, and so on.

As Blustain *et al* point out, the drivers for education are increasingly workforce oriented, although there are still a large number of students who also believe that education should provide them with a meaningful philosophy of life (Blustain *et al,* 1999: 52–3). The fact that there are many such students and that there have been protests against global capitalism in the last few years suggests that education has to seek to re-establish its independent credentials. Since the British government has not shielded higher education from the forces of the market as much as some other governments (Ministry of Education, Finland, 1999) it means that discovering how to play education's more traditional role in the face of market demands is quite a major dilemma, particularly for higher education, to confront in the near future.

Habermas (1972) rightly reminded us that apart from the technical and practical approaches to human enquiry there is another, which he called an emancipatory cognitive interest, which is basically independent evaluative and critical thought. The extent to which this can happen in higher education if it is dependent on corporations for funding is debatable, but what is not debatable is that there has always been an independent critical form of knowledge – it might be called ideological within the present framework but it is no more ideological than many other forms of knowledge. Universities have traditionally embraced this position, seeing themselves as bastions of free speech and critical analysis in democratic society. Universities must not fall into the trap of copying the corporate universities and developing knowledge that serves only the corporations – but at the same time higher education must play a role in servicing the workforce, since this is central to the development of wealth.

Questions about the place of education in the global competitive market must be addressed. Education is faced with the dilemma of both producing recruits to the workforce and of servicing their continuing education. The more it fails to service the corporate sector, the more the corporations will assume that responsibility for themselves. At the same time there is a need to produce a critically aware population able to play their part in ensuring that the world becomes a democratic and humanitarian place in which all people might live. To this end, we might begin to see a greater emphasis being placed on other forms of intelligence in the near future (Gardner, 1983; Goleman, 1996; Zohar and Marshall, 2000)

The future of the learning society

There are always bandwagons in policy, and amongst the present is the idea of the learning society. People have always learnt and always developed themselves as a result of learning, but the word is currently being used with restrictive connotations. Perhaps it will soon rediscover its wider meaning – but we are still faced with the question: after the learning society – what? Education and learning will continue to be important for individual, corporate, social and even universal development, but the significance of arts and humanities might once again be recognized, albeit still in a minor role. We might see the development of more socially concerned subjects within the corporate curriculum, including environmental and ecological issues.

In addition, recognition that we now live in a global society must dominate the future. Significant in this new society is the fact that the state plays a smaller role than it has hitherto. But will corporations rule the world (Korten, 1995)? They are certainly going to dominate, but their concerns are rarely going to be for the socially excluded unless it is in their shareholders' interests. Nevertheless, it is increasingly being recognized that people and even corporations cannot do things by themselves, so that we are beginning to see a greater emphasis placed upon partnership; whether this will ever replace the idea of competition is a moot point. The need for partnership arrangements between the wealth-producers and the other agencies in society might bring about some new social arrangements.

The population in the West is ageing and there will be fewer people in the area to sustain the current emphasis on economic growth, so the focus of a great deal of economic development might move to other parts of the world. There might also be recognition of the positive role of older people, with their emphases in life receiving a more sympathetic hearing.

At the same time, we are seeing greater emphasis being put upon notions of democracy and citizenship and even ethical capitalism and ethical investment, so that the pendulum might swing a little further away from the far right-hand towards the centre – and the dominant discourse might become a little more tempered. The indications are that the other dimensions of humanity, ethical, spiritual, etc, will surely find a greater place in tomorrow's world than they have in that of the modern era. A postmodern world will be a different world – but the mirage of the good society will stretch out in front of us, telling us that we still have not arrived. This is the major function of utopian thinking!

References

Althusser, L (1972) 'Ideology and ideological state apparatuses', in ed B R Cousin, *Education, Structure and Society,* Penguin Books, Harmondsworth

Bauman, Z (1998a) *Globalization: The human consequences,* Polity Press, Cambridge

Bauman, Z (1998b) *World Consumerism and the New Poor,* Open University Press, Buckingham

Bauman, Z (1999) *In Search of Politics,* Polity Press, Cambridge

Beck, U (2000) *What is Globalization?,* Polity Press, Cambridge

Blustain, H, Goldstein, P and Lozier, G (1999) 'Assessing the new competitive landscape', in R Katz and Associates, *Dancing with the Devil: Information technology and the new competition in higher education,* Jossey-Bass, San Francisco, CA

Bourdieu, P and Passeron, J-C (1977) *Reproduction,* Sage, London

Freire, P (1972) *Pedagogy of the Oppressed,* Penguin Books, Harmondsworth

Gardner, H (1983) *Frames of Mind,* Basic Books, New York

Giddens, A (1998) *The Third Way,* Polity Press, Cambridge

Goleman, D (1996) *Emotional Intelligence,* Bloomsbury, London

Habermas, J (1972) *Knowledge and Human Interests,* Heinemann, Oxford

Korten, D (1995) *When Corporations Rule the World,* Earthscan, London

Meister, J (1998) *Corporate Universities,* revised and updated edn, McGraw-Hill, New York

Ministry of Education (1999) *Education, Training and Research in the Information Society,* Ministry of Education, Helsinki

Zohar, D and Marshall, I (2000) *Spiritual Intelligence: The ultimate intelligence,* Bloomsbury, London

Index

Numbers in *italics* indicate figures, graphs or tables
Authors etc mentioned in index may also be found in reference lists

OWNERSHIP,
CONTROL AND SUCCESS
OF LARGE COMPANIES

An analysis of English industrial structure and policy
1936 - 1951

BY

P. SARGANT FLORENCE
C.B.E., M.A.(Cantab.), Ph.D.(Columbia), (Hon.)D.Litt.(Hum.)(Columbia)
Professor Emeritus, University of Birmingham

LONDON
SWEET & MAXWELL LIMITED
11 NEW FETTER LANE
1961

PRINTED IN GREAT BRITAIN
BY
THE EASTERN PRESS LTD.
OF LONDON AND READING

PREFACE

Unlike other fields of human endeavour, company structure, and activities and their consequences, are plentifully indicated in statistical data. The difficulty lies in summing up those data in a form which will be significant both practically to the investor, business executive, or even perhaps the politician, and scientifically to the economist and sociologist. The most significant question to all parties must be who rules the modern company which transacts so much of the business of the country. To this question put in my *Logic of British and American Industry* (p. 215) I hazarded an answer.

Some companies have been manager-led, others large-investors led and in yet others there is a compromise. Indeed the continuing strength of capitalism may lie in this very variety and balance of power allowing the fittest for the given circumstances to dominate.

The prevalence of the *ancien régime* by owner-manager entrepreneur or of a managerial revolution required further testing and the wealth of statistics available points the way. Hence this book. Its findings are not based on theoretical assumption, though some assumptions are tested. Nor are they based on the opinions of business men or questionnaires put to them. Once the range of uncertainty and controversy is narrowed down, specific questions may usefully be put. Where measured data are available to the inquirer, the " narrowing-down " approach that is most productive and economical of effort and frustration is statistical. Such an approach has already been made in America by Berle and Means and the U.S. Temporary Economic Committee, in their analysis of the " corporation ", and in Australia by Mr. E. L. Wheelwright. As realised by the National Institute of Economic and Social Research and by the Cambridge Department of Applied Economics (in the work of Fernstein and Revell on types of shareholder) it is high time England, the grand developer of joint stock, came into line.

This book consists of text and appendices and the relation of the two must be briefly explained. Appendix A1 presents that section of all the basic tables that were prepared, which refers to the hundred or so very large industrial and commercial companies. The basic tables attempted to summarise available objective statistical data significant for the ownership and control, and for certain policies and successes of all large English industrial and commercial companies including the medium and smaller large sample companies (named in Appendix A2) down to a capital in 1951 of £200,000. Altogether with the breweries included, about 1,700 of the largest companies are represented, directly or indirectly, in the basic tables published or unpublished, covering about 40% of all the country's economic activities and a still higher proportion of its industry.

The text consists mainly of generalisations and interpretations of the data in the basic tables, helped by tables analysing and summarising those data. It deals with companies as going concerns, not with their birth, or death, hence the promoter (or the receiver) hardly appears, but only those in control of the live company.

One of the main tasks of my inquiry has been to identify *all* the very large companies and, among the medium and smaller, the *representative* companies in which control seemed by objective tests really, as it is in theory, to be vested in the owners, or at least in the chief owners. The companies so identified numbered 89 and formed about a third of all the 268 representative companies where the relevant data were collected. They are listed in Chapter V and the details on which the identification was based are presented for the very large companies in Appendix B. In these owner-controlled companies the precise owner-ship of the largest shares and votes is obviously important and a statement of the names and holdings of the largest twenty shareholders, as of the directors, is worth giving. They are worth giving, though occupying considerable space, not only to substantiate the generalisa-tions of my text, but also to point to possible further generalisations or to answer or ask further questions. Is it true, for instance, as I suggest, that there is little spreading of risk through investment in the shares of several of the very large owner-controlled companies by any of their twenty largest *personal* holders? My readers may care to look for themselves, but I cannot find in Appendix B personal holders whose names reappear as large holders in the different companies.

When analysing and summarising the data of Appendices A and B and similar but unpublished data for the medium and smaller large companies and all breweries, the tables of the text make use of (and the text refers to) certain statistical measures and devices. To explain these, and make them available to my readers as useful tools for reaching further generalisations and for tackling further data, Appendix C has been added as an illustrative statistical Glossary. It must be stressed here, as in the text, that my research refers to the particular period 1936 to 1951. Someone has to start on *some* particular period but the applicability of the generalisations that arise must, of course, be tested statistically for further periods.

Finally, Appendix D illustrates and shows the inter-relation of the few accounting terms that have been used, and Appendix E is a select list of books for further reading.

Appendices A and B and the same data for the medium and smaller large companies were prepared by G. M. Lawrence, M.A., Miss Irene Bowyer, B.COM., Mrs. Barbara Smith, B.COM., Mrs. Dulcibel Jenkins, B.COM. and Mrs. Lewis Ord, under a grant to the University of Birmingham from funds made available under the Conditional Aid Scheme for the Use of Counter-Part derived from the U.S. Economic Aid. In preparing the text, and the summary tables in the text, I have been greatly helped by Miss Bowyer who is also responsible for the index. Professor Brian Tew, Mr. Robin Marris and Professor David Granick kindly read the text in draft and I am most grateful for their criticisms and constructive suggestions. I also have to thank the editors of the *Journal of the Royal Statistical Society* and the *Journal of Industrial Economics* for permission to reproduce parts of articles I contributed.

Great care has been taken to ensure the accuracy of the data presented in the text and appendices, but the task has not been easy. Voting Rights in certain companies were extremely complicated, for instance, and the twenty largest vote-holders not always easy to find in the Bush House Company Register. This Register, as I argue in my *Industry and the State* (pp. 69–77), is an important element in the defence of the shareholders or potential shareholders and the provision of risk-capital. Not enough use has been made of it by economists and social scientists generally, and I tender no apology for exploring, however inadequately, this *terra incognita* to most of my colleagues; but I must take the responsibility for any inaccuracies that may have arisen.

P. SARGANT FLORENCE.

University of Birmingham.

January, 1961.

CONTENTS

ix

Contents

LIST OF TABLES

xiii

CHAPTER I

IMPORTANCE OF THE LARGE JOINT STOCK
COMPANY

§ 1. PAST AND PRESENT PROGRESS OF COMPANIES

HISTORIANS have taught us to look far back into the eighteenth and even
the seventeenth century for the beginnings of the Industrial Revolution—
a revolution in which England took such a dominating lead.   But it is
not generally realised how recently, compared to the long history of this
revolution, the joint stock principle was accepted in industry on any
wide scale.   Writing in 1776 Adam Smith thought

The only trades which it seems possible for a joint stock company to carry
on successfully, without an exclusive privilege, are those, of which all the
operations are capable of being reduced to what is called a routine, or to such
a uniformity of method as admits of little or no variation.   Of this kind is, first,
the banking trade; secondly, the trade of insurance from fire and from sea risk,
and capture in time of war; thirdly, the trade of making and maintaining a
navigable cut or canal; and, fourthly, the similar trade of bringing water for
the supply of a great city.[1]

Even half-way through the nineteenth century the economist McCulloch
thought that joint stock organisation was only applicable to undertakings
which would " admit of being carried on according to a regular systematic
plan . . ." Companies were in all respects unsuited for the prosecution
of ordinary industrial pursuits, whether belonging to agriculture, manufacture or commerce.[2]

In his *Principles of Political Economy*, published in 1848 and for
many decades the standard textbook on Economics, John Stuart Mill
even compared the joint stock company unfavourably with what is now
known as nationalisation:

Whatever, if left to spontaneous agency, can only be done by joint stock
associations, will often be as well, and sometimes better done, as far as the
actual work is concerned, by the state.   Government management is, indeed,
proverbially jobbing, careless and ineffective; but so likewise has generally been
joint stock management.   The directors of a joint stock company, it is true, are

---

[1] *Wealth of Nations*, Book V, Part III, Art. 1.
[2] Hunt, *The Development of the Business Corporation in England* 1800–67, 1936, p. 132.

1

F.L.   1

always shareholders; but also the members of a government are invariably taxpayers; and in the case of directors, no more than in that of governments, is their proportional share of the benefits of good management equal to the interest they may possibly have in mismanagement, even without reckoning the interest of their ease.[3]

In the middle of the nineteenth century there was, in fact, little joint stock in British manufacturing. In 1875 a whole miscellaneous class of stocks and shares that included manufacturing and public utilities formed

TABLE I A

CAPITAL, INTEREST AND DIVIDEND IN 1951 FOR COMPANY SECURITIES QUOTED ON LONDON STOCK EXCHANGE, DIVIDED INTO SECTORS OF ECONOMIC ACTIVITY

Sector of economic activity	Loan Capital		Preference and Ordinary Share	
	Capital £m (1)	Interest £000 (2)	Capital £m (3)	Dividends £000 (4)
Commercial, industrial, etc.	232·2	9,349	1,817·87	230,032
Breweries and distilleries	93·9	3,621	195·98	25,252
Iron, coal and steel	32·2*	1,096	207·24	22,705
Mines overseas†	17·54	676	127·75	21,791
Oil	8·4	207	135·18	25,418
Public utilities‡	66·6	1,825	138·11	9,129
Shipping	5·8	234	75·50	7,445
{ Rubber	3·0	124	81·41	13,775
{ Tea and Coffee	1·04	51	38·21	5,853
{ Banks and Discount Co.	—	—	146·62	17,108
{ Financial trusts, land and property§	80·0	2,715	165·96	13,816
{ Insurance	1·06	39	39·33	16,496
TOTAL ALL QUOTED COMPANIES	542·0	19,939	3,169·54	408,818
Percentage of first two sectors to Total	60%	65%	63%	62%
Railways: U.K.	2·3	93	11·09	360
Overseas	121·7	3,020	29·37	309
GRAND TOTAL	666·0	23,052	3,210·00	409,487

* In process of nationalisation.
† Including nitrate.
‡ Canals and docks, electric lighting and power, gas, telegraph and telephones, tramways and omnibus, waterworks—most of them overseas.
§ Excludes investment trusts to avoid duplication.

only 4·9% of all securities, including government stock, listed on the London Stock Exchange, amounting to less than a fifth of the railway securities; and in 1885 the total paid-up capital of English and Scottish joint stock companies was only £495m. By contrast, in 1933 the

[3] *Principles of Political Economy*, 1848, V, xi, § 11.

stocks and shares in manufacturing and public utilities alone were
16·5% of all securities amounting to *three* times the railway securities;
and in 1935 the paid-up capital of all joint stock companies was £5,640m.,
more than an elevenfold increase since 1885.[4]   The national income had
in this period only about trebled.

Today the council of the London Stock Exchange publishes its own
statistics.[5]   They show the high proportion of loan and share capital of
companies quoted on the Exchange that is devoted to the industrial
sector of economic activities.   Table I A sums up the statistics for 1951,
the last year of our survey.   The two sections of the Stock Exchange *Year
Book* which this present survey covers, the commercial and industrial
and the breweries sections, accounted for £326m. (or 60%) of the £542m. of
loan capital, £2,014m. (or 63%) of the £3,170m. of share capital of all
quoted companies.   The proportions in these sectors are much the same
if we compare interest on loan capital, namely 65%, or dividends on
ordinary shares—62%.   Companies in British Railways have, owing to
nationalisation, almost disappeared and also in public utilities; and in
iron, coal and steel were in the course of disappearing.   Iron and steel,
though not coal-mining, was later to return to the company fold.

Table I A, together with Tables I B (which gives the census orders in
Roman numerals) and I D, serves to indicate in detail the activities of the
public company with shares quoted on the Stock Exchange which will and
will not be covered in this present survey of industrial and commercial
companies.   "Economic activities" is probably the best term to use in
order to convey any type of work on which people are employed for some
sort of pay.   The industrial tables of the population census cover all
economic activities, classify them into sectors or orders, and form a
useful list for "checking up" exactly which of all the possible activities
are included or excluded in any grouping under discussion.   Recently
a standard industrial classification has been agreed upon by the census
authorities and the various government departments dealing with industry,
such as the Ministry of Labour and the Board of Trade, and it is this
classification with its orders that will be used as our framework of
reference.   Fourteen of the orders refer to manufactures.

Following the Stock Exchange *Year Book*'s "Industrial and Commercial" section, all the orders of manufacturing industries (III to XVI)

[4] G. W. Edwards, *Evolution of Finance Capitalism*, 1938.
[5] *Interest and Dividends upon Securities Quoted on the Stock Exchange*, published annually.

are included in our survey, except oil production, together with Orders XVII building, XX distributive trades, and most of XXIV entertainment (*e.g.*, cinema companies) and catering.

TABLE I B

SEGMENTATION OF HOME ECONOMIC ACTIVITIES BY COMPANIES, NATIONAL BODIES OR PARTNERSHIP AND INDIVIDUALS, 1951

Order no.	Industry	Proportion of taxable trading ("Gross True") income or other measure of extent of activity
I	Agriculture ..	96% of income to individual and partnerships.
II	Mining	Coal mining, nationalised
III—XVI	Manufacturing	73 to 100% of income to companies according to branches of manufacture, except Clothing 65%. Iron and steel nationalised, 1951–52.
XVII	Building	62% of income to individuals and partnerships.
XVIII	Gas, electricity, water	Nationalised, company or municipal.
XIX	Transport and communication:	
	Railways.. ..	Nationalised.
	Road passenger goods by road..	56% of income to individuals and partnerships. Partly nationalised.
	Sea (shipping)	97% of income to companies.
	Air	Nationalised.
	Posts, telephone, etc.	Nationalised.
XX	Distributive trades:	
	Wholesaling ..	80% of income to companies.
	Retailing ..	61% of income to individuals and partnerships.
XXI	Insurance, Banking, Finance and Land	54% of income to companies. (Finance and undertakings abroad 100% to companies.)
XXII	Public administration and Defence.	National. No Trading.
XXIII	Professional services	97% of income to individuals and partnerships.
XXIV	Miscellaneous services	75% of income to companies in entertainments, sports. 78% of income to individuals and partnerships in other services.
All economic activities ..		**55% of income to companies.**

The important exclusions from the *Year Book's* industrial and commercial and brewery sections are Orders I, agriculture; II, mining; XVIII, public utilities; XIX, transport and communication; XXI, insurance, banking and finance; XXII, public administration; XXIII, professional services. The effect of these exclusions upon the size distribution of companies is considered in the Annex to this chapter.

The two main reasons for this exclusion will be found in Table I B, and hinge upon the segmentation of modern industrial government into individual, partnership and nationalised, as well as company segments.[6] The business in the excluded orders was either carried on mainly by individual (sole) traders or by partnership; or had been nationalised. Nationalisation normally takes over an industry completely, but where there is trading and no nationalisation individuals and partnerships compete with companies. The precise share of the market obtained by each can be measured by the division of the taxable trading income reported as the " gross true income " by the Inland Revenue.[7] Table I B states which of the two forms of organisation draws more than 50% of the income, and the precise percentage. The division is fairly close to 50/50 in building, road transport, retailing and finance. In only one manufacturing order did companies account for less than 73% of the income, namely in clothing—65%.

The orders (or parts of an order) where companies predominate and which are outside the industrial and commercial, and breweries section that we survey, are part of XIX, sea transport, and the whole of XXI, insurance, banking and finance, including property owning. Though companies hardly appear at all in *home* agriculture they are plentiful enough in large-scale plantations overseas, particularly in rubber, tea and coffee plantations. Overseas mining, including oil production, form a still wider field for company operation. For its daily Closing Prices, *The Times*, for instance, besides grouping oil companies separately, groups mining companies under six headings, each containing at least fourteen companies: South African Gold Mines; South African Gold and Uranium Mines; South African Finance Companies (financing mines and exploration of mines); Rhodesian and East African Mines; Tin Mines; West African and Other Mines. All these appear in Table I A, but as we have said, neither their capital nor their income is considered in the present survey.

To sum up: There is a wide area of company operation which the present survey does not include, particularly finance, shipping and companies operating in mining and agriculture overseas. But, in fact,

[6] It saves confusion if we restrict " sectors " to refer to type of economic activity, " segments " to types of industrial government. When used, sections refer to the *Year Book*.
[7] Annual Reports of H.M. Commissioners of Inland Revenue.

the incursion of the joint stock company organisation into industry and commerce since the last century has made the industrial, commercial and brewing sections quantitatively more important than all the others put together.

§ 2. THE INEQUALITY OF COMPANY SIZES

So far public companies of all sizes have been considered, provided their shares were quoted on the Stock Exchange. It is, however, the larger companies on which this survey will concentrate. One reason for this concentration is that by studying relatively few companies a very wide extent of business can be covered, and studied intensively.

It is not necessary to go beyond the confines of this present book to appreciate the sharp taper in sizes from the larger to the smaller companies and to realise the force of the rule " the larger the fewer." There are very many more companies (especially if we add private to public) with less than £200,000 of issued capital than companies with larger capital. But the aggregate business they transact or the aggregate assets they own, is very much less. Similarly among the companies with £200,000 or more of issued capital that are surveyed in this book, there is a very sharp taper in issued capital, business assets or income from the largest to the smallest company. The largest company we record is Imperial Chemical Industries with, in 1951, an issued capital of £85,600,000 and net tangible assets of £256,900,000. It had over four hundred times the capital and eight hundred times the assets of the smallest companies that we record. In our basic table (Appendix A) there are, in fact, four companies with issued capital between £200,000 and £230,000 and net tangible assets between £320,000 and £380,000. These companies, however, are still, relatively speaking, large and we are careful to call them " smaller large " companies. The Board of Trade issues statistics of registered companies public and private and in 1951 11,891 public companies (over half of them not quoted on the Stock Exchange) were stated to have a paid-up total capital of £3,917m. thus averaging each £330,000, while 247,180 private companies had a total paid-up capital of £2,305m. thus averaging £9,000. Clearly our lower limit of £200,000 issued capital is a long way above the average size of all companies public or private.

The available statistics indicating most completely the relative importance of the large companies among all business concerns are the assessments of the Inland Revenue of trading profits, referred to already.

Local authorities' and industrial provident societies' "true gross incomes"[8] are lumped in with those of companies for the size-analysis, but form a small enough proportion (about 4%) to be neglected.

Table I C compares the number and gross true income of companies and concerns (including companies) that were assessed for £1,000,000 and for £200,000 and over, with companies and concerns of all sizes. The industrial and commercial sector is in the right-hand columns, "freed" from other sectors, but this can only be achieved for *all* sizes of concerns.

TABLE I C

IMPORTANCE OF LARGE COMPANIES IN ALL ECONOMIC ACTIVITY MEASURED BY ASSESSED GROSS TRUE INCOME, 1951–52*

	All sectors		Industrial and commercial sector	
	No.	Aggregate income (£m.)	No.	Income (£m.)
Largest concerns Income of £1,000,000 and over.				
(1) All concerns ..	300	687·2		
(2) Companies only	300	687·2		
Largest and next largest concerns Income of £200,000 and over			Analysis by size and industry not available.	
(3) All concerns ..	1,700	1195·9		
(4) Companies only	1,700	1193·7		
All sizes of concerns (All ranges of income)				
(5) All concerns ..	1,921,800	3185·2	1,341,850	2,288·6
(6) Companies only	185,122	2168·2	166,217	1,692·3
Ratios:				
1/5 Largest companies to all concerns	0·02%	21·4%		
3/5 Largest and next largest concerns to all concerns	0·09%	37·5%		
4/6 Largest and next largest to all companies	0·92%	55·0%		

* Source: Report of Commissioners of Inland Revenue

In our standard year 1951–52, as the ratios at the bottom of the table show, the 1,700 concerns (consisting practically entirely of companies) with over £200,000 gross true income, though they numbered only 0·09%

---

[8] Income before subtraction of depreciation allowance and allowance for repairs, but after relief for losses and management expenses.

of all the 1,921,800 concerns and 0·92% of all the 185,000 companies, yet had 37·5% of the income of all concerns and 55% of the income of all companies. In 1955–56 the number of large companies had grown—but this inequality was maintained. Companies with over £200,000 income formed 0·12% of concerns but had 45% of the income of all concerns, and formed 1·15% of all companies but had 61·2% of the income of all companies. The inequality of the distribution of sizes of business concerns and companies, indeed, far outreaches the familiar inequality of incomes and is perhaps as wide as any kind of inequality in human affairs.[9]

In this distribution of sizes, companies, partnerships and individuals overlap, but companies are clearly enough larger, on average, than partnerships, and presumably partnerships than individuals.   The average gross true incomes (to the nearest £10) of companies (excluding local authorities) was in our standard year (1951–52) £9,870 and that of partnerships £1,500.[10]   In the size ranges assessed for profits of £200,000 or more, *companies* had an aggregate gross true income of £1,193·7m. and other concerns of only £2·2m.   In calculating the extent of the concentration of business in a few hands it is thus only *companies* that really need attention.

The next chapter explains in detail the methods which were used to select the companies to be surveyed. Briefly, within the sectors of economic activity surveyed *all* the 109 very large companies were analysed with over £3,000,000 of issued capital, 141 medium large with capital between £1,000,000 and £3,000,000 representing about 300 companies of that size and a random stratified sample of 101 " smaller large " representing about 1,300 companies with issued capital between £200,000 and £1,000,000.   In short, approximately the 1,700 largest companies in the industrial and commercial sector were represented either directly or by sample.   What share of all company business, or indeed of all the nation's business, do these comparatively few companies represent?

---

[9] We shall have cause to refer on several occasions to degrees of inequality. Where inequality is extreme, a simple measure of its degree is to state the percentage which 1 % of the relevant units receives, holds or controls of total income, wealth, activity, etc. The familiar distribution of income and of wealth or capital may be taken as types of two distinct degrees of inequality. Mr. H. F. Lydall (*Statistical Journal*, 1959, Part I, p. 14 and privately communicated) estimated that in Britain, 1954:
   1 % of income units received (before taxation) 9·3 % of national income.
   1 % of capital owners held 43 % of net capital.
Now the inequality of the sizes of all concerns (with 0·12 % controlling 45 %) is much more extreme, even than the *capital* distribution, while the inequality of the sizes of companies (with 1·15 % controlling 61·2 % of income) is *slightly* more extreme.

[10] Individual traders were lumped in with private individuals in the relevant table and cannot be separated.

§ 3. THE SHARE OF BUSINESS DONE BY THE COMPANIES SURVEYED

Table I C showed that the largest 1,700 companies accounted (in 1951–52) for 55·0% of the aggregate gross true income of all companies, and 37·5% of all business concerns. The total for all companies, however, included companies not in the industrial and commercial sector. In the Annex to this chapter reasons are given for estimating that to obtain the approximately largest 1,700 companies in the sector which we surveyed, about the 2,000 largest companies in *all* sectors would have to be counted; and that these 2,000 companies probably brought in about 59% of aggregate gross true income of all companies, 40% of all concerns. These percentages appear in columns 3 and 4 of Table I D.

TABLE I D
PROPORTIONATE IMPORTANCE OF LARGE COMPANIES CALCULATED BY VARIOUS MEASURES AND ON VARIOUS BASIC TOTALS (=100)

	1951–53 industrial and commercial sector				Manufacturing sector only
Measure used Limit of size and no. of companies involved	Net assets (1)	Issued (paid-up) capital (2)*	Assessed gross true income (3)†	Rough composite measure (4)	Net output
Largest hundred companies (100)	46%			20%	
Companies of over £2·5m. assets (469)	74%	47·7%‡		32%	
Companies of over £200,000 capital (1,700)			59%	40%	
Total of quoted public companies (3,025)	100	64·5%		44%	50–52%
Total of (public and private) companies (185,100)		100·0	100	68%	
Total concerns (1,921,800)				100	100

* Overestimates business of large companies. They have higher proportion of capital to reserves.

† Possibly overestimates business of concerns that are not companies. They include payment for management in true income.

‡ Estimate derived from net assets and capital percentages, *i.e.*, 74% of 64·5%.

This estimate of the disproportionate importance of a relatively few large companies is supported by other investigations. The most comprehensive estimate of the relative importance of the large company was made by the National Institute of Economic and Social Research in their *Company Income and Finance* 1949–53. The accounts were analysed of all companies quoted on the Stock Exchange except in finance, shipping, overseas undertakings and some less important sectors—a total of 3,025 companies. Among these companies the accounts were also analysed of the hundred companies with the highest assets. In the Institute's earlier *Classified List of Large Companies* engaged in British industry the assets are given (for 1953–54) of 512 companies with over £2,517 of assets. Thus it is possible, after certain corrections are made, to give by various tests the extent of the activities of roughly the largest 100, and 500, and all quoted 3,025 companies, and to compare the extent of their business with the 1,700 companies surveyed here.

Exact agreement between the results of different measures and tests of size cannot of course be expected, and comparisons are further impeded by the different sources of published information, and the different bases adopted on which percentages are formed. Certain propositions can, however, be put forward with some assurance as to the proportional importance of the large companies. The various sets of proportions all appear in Table I D. In each of its columns, 100 indicates the basis or denominator on which the proportions or percentages are formed and the heading of each column states the precise measure of size used and also what sectors are being considered.

(1) The total net assets of the largest hundred companies in the industrial and commercial sector was, in 1953, £3,488·0m. or 46% of the £7,531·3m. total net assets of all the 3,825 companies quoted on the Stock Exchange and tabulated by the Institute.[11]

In the earlier publication of the Institute the total net assets of the largest 512 companies, all the companies with over £2·5m. assets, was found to be £6,159. But in this earlier (though not in the later) publication, companies in shipping and property were included. If these are excluded, the companies in the industrial and commercial sector comparable to those in the preceding paragraph are 469 with total assets of £5,653m.

Thus the proportion of net assets in the hands of the 100 largest, the 469 largest and all the 3,025 *quoted* companies are in the proportion of £3,488m. to £5,653m. to £7,531m. or 46% to 74% to 100. These figures appear in the first column of Table I D.

[11] In what follows " Institute " refers to the National Institute of Economic and Social Research.

(2) The comparison can be extended from the quoted to all public companies and to all companies *private* or public. Though there are many unquoted public companies, the additional business they represent (excluding, of course, unquoted subsidiaries of quoted parent companies) does not appear great. The Stock Exchange *Report on Interest and Dividends* states [12] that " the quoted share capital of these (quoted, public) companies covered 90% of the share capital of all British public companies. Their unquoted share capital accounted for a further 5%." It appears therefore that the quoted and unquoted share capital of the quoted companies was 95% of the share capital of all public companies. Under the circumstances it does not seem worth while entering a separate line in Table I D for all public companies apart from *quoted* public companies.

Comparison may, therefore, be carried from *quoted* public companies to all companies public or private. The National Institute has this to say about the share capital of all companies:

The quoted public companies. . . . accounted for £2,740m. that is 43% of the total of £6,412m. for all companies . . . It must be remembered, however, that a substantial number of public and private companies have their share capital wholly or partially owned by other companies; any total of paid-up capital for all registered companies must therefore involve a certain amount of double-counting (possibly of the order of 15,000 companies) which means that the percentage coverage quoted above errs appreciably in the direction of understatement.[13]

If the 15,000 companies whose capital is owned by other companies are subtracted from the total of companies (of which they form 5·5%) then (assuming these subsidiary companies are neither abnormally small or large) the percentages of quoted companies out of the corrected total capital of all companies free of double counting, will, instead of 43%, be 45·3%.

A further and more important reason for considering the original percentages given by the Institute to be *for our purposes* an understatement, is that the numerator refers to " all quoted companies engaged in industry and trade in this country," the denominator refers to companies engaged in *all* economic activities.

Now Table I A shows that the sector covered by the Institute (the first three groups of activity in the table) included 70% of the paid-up

[12] *Op. cit.* (1955) page 19.
[13] National Institute of Economic and Social Research, *Company Income and Finance*, 1949–53, p. 7.

capital (preference and ordinary shares) of all quoted companies. If this proportion between the sectors holds for all sizes of company, it follows that the 45·3% proportion of quoted companies' capital to all companies (public and private) represents 45·3 × 100/70, *i.e.*, 64·5% of all companies in the industrial and commercial sector. Paid-up capital is, however, a measure that probably overestimates the business done by the quoted companies.[14]

(3) The third column of Table I D gives the estimate worked out already (and derived from the Inland Revenue assessments) of 59% as the proportion of *all company* income received by the 1,700 largest companies represented by our present survey. In the framework of estimates derived from assets and capital it fits fairly reasonably between the 47·7% and the 64·5% of the smaller and larger number of largest companies (469 and 3,025).

(4) The Inland Revenue assessments allow a further extension of comparisons to the business of all *concerns*, including individual traders and partnerships as well as companies, that is, to the entire field of private enterprise. The 1,700 companies we survey had an assessed income, we found, of 40% of *all* concerns. In Column 4 of Table I D, which is a composite of all three sources of estimates, this percentage appears, together with percentages (similarly based on all concerns' business) derived by the chain method from the other three columns.[15] Assessed gross income is a measure that probably overestimates the business done by individuals and partnerships since, in their gross income or profit, there is an element of payment for management not found in, at least, the larger companies. This *over*estimate of the activities of smaller concerns may to some extent offset or overset the *under*estimate of the smaller companies' activities mentioned earlier due to their paid-up capital being only a fraction of reserves.

(5) The results of the calculation show that as more and more companies are included from 100 to 469 to 1,700 to 3,025 to 185,000, the percentages of business they do, rise, of course; but rise only sluggishly compared to the over a thousandfold rise in number of companies, from 20% to 35% to 40% to 44% to 68%, *i.e.*, between three and fourfold.

[14] *Company Income and Finance*, p. 7, " in quoted companies reserves exceeded the paid-up capital, but in unquoted companies (particularly the smaller ones) paid-up capital is often only a small fraction of reserves."

[15] Thus the net assets of the hundred largest companies were 46 % of those of all quoted companies; the income of quoted companies 44 % of that of all concerns. 46 % of 44 % is 20 %.

In short, diminishing returns set in rapidly when studying the tens of thousands of companies beyond the 3,000 largest.

As a further test of the high proportion of business done by relatively few companies, though it can apply only to the manufacturing sub-sector, the net output of factories owned by the companies quoted on the Stock Exchange is compared to the output of all concerns. In manufacturing, larger companies are more frequent than in the other activities of the industrial and commercial sector such as retailing, other services and building. So, again, the 50–52% of all manufacturing, given by the Institute as the proportion of the quoted companies' to all concerns' output, [16] fits reasonably with the 44% found for the whole industrial and commercial sector.

(6) To sum up briefly: 1,921,800 concerns were assessed for trading profit by the Inland Revenue in 1951–52, but the hundred largest industrial and commercial companies, corresponding approximately to our *very large* companies, accounted for 20% of the business of all trading concerns; the 469 largest companies, corresponding approximately to our very large and medium large companies, accounted for 32%; and the 1,700 largest companies that are represented in our very large, medium large and smaller large companies accounted for 40% of the business of all concerns in private enterprise.

§ 4. THE INCIDENCE OF THE LARGE COMPANY AMONG THE VARIOUS INDUSTRIES; CHARACTERISTICS OF LARGE—COMPANY INDUSTRIES

The industry groups where the large companies now seem to flourish can be found in Table I E. A rough indication of the " density " of incidence of large companies within each industry group is obtained by finding the proportion of large companies per 100,000 workers. Large companies, as defined by the National Institute of Economic and Social Research, are those with over £2·5m. of assets in 1953–54; their number appears in column 2. These large companies were further subdivided by the Institute into four sub-sizes. In Table I D, for the sake of brevity, the two sub-sizes are lumped together to form (in column 1) a class of very large companies with more than £10m. of assets in 1953–54. In the comparable branches of industry, commerce and brewing this class proves, in fact, to include much the same number of companies as our own " very large " size class with capital of £3m. or more in 1951, to be discussed later.

---

[16] *Company Income and Finance*, 1949–53, p. 8.

TABLE I E

INCIDENCE OF LARGE COMPANIES IN VARIOUS INDUSTRIES, 1953-54

Industry (Standard Classification) Grouped by Census Orders III to XXIV§	No. of Very Large Co. (assets over £10m.) (1)	Total of Large Co. (with assets over £2.5 m.) (includes Col. (1) (2)	Total of these Assets £m. (3)	No. of Workers in whole industry .000 Sept. 1953 (4)	Ratios per 100,000 employed	
					No. of Large Cos. Cols. (2/4) (5)	Assets (£100m.) of Large Cos. Cols. (3/4) (6)
III { Cement	2	3	61·0	15	20·0	4·1
Other Bldg. Materials Pottery & Glass	1	10	52·1	319	3·1	0·2
IV { Petroleum Refining	5	6	233·5	39	15·4	6·0
Other Chemicals	12	31	852·1	496	6·3	1·7
V { Iron, Steel & Non Ferrous Metal Mfr.	14	43	592·9	543	7·9	1·1
VI { Shipbuilding & Marine Engineering	4	10	83·1	287	3·5	0·3
Non-Electrical Eng'ring	6	44	310·2	1,011	4·4	0·3
Electrical Engineering	12	33	415·8	599	5·5	0·7
VII Vehicles & Accessories	12	29	343·7	1,105	2·6	0·3
VIII & IX { Other Metal & Precision Instruments	2	14	160·3	482	2·9	0·3
X { Cotton	3	14	166·3	289	4·8	0·6
Wool	1	8	52·2	218	3·7	0·2
Rayon	2	4	141·3	91	4·4	1·6
Other Textiles	4	19	160·5	388	4·9	0·4
XI Leather and Fur	0	1	2·8	75	1·3	0·0
XII Clothing & Footwear	1	9	50·7	663	1·3	0·1
XIII { Grain Milling	2	3	56·6	41	7·3	1·4
Sugar Refining	2	2	30·1	22	9·2	1·4
Other Food	6	20	186·7	592	3·4	0·3
Drink	15	50	509·3	162	30·9	3·2
Tobacco	4	4	204·8	42	9·5	4·8
XIV { Wood & Cork Products, Furniture	0	1	3·5	295	0·3	0·0
XV { Paper & Wallpaper	7	11	161·1	85	12·9	1·9
Newspapers and Periodicals	4	15	114·5	109	13·8	1·1
Other Print & Publishing	0	5	15·1	326	1·5	0·0
XVI { Rubber	1	5	102·0	108	4·6	0·9
Linoleum	0	2	13·4	15	13·3	0·9
Other Manufacturing	0	5	21·9	140	3·6	0·2
XVII Building	0	4	20·4	1,321	0·3	0·0
XIX { Shipping	9	24	395·1	168	14·3	2·4
Other Transport & Communications	2	10	178·8	150†	6·7	1·2
XX { Wholesaling	1	23	186·4	} 2,187	2·2	0·2
Retailing	1	24	343·5		2·2	0·2
XXIV { Entertainment & Sport	2	4	69·0	211	1·9	0·3
Catering and Hotels	1	5	44·0	657	0·8	0·1
Other Services‡	1	6	53·7	204	2·9	0·3
TOTAL (All activities excluding Petroleum)*	148	493	6,048·1	13,403	3·7	0·45

* The total corresponds to that in the National Institute's List, except for omitting Land and Property.   † Estimated after subtraction for Nationalisation.
‡ Including Storage and Laundries.
§ Orders omitted are I and II Agriculture and Mining. XVIII Public Utilities and Transport that are Nationalised. XXI Insurance, Banking and Finance.
XXII Public Administrative and Defence. XXIII Professional Services.

The bare number of companies is a useful first approximation, but to lend due weight to the very largest companies the *total of assets* of the companies with assets of £2·5m. or over is given in column 3. Both the number of companies of over £2·5m. assets and the total of their assets in £ million are then expressed as ratios per 100,000 *workers* employed in the industry in September 1954.[17]

Industries are listed according to their " order," which is given in Roman numerals in the standard industrial classification. For greater precision, some of these orders, for instance paper and miscellaneous, are split into their separate sub-industries.

Using both ratio of large companies and of the total of their assets per 100,000 workers employed, a number of industries stand out as having a very heavy incidence of large companies; cement, petroleum refining, drink (mostly brewing), tobacco, paper and newspaper publishing. All six have a ratio to 100,000 workers in the whole industry of at least £110m. of assets in over ten large companies. The heavy incidence of large companies and their assets in brewing formed one reason for adding companies in the brewing section of the *Year Book* to those in the industrial and commercial section.

Next in degree of large-company incidence came chemicals (other than petroleum refining), iron and steel, rayon, grain milling, sugar refining, rubber and linoleum. All seven industries have ratios to 100,000 workers of over four large companies, and £90m. of assets in these companies.

Once the industries with a heavy incidence of large companies (for short, the large-company industries) are identified, we may take a step further which will help in the later discussion of the future development and of the consequences of the large company. We may, in fact, relate the incidence of large companies to measures of two important characteristics of these industries, their capital intensity and the concentration of their business, or parts of their business, into a few hands.

Table I F takes all the thirteen industries appearing in Table I E which have an incidence of large companies with assets per 100,000 workers of £90m. or more.

Column 4 presents two measures of intensity of capital taken from the 1951 census of production, horsepower in use per operative employed and net output per person employed.[18] Each of the thirteen industries

---

[17] *Ministry of Labour Gazette.*
[18] It is advisable to use both measures since (*e.g.*, net output of petroleum) neither is by itself always a reliable index of capital intensity.

TABLE I F

DEGREE OF INTENSITY OF CAPITAL AND CONCENTRATION IN THIRTEEN MOST LARGE-COMPANY INDUSTRIES, 1951–53

(1)	(2)	(3)		(4)	(5)
Number of order	Industry	Measures per 100,000 employed of large company incidence (Table I E)		Horse-power and £ net output per worker	Concentration of employment in three largest business units, 1951, wherever 66% or over (source Evely and Little, *Concentration in British Industry*)
		No. of large Co's	Their assets. £100m.		
III	Cement	20	4·1	25·4 £1,492	Cement 87%
IV	Petroleum refining	15	6·0	9·9 £923 (in 1948)	Petroleum 84%
	Chemicals ..	6	1·7	5·7 £960	Matches 85% Dyes and dyestuffs 89% Explosives 93% Seed crushing 81% Soap and Glycerine 72% Fertilizers 73%
V	Metal manufacture (Iron, steel and non-ferrous)	8	1·1	8·4 £819	Cast pipes, etc. 66% Stoves not for solid fuel 68% Tinplate 71% Tubes, wrought iron and steel 77% Tin 75% Zinc 68%
X	Rayon	4	1·6	2·9 £868	Rayon and nylon yarn 72%
XIII	Grain milling ..	7	1·4	7·6 £946	
	Sugar refining ..	9	1·4	6·5 £985	Beet sugar 100% Other sugar 84%
	Drink	31	3·2	0·7 to 18·8 £1,150	Spirit distilling 80% Spirit rectifying 75%
	Tobacco	10	4·8	0·9 £1,375	Tobacco 70%
XV	Paper (excluding printing)	13	1·9	11·5 £1,034	Wallpaper 86% Writing paper 72% Note paper and pads 66% (Paper and board)
	Newspaper publishing	14	1·1	1·9 £944	
XVI	Rubber	5	0·9	4·7 £766	Rubber tyres and tubes 75%
	Linoleum ..	13	0·9	7·6 £794	Floor covering 75%
	Average of all activities ..	3·7	0·45	3·1 £677	All subdivisions (median) 34%

have either a power ratio OR a net output ratio per worker considerably higher than the average for all manufacturers of 3·1 and £677 respectively—in fact 50% higher than the average horsepower a worker and 20% higher than the average net output a worker. Seven of the thirteen large-company industries, cement, chemicals, metal manufacture, grain milling, sugar, paper and petroleum, qualify as capital-intensive on both counts. In short, large companies appear to get established and survive in the capital-intensive to a much greater degree than in industries generally. This conclusion is important in forecasting (as in § 6 *infra*) the future of the large company in a scientific age requiring more and more costly capital equipment.

Column 5 of Table I F, presents a measure of the concentration of the thirteen industries and their subdivisions in a few business hands, based on Evely and Little, *Concentration in British Industry*,[19] which analyses the results of the 1951 census. It gives for each industry, trade or subdivision the percentage of workers employed by the three largest of its " business units " (probably all of them companies), where these percentages are 66% or over and thus indicate a high concentration of control. This index of concentration has in view the possible disposition of large companies toward monopoly or at least oligopoly, to be discussed later.

Twenty-five high-concentration indices of 66% or more appear in column 5. The total of concentration indices given by Evely and Little as within the large-company industries appearing in Table I F is seventy-eight, and the high concentration indices here therefore form 25/78 or 32% of all indices. In the industries excluded from Table I F as not large-company industries, the high-concentration indices of 66% or over form only about 18% of all indices. Thus the large-company industries tend to contain a disproportionate number of high-concentration trades.

§ 5. THE CONSTITUTION AND PROCEDURE OF THE JOINT STOCK COMPANY

In this work we are concentrating (to give them their full specification) on public joint stock companies with limited liability. Unlimited liability on the shareholder to pay creditors up to the full extent of his wealth and not merely of his investment virtually exists no longer. The main class of company the adjective public excludes are the private companies where (1) the right to transfer shares is restricted, (2) members are restricted

---

[19] Cambridge University Press, 1960.

to fifty, (3) invitation to the public to subscribe for shares or debentures is prohibited and (4) there is no requirement to publish accounts. Members of public companies such as we survey, can, on the other hand, if permission is granted, transfer shares on the Stock Exchange—and membership may be very large.   Our survey is possible for the very reason that prices on the Stock Exchange are " quoted," accounts published, subscriptions invited, and the names of the subscribing members and the extent of their shareholdings duly recorded.

The formal constitution derives from three sources of authority.   The most fundamental of them is the law of the land and its judicial inter-pretation.   The joint stock company is a legal entity endowed with perpetual succession, capable of holding property in its own right, of incurring debts and of suing and being sued as a distinct person, and having limited liability so that in the event of failure members cannot lose more than their original investment in the company.

The legally established constitution of these companies consists in two organs: meetings of shareholders who vote according to the voting rights of the shares they hold, and a board of directors.   The board appoints its own chairman and also the top manager or executive—usually called the managing director.   A company must have a regular (usually annual) meeting of the shareholders which (i) elects a board of directors of not less than a certain number for a specific period, after which directors must be re-elected if they wish to continue, (ii) sanctions and may reduce the rate of dividend, (iii) must be presented with, and may discuss, the results of the year's transactions, particularly a balance sheet,[20] and (iv) under company law all amendments to the constitution, such as a change in the capital, must be sanctioned by shareholders, usually in an extraordinary meeting.

In the formal structure and organisation, within the law, of particular companies two further documents are involved, usually issued by the promoters of the company.   The more fundamental instrument is the memorandum of association which sets forth the name and location of the company, the scope of its objects and the total of its capital, and confirms that liability is limited.   The procedure of government, especially the relations of shareholders and directors, of any one company within the terms of its memorandum is stated in its articles of association. Whether stated in these articles or not, we find for different companies, in

---

[20] A. B. Levy, *Private Corporations and their Control*, 1950, p. 734.

fact, quite a wide variety in the number and type of directors, the qualifying shares they must hold and their tenure of office before re-appointment.
Wide variety will also be found, as described in Chapter III, § 1, in the
division of shares into categories (*e.g.*, the capital structure of ordinary,
deferred, preferred, preference) and in the plan for shares to carry votes
or multiples or fractions of votes.   In *theory* (its observance is examined
later) the shareholders who bear the risks should have the vote that gives
control.

Joint stock government has been pictured as proceeding like the sand
in an hourglass from the wide top (to represent the thousands of shareholders) down through the narrows representing the dozen or so of
directors, and the waist representing the managing director.   From this
point the execution of the shareholders' and directors' policy widens
out again in a hierarchy of ranks and functions.

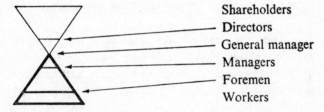

Shareholders
Directors
General manager
Managers
Foremen
Workers

The risk-*bearing* shareholders, in short, are considered in formal
theory also to be the risk-*takers* in the sense of those laying down the
policies of the organisation—policies that will involve various degrees
of risk.[21]   Otherwise, it is thought, excessive risks may be taken by
policy makers, such as the general manager, who are personally often
safe from the direct consequences, owning few shares.   For the sake of
efficiency in government, the powers of appointing top managers, re-
organising the upper management structure and deciding policy are
delegated by shareholders to the board of directors who appear just above
the waist of the hourglass.   The Members of the Board (whose private
interest is supposed to be identified with that of the company by holding
qualifying shares), are, in theory, appointed, and their appointment
periodically reviewed, by the annual shareholders' meeting, which also
decides their scale of remuneration.   Shareholders can check up on
results—in theory again—from the published and duly audited annual

[21] The nature of the risk and the probability distribution and uncertainty of various degrees
of loss is discussed in my *Statistical Method in Economics and Political Science*, Chap. VII,
and illustrated in Chap. VII, § 4, of the present book in discussing the stimulus for risk-
bearing.

balance sheets, and, in fact, will probably occasionally read newspaper comment in the financial columns of their favourite daily newspaper. If a certain proportion of shareholders agree, meetings may be called without reference to the directors. In short, it is the shareholders who, *in law*, appear, at least to some lawyers, as sovereign.

Whether the shareholders are *in fact* sovereign, and the great variety of financial structure and voting rights already mentioned, will be taken up in Chapter III. The number of directors, the proportion of shares they hold, the categories of shares and the total voting rights of shares are recorded for each separate company in basic tables (*e.g.*, Appendix A) together with the number of shareholders—*i.e.*, the top of the hourglass. By a curious coincidence, it is probably no more than that, the total number of shareholders is in many large companies not far from the total number of workers employed. The breadth of the top and the bottom of the hourglass are drawn equal in our diagram, not without reason.

The companies classified as very large in 1951 with over £3m. of capital averaged about 12,000 preference and ordinary shareholders. The companies that were classified as medium and smaller large by reference to their share capital, £1–2·9m. and £0·2–0·9m., had fewer shareholders. Summing up the approximate numbers given in the basic tables of Appendix A, the smaller large companies averaged about 1,750; the medium large companies 4,000.

The evidence points to the shareholdings averaging about the same for all sizes of company. Medium companies have the comparatively narrow limits of share capital of £1m. to just under £3m. If their average size is taken as slightly under £2m. the average shareholding of their 4,000 shareholders may be reckoned in 1951 as slightly under £500 nominal value. And an average shareholding of just under £500 is compatible (though on the high side) with the average of 1,750 shareholders in the smaller companies of £200,000 to under £1,000,000 capital, yielding on average nominal capital per company of under £875,000. For the very large companies an average holding of £500 for the average of 12,000 shareholders would yield an average share capital of £6m. which is about the (median) average size actually found. In short, the average shareholding may well have been about £500 whatever the size of the company.

We must, however, not leave the analysis of the various bodies represented by the hourglass before pointing out the division of economic functions which the existence of those bodies imply. In fact, a great

change has come over " capitalist " organisation in the course of its
history involving a more complex structure. In early capitalism the
dominant figure was the " entrepreneur," though it took some time for
English economists to recognise him. " Undertaker " having too narrow,
or too sinister a meaning, they finally had to borrow a French word for
the purpose. This " entrepreneur " was both the owner of the capital
(or, as Adam Smith had it, the " stock ") employed in industry and its
manager. Owner-managers still, of course, flourish as " sole traders"
in many branches of industry and commerce, notably, as we have seen, in
retailing and building. But in most of industry, " entrepreneurs " have
given way first to partnership where one partner—the " sleeping partner "—
owned but did not manage, and then to the company where the bulk of
the capital owned was not owned by the manager or even the board
of directors, but " sleeping " shareholders. The notion of division of
labour which Adam Smith so rightly considered the foundation of the
Wealth of Nations and described in the very first chapter of his book can
be applied to the evolution of all roles in a large " going concern " and
be represented by the numerous prongs of a fork diagram. In addition
there are the roles of the promoter or innovator to get the concern going,
and of the receiver or reorganiser if it stops going.

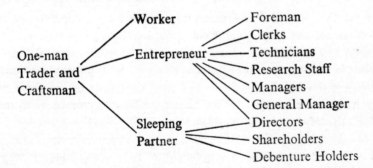

Theoretical economists have again been slow in adapting their
vocabulary to this evolution; the entrepreneur in the old sense of the word
has disappeared, in the bulk of industrial business. His three functions
of providing capital, taking risks with it and managing are now, under
the regime of the large company, performed by a series of people: the
provider of more or of less secure capital—the debenture holder and
the preference shareholder respectively: the provider of risk capital—
the ordinary shareholder: and the managers of various types and ranks.

Management and its auxiliary services have greatly increased if the ever-increasing ratio of salaried staff to wage-earners [22] is taken as a test. In 1924 administrative, technical and clerical staff formed 11·8% of operators, in 1935 15·1%, in 1948 20·0% and by 1951 had risen to 21·6%. The same order of increase has been occurring in the United States.

We are not directly concerned here with middle and lower management and supervision. But the directors are crucial to an analysis of company control. They will figure prominently in later chapters. For the present we need only appreciate that directors own a majority of voting shares, or even a fifth of them, in *very few large companies* [23] as the old entrepreneur owned his stock: and that a problem arises in consequence as to who is in real control—who is actually sovereign.

This book is concerned with the informal but real, the *de facto* and not the *de jure* control and working of the joint stock constitution. Most of the actual facts and patterns will be unfolded in Chapters III and IV devoted to shareholders and directors, and in Chapter V, which attempts to discover the actual seat of control in large companies and to classify them accordingly.

§ 6. THE FUTURE OF THE LARGE COMPANY

Now that the past and present, and the formal constitution and procedure, of the large joint stock company have been reviewed, the question will naturally be asked whether the large company is likely to increase in importance in the future, or even to keep its present importance. To answer this it is necessary to look into the causes of the company's growth up to the present. If the causes are likely to persist or increase in force the large company is, other things equal, likely to grow.

The growth of the joint stock companies has been the result mainly of two connected causes: the increasing size of factories and plants (largely due to the widening markets and sources of raw material following upon mechanisation and cheapening of transport); and the increasing use of special machines, mechanical and chemical processes and other forms of capital equipment, following upon scientific invention and the industrial innovation applying these inventions to industry and requiring finance. Scientific invention can be traced further back to the experimentation of

---

[22] The facts are detailed and the probable causes of this rapid and continuous increase in the staff ratio are discussed in Florence, *Logic of British and American Industry*, pp. 137–40.
[23] The details are given in Chap. V, § 5.

an individual genius or to organised research.[24] Experimentation, organised research and practical innovation involve high capitalisation per worker and require capital savings; but where organised research is financed from the plough-back of company savings a self-reinforcing " feed-back " process—a " virtuous circle "—is attained which borders on perpetual motion and makes continuous industrial development almost a matter of course in countries already developed.

The accompanying diagram sets out the probable train of causation and the virtuous circle involved.   Large joint stock companies " develop " because the " stock " or " capital " of any individual person or a partnership or even of a small company is insufficient to finance the large factories required, combined with the greater " intensity " of capital.

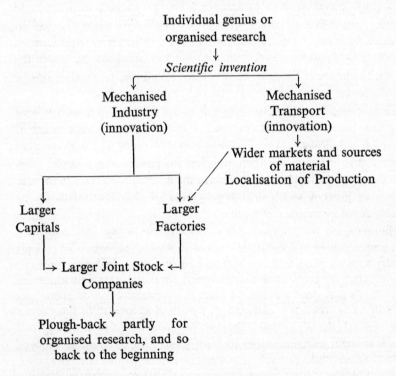

Much of the train of causation suggested in this diagram, can be confirmed empirically.   As pointed out already, a fairly close statistical

[24] See, in particular, Jewkes, Sawers and Stillerman, *The Sources of Invention*, Macmillan, 1958; and for the determinants in general of scientific and technical innovation in British industry, Carter and Williams, *Industry and Technical Progress, Investment in Innovation and Science in Industry*, Oxford University Press, 1957, 1958 and 1959.

association can be established between large companies and mechanisation, most industries with a heavy incidence of large companies are also industries of high horsepower a worker.

Scientific invention and the mechanisation of transport and of industry generally is certainly continuing (horsepower a worker for all manufacturing was 2·4 in 1930, 3·1 in 1951) and today, gives occasion for the new word " automation " and the suggestion of a second industrial revolution. In point of fact, progress and development, apart from some accelerations and decelerations due to trade cycles and wars, has been fairly continuous in the world as a whole ever since the original Industrial Revolution.

With continuously increasing mechanical power statistics also show a continually increasing size of factory. The proportion of workers in factories employing over a thousand has increased since the earliest records were taken. During the period of the present survey it increased from 21·5% in 1935 to 30·1% in 1951.[25] Furthermore, the larger the factory, the larger is likely to be the firm owning and controlling one or more factories.

This development based on research and manifested in greater capital equipment needs funds that only *joint* stock, that is a large number of people all subscribing capital, can supply. Sleeping partners or even private companies with less than fifty shareholders are not enough. It is not artistry but the facts of life that make the hourglass diagram to show at the top as great a width denoting number of shareholders as at the bottom, denoting number of workers.

Though small factories and firms, and factories using little machinery exist, and probably will continue to exist in several industries, large-scale industry appears likely to go on encroaching on them. It does not follow, however, that the joint stock company will similarly extend its influence. Other things may not be equal. In fact the very reduction of operations to " routine or to such a uniformity of method as admits of little or no variation," which Adam Smith thought favoured the joint stock organisation, is thought today, as earlier by John Stuart Mill, to favour schemes of nationalisation and, possibly co-operation. Nationalisation has been applied to public utilities (especially gas and electrical supply), coalmining and railways and temporarily to road transport, but not yet to any manufacturing industry except temporarily in 1951–52, to iron and steel. And

---

[25] Census of production 1951, Summary Tables, Part 1. This is all the more striking since mechanisation, *i.e.*, the substitution of machines for men, would, other things equal, reduce the number of workers.

some manufacturing and many commercial operations included in the present survey of companies have for more than a century been undertaken in Britain by co-operative societies. At present, co-operative societies account for 11% of national retail trade, considerably more in groceries, milk and coal, considerably less in drapery and other durable goods.

What are the prospects that the joint stock companies which have gradually been superseding the individual business and partnership in manufacturing and distributive trades will, in their turn, be superseded by co-operation or nationalisation ? In the last twenty years, two very thorough inquiries have been made into the consumer co-operative societies of Britain, both the retail and the wholesale societies, with the factories they own. In 1938 Sir Alexander Carr-Saunders, Professor Peers and myself [26] saw signs that the advance of co-operation into retailing, wholesaling and branches of manufacturing was coming to a halt. And in 1958 the Independent Commission (with Mr. Gaitskell as chairman, Mr. Crossland as secretary and several economists as members) have confirmed that a halt has in fact occurred. While the capitalist retailing multiples (several of which appear in our list of large companies) have, between 1930–34 and 1952–56, advanced their trade from $14 \cdot 0\%$ to around $21 \cdot 2\%$ of the total national retail trade, the co-operative societies only advanced their proportion from 10 to 11%. It is noteworthy that the chief co-operative success was in groceries, milk and coal distribution—in fact the more routine and uniform trades. Some explanation of this lack of progress is that the co-operatives failed to make provision for the capital requirements of development. The co-operative societies, retail or wholesale, plough back, according to the Independent Commission, very little of their surplus—$7 \cdot 4\%$ as against the companies, $58 \cdot 4\%$ [27] and little, if any, research is undertaken. Even the simplest consumer research, comparing the preferences of panels of consumers for co-operative as against other but similar products at similar prices has been confined to the 1936–38 investigation at the University of Birmingham Faculty of Commerce. [28]

Nationalisation, on the other hand, can provide plenty of capital and has fulfilled to a large extent the intense requirements in that respect of

[26] *Consumers, Co-operation in Great Britain*, Allen & Unwin, 1938.
[27] Independent Commission Report 1958, p. 146. In Chap. VII below a more detailed estimate is made of the plough-back of the large companies.
[28] Carr-Saunders, *et al., op. cit.* Chap. XXIV, esp. § 7.

the public utilities, in particular of the electricity supply and, more recently, the railway industries. Between 1948 and 1956, as shown in Table I G (see below p. 29), the public corporations that governed most nationalised industries invested well over half the amount invested by companies, though the nationalised segment employed only about a fifth of the total employed. Indeed, in the seven years between 1949 and 1955, public corporations invested at the average rate of £270m.[29] a year in the fuel and power industries alone equivalent to £2,430m. in nine years, or one-third in this group of industries, of all the £6,591m. that companies invested in 1948–56.

The wheel has, curiously enough, almost turned full circle from the day of Adam Smith. It is now nationalisation that is advocated as suitable for routine operations while the joint stock company is to be left for the trades needing enterprise and lack of routine. Similarly in raising capital

" where nationalisation is superior to the company is now exactly where the company proved superior to the small capitalist, namely in raising capital and investing in equipment. The dominance of this technical need for capital in an age of applied science has been a logical trend . . . and since the first world war the need for capital has often, paradoxically enough, told against capitalism. British capitalist coal-mining was starved of equipment during the inter-war period, and large-scale investment to the tune of 635 million pounds proposed in the Coal Board's plan of 1950 was not conceivable till after nationalisation. Similarly . . . under a company regime new capital is forthcoming only when large enough profits have been earned in the past or expected in the future to make (a) companies able to reinvest sufficiently and (b) persons and other companies willing to subscribe to new issues. Once an industry's profits fall, a vicious circle is set up whereby low profit and expectation of low profits result in low investment and low investment in still lower profits. Thus, in specific British industries capitalism has been displaced not because it sweated the worker or exploited the consumer, as foretold by some prophets, but because capitalism failed any longer to attract the commodity on which it originally gained power—capital." [30]

Besides its routine nature and the possibility of the government meeting an industry's capital requirements with the state's powers of taxation, other characteristics favour an industry's nationalisation; the fear of a private monopoly power particularly in the basic or common-service industries, for instance, or the need for conservation rather than the immediately profitable exploitation of resources.

[29] *National Income and Expenditure*, H.M.S.O. 1957, p. 31.
[30] Florence, *Logic of British and American Industry*, p. 232.

Apart from the public utilities, however, most manufacturing industries are still variegated, need considerable enterprise (rather than just expertise) and taking of risks and are subject to competition. Even if certain characteristics favouring nationalisation are present in some degree, it does not follow that nationalisation will be applied. Characteristics such as risk, competition and the need for enterprise may outweigh other considerations.[31]

The question is, of course, largely in the lap of the politicians. But the present and future performance of the companies themselves will certainly count. What the national economy needs, if standards of living are to keep on rising, is high capital formation and investment, which depend largely on company and individual savings, and freedom from restrictions on production and development by reason, possibly, of monopoly. Monopoly, investment and personal savings are considered in the next section. Meanwhile a long-run prophecy can perhaps be made, that the medium routine, medium capitalised and less monopolised industries are likely to stay in the hands of private enterprise and probably to shift somewhat from individual and partnerships, more suitable for the less routine and less capitalised activities, to joint stock company control.

§ 7. The Significance of the Large Company to the National Economy

Before passing, in Chapter II, to the methods used in the present enquiry, and in Chapter III onwards, to positive conclusions from the enquiry, a word must be said of the significance of the larger companies to the whole national economy, apart from the quantitative extent of their business operations already estimated. This qualitative significance rests on at least three considerations. One consideration is that the large company may be in a position to dominate an industry as a monopoly; another that the saving of large companies out of their profits is now the main single source of capital formation in manufacturing and some other trades. Finally, and this consideration is nearest to our interest in the individual investors, under continuing inflation the shares of large companies are one of the few remaining sources of *real* security open to the ordinary citizen. Dividends have not risen over the long period

---

[31] For detailed discussion not only of the characteristics of an industry but of the comparative efficiency of nationalisation and company government, see Florence, *op. cit.*, Chaps. V and VI.

and may never rise exactly in conformity with prices, yet do not stay quite fixed in money terms like interest on other (so-called) securities.

(1) the danger of monopoly is the consequence of the extent of business done by relatively few large companies and the usually connected difficulty of entry by new or old firms. The existing size or the growth of large companies does not, in itself, involve monopoly. What at least threatens or gives opportunity for monopoly is the size of one or a few companies *relatively* to the size of the whole industry—when industry is defined as the market for their product and the products of competitors. Mere size is unlikely to involve monopoly if the industry in which the companies operate is large, or if none of the large companies is very large (and there is thus room for a number of moderately large companies to operate) or, again, if, in fact, the industry as recognised by the census includes several markets and the company though large in aggregate has no large share in any one market. For example, in the drink industry (mostly brewing) where Table I E shows the incidence of large companies as highest, the large number of workers employed allows of fifteen not so very large companies with over £10m. net assets. On the other hand, smaller industries, though with a lower incidence of large companies, may, like tobacco, rubber or linoleum, show only one, two or a very few large companies; and this is where the chance of monopoly, or at least a " duopoly " or " oligopoly " (control by two, or a few firms) arises. Attention ought now to be drawn to Leak and Maizel's paper before the Royal Statistical Society in 1945 giving for a great number of industries the percentages of workers who were concentrated in the employment of the three largest business units. There are notable cases of quite a low concentration in the hands of three business units associated with a heavy incidence of large companies. The iron and steel and non-ferrous order has a high incidence of large companies, but its main industry, steel smelting and rolling, had, for instance, only a 27% concentration. Again, brewing, the chief sub-industry of drink, which showed the greatest number of large companies per 100,000 workers, had a concentration of only 23%. Yet a general analysis, as in Table I F, points to a distinct trend for large-company industry to have control concentrated in a few firms.

This is not the place to pursue the implication of concentration of an industry in a few business units for the development of monopoly powers or to ask whether, and if so how, that power is in fact exercised. All we need point out is that in many, particularly in smaller, industries or sub-industries a possibility of monopoly power lies with certain large joint stock companies because the bulk of the industry is concentrated in their hands; they may, at least, be the " leaders " of their industry in pricing and other policies. This constitutes reason enough for investigating large companies. *If concentration of power in the hands of a company within an industry is accompanied by a concentration of power within that company, itself in the hands of one or a few shareholders, there is a double distillation of power. If, on top of that, the one main shareholder is a holding company within which such shares are further concentrated in one or a few hands, a triple distillation of power is effected.* These concentrations of shares will be inquired into in due course.

(2) A further important consequence of large companies to the whole economy, besides the fear of possible monopoly, is the hope of large-scale investment. Companies form the largest single source of funds for industrial investment. The details are shown in Table I G for nine years 1948–56 of industrial and commercial activity.

TABLE I G

GROSS FIXED CAPITAL FORMATION BY COMPANIES AND OTHER BODIES
1948–56

Objects of Investment	Persons and non-corporate business*	Companies	Public corporations†	Central† and local govt. trading	Total (mostly trading)	Central and local govt. (not trading)	Grand total
	£m	£m	£m	£m	£m	£m	£m
Vehicles, ships and aircraft	584	1,649	582	72	2,887	49	2,936
Plant and machinery	1,008	3,238	1,928	732	6,906	274	7,180
Other buildings and works (net)	563	1,704	901	575	3,743	1,423	5,166
Total	2,155	6,591	3,411	1,379	13,536	1,745	15,282
Percent. distribution (1938 distribution)	16% (33%)	49% (45%)	25% (2%)	10% (30%)	100 (100)		
Dwellings	1,313	0	244	2,758	4,315	137	4,452
Grand total invested	3,468	6,591	3,655	4,137	17,851	1,883	19,734

Source: National Income and Expenditure 1957, p. 54

* Individuals and partnerships segment (see Table I B).
† National and nationalised segment (see Table I B).

This table separates off vertically (in the right-hand margin) central and local government investment *not* for trading, and horizontally, in the bottom margin, investment in dwellings. Though not all the " personal " segment in the first column will be industrial, we are left, after subtraction of the dwellings, with investment (*i.e.*, gross fixed capital formation) *mainly* in industrial trading. The total of trading investment given for 1948–56 is £13,536,000,000. Of this outlay companies invested 49%, public corporations 25%, persons 16% and government (local and central trading) 10%.

The role of the company in the capital formation of manufacturing and commerce is, in fact, greater than these percentages suggest. The industry with far the highest gross fixed capital formation in plant, machinery and buildings was electricity supply accounting by itself for £1,532m. All manufacturers put together accounted for £4,793m. and distribution and other services for £1,228m. Thus capital formation in electricity alone was over a quarter of manufacturing and distributive and other service trades put together. Now electricity was supplied in this period by a public corporation, so the preponderance of this one industry explains the unexpectedly high proportion of public corporations' fixed investment.

If we subtract the fixed capital formation (including vehicles) in electricity supply from the data in Table I F and assume it was all attributable to public corporations, the proportions of total fixed investment in trading would become 12% by central and local government, 15% by public corporations, 18% by the personal segment and 55% by companies.

What part of this large contribution by companies to the capital formation of the country is due to their ploughing back their profit; what part to receipts from new issues to the market? An answer can be found in the analysis by the National Institute of Economic and Social Research of the sources and uses of capital funds of all the three thousand companies quoted on the Stock Exchange and engaged in British industry and commerce. During the five years 1949 to 1953 when this analysis was made, it appears that the receipts from the issue of debentures, ordinary and preference shares varied from 37% to 50% of the balance put back to reserves. Thus ploughing back had anything from twice to almost three times the importance of new issues as a source of capital funds. In short the company was not only the main single agent in national capital formation but saved most of its contribution out of its own funds. Later we shall find that the largest companies tended in 1948–51 to plough back more of their profit than the smaller companies. Whether this is true of other years or not, the large companies generally can be said to form a critical source for further industrial investment and we are justified in inserting " plough-back " into the diagram on page 23 as a probable consequence of the larger company.[32]

(3) So far the implication of large companies has been considered upon the policies of the active partners in the company, in particular their possible exercise of monopoly power and their " investment " in the Keynesian sense of capital formation.

Investment requires savings either by the company in the shape of depreciation allowance and ploughing back profits (now the more important source), or by individuals and institutions who can be induced to buy shares in new capital issues.   Inducement to buy shares must depend on the way existing shareholders are treated—the powers and rewards they receive in relation to the risk they run.   Most shareholders, as a result of the division of labour within the company already described, possess little power.   The actual procedure of companies allows people and institutions with money, but without business experience or ability or the desire for engaging actively in business, to be passive lenders of capital, to be bearers not takers of risk.   In exchange for this passivity, however, they are paid dividends which, unlike the interest of debenture holders or of holders of government stock, may rise if circumstances are favourable.   In particular, dividends will tend to rise as profits rise during a period of inflation.   The *real* income of the passive shareholders, unlike that of the holders of fixed interest stock, thus will not necessarily shrink proportionately to the degree of price-inflation.

Now price-inflation has, since, 1936 when the present survey starts, probably proceeded faster than in any similar span of years in English history.   Even at the end of the fifteen years of our survey in 1951 I calculated [33] that the most suitable official indices pointed to a rise of price during the fifteen years as from 100 to 236.   Prices have risen quite as fast since then up to 1958 and the purchasing power of the pound was then about one-third of its 1936 power—a price rise of 100 to 300 for the twenty-two years.

The fifteen-year rise meant that an investor buying stock in 1936 that was redeemable in 1951, would in real terms have got back 42%—the reciprocal of 236%—of his original outlay.   Moreover, if he had bought irredeemable perpetual stock like Consols and sold in 1951 the value of his investment would have fallen from 100 to 78 in money terms alone (the

[32] See also Tew and Henderson, *Studies in Company Finance*, pp. 23–25 and 42 *et seq.*
[33] *Journal of Industrial Economics*, March 1957, p. 100.

price of Consols being that proportion of their price in 1936), and in consequence the total *real* fall in value of his stock would have been as 100 to 42% ×78% or 100 to 32·8—a loss of over two-thirds.

It is true that the investor in the ordinary shares of large industrial and commercial companies would not have kept exactly abreast of the price-inflation. The average gain by appreciation of all the companies surveyed was between 1936 and 1951 as 100 to 180,[34] less by 56% of the original outlay than the rise in prices. But at least the ordinary shareholder would have lost far less in real terms than the investor in fixed interest stock.

Price-inflation has come upon us comparatively so suddenly that many small savers are still perhaps only vaguely aware of their predicament. It was indeed only twelve years ago that so well-known an authority on finance as Hartley Withers could still think the statement worth publishing that " any one who can live comfortably on £800 a year and has got £40,000 in Consols bringing him an income of £1,000 is beyond the slings and arrows of outrageous fortune and need never care about the price at which his stock may happen to stand. His income is assured as well as his income can be." [35]

More of us have by now learned how ephemeral any fixed money income can be in terms of real purchasing power of that income and the joint stock company is giving people the chance to invest *really* more securely than in fixed-interest irredeemable or even long-dated stock. Risks are inherent, as we shall see, in investing in the ordinary shares of any *one* company, and such risks must be spread. The comparatively rich can buy a regular portfolio of shares over different industries and countries and buy, too, at different phases of the general up and down of Stock Exchange prices. The comparatively poor can buy the shares of an investment trust which perform the function for him of spreading risks by holding a great variety of government stock, debentures, preference and ordinary shares.

[34] See below, Chap. VII.
[35] *Stocks and Shares*, 1948 edition, p. 32.

ANNEX TO CHAPTER I

COMPANY PREVALENCE IN THE VARIOUS
ECONOMIC ACTIVITIES

PRIOR to the question of the prevalence in the various economic activities
of the large companies with which this book is concerned comes, logically,
the question of the prevalence of companies generally, large or small.
This Annex is designed to throw light both on this " prior " question and
also on the calculation in Table I D of what proportion of the industrial
and commercial sector of activity is due to large companies.

Public sources of information on companies do not cross-classify
the different activities of the companies by size, but for each size lump
all activities together. Table I A, on the other hand, distinguished
different types of activity, but not sizes, among the public companies
quoted on the Stock Exchange. A more exact analysis according to
activity of all companies, quoted and unquoted, public and private,
but again regardless of size, is provided in the assessment by the Inland
Revenue of the number, and total " gross true " income, of companies
(including the very small proportion (4%) of local authorities, etc.) and
also of all " concerns," including the companies. This information is
detailed for many branches inside, and eight branches of activity outside,
the industrial and commercial sector.

These outside activities have, apart from insurance, banking and
finance at home, either an extremely low or an extremely high proportion
of their total gross true income arising from companies of all sizes rather
than from individuals and partnerships. The average company proportion
for *all* economic activities was, in 1951–52, 76%; but for (1) professional
services it was 3%, for (2) agriculture 4%, for (3) mining 7% and (4)
forestry and fishing 11%. On the other hand, as shown in Table I B,
for (5) shipping, the company proportion was 97% and for (6) finance
abroad and undertakings abroad nearer to 100% than 99%.

If we add iron and steel and road transport (because nationalised in
1951, not covered by our survey), to these six activities, the proportion of
company income to that of all concerns outside the surveyed sector is
found to be 55%—clearly lower on balance than the 76% company
proportion within the surveyed sector.

33

We can now make some attempt to estimate the business done by the 1,700 industrial and commercial companies we have surveyed (directly or by sample) as a proportion (a) of that of all *companies*, (b) of that of all *concerns*, *i.e.*, of the total of private enterprise business of the whole country.

In Table I C (bottom row) it appeared that in 1951–52, the largest 1,700 companies accounted for 55% of total gross true income of all companies; 37·5% of that of all concerns.   But these companies included a certain proportion of companies not in the industrial and commercial sector.   Comparing the two columns of Table I C the proportion for all sizes of company was $(185,122-166,217) \div 185,122 = 10 \cdot 2\%$.   A further proportion of companies was not in our survey for 1951, because of nationalisation.   But according to the Inland Revenue assessment, iron and steel still retained in 1951–52 1·2%, and road transport 2·5% of *all companies*.   Thus to include the 1,700 industrial and commercial companies we surveyed either directly or by sample, it would be necessary to cover $10 \cdot 2\% + 1 \cdot 2\% + 2 \cdot 5\%$ or about 14% more companies—in fact, nearly 2,000.[36]   What approximately is the proportion of total company gross true income brought in by the 2,000 largest companies ?

The proportion of gross true income will of course be more than the 55% of the 1,700 companies, but since income per company tapers off as less large companies are included, it will be less than in the simple proportion of 2,000 to 1,700, *i.e.*, it will be less than 64%.

In 1954–55 when exactly 2,000 companies appeared in the two largest ranges of income (*i.e.*, with over £200,000) their proportion of total *company* income was as 1,703·1 to 2,812·5 or 61% and of total *concern* income as 1,703·1 to 3,983·1 or 43%.   The number of large companies measured in money income had certainly been rising between 1951 and 1955 relatively to small companies, but an estimate of about 59% appears justified (and appears in Table I D) as the proportion of the income of all companies, and 40% as the proportion of the income of all *concerns*. This latter percentage is subject to correction upwards, however, since individuals and partnerships include the pay for management in their " income " and income thus overstates their proportion of business done.

---

[36] This assumes that companies outside our sector averaged about the same size as those inside.   Outside companies were in fact found to have an income (see above) " rather lower on balance."

Chapter II

THE SELECTION OF COMPANIES AND SUMMARY MEASURES OF THEIR CHARACTERISTICS

THE bulk of the information provided by this book is based upon certain summary measurements prepared in a " basic table " for all the companies listed in Appendix A 1 and 2 but published (in Appendix A 1) only for the very large industrial and commercial companies. Before setting forth the various general conclusions that can be drawn from this table, it will be useful not only to describe the sources and methods of computing the summary measurements that are presented, but also to discuss the reasons for presenting these particular measurements. Any analysis of company structure and behaviour is confronted with a wide choice of measures. But the number of measurements chosen must neither be too few, and thus fail to present the situation as fully as possible, nor too many and thus confuse the reader and possibly duplicate information. The statistical analysis of company ownership, control and success is only just beginning and we must avoid being dogmatic about the correct measurements to use. The set of measures presented in the basic tables are believed to be about all that are useful under the limiting circumstances of available data. The value of these particular measurements will, however, be discussed—often critically—and alternative measures suggested.

§ 1. THE CHOICE AND SAMPLING OF COMPANIES AND THEIR INDUSTRIAL GROUPING

This study is based on a sample of public joint stock companies which are registered at the Company Registry Office for England at Bush House, formerly at Somerset House, in London. Scottish companies are thus excluded. We have confined our interest to companies whose particulars are set forth in the commercial and industrial section, and the breweries and distilleries section of the Stock Exchange *Year Book* 1951 [1] and to

---

[1] " Iron, Coal and Steel " forms a separate section in the *Year Book* and is excluded. In 1951 most companies in this section were nationalised or in process of nationalisation.

those whose issued share capitals have a nominal value of £200,000 or more, and which, as already said, may be considered " large." All companies that are subsidiaries have been excluded from the sample if the parent company owning 51 to 100% of its shares has been included, or if 100% (or virtually so) are owned by *any* company. Companies whose activities are principally financial and spread across all industries are also excluded.

The companies studied are classified into three main size groups, denominated very large,[2] medium large and smaller large, according to *issued share capital in* 1951.

Very large:	£3,000,000 or over
Medium large:	£1,000,000 to short of £3,000,000
Smaller large:	£200,000 to short of £1,000,000

In spite of grants in aid of this research it was not possible, with the funds available, to collect information on all the headings and sub-headings of the basic table for large public companies of all sizes. The fullest information available both for 1936 and 1951 was obtained for *all* the *very* large companies, of over £3,000,000 issued capital in 1951. Unavoidable gaps in information occurred, however, and a choice had to be made between leaving out many important very large companies altogether, because some single item was not available, or including all the *very* large companies, and explaining the gaps by means of notes. Though more complicated and burdensome the latter course was adopted. Very few gaps occur in the data for the smaller large companies collected in 1951 and (except for share-concentration) in 1936. For the medium large companies, as shown below, two tables were prepared. One consists of 47 companies where resources allowed full information to be secured for 1951 and (except for share-concentration) 1936; the other of companies where information was collected only on certain aspects, necessary to obtain a sufficient basis for our measurement of distribution policy and success in 1936–51. Company sampling and restricted information for 1936 had to be adopted, as set forth in the following table:

[2] Though perhaps clumsy, " very large " is used rather than the more picturesque " giant," since giant suggests a capital larger than £3m. In our summary (Chap. VIII, § 4) the attribute of " giant " is suggested for companies of (in 1951) £8m. capital or more.

INDUSTRIAL AND COMMERCIAL SECTOR			
	No. listed	Company coverages: ratio of companies measured to all companies	Extent of information
VERY LARGE £3m. Issued Capital or over.	98	All companies measured	All headings in 1936 and 1951
MEDIUM LARGE £1m. Issued Capital to short of £3m.	(A)47 ⎫ ⎬129 (B)82 ⎭	1 in 5 ⎫ 11 in 20 ⎬ representing about 7 in ⎫ 234 com-20 ⎭ panies	(A) *Full information* All headings except concentration of shares in 1936. (B) *Part information* No concentration of shares either in 1936 or 1951. Data only for Gearing, Dividend Policy and Success
SMALLER LARGE £0.2m. Issued Capital to short of £1m.	88	1 in 15 representing about 1,200 companies	All headings except concentration of shares in 1936

Among brewery companies, in order to get a sufficient number (*i.e.*, 11 or 12) in each class of size for purposes of generalisation about concentration of votes, the sampling was more generous. In the medium large class, twelve breweries had the largest twenty shareholders identified, a sample of about 1 in 2, and none was listed that did not have this identification. In the smaller large size again, twelve breweries were listed with identification of the largest twenty shareholders. This was a sample of about 1 in 4. The summary tables presented in Chapters III to VI refer separately to the industrial and commercial and the brewery companies, so that no overweighting of breweries affects the results.

The selected medium large were mainly [3] and the smaller large

---

[3] As among the very large companies, about a 6% proportion (3 out of 47) of the selected medium large companies with full information for 1951 had not been formed, at least as public companies, in 1936.

companies entirely limited to companies who had Stock Exchange prices easily determinable and " Historical Records " available in Moody's *Investors' Services*, for the commencement as well as the ending of our fifteen-year period.   Sources of prices were issues of the *Financial Times* and *Stock Exchange Daily Lists* for late August and early September of 1936 and 1951—trading periods when the market as a whole was relatively quiet and steady in tone.

Within the limits of available prices all the medium large companies were analysed.   Companies with available price data numbered 129 and constituted about eleven in twenty of all the 234 companies in this size group; they included the bulk of the trading on the Stock Exchange. Shares whose prices were not readily available in the official sources of information were shares not traded in commonly, and thus of less interest to investors.   The identification of the largest twenty shareholders and the analysis of vote concentration which used up much time and funds, had to be limited to the sample of forty-seven companies (*i.e.*, just over one in five) stratified to represent the various sizes and industries of the total of 234 companies.   Stratification followed the percentage distribution table below for the drastic operation necessarily applied to the very numerous smaller companies.

The smaller companies were, in fact, sampled for all types of information (including share-concentration in 1951) so as to obtain with brewery companies a sample of about a hundred companies.   The principles of selection to determine which companies should represent the whole population of smaller large companies, were within the limits outlined above, only two:

> (i) the sample was balanced by industrial subdivisions, *i.e.*, following broadly the nomenclature of the *Standard Industrial Classification*, the sample included the proper proportion of companies in the following industrial subdivisions: breweries (tabulated separately), chemicals, distribution (and catering), engineering (sub-groups metal goods, non-ferrous metal manufacture, precision instruments), textiles, paper, food, motors and vehicles (including aviation and accessories) and miscellaneous manufactures, clothing and building materials.
> (ii) Each of these industrial subdivisions must contain an appropriate distribution of companies by issued capital size-classes.

To ensure these results, all the companies in the early pages of the *S.E.Y.B.* sections were listed, nominal share capitals noted and each assigned to one of the industrial subdivisions. A two-way table of identical industrial subdivisions and size classes was thus obtained, which yielded percentages of companies meeting the limits of the enquiry, and which might be expected to be found within each corresponding cell of the sample.

Out of the 2,400 English companies with less than £1,000,000 nominal capital [4] (and not subsidiaries of other listed companies) in the 1951 *S.E.Y.B. Commercial and Industrial Section*, the following table was constructed:

Percentage distribution table of the 2,400 " smaller " companies by size and industry and, italicised, number actually selected for smaller large (capital £200,000 to £1,000,000) [5]

Size in issued capital	Up to £100,000	£100,000 to £249,000	£250,000 to £499,000[6]		£500,000 to £749,000		£750,000 to £1,000,000		Total of percentages in last three columns	Total actually selected
Chemicals	1·8	2·4	·6⌐	*2*	·4	*1*	·3	*1*	1·3	*4*
Distributive Trades ...	4·2	4·4	6·7	*18*	2·0	*6*	·6	*2*	9·3	*26*
Engineering	4·2	7·0	5·2	*13*	2·2	*6*	·4	*2*	7·8	*21*
Food	·4	2·6	2·4⌐	*6*	·4	*2*	·3	*1*	3·1	*9*
Motors	·4	1·2	1·4⌐	*4*	1·4	*4*	0	*0*	2·8	*8*
Paper	1·0	1·8	1·2	*4*	·4	*1*	0	*0*	1·6	*5*
Textiles	2·8	4·0	3·8	*11*	1·4	*4*	·3	*0*	5·5	*15*
Miscellaneous[7] ...	9·9	9·5	6·3⌡	*0*	2·8	*0*	1·9	*0*	11·0	—
Total	24·7	32·9	27·6	*58*	11·0	*24*	3·8	*6*	42·4	*88*

Adding the last three columns, the total percentage of listed (or quoted) companies in the range £250,000 to £1,000,000 is 42·4% of all with under £1,000,000 of issued capital. Companies were sampled, however, below the £250,000 level down to £200,000. The table shows that companies with capital between £100,000 and £249,000 formed 32·9% of all below

---

[4] This number added to the 331 medium and very large companies to make 2,731 is conformable with the 3,025 total of quoted companies given by the National Institute (see above, Chap. 1) since the Institute's list included some 150 breweries, 125 iron, coal and steel companies and also Scottish companies not in these two sections. On the other hand, the *Year Book* included some English companies operating abroad, excluded by the Institute.

[5] Miscellaneous industries were excluded.

[6] Bracket indicates inclusion of a few companies with capital £200,000 to £249,000.

[7] See note [5], above.

£1,000,000 capital.   We may therefore add a number less than a third [8] of this percentage, say 9 or 10%, making a total of 52% of all the 2,400 companies with £200,000 to £1,000,000 issued capital.   This percentage together with about 100 brewery companies of similar small size gives 1,348 companies as the total with issued capital between £200,000 and £1,000,000.   Added to the 258 medium and the 109 very large companies (including breweries), the total of companies represented is thus 1,715, or in round numbers, 1,700.

The sampling of the smaller companies is linked to the type of industry. To secure enough companies to justify generalisation about single industries, sampling was confined to the seven main industries.   Companies in the smaller and more miscellaneous industries are not sampled.   For that and other reasons, we may discuss the industrial grouping at this point, though the " heading " occurs at the bottom of the basic table.

Setting forth the industrial incidences of large companies, the previous chapter has already defined the area of this survey in relation to the standard industrial classification, with its orders.   In addition to the breweries and distillery section, this area is based on the Stock Exchange official *Year Book's* " Industrial and Commercial Section."   This section includes all manufactures except iron, steel, shipbuilding, and oil production, each of which has a separate section in the Stock Exchange *Year Book*.   In addition to manufacturing the section includes building, distributive trades, entertainments and sports, catering and hotels and a few companies in " other transport and communications " and " other services," [9] but excludes land and property and shipping, which have sections to themselves.

Within the area covered by this survey subdivision has been by groups of industry.   To enable reliable conclusions to be reached, the groupings had to be wide enough to include a reasonably large number of companies of each of the three sizes that are distinguished.   Our chemicals, vehicles, [10] textile, paper and distributive trades groups are identical with the standard classification Orders IV (less oil refining), VII, X, XV, and XX, respectively.   The engineering group, however, includes all metal industries, except iron, steel and shipbuilding forming most of Order V; it includes,

---

[8] The number between £200,000 and £300,000 capital would be less than a third because the distribution is not symmetrical, but since there is tapering at both ends asymmetry is not great.

[9] So classified in the Institute's list, but here classified differently, *e.g.*, broadcast relay as engineering and Union International (storage etc.) as food.

[10] Our vehicles companies mostly made parts for or assembled motor-vehicles (including aeroplanes) and have, for short, been designated motors.

in short, the bulk of Orders VI, VIII and IX.   Our food group is not as wide as Order XII, it excludes tobacco (included in miscellaneous industries) and also breweries (which form a separate group), but it includes aerated waters.

The remaining Orders of industry are grouped in " Miscellaneous," which includes a few companies hard to assign to a precise industry. The industries most frequently represented within this group are building materials (eight companies of all sizes), tobacco and clothing (four companies each), but no one industry of this miscellaneous group reaches the minimum number of companies required for generalisation.

As a summing-up, the following table shows the number of companies in each size and each industry that were selected and listed.   For reasons given, however, not every company has information for all the headings of the basic table.   This applies not only to the large " partial information " group of the medium large companies, as already explained, but applies also to a few individual cases which will be duly noted in the tables occurring in the text.

NUMBER OF COMPANIES SELECTED FOR ANALYSIS IN EACH SIZE AND INDUSTRY GROUP					
Issued capital ?	*Very large* £3m. *and over*	*Medium large* £1m. *to short of* £3m.		*Smaller large* £200,000 *to short of* £1m.	*All sizes*	
INDUSTRIAL AND COMMERCIAL		*Total*	*(Full Information)*		*Total*	*(Full Information)*
Chemicals	9	9	(4)	4	22	(17)
Distributive Trades	14	18	(4)	26	58	(44)
Engineering	21	29	(11)	21	71	(53)
Food	12	9	(4)	9	30	(25)
Motor-vehicles	6	14	(7)	8	28	(21)
Paper	9	8	(3)	5	22	(17)
Textiles	12	17	(5)	15	44	(32)
Miscellaneous	15	25	(9)	0	40	(24)
Total	98	129	(47)	88	315	(233)
BREWERIES	11	12	(12)	12	35	(35)
Grand Total	109	141	(59)	100	350	(268)

§ 2. SIZE GROUPS AND YEARS CHOSEN

Since the selection and coverage has had to be different for each size of company and different characteristics appear to attach to different sizes, the companies were (Appendix A 1 and 2) divided into three sections according to the size of the company. Size, as already stated, is measured by issued capital in 1951. Both the criterion of size and the year chosen are, of course, open to criticism. An alternative criterion of size that has been suggested, and tried, is the market value of debentures and shares. But there are grave objections to this measure. Market valuation of shares varies sharply from year to year and even month to month, or day to day, so that size so measured at any one point of time would be most arbitrary. Moreover, as we shall show, market values largely reflect the rates of dividend actually paid and thus more or less expected in the immediate future. The higher the dividend the less, to that extent, the assets ploughed back, so that a size measure depending on dividend might show the very opposite of size measured by assets.[11]

It is, in fact, total assets or, to be more precise, net tangible assets, that is the main alternative to issued capital as a criterion of the size of a company. This is the main measure used in the publications of the National Institute of Economic and Social Research. The net tangible assets of all the companies in our list were calculated both for 1936 and 1951 and when describing and evaluating this measure we shall analyse the difference in the size allocation of companies which its use would entail, as against the use of issued capital.

Issued capital, for reasons given below, is more stable than assets from year to year and looms larger on the horizon of the investor than assets. Other things equal (such as the concentration of shareholding dealt with later), the larger the issued capital, particularly the ordinary shares, the more opportunity for investment. When investigating share prices and dividends paid on shares, it thus seemed relevant to measure size by marketable shares issued.

The year 1951 is that in which most of our measurement was made. Any one year that is chosen could of course be criticised from one or more points of view, but one year or other had to be chosen. The collection of data for our inquiry was completed by 1954 and the data could not be collected further back than 1936. For purposes of comparing events such as prices of shares in the first and last year of the period, years had

---

[11] See below, Chap. VII, § 5.

to be chosen far enough apart to measure true investment rather than speculation, and comparable in the main relevant respects. In September 1936 shares prices reached a peak above 1934 and 1935 prices, on the one hand, and 1937 and 1938 prices on the other. A similar peak within a five-year span occurred in 1951. And when in 1954 the " standard " year had finally to be decided upon, it already appeared that the peak of 1951 was more in the general line of future events than the downward slope of 1952 or the trough of share prices in 1953. The higher peak of July 1955 was in fact building up.

Once a given year, in this case 1951, is agreed upon as a standard point at which to take the fullest possible measurement of the greatest possible number of companies, it is difficult to depart from the rule by classifying companies according to their measurement in some other year, or years, however logical the departure might be, for some specific purpose or other. For instance, in tracing success between 1936 and 1951 and again in studying the distribution of dividend between 1948 and 1951 according to size of companies, it would have been logical to take the 1936 and 1948 measurements of size, respectively, as bases of comparison, thus cutting, however, across the allocation of companies according to the size divisions in the main table, based on 1951. It was felt that several size divisions would be confusing and a compromise between logic and simplicity has been effected by providing estimates, at the relevant points in the discussion, of how far the act of taking the end-year rather than the initial year as the standard has distorted the results, if at all.

Leaving the headings at the top of the table appearing for the very large companies in Appendix A 1, which give the name of the company and the years of survey, the side titles may now be explained in the order in which they appear.

§ 3. CAPITAL AND NET TANGIBLE ASSETS

Capital is divided into ordinary shares, preference shares and loan capital or debentures and the amounts involved are quoted from Moody's *Services' Memoranda.* Deferred shares are included in the ordinary, preferred in preference. Convertible preference shares were, in this period, rare and are included with preference shares.

The division into three sizes of company is based on the issued capital (excluding, of course, debentures) in 1951. Appendix A 1 and Tables V A and V B indicate by brackets where companies very large in 1951 were not so in 1936.[12] Most companies issue their shares in denominations of £1, but some in denominations of 5s. or other fractions of £1. For the sake of comparability, the basic tables (*e.g.*, Appendix A 1 for the very large companies) quote capital always in terms of £000,000.

Net tangible assets is the technical accounting term, sometimes known as net worth, which comprises the issued capital including debentures, already given, together with profit and loss balance and the reserves. In nearly all companies net tangible assets are greater than capital; but in a few, where capital is watered, a debit appears. Net tangible assets correspond on the asset side of the Balance Sheet, as illustrated in Appendix D, to (depreciated) fixed assets, and liquid assets, less current and deferred liabilities and provisions. The asset figures are quoted from Moody's *Services*, which occasionally include goodwill.

Companies, as already suggested, might have been grouped as to size according to their net tangible assets rather than their issued capital. Unlike issued capital, total assets are, however, directly affected year by year by the ploughing back of earnings to form additional assets in the shape of reserves. Net tangible assets during any fairly short period are less stable than the capital and depend immediately on annual profits and the dividend policy allocating the profit. In any case the use of net tangible assets in 1951 will be found to yield a size classification not very different from that based on issued capital, and in the Annex to this chapter a calculation will be made of the differences entailed. In spite of some startling reassignments of individual companies, it is shown that only a small proportion of companies change their size category.

§ 4. SHAREHOLDERS AND CONCENTRATION OF VOTING

The total of shareholders is given only approximately and was estimated for each company by inspection of the Bush House Register of Shareholders. Preference and ordinary shareholders do not add up to the total since many ordinary shareholders will also hold preference shares. Nor does the total vote always correspond to the total of preference and ordinary shares, or even to ordinary shares only. As illustrated in Chapter III most companies do not allow preference shareholders to vote unless their dividends are in arrear—in short, preference shareholders do not normally have *unconditional* rights to vote. And some companies distinguish among their ordinary shares various classes with different

---

[12] Where relevant, companies will be compared according to their size in 1936. See, *e.g.*, Tables III C, III D, IV E, IV G, V C, VII D. See also footnote, p. 53.

voting rights attached.   Some of these ordinary shares may have no
votes at all.

The " total vote " side-title of the basic tables (*e.g.*, Appendix A 1)
is the sum of the votes that can be exercised at a shareholders' meeting,
either in person or by proxy.[13]   If a company has fifty thousand ordinary
shares with ten votes, two million with one, and one million with no vote,
the total vote is given as 2,500,000.   The important fact is, however,
not the total vote but the concentration of votes in a few hands.   We
collected information on the shares and votes possessed by each of the
twenty largest voteholders.   Where for any very large company the proportion of votes in the hands of the largest twenty voteholders was over
30%, and certain other characteristics present, possibly important for
owners' control,[14] the details of these voteholders are given in Appendix B.
For the medium and smaller companies with the same characteristics, the
same details were prepared, but not published.   If concentration was less
than this, the names of the largest voteholders, most of them holding
only a very small proportion of the votes, are not likely to be significant,
for control and details are not given.   But for all companies the basic table
we prepared (*e.g.*, Appendix A 1) gives the percentage of votes held by the
single largest voteholder, and by the total of the twenty largest voteholders.

What are the reasons for picking on the proportion of the total votes
held by the twenty largest voters as an index of concentration of control ?

The sociological basis for the small number is twofold.   First, we must
think of a number of persons not too large to prevent some sort of personal contact and yet large enough to control among companies or corporations a sufficient proportion of votes to give a virtual majority.   The
number hit upon early (about 1937) in my own investigation into British
companies was the twenty largest shareholders, about a normal size for a
committee or board; and significantly enough the same number was picked
in America by the U.S. Temporary National Economic Committee (The
T.N.E.C.).

The bulk of the shareholders with middle-sized as well as small
holdings are usually of such a quantity and quality that they cannot and
do not form a coherent party.   Most of them do not vote and, if and when
they do, their votes are as likely to go one way as another—to be scattered

[13] How far these votes are actually exercised is discussed below.
[14] Specified in full, pp. 130 *et seq*.

indifferently.[15] In this situation the "resolute" person or a small coherent "resolute" group of persons determined on a certain policy or certain key appointments such as that of directors, could win, even with a concentration of a minority of voting shares as low as, say, 10%.

The mathematical basis for this statement is well illustrated by Professor L. S. Penrose [16]:

> In a committee of three people one member will obtain the decision of his choice—that is to say, he will be on the winning side in 75% of the votings, if the other two members vote in a random manner. In a committee of five, the chance that one member will obtain the decision he wishes will be 11/16. . . .
>
> If a committee or electorate consists of two sections, a "resolute" bloc and an "indifferent" random voting group, a small "resolute" group of people who always vote together can exercise a surprisingly powerful control over the whole committee. Thus, three resolute votes can control a committee of twenty-three to the same extent that one vote can control a committee of three. Furthermore, a bloc of twenty-three could control, again to the same extent, an electorate of over 1,000. . . . These blocs have about a 75% chance of carrying the decision in their respective electorates, but, by increasing the size of the resolute bloc, any specified degree of control can be obtained. Blocs three times as great as those mentioned would carry the decisions they desired in nearly 96% of the situations encountered.

Thus in a company or corporation with 1,000 voting shares (and only on the margin of "large") a resolute "bloc" with 20×3 votes or $6 \cdot 0\%$ could, with this 96% probability, carry the decisions they desired.

The important statistical fact which emerges from this discussion is the very high degree of control exercised by a comparatively small resolute group when the indifferent population is very numerous. But before "slickly" applying statistical formulae, a realistic research must be sure that the largest shareholders are fairly co-ordinated and "resolute" toward a common end. Normally the resolute group is the board of directors and their supporters who are likely to include some of the larger shareholders. The successful control of voting by a small minority depends, of course, on the indifference of the remainder of the electorate. A take-over bid offering all shareholders a price higher than the market price will soon change the indifference of the majority and endanger the normal control.

That the twenty largest voteholders is a sufficient number to identify was suggested by the rapid taper which was found to occur when the

---

[15] If there is any bias it will, thanks to the officially sent proxy forms, be in favour of the official policy or nominations.

[16] Elementary Statistics of Majority Voting, *Statistical Journal*, 1946, Part I, pp. 53–54.

percentages of votes from the largest to the twentieth largest were placed in order.   On an average of eighty-two " very large " English industrial companies in 1936 (including breweries and shipping) the largest vote-holder held $10 \cdot 3\%$ of all votes, the second $3 \cdot 0\%$, the third $1 \cdot 85\%$, the fourth $1 \cdot 3\%$, the fifth $1 \cdot 1\%$.   The tenth largest voteholder was down to $0 \cdot 60\%$ of the votes, the fifteenth $0 \cdot 30\%$ and the twentieth $0 \cdot 27\%$.   The average deviation from this sharp taper was calculated by means of quartiles [17] and the taper found to be of a fairly regular pattern.   It would obviously not have been very useful to continue analysis of share-holdings any further when no single holder could add more than $0 \cdot 27\%$ of total voting to any bloc of votes.

The grounds for supposing a probability of concentrated control are not, however, merely quantitative.   The reality of control will depend largely on the *type* of shareholder.   The basic tables classify shareholders into persons, companies, institutions and nominees.

A *personal* shareholder is any shareholder or joint shareholders quoted in the Register by name.   Persons bearing the same names and (unless the name is fairly common) presumably members of the same family may well form a cohesive group for purposes of control.

A *company* holding shares in the industrial or commercial company under analysis is usually another industrial or commercial company. If the holding amounts to over 50% of the votes the shareholding company would legally be a holding company, and the company under analysis a subsidiary company.   There are no such companies in our list, except subsidiaries of companies that are not English or are not industrial and commercial, since, to avoid double-counting, all those subsidiary companies have been omitted whose holding companies are already in the list.   But there are quite a number of companies holding less than 50% of the votes of other companies, yet with enough votes to appear among the twenty largest shareholders.

Institutions include insurance companies, investment trusts and banks. It is important to distinguish these institutions from persons, since institutions are more likely to take a careful interest in the control and management of the company through instructed or expert representatives.

The most frequent class of *nominees* are bank nominees.   A bank's apparent holding may be an aggregate of many small holdings whose beneficiaries are the clients of the bank.   The distinction between an

[17] See Statistical Glossary, App. C § 7, and Florence, *Logic of British and American Industry*, p. 190.

aggregate of many holdings of independent voters and a nominee holding cloaking a single beneficiary has obviously an important bearing upon control which will be discussed in the appropriate chapter. But it may be said, at the outset, that an aggregate of holdings is unlikely to affect control, and single-beneficiary nominee holdings, while introducing an element of uncertainty in the analysis of control, are not as frequent as often supposed.

§ 5. DIRECTORS

Considerable information was obtained on the directors of the companies surveyed and entered in the basic tables. It includes their total number, the percentage of ordinary shares the directors held altogether, the number of them (if any) among the largest twenty holders of voting shares, the number with no more than the minimum share qualification and the number holding directorships in (*i.e.*, interlocking with) other large non-financial companies. The number of directors was obtained from the Stock Exchange *Year Book*; the percentage of their ordinary shares (and the number appearing among the largest twenty shareholders) from the Bush House Register. The point of interest lies here not so much in the votes the directors possess (since directors exercise their power less in voting at shareholders' meetings than in the boardroom) as in their participation in the risk-bearing involved by their decisions as represented by ownership of ordinary shares, regardless of voting rights. Nevertheless if there is a controlling group including all or some of the twenty largest voters it is important to know how many directors may be among them.

In measuring the interlocking of directors, a limit had to be drawn. Obviously directorships in most very small companies, say a local brewery, would have little significance. Consequently we have limited our search to interlocking directorships held in common with directorships in companies of more than £2·5m. assets. Again, directorships of banks, insurance companies and trusts do not interlock industries and are often just a matter of personal prestige. Interlocking is thus confined to interlocking with other large (non-financial and commercial) companies. These limits are obeyed by the large companies listed (for 1953) by the National Institute of Economic and Social Research [18]; it is interlocking with companies in this list to which our basic table (Appendix A 1) refers.

Some of the more important information about directors is at present not obtainable from public sources. For instance, the question of how

[18] A classified list of large companies engaged in British industry. Further details are given below at p. 88.

far a Board consists of professional full-time managers can only be approached indirectly. Though the *total* " emoluments " and fees of the Board are now made public, the direct question how many of the Board have a full-time salary as managers is not divulged. Relying only upon the indirect circumstantial evidence one can say, perhaps, that on the whole, a professional Board is likely to be (1) small, (2) hold relatively few shares, and have few members among the largest shareholders, (3) have many members holding the minimum qualification, (4) have few directors interlocking with other large industrial companies.

§ 6. INVESTORS' SUCCESS 1936–51

Two forms of success were measured: investment success and accounting success. Each of them has two subdivisions: dividend gain and capital or asset gain; both were calculated as a percentage of success between 1936 and 1951 measured on the basis of 1936. The reasons for choosing the two years 1936 and 1951 have already been argued.

If we suppose that investment of funds took place in September 1936 and the investment was sold, *i.e.,* " realised " in September 1951, the capital gain of the investment is measured by the difference in the price at which the shares were bought and were sold, together with the sale price of any bonus shares accruing in the period. The dividend gain is the total of the dividends received on the original and on these bonus shares during the period. The differences in price (*i.e.,* the " capital " gains) are kept distinct from the dividend gains because dividends were taxed in 1936–51, the capital gains were not. The burden of the tax on the dividend varied, under the principle of progressive taxation and surtax, with the total income of the recipient, but at a rough estimate a rate of tax of ten shillings in the £ can be put forward [19] as a general average during the period for the composite of shareholders with various incomes. Though capital gains are thus more valuable than gross dividend gains, it must be borne in mind that dividends are paid throughout any period, while the capital gains, under the circumstances we have assumed, all accrue at the end of the period and are thus subject to discount. Estimates of the correct discount, as of the tax liability of the " average " investor, are uncertain enough to strengthen the case for the separate statement of dividend gain and capital gain. But it must be realised that the investor does look to both gains for his remuneration

---

[19] Florence, " Some Statistical Tests of Stock Exchange Folk-Lore," *Three Banks Review,* March 1958, p. 15.

and therefore a total gain must also be stated. The simplest plan is neither to subtract any assumed average tax liability from the dividend gain nor any discount from the capital gain, and to give the total gain as gross. If he desires so to do, the reader can, from the separate statements of the dividend and the capital gains in Chapter VII, work out a *net* total gain by adding dividend *after* tax, and *discounted* capital gain, according to his own estimate of tax liability and proper rates of discount. In the basic table, therefore, *three* figures were entered under the heading " financial success " and sub-heading " investors' " : the dividend gain, the capital gain and the total gain.

We may vary our original supposition and suppose now that the investment is not necessarily bought in 1936 or sold in 1951. Success can then be measured by the dividend accruing over the period as before, plus the change in the accounting or book value of the assets " behind " the given shares between 1936 and 1951. This is the meaning of the three measures appearing in Appendix A, under " accounting " success corresponding to the dividend, capital and total gain under " investment " success. The two sets of three measures of financial success differ considerably as may readily be understood. The *lower* the proportion of a given profit paid out in dividend over the period and the more ploughed back to assets, the *higher* will become the accounting " book " value of the assets behind each original share. But it by no means follows that the price of the shares will rise accordingly. The price, as will appear later, depends mainly on the (discounted) expectation of future dividends. If the company is thought likely to continue its policy for a long time of ploughing back to reserves much of the profit, the price may not rise in proportion to the plough-back. The asset value of the share will rise, but not to the same extent its price on the market.

Even the two percentage dividend gains differ because the percentage of dividend gain is, for the measure of investment success, based on the funds actually spent by the investor in 1936 when buying the share; whereas, for the accounting gain, it is based on the asset value of the share in 1936. The dividends paid in the course of the period 1936 to 1951 and forming the numerator of the two percentages are the same, but their denominators are different.

The accounting gains are thus far from the same as the total investment (realisation) gains; it is because of their independence that both sets of percentage gains are given in the basic tables.

The accounting gain is a measure at least partially independent, also, of the difference in the figures for net tangible assets, given for the very large companies in the fourth row of Appendix A, for 1936 and for 1951. One reason (explained in Chapter VII § 5) why the accounting gain per share is not the same as the difference is that (unlike bonus shares accruing free to existing shareholders), the shares floated on the market during the period would *add* to the total assets of the company during the period 1936 to 1951 and not just cancel reserves.

Another reason why the difference in assets for 1936 and for 1951 is not the same as the value of the accounting (capital) gain 1936–51 is the consolidation of Accounts which occurred for nearly all companies in the course of 1936–51, and usually about 1948, in consequence of the Companies Act of that year. No correction was made in the figures for net tangible assets in 1936 and 1951 given in company balance-sheets. But an attempt was made to allow for the break in continuity when calculating the percentages of asset gain for the basic table. Briefly stated, the change in assets in the years before and in the years after the year of consolidation were calculated separately, and the year of consolidation " averaged." In detail, the two series of changes were totalled and an average struck for the fourteen years involved. This average, *i.e.*, a fourteenth of the total for the two series of years, was " imputed " to the year of consolidation.

§ 7. THE DISTRIBUTION RATIO

The ratio in which equity profits (*i.e.*, the earnings for ordinary dividend) are distributed to shareholders proves an important measure for a number of reasons.

(1) The ratio separates the portion of equity profits distributed in dividend and the portion ploughed back to reserves. This ploughback, as shown in Table I G, is at present (and must have been for some time) the chief source of funds for industrial investment.

(2) The ratio affects the position of the shareholder and for most companies accounts for his investment success (even over periods of fifteen years) as much, perhaps, as does the total profit of a company. It is usual to say that the price of shares, and in consequence capital gains, depends on expected profit. It would be truer to say that they depend on expected dividends and that dividends are expected on the basis of the existing dividend distribution no less than on the prospect of profit.

(3) The ratio varied radically during the period of the First World War and again during that of the Second World War and its aftermath.

The (Colwyn) Committee on National Debt and Taxation paid considerable attention to company savings. In the report (Cmd. 2800, para. 48) published in 1927 the Committee estimated the ratio of " net reserves " (*i.e.*, profit reserved) to net (total) profit (both after deduction of income tax) to have been: in 1912 33%, 1922 47%, 1923 46%, equivalent to 67%, 53% and 54% in terms of our conversely calculated distribution ratio. The Committee noted that between 1912 and 1922 reserves had managed to keep pace with the rise in prices though profits, and *a fortiori* dividends as a whole, had not.[20]

This pattern of a rise in company savings during the period of the First World War was repeated during the period of the Second World War when, again, a considerable price-inflation occurred.

In this period and its aftermath there was a fairly general drop in the ratio of dividends to profit not only in Britain, where it is often attributed to the official urging of dividend limitation, but also in America. And the considerably lower ratios touched about 1947 have been largely maintained, at least in Britain. Considering large industrial and commercial companies in aggregate, they seem to have changed policy from a fifty-five to forty-five relation of ordinary dividends to reserves ploughed back before the war, towards a reverse relation of about forty to sixty—that is only about 40% of total earnings for dividend is now in fact distributed in dividend. For all companies, large and small, operating in the United Kingdom official returns[21] make the contrast still wider. For the year 1938 the distribution ratio was 56%, for the nine consecutive years 1948 to 1956 the percentages were $30 \cdot 3$, $28 \cdot 7$, $25 \cdot 2$, $26 \cdot 5$, $30 \cdot 1$, $29 \cdot 8$, $29 \cdot 7$, $29 \cdot 0$, $31 \cdot 5$.

Clearly, to judge from past history and present trends, distribution ratios are an important fact to measure for every company on our list.

The form in which the facts are presented is that normally adopted, *e.g.*, by Moody's *Services*, namely after company provision for taxation the annual ratio of ordinary (gross) dividends to earnings for ordinary. The ratios are averaged for the four years 1948–51 — years determined

---

[20] The Committee also compared company savings, or plough-back, with new issues and quotes £194m. as the value (including some miscellaneous items) of profits not distributed by companies and private traders but invested in their own business, as against £89m. of new issues for investment in the United Kingdom.

[21] *National Income and Expenditure*, 1957, Table 26. Dividends on ordinary shares are divided by the total of these dividends and of undistributed income after taxation.

largely by circumstances. Before 1948 there was no legal requirement to consolidate the balance sheets of holding company and subsidiaries[22] and the last year we surveyed was 1951. Hence averaging of the four years between 1948 and 1951 gave the broadest basis that was possible. Occasionally, as duly noted (*e.g.,* in Appendix A 1), consolidation did not occur till 1949 and three years only could be averaged, but no distribution ratio that was used averages less than three years. There is nothing sacrosanct, of course, about the dates 1948–51, and it is to be hoped that subsequent writers will investigate dividend policy in other years.

The distribution ratio denoting the ratio of dividend to net earnings for ordinary dividend is the reciprocal of the stock market's expression " times covered." Thus if an ordinary dividend is said to be three times covered it means that the earnings left after payment of interest on debentures and preference dividend were three times the amount distributed in dividend. For the layman it is probably simpler to express the dividend distributed as a percentage ratio of earnings for ordinary dividend—in this case the distribution ratio is $33 \cdot 3\%$.

---

[22] For this reason caution must always be exercised in comparing the stated net tangible assets of companies in 1936 and 1951, and in using 1936 assets as a measure of size.

ANNEX TO CHAPTER II

THE EFFECT OF ALTERNATIVE CRITERIA OF
SIZE OF COMPANY

SINCE some significant differences will be found in the structure and policy of very large, medium large and smaller large companies it is important to be sure of the basis for classifying companies into these three sizes. As an alternative to issued capital adopted in dividing up our companies, net tangible assets has been suggested. A reasonable threefold classification by net tangible assets would be to count very large companies as those of £6m. of assets, or more[23]; medium large as those of £2m. up to (but not including) £6m. assets; smaller large as those of less than £2m. of assets. It will then be found that there is no overlap at all between the *very* large and the *smaller* large companies, as measured by the two criteria of issued capital and net tangible assets.

A certain interchange occurs between very large and medium large, medium large and smaller large companies. This interchange is shown most simply by the following table. The last column is arrived at by subtracting from the first column the upgraded and downgraded companies in the same row, but adding the companies upgraded from a lower row or downgraded from an upper row. Thus the total of 132 companies classified by the assets test as medium large is arrived at by subtracting from the 141 companies that were medium by the capital test thirteen and twenty-two, and adding sixteen and ten.

In terms of percentages of the original totals, shown in the table by bracketed figures, the displacement is relatively small. Two hundred and eighty-nine companies stayed in the same size-class, sixty-one, or $17\frac{1}{2}\%$ of the total, changed.

Reviewing individual companies, the basic table shows many wide differences of rank according to whether net tangible assets or nominal capital is used as a test of size. Among the very large companies classed in Appendix A 1 by issued capital, Lebus (Harris), for instance, had in 1951 net tangible assets of £3·0m., whereas among the companies classed

---

[23] The £10m. of assets used in Chap. 1, § 4 and table as roughly equivalent to our very large companies with £3m. of issued capital referred not to 1951 but 1953–54.

54

Companies sized by issued capital 1951 (*including breweries*)	If sized by net tangible assets 1951 (*Very large £6m. or over; medium large £2–5·9m.; smaller under £2m.*)			
	Down-graded one size	*Up-graded one size*	*Remaining in same size-class*	*Total (as a result of re-grading by asset size)*
Very large over £3m. 109	16 (15%)	—	93	115
Medium large £1–3m. 141	13 (9%)	22 (16%)	106	132
Smaller large £⅕ to £1m. 100	—	10 (10%)	90	103
Totals: 350	61 (17½%)		289	350

by issued capital as medium large in the table, Chloride Electrical Storage and Brooke Bond had in 1951 assets as large as £11·9m. and £11·7m.

These extreme examples of divergence would involve a difference in the size-*class* of the company according to the criterion used. But most of the divergences in relative size of an individual company due to sizing by issued capital and by assets respectively, did not (since the size-classes were drawn broadly) involve any difference in assignment to a class of size. The interchange in size-class, as already seen, involved in total only about one-sixth of the companies and the change never goes beyond the neighbouring class. The threefold size classification adopted for the basic tables therefore is far from irrational.

CHAPTER III

THE CONCENTRATION OF OWNERSHIP AND VOTES

§ 1. THE CAPITAL-GEARING

THE information in the " basic " tables (Appendix A 1 gives the table for
the very large companies) begins with the Capital Structure; that is,
with the amounts of the debentures, and of the preference and ordinary
shares making up the loan and share capital of the company, and also
with its net tangible assets. This information has a bearing on two
important considerations. One of them, risk, will be considered in
relation to success, the subject of Chapter VII. The other consideration, the concentration of control, will form the subject itself of Chapter V.

Risk is the more familiar preoccupation of economists. Debentures
holders have a legally enforceable right to their stipulated rate of interest;
preference stock a conventional right to the stipulated rate of dividend.
Hence if the debentures and the preference stock are high relatively to the
ordinary shares much of the profit must be paid out to the debenture and
preference holders before anything can be paid in dividend to the holders
of ordinary stock. A company with large priorities of this sort to be paid
out of profit is said to be highly " geared " and the holders of ordinary
stock in such companies run greater risks of non-payment or a low payment of dividend. On the other hand, interest, and rates of dividend on
preference stock, are normally lower than dividends on ordinary stock,
so that capital raised by debentures and preference is cheaper, and when
the profit is adequate more of it is available for the ordinary shareholder
than if all capital were in the form of ordinary shares.

Now the gearing of the different companies on our list varies considerably. We are concerned here, at the outset, with the capital structure
and the relation of ownership of the different categories of share with
control, so that we need take account only of the nominal, not the market,
value of shares. The market values of shares on any particular day do
not, in fact, form part of our basic reference tables. Market values have
been used in Chapter VII, however, to measure the success of companies
and an inquiry based on market value " gearing " ratios is referred to
in the same chapter.

56

The simplest measure of the capital-gearing, used here, is to divide the nominal value of the total loan and share capital (ordinary shares, preference shares and debentures) by the ordinary shares.   An alternative measure used by the Institute of Economic and Social Research is the proportion going into fixed interest and dividend.   This measure will fluctuate with income, and is not like ours directly apparent from the capital structure.   Thus for the Amalgamated Metal Corporation (the second very large company of Appendix A) our nominal gearing ratio in 1936 (and 1951) is seen to be $5 \cdot 3 / 4 \cdot 4 = 1 \cdot 2$.   The expediency of expressing the gearing by this particular ratio is that the higher the gearing the higher the ratio, and that if there is no gearing the ratio will be unity.

TABLE III A

NUMBERS OF COMPANIES OF DIFFERENT SIZE IN 1951 WITH VARIOUS (NOMINAL) GEARING RATIOS

*Industrial and Commercial and Brewery Companies compared**

	Total no. of Co. 1936 & 1951 and % distribution	GEARING RATIOS = (Nominal)				Ord.+Pref.+Debentures / Ord. Shares			
		1936				1951			
		1·0	1·1– 1·9†	2·0– 2·9	3·0+	1·0	1·1– 1·9†	2·0– 2·9	3·0+
Industrial and commercial									
Very large Co. ..	92*	0	46	24	22	0	50	19	23
	100%	0	50%	26%	24%	0	54%	21%	25%
Medium large Co.	125*	17	56	33	19	11	69	27	18
	100%	13%	47%	25%	15%	8%	56%	22%	14%
Smaller large Co.	88	13	40	26	9	13	56	14	5
	100%	15%	45%	30%	10%	15%	63%	16%	6%
All sizes	305*	30	142	83	50	24	175	60	46
	100%	10%	47%	27%	16%	8%	57%	20%	15%
Brewing									
Very large Co. ..	10*	0	3	2	5	0	6	1	4
Medium large Co.	12	0	4	5	3	0	4	5	3
Smaller large Co.	12	1	1	6	4	1	1	5	5
All sizes	34	2	8	13	12	1	11	11	12
	100%	6%	23%	37%	34%	3%	31%	31%	35%

* Excludes companies not formed in 1936.
† Actually, none less than 1.2.

Table III A gives in broad outline the distribution of nominal gearing ratios of the capital for the different sizes of large companies both in 1936 and 1951. Four conclusions can be drawn:

(1) There is a wide variation in the gearing ratios of companies all the way from 1·0, when only ordinary shares have been issued, to 3·0 and over.

(2) The majority of companies, however, have a moderate gearing ratio between 1·2 and 1·9.[1]

(3) The very large companies have on average higher gearing than the medium and the medium a higher gearing than the smaller large companies. All the very large companies have, for both years, some debentures or preference stock and thus a gearing ratio of more than unity and about a quarter of them have a ratio of three or more. Among the smaller large companies, again for both years, 15% had a gearing ratio of unity (*i.e.*, only ordinary shares) and less than 10% a gearing ratio of three or more.

(4) There is not much change between 1936 and 1951 except that fewer of the companies, especially of the smaller size, had in 1951, as against 1936, gearing ratios of 2·0 or more—106 as against 133. High gearing, in short, became less frequent.

Comparing industries it was found that a much greater proportion of companies in the distributive trades were highly geared than among the industrial and commercial companies generally.[2] With two-thirds bearing a ratio of 2·0 or more, against one-third for all industrial and commercial companies, brewing companies were more highly geared even than companies in the distributive trades. This wide difference is true of 1936 as well as 1951 and is amply confirmed by the official Stock Exchange report, as follows:

Loan and Share Capital at end of 1951	(1) *Loan capital*	(2) *Pref- erence shares*	(3) *Ordinary shares*	*Gearing ratio* cols. 1+2+3 / col. 3
Breweries and distilleries	93·9	82·9	113·1	2·56
Commercial, industrial, etc.	232·2	756·8	1061·1	1·92

[1] No examples appear of 1·1.
[2] Among the 14 very large distributive trade companies—9 in 1936 and 12 in 1951—a proportion of 65% in 1936 and 85% in 1951 had gearing ratios of 2 or more as against 50% and 46% for all very large industrial and commercial companies.

A comment on the relatively high gearing of brewery companies by Professor S. R. Dennison [3] throws light on the logic behind the capital structure—a logic derived from the peculiar market and technological and sociological characteristics of the industry:

> There are various reasons for the emphasis on debentures in the brewing industry; they have certain advantages which can offset the disadvantages of having to meet fixed-interest charges. Debenture interest is regarded as a charge against profits liable to profits tax. This advantage is a matter of some importance in brewing in view of the lack of depreciation allowances on licensed properties. Moreover, the industry is one in which family interests are still important, even in the biggest companies, and there may be unwillingness to reduce the extent of control. Although the industry has been declining, profits are not subject to very large fluctuations, so that there is not the same reluctance to accept fixed-interest charges that there is in an industry with less steady rate.
>
> Moreover, the fixed assets are usually highly suitable as security, in a way in which those of many industries are not, so that there is little difficulty in arranging an issue.

Closely connected with the capital structure are the reserves of a company. Reserves were not added to the information in the basic tables since companies often split up reserves into a number of categories somewhat arbitrarily under various provisions. The balance of the profit and loss account would also have to be added for a complete picture. Instead, to represent the entire capital over which control is exercised we give the net tangible assets, which is the conventional measure of the extent of a company's property.[4]

This brings our discussion to the second main purpose for considering capital structure—the degree of concentration of the control over a company's property.

§ 2. THE VOTE-GEARING

The risk-structure of the loan and share capital is built to suit all tastes: debentures for those who want to be assured of a fixed income, preference for those who are prepared to take a slight risk with the prospect of a rather higher income on average, ordinary shares for those ready to take higher risks with a still higher average income to be expected.[5] But parallel to this risk-structure there runs a vote-structure. Capitalism's

---

[3] Tew and Henderson, *Studies in Company Finance*, the National Institute of Economic and Social Research, Cambridge University Press, 1959, p. 151.

[4] The relation of assets to ordinary share value is discussed in Chap. VII, § 5. See also App. D.

[5] The relation of risk to average income during the period 1936–51 is taken up in Chap. VII.

golden rule has been proclaimed that " where the risk lies there the control lies also." [6] This, as we shall see in Chapters IV and V, is not true when the amount of control is considered now exercised by managers and directors without substantial holding of ordinary shares. But while nearer the truth it is not quite true even as between different categories of shareholders. Though for the majority of companies there appears to be a normal pattern in which capital-gearing and what we may call *vote-gearing* is roughly the same, many companies show deviations.

Analysis of concentration of control must begin by considering which among the categories of share capital has what voting rights. The majority of companies give a vote to each ordinary share, and only allow holders of preference shares to vote under specified conditions, particularly when their stipulated dividend is in arrear. This pattern in which only ordinary shares have an unconditional vote will be described as normal. A fairly large minority of companies are, however, not normal. If the normal situation, where only ordinary shares have votes and each ordinary share has only one vote is classified as case A, the main deviations may conveniently be classed as AA, B, C and D, extending from *very* Aristocratic to Democratic. AA is less broad-bottomed in the dispersion of voting than A; B, C and D, more so.   The patterns may be listed, least dispersed or " democratic " first:

AA   Ordinary shares are subdivided into categories each with different voting rights, or no votes at all.

A   (" Normal "). Only ordinary shares carry unconditional votes.
    (1) Ordinary and preference shares issued, but holders of preference shares vote only when their stipulated dividend is in arrear.
    (2) Only ordinary shares issued.

B   *Some* preference shares have unconditional votes as well as all ordinary shares.
Each such preference share may carry a vote
    (1) of less value than the ordinary share,
    (2) of equal value.

C & D *All* preference shares have unconditional vote as well as the ordinary shares.
Preference may (C) have less than an equal vote, (D) have an equal vote.

[6] Robertson, *Control of Industry*, Cambridge University Press, p. 89.

TABLE III B

COMPANIES CLASSIFIED BY VOTING RIGHTS PATTERN, 1951

Ordinary and Preference Shares ; unconditional voting

(Total No.)	Voting of ord. shares differentiated	Preference issued, but only ord. Shares vote	All shares ordinary (gearing = 1·0)	Some pref. vote		All pref. Vote	
				Unequally with ord.	Equally with ord.	Unequally with ord.	Equally with ord.
	AA	A1	A2	B1	B2	C	D
Very large Co. (98)	12	62	0	6	2	9	7
Percent. distribution	12%	63%	0%	8%		17%	
Medium large Co. (129)	14	67	13	2	4	24	7
Percent. distribution	10%	52%	10%	4%		24%	
Smaller large Co. (88)	2	36	12	0	1	19	18
Percent. distribution	2%	41%	14%	1%		42%	
All sizes (315) ..	23	164	25	8	7	52	32

Table III B gives the distribution of companies according to this classification of voting rights. In the degree of dispersion or concentration of the voting among the owners of the share capital, some inclusive " patterns " may quite justifiably be said (since it is a question of votes), to be democratic; others, exclusive, to be aristocratic. Democratic patterns are those where all owners of the share capital vote equally, either because only ordinary shares have been issued or because *all* preference and ordinary shares vote equally—in short, patterns A (2) and D. At the other end of the scale aristocratic patterns are those where part of the capital is in preference shares but these have no vote, or where categories of ordinary shares have been issued with differing voting rights, in short, patterns A (1) and AA. Patterns B (1) and (2) and C fall in the middle of the demo-aristocratic spectrum.

Moving (right to left!) from the democratic D to the aristocratic A and super-aristocratic AA, Table III B allows at least five statements.

1. All the *very large* companies have categories of share-capital besides the ordinary shares. There is no simple A (2) pattern among them.

In most of the characteristics that we shall examine the very large companies show much more variety than the smaller sizes of company. This, however, is not true of their voting pattern.

Nearly two-thirds (63%) of the very large companies follow one pattern, the " A (1)." There are preference shares, but only the ordinary shares have an unconditional vote.

2. Among many of the medium large and still more among the smaller companies, *all* preference shareholders have voting power. In 24% (31 out of 129) of the medium and 42% (37 out of 87) of the smaller large companies they vote unconditionally (though usually not equally) with the ordinary shares. Only 17% (16 out of 98) of the very large companies allow voting by all preference shares.

3. Well over half of all the companies of all sizes issuing preference shares (164 out of 290) give unconditional voting rights only to ordinary shareholders and not to their preference shareholders. This " A (1) " group, excluding the preference shareholders from voting, is relatively more frequent the larger the company.

4. On the other hand, only a very small minority of companies split up ordinary shares into several categories with differential voting rights. This " AA " group hardly exists among the smaller large companies.

5. A substantial number of the smaller and medium large companies allow unconditional voting to their preference shareholders, forming a higher proportion than among the very large companies. The proportion of companies allowing some or all preference shares to vote (columns B (1)+B (2)+C+D) is 25% of the very large, 28% of the medium and 43% of the smaller large; the proportion allowing *all* preference shares to vote (columns C+D only) is, as stated, 17%, 24% and 42% for each size. Thus *the smaller the company the more preference shares appear to vote*.

All five of these findings thus lead toward the conclusion that the smaller the company the more democratic its pattern of voting. And if we join these findings on the voting pattern (*i.e.*, the relative votes per share-unit) to the findings on the capital-gearing (*i.e.*, the relative number of share-units) we can obtain a " vote-gearing " ratio which can measure fairly exactly the greater concentration in power through capital structure and voting rights within the *very large* companies. To illustrate from Tables III A and B. The gearing of the very large companies has a median average of about 1·9 and of the smaller large companies, 1·6. Two-thirds of the very large companies have no unconditional preference vote and the *vote*-gearing here is thus equal to the capital-gearing of 1·9.

Almost half the smaller large companies, however, give votes to the preference shares (though not all in equal measure with the ordinary shares).
It is thus probable that the preference shares have a total of about half
the votes of the ordinary shares and, of course, the debentures have none.
We can estimate that for the smaller large companies the vote-gearing
corresponding to the share gearing of

$$\frac{\text{Ord.}+\text{Pref.}+\text{Deb.}}{\text{Ord.}} \left\{ = \frac{1\cdot6}{1} \right\}, \text{ is } \frac{1+\frac{1}{2}(0\cdot6)+0}{1} = 1\cdot3$$

So far we have established that there is a normal pattern for the three
sizes of large company, both in respect of capital-gearing and voting rights
and, therefore, vote-gearing. Though some medium and smaller companies have no debentures or preference shares, and some very large
companies have particularly high gearing ratios, the majority of companies of all sizes agree in having capital-gearing ratios between $1\cdot2$ and
$1\cdot9$, both in 1936 and 1951. In vote-gearing also, though more of the
smaller and medium large companies than the very large give votes to
preference shares the majority of companies of all sizes follow a specific
pattern—only the ordinary shares voting unconditionally. We may
speak, therefore, of a norm of *vote*-gearing of from $1\cdot2$ to $1\cdot9$, the votes
of the ordinary shares normally controlling the nominal capital up to
almost twice their own nominal value. The deviations from this norm
may well be significant, however.

The deviations may be in the same direction, both toward narrower
concentration of risk and control, *i.e.*, high gearing and aristocratic
voting, or both toward less concentration; or they may be in opposite
directions.

When companies combine an abnormally high gearing ratio and an
abnormally aristocratic voting pattern, power is obviously highly concentrated by means of the capital structure. Thus if debentures, preference
and ordinary shares were each equal in nominal value (giving a gearing
ratio of 3) and preference shares had no votes, any more than, of course,
the debentures, the votes of the ordinary shares would control a capital
of three times their nominal value. On the other hand when gearing,
though high, is combined with a democratic voting pattern, then concentration may be said to be " tempered " as far as control is concerned.
If, in the example just given, the preference shares vote equally with the
ordinary shares, then the ordinary total vote would control capital as 2 to 3

and the gearing " tempered " to result in wider dispersal of control. There appears to be no strong tendency to temper high gearing, however. Of the twenty-three abnormally high-geared very large companies with a 1951 gearing ratio of 3 or over in fact only nine [7] were at all tempered. Of the eighteen similarly highly geared medium and five smaller large companies in 1951 (counting down Table III A last column), only six were " tempered " by any democratic voting pattern (B or C). This is logical enough, since in highly geared capital structures due to much preference stock, the preference shareholders though bearing little risk might, if given equal voting rights, outvote the ordinary shareholders. Whatever the reason, there was certainly no company where the number of preference exceeded the ordinary shares and the preference had, on pattern D, democratic equal voting rights. In general, it can be said that the gearing of the votes tends to follow the pattern of the capital-gearing, and is almost as concentrated.

In consequence of the various gearing ratios and various voting rights of the different categories of capital, the figures for the *total votes* recorded in the basic tables (*e.g.*, Appendix A I) often differ from the figures for the share capital or any item of it. Moreover, shares are quoted in the basic tables in £ values, votes by units. In very many companies shares are, for instance, quoted in 5s. units. In the majority of companies, votes will be found (where pattern A is followed) either to be equal to the ordinary shares or to be a multiple of the ordinary shares (*e.g.*, of 5s. shares, four times); or else (where pattern B (2) is followed) to be equal to, or a multiple of ordinary *and preference* shares. If these normal patterns of voting are not followed, however, the figure in the basic tables for total votes (*e.g.*, in Appendix A I) cannot be derived by eye from the figures for the ordinary or ordinary and preference shares.

§ 3. Concentration in the Ownership of Voting Shares

We now turn from companies' capital structure, that is, the quantitative relations between debentures, preference and ordinary shares with or without full votes, exclusively to the holders of the voting shares. One of our main concerns is the degree of control exercised by shareholders through their voting power and, particularly, as we shall see, through the concentration of this power in a few hands. It is the holding of votes that is here of interest, rather than the number of ordinary shares held. In

---

[7] Beecham, International Tea, Lever, Sears, Lewis Investment, Patons & Baldwins, Rowntree, U. Dairies, Winterbottom Book Cloth.

the majority of companies it has been shown that ownership of ordinary shares is equivalent to ownership of votes and we may speak of share concentration as equivalent to vote-concentration.[8] But to cover all cases, vote-concentration is the more exact expression.

For reasons explained in Chapter II, a special investigation was necessary of all the shareholders registered to find the largest share- or rather vote-holders. Such an investigation, even when confined to dis-covering only the *twenty* largest share- or vote-holders, takes considerable time and it was not possible to analyse all the companies in 1936 and 1951. Priority was given to the larger companies and the later date. Accord-ingly, as already explained, out of all the companies listed in the basic tables, those analysed for the ownership of the largest voting-power were:

1. All the very large industrial and commercial, and brewing com-panies (with £3m. or more) in 1951 and 1936—a total of ninety-eight and eleven respectively.
2. All the listed smaller large " industrial and commercial " and brewing companies in 1951, a total of eighty-eight and twelve respectively.
3. A sample (just less than two in five) of the medium large industrial and commercial companies, forty-seven out of 129 listed;[9] and all the twelve listed medium large brewing companies.

The purpose of the analysis of voting power was to find the degree of its concentration in a few hands. For reasons set forth in Chapter II and mainly concerned with the possibility of close personal contact " few " is interpreted as twenty.   In the basic table particulars were given, for every one of these companies, of the percentage of the total vote held by the largest single and by the largest twenty vote owners. These particulars enable companies to be graded along a fairly simple scale of vote-concentration as follows:

Grade   I. Companies where the single largest voteholder owns more than 50% of the votes.

Grade   II. Companies where the single largest voteholder owns 20 to 50% of the votes.

Grade III. Companies, apart from those assigned to Grades I and II, where the twenty largest voteholders own more than 50% of the votes.

---

[8] *i.e.*, in patterns (see above p. 60) A (1) and (2).
[9] In stratification by industries the sample represented all the medium large industrial and commercial companies, rather than the listed 129.

Grade IV. Companies, apart from those in Grade II, where the twenty
largest voteholders own 30 to 50% of the votes.

Grade V. Companies, apart from those in Grade II, where the twenty
largest voteholders own 20 to 30% of the votes.

Grade VI. Companies where the twenty largest voteholders own
10 to 20% of the votes.

Grade VII. Companies where the twenty largest voteholders own less
than 10% of the votes.

Looking back to the previous section, however, it may well be asked
whether any particular relation subsists between the abnormal concentration of power over a company's property through gearing and differential
voting rights (in short, vote-gearing) on the one hand and, on the other,
through *vote-concentration* among those who have the votes. Two
opposite possibilities are that vote-concentration among voters com-
pensates, or that it reinforces vote-gearing. If the two forms of
power-concentration tended to compensate, the companies of more vote-
concentrated grades (*i.e.*, I to IV) would relatively frequently be lower
vote-geared; if the two forms of power reinforce one another, the companies of vote-concentrated grades would tend also to be high vote-geared.
On the whole (though not to any very marked extent) it is this latter
possibility of the mutual reinforcement of vote-gearing and vote-concentration that appears from certain calculations to prevail at least among
the very large companies and more so in 1951 than in 1936.[10]

The salient characteristic disclosed by the facts of vote-concentration
among voters is the extreme inequality of holdings and votes in the
typical large company. The (median) average of the number of shareholders (given in the fifth line of Appendix A) was about 10,000 for the
fifty-three very large companies where it was available in 1936 as well as
1951, but only forty of these companies were very large in 1936 as well as
1951, and their average was 14,250. We may take as representative in
round figures, 12,000. Twenty voteholders thus formed about one-sixth
of 1% of all shareholders, and yet they held on average (again, in round

---

[10] For readers interested in the details, the calculations from the facts are as follows:
Among *all* the very large industrial and commercial companies the ratio in the top-
concentrated grades I to IV has been found (see Table III C) to be 0·54 in 1936, 0·38 in
1951. Among the high-geared, very large companies only (gearing 3 or over and voting
equally) the ratio of top vote-concentrated grades to all grades was in each year, higher;
in 1936, 0·63 and in 1951, 0·52. In short, the two forms of power-concentration by
gearing and differentiated voting rights and by concentration of votes, tend to reinforce
one another. Among the medium and smaller large companies in 1951 there appears
little bias either toward reinforcement or compensation.

figures) about 30% of the votes.   This represents far greater inequality than that of *incomes* for the country as a whole, even before taxation, and is similar to the extreme type of inequality shown by the national distribution of *wealth*.[11]   The similarity of the distribution of capital ownership within a company and of capital ownership within a whole country may or may not be a coincidence.[12]

This extreme inequality in the vote-distribution of large companies extends as I have pointed out [13] right up into the largest holdings of voting shares.   There is an extreme " taper " even among the largest twenty voteholders: the very largest has twenty-five to fifty times the vote of the twentieth largest.   To put this inequality among the largest twenty voteholders in another way it appears that the single largest (*i.e.*, 5% of them) held on average just over 40% of these total votes.   Referring to the same estimates of national income distribution as before,[14] the top 5% of income-units received, even before taxation, not 40%, but only 29% of total income in 1938.

The different types of voteholder will be discussed later, in Chapter V. But it may be observed here that if the largest shareholder holds 50% of votes and is another (a " parent ") *company*, Grade I of concentration defines the company under consideration, legally, as a subsidiary.   As set forth in Chapter II, our survey only excludes a subsidiary company if all (or virtually all) its shares are owned by the parent and there is therefore no market in its shares, or (to avoid duplication) if the parent company, owning less than 100% of shares down to 50%, is also in our list.

The list thus contains several subsidiaries of foreign parent companies, not in that list.   If the largest voteholder holding 50% of the votes is a *person*, thus combining ownership and control, he is in the position of the owner-manager " entrepreneur " who is so constantly referred to by economists.   Companies assigned to Grade II, though not controlled absolutely by one shareholder, are virtually so owned, for reasons given in Chapter II.   One " resolute " owner even with only 20% of the votes will probably carry his point if the other owners all have relatively few

---

11 See footnote 9, Chap. I, § 2, p. 8.

12 Extreme inequality of capital within large companies is true of other countries, too. For a recent study in Australia, see E. L. Wheelwright *Ownership and Control of Australian Companies* 1957, Chap. 3 and Summary, p. 1.

13 See above, Chap. II, § 4, and Florence, *Logic of British and American Industry*, frontispiece (in graph form) and Table V D, p. 190.   Brewery and shipping companies were included in the calculation with industrial and commercial companies.

14 H. F. Lydall, " The Long-Term Trend in the Size Distribution of Incomes," *Statistical Journal*, 1959, Part I, p. 14.

TABLE III C. NUMBER OF COMPANIES IN EACH OF SEVEN GRADES OF VOTE-CONCENTRATION FOR VARIOUS INDUSTRIES AND SIZES OF COMPANY 1936 AND 1951.

	Number of com-panies	GRADES OF VOTE-CONCENTRATION							Top grades ratio $\frac{\text{I-IV.}}{\text{I-VII}}$	(Median) Average % of vote held by largest 20
		Largest holding % of Vote		Largest twenty holdings			% of Vote			
		I	II	III	IV	V	VI	VII		
		50% or more	20-49%	50% or more	30-49%	20-29%	10-19%	0-9%		
VERY LARGE CO. (£3m. and over) of 1951.*		(Co. under £3m in 1936 in brackets)				DISTRIBUTION in 1936			(See Table V A)	
Engineering .. .. :	20(-9)	1(-1)	2	3(-3)	3(-1)	4(-2)	5(-2)	2	·45	27%
Distributive .. :	13(-3)	3(-1)	1	3(-1)	1(-1)	1	2	2	·62	50%
Textiles .. .. :	12(-1)	0	1	1	2(-1)	2	4	2	·33	20%
Food .. .. :	11(-1)	0	1	4 (-1)	0	2	0	3	·55	40%
Motors .. .. :	5(-3)	2	1 (-1)	0	1(-1)	1(-1)	0	0	·80	50%
Chemical .. .. :	9(-5)	1(-1)	1 (-1)	1	2(-1)	2(-1)	2(-1)	0	·56	35%
Paper .. .. :	9(-3)	1	2 (-1)	1(-1)	2	3(-1)	0	0	·57	43%
Miscellaneous .. :	13(-3)	1	4 (-1)	1	2(-1)	2(-1)	2	1	·58	42%
Total Industrial and Commercial .. :	92(-28)	9	13	15	13	17	15	10	·54	35%
Co. over £3m. in 1936†	64	7	8	9	7	11	12	10	·52	30%
Breweries .. .. :	10*	1	1	3	2	3	0	0	·70	50%

VERY LARGE CO. (£3m. and over) of 1951*

(Co. under £3m. in 1936 in brackets) — DISTRIBUTION in 1951 — (See Table V B)

	Total									
Engineering	20(−9)	2(−1)	2(−1)	0	2(−1)	4(−2)	8(−4)	2	·30	20%
Distributive	13(−3)	3(−1)	1	0	3(−2)	0	3	3	·54	33%
Textiles	12(−1)	0	0	0	2(−1)	2	6	2	·17	17%
Food	11(−1)	1	2(−1)	2	2	1	1	3	·55	35%
Motors	5(−3)	0	0	0	1(−1)	1	2(−2)	0	·40	25%
Chemical	9(−5)	0	0	1(−1)	2(−1)	1(−1)	1(−1)	4(−1)	·33	15%
Paper	9(−3)	0	1	1	2(−1)	4(−1)	2(−1)	0	·33	27%
Miscellaneous	13(−3)	0	4(−1)	2	1	0	4(−2)	3	·42	18%
Total Industrial and Commercial	92(−28)	6	10	4	15	13	27	17	·38	22%
Co. over £3m. in 1936†	64	4	7	3	8	9	17	16	·34	19%
Breweries	10	1	0	1	3	2(−1)	1	2(−1)	·50	30%

MEDIUM AND SMALLER LARGE CO. (£0·2—2·9m.) of 1951

DISTRIBUTION in 1951

	Total									
Engineering	32	0	5	3	7	12	5	0	·47	28%
Distributive	30	0	3	3	6	7	9	2	·40	26%
Textiles	20	0	0	2	7	7	3	1	·45	29%
Food	13	0	2	1	2	1	5	2	·38	19%
Motors	15	1	1	1	4	4	4	1	·40	26%
Chemical	8	0	0	0	2	2	2	1	·37	25%
Paper	8	0	1	1	1	3	2	0	·37	26%
Miscellaneous	9	0	0	2	2	1	2	2	·44	25%
Total Industrial and Commercial	135	1	12	13	31	37	32	9	·42	28%
Breweries	24	0	0	0	5	10	7·	2	·21	23%

* Excluding companies not formed in 1936.

† Subtracting bracketed figures. Two, medium by 1951, excluded, out of total 66.

votes and are not resolute in voting against him. The whole question of control does not depend only on concentration of votes, however, and will not be taken up systematically till Chapter V, after the discussion of directorships and of various types of shareholder.

The predominance of the single largest shareholders' vote in 1936 in very large companies, quoted from published sources, included brewing and shipping as well as industrial and commercial companies. But the same situation is disclosed if we confine attention to the very large industrial and commercial companies. Appendix A I, though it excludes 100% subsidiaries, shows the single largest share- (or, to be exact, vote-) holders to have varied in 1951 all the way from one case of 0·5% and three of 0·7% (Liebig, Courtaulds, Harrods and United Molasses) to 69·0% and 79·2% of the total vote (British United Shoe Machinery and M. Burton).

Table V A in Chapter V shows that in 1936 out of the sixty-six companies *then* with £3m. capital or over, ten companies had their largest single shareholder holding over 50% and in eleven further companies from 20 to 50% of the votes. The change in inequality from 1936 to 1951 may now be discussed.

§ 4. The Change in Vote-Concentration 1936–1951

All large companies have an unequal distribution of votes, but some are more unequal than others. Moreover the degree of inequality seems to have changed markedly between 1936 and 1951. Tables V A and V B in Chapter V give in their bottom line for the two years the number of the *very large* companies assignable to the various grades of inequality or concentration that have been distinguished. Considerable detail is given in these tables for the purpose of finding the real seat of control but the bare frequency of companies in each grade of vote-concentration may be compared, for the two years, in Table III C. It is important for a true basis of comparison to distinguish those companies which were rated as very large (*i.e.*, had a capital of £3m. or over) in 1951, those rated very large in 1936 and those rated so in both years. It happens, however, that only three companies out of the sixty-six with £3m. capital or over in 1936 did not have £3m. or more in 1951 [15] and it is not worth giving a

---

[15] The three companies which qualified as very large in 1936 but failed to do so in 1951 were Amalgamated Cotton and Platt Brothers, the capital of which was reduced below £3m. in 1951 and which therefore appear in the medium-large companies, and Imperial Smelting which became a subsidiary of Consolidated Tin Smelters. See below, p. 170, for subsequent degree of success.

separate table grading the companies very large in 1936 but not 1951. The three companies appear in brackets in their grade for 1936.

The average shareholders in a company did not change much between 1936 and 1951 when the (median) average for the same companies very large in both years remained about 14,250, but whatever series of companies we compare, whether the very large only in 1951 or in both 1936 and 1951, it is evident that concentration of voting diminished greatly between 1936 and 1951.

If for summary purposes we take a concentration of 30% of votes among the twenty largest voteholders as a dividing line, thus contrasting Grades I to IV with Grades V to VII, then, of all the ninety-two companies formed in 1936 and very large in 1951, fifty, equivalent to a ratio of ·54 (in the last column but one) were above this level of concentration in 1936, but only thirty-five, equivalent to a ratio of ·38, in 1951. Again of the older very large companies (very large both in 1936 and 1951) thirty-one (Grades I to IV, 7+8+9+7) fell above this level of concentration in 1936, but only twenty-two (Grades I to IV, 4+7+3+8) in 1951. It may be observed that the fall in concentration is greater among the older companies than among very large companies generally. This observation will be taken up shortly.

The change toward less concentration of votes is equally evident in the percentage of votes held by the single largest shareholders. The evidence is plain from Tables V A and B. In 1936 as already pointed out the largest single shareholders owned over 50% of the votes in nine of the very large companies; by 1951 only six such companies showed this extreme concentration. In a further thirteen of the companies the largest single vote-owner held in 1936 from 20 to 50% of the total vote. But in 1951 only ten of these companies showed such concentration.

Another, and more conventional, means of summary comparison is to compare averages. The last column of Table III C gives the (median) average percentage of votes held by the twenty largest voteholders. The median is a form of average explained in the Statistical Glossary (Appendix C § 3) and used here because it is not affected by a few extreme cases. Apart from Grade II, all the grades in Tables V A and B are, or can be, expressed in terms of the percentage of votes held by the largest *twenty* voteholders. Obviously if one shareholder holds 50% or over of the votes, the largest twenty will do so too. So Grade I is merely a special case of Grade III.   Grade II, however, is, so to speak, out of line.[16]   If the largest shareholder holds from 20 to 50% of votes, the largest twenty holders might hold any proportion from just above 20% and the company concerned might be classifiable either in Grade III (where the largest twenty shareholders held 50% or over) in IV or even possibly in V where the twenty largest voteholders held respectively either 30 to 50% or 20 to 30%.[17]   To find the average (median) concentration it may be necessary therefore to reallocate the companies in Grade II according to the percentage of the vote actually concentrated in twenty hands.   Normally, however, *all* Grade II companies will have concentrations above the median and reallocation will be unnecessary.

When the median concentrations have been calculated, they tell the same story as the distribution of companies.   The median percentage of votes held by the largest twenty shareholders in the sixty-four companies that were very large in 1936 was, in 1936, 30%; in 1951 19%.   Among the ninety-two companies very large in 1951 but not necessarily so in 1936, the median percentage of votes held by the largest twenty voteholders was in 1935, 35%; in 1951 22%.

The distribution of the very large companies over grades of vote-concentration and the (median) average of votes owned by the twenty largest vote owners both measure a fall, on the whole, in vote-concentration between 1936 and 1951.   But what of the history of the companies individually ?   Table III D answers the simple question of how many companies fell in vote-concentration, how many rose between 1936 and 1951.   Of the total of ninety-two companies that were very large in 1951 (*i.e.*, had £3m. capital or over) and were formed in 1936, seventy-one had fallen in concentration, twenty-one risen.

If we split these companies up, a further trend can be observed which throws light not merely on the change toward less concentration but on the process whereby this change has come about.   Table III D distinguishes (in row 5) as did Table III C, the total of companies of £3m. capital or over in 1951, and (in row 1) all companies of that size in 1951 and 1936.   But among the latter companies this table makes a further

---

[16] This deviation from a neat grading scale is necessary, however, because concentration of votes in *one* hand, even if the concentration is, say, only 20 %, carries more significance than concentration even of 50 %, in twenty hands.   The twenty largest vote-owners may be at sixes and sevens, and it is only a presumption that they, or the bulk of them, form a coherent group in personal contact.

[17] App. A 1 shows, in fact, an equal number (5) classifiable (if it were not for the holding of their largest holder) in Grades III and IV, none in Grade V.

distinction between (row 3) growing companies increasing and (row 2) static companies not increasing their capital between 1936 and 1951. It then appears that *the companies most prone to fall in concentration are the growing companies*. Among the companies very large in 1936 and 1951, eighteen out of twenty-nine (or 62%) of the static companies fell in concentration, but thirty out of thirty-five (or 86%) of the growing

TABLE III D

NUMBER OF VERY LARGE COMPANIES RISING OR FALLING IN VOTE-CONCENTRATION BETWEEN 1936 AND 1951

	Falling in degree of concentration (and percentage of total)	Rising in degree of concentration	Total
(1) *Co. with £3m. or more capital** .. (both in 1936 and 1951)	48 (75%)	16 (25%)	64
(2) Capital same in 1951 as 1936 (" static " Co.)	18 (62%)	11 (38%)	29
(3) Capital increased between 1936 and 1951 (" growing " Co.)	30 (86%)	5 (14%)	35
(4) *Co. with £3m. or more capital* .. .. in 1951, *less in* 1936 (Co. growing sufficiently to be " promoted " Co.).	23 (85%)	4 (15%)	27
(5) Total of companies with £3m. capital or over in 1951	71 (78%)	20 (22%)	91†

* Of Co. with £3m. or more capital in 1936, all except three remained independent with £3m. capital or more in 1951.
† One Co. (Tobacco Securities) data not available.

companies. Moreover of the twenty-seven companies (row 4) with capital below £3m. in 1936 who grew sufficiently to reach a capital of £3m. or more in 1951 and be " promoted " into the very large class, twenty-three or 85% fell in concentration. The conclusion to be drawn appears to be that when a company grows as a result of additional capital that capital (or at least the voting capital) is usually not added proportionately to all holdings, but the large holders get proportionately less.

§ 5. DIFFERENCES IN CONCENTRATION ACCORDING TO
SIZE AND INDUSTRY OF COMPANY

The distribution of companies into the seven grades of vote-concentration was analysed in Table III C according to size and industry

and in the last column a (median) average percentage of vote-concentration
in twenty hands was calculated.   As a further summary measure the ratio
was also given of the number of companies in the four top grades I–IV
to companies in all seven grades.   This ratio may be called, for short,
the *top grades ratio* and forms a simple and useful summary index of
concentration which can be derived from the details in Table III C almost
by eye.

TABLE III E

**SIMPLIFIED FORM OF COMPARISON IN VOTE-CONCENTRATION OF
COMPANIES IN VARIOUS INDUSTRIES**

	Degree of concentration in companies very large in 1951.		Companies medium and smaller large 1951	Companies all sizes in 1951 Average (if col. 2 and 3 agree sufficiently)
	Concentration in 1936	Concentration in 1951		
	(1)	(2)	(3)	(4)
Engineering ..	Mod. high	Mod. low	Moderate*	Mod. low
Textiles ..	Mod. low	Low	Mod. high	(?Mod. low)
Distributive ..	Very high	Mod. high	Mod. low	Moderate
Food	High	High	Mod. low	(? Mod. high)
Motors	Very high	Low	Mod. low	Low
Chemical ..	High	Mod. low or low†.	Mod. high	Moderate
Paper	High	Low or mod. high†	Mod. high	(?Moderate)
Miscellaneous ..	High	Moderate	Mod. high	Mod. high
Average for all industries ..	High	Mod. low	Moderate	
Breweries ..	Very high	High	Low	

* Medium, low; smaller, high.
† Two measures disagree widely, both stated.

Table III E presents the comparison between industries of Table III C
in a much simplified form.   The degree of vote-concentration is not
presented by any ratio or average but rated as very high, high, moderately
high, moderately low, or low.   This fivefold rating is not, however,
arbitrary, but is obtained primarily from the top-grade ratios.   Ratios
of over 0·6 are rated " very high," of 0·5 to 0·6 as " high," between a
third and a half " moderately high," between a quarter and a third
" moderately low," and a quarter or under " low."   The five ratings

agree also with the medians of concentration in most cases.[18]   Very high for medians above 35%; high, for medians of 32 to 35%; moderately high, of 26 to 32%; moderately low, of 18 to 25%; low, of 0 to 18%. At least four conclusions can be drawn from Table III E and the more detailed Table III C.

1. The fall in vote-concentration found on average and for the majority of very large companies between 1936 and 1951 is seen by comparison of columns 1 and 2 of Table III F to be true of all industries separately, except food, where the degree of concentration remained about the same.   The fall in concentration is particularly marked in the paper and chemical and (though its companies are few) in the motor industry.

2. Comparing sizes in Table III C, it must be remembered that all very large companies except complete subsidiaries were included in our list, but among the medium and smaller large companies only those were included where a quotation of the price of shares was available.   The closer-held, more share-concentrated, medium and small companies are likely, therefore, not to appear, and the listed companies of these smaller sizes might be expected to show, on average, lower vote-concentrations. In fact they show slightly higher concentrations.   Their " top grades " ratio was ·42 and their concentration was on average 28% as against a ratio of ·38 and an average concentration of 22% for the very large companies.   It may be concluded, therefore, that if all the medium and smaller large companies had been included, their share and vote-concentration would have been, on average, *considerably* higher than the average concentration for the very large companies.   This conclusion from the facts is reasonable, since with a given amount of money it is easier to buy a high proportion of voting shares in a smaller, than in a larger company.

3. Comparing columns (2) and (3) of Table III F the higher vote-concentration of the medium and smaller large companies is seen to be true of six out of the nine industries taken separately.   In paper and in textiles, the higher concentration of the medium and smaller companies is particularly evident.   On the other hand, the vote-concentration is lower in the medium and smaller companies of the distributive and food industries and especially in brewing.

4. In consequence of the divergence pointed out in (3) between the degree of vote-concentration in the very large and the medium and smaller

---

[18] One wide disagreement is noted in the Table.

large companies of certain industries, a characteristic vote-concentration (for all company sizes) can be established only for the engineering, distributive, motor, chemical, and miscellaneous groups of industries. The average rating of vote-concentration applying to companies of all sizes is given in column 4 of Table III E, but in the other industry groups (textiles, food, paper and breweries) their average would be an arbitrary splitting of differences between columns 2 and 3 and it is put in brackets with a question mark.

On the whole, for all sizes together, the particular industry involved appears not a very important factor in directly influencing the vote-concentration of companies.[19] This conclusion, however, is largely due to the medium and smaller companies where the differences between industry averages were rather narrow.   In these sizes (the data are summed up at the bottom of Table III C) the different median vote-concentrations for the several industries ranged only from 19 to 29%, the top-grade ratios only from ·37 to ·47.

Among the very large companies, even if we omit motor companies as too few, the industry medians and ratios, however, differed widely. The medians are seen at the top of Table III C to have ranged in 1936 from 15 to 35% and in 1951 from 20 to 50%, and the top-grade ratios from ·33 to ·55 in 1936 and from ·33 to ·62 in 1951.

For the *very large* companies, then, it is possible to recognise from Tables III C and D four distinct patterns of vote-concentrations for the eight different industry groups that had sufficient numbers of companies in 1936 and 1951.

1. *High percentage vote-concentration, both years:* Medians over 33%; top-grade ratios over ·50
    Distributive trades,
    Food,
    Brewing.

2. *Moderate percentage vote-concentration, both years:* Medians 27% and 20%; ratios ·45 and ·30
    Engineering.

3. *Low vote-concentration, both years:* Medians 20% and 17%; ratios ·33 and ·17
    Textiles.

---

[19] It has more influence upon the number, type and shareholding of directors, as shown in Chap. IV.

4. *Vote-concentration falling* 1936 *to* 1951: Steeply from high to moderate and low. Medians from 35–43% to 15–27%; ratios from ·56–58 to ·33–42.

        Chemicals,
        Miscellaneous,
        Paper.

These different patterns will, in the next chapter, be connected up with the degree of share-ownership by directors and with differences in the financial and market situations of the different industry groups.

CHAPTER IV

THE DIRECTORS

§ 1. Position of the Director and his Relation to Management

THE board of directors is the link in the joint stock company between shareholders and the operating staff. Or, in terms of the metaphor used earlier (page 19), it is at the waist of the hourglass—a waist that represents the concentration before the delegation of power in the company. In theory the shareholders or, at least, the ordinary shareholders with votes at their periodical meeting, approve policy and appoint the directors, who in turn appoint and give orders to the managers who, in their turn, appoint the staff and the foremen who give orders to the operator. The grains of sand falling through the hourglass represent the process of appointment and of deciding policy first concentrated into the hands of the board of directors then scattered through the executive ranks of the organisation.

The width of the hourglass represents the numbers of persons engaged at each of the processes. The waist of the diagram is proportionately very narrow compared to the shareholders and workers, since it usually consists in one man, the managing director, as against the tens of thousands of shareholders and employees in a typical large company. Just above the managing director in the hourglass comes the board of directors with, as we shall see, usually four to nine members, varying with the size of company. But even so, the concentration of power is narrow, a wasp-waist, compared to the wide spread of the shareholders above and the administrative staff and workers below.

The persons and bodies within the company organisation associated with the activities of the top control and decision-making can best be discovered by focusing on the area just above and below the waist of the hourglass. Here there are three intersecting groups, including a not dissimilar number of persons: the large shareholders likely to affect policy, the directors, and the top managers. The degree of intersection will be ascertained more exactly from our present survey,[1] but may first

---

[1] The findings are given in the Summary of Conclusions, Chap. VIII, § 4.

be represented by the superimposition of three equal circles.   The largest
shareholders are identical to *some* extent with directors and are shown to
intersect, but top management and directors intersect still more, as
represented by full-time managing directors.   On the other hand there
are probably few large shareholders who are full-time managers.   Neither
the circles or their intersection determine completely the real seat of
control, but that seat is very likely to be somewhere in the intersections
as shaded in the diagram.

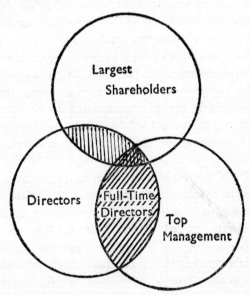

The most likely persons to be in control are those that are both large
shareholders *and* directors, or directors *and* top managers.   But not all
persons at these intersections are *ipso facto* the real top rulers; nor are
directors, largest shareholders, and top managers with no other qualification (*i.e.*, not at intersections) altogether excluded from the possibility
of real power.

Thanks to the present survey it is possible to be numerically more
accurate in this intersection of directors, large shareholders and top
managers—an intersection so vital to the question of who controls and
makes the top decisions.   But further evidence has to be sifted, specially
on the size, composition and shareholdings of boards and the statement
of the full conclusion will be postponed to the summary chapter, where
it appears (on page 191) in the form of a diagram illustrating the

position for the average very large company as established, partly at least, from our statistics. We may, however, anticipate here to some extent. The average size of the board of the very large companies is found statistically to be nine. The twenty largest holders, shown [p. 191] p193 in the diagram as a column of twenty (shaded) units, are seen (as our statistics indicate) to have only, on average, one and a half of these twenty within the nine-unit square representing the directors. But the eight top managers (indicated by a circle within each unit) are deduced (but not *statistically* proven) to have four of their number among the directors. These figures of 4 and $1\frac{1}{2}$ correspond in the intersecting circles shown on page 79 with the greater area of intersection between top management and directors than between top-management and the twenty largest shareholders. The later, full, diagram presents additional facts about the composition of the average board that are found statistically, particularly the average number of directors holding no more than qualifying shares and holding other (possibly " interlocking ") directorships. Conclusions on these heads are, however, postponed till later.

The seat of *real* control will be discussed in the next chapter: here we can only begin by elucidating the formal and informal relations of directors to managers. Of the three groups shown by the circles, the directors are clearly, indeed *legally*, defined. But what is required for realistic exposition beyond the formal organisation are terms to refer (a) to the full-time top executives (in the lower circle) whether on the board or not and (b) to the whole set of persons in top authority, whether in name (middle and lower circle) or nearer reality (mainly in the shaded area). In this chapter we can only lay the foundations and confine attention to the duties and activities of directors particularly in relation to and contrasted with those of managers. The position is complicated of course by the fact that many directors are also full-time executive managers, but their two capacities can be distinguished.

The distinguishing mark of members of the executive group is that they are in continuous session, " on location " like all the staff below the waist of the hourglass. *The word " management " appears the best " fit " for this continuous work*. Continuity naturally affects the type of duties managers are called upon to perform. In contrast, directors, as such, only meet at intervals and may hold directorships in other companies, *e.g.*, may be interlocking directors. This discontinuity will, in turn, naturally affect the duties directors are called upon to perform.

Considerable thought and analysis has been devoted to the real
" functions " of the director, particularly in America.   Among the books
listed in our bibliography we may pick out Chester Barnard's *The Functions
of the Executive*, published in 1938, John C. Baker's *Directors and their
Functions*, published in 1945, R. A. Gordon's *Business Leadership in the
Large Corporation* and Copeland and Towl's *The Board of Directors and
Business Management*.   On the basis of these and my own analysis
it is possible to list at least nine types of work which the directors are
usually found to perform as distinct from either the shareholders at their
meetings or the top management.

The board of directors, we said, formed the link between shareholders
and the executive staff.   Some of these " functions " are mainly relations
with the shareholders and " financial," others are relations mainly with
the management and in the list of nine specific activities of directors that
follows, we move, on the whole, from relations with the financial world
and the shareholders to relations with (and action upon) the managing
staff.   Activities 1 and 2 are directly financial; 3 and 4 and 5 inspect and
co-ordinate the management largely on behalf of shareholders; 6, 7, 8
and 9 involve direct action upon and giving orders to the management.

§ 2.   The Main Activities of Directors Listed

1. Deciding the rate of dividend to be declared on the ordinary shares.
Shareholders may reduce, but not increase the rate.

2. Proposing any new capital structure such as the issue of shares on
the market, bonus shares, preference shares or debentures.   Advice on
this activity is usually sought from financiers who may be on the board.
Proposals have to be confirmed at a shareholders' meeting.

3. Reviewing and " checking up on " the work of the management,
particularly as the trustee of the shareholders.

4. Asking " discerning questions " of the management.   Here the
outside part-time director plays a special role.

5. Forming a link between different companies by interlocking, *i.e.*,
by holding directorships in more than one company.   Here two different
situations must be distinguished according as (a) the companies interlocked
are otherwise independent, or are (b) the subsidiaries or parent and subsidiary.   It is often found convenient for a large company with scattered
interests to split them formally by organising a separate company with
some, but not necessarily all, of the directors different.

6. Appointing the top managers and, if necessary, dismissing them.

7. Determining the salaries and other " emoluments " of these top managers.

8. Organising new (or closing or adapting old) posts at the top of the management structure.   In short, restructuring.

9. Deciding on general lines of policy such as what to make, how much of it at what price with what investment.   Here the board of directors as a whole is possibly less important than the managing director and chairman.   All the board can do, meeting, as it does only at intervals, is to " order continuation or change in the *direction* of the ship of business from time to time."   In short to issue " directives."   The interpreting of these directives and the actual day to day management in the words of R. A. Gordon is for the board a mere " approval function." [2]

§ 3.   INDICATIONS OF THE PRESENT SURVEY

The indications about the activities of directors that follow from the present survey of large companies relate to the size of a company's board of directors, the shareholdings of its directors in the company and their interlocking with other companies.   Three measures are taken of directors' shareholdings: the shareholding of the whole board as a proportion of total shares, the number of directors among the twenty largest holders of voting shares and the number holding no more than the minimum share qualification.   Two measures are taken of interlocking directors: the number of such directors and the total of their interlocks.   The resultant six objective measurements (size of board, proportion of directors' shares, large and minimum shareholding directors, interlocking directors and total of interlocking) throw considerable light on the actual power, functions and policy of the board.

If directors of any company are found on the boards of other companies it may indicate the importance of the function or activity just listed fifth.   A significant " interlocking " of interests cannot be assumed, however, till we know the relationship of the two companies and for that reason, as explained later, it is safest to use in the first instance the phrase director-in-common.   A man may be a director-in-common because he is known as a shrewd counsellor of wide experience whom several companies (in common) wish to have on their boards simply for that reason and not to interlock.

The other measures recorded in the basic table also throw light on the powers and activities of the board of directors, though less directly.

---

[2] A tenth activity might be added, internal to the board—that of *co-option* of new directors—by which boards are virtually self-perpetuating.

There is no direct information available of who is a full-time working director concerned particularly with the policy activities (listed ninth), and who is not. But there are indirect indications.

A small size of board and little interlocking probably indicate a " working board," most of whose members are full-time managers. Directors working full-time with the company, though they might be found on the boards of banks, insurance and other finance companies, are not likely to be directors of other *non-financial* companies. Directors who are large shareholders are likely to be concerned with the financial function listed first and second and, together with " outside " part-time directors, concerned with the reviewing and questioning activities listed third and fourth.

The three sections which follow, measure and analyse by size and industry of company, the characteristics of directors and boards of directors that could be directly measured:

(§ 4) Sizes of boards of directors and, for the very large companies, the number of directors in common with other large non-financial companies.

(§ 5) The ordinary shares held by directors, measured by the proportion of total shares held by the board and by the number of directors among the twenty largest voteholders, and the number holding no more than the minimum qualifying shares.

(§ 6) Changes in size of board and directors' shareholding, 1936 to 1951.

§ 4. The Size of Boards of Directors and Number of Directors-in-Common

The companies with various numbers of directors from three to nineteen and over is given in Table IV A for different sizes of company and different industries. Nineteen and over is an exceptional size and the companies concerned may be discussed individually. Boards as large as this are relatively much more frequent in financial activities such as banking where various connections and contacts are sought, where, in fact, that function is important which has just been enumerated as (5) " interlocking."

The six industrial companies with a board of nineteen or over may be set down in detail and compared with the " Big Five " banks.

TABLE IV A. DISTRIBUTION OF COMPANIES BY SIZE OF THEIR BOARDS

Number of directors on the board	3	4–6	7–9	10–12	13–15	16–18	19+	Total of companies	Percentage of companies with boards of 10+	Average (median) size
Industrial and commercial										
Very large	1	17	33	25	10	7	5	98	48%	9
Medium large	1	17	24	4	1	0	0	47	11%	7
Smaller large	2	62	22	1	0	0	1	88	3%	5
TOTAL	4	96	79	30	11	7	6	233	23%	7
Engineering	2	19	20	7	4	1	0	53	23%	7
Textiles	0	14	11	2	1	1	3	32	22%	7
Distribution	0	24	16	3	0	0	1	44	9%	6
Food	1	14	7	1	2	0	0	25	12%	6
Motors	1	9	8	3	0	0	0	21	14%	7
Chemicals	0	2	5	6	2	1	1	17	59%	10
Paper	0	5	5	4	1	2	0	17	41%	7
Miscellaneous	0	9	7	4	1	2	1	24	33%	8
Breweries	1	20	9	3	2	2	0	35	14%	6

*Comparison of the six industrial and commercial companies having the
largest boards with the " Big Five " banks, 1951*

	£m. Capital	No. on Board		£m. Capital	Rank	No. on Board
Barclays	15·9	31	Bleachers Assoc.	4·4	(53rd)	21
Westminster	30·5	33	Fine Cotton Spinners	8·6	(16th)	23
Midland	42·4	30	Lyons, J.	9·5	(12th)	21
National & Provincial	60·0	24	Imperial Tobacco	50·1	(3rd)	34
Lloyds	73·7	33	Lever Bros.	73·5	(2nd)	24
	—		British Cotton and			
Average (a.m.)		30	Wool Dyers	0·8	(smaller group)	19

The larger boards are associated to some extent with industrial companies of larger capital though not universally so. Listed companies with the second and third largest capital—Lever, and Imperial Tobacco—appear in the table with boards of twenty-four and thirty-four. The company with the largest issued capital (Imperial Chemicals) had in 1951 eighteen directors and the fourth largest (Courtaulds) also had eighteen. Thus the four largest companies in our list all had boards of eighteen or more. But the fifth, sixth, seventh, eighth, ninth, tenth and eleventh[3] largest companies all had boards of fourteen or under; and, as the table shows, one very large board is that of the Bleachers Association, a company as low as fifty-third in order of share capital. Another is actually the board of a smaller large company (British Cotton and Wool Dyers) with capital under £1m.[4]

The partial association of larger boards with large capital can be demonstrated further by comparing the very large companies as a whole with the medium and smaller large. The (median) average size of board of the very large companies (as shown in the last column of Table IV A) is nine; that of the medium and smaller large companies seven and five.[5] But the capital of the very large (over £3m.) is at least three times that of the smaller companies so that the size of board is far from increasing proportionately to the size of the capital.

---

[3] Woolworth, Dunlop, Union International, Ford, B.I.C.C., British Celanese, G.E.C.
[4] It is noticeable that, relatively to their size, several textile companies have very large boards. This may be due to the companies concerned having been formed as associations of firms each requiring some representation on the board.
[5] These approximate medians are " pinpointed "; see App. C, § 3.

In most of their characteristics companies have shown wide variation; but in size of the boards there is considerable uniformity. Sixty-two out of the eighty-eight smaller large companies are seen in Table IV A to have boards with from four to six members. If we analyse these sizes in greater detail we find twenty-six companies with four, seventeen with five, nineteen with six and eleven with seven members. In short, seventy-three out of the eighty-seven smaller companies (or 84%) have boards from four to seven members. This is a narrow range considering that these smaller large companies range so widely in their capital—from £0·2m. up to £1·0m.

For comparing the size of boards of different industries, a simple measure, given in Table IV A, is the ratio of boards of ten or over to all boards. This measure brings out very clearly the effect of the type of market. Industries serving or making products for the final consumer, like distribution, food, motors and brewing, have fewer large boards. Industries making products for other industries like engineering, textiles (making mainly for the clothing industries, or spinning for the weaving section), paper and, above all, chemicals, have larger boards. Chemical companies, indeed, have ten as their (median) average size of board [6] as against the narrow range of six to eight within which the all-size averages of other industries fall.

The larger size of the chemical companies' boards may be due, also, to the need of scientists (or at least of persons with some knowledge of science) as directors, a matter to be referred to later in Chapter V. But the main feature to notice here is the relative infrequency generally of large boards of industrial and commercial companies compared to that of insurance companies, banks, or the railway companies previous to nationalisation.

Compared to our very large companies averaging in 1951 nine board members, the " Big Five " banks then averaged, as already noted, over thirty members; the nine insurance companies with over £3m. capital averaged 17·7. In 1936 the " Big Four " railway companies averaged twenty members on their boards.

The logic of this difference may, as a hypothesis, be traced to the greater need for outside contacts in what are essentially " service " industries. This consideration brings up, as a possible test of the need of

---

[6] Miscellaneous industries are not represented in the small companies where boards are small and for this reason their distribution in respect of size of board is not comparable with that of companies in other industries.

contacts, some measure of interlocking directors or, to be more exact, the number of directors any company has in common with other companies. Such directors in common are often referred to as multiple or plural, with a somewhat indiscriminating allusion perhaps to the pluralist priests of the Middle Ages. Here, however, to be as objective as possible, we shall speak of " directors-in-common," particularly with other large non-financial companies. My original article on Company Control,[7] published in 1947, summarised work done at Birmingham University by Dr. J. Siviter and Dr. W. Baldamus:

From a random sample of all trading companies in the *Stock Exchange Year Book* it appears that the directors of large companies hold more directorships on the average than directors of small companies. Half the directors of the smaller companies were pluralists; 12% held six or more directorships, and 4% over ten. But three-quarters of the directors of the *larger* companies (of £0·5m. or over in 1936) were pluralists, with 30% holding six or more directorships and 13% over ten. This situation seems at first sight contrary to logic, since it might be expected that the direction of larger companies would involve greater responsibility, time and energy, and thus be less frequently multiplied, than the direction of smaller companies.

Part of the explanation of this paradox fits in with our assumption that plural directorships are a sign of divorce of control from ownership. The control of larger companies is more divorced from ownership and their directors are not tied down to directing only where they own substantial capital, but can pay attention, promiscuously, to one company after another.

This early inquiry looked to directorships held in common with companies of all sizes. For our present limited purpose of testing how far directors-in-common are a mark of service industries requiring contacts, the enumeration of directorships is limited to those held in the larger non-financial industrial companies. Here we found small boards with each director presumably fairly engrossed. Holding several such directorships is thus significant. A business man might well be a director of several *small* local companies, however, without much significance. But if limits are placed on size, no limit must be placed on the *type* of industry. In enumerating directorships held in common with our industrial and commercial companies, we have ranged over companies other than those in the industrial and commercial section of the Stock Exchange *Year Book.* We have ranged, in fact, into iron and steel, shipbuilding, building, land and property, shipping and other transport, and communications, using as our guide the *Classified List of Larger Companies Engaged in British*

---

[7] *Statistical Journal*, 1947, Part I, p. 14.

Industry published by the National Institute of Economic and Social Research. This list includes all companies, not subsidiaries, operating in Great Britain except those engaged in banking, insurance, finance and agriculture. It defines as " large " any company of over £2·5m. assets in 1953–54 quoted on the United Kingdom Stock Exchange. 512 companies are included and the size limits in terms of assets are slightly wider than those for our very large and medium large companies, defined in terms of capital.

Directorships-in-common in several companies were found in 1936 to be relatively more frequent in the larger than the smaller companies and our inquiry was accordingly confined to the directors in our very large companies. The details analysed by industry are given in Table IV B.

TABLE IV B

INDUSTRIAL GROUPING OF VERY LARGE COMPANIES HAVING VARIOUS NUMBERS OF DIRECTORS IN COMMON WITH OTHER LARGE NON-FINANCIAL COMPANIES

Industry group (and) no. of Cos.	No. of directors-in-common	0	1	2	3	4	5	Average number (arithmetic mean)
Total industrial and commercial	(98)	42	23	11	10	8	4	1·3
Engineering	(21)	3	6	6	3	2	1	2·0
Textiles	(12)	8	1	2	1	0	0	0·7
Distributive	(14)	8	2	0	3	0	1	1·1
Food	(12)	8	3	0	0	1	0	0·6
Motors	(6)	4	1	0	1	0	0	0·7
Chemical	(9)	2	3	2	1	1	0	1·6
Paper	(9)	4	4	0	0	0	1	1·0
Miscellaneous	(15)	5	3	1	1	4	1	1·9
Breweries	(11)	5	4	2	0	0	0	0·7

Three conclusions may be drawn from the table:

(1) Wide differences exist between one and another of our very large industrial and commercial companies in respect of the directors they have in common with other very large and medium large non-financial companies (*i.e.*, of over £2½m. assets). Almost half the companies have no such directors-in-common—in great contrast to insurance and banking companies. But a certain number, twenty-two out of ninety-four had in 1951 as many as three directors-in-common.

(2) The differences in the number of directors-in-common between our companies are partly due to their industry;—there is considerable contrast between the different industry groups. Engineering companies stand out, followed by chemical, as much more inclined to have directors-in-common with other large companies. The logic of this, as it was of the preceding conclusion, is that engineering, and to a less extent chemistry, like banking, shipping and insurance, are industries rendering services to other industries and requiring some " interlocking " (in the strict sense) to obtain business from, or at any rate to co-ordinate with, those other industries.

(3) Sharing directors least in common are the large companies in the distributive, the food, the brewing and the motor industry. These industries make, or mainly make, consumers' goods and do not require to " interlock " so much with other industries.

Some directors who held a directorship in another large company might, of course, hold further directorships in three, four or more large companies. The extent of this multiplication of directorships was investigated, and our very large industrial and commercial companies were found to be distributed as follows in respect of aggregate numbers of other large companies in which their directors held directorships compared to the plain number of directors-in-common.

Distribution of ninety-four very large companies in 1951 according to their directorships-in-common with other large [8] non-financial companies:

	0	1	2	3	4	5 or more	Total
No. of companies with above-stated number of directors-in-common ...	42	22	10	9	8	3	94
No. of companies with above-stated *total* of other large companies in which directorships held by their directors	42	15	15	9	5	8	94

The figures need little explanation. Obviously if companies had no director-in-common with other large non-financial companies the same number of companies (in our case forty-two) would show no companies having directorships-in-common. But if they had one director-in-common, as had the twenty-two companies in our table, he might, and often did, hold more than one directorship in other large companies. Seven (*i.e.*, 22 minus 15) of our companies are in this case. On the whole, however, companies are not distributed very much more widely

[8] Not all the probable directorships of directors in four of our 98 companies were available.

NUMBER OF COMPANIES GROUPED BY SIZE AND INDUST
% OF ORDIN

	(1) Total number	(2) Less than ½%	(3) ½%+	(4) 1%+	(5) 2%+	(6) 3%+	(7) 5%+	(8) 10%+	(9) 20%+
Industrial and Commercial									
Very large	98	27	17	12	11	9	4	5	13
Medium large	47	5	11	8	4	5	8	0	6
Smaller large	88	12	7	13	12	13	13	11	7
TOTAL	233	44	35	33	27	27	25	16	26
Engineering (E)	53	12	9	7	9	8	4	3	1
Textiles (T)	32	2	4	9	6	3	6	0	2
Distributive (D)	44	8	6	7	1	6	5	4	7
Food (F)	25	6	5	1	0	2	6	0	5
Motors (Mo)	21	8	3	2	3	0	0	2	3
Chemical (Ch)	17	2	3	2	3	2	1	2	2
Paper (Pa)	17	2	2	2	4	1	1	3	2
Misc. (X)	24	4	3	3	1	5	2	2	4
Breweries									
Very large	11	1	0	1	0	2	4	1	2
Medium large	12	2	0	1	2	3	4	0	0
Smaller large	11	1	1	0	3	4	1	1	0
TOTAL	34		7		5	9	9	2	2

* Summary of information from Table IV D.

IV C

RY IN WHICH THE BOARD OF DIRECTORS HELD STATED
ARY SHARES, 1951

Name of Co. (and size, if medium or smaller large, M-L or S-L) and exact %	(10) Ratio cols. 5–9 $\frac{}{2-9}$	(11) Boards average (median) % of shares	(12)* Average (A. mean) no. of directors among twenty largest holders	(13)* % of such directors among all directors	(14)* % of Cos. with no minimum holding directors
	·43	1·5%	1·5	16%	35%
	·49	2·0%	1·4	20%	47%
	·63	2·9%	2·0	37%	42%
	·52	2·3%	1·7	25%	40%
Carrier (S-L) 41·0%	·47	1·8%	1·2	17%	34%
Keystone (S-L) 32·5%, Wolsey (M-L) 21·7%	·53	2·2%	1·7	24%	61%
Burton 69·3%, Gieves (S-L) 27·3%, Lewis, J. 66·6%, Reed, A. (M-L) 37·8%, Upson (M-L) 20·0%, Vavasseur (S-L) 31·1%, Yeo (S-L) 25·6%	·52	2·0%	1·7	28%	53%
B. Cocoa 32·2%, Colman 27·5%, Hampshire (S-L) 22·1%, Hartley (M-L) 40·0%, Ranks 33·3%	·52	2·5%	1·8	30%	60%
Bristol Aero 24·9%, Morris 28·3%, Rootes 30·6%	·38	1·0%	1·3	14%	38%
Albright & W. 30·0%, Lever 23·2%	·59	2·5%	1·8	18%	35%
Ill. News 39·6%, Oakey (S-L) 25·4%	·65	2·7%	1·9	27%	47%
Lebus 28·0%, Morgan C. 20·2%, Norvic (M-L) 27·7%, Times Furnish (M-L) 29·7%	·58	2·5%	2·7	34%	46%
Smith (Tad.) 69·5%, Walker & Cain 20·8%	·80	7·5%	3·2		
	·75	4·0%	1·7		33%
	·58	3·7%	1·4		
	·78	4·3%	2·1	35%	41%

when classed by the aggregate number of other large companies in which directorships are held by their directors than when classed by the bare number of such directors, and it is not worth repeating any detailed analysis by industries.

§ 5.　DIRECTORS' SHAREHOLDING

Both Adam Smith and John Stuart Mill, we saw, thought companies unsuitable for carrying on trade that was not just routine, and that required some management.　Adam Smith indeed described competitive (foreign) trade as " a species of warfare, of which the operations are continually changing and which can scarce ever be conducted successfully without such an unremitting exertion of vigilance and attention as cannot long be expected from the directors of a joint stock company." [9]　He, like Mill, assumed that without full ownership and, as Mill put it, " their proportional share of the benefits of good management," managers would soon take their " ease."

A question that classical economists would pick as of main importance would thus be the extent to which directors participate in the risks and successes of the shareholders whom they are supposed to represent, in short, how far control, as embodied in the directors, is divorced from ownership of the risk-capital.　The proportion of *votes* directors hold is of less importance since, once they are directors, they exercise control more by the very fact that they are directors and less by ownership of votes.　And directors' holding of preference stocks is less important since these stocks are not greatly subject to risk of losses and uncertainty of gains.　The extent of the holding of ordinary shares by directors will be measured in three ways, two of which do not directly involve the voting power: the proportion of all ordinary shares held by the boards as a whole; the number, if any, of directors among the twenty largest voteholders; the number, if any, of directors holding no more than the minimum qualifying shares.

The first two tests are, of course, likely to agree to some extent and will be denoted as AA and A; the third test, the absence of large shareholders among directors, is likely to show results opposite to AA or A and will be denoted B.

This is a long section and will be conveniently subdivided by describing separately these three tests *and their interrelations*.　Subsections will,

---

[9] *Wealth of Nations*, Book V, Chap. I, Part III, art. 1.

accordingly, be headed Test AA; Test A; Tests AA and A; Test B; and
Tests A and B.

Test AA (*the board's proportion of shares*).   Table IV C gives, for the
three sizes of company and the different industry groups, the number of
companies in which the board as a whole holds stated proportions of the
total of ordinary shares.   Where the proportion is 20% or more, the name
of the company is given.   It appears from the ratios in column 10 that the
boards of only just over half the companies (53%) hold a total of 2%
or more of all the ordinary shares.[10]   Among the very large companies
this ratio is as low as 43%; among the medium and the smaller large it is
49% and 63%.   In short, *the larger the company, the lower the proportion
of ordinary shares held by the board.*

Test A.   Columns 12 and 13 of Table IV C sum up briefly the results
of the second test of directors' shareholding, namely *the number of directors
among the twenty largest voteholders.*   This number was found to vary
from individual company to company (as may be seen below in rows A
of Table IV D) quite as widely as the percentage of the total ordinary
shares owned by the whole board.   In 1951 almost a third of all sizes of
our industrial and commercial companies (seventy-four out of 233) had
no directors at all among their largest twenty voteholders and a further
quarter (fifty-nine) only one.   At the other end of the scale twenty-one
had four such directors each and seventeen, five or more.   For the groups
of companies of separate sizes and industries, column 12 of Table IV C
gives an ordinary arithmetic mean average of directors among the largest
twenty holders, and column 13 the percentages of such directors
among all directors.   A further index of directors' holdings is given in
column 14, to be used later, mainly in Chapter V, to compare sizes.[11]
It is the proportion of companies with no directors holding no more than
minimum qualifying shares—for short, with no " minimum-holding "
directors.

The second set of measures of directors' shareholding, based on the
number of directors among the largest twenty voteholders, is separately
given in Table IV D, rows A for different sizes of company.   It is important as an independent test of the evidence of the board's percentage
of total ordinary shares already presented.   Tests AA and A, the two
sources of evidence, are independent to the extent that one deals with

[10] This low percentage is all the more remarkable since joint holdings of a director with
others are all, for want of any further detail, attributed to him.   See App. B for particular
cases.   Some of these joint holdings (*e.g.*, in British Cocoa and Chocolate) may be
charitable trusts.

[11] The differences *between industries* are slight.   Only engineering (with 34%) shows any
marked variation from the general average of 42% for all industries.

DISTRIBUTION OF COMPANIES OF DIFFERENT SIZE ACCORDING
AND (B) WITH NO MORE THAN MINI

	All Cos.	Number of companies with		
		0	1	2
Industrial and Commercial Cos.				
No. of very large Cos. (and total of directors involved) with No. of directors each as stated in top row.				
(A) Among twenty largest holders	97*	37	26 (26)	12 (24)
(B) With no more than min. qualifying shares ..	98	33	17 (17)	6 (12)
No. of medium large Cos. (and total of directors involved) with No. of directors each as stated in top row.				
(A) Among twenty largest holders	47	18	14 (14)	4 (8)
(B) With no more than min. qualifying shares ..	47	22	9 (9)	7 (14)
No. of smaller large Cos. (and total of directors involved) with No. of directors each as stated in top row.				
(A) Among twenty largest holders	88	19	19 (19)	21 (42)
(B) With no more than min. qualifying shares ..	88	37	22 (22)	11 (22)
All sizes				
Total of (A)	232	74	59 (59)	37 (74)
Total of (B)	233	92	48 (48)	24 (48)
Breweries (All sizes)				
As (A) above	34	5	13 (13)	4 (8)
As (B) above	34	14	10 (10)	4 (8)

* One company (Tobacco Securities) not available.   ‡ See footnote to Table IV F

IV D

TO NUMBER OF DIRECTORS (A) AMONG LARGEST HOLDERS
MUM SHARE QUALIFICATIONS IN 1951

stated No. of directors (A) or (B). Consequent total of directors in brackets.					Cos. with two or more directors (A) or (B)	% of all Cos.	Average a company (and total) of directors (A) or (B) ..	
3	4	5	6	7+				
9 (27)	7 (28)	2 (10)	0	4 (31)	34	35%	1·5	(146)
6 (18)	7 (28)	11 (55)	7 (42)	11 (92)‡	48	49%	2·7	(264)
4 (12)	3 (12)	3 (15)	1 (6)	0	15	32%	1·4	(67)
6 (18)	2 (8)	1 (5)	0	0	16	34%	1·1	(54)
11 (33)	11 (44)	2 (10)	3 (18)	2 (14)	50	57%	2·0	(180)
8 (24)	4 (16)	6 (30)	0	0	29	33%	1·3	(114)
24 (72)	21 (84)	7 (35)	4 (24)	6 (45)	99	43%	1·7	(393)
20 (60)	13 (52)	18 (90)	7 (42)	11 (92)	93	40%	1·9	(432)
6 (18)	3 (12)	2 (10)	1 (6)	0	16	47%	2·0	(67)
4 (12)	1 (4)	1 (5)	0	0	10	29%	1·1	(39)

votes the other with risk-capital. Nevertheless the findings of each of the two measures are roughly similar.

Tests AA and A

1. There are wide differences between the companies generally within each of the three sizes of company and within each industry. The wide variety is particularly noticeable in the *very large* industrial and commercial companies, in twenty-seven of which the board owns less than ½% of the shares and in thirty-seven no director is even the twentieth voter; it is least noticeable in breweries which present more of a uniform pattern in directors' shareholding. Twenty-eight companies with over 20% shareholding by directors (of which two are very large brewery companies) are all mentioned by name in Table IV C. Most of them will be referred to later in discussing owner-control generally in Chapter V.

2. On the whole, however, a wide prevalence of divorce of directors' control from ownership is amply demonstrated. As already said, and shown in column 10 of Table IV C, only in a bare majority of industrial and commercial companies do the directors own between them even 2% of the ordinary capital; and a clear minority of only ninety-four out of 233 (or 40%) own 3% or more of the ordinary shares.

The directors, it must be remembered, have the function of representing the interests of the shareholders. If for a more realistic representation of the controlling group top managers who were *not* directors were added to the directors the divorce of control from ownership would be still more startling.

3. Comparing sizes of industrial and commercial companies the first feature of Table IV C to strike the eye is the much wider dispersion of the directors' proportion of holdings among the very large than among the medium and smaller large companies. There is a much higher number of very large companies, absolutely and relatively, both where the boards hold less than ½% of the total shares and where they hold over 20%. The extreme range of variation in directors' holdings is from 0% to 69·3%, but even if we subtract the lowest and highest tenths to find the interdecile range (see Appendix C, § 7) the range still extends for the very large companies from under ¼% to over 20%. Thirteen companies (14%) are named as having boards holding 20% or more of the ordinary shares. Among all the medium and smaller large companies put together there were only thirteen (or 9½%) of such named companies.

4. On average, the boards of directors of very large companies appear

to own a lower proportion of the ordinary shares than the boards of the medium large companies, and, again, the boards of the medium own a less proportion of the shares than the boards of the smaller large companies.   In short, the larger the company the less, relatively, the holdings of the board and this in spite of the fact that, as we have seen, the boards of the larger companies are larger.

The effect of the size of the board does however appear to make itself felt (see column 12) in the average number of directors among the largest twenty voteholders.   The boards of the medium large companies average slightly *fewer* directors (1·4) among their twenty largest voteholders than the very large companies.   If, however, we consider the difference in the average size of these boards (given in Table IV A) and work out a percentage of these top-holding directors among all directors, the percentage is distinctly higher for the medium than the very large companies—20% as against 16%—and very much higher for the smaller than for the medium large companies (37% as against 20%) [12]   Thus the rule that the smaller the company the less the divorce of directorship from ownership still holds.

5. Comparing industries it is at once apparent that among the brewery companies as a whole divorce of control from ownership has not gone nearly so far as among the industrial and commercial companies. All indices agree here.   In 78% of the thirty-four brewery companies (column 10) the boards owned at least 2% of the ordinary shares (as against only 52% for the industrial and commercial companies); the (median) average of shares held by directors was 4·3% as against 2·3%, and the average number of directors among the largest twenty voteholders was 2·1 against 1·7 for the 233 industrial and commercial companies.

Comparing the various specific industry groups besides brewing there is some disagreement between the four indices shown in columns 10, 11, 12 and 13, but also considerable agreement.   All four indices are expressed in such a way that a low figure signifies wide prevalence of divorce of directorships from ownership, a high figure a high prevalence of " marriage."   Engineering and motor companies show low indices and signs of wide prevalence of divorce of director-control from ownership; such divorce seems least prevalent, after brewery, among food, paper and

---

[12] The detailed calculation, dividing the averages in column 12 of Table IV C by those of the last column of Table IV A calculated to one place of decimals, is: very large Co. 1·5 ÷ 9·3 = 16%; medium large Co. 1·4 ÷ 7·2 = 20%; smaller large Co. 2·0 ÷ 5·4 = 37%.

chemical companies, where at least three of the four indices run comparatively high.

6. These differences between companies of various sizes and industries in the prevalence of the divorce of directorship and ownership follow to some extent the pattern of capital- and vote-gearing and of vote-concentration discussed in the last chapter. Brewing companies are outstanding both for a low divorce prevalence and a *high* gearing. There is, perhaps, some logical connection, not necessarily one of direct cause and effect; but both vote-gearing and the divorce of directors' control from ownership may well be results of a common cause. Such a cause might be the technological and marketing conditions of the industry. Engineering is here in marked contrast to brewing. As against brewing's stable though declining consumers' market and high capitalisation the market for engineering is a producer's market, growing but subject to fluctuations and uncertainty, while the value of its capital equipment is comparatively low. In 1951, for instance, the ratio of fixed to total net tangible assets was for all the engineering group of companies [13] quoted on the Stock Exchange 31·5%. For drink, mainly breweries, the same ratio was as high as 75%. Of the other industry groups which we have distinguished some, like motors, seem to approach the engineering type or " pole " in most characteristics, others, like food and distribution, the brewery type both in fixed asset ratio and market conditions and results. Textiles during the period 1936 to 1951 were undergoing such market convulsions (fluctuations is hardly a strong enough word) that significant comparison is difficult in respect of the long-period " structural " characteristics such as capitalisation and market situation.

Test B

The third test to be used of directors' shareholding is the number holding no more than the minimum shares qualifying them as directors. Fearing the possible lack of incentive in the absence of any direct economic interest in profits and dividends from shares on the part of directors and top management, some companies have instituted forms of profit-sharing for management. Too much stress, however, must not be laid upon the share (*i.e.*, the proportion) of shares owned by a director as a personal incentive or lack of incentive, and more perhaps on the absolute amount

[13] *Company Income and Finance* 1949–53, National Institute of Economic and Social Research. Our engineering group corresponds approximately to the sum of the Institute's three groups: shipbuilding and non-electrical engineering; electrical engineering and electrical goods; other metal goods.

he owns.   Among the very large companies a quite small proportion may yet mean a large absolute sum which might conceivably be more important financially to a director or manager than his fee or salary.   But on the whole the evidence is that the average director, and certainly a director working full time for a company, will receive considerably more by way of fee or salary than as an owner of capital.   Of the total of about 925 directors in the very large industrial and commercial companies, only 146 were among the twenty largest voteholders in their company and about 260 held no more than *minimum qualifying shares*.   The number of these minimum holding directors is included in the information in our basic tables (*e.g.*, Appendix A 1), and Table IV D sums up in the rows marked B the distribution of companies according to the number of their directors holding no more than the minimum qualifying shares.   This measure is not ideal, since companies vary widely in the share qualification for directors.   It is, however, exceptional, as Appendix B illustrates, for this qualification to be more than £1,000—a capital sum which would presumably not yield a large proportion of directors' total income.

The different industries do not show any wide differences [14] except engineering, which had relatively numerous very large companies with many directors owning not more than the minimum qualifying shares. Though confined to a comparison of company sizes, Table IV D points to several important conclusions.

(1) On the average, almost two directors in every company have no more than qualifying shares (432 in 233 companies).

(2) The average proportion of such directors is highest in the very large companies where it is about five for every two, *i.e.*, 264 directors for the ninety-eight companies, and least in the smaller companies where it is about five for every four companies (114 for the eighty-eight).

(3) These averages are by no means representative because of the wide divergence in the number of directors concerned.   This divergence is particularly marked among the larger companies.   While 47% (forty-one out of eighty-eight) of the smaller large companies had about the average number of minimum-holding directors (*i.e.*, one to three), of the very large companies only twenty-nine out of ninety-eight (or 30%) were in this " typical " range.   Eleven very large companies had in 1951 seven or more directors holding no more than the minimum qualifying shares.

[14] And the industrial analysis is not worth presenting in a detailed table.

Tests A and B

Table IV D compares in detail for the three sizes of company (a) the number of directors among the largest twenty voteholders, and (b) the number owning no more than the qualifying amount of ordinary shares. The comparison reinforces the trend already observed for the directors of the larger companies to own less of the capital. The total number of directors owning no more than the qualifying shares is much greater than that of directors among the largest shareholders for the very large companies, rather less for the medium large, and much less for the smaller companies.

What is the relation between the results of the two tests? On the whole there is a consistency in the shareholding of any company's directors. Where two or more directors hold a large number of votes there will usually be no more than one director with no more than the minimum qualifying shares. This consistency holds true of medium and small as well as the very large companies. We can thus draw a useful distinction between companies where directors' control is divorced from ownership and companies where the two are " married " with at least two directors owning large blocs of shares. Here, the big contrast between sizes is that of the smaller as against the very large and medium large companies. Far more smaller companies have (in spite of their smaller boards) two or more directors among their largest twenty holders, and fewer have boards with two or more directors holding no more than qualifying shares. This confirms in a striking way the much wider divorce of control and ownership among the larger, compared with the smaller, companies.

The smaller companies, it is true, tend to have the smaller boards. To that extent they might, in the nature of things, be expected to have fewer directors among their largest twenty shareholders as well as a lower proportion of shares owned by the board. On the other hand, it is also in the nature of things easier for a director to be among the largest twenty shareholders and for the board to hold a higher proportion of shares of a company with smaller capital since a lower individual investment is required. On balance, the indices of directors' shareholding that we use are probably not unsatisfactory for comparing sizes.

§ 6. CHANGES IN THE CHARACTERISTICS OF THE
BOARD OF DIRECTORS, 1936–51

What has been the direction of change, if any, between 1936 and 1951 in the size of boards and the shareholding of directors?

TABLE IV E

CHANGE IN SIZE OF BOARDS OF VERY LARGE COMPANIES
1936–51

Size of board	Distribution of Co. very large in 1936 among stated sizes of board		Distribution of Co. very large in 1951 (and existing in 1936) among stated sizes of board	
	1936	1951	1936	1951*
3	0	0	1	1
4– 6	11	7	21	17
7– 9	25 } 36	20 } 27	36 } 58	30 } 48
10–12	14	19	17	23
13–15	5	8	8	9
16–18	5 } 30	7 } 39	3 } 34	7 } 44
19+	6	5	6	5
All sizes	66	66	92	92
Median average size	9	10	8	9

* As Table IV A, first row, less the six companies not formed in 1936.

Comparing the columns in Table IV E it appears that the size of the boards increased slightly on the whole; for the companies very large in 1951 from a median average of about eight to nine; for the companies very large *in 1936* from about nine to ten. This difference is according to expectation. About a third of the companies very large in 1951 (*i.e.* with £3m. capital or over) were not so in 1936 and their growth was accompanied by a growth in the size of their board. And most of the companies very large both in 1936 and 1951 had also been growing. It is indeed, on the whole, surprising that the size of boards did not tend to grow more. There is little sign of any Parkinson's Law here. In particular Table IV E shows that though there were in 1951 fewer very small boards of nine members or under, the very large boards of nineteen or more members were less numerous than in 1936. Two companies increased their boards up to, three reduced them from, that range.

Though there was little change in the size of boards there appeared to be some increase in the number of directors in common with other large companies. It was not possible to apply the same test in 1936 as in 1951 of other large companies since the National Institute's list of large companies referred only to 1953. But a random sample of the very large companies in 1936 seemed to show fewer directors in common with the

TABLE IV F

DISTRIBUTION IN 1936 AND 1951 OF COMPANIES VERY LARGE IN 1951* ACCORDING TO NUMBER OF DIRECTORS (A) AMONG LARGEST VOTEHOLDERS, AND (B) HOLDING NO MORE THAN MINIMUM SHARE QUALIFICATION

Number of directors	0	1	2	3	4	5	6	7+	Total of Co. (and of directors)	Average per Co.
				(Total of directors involved in brackets)						
A Among twenty largest holders										
1936	34	11 (11)	15 (30)	10 (30)	9 (36)	3 (15)	4 (24)	5† (41)	91‡ (187)	2·0
1951§	36	25 (25)	12 (24)	8 (24)	5 (20)	2 (10)	0 (0)	3‖ (22)	91‡ (125)	1·4
B Holding no more than minimum share qualification										
1936	22	19 (19)	14 (28)	13 (39)	12 (48)	5 (25)	2 (12)	5¶ (43)	92 (214)	2·3
1951§	30	17 (17)	6 (12)	5 (15)	7 (28)	9 (45)	7 (42)	11** (92)	92 (251)	2·7

Bracketed group totals: 1951§ (A) — 31 (146) and 18 (76). 1951§ (B) — 12 (80) and 27 (179).

* and formed in 1936.
† 7, 7, 7, 7 and 13 respectively.
‡ One Co. data not available. (Tobacco Securities Trust).
§ Figures correspond to those of the 1st and 2nd lines of Table IV D except that the six companies not formed in 1936 are here omitted for the comparison of 1936 with 1951.
‖ 7, 7 and 8 respectively.
¶ 7, 7, 8, 10 and 11 respectively.
** 7, 7, 7, 7, 7, 8, 8, 9, 9, 10 and 13 respectively.

Institute's list than would be accounted for by *some* companies on this list being, in 1936, considerably smaller than in 1951. Further work should be done on directors-in-common, tracing, in particular, the technical relation between the companies having directors-in-common.[15] For instance, is a brewery company likely to have a director who is also a director of an hotel company, and is this form of " vertical " integration increasing? Is integration through the method of directors-in-common growing in other directions, particularly diagonal or " service " integration,[16] for instance marine insurance companies having directors on shipping companies' boards.

These possible forms of interlocking in the true sense lie outside the main scope of the present book and we must return to the changes in the shareholding of directors.

Since both measures refer to the number of directors a company, one table, IV F, can conveniently sum up for the very large companies the change (row A) in directors among the largest twenty voteholders and (row B) in directors holding no more than minimum qualifying shares.

The 1951 distribution of companies reproduces the first row of Table IV D except that the six companies that did not exist in 1936 have, for fair comparison of the two years, been excluded. Between 1936 and 1951, it will be seen, the relative frequency of companies with three directors or over among the twenty largest holders fell very much, in fact from thirty-one to eighteen, while the number with only one such director increased from eleven to twenty-five. Less change, however, occurred in the frequency of companies with several directors holding no more than qualifying shares. The company average of such directors was 2·3 in 1936, 2·7 in 1951. More significant perhaps of the increasing divorce of control from ownership than this slight rise is the fact that whereas in 1936 twelve companies only had five or more directors apparently with no more than minimum qualifying shares, twenty-seven companies had this characteristic in 1951.

Table IV G uses, to measure the change, more comprehensive measures of the percentage of ordinary shares held by the whole board. Here, in order to trace any difference between growing companies that had a capital of £3m. or more in 1951 but less in 1936, the very large companies

[15] An inquiry of this sort is being undertaken by Dr. Michael Beesley at the University of Birmingham.
[16] For the various directions of integration see Florence, *Logic of British and American Industry*, pp. 44–47.

TABLE IV G

DISTRIBUTION IN 1936 AND 1951 OF COMPANIES VERY LARGE IN 1936 AND 1951, ACCORDING TO THE PERCENTAGE OF ORDINARY SHARES HELD BY THE WHOLE BOARD

(1) % of ordinary shares held by total board	(2) Less than ½%	(3) ½%+	(4) 1%	(5) 2%	(6) 3%	(7) 5%	(8) 10%	(9) 20%	Total	(10) Ratio cols. $\frac{5-9}{2-9}$	(11) (Median) Average % of shares held
"Very large" Co. with £3m. capital or more in 1936* — Distribution (1) in 1936	20	3	5	10	9	6	5	7	65	·57	2·4%
— Distribution (2) in 1951	22	10	9	8	4	1	3	8	65	·36	1·0%
"Promoted" Co. with £3m. capital or more in 1951, but less in 1936 — Distribution (3) in 1936	1	4	3	1	5	4	4	5	27	·70	3·5%
— Distribution (4) in 1951	4	5	3	3	5	2	2	3	27	·56	2·7%
Total industrial and commercial Co. very large in 1951 (excluding Co. not formed in 1936) — Distribution [(1)+(3)] in 1936	21	7	8	11	14	10	9	12	92	·61	2·8%
— Distribution [(2)+(4)] in 1951†	26	15	12	11	9	3	5	11	92	·42	1·5%
Total of brewing Co. very large in 1951 (1936)	1	0	0	0	0	3	1	5	10	·90	20%
(1951)	1	0	1	0	2	3	1	2	10	·80	8%

* Excluding three companies very large in 1936 but not in 1951.

† This row corresponds to the top row of Table IV C except that the six companies not formed in 1936 are omitted.

of 1951 are split into two parts. Those with £3m. or more in 1936 [17] are to be found in the first two rows. The same trend can be detected, in both divisions, toward more divorce of control from ownership. Among the growing companies (in the third and fourth rows) " promoted " from medium or smaller large to the very large size, the average percentage of shares held by the board fell from about 3·5% to 2·7%; among companies already very large in 1936 (in the first and second rows) the average percentage fell from 2·4% to 1·0%. In both divisions, too, the ratio of companies with a high-sharing board of directors (2% held or above) fell considerably. Proportionately, however, the fall in directors' shareholding was less in the " promoted " companies. Brewing companies had in both years much higher percentages of the shares held by the board but here also divorce of ownership from control appeared to be growing. Instead of five of the ten very large brewery companies having a board owning 20% or more of the ordinary shares, the bottom row of Table IV G shows that only two were left in 1951 ; the average percentage of ordinary shares held by the whole board fell from 20% to 8%.

By all measures, then, directors' share holdings in the industrial and commercial and in brewery companies are seen to have diminished. In 1951 the boards held a lower percentage of shares; fewer companies had two or more of their directors among the twenty largest shareholders, the number of directors holding no more than minimum qualifying shares had (slightly) increased and the number of companies with five or more such directors had increased considerably.

§ 7. The Grounds for the Appointment of Directors

Before concluding this chapter on directors we must put their relation to shareholding in correct perspective. We have found that the great majority of directors are not among the largest shareholders and many own no more than the minimum of shares to qualify as directors. Most of these relatively shareless directors are probably full-time " inside " executive officers of the company and the holding of office is certainly a more frequent ground for appointment to directorships than shareholding, particularly where boards are small.

If directors are not appointed by reason of their executive position in the company nor yet by reason of large shareholding, what other reason may account for their position? Professor R. A. Gordon quotes

---

[17] As said elsewhere (p. 70), only three of the very large companies of 1936 were not very large also in 1951.

an illuminating analysis of all the main reasons for appointing 1,868 individual directors of American manufacturing companies.[18]   For just over a quarter of all the directors (527 or 28%) the main reason was knowledge of the technical details of the business and, as Gordon says, this would refer chiefly to full-time working directors; and a further thirty (or 3%) explicitly gave as reason " executive office."   Two other main reasons adding up to 408 (or 22%) are connected with ownership: " shareholder or represents important shareholder."   The remaining reasons can be grouped as follows:

		No.	*% of All grounds*
Retired or former official of company	...	78	4%
Specialised counsel or knowledge ...	...	328	18%
Sound executive judgment	... ...	350	19%
Represents customers, allied interests, banks or financial interest	... ...	105	6%
Total		861	47%

This group accounts largely for the outside director who holds few shares and no office.   Apart from the former officials, the outside director will often be loosely called interlocking since more than one company may need " specialised counsel or knowledge "—legal, accounting, technical, and need men of " sound executive judgment."   But the more particular reason for directors common to more than one company lies probably in the group representing " customers, allied interests, banks or financial interest."   Directors appointed for this reason may be correctly called " interlocking."

Unfortunately, only small-scale analysis of the appointment of directors has been carried through in England.   This book is not concerned with directors as such, and this chapter must therefore end with only a brief summary of the more important findings.

The most important single piece of information to secure would be the proportion of directors of any company or group of companies that worked full time.   At present this can only be guessed at by the characteristics we have already measured.   A smaller board, for instance, probably

---

[18] *Business Leadership in the Large Corporation*, p. 127, reproduced from the National Industrial Conference Board, quoted in my *Logic of British and American Industry*, p. 207.

portends that it is a working board, a director also a director of another large company that he is *not* a working director of any one company.[19]

In my paper to the Royal Statistical Society meeting in 1947 [20] I reported upon a sample of companies drawn from the iron, coal and steel, the industrial and commercial and the brewery sections of the Stock Exchange *Year Book* for 1936.   This sample, of one in ten, was examined by Baldamus, Siviter and myself to find the antecedents and qualifications of directors, and the possible effect of such antecedents upon company policy.

On the Boards of 436 sample English trading companies we traced at least 127 accountants, 58 lawyers, and 88 men with some admitted technical qualifications.[21]   The number of the accountants and technicians among the directors, though not the lawyers, increased with the size of the company.   For companies with capital below £100,000, technical men numbered $2 \cdot 6\%$, accountants $3 \cdot 2\%$ of all directors, roughly eleven and fourteen per hundred companies.[22] For companies with capital between £100,000 and £500,000, technical men numbered $4 \cdot 7\%$, accountants $5 \cdot 0\%$, of all directors, roughly twenty-three and twenty-five per hundred companies.   While for large companies with capital above £500,000 technical men were $4 \cdot 2\%$, accountants $7 \cdot 6\%$ of all directors, roughly twenty-nine and fifty-three per hundred companies. . . .

The random sample of English companies disclosed 172 directors with a title, forming over 8% of all directors.   Titled directors were particularly frequent in the largest companies; among the sample companies with over £500,000 capital they numbered almost 15% of all directors; indeed 48% of all these large companies had some titled director on its board, and in the iron, coal and steel section all the sample companies of this size had this distinction.   At a rough estimate almost half the titled directors inherited their title or acquired it by prowess in the fighting services or sport and not in business and can be considered as probable guinea-pigs.

In 1955 D. P. Barritt [23] surveyed 500 firms of all sizes of which 375 had assets of more than £500,000 and would be comparable to, and indeed include, many of the companies surveyed in this book.   The question Mr. Barritt sought to answer was the average number of directors *per firm* who possessed formally stated qualifications either by reason of university

---

[19] A further test would of course be the remuneration of the directors. At present, however, only the remuneration for the whole board is given under headings that often vary from company to company.

[20] "The Statistical Analysis of Joint Stock Company Control." *Statistical Journal*, 1947 Part I.

[21] Since experts on the board of a company are likely to pull more weight than non-expert directors, their number per hundred companies is more significant than their proportion to total of directors.

[22] See note [21].

[23] *Journal of Industrial Economics*, July 1957, pp. 220–224.

degrees or professional, financial or other " paper " qualifications or both. The answer he found was 1·39 for firms of £500,000 to £2,000,000 assets (equivalent to our smaller large companies) and 2·05 for firms of assets over £2m. (equivalent to our medium and very large companies). Considering the differences in the total membership of the board the proportion of directors so qualified would be much the same in both sizes of firm—in fact about a quarter of the directors. Comparing industries, Barritt found " the average number of ' qualified ' directors on boards was greatest in engineering and motor (vehicles) firms—over a third in fact; and was lowest, only about a sixth, in textiles and paper."

For industry generally Barritt found a higher proportion of qualified directors in 1955 than I and my colleagues found in 1936 and this may, as he suggests, be due partly to a real trend toward appointing qualified men (or greater ease in acquiring qualifications). But it may also be due to the rather more stringent test of qualification in the sources we used.

The evidence of Mr. Bosworth Monk may be cited against any real trend toward more technically qualified directors. Confining himself to the engineering industries (including motors and shipbuilding) Bosworth Monk [24] found 21·5% as the proportion of technically qualified directors in 1952 with the highest proportion (42·5%) in aircraft and components, and the lowest (9·5%) in office equipment companies. Judging from the proportion of members of the Council of the Institution of Mechanical Engineers holding directorships he sees reason to speak of the professional engineer suffering " something of an eclipse " in the last seventy years. According to his calculation the proportion had fallen from 51·5% in 1882 to 29·5% in 1952.

The reasons for men being in control of large companies in England and the characteristics of such " leaders," whether or not they are directors, will be briefly considered at the end of the next chapter—devoted to Control. Knowledge is gradually being accumulated, but we can do no more than refer readers to such works as G. H. Copeman, *Leaders of British Industry* (Gee, 1955), R. Stewart, *Management Succession* (Acton Society Trust, 1955), A. V. Clements, *Managers* (Allen & Unwin).

---

[24] Paper read before Section G, British Association for the Advancement of Science, Sept. 7, 1954, published in *Engineering*.

Chapter V

OWNERSHIP AND THE SEAT OF CONTROL

§ 1. The Pilot Inquiry of 1936

ONE of the main reasons for analysing the concentration of voting powers and the types of directors in Chapters III and IV was to reach some conclusion as to the seat of control in the large companies. Perhaps the first attempt to do this for English companies was contained in my article in the 1947 (Part I) *Journal of the Royal Statistical Society* on the " Statistical Analysis of Joint Stock Company Control." This article reported a small pilot inquiry into the 1936 position in twenty large companies, undertaken to ensure that the analysis of larger numbers of companies would not be too abstract and removed from the facts and the possibilities of measuring the facts in its assumptions and classifications.

In this pilot inquiry types of control were classed by three tests. The principal test was the degree of concentration of voting shares, discussed in Chapter III; a further test was the shareholding of directors; and a third test the type of large shareholders and possible connections between them.

As far as concentration of shares went, all the " pilot " companies showed some degree of divorce of management from control. None of the twenty companies had one shareholder owning 50% or more of the stock and thus constituting a form of control in which ownership of capital was clearly dominant. Thus the case of the owner-manager entrepreneur, assumed as normal at least for the sake of argument by so many economists, did not appear at all at first sight. However, as I then wrote, " Undoubtedly . . . there are such cases even among large companies." I went on to stretch a point by extending the notion of an entrepreneur from a person to a company. " For a subsidiary with all or the majority of its stock owned by a single parent company, the parent company is the classical type of entrepreneur, both owning and managing the subsidiary. It still remains a question, of course, whether there is any such entrepreneur (company or person) for the parent company."

Subsequent investigation of all large English industrial and commercial companies had confirmed that there are cases of one-shareholder control; but that they are relatively few and are diminishing in number. It was shown in Chapter III that, excluding completely subsidiary companies with 100% of votes in the hands of a parent company there were in 1936 seven very large companies with a single shareholding 50% or over of votes and in 1951 also seven. But in the average very large company the largest shareholder held not 50% but about 10% of the votes.

This rarity of the one-man owned company and the much lower than 50% of votes held by any *one* shareholder reduces the utility and significance of any analysis based on the proportion of shares held by a single owner. Our statistical approach to control, for reasons given in Chapter II, will mainly turn on the proportion of votes owned by the twenty largest shareholders. This criterion was adopted in my original pilot inquiry, was used in the (later) large-scale American investigation of the Temporary National Economic Committee, and was continued in my further inquiries reported in *Logic of British and American Industry*.

The pilot inquiry into the twenty large companies found that in three companies the twenty largest shareholders held less than 10% of votes and in another three they held 10–19% of votes. These shareholdings, it was thought, gave little control. The remaining fourteen companies, where twenty shareholders held 20% or more of votes, were divided into nine companies probably shareholder-controlled and five uncertain in control.

Subdivision of fourteen companies where largest twenty shareholders own 20% *of votes.* Pilot Inquiry, 1936

Connected persons among twenty largest hold 20% of votes or over	3	} probably shareholder-controlled
Companies among twenty largest hold over 20% of votes.	5	
Twenty largest shareholders consist of connected persons AND companies ..	1	
Twenty largest shareholders neither companies nor apparently connected ..	2	} Control uncertain
Largest shareholder a nominee	1	
Too many nominees among largest twenty ..	2	

§ 2. THE FULL-SCALE INQUIRIES OF 1936 AND 1951

Extensive inquiries were undertaken subsequent to the pilot study. They made use of the pilot analysis but introduced a finer classification in the proportion of the total votes owned by the largest or by the twenty largest voteholders. The distribution of companies in 1936 and 1951 according to this classification or grading has already been reported in

Chapter III.   Now, however, we can bring in two further tests of possible control besides the tests by the voting powers of the largest and of the largest twenty voteholders.

Companies may in fact be picked out as possibly controlled by vote-ownership through four statistical tests or criteria.

A. That the single largest shareholder has 20% of the votes or over.

B. That the largest twenty shareholders have 30% of the votes or over.

C. That if A or B are true, these shareholders are companies (C) or, if persons (P), are connected, rather than institutions (I) or nominees (N).

D. That the directors, between them, hold 5% or more of the ordinary shares.

Tests A and B were further subdivided as described in Chapter III. Test A divides companies into Grades of Concentration I or II, according as the largest shareholder owns 50% or over, or 20 to 50% of the votes.

Test B divides companies into Grades of Concentration III, IV, V, VI and VII according as the largest twenty shareholders have 50% or over, 30 to 49%, 20 to 29%, 10 to 19%, and under 10% of the votes.[1]

The question to be finally settled here is what precise proportion of votes below 50% should be considered to give the single or the twenty largest shareholders virtual control.   In short, if we call the rare companies having one shareholder with over 50% of votes as first-degree shareholder control, what should constitute lesser degrees of shareholder control?   Based merely on quantitative statistical data, 20 to 50% of votes for a single holder and a clear majority of over 50% of votes for the twenty largest shareholders (Grades II and III) may be classed prima facie as second and third degree shareholder control.

At the other end of the scale, companies with 10–20% or less than 10% of votes for the twenty largest shareholders (Grades VI and VII in Tables IIA and B) may prima facie be considered as without shareholders' control.   In the middle of the scale, shareholders' control may be considered very doubtful in companies of Grade V where the twenty largest vote-owners (not necessarily in communication or jointly resolute) hold 20 to 30% of the votes, and no single owner has 20% or more.   But in Grade IV, where the twenty largest vote-owners hold from 30 to 50% of

---

[1] Many companies will respond positively to *two* tests.   Obviously a company which is, on Test A, in Grade I—the largest shareholder owning 50% of the votes—will also be in Grade III, since the twenty largest shareholders will have 50% or more of votes.   Such companies are graded according to the more severe test and put in the higher of the two grades—in this case, Grade I.

TABLE V A

NAMES AND NUMBER OF THE VERY LARGE COMPANIES IN EACH OF SEVEN GRADES OF VOTE-CONCENTRATION, AND TYPE OF LARGE HOLDER IN THE FIRST FOUR GRADES: 1936

Brackets refer to size: Capital less than £3m: [Square] in 1951; (Round) in 1936

Grade:	I	II	III	IV	V	VI	VII
Main category of bloc holders	Largest holding 50% or more	*percentage of vote* 20–49%	50% or more	*Largest twenty holdings: percentage of vote* 30–49%	20–29%	10–19%	0–9%
(P) Personal	(Albright & W.) Burton Carreras Illus. News (Lewis, J.) Morris	(Austin) Ranks	B. Cocoa Colman (E. Electric) Lewis Inv. Marks and S. (Metal Box) Morgan C. (Robinson) (Rowntree) Tate and Lyle Union International	(Bristol Aero) (Fison) Paton and B. Reckitt (Winterbottom)			
(C) Company	(B.U. Shoe Mach.) Ford Woolworth	Ass. B. Pictures Ass. Electric Tobacco Securities		Amal. Metal			
(I) Institution	Ass. News B–A Tobacco Lancs. Cotton Selfridge		Boots				

(N) Nominee	Con. Tin Smelt (Bowater) (B. Oxygen) (Tunnel P.)	B. Celanese (Crompton P.)	Amal. Press (Gt. Univ. Stores)	Shareholding all relatively small and not categorised		
(M) Mixed		Lyons	B. Match, Kemsley News, (London Brick), (Lucas), Tube Invest.			
				[Amal. Cotton]	Ass. P. Cement.	B.S.A.
				(Beecham)	B. Aluminium	Bleachers Assn.
				(B. Plaster Bd.)	Bradford Dyers	Bovril
				(B. Ropes)	(Brush Elec.)	Dunlop
				Courtaulds	Calico Print.	E. Sewing Cotton
				(Dickinson)	Debenham	Harrods
				Elec. and Mus.	Fine Cotton	Harrods B.A.
				(Hawker S.)	G.E.C.	Liebig
				Home & Col.	Goodlass Wall	Radiation
				Lever	I.C.I.	U. Dairies
				[Platt Bros.]	Imp. Tobacco	
				Sears	Int. Tea	
				Siemens	(Pinchin J.)	
				(Smith S.)	(Ruston & H.)	
				Spillers	Rylands	
				Turner & N.		
				U. Molasses		
				Wallpaper		
				Wiggins T.		
TOTALS: (94)	13	15	13	19	15	10
without sq. brkts. (92)	13	15	13	17[+2]	15	10
without all brkts. (65)	9	10	7	11[+2]	12	10

9
9
6

TABLE V B

NAMES AND NUMBER OF THE VERY LARGE COMPANIES IN EACH OF SEVEN GRADES OF VOTE-CONCENTRATION AND TYPE OF LARGE HOLDER IN THE FIRST FOUR GRADES: 1951.

Brackets refer to 1936: [Square] Co. not formed; (Round) Co. less than £3m. capital

Grade: Main category of bloc holders	I	II	III	IV	V	VI	VII
	Largest holding percentage of vote		*Largest twenty holdings: percentage of vote.*				
	50%+	20—49%	50%+	30—49%	20—29%	10—19%	0—9%
(P) Personal	Burton (Lewis, J.)	Carreras (Crompton P.,) Illus. News Ranks (Rowntree) [Smith, W. H.]	(Albright & W.) B. Cocoa [Lebus] [Rootes]	Marks & Spencer Morgan C. (Bristol Aero) Colman (Robinson)			
(C) Company	(B.U. Shoe Mach.) Ford Woolworth	Ass. Elec. Tobacco Securities	[B. Sugar]				
(I) Institution		Ass. B. Pictures		Lyons			
(N) Nominee	Cons. Tin.	Home & Colonial (Tunnel Portland)		B. Celanese Electrical & M. (Gt. U. Stores) [Odeon]			
(M) Mixed			Sears Union Int.	Bovril (B. Oxygen) B. Match (Brush Elec.) Kemsley News (Winterbottom)			

Shareholdings all relatively small and not categorised

	Amal. Press	Amal. Metal	Ass. P. Cement.
	Ass. News	(Austin)	(Beecham)
	B. Aluminium	Bradford Dyers	B.S.A.
	Courtauld	[B.I.I.C.]	Bleachers
	(Dickinson)	(B. Plaster Bd.)	Boots
	(Fison)	(B. Ropes)	B.A. Tobacco
	(Lucas)	(Bowater)	Debenham
	(Metal Box)	Calico Prints	Dunlop
	Morris	(E. Electric)	Fine Cotton
	Rylands	E. Sewing Cotton	Harrods
	Tate & Lyle	G.E.C.	I.C.I.
	Tube Inv.	Goodlass, Wall	Lever
	Wiggins T.	Harrods B.A.	Lewis Inv.
		(Hawker S.)	Liebig
		Imp. Tobacco	Radiation.
		Int. Tea	U. Dairies
		Lancs. Cotton	U. Molasses
		(London Brick)	
		Paton & B.	
		(Pinchin J.).	
		Reckitt.	
		(Ruston & H.)	
		Selfridge	
		Siemens	
		Spillers	
		(Smith S.)	
		Wallpaper	
		Turner & N.	

TOTALS: (98)	6	11	7	16	13	28	17
without sq. brkts. (92)	6	10	4	15	13	27	17
without all brkts. (65)	4	7	3	9	9	17	16

the total vote, the criteria (C) and (D), referring to the type of shareholder and the shareholding by directors, must be brought into use.

Wherever there is high concentration of votes among a few shareholders, the question of the type of large shareholder is important in its own right. It is given a prominent place in Tables V A and B for the high-concentration Grades I, II, III and IV. These tables give all the very large companies by name, and place those in Grades I to IV into four subdivisions, according as these twenty largest voteholders are (P) persons, (C) companies, (I) institutions, such as insurance companies or investment trusts, (N) nominees or (M) mixed. Thus in Grade IV, where the degree of shareholder control is uncertain and depends particularly on the type of shareholder, companies in subdivisions IV P, IV C or IV I are those that have a high proportion of the 30% to 49% of votes held (P) by personal holders often connected through family ties or (C) or (I) by companies or institutions. Companies in subdivision IV M have a mixed bag of large personal, company or other shareholders, while companies in subdivision IV N suffer further uncertainty as to control due to a high proportion of nominee shares. In Grades I and II there is only one—the largest—voteholder involved so there *is* no mixed subdivision (M). In Grades III and IV however it is not always easy to decide whether the twenty largest voteholders are mainly of one type or mixed. The rule adopted is to assign to one type where 20% or more of the total vote is of that type and of no other.

The fourth criterion of the seat of control, that of directors' shares, will be taken up in the next section.

§ 3. The Type of Large Shareholder: Effect on Control

This cross-division by type of shareholder is undoubtedly important in the analysis of company control. An industrial company is more likely to hold a given large block of shares for the purpose of control, than an institution like an insurance company or an investment trust. This probability can be tested by investigating the number of large companies in which any given large shareholder will hold shares. The shareholder who wants to spread his risks, rather than control any one company, will presumably invest in many companies. One inquiry in fact concluded that [2] the average shareholder held shares in about eight companies.

---

[2] Ellinger and Carter, *Financial Times*, March 2, 1949. Though the total of shareholdings in Britain may have run to ten millions and over, the authors estimated that there were in 1941 only a million and a quarter shareholders.

His investments being thus split up, a given shareholder is most unlikely to appear among the largest twenty shareholders of more than one large company unless he is a multimillionaire.

In view of post-war levels of income tax it can be held with some confidence that no *private person who spreads his risk* will in recent years have appeared among the largest twenty shareholders of a large company; but it is quite possible that the larger insurance companies and investment trusts, though their main object is to spread risk, will so appear. They have such large funds to invest that in spite of investing in many companies they may yet appear repeatedly among the largest twenty voteholders. The following table provides the direct evidence.

Reappearances of certain insurance companies among largest holders in the very large industrial and commercial companies, 1951

Insurance companies	No. of appearances among largest twenty voteholders of the ninety-eight very large companies	No. of such appearances holding more than 2% of voting stock
Prudential	47	6
Pearl	33	2
Royal London Mutual ..	27	2
Refuge Assurance ..	18	1
U.K. Temperance & General	16	1
Royal Exchange	15	1
Equity	10	3

The Prudential Assurance Co. appeared, in 1951, as one of the twenty largest voteholders in forty-seven out of the total of over ninety-eight very large companies where the concentration of votes could be analysed. The frequency of reappearing insurance companies in 1951 compared to persons can be tested by inspection, in Appendix B, of the lists of largest holders.

The bona fide investment trusts may be said to exist for the very purpose of spreading risks, not primarily at least for control of a single company. They may be expected to appear and reappear among the shareholders of the large companies even more extensively than the insurance companies. But for the very reason that they spread their net wide and do not confine investment to the large companies, their holding of shares in any one large company is not so likely as insurance company shares to be among the *twenty largest* shareholders of the very large companies. Moreover, the total of the holdings of investment trusts is generally smaller than that of insurance companies.

Among financial institutions that can invest in ordinary shares, the insurance companies are outstanding in the extent of their assets. In 1958, according to the Radcliffe Committee Report, the insurance companies established in Britain had assets of £5,990m. (£1,740m. in 1937). Superannuation funds came second with £2,500m. and investment trusts, quoted in the London Stock Exchange, only third with (in 1957) £710m. We therefore limit detailed analysis of institutions and trusts to the insurance companies.

From the standpoint of control, however, nominee shares must be distinguished from the shares of all other types of holder. Their purposes are various and sometimes uncertain. At the time of my pilot inquiry in 1947, I expected to find that nominee shares existed for the very purpose of obscuring the real seat of control and that their presence among the largest twenty holdings might well make it impossible, at the very outset, to assign the company to any one type of control.[3]

Subsequent investigation and discussion, however, has made this obstacle appear less formidable. Certain nominee companies were found to appear and reappear among the twenty largest shareholders of company after company, like the insurance companies and investment trusts. Many nominees, particularly the bank nominees, seem to act as intermediaries for a number of beneficiaries.[4] It is these nominees that appear and reappear, particularly often among the largest twenty shareholders. Confining attention to the very large companies in 1951, I found the names of the same twelve nominees appearing in this way at least five times.

The upshot of these findings is that the nominee holdings are probably only exceptionally a device for hiding the real control of a company. Most of such holdings are in the name of some agency often connected with a bank which will transact business for a number of beneficiaries. In so far as the beneficiaries retain their right of voting, these " composite " nominees should not really appear among the twenty largest voteholders at all. However, it is not possible to distinguish such composite nominees from nominees that are a single voting unit.

---

[3] See Florence, " The Statistical Analysis of Joint Stock Companies," *Statistical Journal,* 1947, Part I, pp. 6, 7.

[4] See Cohen Committee report, 1945, para. 78, for sample analysis of beneficiaries and para. 81 for legal procedure.

Of the twelve nominees whose names reappeared so often among the twenty largest shareholders of very large companies, six owned no holdings forming 2% or more of any company's total vote. But the remaining six nominees (lettered " A " to " F ") owned a number of holdings in different companies, each amounting to over 2% of the total vote. Details appear in the following table:

	Total Holdings	Under 2%	2–5%	5–10%	Over 10%
Nominee Co. " A "	11	8	1	1	1
" B "	20	16	2	2	0
" C "	24	21	3	0	0
" D "	5	4	1	0	0
" E "	12	9	0	2	1
" F "	9	7	0	0	2
Total	81	65	7	5	4

In four companies, nominee holdings appear with over 10% of the vote. These companies were Associated Picture in which nominee "A" held 25·1% of the vote, Electric and Musical, in which nominee " E " held 37·3% of the vote, and Tunnel Portland Cement and Great Universal Stores in which nominee " F " held 22·2% and 16·2%.

§ 4. ANALYSIS OF COMPANIES BY VOTE-CONCENTRATION AND TYPE OF TOP VOTEHOLDER

The third test of owner control depends on the type of shareholder, and we have considered the institutional type, such as insurance companies and also the nominee shareholder as well as the personal and industrial company shareholder. It is reasonable to suppose that an industrial company acquires a large block of shares for the sake of control, that a person or his nominee does so less certainly for that purpose, and an institution such as an insurance company or investment trust least certainly, if at all. Whatever the motive of the various bodies for acquiring and holding large shares, it is important in all companies where concentration of votes is considerable, to find out the precise type of these large investors.

A considerable concentration of votes may be taken to mean all cases where the largest twenty holders own at least 30% of the total vote, or the single largest 20%.   This definition covers the Grades of vote-concentration I to IV that have already been distinguished.   In Tables V A and V B accordingly, all very large companies in these four top grades of vote-concentration are classed (P), (C), (I), (N), according to the predominance of one or other of the four main categories of largest vote-holders, or (M) a mixture of them.   The classification by type presents, of course, no difficulties in Grades I and II, where the single largest holder involved must be of one category or another, and there are no mixed category companies.   In Grades III and IV, referring to the twenty largest holders, the guiding principle has been to class the company in that category out of the four that has 20% of the total vote.   The percentage of the total vote held by the total of shareholders of each category is recorded (*e.g.*, Appendix A 1) for every company in our list.   If there is more than one such category or no particular category with over 20% of the vote, the company is classed as mixed.

Table V A refers to 1936, Table V B to 1951.   Both tables contain the names of all companies that were very large (*i.e.*, with £3m. capital or over) in 1951.   Companies not of this size in 1936 are enclosed in round brackets.   Companies not formed in 1936 are enclosed in the 1951 table in square brackets.   Companies (there are only two of them) [5] very large in 1936 but not in 1951, are enclosed in square brackets in the 1936 table. They appear for 1951 among the medium large companies in Table V C. Thus it is possible when looking into changes between 1936 and 1951 to compare companies classified by size, either as in 1936 or 1951.

In my *Logic of British and American Industry* [6] a classification was made for eighty-two companies very large in 1936 (including shipping and brewing companies as well as industrial and commercial) according to concentration of votes and type of holder in particular persons and companies or financial institutions.   The classification was designed to discover how companies were distributed into companies with a dominant interest based on shareholding, companies with no dominant interest or companies that were marginal.   I wrote at the time: " Research is still proceeding on the large English industrial companies and it is safer to declare many companies marginal in their assignment."[7]   On the whole this research has shown that in 1936 a larger proportion of companies had no dominant interest than originally assigned, mainly owing to the

[5] See footnote, Chap. III. p. 70.
[6] Chap. V, § 3, p. 202.
[7] *Op. cit.* p. 202.

TABLE V C

DISTRIBUTION OF COMPANIES WITH TOP GRADES (I to IV) OF VOTE-CONCENTRATION ACCORDING TO CATEGORY OF PREDOMINANT VOTEHOLDERS

	Total in Grades I to IV	Personal	Company	Institutions	Nominee	Mixed	Ratio of personal to total
Companies very large as of 1936							
1. Distribution in 1936*	32	14	6	5	3	4	·44
2. Distribution in 1951†	23	8	4	2	4	5	·35
Companies of various sizes as of 1951							
3. Very large*:							
Distribution in 1936 ..	50	24	7	5	8	6	·48
4. Very large†:							
Distribution in 1951 ..	40 ⎫	17 ⎫	6	2	7	8	·42
5. Medium large:							
Distribution in 1951 ..	16 ⎬ 99	8 ⎬ 48	2	1	3	2	·50
6. Smaller large:							
Distribution in 1951 ..	43 ⎭	23 ⎭	4	4	2	10	·54

* See table V A
† See Table V B

test then adopted. My present standard of "dominant interest" is stiffer. 100% subsidiaries of companies, even if the parent company was not on our list, were excluded and the twenty largest shareholders were required to have 30% or more of the total vote, rather than 20%, *i.e.*, Grade V is excluded. On the other hand, more of the largest holders concentrating a 30% vote have been definitely classified, so that we now have fewer marginal cases.

Comparing Tables V A and B, it is possible to trace the change in types of predominant holders in the companies of Grades I to IV of vote-concentration between the years 1936 and 1951. The numbers of companies involved are given in the first column of Table V C which also allows for comparisons between companies of different size in 1951. As already said, in Chapter III, there was a decline in vote-concentration, and this now appears (by comparing rows 1 with 2, and 3 with 4) to have been mainly in personal and institutional concentration of voteholding, rather than in company or nominee concentration. Among the companies very large in 1936, the companies with mainly personal concentration fell from thirteen to eight, and among those very large in 1951, fell from twenty-four to seventeen. The companies mainly with institutional concentration that were very large either in 1936 or 1951 fell from five to two.

For the details of holdings in 1951 in the very large companies readers should refer to Appendix B, where the twenty largest voteholders are named wherever the company was in the top four grades of vote-concentration and had certain other characteristics specified later (§ 6), and thus wherever ownership of votes was likely to have an important influence on control and policy.

No formal statistical analysis has been made of these names, but it is evident that most of the companies whose owners appear to be in control fall into specific categories. Family control certainly forms the majority among the smaller large owner-controlled companies, as evidenced by the repetition of the same family name among the largest twenty voteholders. But it is also noticeable that if one company, one institution (such as an insurance company) or even a nominee appears amongst the largest twenty voteholders of any given company, so, respectively, will other companies or institutions or nominees. "Birds of a feather" seem to flock together. Examples in Appendix B are Associated Electric, Bovril, British Match, and Ford and the same flocking together is found in medium and smaller companies.

The number of holdings by institutions is much greater than holdings by companies. But the company holdings are on average larger and are more significant for control. Apart from the " subsidiary " companies (graded I C) where another company, not already on our list, has 50% or more of the votes and is a legally recognised holding company, there are several listed companies that are, in fact, probably subsidiary to one or more other companies.

Owner control cannot here be tested by directors' shares, since companies cannot be directors. But certain companies have among their shareholders several companies holding between them a majority, or a large proportion, of the votes.[8] As pointed out in my pilot inquiry,[9] this device probably indicates that the several companies each desire a " finger in the pie," thus co-ordinating their interests; or, at least, want some power of veto. Whatever the motive for ownership, these " company-owned companies " are of considerable interest for control, and, however hard it sometimes is to analyse their vote-concentration and directors' interests, they must not be omitted from consideration.

The medium and smaller large companies were studied for 1951 but not 1936 and the results appeared in Table III C as far as the number of companies in various vote-concentration grades were concerned. These companies, less well known and, in any case, samples, are not tabulated by name. The numerical distribution of those in the top four grades of vote-concentration I to IV, according to the predominant category of voteholder appears in Table V C. The salient features of this distribution as far as 1951 is concerned are that the smaller and medium, compared to the very large companies, have relatively more concentration in personal voteholding; about the same proportion in institutional and mixed; but considerably less concentration of company and nominee holdings. Since concentration of voteholdings in personal hands was the most frequent case, even in the very large companies, this means that for companies of all sizes, concentration of votes in personal holdings is by far the most frequent case. In fact, in 1951, it accounted for nearly half, forty-eight out of all the ninety-nine companies, with vote-concentration of Grades I to IV.

---

[8] Notably, among the *very large companies* (see App. B): Associated Electric; Tobacco Securities; among the *medium large companies*: British Timken; Sunday Pictorial Newspapers; among the *smaller large companies*: Colthrop Board; Peek Bros.; Telegraph Construction; Wallis Tin Stamping.

[9] *Statistical Journal*, 1947, p. 11.

§ 5. ASSOCIATION OF VOTE-CONCENTRATION AND
DIRECTOR SHAREHOLDING

The main characteristics that have been singled out as tests of control by share-ownership are (1) vote-concentration of Grades I to IV, (2) particularly in the hands of persons or companies, and (3) substantial ownership of ordinary shares by the board of directors. The important question now to be asked is how far these characteristics are found combined or associated in the same companies in a " syndrome " that would establish them as definitely owner-controlled.

We can assume that companies in Grade I of vote-concentration, where more than 50% of votes are owned by one person or body of persons, are controlled by that ownership. In companies of the other grades of vote-concentration, the seat of control, is not, however, prima facie established. But in so far as votes correspond to ordinary shares, control through ownership is the more probable the higher the grade of vote-concentration, and the more shares that directors own. If both characteristics are present, that is, if a company is in, say, Grades II to IV and has a board of directors holding relatively a high proportion of the ordinary shares, then control through ownership may well be surmised.

We will begin by combining the tests of vote-concentration and directors' shareholding for the very large companies in 1951. If we compare Tables V B and IV C in each of which the relevant companies are given by name, we shall find that nine of the very large companies had both a high vote-concentration (Grades II to IV) and a board owning as high a proportion of the ordinary shares as 20% or over. To these companies may be added four with the same vote-concentration but 10–19% share-ownership by the board of directors. Here is the list:

*Companies with board of directors holding stated percentage
of shares in 1951*

Grade II of vote-concentration

Associated British Picture	..			12·9%
Illustrated Newspapers	..			39·6%
Ranks ..	..	..	..	33·3%

Grade III of vote-concentration

Albright & Wilson	..	..		30·0%
British Cocoa & Chocolate	..			32·2%
Lebus (Harris)		..	..	28·0%
Rootes Motors		..	..	30·6%

Grade IV of vote-concentration

Bristol Aeroplane	..	..	24·9%
Colman	..	..	27·5%
Kemsley Newspapers	..	..	18·5%
Marks & Spencer	..	..	14·9%
Morgan Crucible	..	..	20·2%
Robinson (E. S. and A.)		..	12·6%

These thirteen companies, with considerable director-ownership among them compare with twenty-one companies in the same top grades (II, III and IV) of vote-concentration where the board of directors owned 10% or less of shares. In contrast to this almost two-to-three relation we find among the companies in the lower grades of concentration, V to VII, only three companies [10] where the board owned 10% or more of shares, but as many as fifty-five where it owned less than 10%. This cross-classification of companies can be conveniently tabled as follows:

		Vote-Concentration Grades	
		II–IV	V–VII
% of Shares owned by the	0–10%	21	55
Board of Directors	10%+	13	3
Total		34	58

It is clear that among the very large companies in 1951 [11] low share-owning by the board of directors was strongly associated with low vote-concentration of Grades V to VII. To be precise (see Appendix C, § 12) the coefficient of association is $+·85$.

The close association (among the various sizes of company) between the board's ownership of shares and the concentration of shareholders' votes is possibly partly due, however, to the two associated characteristics not being altogether independent. If, for instance, the total votes of the twenty largest shareholders are 10% or less of the whole vote, a board of, say, nine directors is not likely, considering the close relation of shares and votes, to have more than 5% of the shares. There are, it is true, comparatively few cases of such low vote-concentrations. A consideration of wider import is that if there is concentration of votes in a few hands there will probably also be share-concentration, and some of these hands will

---

[10] Debenhams, Levers, Morris.
[11] The total involved is 92, *i.e.*, minus six in Grade I.

TABLE V D

ASSOCIATION OF VOTE-CONCENTRATION AND NUMBER OF DIRECTORS AMONG TWENTY LARGEST HOLDERS SHOWN IN 1951 BY VERY LARGE COMPANIES EXCLUDING GRADE I*

Directors among twenty largest voteholders	Grade of vote-concentration					
	II	III	IV	V	VI	VII
Two or more	Ass. P. Pictures	Albright & W.	Bovril	Dickinson	B. Plaster Bd.	Fine Cotton Spinners
	Carreras	B. Cocoa	Bristol Aero	Metal Box	Calico Print.	Lewis Invest.
	Crompton P.	Lebus	B. Match	Morris	Imp. Tobacco	
	Illus. News	Rootes	Colman		London Brick	
	Rank	Union Int.	Kemsley News.		Paton & B.	
	Smith, W. H.		Marks & Spencer		Reckitt	
			Morgan Crucible			
			Odeon			
			Robinson			
			Winterbottom			
Total Co. 32	6	5	10	3	6	2
(excluding Grade I)		21			11	
One or none	Ass. Electric (C)	B Sugar (C)	B. Celanese			
	Home & Colonial	Sears	B. Oxygen			
	Rowntree (C)		Brush Electric			
			Electr. & Mus.			
			Gt. Univ. Stores			
			Lyons			
Total Co. 59	4	2	6	10	22	15
(excluding Grade I)		12			47	

C = Mainly company-held.
* and Tobacco Securities where largest twenty holders not known.

in the natural course of events be directors'.   Directors, in short, tend to own more shares by the very fact of vote-concentration.

The presence of directors among the largest twenty voteholders is, however, free from this bias.   Wherever there are more than twenty voteholders there must always be twenty largest voteholders, and directors are as likely to be among them, whether the vote-concentration be high or low.

We must, therefore, fall back on our secondary test of directors' share-owning, namely, the number of them among the largest twenty voteholders.   Let us take *two or more* such directors, as the " index " of " top holding " directors.

There were in Grades of vote-concentration II–IV, twenty-one very large companies with two or more directors among the twenty largest voteholders in 1951.   All the thirteen companies with directors holding at least 10% of ordinary shares that have been listed are included, and eight others, as follows:

> *Grade II of vote-concentration*
> Carreras
> Crompton Parkinson
> Smith, W. H.
>
> *Grade III of vote-concentration*
> Union International
>
> *Grade IV of vote-concentration*
> Bovril
> British Match
> Odeon
> Winterbottom Book Cloth

The total of twenty-one companies appear in the top left quartering of Table V D under their respective grades of concentration.

The table also covers all the other companies with two or more directors among the largest twenty voteholders; they fall into Grades V to VII of vote-concentration in the right top quartering of the table and numbered eleven in all.   Thus out of a total of thirty-two companies with two or more top shareholding directors, twenty-one or 66% are in Grades II to IV of vote-concentration, only eleven or 34% in Grades V to VII.

The remaining fifty-nine companies (excluding the six in Grade I and Tobacco Securities Trust, where the largest twenty voteholders are not known) have only one or no director among their twenty largest holders; of these only twelve (or 21%) were in the top vote-concentration

Grades II to IV, but as many as forty-seven, or 79% in Grades V to VII. The numbers in the four quarterings of Table V D are, in short, as follows:

All very large companies excluding breweries 1951		*Vote-concentration*	
		Grades II–IV	*Grades V–VII*
Directors among ⎤ Two or more		21	11
largest twenty ⎬			
vote-holders ⎦ One or none		12	47

A close positive association again appears between vote-concentration and shareholding of directors, and this time there is no inherent dependence between the two measures. The coefficient of association is as high as $+\cdot76$ and is significant.[12]

There is, however, a further consideration. Where the concentrated vote is predominantly in the hands of a company and, as already said, control is likely to be the aim, that control exercised by the company holding the large block of votes will be through some director who is not necessarily (in fact probably not) a large holder. Accordingly, since control has here little to do with directors' shareholding, those two companies ought to be withdrawn from consideration where the high vote-concentration (Grades II to IV) is mainly in the hands of companies.[13] In Tables V A and B these partially subsidiary companies were indicated by appearing in the " C " row.

If we include the very large breweries, the inclusive " net " association table for all Grades, less I and II to IV C, is as follows:

Companies very large in 1951 *including breweries, excluding company-controlled co.*		*Vote-concentration Grades*	
		Grades II–IV	*Grades V–VII*
Directors among ⎤ Two or more		25	15
twenty largest ⎬			
holders ⎦ one or none		10	48

yielding a significant coefficient of association of $+\cdot78$.[14]

---

[12] See App. C, § 12. A standard method has been worked out by statisticians to test the significance or reliability of this coefficient. The formula for this " standard error " is:

$$\frac{1-Q^2}{2} \sqrt{\frac{1}{a} + \frac{1}{b} + \frac{1}{c} + \frac{1}{d}}$$

where Q is the coefficient and a, b, c, d the figures in each of the four cells of the association table. In the present case the standard error is therefore,

$$\frac{1-(\cdot76)^2}{2} \sqrt{\frac{1}{21} + \frac{1}{12} + \frac{1}{11} + \frac{1}{47}} = \cdot11 .$$

To be significant the coefficient should be at least twice its standard error. Here it is nearly seven times its standard error.

[13] Associated Electric and British Sugar Corporation. Tobacco Securities already withdrawn.   [14] The standard error (see above) is $\cdot19$.

A similar net inclusive association table was worked out for the companies that were found very large *in 1936, i.e.,* had a capital of £3m. or more, including breweries and excluding, as before, the companies with vote-concentrations mainly by other companies and all Grade I.

Companies very large in 1936 *including breweries, excluding company-controlled co.*	*Vote-concentration*	
	Grades II–IV (excluding C)	*Grades V–VII*
Directors among twenty largest holders — Two or more	18	14
Directors among twenty largest holders — One or none	6	21

This yields a significant coefficient of association of + ·64 [15]

The association between vote-concentration and directors among the largest twenty voteholders appears to have been close in 1936 as well as 1951, but to have increased somewhat between the two years.

For the *medium and smaller* large companies in 1951, again including breweries and excluding apparently company-dominated companies, the standard association table was as follows:

Medium and smaller large companies, 1951	*Vote-concentration*	
	Grades II–IV (excluding C)	*Grades V–VII*
Directors among twenty largest holders — Two or more	35	36
Directors among twenty largest holders — One or none	22	61

This yields a significant coefficient of + ·46, not as high as for the very large companies but still demonstrating some positive association between a concentration of voting power and control by directors with capital interests.[16]

The question these association tables set out to answer was how far the inequality and concentration of voteholding could be linked with directors' ownership of ordinary shares as corroborative evidence of owner control. It would be possible for such concentration to be the chance result of the inequality of wealth among the shareholders or of the past history of the company. But the answer arising from these associations, with significant positive coefficients, is that there is some ground for supposing that *high vote-concentration among owners of shares is in fact usually connected with control by directors who themselves have large holdings of ordinary shares.*

[15] The standard error (see above) is ·17.
[16] The standard error is ·14.

§ 6. IDENTIFICATION OF THE OWNER-CONTROLLED COMPANIES

Apart from the significance to the question of control by ownership of the association of vote-concentration and directors' ownership of shares, it is evident that there is a distinguishable group of companies with the two characteristics that they have (a) a relatively high concentration of votes in a few hands, and (b) a considerable ownership of shares by directors. The fact that out of thousands of the shareholders found in most large companies (all qualified by share-ownership for the position), many of the mere twenty largest shareholders become directors is strong evidence that large ownership of shares is an important means of control. But two further sources that we have discussed may supply useful corroboration or disproof, namely the type of top vote-holder and the *vote-gearing*.

The type of large voteholder is particularly significant where there are a few relatively very large voteholders, *i.e.*, where there is high vote-concentration. In Table V A and B the usual letters P, C, I, N are given for all companies in the four top grades of vote-concentration to denote the prevalence of personal, company, institutional and nominee type of shareholders. A company " C," as already said, if it holds a large block of votes in another company probably does so for purpose of control rather than income, but the motives of the other types of shareholder are less certain *a priori*. As for persons, one test is the spreading of risks. We have found that few persons appear twice among the largest twenty voteholders of our companies which (since voting rights are so closely connected with risk) they logically should do, if they were spreading their risks. We may presume *a posteriori* that the large investment put as it is all in one basket is for purposes of control. On the other hand, the same institutions, particularly insurance companies, do appear many times over among the largest holders in various companies and maximum income with security is the probable motive rather than control.

Where the seat of control is definitely ownership, as in companies where a single holder has more than 50% of the votes, gearing does not affect the issue. High gearing will merely represent an attempt to extend the owner's power over more of the capital. But where the other tests of the seat of control are not so certain some weight may well be attached to gearing devices for granting certain owners differential voting powers.

In Table V E, a list is set out in alphabetical order of the very large industrial and commercial and brewery companies which show multiple

TABLE V E

**LIST OF VERY LARGE COMPANIES WITH RELEVANT TESTS
WHERE CONTROL PROBABLY VESTED IN CONCENTRATED
OWNERSHIP**

COMPANY	Grade of vote concentration	Type of predominant holder	Where not Grade I % of ord. shares owned by directors (No. among largest twenty voteholders)	Capital gearing ratio (No company in the list has equal voting)
INDUSTRIAL AND COMMERCIAL				
Albright & Wilson	III	P	30·0% (7)	2
Associated B. Picture	II	N	12·9% (2)	3+
Bovril	IV	M	0·1% (2)	3+
Bristol Aeroplane	IV	P	24·9% (4)	1·2
B. Cocoa & Chocolate	III	P	32·2% (8)	1·2
B. Match	IV	M	3·8% (3)	1·1
B. U. Shoe Machinery	I	C		
Burton, M.	I	P		
Carreras	II	P	8·3% (5)	1·4
Colman	IV	P	27·2% (4)	1·8
Consol. Tin Smelters	I	N		
Crompton Parkinson	II	P	2·8% (4)	1·2
Ford	I	C		
Illustrated Newspapers	II	P	39·6% (4)	2·4
Kemsley Newspapers	IV	M	18·5% (3)	3+
Lebus (Harris)	III	P	28·0% (4)	1·5
Lewis, J.	I	P		
Marks & Spencers	IV	P	14·9% (4)	3
Morgan Crucible	IV	P	20·2% (8)	1·8
Odeon Theatres	IV	M	0·9% (9)	3
Ranks	II	P	33·3% (4)	1·6
Robinson (E. S. A.)	IV	P	12·6% (3)	3
Rootes Motors	III	P	30·6% (4)	3
Smith, W. H. & Son	II	P	1·8% (3)	2
Union International	III	M	0·0% (2)	3+
Winterbottom Book Cloth	IV	M	5·5% (4)	3
Woolworth	I	C		
BREWERIES				
Bass	IV	P	6·9% (5)	1·7
Charrington	III	P	7·2% (4)	2·1
Guinness	IV	P	17·9% (4)	1·3
Smith's (Tadcaster)	I	P		
Walker Cain	IV	P	16·4% (3)	1·9
Wilson & Walker	III	P	8·4% (4)	1·6

evidence of being controlled by ownership. The evidence supplied includes the two additional tests of the type of holder and the gearing as well as the original tests of vote-concentration and directors' shares.

The higher the grade of vote-concentration the greater the likelihood of owner-control. The seven companies in Grade I (one is a brewery) with 50% or more of their votes controlled by one owner need no further proof of owner-control, and the table omits for them any further details. The six companies in Grade II with 20% to 50% of their vote controlled by one owner (in five companies a person, in one a nominee) need only a little further proof of owner-control—in fact probably none if the main owner is another company which owns more than 20% of the vote. The table shows five companies that have a high percentage of directors' votes (at least three directors among the largest shareholders). The other company has a high gearing.

The twelve industrial and commercial companies and five breweries in Grades III and IV (where twenty holders, not just one, are involved in the vote-concentration) certainly require more proof of owner-control. Of the seven companies in Grade III (two of them breweries), two have very high gearing ratios of three or more, and the rest have very high percentages of shares owned by directors, or four or more top-holding directors, or both. Of the thirteen companies in Grade IV (three of them breweries), five have the high gearing ratio of three or more, and another seven very high percentages of shares (15% or over) owned by directors or five or more top-holding directors or both. The only company in the list perhaps not passing enough of these statistical tests of owner-control is British Match and we may consider that company to have been in 1951 on statistical grounds the least probably owner-controlled.

The outcome of these tests of owner-control is that among the very large companies a certain group can be fairly definitely distinguished at one end of the scale as controlled by virtue of the ownership of shares carrying votes. At the other end, there are the companies in concentration Grades VI and VII where the twenty largest shareholders held less than 20% of the vote. In the middle of the scale may be placed companies which though in Grades II to IV of vote concentration had a rather low percentage of director-owned shares and failed in other tests of owner-control. They appear in the lower left quartering of Table V D. We should also, perhaps, include in the middle of the scale companies in Grade V where the twenty largest voteholders have 20 to 30% of the votes. In my earlier work I took companies with this degree of concentration as probably owner-controlled, but it is safest to consider their control doubtful.

In identifying the medium and smaller large companies where control appears from the statistical tests definitely to be vested in the owners, we shall not go into the same detail that was applied to the very large companies. It will suffice to list those companies which are either in Grade I or show similar characteristics to those mainly qualifying the very large companies for Table V E, namely:

(1) vote-concentration Grades I to IV; and *either*

(2) 10% or more shares owned by the board; *or*

(3) two directors or more among the largest twenty shareholders.[17]

In the following list of medium and smaller large companies that are probably owner-controlled, their industry is denoted by capitals, as in Appendix A2, preceding the name. E stands for Engineering, D for Distribution, T for Textiles, F for Food, Mo for Motors, Ch for Chemicals, Pa for Paper, X for Miscellaneous. The predominant type of owner holding 20% of votes or more is denoted by capitals in brackets following the name of the company. (P) stands for Persons, (C) for Companies, (I) for Institutions, (N) for Nominees, (M) for Mixed, where no one type holds 20% or more.

The great majority in this list of companies have votes concentrated in the hands of persons (or less often in mixed hands), gearing ratios of 1·6 or more, and inequality of voting rights as between preference and ordinary shares. The gearing and voting rights are stated wherever gearing was less than 1·6% and voting rights were equal.

Medium large companies (11 out of 47) + 1 brewery

E:	Falk Stadelmann (N and P)
F:	Hartley, Wm. (P)
Ch:	Monsanto Chemicals (C) [Grade I of vote-concentration]
X:	Norvic Shoes (P)
X:	Prices Trust (P)
D:	Reed, Austin (P)
X:	Times Furnishing Holdings (P)
E:	United Gas Industries (P)
D:	Upsons (P)
T:	West Riding Worsted Woollen Mills (N)
T:	Wolsey (P)
Brewery Co.:	Brickwood (P)

Smaller large companies (27 out of 88):

T:	Ballito Hosiery (P)
F:	Bassett (gearing 1·4)
D:	British Home Stores (P)
E:	British Vacuum Cleaner (I)

---

[17] Only one Grade I company appears among the medium and smaller, and characteristic (2) includes only a few additional companies beyond characteristics (1) and (3) between them. In consequence the total number of companies on this list, 38, is only a little higher than the 35 in the association table (p. 129) of the preceding section.

E:	Carrier Engineering (P)
F:	Chaplin Holdings (P) (gearing 1·4)
Pa:	Colthrop Board and Paper
Pa:	Cropper (P) (equal voting rights)
Mo:	Currys (P) (gearing 1·5)
T:	Derby Midland Mills (P) (gearing 1·4)
D:	Easterns (M)
F:	Foster Clarke (P) (gearing 1·2)
D:	Gieves (P) (equal voting rights)
E:	Glacier Metals (P)
F:	Hampshire, F. W. (P) (gearing 1·3)
Mo:	Jaguar (N)
T:	Keystone Knitting Mills (P)
Mo:	Mann, Egerton (P)
D:	Mann & Overton (P)
D:	Metal Agencies (P)
Pa:	Oakey, J. (P) (equal voting rights, gearing 1·4)
D:	Peek Bros. & Winch (C) (gearing 1·4)
Ch:	Reeves & Sons (P) (equal voting rights)
E:	Revo (P) (gearing 1·0)
D:	Vavasseur (P) (gearing 1·3)
E:	Wallis Tin Stamping (P and C)
D:	Yeo, John (P)
Brewery Co.:	Groves (P)

Though there were relatively many *very large* brewery companies qualifying for the owner-controlled list, there are few so qualifying among the twenty-four *medium and smaller large* breweries sampled. In fact, only two are relatively vote-concentrated, with two or more directors among the largest twenty holders or more than 10% of the shares owned by the board.

The list of companies probably owner-controlled can of course be extended either by easing the requirements on vote-concentration or on the director shareholding. For instance companies in Grade V of vote-concentration which had half or more of its directors among the largest twenty shareholders might be considered " marginally " owner-controlled. Or the directors' shareholding requirements could be eased if the degree of vote-concentration were high enough, say of Grade II, and the type of shareholder with 20% concentration of votes were either a company or a person with other persons of the same family holding further large votes and therefore likely to exercise control.

The result of these two easements would place the following of our companies among the marginally owner-controlled.

Companies with Marginal Probability of Owner-Control

Easement of Test	Very Large	Medium Large	Smaller Large
Directors Shareholding insufficient but grade II *and company* or *family group* predominating among shareholders	E: Associated Electrical Industries F: Rowntree X: Tobacco Securities Trust	E: British Timken Pa: Sunday Pictorial	E: Telegraph Construction
Grade V in vote-concentration but half or more of the directors among twenty largest shareholders	(None)*	E: Lister, R.A.	C: British Glues Chemicals D: Holborn & Frascati D: Jones & Higgins E: Metal Closure D: Travers, J. & Sons Pa: R. Tuck T: Wardle & Davenport B: Boddington B: Chesters
Total	3	3	8+2 Breweries

* If just below Grade V of vote-concentration, *i.e.* 29·7%, be allowed with directors' holdings as high as 28·3%, then Morris Motors should be included.

Easing the tests, it will be noticed, brings in more of the smaller large companies and points to a greater proportion of the smaller companies being owner-controlled.

The aim of the two lists (in Table V E and on pp. 133-4) has been to identify by strict objective tests and yet with fair probability the owner-controlled companies. Very possibly other companies are owner-controlled. Their absence from our list must not be taken to imply that they are not so, but merely that they cannot be shown to be so by strictly objective statistical measures.

The two lists of very large (Table V E) and of medium or smaller large companies (pp. 133-4) probably owner-controlled, together with the list (above) of the marginally owner-controlled, comprise (as noted more particularly below) the companies whose twenty largest voteholders and all directors with

*their shares were recorded in detail. Appendix B presents these details for
the very large companies.* It will be noticed from the data in this Appendix
that most of the companies where the prevailing large shareholders are
not Companies (C), Institutions (I) or Nominees (N), but Persons (P),
have in fact many persons who bear the same family name. In short, most
of these companies marked P in Table V B, and not C, I or N in the
owner-controlled lists of Table V E and the present section, appear to be
family firms. The fall in the number of companies where large personal
shareholding prevails was brought out in Chapter III, § 4, and thus also
marks a fall in the importance of family control. Nevertheless Appendix
B is witness to the fact that, in 1951, many family firms still existed among
very large English companies, notably Albright & Wilson, British Cocoa
and Chocolate, Colman, H. Lebus and E. S. & A. Robinson. A still
higher proportion of family firms were found among the medium and
especially the smaller owner-controlled companies.

The late Sir Hubert Henderson defined entrepreneurs as men who
combined " three functions." [18] " They perform to a large extent the
work of management; they supply capital on what may be a considerable
scale; but it is the taking of a business risk which is perhaps their most
characteristic function." The present position, where management and
directorship is usually divorced and more and more frequently divorced
from ownership of the ordinary risk-capital may, perhaps, not inaptly,
be summed up as the twilight of the entrepreneur.

The frontier between companies probably managed and controlled
by the owners of the risk-capital—*i.e.*, by entrepreneurs—and NOT
owner-controlled seems at first sight hard to draw and it is for this reason
that we have constituted a class of " marginally " owner-controlled
companies. We could add to these marginal cases companies with high
vote-concentration (*i.e.*, in Grades II or III) but no other sign of owner-
control. The few very large companies involved can be read off in
Table V B.[19] The medium large companies concerned are Fisher and
Ludlow and Mitchell Coutts, and the smaller large would include William
Goodacre and Greeff Chemicals and Coventry Tool. In many of these
companies the votes of institutions or nominees prevail and thus add to
the difficulties of analysis.

[18] *Supply and Demand*, 1922, p. 116.
[19] Subtracting companies already assigned as owner-controlled, British Sugar Corporation,
    Home and Colonial Stores, Sears, and Tunnel Portland Cement only remain. Of these
    all but the Sugar Corporation have a high proportion of nominee holdings which renders
    any assignment the more uncertain.

The surprising fact is, however, that whatever reasonable test of a *marginal* case is adopted, not many companies answer to it. In short, a relative gap appears between probably owner-controlled and the probably not owner-controlled companies.

Our immediate problem is to decide which are important enough owner-controlled companies to claim the considerable space required for naming their largest twenty voteholders and their directors that hold more than qualifying shares. We have had to confine publication to the companies that were very large in 1951. In selecting the entries for Appendix B *all* the probably and marginally owner-controlled companies in the industrial and commercial sector are included—a total of thirty.

§ 7. Some Grounds for Predicting Policy

As a final comment, if not a caution, on the last as well as this chapter, we must disclaim any assertion that large shareholding together with a directorship will be sure to identify the real leaders or " top ruler " of a company—the men who finally make the important decisions. The formal test by ownership or office most likely to approach reality is the office of chairman or managing director. But strong personalities among the directors or large shareholders, or even top managers who are not directors, may well be the decision-makers, either singly or in small groups. All that can usefully be claimed here is that holding a directorship or a large proportion of the voting shares and, in particular, both, put a man—so to speak—*on the short list* in the search for the top decision-maker.

This search is of national importance since we cannot assess the ability, or appeal to the motives or predict the behaviour of our industrial leaders till we know who they are. Decisions on the policy of large companies, it must be remembered, often have important results on the whole of its industry and sometimes on the whole national economy and it is certainly of value to be able to predict this policy.

At the end of the last chapter we considered the ground, in general, for the appointment of directors, and in particular what other characteristics besides, or in lieu of, large ownership of risk-capital and being a top manager appeared to qualify for *directorship*. At the end of this chapter we must broaden out the inquiry and ask what characteristics besides, or in lieu of, being a director appear to predispose a person to be in *real control*, and to make the top policy decisions.

Elsewhere I have pointed out [20] that though we cannot identify most of them individually, the men making the top decisions in industry appear to fall into four main types whose experience and incentives will vary, and their policies accordingly, and that to some extent their type can be identified. They may or may not be directors.

(i) The entrepreneur type, the owner-manager using his own capital who is now mainly confined to small business. The director of a large company, however, who is a large shareholder may well have the same attitude and incentives as the self-made, or head of a family business, entrepreneur.

(ii) The financier, who may make the top decisions, is not necessarily a director but may temporarily at least hold a large shareholding or may represent a firm doing so. His economic interest in the company is often only temporary and he may have no other interest but the directly economic.

(iii) The part-time director who, as already said, may hold interlocking directorates or be a professional expert, but probably does not hold any large number of shares.

(iv) The full-time executive, who is not necessarily a director. If, as is usual, he has no large shareholding, we cannot look to a direct personal economic motive, except perhaps promotion and a possible rise in salary. Instead the motives actuating him may be *esprit de corps*, loyalty to or " identification " with the organisation,[21] interest in work, desire for independence, fame or other non-economic aim.

Of these four broad types the first three can be traced by way of a statistical analysis of shareholding and directorships such as we have made. The last type will make decisions largely according to his antecedent conditioning and experience. In the work referred to already, I considered the different motives and capacities likely to be associated with ex-foremen or clerks, technicians, trained accountants or professional men. While accountants might, for instance, aim at liquidity in a balance-sheet, engineers might be expected to have a bias toward investing in machines and fixed assets generally.

We now turn from questions, largely sociological, of who owns and controls large companies to questions more economic in nature, such as how much of the profit is distributed in dividend or ploughed back into

---

[20] *Logic of British and American Industry*, 1953, pp. 299–315.
[21] See H. A. Simon, *Administrative Behaviour*, 1948, Chap. IX.

the business, and what financial success investors met with in the several companies between 1936 and 1951. Answers to these two questions appear separately in the next two chapters, but they are interconnected through the link of incentives, attractives and repellants. Dividend policy, discussed in Chapter VI, will directly and also indirectly by affecting his capital gains and losses influence investors' financial success discussed in Chapter VII, and will thus offer in the face of the risks entailed, sufficient or insufficient inducement to invest.

CHAPTER VI

DIVIDEND POLICY

§ 1. THE IMPORTANCE OF THE DISTRIBUTION RATIO

THE " distribution ratio " of a company's ordinary dividend to earnings for ordinary (averaging 1948, 1949, 1950 and 1951) was entered as one of the measured characteristics in our basic tables, for reasons stated in Chapter II. The portion of the profit not distributed in dividend is now the chief source of all national industrial investment in capital formation. Table I G has shown resources ploughed back by companies to be as great as personal saving and government finance (including that of public corporations) put together.

Dividend payment moreover has greatly affected investors' success. The distribution ratio is the proportion of earnings left for ordinary shares (after payment of preference dividends) which is actually distributed in dividends. Recent investigation into changes in share prices and capital gains over a middle-range period of fifteen years has shown the importance of the dividends paid in accounting for these changes rather than merely the profits earned. The gains or losses of the ordinary shareholder were found to depend on the policy of its directors when declaring dividend quite as much on the total of the earnings or profits.[1]

Capital appreciation and dividend have been found closely associated in the fifteen years from 1936 to 1951. Of the companies with below-average dividend gain to the 1936 investor 79% had below-average capital gains (i.e., appreciation on Stock Exchange price). And of the companies with above-average dividend gains, 81% had above-average capital gains. The coefficient of association (see Appendix C, § 12) between dividend and capital gain was in fact as high as $0 \cdot 89$ on a scale where 0 measures no association, 1 complete association.

For the view generally held that share prices depend upon the expectation of future profits, it would be more accurate to read " dividends " for " profits." The two, though related, are far from being one and the same, considering the wide variation that we shall show in the proportion of profits declared as dividends.

[1] See Florence, " Tests of the Validity of Some Stock Exchange Folk-Lore," *Three Banks Review*, March 1958. See also below, Chap. VII, § 5.

The importance of prospective dividend policy in addition to prospective earnings has been unduly neglected by economists. In the twelfth chapter of his *General Theory*, Keynes " digresses " to a lower " level of abstraction," in discussing the considerations which enter into the market valuation of the yield of an investment.[2] He emphasises the precariousness of this valuation when based on the convention that the existing state of affairs will continue indefinitely and lists several important factors which accentuate this precariousness; but the uncertainties of directors' dividend policies do not appear among the factors.

A third reason for measuring distribution ratios, beside their effect on capital formation and investors' success, is that they vary so widely, both from time to time and company to company. About the year 1947 they were on average greatly diminished, as briefly described in Chapter II. The distribution ratios presented in this book, because of circumstances (*e.g.* the 1948 Act, see p. 53), refer to 1948–51, after the new level was established.   But a further reason for studying distribution ratios is their great variety, comparing one company with another, even in the same years.

§ 2.   Variety of Dividend Policy; The Influence of Industry and Size

Table VI A presents the full set of distribution ratios measured, as described in Chapter II, § 7, for all the companies where available in the years 1948–51.   The table is arranged by size of company and by industry.   Within the size and industry groups the company's distribution ratios are arranged in order of magnitude.

The wide variation in distribution ratios is particularly remarkable when it is borne in mind that for each company the ratios are averages, normally, of the same four years, 1948, 1949, 1950 and 1951, during the same business " conjuncture," and borne in mind also that companies suffering a loss in more than one year are excluded (only a few cases occurred) and that ratios, in any case, cannot exceed 100 very long without bankruptcy.

For all the large industrial and commercial companies in our list (excluding breweries) the average proportion of " earnings for ordinary " distributed was $40 \cdot 5\%$.   The total range extended from 0 to $138 \cdot 4\%$, but the range is usually wide, even within one industry for one size only.

The wide variation between individual companies can, however, be reduced to a certain order.   The averages for different sizes and for

---

[2] *The General Theory of Employment, Interest and Money*, 1936, pp. 153–158.

TABLE VI A

RATIOS OF ORDINARY DIVIDEND TO NET EARNINGS FOR INDIVIDUAL COMPANIES 1948–51 CLASSIFIED BY SIZE AND INDUSTRY

Very large companies (capital £3m. and over in 1951)

Industry													
Distributive trades	12·8	22·6	25·5	31·7	37·3	34·2	39·0	42·9	43·1				
	44·7	56·1	65·3	19·4	19·2		20·9	21·4	24·4				
	12·5	14·0	17·2	18·8	35·8	19·2	35·8	37·9	40·7				
	26·5	27·4	30·2	33·5	34·2	34·2	36·6						
	42·6	55·0	62·7										
Food	5·7	9·8	30·8	32·2	36·8	36·8	45·8	48·9	56·1				
	69·8						39·0						
Motor vehicles	17·3	18·7	27·5	46·9	48·0								
Textiles	11·5	12·2	15·2	16·9	17·6	17·6	19·8	23·5	32·8	35·7			
	39·8	43·3	49·0										
Other industrial and commercial*	11·0	11·7	12·5	17·5	19·4	19·7	20·6	23·9	28·9				
	29·4	29·9	30·9	31·0	32·8	33·5	40·0	41·4	43·2				
	46·4	50·9	53·5	60·2	61·3	62·1	65·8	67·8	69·2				
	80·5	86·7	87·1	87·6									
Breweries	41·8	42·1	43·5	46·7	52·8	57·5	62·0	62·5	64·6				
	67·9	72·6	82·5										

Medium large companies (capital £1m. up to £3m. in 1951)

Industry										
Distributive trades	9·7	15·6	21·5	27·5	28·8	32·7	34·0	37·4		
	37·4	38·6	44·3	58·8	69·3	93·6	98·6	100·0		
	138·4			67·0						
Engineering	0·0	6·2	12·8	16·9	17·6	17·9	18·7	19·5		
	20·8	21·0	29·6	30·2	31·5	32·1	32·3	35·9		
	37·2	39·2	39·6	39·9	40·5	41·6	49·6	52·8	63·7	
	101·3									
Food	16·1	16·7	25·4	29·8	35·8	36·1	49·5	56·9	68·4	
	72·9									

TABLE

AVERAGE DIVIDEND RATIO 1948–51 BY SIZE AND
INDUSTRY OR COMPANY

Average ratios, all sizes ... for ordinary ... number of companies ...

Large companies

Industry								
Motor vehicles	19·1	24·6	26·1	29·5	32·1	34·5	35·0	41·0	41·7
Textiles	46·7	46·9	47·2	49·6	70·8	20·6	25·5	25·5	25·5
Other industrial and commercial*	11·3	13·5	14·9	16·0	16·5	49·8	56·6	71·3	23·2
paper	31·1	31·7	34·4	36·5	39·5	21·6	22·0	22·6	29·7
chemicals	13·6	14·9	15·7	17·4	21·2	26·0	27·7	28·7	47·9
Breweries	23·5	23·6	24·1	24·9	25·7	41·2	41·5	44·3	69·8
	35·6	37·0	42·5	43·5	44·7	45·2	49·8	53·6	54·3
	50·3	58·8	65·1	65·2	68·3	68·7	68·8	69·1
	75·0	79·4	80·0	87·6	90·3

Smaller large companies (capital £0·2m. up to £1m. in 1951)

Industry								
Distributive trades	21·8	23·5	27·3	30·2	31·8	32·6	33·2	34·9
	43·8	53·3	53·7	54·0	56·3	57·2	61·9	69·2
Engineering	6·8	11·9	22·3	24·4	25·2	28·9	31·0	31·4
	33·9	35·0	35·2	35·4	35·6	39·8	47·5	53·8	64·4
	69·8	70·5	77·9	79·9	93·9	103·1	112·4	115·5
Food	57·4	60·0	62·3	71·9	76·8	77·9	78·9	115·5
Motor vehicles	26·0	30·1	38·6	50·0	70·3	98·6	27·0	28·8	30·8
Textiles	14·9	19·2	34·1	34·3	56·9	59·7	85·7	89·3	23·6	24·2	26·0
Other industrial and commercial†	*10·8*	*16·9*	*19·7*	*32·4*	*34·3*	*48·6*	*46·0*	*61·0*
	18·5	*33·7*	*37·3*	*40·1*	*42·2*	*43·0*	*44·2*	*46·9*	*51·2*
Breweries	51·9	64·9	69·2

* Includes industries with less than twenty-five companies altogether and less than five in any one size class, *i.e.*, paper, chemicals, tobacco, building materials, clothing, miscellaneous manufactures and services. Paper and chemicals are in italics.

† Paper and chemicals only.

different industries given in Table VI B suggest that industry and size both have some influence over the dividend ratios. Distributive trades averaged highest, with food and motor vehicles ratios definitely higher than textiles, and engineering somewhere in between. And if, for the moment, we turn attention to brewery shares, their dividend ratios are found to have been, on average, as liberal to their shareholders as the distributive trades' at 50·4%, as against the textiles' " stingy " 31·0% at the other end of the scale.

TABLE VI B

AVERAGE DIVIDEND RATIOS 1948–51 BY SIZE AND INDUSTRY OF COMPANY

Size of company Industry group	% ratios of ordinary dividends to net earnings for ordinary (number of companies in brackets)*			Average ratios, all sizes	
	Very large capital £3m. +	Medium Large capital £1–3m.	Smaller Large capital £0·2–1m.	Weighted, *i.e.*, all companies equally	Unweighted, *i.e.*, equal weight to each size
Engineering	(21) 30·0	(28) 31·8	(22) 41·9	34·4	34·6
Distributive trades	(12) 37·9	(19) 51·5	(26) 57·8	51·6	49·1
Textiles	(12) 26·4	(17) 30·5	(15) 38·5	32·2	31·8
Food	(10) 37·5	(10) 40·8	(5) 56·5	42·6	44·9
Motor vehicles	(5) 31·7	(14) 39·1	(8) 54·0	42·1	41·6
Average of companies in five homogeneous industries	(60) 32·3	(88) 38·0	(76) 49·0	40·4	39·8
All industrial and commercial Co.	(91) 36·2	(127) 38·9	(85) 47·1†	40·5	40·7
Breweries	(12) 58·0	(11) 52·4	(12) 45·3	51·9	51·9

* Several companies did not consolidate their accounts for the required three years minimum and their ratios are omitted. One company is included (Sena Sugar) which had data for the required ratio, but little other data; it appears in section 3b of Appendix A 2.

† Besides the five homogeneous industries no other industries are included in the sample of smaller large companies except paper and chemicals. Companies in these seven industries only, have, for the three sizes, average ratios of 33·4%, 38·9% and 47·1%.

In this scale of liberality and stinginess the size of company also appears to have considerable influence. Since the nature of the industry makes a difference, it is important to isolate the industry factor as far as possible. The five industry groups distinguished in Table VI B are homogeneous enough and are represented by enough companies of each size to make comparison between the averages for each size worth considering. In *all* these five industry groups, given separately and together in Table VI B, the average dividend ratio invariably rises as we pass from very large to medium large, and from medium large to smaller large companies. The unweighted average (not given in the table) for these five homogeneous and sufficiently-represented industries rises from 32·7% for the very large to 38·8% for the medium large to 49·5% for the smaller large companies. When weighted according to the number of companies in each industry as in the table the average rises in much the same way from 32·3% to 38·2% to 49·4%.

No other industrial and commercial groups except the five appearing in Table VI B, contain a total of as much as twenty-five companies altogether and of at least five companies in every one of the size-classes. The two industries, paper and chemicals, which are nearest to providing such a " quorum " are moreover far from homogeneous. Paper includes many newspaper publishing companies as well as pulp and paper manufacturing; chemicals include heavy chemicals and paint manufacturers as well as pharmaceutical companies with a retailing business attached. For more strict comparison with the smaller large companies which were selected from no " other industries " except these two, paper and chemicals are added to the homogeneous five large-industry group to form a seven specified-industry " ensemble." In these comparable seven industries the average distribution ratios are 33·4% for the very large companies, 38·9% for the medium large and 47·6% for the smaller large.

Table VI B presents, in short, a coherent picture of the very large companies saving and ploughing back more and distributing less to their shareholders than the medium large and similarly the medium large than the smaller large.

Readers who want to know how far the industrial size differences shown in Table VI B are statistically significant and the differences when size is measured by assets in 1948, the opening year, may refer to my " Size and Other Factors in Dividend Policy " (*Statistical Journal*, 1959, Part I [3]) where the differences between the averages are compared with the dispersion, or " deviation " (see Appendix C § 6) of the individual companies' ratios making up those averages. It was found possible to state that in the distributive trades the difference between the very large companies' average rates of 37·9% and the smaller large companies' 57·9% was

---

[3] The use of issued capital rather than assets as a criterion of size is also discussed in this article.

wider than was possible on the basis of a mere chance fluctuation. A somewhat similar though less certain significance was found to attach in the textiles group to the difference of $38 \cdot 5\%$ and $26 \cdot 4\%$ between the very large and the smaller large companies and also to the difference of $41 \cdot 9\%$ and 30% between the very large and the smaller large in the engineering companies. The difference between the low average distribution ratios of the very large and the smaller large companies is also wide in food and in motor-vehicles; $37 \cdot 5\%$ to $56 \cdot 5\%$ and $31 \cdot 7\%$ to 54%; but there are insufficient companies to establish the significance of the difference very securely on a statistical basis.

Some of the industries also seem to show different levels of dividend distribution, in the same size of company, fairly significantly and consistently. Textiles had in 1948–51 the lowest dividend distribution for every size and, apart from brewing, the distributive trades the highest. The differences between the average distribution ratios of the very large textile and the very large distributive companies $26 \cdot 4\%$, as against $37 \cdot 9\%$— and also between the smaller large textile and the smaller large distributive companies—$38 \cdot 5\%$ as against $57 \cdot 8\%$, was found statistically significant. The difference between the average distribution ratio of 58% among the very large breweries and that of very large companies in all the other industries tabulated is, however, the most outstanding in significance.

Industrial and size differences in the circumstances and behaviour of companies are summed up in Chapter VIII, §§ 3 and 4. Interpreting provisionally the differences just found in dividend policy we can say that as between sizes of company they are compatible with the economist's theory that large size carries an advantage in case of borrowing and financial costs.[4] The very large companies paid their shareholders less of the profit, less on the assets and *also* less, as the next chapter will show, on the initial investment. The differences between industries are on the whole compatible too, with the notion of certain " growth " or " development " industries, like engineering or chemicals, that plough back considerably more than stationary industries like brewing or the distributive trades.

§ 3. Possible Principles in Distribution Policy

The industry and the size of the company appear to some extent to affect the ratio of dividend to earnings. Judging, however, from the wide variety of dividend ratios of individual companies *within* the same

[4] E. A. G. Robinson, *Structure of Competitive Industry*, Chap. IV, § 4.

size and industry group shown in Table VI A, and measured summarily in Table VI B, other factors besides size and industry are at work. The brewing industry was found to stand apart in its dividend policies and, for the present, attention will be confined to the main group of industrial and commercial companies. Can we perhaps discover certain principles connected with the dividend policy of the individual boards of directors that might account for this variety ?

The principles underlying the policies of boards of directors of in-dividual companies in allocating to dividends a proportion of the net earnings at their disposal, might be of at least three kinds.

(1) A certain definite amount or proportion of assets may be con-sidered to be required regardless of profit for allocation to reserves in view of the technical and market conditions of different industries. Some industries, as already noted, show, on average, significantly different levels in the distribution of earnings between dividends and reserves, and within an industry individual companies may have to meet particular technical and market requirements. This policy may be called the " required re-investment " type of allocation. Its allocation to reserve may act as an extension of depreciation.[5]

(2) A certain specific proportion may be considered " fair shares " as between dividends to shareholders and allocation to reserves, and a policy followed aiming essentially at earnings-sharing at a fixed proportion throughout. The principle is not just a theoretical possibility. In America, according to Graham and Dodd,[6] " 10% as the proportion of total earnings to be retained in the business, reflects the average practice of independent operating electric utilities over a period of years." The authors generalise later that " in the case of industrial and railroad companies an average pay-out (in dividends) of about two-thirds of earnings may be considered as normal and appropriate, and that for soundly capitalised public utilities the desirable pay-out ratios might be set as high as 85%."

(3) A stable rate of dividend on the nominal capital (or on assets) ay be favoured—constituting a " dividend rate stability " type of policy.

---

[5] It is a possibility which must not be overlooked that of the different companies within the same industry some may allow proportionately more and some less for depreciation, according to the age of their equipment and to their policy in meeting the accounting problems of inflation, particularly the divergence of replacement from the historical cost of fixed assets. Companies allowing less and perhaps not enough for replacement and maintenance of their capital might compensate themselves by ploughing back more out of their net earnings than the other companies in the same industry.

[6] *Security Analysis*, 1951, pp. 274–275 and 436.

This principle, too, is not just a theoretical possibility. Many famous American and British companies have treated their ordinary shares as though they were preference shares or debentures, to be paid a fixed income. The American Telephone and Telegraph Company, for instance, paid 9% for very many successive years, and the Bank of England, before it was nationalised, paid its shareholders 9% for the ten successive years 1904 to 1913 and 10% for the seven years from 1914–15 to 1920–21. This policy is sometimes spoken of as " institutionalising " a company.

Several examples of long stability in dividends occurred among the companies we surveyed. Among the very large companies the following paid the same rate of dividend on ordinary shares for at least ten years running, out of the fifteen, 1936–51, surveyed.

Associated Electrical Industries	10·0%	1936–45
Birmingham Small Arms	7·5%	1940–49
Bristol Aeroplanes	10·0%	1939–49
British United Shoe Machinery	13·5%	1941–50
English Electric	10·0%	1937–49
General Electric	17·5%	1941–50
Hawker Siddeley	32·5%	1937–50
Imperial Chemical Industries	8·0%	1936–45 [7]
Joseph Lucas	15·0%	1936–46
Reckitt & Sons	22·5%	1936–51
Ruston & Hornsby	12·5%	1939–50
Siemens Bros.	7·5%	1937–49
Spillers	15·0%	1936–48
Tate & Lyle	13·5%	1939–48
Union International	10·0%	1939–51

Do any of these three principles apply, singly or in combination ? For the principles affected by depreciation, consideration of assets was involved. Testing for the applicability of these principles therefore meant working out rates of equity profit and of dividends based on net tangible assets. And since the period involved was the four years 1948–51, net tangible assets for 1951 alone, as given in the main table, had to be extended to the average for 1948–51.

§ 4. ACTUAL PRINCIPLES ADOPTED 1948–51;
THE STABILITY OF DIVIDEND

In the light of the wide variety of dividend-to-earnings ratios disclosed in Table VI A it is evident that policy (2), subscribing, for a whole industry or size-group, to a common notion of a fair earnings-sharing between

[7] 8·5% in 1937 (after consolidation).

dividends and reserves, is not the principle mainly adopted in any crude form. If it were, a closer approximation of company results to a representative average ratio would appear, at least for each row of figures. The nearest approximation to uniform shares is in the brewing industry and this may portend some strength in the earnings-sharing principle in that industry.   In the absence, among other industries, of any approach to uniformity in the dividend-earnings ratios the predominant principles of the three suggested might be either of type (1) or (3).   Evidence from various sources appears to point to the stabilising of the rate of dividend as perhaps the principle mainly actuating directors of large companies, leading them to withhold the full benefit of upward profits from shareholders.

TABLE VI C

RELATION OF RATES OF EQUITY PROFIT AND OF DIVIDEND ON NET TANGIBLE ASSETS 1948–51

% range of equity profit on assets (1)	(No. of companies)	Average % rate of dividend on net tangible assets 1948–51 (2)	Average % rate of equity profit left for reserves and investment* (3)	Average distribution ratio (2) ÷ midpoint of range in (1) (4)
0– 0·9	(3)	0·50	0·00	100%
1– 1·9	(10)	1·17	0·33	80%
2– 2·9	(14)	1·26	1·24	50%
3– 3·9	(15)	1·84	1·66	53%
4– 4·9	(23)	2·18	2·32	48%
5– 5·9	(35)	2·29	3·21	44%
6– 6·9	(37)	2·47	4·03	39%
7– 7·9	(36)	2·91	4·59	39%
8– 8·9	(14)	2·53	5·97	30%
9– 9·9	(21)	2·87	6·63	30%
10–11·9	(37)	3·00	8·00	28%
12–13·9	(25)	3·91	9·09	30%
14–15·9	(18)	2·97	12·03	20%
16+	(15)	5·06	13·94	27%
	(303)			

* Calculated from the midpoint of range of equity profit in column 1.

This stabilising principle is brought out by the figures in Table VI C where companies (their numbers appear in brackets) are classed into fourteen rates of equity profit in 1948–51 on net assets.   The ratios of dividends to earnings are in the last column averaged for each of these fourteen classes of rates of equity profit.   A fairly continuous downward trend then appears in the dividend ratio associated with higher and higher

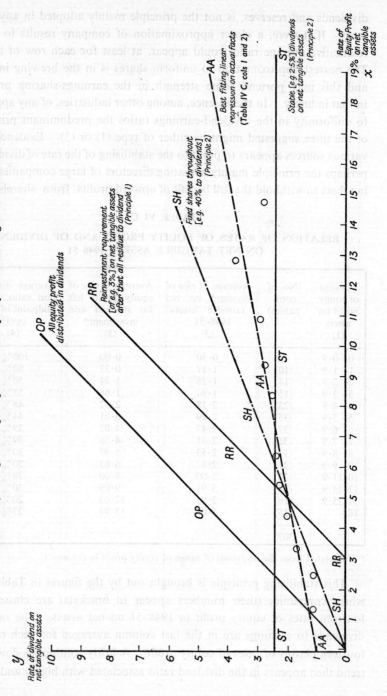

TABLE VI D

RELATION OF DIVIDEND POLICY TO EQUITY PROFIT

Illustration of three plausible principles in dividend policy and actual regression line 1948–51.

rates of equity profit.   All classes of rates of equity profit of 8% or over have average dividend to earnings ratios of 30% or less.

In the middle columns of Table VI C dividends are, like the equity profits, expressed as a rate on the net tangible assets.   It then appears that the rates of dividend on these assets tended to rise from a certain minimum as rates of equity profits rise from 1% to 15·9%, but at such a regularly diminishing pace that they can be called relatively stable.   Except for the class with the lowest equity profit, there are enough companies in each class (ten or over) to allow generalisation.   The rate of dividend only rises from 1·17 to 2·97% as equity profit rises from 1 to 15·9%. There is some manifestation of the sharing principle, though a niggardly sharing.   But in addition to sharing, investors seem to get a certain minimum dividend rate on the assets regardless of profits (above very low profits or near losses).   In fact, as worked out statistically, the line which is the best fit is a minimum dividend (whatever the profit) of 1·1% on the net tangible assets plus rather less than a fifth (a 19%) share of the equity profit.   For instance, among the twenty-one companies with equity profits of 9 to 9·9% with a midpoint of 9·5%, the rate of dividend according to the linear trend should be 1·1%+(19% of 9·5%)=1·1+1·8=2·9% of net tangible assets.   In fact the average of the actual rates of dividend paid was 2·87%.   A diagram is appended (Table VI D) to show not only the actual application of principles, but to illustrate singly the three possible, indeed plausible, principles that might guide dividend policy.

The plausible principle under conditions of inflation, of ploughing back, as a first claim on profit, a certain fixed proportion of the net assets does not seem to have entered actual practice in 1948–51.   If it had been, the average rates of dividend should have been very low or non-existent when profits on assets were low.   All the available profit might, under this principle, go to reserves up to say 2 or 3 or 4% of assets, and the first four items of column (2) (giving the average rates of dividends) instead of 0·50, 1·17, 1·26 and 1·84 as might be expected, would read something like 0·0, 0·0, 0·0, 0·0.   After that, with higher profits some steep jump up in dividends rates as the asset requirements got satisfied might have been expected.   Instead, the *actual* rates of dividend starting at an almost fixed minimum, even when there is less than 2% of profit, rise, as we have said, steadily but slowly, as profit rates rise.   This fixed minimum presents an interesting parallel to the practice of paying wage-earners on piece-rates a minimum " fall-back " wage and lends point to J. A. Hobson's view of shareholders as a great capitalist proletariat.

In consequence, the *plough-back to reserves*, instead of starting at a certain minimum requirement when profits are low and then when requirements are satisfied rising if at all only slowly, behaves contrariwise. Approximate rates of plough-back on assets can readily be obtained by subtracting the rates of dividend from the midpoint of the ranges of equity profit on assets. As shown in column (3) they start low or at nothing and, with rising rates of profit, rise very steeply from 0 and $0\cdot33\%$ to $12\cdot0\%$ and $13\cdot9\%$.[8] The amount ploughed back rather than the return to shareholders appeared in fact to be the ultimate residual, and the reserves withheld from dividend varied from year to year even more than equity profit.

The element of stability in the actual policies pursued now becomes evident. The long stretches, year by year, of stable dividend on the ordinary shares which we have quoted as the policy of certain leading companies appear as the fairly general policy of the majority of companies though they may not all find it possible to keep up such long stretches. Analysing the year to year rates of dividend from 1948 to 1951 on the ordinary capital of all our companies, I found that *rates persisted in the great majority of years in spite of bonus shares and the issue of shares on the market*, both of which are, in theory or, at least, in folklore, expected

TABLE VI E

FREQUENCY OF VARIOUS DIVIDEND-RATE POLICIES (PUT UP, STABLE OR PUT DOWN) WHEN EARNINGS WERE RISING, STABLE OR FALLING: 1948–49, 1949–50, 1950–51

Equity profit *i.e.*, earnings for ordinary dividends Ordinary dividend rate	Put up	Stable	Put down	All policies
Rise 10% or more	163	230	35*	428
Stable within 10%	47	163	22	232
Fall of 10% or more	7	135	48	190
Total	217	528	105	850

* Bonus shares issued on 28 out of the 35 occasions.

[8] Table V C is given in greater detail as Table 6 A in my " Size and Other Factors in Dividend Policy," (*Statistical Journal*, 1959, Part I), with separate results for the different *sizes* of companies. Apart from the greater generosity to shareholders of the smaller companies the trends are similar for all sizes of company. Since this article was written my attention has been drawn to comparable results found in America by Dobrovolsky (*Corporate Income Retention* 1915–43) and Meyer and Kuh (*The Investment Decision*).

to unsettle dividend rates.[9]   Adding to the total of shares by means of a bonus issue should (assuming profits to be unaffected) reduce dividend rates proportionately, since the shares entitling to the same total of profit are then increased.   And when new issues are contemplated for sale on the market, it is usually thought that the dividend rate will be increased so as to raise the sale price.

Bonus shares and new issues are, however, comparatively isolated events and the main determinant of the rate of dividends is expected to be the amount of profit.   In spite of *greatly fluctuating profit* year by year, a high persistence was recorded in dividends.   The test, adopted in Table VI E, was to compare for all the companies the change from 1948 to 1949, 1949 to 1950 and 1950 to 1951 in their equity profits (*i.e.*, their earnings for ordinary) and in their rates of dividend.   Equity profits are, of course, liable to an almost infinite variety of changes and will never, except by sheer coincidence, be exactly the same from one year to another.   Dividends, on the other hand, if they changed at all were found to change in fairly regular steps about 10% apart, *i.e.*, $4\frac{1}{2}\%$, 5%, $5\frac{1}{2}\%$ on the capital. Changes in profit were accordingly classified into rises of 10% or more: *stable within 10%*, plus or minus; and falls of 10% or more.   Among the 850 year to year " occasions " available, a stable dividend rate was found to have been declared on 528 occasions or 62%, but the equity profit had only been " stable," even within the wide limits, on 232 or 28% of occasions.

As Professor Brian Tew has suggested to me, a dividend policy seems to be a ratchet mechanism.   A board does not increase dividends unless it can be sure that the higher level can be maintained in the indefinite future.   Then, if it is sure, it increases the dividends less by changing the rate than by keeping it constant and giving a bonus issue.

§ 5.   The Use and Future of Undistributed Reserves; Institutional Factors Involved

The significance of differences in distribution ratios may well extend beyond the generalisations that can be derived from the main table of measured characteristics.   Further conclusions must wait upon investigations in greater detail or undertaken for further sets of years, or both.   All that can be said at present is by way of possible hypotheses for which there is some, but not conclusive, evidence, first on the use of

---

[9] I analysed the effect on rates of dividend of the issue of bonus shares in the *Statistical Journal*, 1959, Part I, Table 7.

reserves, secondly on the future of reserves and finally on the motives and institutional factors and changes behind distribution policy.

(1) Undistributed profits put to reserve are not, of course, necessarily " invested " in the sense of forming fixed capital, but evidence points to the conclusion, comparing the largest hundred companies and the remaining companies quoted on the Stock Exchange,[10] that very large companies had a lower proportion of liquid to total assets than all the 2,800 (smaller) remaining companies.

Though in 1953, for instance, the aggregate net assets were as close as £3,488m. for the 100 largest companies and £4,043m. for the remaining companies, their liquid assets were £588m. and £833m. respectively. In short, the liquid assets were 17% of the aggregate net assets of the 100 largest companies; 21% of the smaller companies. If the 1,600 companies we surveyed, excluding the 100 or so very large, behaved on this pattern, it would appear that they not only put less to reserve out of profit in 1948–51 but that less of their reserves found its way into capital formation. This supposition tallies with the statistics of the use of funds for liquid assets in 1948–53. For the five years, the 100 *largest* companies, analysed by the Institute,[10] increased their liquid assets by £152·3m., and spent on fixed assets £1,001·7m. The total of companies increased liquid assets by £365m., and spent on fixed assets £1,958m. Thus subtracting the largest companies from the total we find that the smaller companies increased liquid assets by £212·7m., spent on fixed assets £95̸3m. (956·3) The proportion of increase of liquid to spending on fixed assets was thus 15·2% for the 100 largest companies, 22·3% for the smaller companies.

(2) The future trend of the distribution ratios will depend on the trend of prices and of taxation. The Colwyn Committee noted that in the inflation of 1912–22 the *real* values of reserves was maintained. Much the same seems to have been happening in the inflation of 1936–51. Reserves, on the whole, maintained their real value though the market value of shares had not. Between 1936 and 1951 the average capital gain for shareholders in all sizes of company had, in money terms, risen (as detailed in the next chapter) + 80%, accounting gains (*i.e.*, the asset value of the shares) about + 150%.[11] Prices had risen + 136%.

State encouragement or discouragement has certainly played some part in companies' dividend policy. We have already mentioned the

[10] National Institute of Economic and Social Research, *Company Income and Finance, 1949–53.* Liquid here denotes mainly cash and marketable securities.
[11] See next chapter, § 5.

Labour Government's urging of dividend restraint in 1947, which may have accounted for some of the low distribution ratios and the stability of dividends found in 1948–51. In America, however, where there was no such state hortative, similar restraint and stability in dividend policy has been evident, at least up to 1953. Moreover, as we have said, this restraint lasted in England beyond 1951 when state hortatives to restrain dividends were given up.

The state, however, has gone beyond hortatives in its taxing capacity and, till 1958, put a higher tax on distributed than on undistributed profits. The differential was abolished in 1958 in accordance with the recommendations of both the majority and minority reports of the Royal Commission on the Taxation of Profits and Income. These recommendations were based on the supposition that shareholders would reinvest the additional dividends they received in other companies and would distribute these investments at least as rationally as the distributing company would reinvest its resources. Most economists, indeed, point to the danger of " ossification " of the national economy if investment is mainly just reinvestment by companies in their own line of business.

This point of view neglects, however, the now widespread practice by the large companies of integrating many activities and investing in industries other than their original industry; and some economists doubt whether most shareholders would invest any additional dividends they received at all. They might, after all, consume them.[12]

This disagreement among economists may well affect state policy in the future. In fact, the Labour Party still favours a differential tax on distributed profits. Consequently, in so far as special taxation of dividends affects companies' distribution policy, any firm forecast of future distribution ratio would be rash.

(3) The third set of hypotheses, for which there is some evidence and which appears worth following up further, concerns the motives and institutional factors associated with distribution policy. The specific question is how far, if at all, differences in dividend policy can be traced to differences in the seat of control. And the main hypothesis, for which there appears considerable evidence, shortly to be cited, is that where control is concentrated in the hands of shareholders and shareholding directors, the distribution policy is likely to be " liberal " on dividends. This is not as obviously rational behaviour for economic men as it sounds.

---

[12] See, for instance, T. Balogh, " Differential Profits Tax," *Economic Journal*, Sept. 1958.

On the contrary, the sophisticated usually suppose that the large share-holder is likely to favour a high plough-back and low dividends because he is super-taxed on the dividends, but not taxed at all on capital gains. Yet the obvious hypothesis seems nearer the truth than the sophisticated. If, as we argue, prices of shares depend largely on the rate of dividend,[13] the capital gain which the large shareholder wants may not be obtained without a liberal dividend policy. All shareholders, small and large, are thus probably interested in higher dividends. With less shareholders' control shareholders' interests are likely to suffer as against management interests and shareholders without control seem content with comparatively fixed dividends, allowing directors to plough back most of the residual of profits fluctuating from year to year, even when profits were high and increasing over the years.

Where shareholders are not in control, and failing any sign of take-over bids, the existing management may continue to put most of the big profits back to company assets as reserves. It may or may not consciously admit " loyalty " to the " company "; and continuance of this policy certainly serves the interest of the " company," in so far as company can be distinguished from shareholder interests. Whether this high plough-

TABLE VI F

RELATION OF TWO MAIN TESTS OF DEGREE OF OWNER-CONTROL WITH DIVIDEND POLICY: 1936 AND 1951 AND BY SIZE OF COMPANY

	Test of Vote-concentration (see Table III C)	Test of directors' shares (see Table IV C)	Dividend ratios
COMPARING 1936 with 1951			
All very large companies ..	High	High	High
COMPARING SIZES of companies			
Industrial and commercial			
Very large	Low	Low	Low
Medium and smaller large ..	High	High	High
Breweries			
Very large	High	High	Very High
Medium and smaller large ..	Low	Low	Mod

back serves the interest of the country must depend on what is done by the company, or would have been done by the shareholder, with the critical portion of the profits in dispute. As Samuelson remarks,[14]

[13] Florence, " Tests of the Validity of Some Stock Exchange Folk-Lore," *Three Banks Review*, March 1958, and below, Chap. VII.
[14] *Economics*, 1948, p. 131.

" . . . the managers of every organisation have an innate tendency to
try to make it grow and perpetuate itself.   There is reason to question
whether profits are not ploughed back into a company when the same
could better be invested by the stockholders elsewhere, or be spent upon
consumption."

What is the evidence in support of this hypothesis of an innate
tendency ? Let us compare years and size of company first.   Set forth
in Table VI F, the *lower* dividend ratios were found in (1) the very large
industrial and commercial companies, (2) the medium and smaller among
the breweries (*reversing situation* (1)) and also (3) in 1951 generally as compared with 1936.   Now the majority of these areas exhibit, as pointers to
weak owner-control, a low vote-concentration and a lower proportion of
directors' shares.   In this sense some particular forms of control seem
associated with some particular forms of policy.   A low dividend policy
(or high plough-back) is associated in fact with the two main measures of
a low concentration of owners' power and probably a greater freedom
for managers.   High dividend policy on the other hand is associated with
both main measures of a high concentration of owners' power, in short
with owner-control.   The brewery associations are particularly significant.
The general dividend policy is reversed, the smaller breweries pay out least.
and the control situation is *also* reversed, the *smaller* breweries are least

TABLE VI G

**RELATION OF TEST OF DEGREE OF OWNER-CONTROL WITH DIVIDEND
POLICY IN RANKING OF INDUSTRIES**

Industry	(1) All companies where ownership analysed	(2) Number pro-bably owner-controlled or marginally so*	(3)=(2)÷(1) % owner-controlled	Rank	(4) Average dividend ratios %†	Rank
Engineering (E)	53	14	26·4%	2nd	34·6	2nd
Distributive trades (D)	44	18	39·0%	6th	49·1	8th
Textiles (T)	32	7	22·0%	1st	31·8	1st
Food (F)	25	11	44·0%	7th	44·9	6th
Motors (M)	21‡	7	33·3%	4th	41·6	5th
Chemical (C)	17	5	29·4%	3rd	37·1	3rd
Paper (P)	17	8	47·0%	8th	37·3	4th
Miscellaneous (X)	24	9	37·3%	6th	45·3	7th

* See Table V E and Chapter V, pp. 133–35.
† See Tables VI A and B.   Chemical, paper and miscellaneous, classified together in
that Table, are calculated separately from the original data.
‡ Including Morris Motors, see note to table, p. 135.

vote-concentrated and director-owned. This double reverse supplies a particular confirmation of the hypothesis that owner-control is associated with higher, management control with a lower, distribution of dividends.

And now to compare industries. Table VI G sets forth the relation industry by industry between the degree of owner-control and dividend policy in a much simplified form. The list of companies given (in Table V E and Chapter V, pp. 133–5) as probably owner-controlled in 1951, is used to calculate the percentage these companies formed of all companies in the same industry. These percentages indicating an industry's degree of owner-control are ranked and placed alongside the (unweighted) average dividend ratios for each industry in 1948–51[15] which are also ranked. The rankings are then seen to be remarkably alike. The coefficient[16] measuring the correlation of rankings is as high as +·73, indicating a strong tendency for the dividend ratio to be generous in those industries within the industrial and commercial sector where companies are most owner-controlled. It will be seen that only one industry is out of line. The paper industry is eighth (*i.e.*, highest in the proportion of owner-controlled companies) but midway (fourth) in stinginess of dividend policy.

TABLE VI G

RELATION OF TEST OF DEGREE OF OWNER-CONTROL WITH DIVIDEND POLICY IN RANKING OF INDUSTRIES

Industry	(1) All companies	(2) Number probably owner-controlled or marginally so	(3) % owner-ship marginally so	Rank	(4) Average dividend ratios (%)	Rank
Engineering	41	11	26·7	2nd	24·6	2nd
Durable-goods (D)	44	13	29·1	6th	19·1	8th
Textiles	32	7	22·0?	1st	21·8	1st
Food	26	11	44·0?	7th	44·0?	6th
Motors (M)	21	8	23·3?	5th	21·3	5th
Chemical	11	5	19·9?	3rd	19·9?	3rd
Paper	17	8	47·0	8th	47·0	4th
Miscellaneous (X)	24	9	17·3?	6th	17·3?	7th

Chapter VII

INVESTORS' FINANCIAL SUCCESS IN 1936–51

§ 1. The Meaning of Success

SUCCESS is used in this chapter, as in the title of this book, in preference to efficiency, in order to indicate the limited but definite nature of the issue involved. Success [1] is usually defined as referring to the attainment of some specific object; the object kept in mind here is limited to the interest of the investor. The object of the normal investor is frankly economic, to make money at least cost; consequently the first consider-ation in success is measured by his income or the capital gains accruing during the period under review. But two secondary considerations, less obvious and less measurable, must nevertheless arise in the minds of investors. What are the prospects of future income and gain at the end of the period; and what are the costs involved ?

These secondary considerations will be taken into account in the last two sections (4 and 5) of the present chapter. Meanwhile, in the material, measurable income and capital gains between 1936 and 1951 of invest-ment in the 300 or so companies will be summarised first (§ 2) by individual companies generally; then (§ 3) by industrial and size-groups. Fifteen years has been taken as an average period of the tenure of single investment, as against a speculation for immediate profit.[2]

At the outset, it is important to realise that incomes from dividend and capital gains are not necessarily contrasting and opposite methods of making money, but, for the period 1936–51 at least, were closely correlated. Elsewhere [3] I divided all the 304 companies into four sections; companies (i) with below-average dividend gain and capital gain, (ii) with below-average dividend but above-average capital gain, (iii) with above-average dividend gain but below-average capital gain, (iv) with above-average dividend gain and capital gain. Far more companies fell into the sec-tions (i) and (iv) where the two gains agreed than into the sections (ii) and (iii) where they disagreed: the agreeing companies were (i) 120 and

---

[1] Success: " Accomplishment of end aimed at," *The Concise Oxford Dictionary.*

[2] Florence, " The Reward for Risk-bearing by Shareholders in Large Companies." *Journal of Industrial Economics*, 1957, p. 83.

[3] Florence, " Tests of the Validity of Some Stock Exchange Folk-Lore," *Three Banks Review*, March 1958.

(iv) 123 as against the disagreeing companies (ii) 28 and (iii) 33. The coefficient of association (see Appendix C, § 11), measuring the degree of agreement, was as high as $+0 \cdot 89$ where $+1$ indicates complete agreement, 0 no association and -1 complete disagreement. This result should by no means be surprising, since both capital gains and dividends depend in the long run, and to some extent, upon the comparative prosperity of the company.

Connected with the current misconception of the relation of capital and dividend gains is the belief, referred to in Chapter II, § 6, that they must be kept separate. It is true that capital gains were not taxed in this period whereas income from dividend was heavily so. But for a period as long as fifteen years the capital gains coming at the end of the period must be heavily discounted, and though the discount will in most cases not be as great as the tax, the two gains were not so very different in importance. In any case the normal investor looks to both income and capital appreciation and thus it is not unrealistic to think and write of a " total investors' gain " as well as of its two components, capital gain and dividend gain.

The measurement of varying success has been discussed without reference to the possibility of varying costs. But in fact we should speak of a net success as well as a gross success. When considering the earnings of labour, economists have made us familiar with the *net advantages* of an occupation in which certain costs such as the expenses of training, fatigue, unhealthiness or low social position [4] are set against the earnings. Relatively high gross earnings might turn out to have relatively low net advantages if the occupation involved long training, long hours of work and the risk of accident or disease. Similarly, relatively high gross gain on investment in a risky industry or a risky size-class of company might be considered only a low net success. The average investor is presumed to have as his objective the highest gain compatible with high security. A high gain achieved from an investment in a class of company fraught with great insecurity should thus count as less of a net success than the same rate of gain in a class of investment of high security. It is possible by statistical measures of the dispersion of the data here considered to make a preliminary assessment of the degree of security, and later degrees of security will be compared with degrees of gain on certain classes of investment.

---

[4] Marshall, *Principles of Economics*, 6th ed., VI, vii 8.

Up to the present the investor's success has been reckoned somewhat narrowly, perhaps, on his actual " take-home " dividends during the fifteen-year period, and the capital gain or loss that would be incurred by sale of the investment at the end of the period.   The usual test of a company's success, its profit or net revenue, contains, however, other elements besides dividends, in particular the amount ploughed back to reserves as described in Chapter VI.   These reserves add to the assets and if we wish to take account of the sums put to reserves over the fifteen years we may compare the assets in 1936 with assets in 1951.   It is not the company's success that is being here assessed, but the shareholders', consequently the assets must be allotted to the shares originally held. This measure, in fact, gives some assessment of the success of the investor *not* selling out at the end of the fifteen-year period.   Success in this case can be measured to some extent by the increase during the period in the assets represented by his shares.   These assets are legally the property of every shareholder and the increase in assets due to his shares marks the accumulation in the " book " or accounting value of his property.   The relative total " accounting " success of an investment over a period is, then, the dividend received during the period *plus* the increase in the asset value of the share, all expressed as a percentage of the original asset value.   The varying accounting success of the three-hundred-odd companies is discussed in § 5 of this chapter.

To sum up, the financial success in the larger industrial and commercial companies during the period 1936 to 1951 will be assessed by taking four main points into consideration:

(1) The dividends paid to shareholders (including dividends on bonus shares allotted during the period).

(2) The capital gain accruing to shareholders on the original and bonus shares, if they had bought the shares in 1936 and sold in 1951.

(3) The risks involved in the different classes of investment; and

(4) the gain in the asset or accounting value of the investment.

§ 2.   INVESTMENT SUCCESS IN INDIVIDUAL COMPANIES

A detailed account has already been published of the widely scattered results for investors in the dividends paid and capital accruing according to the company in which they invested in 1936.[5]   This account was based

---

[5] Florence, " The Reward for Risk-bearing by Shareholders in Large Companies," *The Journal of Industrial Economics*, March 1957, Vol. V, No. 2, pp. 81–111.

on such of the listed industrial and commercial companies that had the required information, 304 in all,[6] and success was measured by the percentage which the income from dividends and the capital gain between 1936 and 1951 formed of the 1936 purchase price.

These results may here be summarised, together with some other published results under headings (a) to (f).

(a) The outstanding feature of the dividends paid and particularly of the capital gains accruing was their wide dispersion. For all the 304 companies the dividend income, hereafter referred to as the dividend gain, ranged from 0 to 429% of the original investment and the capital gains from –86% to +1,106%. Among very large companies the extremes in the dividend gain can be seen in Appendix A to have ranged from 0 to 223%; the extreme capital gains and losses to have ranged from –52% to +438%.

Even if the 10% lowest and highest gains are excluded the resulting " interdecile " range (see Appendix C, § 7) for companies of all sizes was still from 44% to 172% for the dividend gain and from –27% to 244% for the capital gain.

If the conventional measures of variation are used for comparisons with other instances of wide variation, the coefficient of variation [7] for the dividend gains of all 304 companies will be found to be 29% and the capital gain 80%. Both measures show a greater variation than the English outdoor temperature throughout the year. For English noon temperatures week by week throughout five years (taken at Chester), the coefficient of variation was 18·6% !

A picture of the wide splay or fanning out of capital growth (of share values) in the very large companies is presented in Table VII A. This gives the percentage of the Stock Exchange price in 1951, on the 1936 purchase price (taken as a hundred), of the extremes, the decile, the quartiles and the (median) average. No attempt is made to show the position of the " fan " in intermediate years (except for the graph of Moody's index number of average prices, based on a sample of companies); the prices for 1936 and 1951 are simply joined by a straight line.

---

[6] A few of the total of 317 industrial and commercial companies did not have the price of their shares recorded in 1936. They were in fact close-held and not easily purchased then. On the other hand one smaller company (Telephone Condenser) was included in the success calculations, though, owing to paucity of all other data, omitted from the basic data.

[7] According to the first formula, based on the quartiles, the skew was $\dfrac{170 + 89 - 2\,(117)}{170 - 89}$ = +·31.

TABLE VII A

A FANNING OUT OF CAPITAL GROWTH 1936-51 ON SHARES OF INDIVIDUAL VERY LARGE COMPANIES

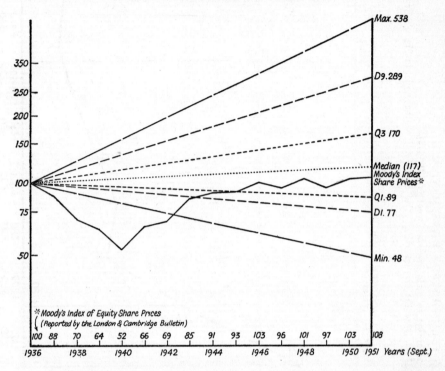

(b) In distribution the fifteen-year gains were noticeable also for their " skew." By skew is meant that the variations were not disposed symmetrically about their average, but were lop-sided.[7] The skew was positive, that is, the upward deviations from average were greater than the downward. For the *total* gains it is clearly presented by Table VII B, a chart drawn according to the statisticians' standard practice. The frequency of cases is shown vertically, the percentages of total loss or gains shown laterally. The most frequent case or " mode " (namely sixty-five companies) was a total gain, over the fifteen years, of between +50 and 100%, but the median and arithmetic mean averages were higher. This and the unequal distances of the deciles from the median are manifestations of the positive skew stretching cases out to the right of the diagram. The skew is also evident from Table VII A in the greater distance of maximum capital gain and the upper decile, D9, from the median of 117 than the

TABLE VII B

THE SHAPE OF THE INDUSTRIAL INVESTMENT RISK

The frequency distribution of 304 large companies according to their investors' total gain 1936–51. Frequencies have been grouped for equal intervals of 50, from the original data. The shape follows the model in Pigou's *Economics of Welfare*, ed. 1920, p. 918.

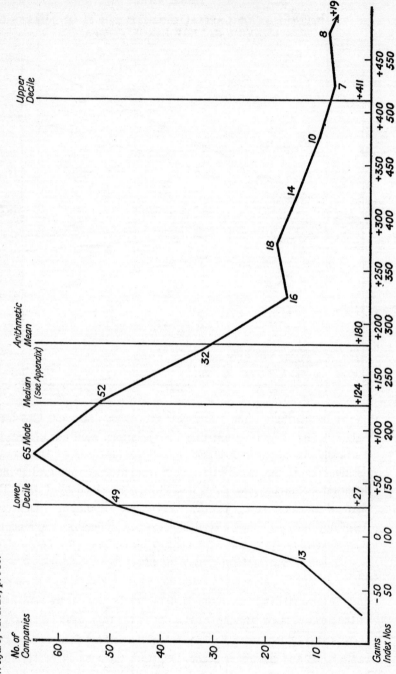

minimum gain and the lower decile, D1. This difference appears in spite of the fact that Table VII A is drawn to a logarithmic (or geometrical progression) scale. For example, the 50-point interval from 50 to 100 is made equal not to that from 100 to 150 but to that from 100 to 200, since 50 to 100 and 100 to 200 both represent doubling.

(c) Though individual gains stretch further on the positive than the negative side, yet it is probable that the fear of losses outweigh in the investor's mind the chances of gain. By a loss most investors probably think not just of an " absolute " loss due to a fall in the price obtained in 1951 compared with 1936 (even when the dividends occurring in the interval are added) but to a loss relative to the gain obtainable if the money had been put in a completely safe investment.

If, for instance, £100 had been put in the Post Office Savings Bank in 1936, £100 could have been drawn out at any time plus the interest at $2\frac{1}{2}\%$ a year. In fifteen years, even if compound interest is not reckoned, the investor would have made a total gain of $37\frac{1}{2}\%$ on his original investment. Now one-tenth of all the 304 industrial and commercial companies made a total gain as low as 27% or less.[8] If brewery shares are added to the industrial and commercial it was found that exactly *one-sixth* of the 340 companies included had a total gain in 1936–51 of 37% or less, *i.e.*, below that of secure Post Office savings. A one to five chance of making *less* in an unsecure than a perfectly secure investment might well deter some investors, however much higher the average reward for risk-bearing.

(d) Comparing capital with dividend gain, it appears that, over the fifteen years,[9] capital gains were less on the average than dividend gains and that they were more dispersed. The arithmetic mean of capital gains of all sizes of company was 80% as against 100% for dividend gain. But capital gains were more widely dispersed and the more numerous losses and very low gains were clearly counterbalanced by some capital gains much higher than any dividend gains. A tenth of the capital gains were +244% or over, but a tenth of the dividend gains only +172% or over.

This points to the relative equality of dividend yields as between companies. The coefficient of variation is low for the dividend gains on

---

[8] *Op. cit.* Table I, col. 4.
[9] Dividend gain is a function, of course, of the number of years, increasing with time; capital is not necessarily so.

purchase price, namely 29% for all sizes, when compared with that of 80% for the capital gains.

If we compare the " bulk " of companies excluding the top and bottom tenth of gainers in an interdecile range (Appendix C, § 7) the same tale is told. For all sizes, eight-tenths of dividend gains lie between +44 and +172%, eight-tenths of capital gains between the much wider limits of –27 and +244%.

(e) The scatter and differentiation of capital gains over the fifteen years of the individual companies is far wider than the more publicised fluctuation from time to time in the average price of shares. As an illustration we may take the *monthly* fluctuations during these fifteen years, a total of 180 quotations. The resultant frequency distribution of month-to-month general indices of share prices is much less widely scattered than the prices of even the individual *very large* companies. The coefficient of variation is 19·6% compared with the 61% for that of the capital gains. Yet the period 1936–51, including as it did the month of Dunkirk, was far from a particularly stable fifteen years for the general index of share prices.

It would thus appear that the dreaded variability or fluctuation of share prices from time to time is far less wide than the variability of the shares of one company rather than another over a fifteen-year period. This fact points to the greatly increased security obtained in " spreading " the risks by investing in a number of companies. It is a point to remember in any policy to encourage the small investor with insufficient funds to spread risks for himself.

(f) Hitherto only monetary gains have been considered, but it must not be forgotten that between 1936 and 1951 great changes took place in the real value of money and also in taxation.

The index of consumer prices rose from 100 to 236 between 1936 and 1951 and thus the purchasing power of money fell by 58%. For the slightly different period 1938–55 we have the authoritative statement of the White Paper on the *Economic Implications of Full Employment* issued in March 1956 that " the real value . . . of dividends has decreased by 30 per cent. while the real value of wages and salaries increased 40 per cent." Even the increase in average *capital* value between 1936 and 1951 for all 304 companies from 100 to 180 is less than the rise in consumer prices.[10] Compared, therefore, to other factors of production the

---

[10] Capital values are notoriously unstable from year to year. But it must be recalled that 1936 and 1951 were chosen for the period of fifteen years (see Chap. II) because both years showed a peak in Stock Exchange prices compared to the two years on either side.

TABLE VII C
INVESTMENT SUCCESS AND VARIATIONS IN SUCCESS ACCORDING TO SIZE AND INDUSTRY OF COMPANY IN 1951

	Total gain		Capital gain		Dividend gain	
	Average (and rank, highest first*)	Coefficient of variation (and rank, lowest first*)	Average (and rank, highest first*)	Coefficient of variation (and rank, lowest first*)	Average (and rank, highest first*)	Coefficient of variation (and rank, lowest first*)
Different sizes of co. all industries (excluding breweries)						
Very large	+129% (3)	53% (1)	+50% (3)	61% (1)	+79% (3)	21% (1)
Medium large	+188% (2)	62% (2)	+85% (2)	72% (2)	+103% (2)	28% (2)
Smaller large	+201% (1)	81% (3)	+93% (1)	96% (3)	+108% (1)	35% (3)
Different industries; all sizes of Co.						
Engineering	+159% (3)	48% (2)	+61% (3)	52% (2)	+98% (2)	24% (3)
Textiles	+321% (1)	63% (4)	+180% (1)	70% (4)	+141% (1)	35% (6)
Distributive	+177% (2)	79% (6)	+82% (2)	101% (6)	+95% (3)	29% (5)
Food and tobacco	+145% (4)	67% (5)	+58% (4)	80% (5)	+87% (4)	27% (4)
Motors	+118% (5)	51% (3)	+34% (5)	56% (3)	+84% (5)	21% (2)
Breweries	+73% (6)	34% (1)	-4% (6)	41% (1)	+77% (6)	12% †(1)
Sizes within industries:‡						
Textiles						
Very large	+250% (3)	50% (2)	+151% (2½)	59% (2)	+99% (3)	23% (1)
Medium	+289% (2)	47% (1)	+151% (2½)	53% (1)	+138% (2)	37% (3)
Smaller large	+409% (1)	70% (3)	+234% (1)	80% (3)	+175% (1)	35% (2)
Distributive trades						
Very large	+86% (3)	52% (1)	+22% (3)	53% (1)	+64% (3)	21% (2)
Medium	+200% (1)	60% (2)	+98% (1)	78% (2)	+102% (1)	20% (1)
Smaller large	+190% (2)	95% (3)	+90% (2)	92% (3)	+100% (2)	29% (3)
Engineering						
Very large	+141% (3)	48% (2)	+60% (2)	52% (2)	+81% (3)	19% (1)
Medium	+149% (2)	35% (1)	+56% (3)	51% (1)	+93% (2)	26% (2)
Smaller large	+186% (1)	51% (3)	+68% (1)	55% (3)	+118% (1)	28% (3)

* For the purpose explained on page 174.

‡ Only these three industries have over ten companies of each size.

Source: Florence, "The Reward for Risk-bearing by Shareholders in Large Companies," *Journal of Industrial Economics*, March 1957, tables on pages 84, 86, 87 and 94.

† Source corrected.

average risk-bearing shareholder cannot at first sight be considered successful in real terms during this period.

Against this unfavourable comparison must be set the fact that capital gains were not taxed and that the investor in ordinary shares was more successful than the investor in fixed interest stocks. Since many industrial investors would be subject to surtax an overall average rate of tax on dividends for the period 1936–51 might well be taken as 50%. In that case, any given capital gain is in net reality twice as valuable as a similar dividend gain. On the other hand as we have seen, capital gains accruing after fifteen years must be discounted and are far more risky *and uncertain!*

§ 3. Investors' Success in Industrial and Size Groups of Company

Individual company results are in Table VII C grouped into industries, wherever a sufficient number of companies were included, and also into sizes. The six industries with sufficient total of companies (all of them over twenty-eight) are ranked in order of the total gain as averaged for the group, and discussion will in this section be limited to average gains— the measure of variation being left to § 4. It is evident that gains—total, dividend and, particularly, capital gains—were widely differentiated for the different industries. The order or rank of industries in average dividend and capital gains is exactly the same as the total gains (the ranking is given in brackets) except that distributive companies are third and engineering companies second in capital, but vice versa in dividend gains. This conformity is further evidence of the close correlation of capital and dividend gains and we need not discuss separately the three forms of gain.

The most surprising difference between industries is the high gains in 1936–51 obtained by investors in the textile companies. This was due mainly to the low price level of textile shares in September 1936 (due, in turn, largely to the passing of dividends by textile companies) when other shares were at a peak, and to their relatively high level in 1951 due largely to the absence of foreign competition. Gains did not differ significantly as between the different branches of the textile industry.

Comparing the three sizes among the companies, it appears that the very large companies had on average considerably lower total gains than the medium large companies—their arithmetic mean total gain was 129% against 188%. The medium large companies in turn have a slightly lower average total gain than the smaller large companies, 188% as against

201%. This trend among large companies of a higher investment gain the smaller the company size is true of dividend and capital gains separately. But the larger companies show less extremes.

In capital gain the least successful very large companies were not so unsuccessful as some of the medium and especially the smaller large companies. Among very large companies the lowest-gain company *lost* less (*i.e.*, 52%) than the corresponding medium and smaller large companies (*i.e.*, 86% and 74%). And 10% of the very large and medium large companies lost less (*i.e.*, 23%) than 10% of the smaller large companies (*i.e.*, 34%). On the other hand the highest-gain company and 90% of companies among the medium and smaller large companies *gained* far more than the corresponding company or companies among the very large. The highest capital gain, one of +1106% was made by a medium large company.

It is possible that the differences apparently due to size were in fact due to the industrial composition of each size-class. The results on very large companies might, for instance, be due to the type of industry in which very large companies might tend to specialise. It is prudent therefore, to isolate the factor of size (as well as other factors) by grouping companies into our three standard sizes *within one industry group*. In many industries there are not enough companies to make valid comparisons, but three industry-groups, namely distribution, engineering and textiles, contain enough companies (*i.e.*, over ten) in *every* size grade to make comparison between these subdivisions fairly reliable.

Comparing sizes within each of the three large industry groups the trend remains true that the larger the company the lower the average gain, whether total, capital or dividend gain. There is only one exception in comparing very large to medium large companies (the medium companies had a lower average of capital gains in engineering), but three (all types of gain in distributive trades) in comparing smaller to medium large companies.

In our analysis of the comparative success of investment in large companies we have taken the standpoint of the potential investor contemplating the situation in September 1951 and judging the success of existing large companies from the experience of their investments during the past fifteen years—in short, judging future prospects from past " form." Losses may however, be underestimated since, by this approach, any companies not surviving the fifteen years, or so reduced in nominal capital as no longer to be included among large companies, are omitted.

This source of error is especially relevant when comparing size-groups. The very large group, in particular, might show high success because the failures falling below £3m. capital between 1936 and 1951 were omitted.

It is necessary therefore to note any industrial and commercial companies which had above £3m. capital in 1936 but not in 1951. Only three fit this bill among the very large companies.[11]   One, the Imperial Smelting Company, became a subsidiary of Consolidated Zinc, all its ordinary and preference shares being taken over by this new company formed in 1945.   The other two, Platt Bros. (Holdings), and Amalgamated Cotton Mills Trust became, in 1951, by capital reorganisation, only *medium* large companies under our grading of size by nominal capital.

The price paid by a would-be holding company in buying the shares of another company (unless the shares were bought up after liquidation) is usually higher than market price, and shareholders are likely to fare better than average in a company like Imperial Smelting that becomes a subsidiary.   The fortunes between 1936 and 1951 of shareholders in the two " degraded " companies (included in among the medium large companies of 1951) were, in Platt Bros. (Holdings), a dividend gain of 98% and a capital gain of 134% and thus a total gain of 232%; and in Amalgamated Cotton Mills Trust a dividend gain of 65%, a capital gain of 98% and thus a total gain of 163%.   These total gains are all above the arithmetic mean gain for the very large companies.

Among the medium large companies in 1936, again, non-survivors to 1951 formed only a small proportion—five compared to the 109 survivors. One of these became a subsidiary but investors in two probably, and in two others *certainly*, suffered a loss.

A further precaution must be taken before we can definitely conclude that investors in the very large companies gained less during 1936–51 than those in the medium large, and those in the medium less than those in the smaller large companies.   We must in fact contemplate the situation as it was in 1936 and allot companies to the three size-classes according to their issued capital in 1936.   The majority of the companies did not in fact change in class of size between 1936 and 1951.   Out of the ninety-eight companies very large in 1951, twenty-one had been medium in 1936 and five smaller large.   Out of the 134 medium large in 1951 forty-two had been smaller large in 1936, and two, as already mentioned, very large.

[11] For details see Florence, *op. cit.* pp. 96–97, and above, p. 70.

TABLE VII D

TOTAL INVESTMENT AND TOTAL ACCOUNTING SUCCESS AND ASSET GAINS 1936-51 OF INDUSTRIAL AND COMMERCIAL COMPANIES GROUPED BY SIZE IN 1951 AND IN 1936

	Companies with data for success of EITHER TYPE					The same companies with data for BOTH types of success		
	(1) No. of Co. (see Table VII C)	(2) Total investment success	(3) No. of Co.	(4) Total accounting success	(5) Asset gain only	(6) No. of Co. with both data	(7) Total investment success	(8) Total accounting success
Very large Co. with £3m. capital or more in 1951	81*	129%	88	409%	203%	79	131%	392%
Very large Co. with £3m. capital or more in 1936	58	138%	61	358%	173%	56	139%	342%
Medium large Co. with £1–2·99m. capital in 1951	134†	188%	121	301%	130%	119	194%	297%
Medium large Co. with £1–2·99m. capital in 1936	104*†‡	170%	98	332%	159%	93	174%	331%
Smaller large Co. with £0·2m.–0·99m. capital in 1951	89	201%	89	301%	126%	89	201%	301%
Smaller large Co. with £0·2m.–0·99m. capital in 1936	136§‖	188%	133‖	310%	130%	132‖	197%	306%
All Cos. listed { in 1951	304	180%	298	333%	153%	287		
All Cos. listed { in 1936	298‖	—	292	—	—	287‖		

	(1)	(2)	(3)	(4)
‡ Of these, promoted into very large by 1951.	22	103%	22	554%
§ { Of these, promoted into medium large.	37	195%	45	367%
§ { Of these, promoted into very large	5	66%	5	306%

* Omits six companies not formed in 1936 and eleven further companies with share quotation not available in 1936.

† Includes companies in 3 (b) of Appendix A (2).

‖ Excluding six companies with less than £0·2m. in 1936.

Of the eighty-nine smaller large companies only six had an issued capital of less than £·2m. (and therefore not large in any sense) in 1936.   However, the number of companies that changed in size-class is sufficient to justify separate analysis on a 1936 size classification, particularly as a bias might be expected in that the companies promoted in size-class would presumably also be the companies more successful for their investors.   Table VII D gives in heavy type in columns (2) and (7) the total investment success (or gain) averaged for the companies that were (according to their then capital) very large, medium and smaller large in 1936.   The total gain averaged for the 1951 size-classes is copied (in column 2) from Table VII C for the sake of comparison.

The differences due to reclassification are seen not to be great and run somewhat contrary to the presumed bias.   The average gain appears higher for the companies that were very large in *both* 1936 *and* 1951 (only two, as said already, were very large in 1936 but not 1951) than for all companies very large in 1951.   This implies that for the twenty-seven companies growing in capital sufficiently to be promoted from medium or smaller large in 1936 to very large in 1951, the average gain for investors was relatively low!   As indicated by a footnote to the table their investors' total gain in companies promoted from medium and from smaller large averaged, in fact, only 103% and 66% respectively as against 138% for the sixty-three companies already very large in 1936.   Some explanation will be offered later of this unexpected tendency for the growing companies to be, for investors, the less successful.   In the thirty-seven companies growing from smaller in 1936 to medium large in 1951, the total gain for investors is according to presumption, higher, though not much higher, than for all companies starting in the smaller size—195% as against 188% and in the five growing fastest, from smaller to very large, investors' success was as said already only 66%.

To sum up.   Grouping the individual companies by industry or size shows certain group differences in investors' gains for 1936–51 and suggests that the circumstance of a particular industry or size of company may have been a general factor influencing the specific fortunes of the investors involved.

§ 4.   SUCCESS IN RELATION TO RISK

A glance at Table VII C makes it evident that the relative total gains of investment in the several industries bear some relation to the variability of those gains.   Investors in breweries had much the lowest average gain and also much the lowest measure of variability and, in general, the order of gains given in the table is not very different from the order of variability.

This agreement also holds when comparing the three size-groups of company. The very large companies had in 1936–51 the lowest average of total gains, capital gains and dividend gains; and they also had the lowest coefficient of variation. The medium sized companies had medium average gains of each type and medium variation. The smaller large companies, the highest gains of each type and the widest variation.

In short, the average gains which represent the normal pay for the shareholder in any given group of companies appear roughly proportionate to the risks involved. The groups where the individual companies varied widely in their investors' gains, like the distributive trades or the smaller companies, were the groups where the average gains tended to be highest and vice versa. Thus the shareholders' gain appears as a compensation for risk and the economist's analysis of the investor's function, as peculiarly one of risk-bearing, is confirmed, at least for the period under review.

Elsewhere I have shown that this relation of average gain to variability in gains is also true when comparing companies grouped into five degrees of gearing in their capital structure: not geared at all, low, medium, highly and very highly geared.[12] The very highly geared companies in 1936 showed a wide spread in their capital losses and gains between 1936 and 1951, while most of companies less highly geared or not geared at all showed middle ranges of gain. The average level of capital gains of these less variable groups of company was definitely lower than that of the more variable companies in the high-geared group.

Comparing industries, however, certain deviations from this tendency can be detected in Table VII C. These deviations (as already suggested in § 1) may be taken as a measure of *net* success (or ill success). Textile companies with the highest average total gain of +321% did not have the highest coefficient of variation, and engineering companies with a *medium* average total gain had a relatively low coefficient. These industries turned out to be relatively safe yet paid their investors relatively well, and in that sense investors in textiles and engineering companies scored a net success. On the other hand companies in food and tobacco experiencing between 1936 and 1951 wide differences in gains for their

---

[12] Florence, " Tests of the Validity of Some Stock Exchange Folk-Lore," *Three Banks Review*, March 1958, pp. 3–20. The degree of gearing was here measured by the aggregate market value of a company's preference and debenture stocks divided by that of its ordinary shares.

investors, for which they should have been additionally compensated, achieved, instead, a low average gain and thus may be considered to have had a relatively low net success.   It is not possible yet to determine what precise degree of variability requires, for its compensation, what amount of gain, but it is possible to derive from Table VII C a rough composite index of the comparative net success of investors, in companies of different industries and sizes.   The table ranks industries according to their average gain, *first rank being accorded to the highest gain.*   It also ranks the co-efficients of variation, *first rank being accorded to the lowest or narrowest variation.*   This apparently perverse procedure is perpetrated for a purpose.

If the six industries were compensated strictly according to their variability (the wider the variation, the greater the gain), then the first in gain should be ranked sixth in variation, the second in gain fifth in variation and so on.   In short, adding the two ranks, *each industry if compensation were " fair " in respect of risk should get seven points.*   In fact, for the three forms of gain—capital, dividend or total—appearing in Table VII C, the six industries show a *net* success rank index no more than one point away from the seven, in eleven of the possible eighteen cases.   No form of gain was, for any industry, more than two points above what may be called this norm of seven points.   For food (and tobacco) in total gain and capital gain the composite rank index was $4+5=9$, indicating a net ill success.   For textile companies total and capital gains and for engineering companies, total, capital and dividend gains, the composite rank index was five, indicating a net success. Similarly, comparing the three sizes of company ranked 1, 2 or 3 in respect of the average, and the variation, of the three gains, the norm is 4.   All nine cases show a composite rank index of 4 and thus show a normal relation of average gain and variability.

The averages and dispersion measures of Table VII C summarising the actual course of events from 1936 to 1951, bring home the importance of the notion of a *net* success.   It would certainly not be common sense to say, for instance, that the very large companies were less successful than the smaller just because the gross gains of their investors were lower. The lower risk these investors bore must obviously be taken into account. But though the notion of net success, taking risk into account, is sound enough, the particular measure of risk that is used—the coefficient of variation—is by no means sufficient.

The data on which the coefficient of variation is calculated should in the first place not be confined to the same period as that in which the average gains were calculated, since expected risks in a given industry or size of company are formed on past rather than current experience.[13] This criticism has less force when the period chosen is as long as fifteen years because there is then considerable time for expectations to have been formed and acted upon.   For instance, if any particular industry shows in the first few years comparatively wide variation in the gains of its companies, a comparatively high average compensation will be expected in the remaining years.

In the second place, it is not just the probability of a deviation or variation that affects the real cost (*e.g.*, the anxiety and lack of security) for which compensation is paid, but the " probability of that probability " —in other words, the reliability or uncertainty of a particular degree of deviation that was observed or sampled being representative.   Here some statistical measurement is possible, since the degree of reliability of an average or standard deviation or coefficient of variation depends on the number of items observed.[14]

When the past " form " of whole groups of companies is being studied the number of items may be considerable.   Moreover, we must bear in mind precisely who it is that we are discussing.   It is not investors in the economist's sense of entrepreneurs taking a risk by a decision to commit resources to a particular and irrevocably fixed capital asset that are in question,[15] but investors in the more commonly used sense of purchasers of units of the shares of companies that have already been tested in the market.   The weight of the risks that are thus " borne " rather than " taken " will, to be sure, conformably with their personality, be felt more by some investors than others and the compensation to induce investment

[13] Some authorities, notably Professor Shackle, hold that investment decisions involving expectation of risks are not formed on statistical experience past *or* present. He is thinking, however, of a single, possibly unique, decision by a firm to invest in particular capital equipment, not of the many similar Stock Exchange transactions dealt with here.

[14] The formula generally used is the standard error, *i.e.*, the coefficient of variation (App. C, § 9) divided by the square root of twice the number of items.   For the several meanings of probability see Florence, *Statistical Methods in Economics and Political Science*, Chap. VII.

[15] G. L. S. Shackle, *Uncertainty in Economics*, 1955 (Cambridge Press); L. M. Lachmann, *The Structure of Capital*, 1956 (Bell).   For realistic and recent discussions of that question, readers may be referred to Carter and Williams, *Investment in Innovation*, 1958 (Oxford Press), esp. Chap. III; E. Penrose, *The Theory of the Growth of the Form*, 1959 (Blackwell), esp. pp. 56–64; Bowman (Editor), *Expectations, Uncertainty and Business Behaviour*, 1958 (New York, Social Science Research Council).

will vary accordingly. In this sense they are " subjective," felt as " uncertainties " and not measurable.[16] Statistical information, however,
such as is given here should help make events less uncertain and expectation more accurate.

Evaluation of the risks of investing in companies of different size or
in different industries must also depend, in the third place, on considerations other than the statistical experience, *in any period*, of variation
in the distribution of gains. The textile industry, for instance, certainly
presented a risk in 1936—or 1951—greater than appears from its actual
statistical experience of 1936–51. The statistical experience of, say,
1918–36 would have to be added. And in addition to such an extension
of the statistical experience, factors would have to be considered such as
foreign competition or old-fashioned machines, organisation and management in some companies—factors probably leading not only to a forecast
of a wide scatter of gains but also making for uncertainty in that forecast.

Nevertheless, the coefficients of dispersion for 1936–51 measure a
large element in the risk and in the consequent net success. And thus
the notion of net success appears no mere academic hairsplitting, but has
a practical bearing on the important question of the direction of investment and the distribution of resources. When the capital and dividend
gains in a particular industry or a particular size of company are expected
to be more variable and the investor's risk is greater, then as an incentive
to enter, or stay in, that industry, gains greater than the average for all
industries or sizes should accrue. If investors, taking these greater risks,
gain no more than average, then other investors will not think of them
as successful and will be deterred from entering that industry or size-
group.

§ 5. ACCOUNTING SUCCESS; GROWTH OF ASSETS PER SHARE

Hitherto we have analysed, as was the main purpose of this chapter,
the gains (or losses) to those persons, companies, institutions or other
investors who risk capital by investing money in (*i.e.*, buying and selling)
the ordinary shares of industrial companies. These gains and losses
measured what may colloquially be termed the " take-home " success of
the investment. But the financial success of a company lies not merely

---

[16] Subjective considerations have been borne in mind by economists at least since Adam
Smith in his *Wealth of Nations* (Book I, Chap. X), thinking of lotteries, wrote of the
" absurd presumption " of the greater part of men " in their own good fortune." " The
chance of loss is by most men under-valued, and by scarce any man, who is in tolerable
health and spirits, valued more than it is worth."

in the realised or even realisable gains of their shareholders over a given period. As we have found, and have described in Chapter VI, the dividends paid to shareholders each year vary widely as a proportion to net earnings, and these earnings or " equity profits " might well be taken as a more genuine test of success than, at least, the dividend gains of the ordinary investor.

The investor's total gains that we have recorded included capital as well as dividend gains. These capital gains (or losses) were the difference between the Stock Exchange price of an investor's shares in September 1936 and 1951 (allowing for bonus shares accruing in the period), and it might be thought that the movement in these share prices would reflect the earnings attributable to the shares fairly closely. If they have not in fact reflected earnings, a separate additional measure of a company's success must perhaps be calculated which does so.

The first question, then, is how far the investors' share of earnings and investors' take-home gains between 1936 and 1951 were, in fact, correlated.

Net earnings or equity profit (*i.e.*, profit less depreciation, taxation and prior charges on debentures and preference shares) are allocated each year as described in the last chapter, either to ordinary dividends or to reserves. These reserves appear in the company balance-sheet together with the capital (*i.e.*, the nominal value of debentures, preference and ordinary shares) and the current balance of profit and loss (as in Appendix D) opposite the assets. When bonus shares are issued part of the reserves reappear as share capital, but the *total* of resources and capital is unchanged. The increase in the share capital is exactly equivalent to the decrease in reserves.

When other items remain constant and no new issues are floated on the market, it follows from these conventional accounting practices that the growth in the total net assets of a company over any period will equal the reserves allocated out of earnings over that period. And if the dividends declared (on original and bonus shares) in that period be added, we arrive at the total of earnings over the period. The question of the correlation of earnings and of investors' gain can thus be resolved by correlating with investors' total (*i.e.*, capital and dividend) gain investors' asset gain plus dividends (which we term his total accounting gain). The percentage increases in investors' asset and dividend gain, based on assets value of shares in 1936, appear for very large companies in Appendix A.

Table VII D, already discussed, compares the two forms of success over the period 1936–51 for the three sizes of company. On the left side of the table the two types of success are compared for all companies where the data of either type are available. On the right side the two types of success are more strictly compared—only those companies being selected where *both* types of data were available. The results are surprising. In the first place the investment gains of the industrial and commercial companies formed, on average, a much lower percentage of the 1936 value than did the accounting gains. Instead of a total investment gain averaging for all available companies +180%, the average accounting gain for all available companies was +333%. The difference was little less when exactly the same companies were compared, which had both investment and accounting gains available. Though at a lower level, the same difference appeared for brewery companies between an average investment gain of +73% and an average accounting gain of +191%.

This difference was mainly due to the greater proportionate growth of the value of the assets during this period than of the market capital. A survey of the capital structure and the value of net tangible assets of the industrial and commercial companies of all sizes (the very large are given in Appendix A) shows very few with the same or diminished *assets*, but a considerable number with the same, and quite a few with diminished,[17] share capital in ordinary and preference shares. Thus:

Comparing 1951 with 1936, companies with same or less	Very large co.	Medium large co.		Smaller large co.	Total
		Full inform.	*Part inform.*		
Share capital ..	31	15	27	34	107
Net tangible assets ..	3	6	1	6	16

This marked deviation of assets growth from capital growth implies a great increase in assets per unit of capital.

But more interesting and surprising are the results of comparing sizes. We have found the percentage investment gains tended to be lower on average for the very large companies than for the medium large, and lower for the medium large than for the smaller large. This tendency we found to hold good (Table VII D, col. 1) whether companies were classified by size according to their capital in 1951 or in 1936. But the trend of the

[17] Diminutions in share capital were due to financial reorganisation at some time or other between 1936 and 1951.

accounting gains is the precise opposite. The *larger* the company the
greater the 1936–51 accounting gains per share.

Considerable difference might be expected here according as the
classification was by the 1936, or by the 1951 size of capital; though not,
perhaps, as great a difference as sometimes thought. On the one hand
increase in the assets of a company usually results in increase in capital,
so that companies promoted between 1936 and 1951 from smaller to
medium large, or from medium to very large, as measured by capital, will
tend to be companies which have increased their assets considerably.
On the other hand, there is often a long lag between growth of assets and
issue of new capital (*i.e.*, reserves are allowed to accumulate), and when
the share capital *is* increased the given total of assets *per share* will, of
course, fall.

Turning from theory to the facts displayed in Table VII D, and concentrating attention on the size grouping of *1936*, printed in heavy type,
we find it still remains true that the trend of accounting success, size by
size, was the opposite of that of investment success. Companies very
large in 1936 grew more in assets a share, than the then medium large.
The percentage total accounting gain of the investor (which includes his
dividends) for 1936–51 based on 1936 averaged 358% for the companies
very large in 1936, 332% for those medium large in 1936, and 310% for
those smaller large in 1936.[18] If the dividend gain is subtracted from
the total investment and the total accounting gain, the relative differences

TABLE VII E

**RANKING OF INDUSTRIES BY INVESTMENT AND
ACCOUNTING SUCCESS 1936–51**

Average of companies in	Total investment gain on 1936		Total accounting gain on 1936		Difference in rank
	%	Rank	%	Rank	
Engineering	+163	4th	+406	2nd	2
Distribution	+175	3rd	+265	7th	4
Textiles	+322	1st	+282	6th	5
Food (excluding tobacco)	+135	5th	+408	1st	4
Motors	+107	8th	+339	4th	4
Chemical	+129	7th	+402	3rd	4
Paper	+217	2nd	+259	8th	6
Miscellaneous (including tobacco)	+143	5th	+313	5th	0

[18] Breweries showed the same trend (opposite to that of investment gains) for the 1936
sizes. Total accounting gains averaged 281 % for the then very large, 178 % for the medium
and 147 % for the smaller large companies.

between the sizes in the remaining " asset " gains become still wider. This is shown in column 5 of Table VII D. Based on size in 1936 the very large companies show a rise in assets per share of 73%, the medium large of 159% and the smaller large of 130%. The same opposition in size by size trends is shown when (Table VII D last 3 columns) exactly the same companies are compared.

Where industries rather than sizes are compared, the same opposition appears between the investor's accounting and his investment success. The relative investment success of the different industries has been set forth in Table VII C, and in the first two columns of Table VII E somewhat similar figures and ranks appear. They are " somewhat similar " only because, for strict comparison with accounting success, a few companies had to be omitted for which accounting gains were not available. Moreover, for a full comparison the less-represented paper and chemical industries were here (unlike Table VII C) brought in, and tobacco had to be excluded from food companies.

Against the total investment gain averaged by the companies of each industry is set their total accounting success. In spite of a common factor in the dividend gain, the two forms of success show a striking opposition when ranking the industries. Textiles and paper, with the greatest investment gain, come only 5th and 7th out of the seven specific industries for accounting success. The rank correlation coefficient for the different industry groups between the two forms of success is, in fact, fairly strongly negative.[19]

The two main factors underlying this surprising failure of accounting and investment gains to correlate positively have already been discussed. They are:

(1) the higher proportion of equity profit allocated to dividend by the smaller companies, evident in Table VI B, and

(2) the correlation between investor's capital gain and dividend gain already suggested in Table VII C, which must be now further analysed.

The investors' dividend gain in a company is, by definition, determined by the *net* earnings (*i.e.*, profit after deduction of depreciation, taxation and the " prior charges " of debenture interest and preference dividends) and the proportion of net earnings allocated to reserves, as detailed in Chapter VI. But the capital gain, that is the difference between the Stock Exchange prices of the ordinary shares in 1936 and 1951, is not so

[19] Namely −0·57. See App. C, § 14.

definitely determined.   It depends on the stock market valuations at the two moments of time, and the underlying question is on what factors these valuations depend.

To probe for an answer or answers to this question capital gains 1936–51 was correlated company by company on two alternative hypotheses: (a) that changes in the Stock Exchange valuations of a share depended on changes in the net assets of a company behind this share; (b) that they depended on the dividend gains during the period.   Since merely a preliminary probing was attempted, the correlation was based simply on the rank of each company when ranked in order of capital gain, of dividend gain and of change in assets per share.   To isolate the factors at issue and to eliminate the possibly disturbing factors of industrial differences, companies in different industry groups were considered separately.

TABLE VII F

CORRELATION BETWEEN THE CAPITAL GAIN (1936–51) OF INVESTORS IN COMPANIES IN THE SEVERAL INDUSTRIES AND (1) THEIR DIVIDEND GAIN, (2) THEIR ASSET GAIN

	Coefficient of Rank Correlation of investment capital gain with dividend gain	Coefficient of Rank Correlation of investment capital gain with assets gain per share
Engineering	+0·77	+0·29
Distribution	+0·87	+0·42
Textiles	+0·71	+0·15
Food	+0·59	+0·38
Motors	+0·75	+0·43
Chemicals	+0·67	+0·35
Paper	+0·73	+0·20
Miscellaneous	+0·76	+0·53
Brewing	+0·75˙	+0·37

It is evident from Table VII F that in each of the eight industry groups (miscellaneous is excluded) investors' capital gains in 1936–51 are far more closely correlated with dividend gains than with gains in net assets.   To be exact, the rank of companies in respect of capital gain was much closer to their rank in respect of dividend, than of asset gain.   In all the industry groups, the capital and asset gain coefficients of correlation, though positive, are so low (all are below 0·44) that any significant correlation is doubtful.   In two industries (paper and textiles) the correlation coefficients between capital gains and accounting gains were as low as 0·20 and 0·15.

All the correlation coefficients between capital gains and dividend on the other hand (except for food, 0·59) were above 0·66.

The conclusion must be drawn that changes in the Stock Exchange valuation in 1951 as against 1936 were determined by the dividends paid between the two years far more than by the increase in assets per share, and the allocation of profits to reserves and reinvestment which that increase implies.

If this conclusion is correct, at least for 1936–51, we can tackle the question why the larger companies, though they had the larger increase in assets per share, had the smaller increase in Stock Exchange prices and capital gains for the investors. A good part of the answer seems to lie in the different allocations to reserve which, on average, the larger companies were found to make as compared to the smaller. The very large companies (as told in Chapter VI, § 2) distributed in 1948–51 a lower proportion to dividends than the medium large companies, except in textiles; and medium large companies distributed a lower proportion than the smaller large companies, except in breweries. In short, the larger the company the less generous was it to shareholders. Since, as just shown, share prices are fairly highly correlated to dividends paid, it follows that the Stock Exchange prices for the share of the more generous smaller companies rose more between 1936 and 1951 than the prices for the shares of the less generous larger companies, *in spite of* the larger companies' greater growth in assets per share. It must be repeated, however, that 1936–51 may not have been a typical period. Indeed, *no one period will probably ever be found that is typical and, before wide generalisations are drawn, many more periods will have to be studied.*

One feature in particular of the 1936–51 period must be mentioned as probably affecting companies of different size. Stock Exchange values depend largely on immediate prospects and in 1936 there was still some 10% of unemployment, and the Great Depression had left behind a feeling of insecurity about immediate prospects in which paper asset values counted less than the actual dividends paid out. With the wider dispersion in their gains (see Table VII C), investors in *smaller* companies are peculiarly subject to feelings of insecurity. Therefore, in times of industrial depression the prices of their shares are likely to be lower in relation to their assets per share when compared with the prices of the shares of larger companies in relation to their net assets per share. In 1951, on the other hand, with full employment of men (and fuller use of the fixed assets) and with more industrial stability, share prices and net assets per share became more closely correlated, and the smaller companies' share prices pulled up from their 1936 prices, depressed by their peculiar insecurity. This interpretation requires further testing, but it may, partly at least, account for the increased Stock Exchange prices of the smaller as against the larger companies' shares, a relative increase not justified by any relative increase in their net assets.

Chapter VIII

A SUMMARY OF CONCLUSIONS

THE coverage of the survey upon which this book is based is about 1,700 of the largest English public joint stock companies drawn from the industrial and commercial and the brewery sections of the Stock Exchange *Year Book*. The two sections are treated separately. The " very large " companies with capital in 1951 of £3m. or over are all represented; the medium large with a capital of £1m. to £3m. are represented by a sample of one in two; the smaller large with a capital of £0·2 to £1·0m., by a duly stratified sample of one in fifteen.

For the very large companies more information for 1936 was obtained than for the others. The period of this survey was from 1936 to 1951, both of them years when the Stock Exchange prices were at a peak. A fifteen-year period was chosen as representing a fairly average duration of non-speculative investment.

Summaries of particular parts of the inquiry will be found in the appropriate chapters of the text.[1] This present summary cuts across the chapter headings and is divided into four sections: § 1, General indications; § 2, The trend 1936–51; § 3, The influence of the nature of the particular industry; § 4, The influence of the size of the company.

§ 1. GENERAL INDICATIONS

·1 The outstanding feature appearing from the survey and analysis is the wide variety displayed in the structure, policy and success of the individual companies. Wide variety in success, forming the basis of the risks they bear, was to be expected in tracing the fortunes of investors in ordinary stock; but the variety of structure and policy is unexpected and may perhaps be a sign of the adaptability of the company to differing circumstances.

·2 In the structure of ownership all companies showed inequality in holdings. The degree of inequality was beyond that even of the distribution of wealth, let alone income. But some companies were more unequal than others.

---

[1] Notably Chap. III, § 2 (p. 62), § 5 (p. 75); Chap. IV, § 5 (pp. 93–100); Chap. VI, § 5 (pp. 154–8); Chap. VII, § 2 (pp. 162–8).

On average, the twenty largest voteholders in the *very large* companies (about 0·02% of all voteholders) held about 30% of the votes, but in a substantial proportion they held 50% or more. Moreover, the voteholders as a whole, owing to the capital-gearing and vote-gearing, often held only a small proportion of the total capital.

·3 The structure of the board of directors showed more uniformity than that of the share ownership. The sizes of the boards were seldom over twelve, in wide contrast to the boards of banks and insurance companies. Even among the very large companies, including breweries, over two-thirds had either *no* director, or only one, who was also a director of another large non-financial company.

The most surprising fact was the small proportion of ordinary shares owned by the boards as a whole, and the small number of directors found among the largest twenty shareholders. For the companies of all sizes and industries, excluding breweries, the average percentage of the ordinary shares owned by the total board was, in 1951, 2·3% and the number of directors among the largest twenty shareholders only three for every two companies. The trend 1936 to 1951 among the very large companies and the differences in shareholding by the board for different sizes of company and for different industries are summed up later.

·4 Combining the test of vote-concentration and gearing, the type of predominant voteholder and the proportion of ordinary shares owned by directors, a certain number of large companies can be identified as probably owner-controlled or marginally so. Thirty very large and forty-nine medium and smaller large industrial and commercial companies, together with six very large and four medium or smaller breweries, were so identified. The proportion of these eighty-nine to the total of 268 companies fully analysed is 33%. Two-thirds of the large companies in 1951 were thus probably not owner-controlled.

·5 One important company policy could be measured, namely, the proportion of the equity profit allocated to ordinary share dividends, and consequently the proportion ploughed back as reserves. The ratio of the dividend distributed to the total equity profit showed surprising variation even as between companies of the same size and the same industry. At the end of our period, after the consolidation of accounts was made obligatory in 1948, it was found possible to test on what principle directors distributed various ratios of profit as profit was higher or lower. This is summed up in § 2·5.

·6　The success of companies between 1936 and 1951 relates to the investors' (*i.e.*, the proprietors') gain.　This was measured in two ways: the realised investment gain by receipt of dividends and capital appreciation of a given holding of shares bought in 1936 and sold, together with bonus shares accruing, in 1951; and (added to the receipt of dividends) the book or accounting gain in assets represented by such a shareholding between 1936 and 1951.　Both measures of success showed results differing widely between individual companies and between companies grouped by size and by industry, thus indicating the risks involved by investing in any one company.　A surprising difference was shown between the two measures in general average trend.　Accounting gain rose proportionately much higher than realised investment gain and, comparing the relative success of different sizes of company and different industries, the order of accounting success was almost the reverse of the order of investment success.　The main results of these comparisons between sizes and industries are summed up in §§ 3 and 4.

·7　On investments in their ordinary shares bought in 1936 and sold in 1951 one-sixth of all companies (including breweries) showed less total gain success than straight investment in Post Office savings.　On the other hand one company showed a capital gain alone of 1,106%.　This wide fanning out from 1936 into losses and gains to the shares of different companies shows by 1951 a wider scatter than the more publicised price fluctuations over time of an average of companies' share-prices, and stresses the need for an investor to spread investments.　The shape of the scatter which is by no means symmetrical, was examined in detail.

§ 2.　The Trend 1936–51

·1　Though a certain proportion of the large companies did not appear to have their control divorced from ownership, the trend toward such divorce was clear for the very large companies (which were surveyed in 1936 as well as 1951).　In particular, the proportion of votes in the hands of the largest twenty shareholders fell on average, and for the great majority of companies.　This fall in concentration was common to practically all industry groups.

In 1936 the average proportion of the total votes held by the largest twenty shareholders was 30%; by 1951 19%.　Forty-eight of these very large companies showed a fall in this measure of concentration; only sixteen showed a rise.

The fall in concentration was greatest for the growing companies. When additional capital is issued the larger shareholders appear to get less than their original proportion.

·2 The type of shareholders holding a lower proportion of votes in 1951 than in 1936 is mainly the individual person.

·3 The proportion of shares held by directors in the very large companies fell between 1936 and 1951 and also the number of directors among the largest twenty voteholders. More directors appeared holding no more than their minimum share qualification.

·4 Possibly connected with these signs of a managerial evolution, if not revolution, is the trend generally observed and recorded toward a much higher proportion of plough-back. The proportion ploughed back of one-third of the equity profit in the thirties changed to two-thirds of that profit in the fifties. Though no doubt triggered off by the hortatives of the Labour Government, the high plough-back of 1948 has persisted (and also occurred in America). It might plausibly be connected with the rise of the price of replacements of equipment, for which conventiona rates of depreciation on fixed assets are insufficient.

·5 However, analysis of the proportion of equity profit ploughed back in 1948–51 at different rates of profit showed that not the assets but the shareholders had priority and that the assets were the residuary legatee. Shareholders were not paid all the profit once the requirements for re-placement of assets and new investment were met; nor were they paid specific shares of the equity profit, whatever the total profit. The prin-ciple actually adopted by 1948–51 appeared to be for a company to distribute to shareholders just over 1% of assets whatever its profits, and for companies making higher profits to allow their shareholders in addition only about a fifth share of the profits. This policy resulted in a certain stability of dividend but violently fluctuating plough-backs. Stability of dividend and a low distribution of profit but not below a certain minimum appears the dominating principle at the end of our period. The amount of the plough-back to reserves and consequent investment thus seems to depend almost wholly on the opportunity offered by the amount of the profit of the preceding period.

§ 3. THE INFLUENCE OF THE NATURE OF THE PARTICULAR INDUSTRY

·1 Companies *generally*, small or large, prevail over sole traders and partnerships in most economic activities today, except agriculture, build-ing, road transport, retailing, professional and other services. Among branches of manufacturing, the lowest proportion of company activity is in clothing with 65%; no other branch of manufacture derives less than 73% of its income from companies.

·2 Relatively large manufacturing companies of over £2·5m. assets prevail particularly in chemicals, oil refining, cement, heavy metal "manufacture," rayon, grain milling, sugar refining, drink (mainly breweries), tobacco, paper and newspaper publishing, rubber and linoleum.

·3 Conclusions 1 and 2 are consistent with the hypothesis that company, and particularly large company organisation, is largely a result of the capital intensity of the industry either directly or because capital intensity influences size of plant, and size of plant size of company. Associated with its relatively low company incidence, for instance, clothing had the particularly low capital intensity, measured by horse-power and net output a worker, in 1951, of only 0·2 and £414. On the other hand, all the branches of manufacture mentioned (in conclusion 2) had, in 1951, either a horsepower of 4·7 and over, or net output a worker of £868 and over; while the all-manufacture averages were respectively 3·1 and £677. Innovation and the continued application of science to industry is likely to increase capital intensity and therefore the prevalence of companies, and particularly large companies.

·4 The particular nature of the industry concerned affects also relations within the large company. Among the *very large* companies contrasts were especially marked between the two poles of the engineering and the brewing industries.

Engineering companies had distinctly larger boards and more directors in common with other large non-financial companies, and showed signs of a wider prevalence of divorce between ownership and control in a low proportion of shares held by directors, and few directors among the largest twenty shareholders.   The vote-concentration also was particularly low in the very large and medium large engineering companies though not in the smaller large companies. Engineering companies (particularly the larger) practised a high ploughback of profit.

The very large brewery companies, on the other hand, had distinctly higher capital and vote gearing, high vote-concentration, small boards and little interlocking of directors, higher share-owning by directors and other signs of more " marriage " of ownership and control. In contrast to engineering, brewing companies, particularly the very large, are relatively liberal in dividend distribution.

·5 This contrast may probably be explained logically by certain facts of the market and technical situation. The engineering group pre-eminently:

   (a) makes producers' not consumers' goods and renders services to other industries;
   (b) requires scientifically trained directors even though they hold few shares;
   (c) is a growing industry requiring reinvestment of capital.

On the other hand, brewing pre-eminently:

   (a) is a consumer industry;
   (b) has marketable assets suitable for use as security, especially public houses and their sites;
   (c) is fairly stationary, both in the sense of not growing and not being subject to much fluctuation.

·6 These logical explanations fit the way in which the larger companies in the other industry groups follow either the engineering or the larger brewery patterns.

The distributive trades and the food industry, like brewing, provide consumer goods and services, and the distributive trades, at least, have similar marketable assets. Both are fairly stationary. They follow, as is logically to be expected, the large-brewery pattern of high gearing and vote-concentration, smaller boards of directors, little interlocking and a relatively large shareholding by directors. Again, like breweries, companies in these industries declared relatively high dividends and low plough-back.

The chemical industry is most like engineering in providing producers' goods subject to some risk of slumps, requiring scientific directors and growing in the long run. As logically to be expected, its companies had large boards and considerable interlocking and follow the engineering pattern of low gearing and vote-concentration. Like engineering companies they declared a lower than average dividend ratio.

The other industries—motors, textiles and paper—occupy middle positions in their technical and market circumstances, in their ownership and control, and in their dividend policy. Thus the technique of the motor industry is much like engineering and likewise the industry is growing. On the other hand, its market is the final consumer, rather than the producer. Its companies have, like the larger breweries, small boards and little interlocking with other large producers and have a relatively low prevalence of divorce of ownership from control.

·7 The two industrial characteristics, one on the technical—*i.e.*, intensity of capital, the other on the market side—*i.e.*, fluctuations of demand, probably also influenced the pattern of ownership, control and policy. Both characteristics may have affected relative dividend policy. Comparatively low dividend ratios are consistent with plough-back for the intensive capitalisation of the paper and chemistry industries, or for the liquidity against the risks of fluctuation of the textile industry.

The factor of intensity of capital which was found so important in conclusions 1–3 for the differing incidence of companies, and especially large companies, in different industries did not apparently affect the ownership and control patterns of companies except in the shareholding of directors. The more intensely capitalised industries, chemicals and paper, and to a less extent textiles, were industries in which directors owned a proportion of their company's shares greater than average, and in this characteristic followed the highly capitalised breweries, rather than the lower capitalised engineering.

·8 The association of structure and policy (conclusions 6 and 7) whereby the sizes of companies and the industries that are more owner-controlled—brewing, food and the distributive trades—were found to be those where policies of high dividend ratios occur, is particularly evident from comparing the brewing with other industries. Comparing brewing company *sizes*, the trend in both their structure and their policy is the reverse of the trend in other industries. *Both* dividend ratios and owner-control are particularly high in the very large breweries; *both* particularly low in the very large companies of the industrial and commercial group as a whole. Moreover the several industries within this group tend to follow the same ranking, both for degree of owner-control and for dividend distribution. Which is cause, which effect, cannot, however, be laid down. Dividends may be kept low because managers, not owners, are in control; or managers may be in control in certain industries because low dividends and a high plough-back have proved more successful there for survival and growth. Both trains of causation may, indeed, be at work and thus mutually reinforce one another.

·9 The success achieved varied widely between companies in different industries, measured either by investment or by accounting and asset gains, though industries showing the highest investment gains, like textiles, were not those showing the highest accounting gains. The highest investment gains in the textile industry were balanced by its contemporary risks. And, generally, as between industries and sizes, gains were found to be balanced by the risks measured in the variation between individual companies, again confirming the economist's view that profits (or, more accurately, dividends) are a compensation for risk.

§ 4. INFLUENCE OF THE SIZE OF COMPANY

·1 The larger the company the greater its capital-gearing and vote-gearing and the greater, on the whole, its concentration of voteholders. Thus the concentration of power over all capital owners (debenture, preference and ordinary) and as between the voteholding ordinary shareholder is more intense, the larger the company.

·2 The larger the company, the larger its board of directors, though less than proportionately larger to the capital; there are more directors in common (*e.g.*, interlocking) in the very large companies.

·3 Control is divorced from ownership in more of the very large companies. Among these companies, the proportion of shares owned by the board is lower, fewer have directors among their largest twenty shareholders, and more have directors holding no more than qualifying shares. To be exact, these three tests of directors' shareholding compare as follows for the industrial and commercial companies:

Average percentage of ordinary shares owned by the board: 2·9% for the smaller, 2·1% for the medium and 1·5% for the very large. Proportion of directors among the twenty largest shareholders: 30% for the smaller, 21% for the medium and 16% for the very large companies. Proportion of companies with *no* directors holding no more than minimum qualification: 47% for the smaller, 47% for the medium and 27% for the very large.

·4 The membership of the board and its relation to shareholding, interlocking, and management is so distinct in the *very large* companies that its " pattern " is in the literal sense worth depiction on a diagram.

On average, the board of a company with over £3m. capital in 1951 consisted of nine directors. Of the directors three in every two companies (*i.e.*, 1½ on average) are among the twenty largest shareholders. On the other hand, five directors in every two very large companies (*i.e.*, 2½ on average) hold no more than a qualifying share. Three directors out of every two companies (*i.e.*, again 1½ on average) hold a directorship in another large non-financial company, but some of these " directors-in-common " are likely also to have no more than the minimum qualifying share and thus to overlap to some extent, say on average half a director. Finally, we may estimate that, of the eight top managers, four may well be directors with (again an overlap) perhaps two of them holders of not more than minimum qualifying shares.

The picture that emerges may replace the overlapping equal circles in Chapter IV, § 1, as more statistically established in its dimensions; though deductions still enter into some of the calculations.

·5. In the period 1936–51, the larger the company, the greater the plough-back of profits to reserve and the lower the dividend.

·6 Partly in consequence of (5) the success of investors between 1936 and 1951 averaged higher in the smaller companies as measured both by the investment gain from dividends and the capital gain. Looking at the result from the company standpoint more was paid out in dividends for a given investment in 1936. But the dispersion of gain or risk of investment in the smaller companies was greater. Thus, as between sizes of companies the economist's expectation is again supported that investors' gains compensate for their degree of risk-bearing; and his theory is also supported that the financing of the larger company is cheaper.

·7 Also in consequence of (5) the accounting gain of the three size-groups of companies (measuring dividend and change in asset value as a percentage of the asset value of shares in 1936) differed in the opposite direction to the investment gain. The very large companies as of 1951 or 1936 showed on average a greater accounting gain than the medium, and the medium than the smaller large companies.

·8 These comparisons were made between three size-groups of large company, of which the very large included all companies in a very wide range with over £3m. capital in 1951. Companies with (in 1951) over £8m. capital, of which there were seventeen, might be considered as " giant " companies in another category of size altogether. Wherever these giant companies were distinguished, *e.g.*, in size of board or divorce of control from ownership, their average did not appear to vary significantly from the other very large companies, except perhaps in one particular— the type of prevalent shareholders.

Five of these seventeen " giant " companies were in our owner-controlled lists—Associated British Pictures, Ford Motor, Kemsley Newspapers, Union International and Woolworth—a proportion of about 30%, very close to the proportion for *all* the very large companies. But in none of these five " giant " companies did persons appear to prevail among the controllers, whereas for very large companies generally persons prevailed in over half (sixteen out of the twenty-eight). It looks as though control by personal or family ownership were not possible beyond a certain size of company.

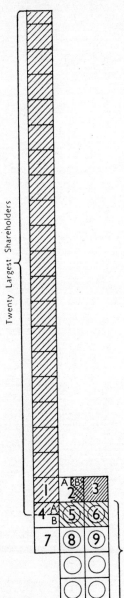

Twenty Largest Shareholders

Diagram Illustrating Average Identification and Interrelation of Directors of the Very Large Companies with the Twenty Largest Vote Holders and Minimum Shareholdings, Top Managers and Directors in Common.

One large square = One Person

Out of 9 Directors, numbered 1, 2, 3, 4, 5, 6, 7, 8, 9 :

    Total of 1½*. Nos. 1 and top half of 4 (4a), are among largest twenty vote holders.

    Total of 4, Nos. 5, 6, 8, 9, are among top eight managers.

    Total of 1½*. Nos. 3 and right half of 2 (2b), are directors in common with other large companies.

    Total of 2½*. Nos. 5, 6 and same half of 2 (2b), have minimum qualification in shareholding.

    Total of 2, Nos. 7, 4b and 2a, have no specifications.

    Subtract 2½, Nos. 5, 6, 2b, overlapping.

    Net Total 9

1½ Directors in common

2½ Minimum Share Directors

8 Top Managers

* Established by statistical analysis.

APPENDICES

Appendix A 1 and A 2: The Basic Tables

A 1 is the full basic table for all the very large industrial and commercial companies in 1936 and 1951; A 2 gives the names and industries of the sample of medium and smaller large companies in 1951, and also the very large breweries, for which basic tables were prepared but which for reasons of space are not published. The numbers of shareholders given in A 1 are only approximate and for those companies, limited in number, where they were obtainable in 1936, the shareholders are printed in brackets.

Appendix A

FULL ANALYSIS OF VERY LARGE COMPANIES (CAPIT

(1936) in brackets if companies had less

	Albright & Wilson		Amalgamated Metal		Amalgamated Press	
	(1936)*	1951	1936	1951	1936	1951
Capital £m.						
Ordinary shares	0·4	2·0	4·4	4·4	1·2	1·8
Preference shares	1·0	2·0	0·9	0·9	4·5	4·5
Debentures	0·0	0·0	0·0	0·0	2·5	0·0
Net Tangible Assets £m	N/A	6·7	5·4	7·2	9·5	14·2
Shareholders (00's)	(0, 1)	3, 0	—	7, 5	(23, 5)	21, 7
Voting						
Total (000,000's)	0·4	8·1	4·4	4·4	2·4	3·6
% of total vote						
largest 20 holders	90·3	51·8	40·4	17·2	66·6	26·7
Breakdown by type:						
Personal (P)	90·3	50·6	5·5	1·5	27·5	5·9
Company (C)	0·0	0·0	26·9	0·5	0·0	0·4
Institution (I)	0·0	1·2	5·2	13·2	4·0	3·8
Nominee (N)	0·0	0·0	2·8	2·0	35·1	16·6
largest single holder	17·8	8·8	11·3	6·2	15·7	5·0
his type	P	P	C	I	N	N
Directors						
Total	7	8	16	10	10	13
% of Ordinary shares held	48·8	30·0	4·8	0·2	11·4	2·6
No. among largest 20 holders	6	7	1	0	5	1
No. interlocking with other large companies	0	1	6	2	2	0
No. holding only minimum share qualification	0	0	4	9	4	6
Financial Success 1936-1951						
Investors' success on 1936						
% Dividend gain	N/A, Not		61		223	
% Capital gain	public co.		−21		160	
	before 1948		—		—	
%Total gain			40		383	
Accounting success on 1936						
% Dividend gain			90		252	
% Asset gain			13		161	
			103		—	
%Total gain			—		413	
Distribution ratio 1948-1951	29·4		62·7		12·5	
Industrial Group	Chemical		Engineering		Paper	

NOTES
* 1937.

DIX A 1

AL £3M. OR MORE IN 1951) FOR 1936 AND 1951

than £3m. share capital in 1936

Associated British Picture Co.		Associated Electrical Industries		Associated Newspapers		Associated Portland Cement Mfrs.		Austin Motors		Beecham Group	
(1936)	1951	1936	1951	1936	1951	1936	1951	(1936)	1951	(1936)	1951
1·5†	2·0	4·9	6·0	2·8	2·8	3·5	4·0	1·2	1·8	0·2	1·5
2·0	7·0	1·2	2·7	1·1	1·1	2·5	2·5	1·4	2·9	2·0	3·5
3·5	0·0	0·0	4·0	1·0	0·5	3·6	2·1	1·1	0·0	0·0	10·0
8·3	14·3	8·4	34·7	6·0	7·1	9·7	18·8	5·0	11·9	2·4	12·3
—	14,5	—	12,0	—	17,9	(18,3)	25,9	—	22,8	—	33,4
6·2	8·0	5·5	7·3	11·1	11·0	3·5	4·0	1·4	4·3	1·4	3·1
60·1	51·6	53·0	35·6	61·2	21·6	16·5	9·3	35·3	11·5	22·6	4·6
1·3	21·0	0·3	0·0	2·7	8·4	4·0	1·1	28·2	1·7	4·0	1·1
11·3	0·0	35·4	29·1	2·5	0·0	0·0	0·0	0·3	0·0	0·0	0·0
28·5	2·4	1·9	5·0	43·3	4·2	2·4	2·7	0·7	2·7	3·3	1·1
19·0	28·2	15·4	1·5	12·7	9·0	10·1	5·5	6·1	7·1	15·3	2·4
25·8	25·2	21·3	29·1	40·9	5·0	2·5	1·6	22·4	1·4	13·1	1·0
I	N	C	C	I	N	N	N	P	N	N	N
6	5	11	13	12	10	9	15	7	5	6	9
1·0	12·9	0·5	0·2	0·5	0·4	1·4	0·6	12·4	0·1	6·3	2·2
0	2	1	0	0	0	0	0	1	0	2	1
1	0	2	1	0	1	3	4	0	0	0	2
1	0	4	7	3	2	2	9	1	0	0	0

89	75	55	52	51	164
−19	69	−13	2	3	83
70	144	42	54	54	247
152	133	218	262	292	1133
102	217	41	242	327	1050
254	350	259	504	619	2184
67·8	18·8	62·1	30·9	27·5	46·4
Misc.	Engineering	Paper	Misc.	Motors	Chemicals

† Excluding stock held by group.

Appendix A

FULL ANALYSIS OF VERY LARGE COMPANIES (CA

(1936) in brackets if companies had

	Birmingham Small Arms		Bleachers' Associations		Boots Pure Drug	
	1936	1951	1936	1951	1936	1951
Capital £m.						
Ordinary shares	2·8	2·8	3·8	1·9	1·6	1·9
Preference shares	0·6	0·6	2·5	2·5	1·4	1·4
Debentures	1·6	1·1	2·2	2·2	0·0	0·0
Net Tangible Assets £m.	5·1	9·9[1]	9·8	8·4	5·5	9·9
Shareholders (00's)	(12,0)	13,5	—	19,7	(23,0)	39,0
Voting						
Total (000,000's)	2·8	2·8	3·8	3·8	6·4	7·1
% of total vote						
largest 20 holders	7·9	6·9	8·9	8·1	58·4	8·8
Breakdown by type:						
Personal (P)	3·4	1·5	6·6	5·9	5·9	1·3
Company (C)	0·0	0·2	0·3	0·0	15·7	0·2
Institution (I)	0·0	2·5	0·7	0·6	21·9	5·8
Nominee (N)	4·5	2·7	1·3	1·6	14·9	1·5
largest single holder	1·1	1·8	1·3	1·1	13·2	2·3
his type	P	N	P	P	C	I
Directors						
Total	8	7	22	21	12	10
% of Ordinary shares held	0·7	0·9	3·2	1·3	2·5	0·9
No. among largest 20 holders	1	1	2	1	0	1
No. interlocking with other large companies	3	5	0	0	0	0
No. holding only minimum share qualification	1	4	10	5	2	0
Financial Success 1936-1951						
Investors' success on 1936						
% Dividend gain		155		48		49
% Capital gain		208		63		–9
% Total gain		363		111		40
Accounting success on 1936						
% Dividend gain		143		11		218
% Asset gain		164		43		108
% Total gain		307		54		326
Distribution ratio 1948-1951		24·4		23·5		43·2
Industrial Group		Engineering		Textiles		Chemicals

NOTES

[1] Includes goodwill since 1937.

DIX A 1

PITAL £3M. OR MORE IN 1951) FOR 1936 AND 1951

less than £3m. share capital in 1936

Bovril		Bowater Paper Corporation		Bradford Dyers' Association		Bristol Aeroplane		British Aluminium		British American Tobacco	
1936	1951	(1936)	1951	1936	1951	(1936)	1951	1936	1951	1936	1951
1·0	1·0	0·7	2·7	2·3	2·3	0·6	3·3	2·0	3·6	23·7	23·8
2·3	2·4	1·1	2·8	2·5	2·5	0·6	0·6	1·5	1·5	10·5	10·5
0·0	0·0	1·0	3·2	1·5	1·1	0·0	0·0	3·5	5·0	0·0	0·0
4·3	7·0	3·5	18·9	6·6	8·5	1·3	8·0	8·5	18·8	39·2	143·2
—	10,6	(8,9)	11,7	—	17,1	(3,0)	8,2	(8,6)	15,7	(35,2)	72,8
3·2	3·2	0·5	1·8	2·3	2·3	1·2	6·6	2·2	3·0	23·7	23·8
8·4[2]	30·4	71·8	19·6	15·7	11·7	39·0	47·4	12·8	21·8	34·2	4·6
5·4	14·7	10·8	2·0	11·5	2·6	35·3	43·4	4·1	0·5	2·3	0·5
0·2	0·0	0·0	0·0	2·3	1·7	0·2	0·6	0·0	0·0	28·3	0·0
2·8	15·5	2·6	4·9	0·4	1·6	0·4	1·3	3·5	18·6	2·5	2·3
0·0	0·2	58·4	12·7	1·5	5·8	3·1	2·1	5·2	2·7	1·1	1·8
2·6	7·1	29·6	3·2	3·2	1·8	11·5	8·7	1·9	3·7	27·5	1·1
P	P	N	N	P	N	P	P	P	I	C	I
5	6	8	10	26	13	4	8	7	11	20	17
0·7	0·1	5·1	1·2	0·8	2·6	41·8	24·9	0·2	0·2	1·7	0·2
2	2	1	1	2	1	3	4	0	0	3	0
0	1	0	1	0	0	0	0	2	3	0	0
1	0	3	0	4	2	0	0	3	7	4	0

Bovril	Bowater Paper Corporation	Bradford Dyers' Association	Bristol Aeroplane	British Aluminium	British American Tobacco
148	43	152	55	80	54
54	95	338	−34	4	−11
202	138	490	21	84	43
900	39	55	164	98	278
20	93	127	149	71	236
920	132	182	313	169	514
36·8	11·7	17·6	46·9	34·2	28·9
Food	Paper	Textiles	Motors	Engineering	Misc.

[2] Largest 15 shareholders only.

FULL ANALYSIS OF VERY LARGE COMPANIES (CA

(1936) in brackets if companies had

				British Celanese		British Cocoa and Chocolate		British Insulated Callenders Cables	
				1936	1951	1936	1951	1936[1]	1951
Capital £m.									
Ordinary shares	..	..	..	2·2	2·2	2·7	5·4		9·2
Preference shares	..	..	..	6·7	7·7	0·8	0·8		2·0
Debentures	..	..	..	3·5	3·2	0·0	0·0		0·0
Net Tangible Assets £m.	..	..	..	11.5	18·5	N.A.	22·9		23·4
Shareholders (00's)	..	..	..	—	25,1	(0,5)	0,9		21,0
Voting									
Total (000,000's)	..	..	..	4·4	4·4	2·7	5·4		9·2
% of total vote									
largest 20 holders	..	..		56·4	43·4	78·8	66·1		10·1
Breakdown by type:									
Personal (P)	..	..	..	8·8	6·0	78·8	61·2		2·4
Company (C)	..	..		1·8	1·6	0·0	0·0		0·4
Institution (I)	..	..		0·0	0·5	0·0	4·9		6·1
Nominee (N)	..	..		45·8	35·3	0·0	0·0		1·2
largest single holder	..	..		9·8	16·9	15·1	12·7		1·3
his type	..	..		N	N	P	P		I
Directors									
Total	..	..	..	9	10	17	11		13
% of Ordinary shares held	..	..		5·7	4·4	49·6	32·2		0·6
No. among largest 20 holders	..	..		1	1	13	8		1
No. interlocking with other									
large companies	..	..		1	0	0	0		2
No. holding only minimum									
share qualification	..	..		3	0	1	0		5
Financial Success 1936-1951						N.A.		N.A.	
Investors' success on 1936									
% Dividend gain	..	..	..	67					
% Capital gain	..	..	..	212					
% Total gain	..	..	..	279					
Accounting success on 1936						N.A.		N.A.	
% Dividend gain	..	..	..	69					
% Asset gain	..	..	..	2678					
% Total gain	..	..	..	2747					
Distribution ratio 1948-1951	..	..	..	11·5		30·8		17·2	
Industrial Group	..	..	..	Textiles		Food		Engineering	

NOTES

[1] Company formed since 1936.

DIX A 1

PITAL £3M. OR MORE IN 1951) FOR 1936 AND 1951

less than £3m. share capital in 1936

British Match Corporation		British Oxygen		British Plaster Board		British Ropes		British Sugar Corporation		British United Shoe Machinery	
1936	1951	(1936)	1951	(1936)	1951	(1936)	1951	1936²	1951	1936	1951
6·2	6·2	1·9	4·2	0·7	2·9	1·0	2·3		5·0	2·8	2·8
0·5	0·5	0·5	2·5	0·1	0·1	0·6	1·3		0·0	0·4	0·4
0·0	0·0	0·0	4·0	0·0	0·0	0·8	0·0		3·5	0·0	0·0
7·2	12·7	3·6	17·8	1·2	4·2	2·6	6·3	N.A.		3·4	7·4
—	5,4	(8,5)	18,4	(5,4)	15,3	—	11,1		3,2	—	2,0
6·2	6·2	1·9	3·5	2·7	11·6	3·7	18·9		5·0	2·5	2·8
41·0	39·3	52·1	34·0	28·5	17·8	28·7	16·2		68·2	89·8	86·5
9·5	6·7	0·4	1·2	13·7	5·1	15·5	4·9		17·9	9·7	5·2
12·9	12·9	0·0	0·2	0·0	0·3	0·0	0·6		29·6	79·5	79·5
16·8	18·4	2·1	3·2	1·1	0·9	1·3	5·2		17·9	0·6	0·9
1·8	1·3	49·6	29·4	13·7	11·5	11·9	5·5		2·8	0·0	0·9
16·2	12·9	41·9	27·3	3·6	8·6	3·0	2·7		15·0	79·1	79·2
I	C	N	N	P	N	N	N		I³	C	C
12	12	7	12	15	18	6	11		9	14	17
3·0	3·8	0·6	0·7	3·6	2·4	6·4	3·1		0·2	3·1	2·3
3	3	0	1	0	3	5	1		0	4	3
1	1	0	1	0	3	0	0		0	0	1
2	5	3	6	2	0	0	1		5	4	8
								N.A.			

British Match Corporation	British Oxygen	British Plaster Board	British Ropes	British Sugar Corporation	British United Shoe Machinery
68	51	90	106		38
−7	−18	−1	96		−1
61	33	89	202	N.A.	37
123	241	579	398		233
40	157	203	648		129
163	398	782	1046	N.A.	362
50·9	40·0	69·2	26·5		42·6
Chemicals	Chemicals	Misc.	Engineering	Food	Engineering

² Company formed since 1936.   ³ Solicitor for H.M. Affairs.

Appendix A

FULL ANALYSIS OF VERY LARGE COMPANIES (CA

(1936) in brackets if companies had

				Brush Electric		Burton (Montague)		Calico Printers Association	
				(1936)	1951	1936	1951	1936	1951
Capital £m.									
Ordinary shares	..	..	..	0·5	2·4	2·0[1]	2·2	2·0	2·0
Preference shares	..	..	..	0·0	1·0	3·0	3·0	3·0	3·0
Debentures	..	..	..	1·7	0·0	3·7	3·9	3·2	3·2
Net Tangible Assets £m.	..	..	..	0·6	6·1	9·5	15·5	9·9	15·4
Shareholders (00's)	..	..	..	(2,6)	9,5	(14,5)	30,3	(9,8)	14,8
Voting									
Total (000,000's)	..	..	..	4·9	2·4	4·2	4·5	2·0	2·0
% of total vote									
largest 20 holders	..	..	..	19·3	39·8	79·2	72·8	15·9	19·2
Breakdown by type:									
Personal (P)	..	..	..	7·2	19·3	71·5	70·3	7·7	4·5
Company (C)	..	..	..	0·6	0·0	0·0	0·0	4·7	0·9
Institution (I)	..	..	..	2·6	4·5	3·3	1·5	0·7	7·9
Nominee (N)	..	..	..	8·9	16·0	4·4	1·0	2·8	5·9
largest single holder	..	..	..	5·1	18·7	66·4	69·0	4·4	4·9
his type	..	..	..	N	P	P	P	C	I
Directors									
Total	..	..	..	3	12	7	8	7	7
% of Ordinary shares held	..	..	..	0·2	0·3	68·7	69·3	2·9	1·8
No. among largest 20 holders	..	..	..	0	1	0	1	2	2
No. interlocking with other large companies	..	..	..	0	8	1	0	0	0
No. holding only minimum share qualification	..	..	..	1	8	1	1	5	0
Financial Success 1936-1951									
Investors' success on 1936									
% Dividend gain	..	..	..	44		57		104	
% Capital gain	..	..	..	23		6		438	
% Total gain	..	..	..	67		63		542	
Accounting success on 1936									
% Dividend gain	..	..	..	24		98		23	
% Asset gain	..	..	..	34		185		95	
% Total gain	..	..	..	58		283		118	
Distribution ratio 1948-1951	..	..	..	19·2		31·7		12·2	
Industrial Group	..	..	..	Engineering		Distribution		Textiles	

NOTES

[1] Excludes holding of subsidiary companies.

DIX A 1

PITAL £3M. OR MORE IN 1951) FOR 1936 AND 1951

less than £3m. share capital in 1936

Carreras		Colman J. J.		Consolidated Tin Smelters		Courtauld		Crompton Parkinson		Debenham's	
1936	1951	1936	1951	1936	1951	1936	1951	(1936)	1951	1936	1951
1·8	3·7	2·0	2·0	2·0	2·0	24·0	24·0	0·5	3·1	0·5	2·0
1·3	1·3	1·5	1·5	1·3	1·3	8·0	8·0	0·7	0·7	5·7	5·7
0·0	0·0	0·0	0·0	0·0	0·0	0·0	0·0	0·0	0·0	2·9	1·8
5·5	11·6	4·3	5·1	3·5	4·9	42·7	63·1	1·8	5·9	9·9	23·2
(29,0)	34,1	(2,7)	6,1	—	1,0	(34,8)	89,3	—	10,0	—	30,0
0·2	0·2	2·0	2·0	1·9	2·0	24·0	24·0	0·4	0·4	17·4	17·5
84·6	84·1	81·8	49·2	85·1	90·5	21·0	7·1	75·5	49·4	13·5	9·4
77·2	82·4	77·0	41·0	5·3	1·6	16·7	4·4	27·9	44·0	5·9	2·2
0·0	0·0	0·4	0·0	28·0	19·8	0·0	0·0	0·0	0·0	0·7	0·0
6·8	1·4	1·2	6·9	0·3	7·4	1·0	1·3	1·2	2·3	1·0	2·1
0·6	0·3	3·2	1·3	51·5	61·7	3·3	1·4	46·4	3·1	5·9	5·1
52·9	26·7	11·6	7·4	43·7	50·0	2·6	0·7	42·1	34·5	2·1	0·8
P	P	P	P	N	N	P	P	N	P	N	N
6	9	7	7	8	9	14	18	6	12	15	12
36·5	8·3	52·9	27·5	0·2	0·4	3·3	1·2	26·1	2·8	3·2	10·0
4	5	7	4	0	0	2	1	1	4	3	0
1	1	0	0	1	2	0	1	0	2	0	0
0	0	0	1	5	5	2	7	3	7	0	4

Carreras	Colman J. J.	Consolidated Tin Smelters	Courtauld	Crompton Parkinson	Debenham's
105	64	N.A.	43	43	156
28	−2		−11	−32	212
133	62		32	11	368
407	190	65	82	320	245
144	10	64	76	234	351
551	200	129	158	554	596
60·2	N.A.[2]	35·8	35·7	55·0	39·0
Misc.	Food	Engineering	Textiles	Engineering	Distribution

[2] Reorganisation in 1948-51.

Appendix A

FULL ANALYSIS OF VERY LARGE COMPANIES (CA

(1936) in brackets if companies had

				Dickinson (John & Co.)		Dunlop Rubber Co.		Electric & Musical Industries	
				(1936)	1951	1936	1951	1936	1951
Capital £m.									
Ordinary shares	..	..	..	1·4	2·9	7·9	12·9	2·9	2·9
Preference shares	..	..	..	0·3	0·4	4·4	4·4	0·5	0·5
Debentures	..	..	..	0·8	0·7	3·5[1]	5·6[1]	0·0	2·0
Net Tangible Assets £m.	..	..	..	3·3	8·4	20·6	51·5	3·6	8·7
Shareholders (00's)	..	..	..	(4,8)	5,0	(85,8)	45,5	(15,0)	12,4
Voting									
Total (000,000's)	..	..	..	1·4	2·9	25·3	38·6	5·8	5·8
% of total vote									
largest 20 holders	..	..	..	25·9	28·0	5·1	9·6	25·3	41·0
Breakdown by type:									
Personal (P)	..	..	..	18·6	10·3	1·2	0·2	7·4	0·3
Company (C)		..	..	0·6	0·5	0·3	0·0	0·0	0·0
Institution (I)		..	..	5·3	16·3	1·5	4·1	2·5	1·4
Nominee (N)		..	..	1·4	0·9	2·1	5·3	15·4	39·3
largest single holder	..		..	3·4	8·6	0·6	2·3	10·0	37·3
his type	..		..	I	P	I	I	N	N
Directors									
Total	..	..	..	7	5	8	10	10	6
% of Ordinary shares held		..	..	4·4	1·9	0·09	0·03	0·13	0·3
No. among largest 20 holders		..	..	2	2	0	0	0	0
No. interlocking with other									
large companies	..	..	..	0	1	2	5	1	4
No. holding only minimum									
share qualification	..	..	..	1	0	1	1	0	0
Financial Success 1936-1951									
Investors' success on 1936									
% Dividend gain	..	..	..		95		106		50
% Capital gain	..	..	..		126		91		−6
% Total gain	..	..	..		221		197		44
Accounting success on 1936									
% Dividend gain	..	..	..		200		114		105
% Asset gain	..	..	..		230		112		103
% Total gain	..	..	..		430		226		208
Distribution ratio 1948-1951	..	..	..		17·5		31·1		36·6
Industrial Group	..	..	..		Paper		Misc.		Engineering

NOTES

[1] Less held by subsidiary company.

DIX A 1

PITAL £3M. OR MORE IN 1951) FOR 1936 AND 1951

less than £3m. share capital in 1936

English Electric Co.		English Sewing Cotton Co.		Fine Cotton Spinners Doublers Assocn.		Fisons		Ford Motor Co.		General Electric Co.	
1936)	1951	1936	1951	1936	1951	(1936)	1951	1936	1951	1936	1951
1·4	4·1	2·0	2·0	4·4	5·6	0·7	4·4	9·0	9·0	3·8	4·2
1·1	2·6	1·0	1·0	3·9	3·0	0·2	3·3	0·0	2·9	3·6	5·6
1·1	3·9	0·91	0·9	2·7	1·9	0·2	3·5	0·0	0·0	0·0	8·0
3·7	16·9	5·1	7·5	11·9	19·9	1·5	14·3	12·4	34·9	11·6	36·8
—	14,3	—	12,7	(27,2)	30,2	(3,0)	5,4	(10,0)	12,0	—	29,7
1·4	4·1	2·0	2·0	5·3	5·6	0·9	4·4	9·0	9·0	5·0	4·2
60·4	15·2	12·0	11·9	11·4	6·8	33·3	20·3	80·7	72·4	14·9	13·3
27·7	0·5	3·9	2·5	6·6	2·4	28·1	3·1	0·2	0·3	3·3	2·7
8·3	0·0	1·8	0·5	2·0	1·4	0·0	6·2	57·9	59·2	1·0	0·3
11·7	6·3	3·3	3·1	0·4	0·4	2·7	5·1	0·1	1·4	4·1	6·2
12·7	8·4	3·0	5·8	2·4	2·6	2·5	5·9	22·5	11·5	6·5	4·1
20·8	2·8	3·0	2·4	3·0	0·8	5·9	6·2	57·9	59·1	2·6	3·2
P	N	N	N	P	C	P	C	C	C	N	I
7	8	8	8	21	23	12	10	7	11	17	14
0·8	0·6	1·2	0·7	1·9	1·5	5·6	0·9	1·4	0·2	3·2	0·2
0	1	2	1	4	2	3	1	0	0	3	0
0	3	1	2	1	1	0	2	1	3	2	2
5	3	4	0	11	6	1	3	1	2	3	9
120		59		166		77		80		63	
152		17		309		−23		76		4	
272		76		475		54		156		67	
164		79		56		111		89		138	
126		75		42		83		103		150	
290		154		98		194		192		288	
30·2		16·9		32·8		61·3		17·3		27·4	
Engineering		Textiles		Textiles		Chemicals		Motors		Engineering	

Appendix A

FULL ANALYSIS OF VERY LARGE COMPANIES (CA

(1936) in brackets if companies had

				Goodlass Wall & Lead Industries		Great Universal Stores		Harrods	
				1936	1951	(1936)	1951	1936	1951
Capital £m.									
Ordinary shares	..	..	..	1·2	1·7	0·3	1·3	2·2	2·2
Preference shares	..	..	..	1·8	1·3	0·7	2·2	4·0	4·0
Debentures	..	..	..	0·0	0·0	0·0	0·0	0·0	0·0
Net Tangible Assets £m.	..	..	..	3·1	8·7	1·4	14·4	7·5	10·2
Shareholders (00's)	..	..	..	(11,8)	7,8	—	16,8	(31,5)	13,3
Voting									
Total (000,000's)	..	..	..	3·3	3·3	1·2	5·3	6·2	6·2
% of total vote									
largest 20 holders	..	..	..	36·4	17·3	39·2	31·9	4·6	6·2
Breakdown by type:									
Personal (P)	..	..	..	5·5	3·2	4·2	5·5	2·4	0·9
Company (C)	..	..	..	12·7	6·3	0·0	0·5	0·0	0·0
Institution (I)	..	..	..	11·8	3·2	0·4	3·1	1·1	3·7
Nominee (N)	..	..	..	6·4	4·6	34·6	22·8	1·1	1·6
largest single holder	..	..	..	12·7	12·6	25·9	16·2	0·5	0·7
his type	..	..	..	C	C	N	N	I	N
Directors									
Total	..	..	..	12	11	6	4	8	9
% of Ordinary shares held		..	..	1·6	1·3	0·6	0·9	2·1	0·2
No. among largest 20 holders		..	..	3		2	1	1	0
No. interlocking with other large companies		..	..	2	1	0	0	3	0
No. holding only minimum share qualification		..	..	1	1	0	0	0	5
Financial Success 1936-1951									
Investors' success on 1936									
% Dividend gain	..	..	..	122		95		55	
% Capital gain	..	..	..	266		35		−22	
% Total gain	..	..	..	388		130		33	
Accounting success on 1936									
% Dividend gain	..	..	..	143		459		143	
% Asset gain	..	..	..	450		752		33	
%Total gain	..	..	..	593		1211		176	
Distribution ratio 1948-1951	..	..	..	12·5		22·6		43·1	
Industrial Group	..	..	..	Engineering		Distribution		Distribution	

DIX A 1

PITAL £3M. OR MORE IN 1951) FOR 1936 AND 1951
less than £3m. share capital in 1936

Harrods (Buenos Aires)		Hawker Siddeley Group		Home & Colonial Stores		Illustrated Newspapers		Imperial Chemical Industries		Imperial Tobacco	
1936	1951	(1936)	1951	1936	1951	1936	1951	1936	1951	1936	1951
2·4	2·4	1·5	5·8	2·3	2·3	1·4	1·4	49·2	60·6	37·6	37·6
2·9	2·9	1·4	2·0	2·0	2·0	1·8	1·8	22·7	25·0	12·9	12·9
0·0	0·0	0·0	2·9	0·0	0·0	0·3	0·2	0·0	20·0	0·0	0·0
5·6	7·9	3·7	20·9	7·7	13·0	3·5	4·6	87·9	256·9	58·0	123·3
(24,3)	20,0	—	23,0	(14,6)	34,4	(10,0)	8,2	(199,0)	200,0	(105,6)	163,4
7·3	7·2	1·0	5·8	3·5	3·5	1·4	5·6	51·4	63·0	37·5	37·6
7·1	12·5	23·1	14·0	29·7	49·2	59·3	47·2	10·1	9·3	19·0	15·8
3·0	5·5	0·2	0·4	8·6	0·7	55·3	46·3	1·1	0·1	14·6	10·2
0·0	0·0	0·0	0·0	7·7	0·0	0·9	0·0	5·1	0·0	0·0	0·0
2·6	2·3	1·4	5·2	1·8	1·5	0·0	0·1	1·1	2·8	4·4	4·0
1·5	4·7	21·5	8·4	11·6	47·0	3·1	0·8	2·8	6·4	0·0	1·6
1·2	2·8	6·9	2·4	9·4	45·6	53·5	22·8	5·1	4·4	3·9	3·0
P	P	N	I	N	N	P	P	C	N	P	P
6	6	6	5	8	7	6	8	16	17	35	34
0·09	0·2	1·7	0·2	0·4	0·2	0·64	39·6	0·2	0·1	10·4	4·2
0	0	0	0	0	0	0	4	0	0	7	4
3	1	0	1	0	0	3	0	2	4	0	1
1	1	2	1	3	1	4	2	5	2	2	6
0		N.A.		61		125		72		65	
−49				25		151		29		−39	
−49				86		276		101		26	
0		255		33		27		127		455	
21		316		67		64		226		76	
21		571		100		91		353		531	
12·8		18·7		26·1		19·7		29·9		80·5	
Distribution		Motors		Distribution		Paper		Chemical		Misc.	

APPEN

FULL ANALYSIS OF VERY LARGE COMPANIES (CA

(1936) in brackets if companies had

	International Tea Co. Stores		Kemsley Newspapers		Lancashire Cotton Corporation	
	1936	1951	1936	1951	1936	1951
Capital £m.						
Ordinary shares	1·5	1·5	2·0	2·5	0·7	3·9
Preference shares	3·6	3·6	6·7	6·7	4·3	0·1
Debentures	0·0	0·0	3·5	3·2	6·5	0·0
Net Tangible Assets £m.	6·9	9·5	13·7	19·2	10·1	12·8
Shareholders (00's)	(30,0)	27,0	—	20,9	(23,2)	10,9
Voting						
Total (000,000's)	2·9	8·6	2·0	2·5	9·7	1·4
% of total vote						
largest 20 holders	13·9	12·5	38·0	32·1	50·7	14·3
Breakdown by type:						
Personal (P)	4·9	2·2	18·6	18·2	5·5	0·9
Company (C)	0·0	0·3	0·6	0·6	5·3	0·4
Institution (I)	5·5	7·4	0·8	2·5	21·5	4·7
Nominee (N)	3·5	2·6	18·0	10·8	18·4	8·3
largest single holder	2·2	1·7	12·4	9·6	20·7	5·4
his type	P	P	N	P	I	N
Directors						
Total	7	8	11	18	7	7
% of Ordinary shares held	2·3	0·5	9·5	18·5	0·01	0·4
No. among largest 20 holders	0	0	6	3	0	0
No. interlocking with other large companies	1	0	3	0	1	2
No. holding only minimum share qualification	1	0	4	10	6	1
Financial Success 1936-1951						
Investors' success on 1936					N.A.	
% Dividend gain	43		91			
% Capital gain	−36		−23			
% Total gain	7		68			
Accounting success on 1936						
% Dividend gain	109		73		94	
% Asset gain	77		58		171	
% Total gain	186		131		265	
Distribution ratio 1948-1951	25·5		33·5		15·2	
Industrial Group	Distribution		Paper		Textiles	

NOTES

[1] Company not formed in 1936. [2] Limited votes for any one holder, figures estimated.

DIX A 1

PITAL £3M. OR MORE IN 1951) FOR 1936 AND 1951

less than £3m. share capital in 1936

Lebus (Harris)		Lever Bros. and Unilever		Lewis (John) and Co.		Lewis Investment Trust		Liebigs Meat Extract		London Brick Co.	
1936[1]	1951	1936	1951	(1936)	1951	1936	1951	1936	1951	(1936)	1951
	2·0	8·5	13·6	0·9	0·9	1·2	1·2	2·0	2·0	1·6	2·6
	1·0	52·8	56·0	1·7	2·2	1·9	2·0	1·0	2·0	0·4	0·4
	0·0	0·0	0·1	1·0	0·0	2·2	1·4	0·0	0·0	0·0	0·0
	3·0	80·5	193·7	3·6	5·1	4·9	8·9	4·2	7·6	2·3	4·8
	2,2	—	192,9	(3,3)	8,3	(6,2)	9,0	—	3,4	(5,3)	8,8
	2·0	6·1	70·1	1·0	1·1	1·4	14·4	·01[2]	·01[2]	1·6	10·4
	72·4	20·4	7·6	85·5	81·0	58·9	6·8	5·8	8·8	32·2	14·9
	59·6	2·3	4·7	56·1	53·4	41·0	3·6	3·4	1·2	19·3	7·0
	0·0	16·7	0·0	18·8	17·8	0·0	0·0	0·0	0·0	0·0	0·0
	5·8	1·4	2·0	1·2	0·8	11·2	1·5	2·0	3·9	1·2	5·8
	7·0	0·0	0·9	9·4	9·0	6·7	1·7	0·4	3·7	11·7	2·1
	13·1	8·5	4·3	55·8	53·3	14·7	1·8	0·5	0·5	4·9	1·8
	P	C	P	P	P	P	P	P	N	P	P
	10	18	24	9	8	9	10	4	6	7	7
	28·0	7·2	23·2	66·6	66·6[3]	24·7	1·1	2·6	0·8	52·6	3·5
	4	0	0	1	1	3	3	0	1	6	3
	0	0	0	0	0	0	3	0	0	0	1
	0	7	13	5	6	0	7	2	0	0	1
			N.A.								
		30				63		65		59	
		51				16		—16		—16	
		81				79		49		43	
		N.A.									
				151		237		122		158	
				323		100		19		31	
				474		337		141		189	
53·5		20·6		34·2		37·3		69·8		87·6	
Misc.		Chemical		Distribution		Distribution		Food		Misc.	

[3] Joint holding, three persons, one a director.

Appendix A

FULL ANALYSIS OF VERY LARGE COMPANIES (CA

(1936) in brackets if companies had

					Lucas (Joseph)		Lyons J. & Co.		Marks & Spencer	
					(1936)	1951	1936	1951	(1936)	1951
Capital £m.										
Ordinary shares	..	..	..	..	2·0	6·3	2·9	2·2	1·4	2·2
Preference shares	..	..	..		0·2	0·5	6·6	6·6	1·3	1·3
Debentures	..	..	..		0·0	0·0	1·7	2·7	1·0	3·2
Net Tangible Assets £m.	..	..	..		2·9	16·5	13·1	20·2	5·0	16·2
Shareholders (00's)	..	..	..		—	8,5	—	32,5	—	25,9
Voting										
Total (000,000's)	..	..	..		1·9	6·3	1·3	1·3	2·4	1·2
% of total vote										
largest 20 holders	..	..	..		32·3	20·2	54·0	37·0	64·3	43·9
Breakdown by type:										
Personal (P)	..	..	..		12·7	3·5	24·8	1·6	52·9	28·8
Company (C)		..	..		0·5	0·0	0·7	0·1	0·0	0·0
Institution (I)		..	..		2·9	6·6	0·8	34·3	10·6	15·1
Nominee (N)		..	..		16·2	10·1	27·7	1·0	0·8	0·0
largest single holder	..	..	..		11·9	5·3	12·6	33·3	10·4	10·5
his type	..	..	..		N	N	N	I	P	I
Directors										
Total	..	..	..		6	9	13	21	6	8
% of Ordinary shares held	..	..			4·4	2·1	3·8	1·1	9·2	14·9
No. among largest 20 holders	..	..			0	1	7	1	4	4
No. interlocking with other large companies	..	..			0	3	0	5	0	1
No. holding only minimum share qualification	..	..	..		0	3	5	5	2	2
Financial Success 1936-1951										
Investors' success on 1936										
% Dividend gain	..	..	..			72		50		42
% Capital gain	..	..	..			70		–24		57
% Total gain	..	..	..			142		26		99
Accounting success on 1936										
% Dividend gain	..	..	..			196		N.A.		293
% Asset gain	..	..	..			421				193
% Total gain	..	..	..			617				486
Distribution ratio 1948-1951	..	..	..			14·0		56·1		42·9
Industrial Group	..	..	..	..		Engineering		Distribution		Distribution

NOTES

[1] Company not formed in 1936.   [2] Company controlled by one person.

DIX A 1

PITAL £3M. OR MORE IN 1951) FOR 1936 AND 1951

less than £3m. share capital in 1936

Metal Box Co.		Morgan Crucible Co.		Morris Motors		Odeon		Paton & Baldwins		Pinchin Johnson & Associates	
(1936)	1951	1936	1951	1936	1951	1936[1]	1951	1936	1951	(1936)	1951
1·0	3·6	2·2	2·5	2·2	2·6		0·9	1·6	2·6	1·7	2·6
1·0	2·4	2·1	2·1	3·0	3·0		2·7	1·4	4·4	0·8	0·8
0·8	0·0	0·2	0·0	0·0	0·0		0·0	0·5	3·0	0·0	0·0
3·2	11·5	4·6	6·7	8·7	15·0		4·7	4·3	17·7	3·4	7·4
(3,6)	6,4	(3,1)	4,9	(10,9)	13,3		6,2	(6,9)	17,0	—	19,6
1·0	3·6	2·3	2·4	4·5	5·3		3·8	1·8	2·9	3·3	5·2
61·5	23·2	82·5	37·2	99·9	29·7		41·3	36·5	14·4	15·8	11·4
32·5	10·4	74·6	33·7	99·9	28·3		1·5	30·8	4·2	5·6	1·2
17·9	0·8	7·9	0·0	0·0	0·0		0·0	0·0	0·0	0·0	0·0
6·0	9·1	0·0	3·5	0·0	0·5		0·8	0·5	7·5	2·4	4·0
5·1	2·9	0·0	0·0	0·0	0·9		39·0	5·2	2·7	7·8	6·2
13·3	5·1	8·0	6·4	99·9	18·8		38·3	5·9	3·5	3·0	1·9
C	I	P	P	P[2]	P		N	P	I	N	I
9	9	8	11	10	9		12	12	10	8	10
14·7	3·2	34·2	20·2	0·1	28·3		0·9	16·1	2·4	1·9	6·8
4	2	7	8	0	2		9	4	2	2	0
0	1	0	1	0	0		4	0	0	0	3
2	1	0	0	7	4		3	1	1	0	0
74		N.A.		97		N.A.		75		57	
37				23				9		11	
—				—				—		—	
111				120				84		68	
201		95		140		N.A.		166		185	
245		72		44				155		29	
—		—		—				—		—	
446		167		184				321		214	
37·9		41·4		48·0		0·0[3]		39·8		65·8[4]	
Engineering		Misc.		Motors		Misc.		Textiles		Chemicals	

[3] No profits. [4] Three years only.

Appendix A

FULL ANALYSIS OF VERY LARGE COMPANIES (CA
(1936) in brackets if companies had

Capital £m.				Radiation		Ranks		Reckitt & Sons	
				1936	1951	1936	1951	1936	1951
Ordinary shares	..	..	..	2·3	2·3	3·1	3·5	3·7	3·6
Preference shares	..	..	..	1·1	1·1	4·2	2·2	1·4	1·4
Debentures	..	..	..	0·0	0·0	0·0	0·0	0·4	0·2
Net Tangible Assets £m.	..	..	..	3·7	6·9	7·4	25·6	7·1	7·5
Shareholders (00's)	..	..	..	(10,5)	10,3	—	13,0	(13,0)	7,1
Voting									
Total (000,000's)	..	..	..	2·3	2·3	12·3	13·8	0·3	0·4
% of total vote									
largest 20 holders	..	..	..	8·0	9·9	93·1	100·0	35·0	18·5
Breakdown by type:									
Personal (P)	..	..	..	3·8	3·4	91·3	100·0	32·3	14·1
Company (C)		..	..	0·0	0·0	0·0	0·0	0·0	0·0
Institution (I)		..	..	0·2	5·1	0·4	0·0	1·8	3·5
Nominee (N)		..	..	4·0	1·4	1·4	0·0	0·9	0·9
largest single holder	..	..	..	1·3	1·5	28·4	36·4	8·7	2·5
his type	..	..	..	N	I	P	P	P	P
Directors									
Total	..	..	..	9	8	4	3	9	6
% of Ordinary shares held		..	..	0·3	0·2	85·0	33·3	13·1	3·2
No. among largest 20 holders		..	..	0	0	4	3	4	2
No. interlocking with other large companies		..	..	1	0	0	1	0	0
No. holding only minimum share qualification	..	..	..	4	5	0	0	2	1
Financial Success 1936-1951									
Investors' success on 1936									
% Dividend gain	..	..	..	48		69		61	
% Capital gain	..	..	..	–14		8		–11	
% Total gain	..	..	..	34		77		50	
Accounting success on 1936									
% Dividend gain	..	..	..	149		254		245	
% Asset gain	..	..	..	51		102		2	
% Total gain	..	..	..	200		356		247	
Distribution ratio 1948-1951	..	..	..	40·7		48·9		121	
Industrial Group	..	..	..	Engineering		Food		Misc.	

NOTES

[1] Company not formed in 1936. [2] Excludes amount held by subsidiary

DIX A 1

PITAL £3M. OR MORE IN 1951) FOR 1936 AND 1951

less than £3m. share capital in 1936

Robinson E.S. & A.		Rootes Motors		Rowntree & Co.		Ruston & Hornsby		Ryland		Sears J. Co. (Trueform)	
(1936)	1951	1936[1]	1951	(1936)	1951	(1936)	1951	1936	1951	1936	1951
0·7	2·2		1·0	0·2	0·5	1·2	4·4	2·0	2·0	0·6	0·6
1·2	2·3		2·0	2·2	2·5	0·4	0·4	1·0	1·0	2·4	2·8
0·1	0·1		0·0	0·0	0·0	0·5	0·3	0·0	0·0	1·7	1·7[2]
2·0	7·7		8·4	2·9	7·4	2·3	8·8	3·2	4·6	5·4	7·1
(1,6)	7,7		5,0	(8,8)	9,0	—	8,2	(6,9)	7,4	(14,0)	14,1
0·6	2·2		5·0	1·7	2·0	0·1	0·4	2·0	2·0	0·5	0·5
52·2	33·5		55·0	40·7	73·1	10·2	15·0	7·7	23·8	25·4	75·1
50·2	29·8		34·4	40·7	61·2	7·2	1·0	3·1	9·5	10·9	8·0
0·0	0·0		0·0	0·0	0·0	0·0	0·3	0·0	9·7	0·0	0·0
0·0	1·8		15·7	0·0	11·9	1·5	7·8	0·0	2·0	3·1	35·7
2·0	1·9		4·9	0·0	0·0	1·5	5·9	4·6	2·6	11·4	31·4
8·0	7·0		18·7	27·1	43·8	1·1	2·9	3·8	9·7	4·4	19·9
P	P		P	P	P	I	I	N	C	N	I
12	9		9	9	9	9	11	7	6	6	6
11·8	12·6		30·6	12·1	0·8	1·2	0·2	0·7	0·9	2·3	2·3
6	3		4	2	1	0	0	0	0	2	0
0	0		0	0	0	0	1	0	0	0	0
4	0		0	3	5	1	6	3	0	0	0
N.A.				N.A.							
						138		137		79	
						177		181		11	
						315		318		90	
439				53		172		39		163	
553				217		244		68		220	
992				270		416		107		383	
23·9		14·5		9·8		20·9		43·3		19·4	
Paper		Motors		Food		Engineering		Textiles		Misc.	

Appendix A

FULL ANALYSIS OF VERY LARGE COMPANIES (CA

(1936) in brackets if companies had

				Selfridge Holdings		Siemens Bros. & Co.		Smiths & Sons (England)	
				1936	1951	1936	1951	(1936)	1951
Capital £m.									
Ordinary shares	..	..	..	1·8	1·0	2·4	2·4	0·8	1·7
Preference shares	..	..	..	1·3	2·3	0·6	1·5	0·1	1·4
Debentures	..	..	..	0·0	0·0	0·0	0·0	0·0	0·0
Net Tangible Assets £m.	..	..	..	4·4	4·2	4·0	8·0	1·6	5·7
Shareholders (00's)	..	..	..	—	16,0	(7,1)	7,3	(8,1)	8,3
Voting									
Total (000,000's)	..	..	..	3·1	1·0	3·0	3·0	1·9	8·4
% of total vote									
largest 20 holders	..	..	..	40·4	19·9	21·4	11·3	20·6	19·5
Breakdown by type:									
Personal (P)	..		..	4·6	0·3	0·4	0·2	1·5	0·0
Company (C)		..	..	0·1	0·0	0·7	0·0	0·5	0·5
Institution (I)		..	..	35·7	5·7	16·3	9·0	8·7	10·4
Nominee (N)		..	..	0·0	13·9	4·0	2·1	9·9	8·6
largest single holder	..		..	34·9	5·5	15·0	2·0	7·0	5·4
his type	..		..	I	N	I	I	I	N
Directors									
Total	..	..	..	7	6	8	8	6	6
% of Ordinary shares held		..	..	0·0³	0·3	0·3	0·2	0·7	0·9
No. among largest 20 holders		..	..	0	0	0	0	1	0
No. interlocking with other large companies	..		..	0	3	2	1	0	2
No. holding only minimum share qualification	..		..	3	3	6	4	2	0
Financial Success 1936-1951									
Investors' success on 1936				N.A.					
% Dividend gain	..	..	..			76		67	
% Capital gain	..	..	..			49		−8	
% Total gain	..	..	..			125		59	
Accounting success on 1936									
% Dividend gain	..	..	..	N.A.		85		190	
% Asset gain	..	..	..			89		192	
% Total gain	..	..	..			174		382	
Distribution ratio 1948-1951	..	..	..			33·5		19·4	
Industrial Group	..	..	..	Distribution		Engineering		Engineering	

NOTES

[1] Co. not formed in 1936   [2] See Appendix B.   [3] Directors hold preferential and staff shares.

DIX A 1

PITAL £3M. OR MORE IN 1951) FOR 1936 AND 1951

less than £3m. share capital in 1936

	Smith W. H. & Son (Holdings)	Spillers		Tate & Lyle		Tobacco Securities Trust Co.		Tube Investments		Tunnel Portland Cement	
1936¹	1951	1936	1951	1936	1951	1936	1951	1936	1951	(1936)	1951
	3·0	2·7	3·0	4·8	5·2	4·9	4·9	2·3	3·3	0·7	1·2
	3·0	1·1	1·1	1·1	1·1	0·0	0·0	0·8	0·8	0·2	2·4
	0·0	0·0	0·0	1·7	0·5	0·0	0·0	0·0	0·0	0·0	0·0
	6·0	6·7	12·5	8·9	11·0	5·2	15·5	4·5	29·7	2·1	7·2
	24,4	(8,0)	10,5	—	21,1	—	18,2	(7,0)	10,8	—	4,0
	5·0	3·8	4·1	3·4	5·2	4·7²	4·7²	4·1	4·2	0·6	2·4
	45·5	21·0	11·9	64·9	27·2			33·0	24·4	98·3	74·0
	38·2	12·3	5·9	59·4	22·0	Two Cos.		6·1	2·0	10·8	6·5
	0·0	0·0	0·0	3·6	3·3	and one		16·7	12·3	38·1	9·8
	5·6	6·2	3·8	0·0	0·6	nominee hold		2·3	6·4	5·7	15·7
	1·7	2·5	2·2	1·9	1·3	bulk of vote²		7·9	3·7	43·7	42·0
	24·3	3·4	1·2	6·0	10·6			14·4	11·8	43·6	22·2
	P	P	P	P	P	C	C	C	C	N	N
	7	6	5	14	13	7	8	12	13	7	6
	1·8	1·3	1·6	45·5	4·9	0·3	0·2	3·5	0·7	2·5	4·8
	3	0	1	5	0	—⁴	—⁴	2	0	2	1
	0	0	0	0	0	0	4	1	4	0	2
	0	0	2	1	1	2	5	0	4	4	0
N.A.		102		67		29		97		58	
		63		26		−52		69		6	
		165		93		−23		166		64	
N.A.		148		244		105		278		121	
		60		59		2		592		93	
		208		303		107		870		214	
N.A.⁵		56·1		45·9		86·7		21·4		32·8	
Distribution		Food		Food		Misc.		Engineering		Misc.	

⁴ Largest twenty not known. ⁵ Only two years consolidated accounts.

FULL ANALYSIS OF VERY LARGE COMPANIES (CA

(1936) in brackets if companies had

	Turner & Newall		Union International Co.		United Dairies	
	1936	1951	1936	1951	1936	1951
Capital £m.						
Ordinary shares	5·1	5·3	1·0	1·0	2·5	4·4
Preference shares	1·4	1·4	11·0	11·0	3·2	3·9
Debentures	0·0	0·0	0·0	0·0	0·0	0·0
Net Tangible Assets £m.	8·3	25·6	12·2	28·5	6·8	14·5
Shareholders (00's)	(15,0)	19,1	—	1,0	—	22,3
Voting						
Total (000,000's)	4·8	5·3	2·0	2·0	5·7	8·3
% of total vote						
largest 20 holders	20·4	11·2	79·4	80·3	9·1	7·1
Breakdown by type:						
Personal (P)	14·5	1·8	67·6	49·1	5·2	0·5
Company (C)	0·0	0·0	7·3	0·0	0·6	0·6
Institution (I)	2·9	3·9	4·5	5·3	2·1	4·8
Nominee (N)	3·0	5·5	0·0	25·9	1·2	1·2
largest single holder	4·5	1·2	17·5	17·5	1·7	1·2
his type	P	N	P	N	P	I
Directors						
Total	12	7	5	6	15	13
% of Ordinary shares held	10·9	1·0	0²	0²	2·5	0·9
No. among largest 20 holders	4	1	0	2	2	0
No. interlocking with other large companies	0	0	0	1	0	0
No. holding only minimum share qualification	0	4	2	1	3	1
Financial Success 1936-1951						
Investors' success on 1936			N.A.			
% Dividend gain	54				72	
% Capital gain	3				47	
% Total gain	57				119	
Accounting success on 1936						
% Dividend gain	185		1103		160	
% Asset gain	294		949		65	
% Total gain	479		2052		225	
Distribution ratio 1948-1951	19·8		5·7		32·2	
Industrial Group	Textiles		Food		Food	

NOTES

[1] Limited votes for any one holder, figures estimated.   [2] Directors hold preference stock.

DIX A 1

PITAL £3M. OR MORE IN 1951) FOR 1936 AND 1951

less than £3m. share capital in 1936

United Molasses Co.		Wallpaper Manufacturers		Wiggins Teape & Co.		Winterbottom Book Cloth Co.		Woolworth F. W.	
1936	1951	1936	1951	1936	1951	(1936)	1951	1936	1951
1·9	2·0	3·9	3·9	1·6	3·9	1·5	2·1	3·7	15·0
1·2	1·2	0·0	0·0	1·4	1·9	0·7	1·2	5·0	5·0
0·0	0·0	2·6	2·6	1·2	1·9	0·0	0·0	0·0	0·0
3·4	13·7	7·4	12·5	5·0	10·1	3·1	6·0	15·5	26·7
—	17,6	—	14,0	(7,3)	7,9	—	4,3	(12,2)	74,6
5·8	17·6	3·9	3·9	2·9	5·8	0·3	0·3[1]	3·7	60·0
22·5	4·0	23·9	14·5	25·7	21·2	38·9	32·0	87·5	66·3
1·1	0·0	18·8	7·3	16·8	6·5	35·5	20·0	2·6	4·4
1·3	0·4	0·0	0·0	0·0	0·0	0·0	0·0	67·1	52·7
0·8	1·1	0·0	3·6	5·1	10·6	2·6	9·8	12·7	5·4
19·3	2·5	5·1	3·6	3·8	4·1	0·8	1·2	5·1	3·8
4·7	0·7	3·4	1·8	3·4	3·3	12·1	8·4	52·7	52·7
N	N	P	N	P	N	P	P	C	C
6	9	24	17	11	11	8	9	9	12
0·1	0·4	3·7	1·1	4·1	2·5	3·5	5·5	2·8	0·1
0	0	0	0	3	1	3	4	1	0
1	4	0	1	0	5	0	3	0	3
0	4	2	6	1	0	2	0	0	3
109		48		76		90		70	
189		4		74		57		30	
298		52		150		147		100	
343		90		105		178		676	
325		161		175		100		111	
668		251		279		278		787	
39·0		11·0		87·1		49·0		65·3	
Food		Paper		Paper		Textiles		Distribution	

APPENDIX A 2

NAMES AND INDUSTRY OF COMPANIES ANALYSED PARTLY OR FULLY (AS APPENDIX A 1 FOR VERY LARGE INDUSTRIAL AND COMMERCIAL COMPANIES)

1. Very large breweries fully analysed

Ansell's.
Bass Ratcliffe
Charrington
Guinness
Ind Coope
Mitchell and Butler

Smith's Tadcaster
Walker Cain
Watney Combe & Reid
Whitbread
Wilson and Walker

2. Medium large companies (breweries in italics) fully analysed

Aerated Bread (F)
Associated Commercial Vehicles (Mo)
Barclay Perkins (*B*)
Barry & Staines (X)
Benskins Watford (*B*)
Brickwood (*B*)
Bristol Brewery (*B*)
British Timken (E)
British Tyre & Rubber Co. (X)
Brockhouse (J.) (E)
Brown (*Matthew*) (*B*)
Crosse & Blackwell (F)
Daily Mirror Newspapers (Pa)
De Havilland Aircraft (Mo)
Denny Mott & Dickson (D)
Enfield Cables (E)
English China Clays (X)
Falk Stadelmann (E)
Fisher & Ludlow (Mo)
Fremlins (*B*)
Gestetner (E)
Glaxo Laboratories (Ch)
Gordon Hotels (X)
Hammonds United Breweries (*B*)
Hartley Wm. (F)
Howard & Bullough (Securities) (E)
International Paints (Ch)
Johnson & Philips (E)
Lansil (T)
Laporte Chemicals (Ch)

Leyland Motors (Mo)
Lister (T)
Lister (R.A.) (E)
Mather & Platt (E)
Mitchell Cotts (D)
Monsanto Chemicals (Ch)
Meux's Brewery (*B*)
Norvic Shoe (X)
Odhams Press (Pa)
Olympia (X)
Pressed Steel Co. (Mo)
Prices Trust (X)
Reed (Austin) (D)
Rolls Royce (Mo)
Salts (Saltaire) (T)
Savoy Hotel (X)
Schweppes (F)
Simonds H. & G. (*B*)
Standard Motor (Mo)
Sterling Industries (E)
Sunday Pictorial Newspapers (Pa)
Taylor Walker (*B*)
Threlfall's Brewery (*B*)
Times Furnishing (X)
United Gas Industries (E)
Upsons (D)
W. Riding Worsted & Woollen Mills (T)
Wolsey (T)
Wolverhampton Brewery (*B*)

B = Breweries
Ch = Chemicals
D = Distribution Trades
E = Engineering

F = Food
Mo = Motors and other vehicles
Pa = Paper
T = Textiles

X = Miscellaneous

3. Medium large industrial and commercial companies not fully analysed

(a) *Partially Analysed*

Agar Cross & Co.   (D)
Allied Bakeries   (F)
Amalgamated Cotton Mills Trust   (T)
Amalgamated Dental Company   (E)
Amalgamated Road Stone
    Corporation   (X)
Aspro   (Ch)
Associated Fisheries   (F)
Automatic Telephone Electrical
    Company   (E)
Avery (W. & T.)   (E)
Barker (John) & Co.   (D)
Barrow, Hepburn & Gale   (X)
Birmingham Railway Carriage &
    Wagon   (Mo)
Booker Bros. McConnel & Co.   (D)
Borax Consolidated   (Ch)
British Drug Houses   (Ch)
British Enka   (T)
Broadcast Relay Service   (E)
Brooke Bond   (D)
Brown Bros.   (Mo)
Cape Asbestos   (X)
Carpet Trades   (T)
Cementation   (X)
Cerebos   (F)
Chloride Electrical Storage   (E)
Cook, Son (St. Paul's)   (D)
Cooper McDougall & Robertson   (Ch)
Cow & Gate   (F)
Crittal Manufacturing   (E)
Crosses & Heatons   (T)
Eastwoods   (X)
Ever Ready (Gt. Britain)   (E)
Fairey Aviation   (Mo)
Financial Times   (Pa)
Finlay (James)   (D)
Gloucester Railway Carriage and
    Wagon   (Mo)
Greyhound Racing Association
    Trust   (X)
Grosvenor House (Park Lane)   (X)
Harrisons & Crosfield   (D)
Henley's (W.T.) Telegraph Works   (E)

Henry (A. & S.)   (T)
Hollins (W. H. & Co.)   (T)
Hoyle (Joshua) & Sons   (T)
Ilford   (X)
Initial Services   (X)
International Combustion (Hlds.)   (E)
Lines Bros.   (X)
London Electric Wire, & Smiths   (E)
London Express Newspaper   (Pa)
Lovell & Christmas   (D)
McDougall's Trust   (F)
Maple   (D)
Mappin & Webb   (D)
Marley Tile (Holdings)   (X)
Marshall Sons   (E)
Millar's Timber & Trading   (D)
Murex   (E)
Nairn (Michael) and Greenwich   (X)
Newnes (George)   (Pa)
Parkinson & Cowan   (E)
Phillips (Godfrey)   (X)
Platt Bros. Holdings   (E)
Porrits & Spencer   (T)
Raleigh Industries   (Mo)
Ransome & Marles Bearing   (E)
Reed (Albert E.)   (Pa)
Renold & Coventry Chain   (E)
Reyrolle (A.)   (E)
Rio de Janeiro Flour Mills
    & Granaries   (T)
Rugby Portland Cement   (X)
Sangers   (Ch)
Stoll Theatre Corporation   (X)
Swears & Wells   (D)
Tecalemit   (Mo)
Thompson (John)   (E)
Tootal Broadhurst & Lee   (T)
United Drapery Stores   (D)
United Glass Bottle Makers   (X)
Waterlow & Sons   (Pa)
Westinghouse Brake & Signal   (Mo)
Whites (Timothy) & Taylor   (D)
Whitworth & Mitchell   (T)
Wool Combers   (T)

B   = Breweries
Ch = Chemicals
D   = Distribution Trades
E   = Engineering
F   = Food
Mo = Motors and other vehicles
Pa = Paper
T   = Textiles
X   = Miscellaneous

(b) *Data only for investment success*

Burberry's (X)

Caribonum (X)

Coalite & Chemical Products (Ch)

Egyptian Salt & Soda (Ch)

Griffiths Hughes (Ch)

Johnson Bros. (X)

Mackintosh (John) & Sons (F)

Sena Sugar Estates (F)

Whiteway Laidlaw (D)

4. Smaller large companies (breweries in italics) fully analysed

Alvis (Mo)

Apollinaris Presta (F)

Aristoc (T)

Army and Navy (D)

Associated Auto Machine (E)

Ault and Wiborg (Pa)

Ballito (T)

Bartholomew (D)

Bassett (F)

Boddington (B)

Boulton & Paul (Mo)

Bradbury Greatorex (D)

Bradley (Chepstow Place) (D)

Brampton (B)

British Cotton & Wool Dyers (T)

British Glue and Chemical (Ch)

British Home Stores (D)

British Industrial Plastics (Ch)

British Vacuum Cleaner (E)

Broom and Wade (E)

Bullard (B)

Burt, Boulton & Haywood (Ch)

Carrier Engineering (E)

Chaplin Holdings (F)

Chesters Brewery (B)

Cole, E. K. (E)

Colthrop Board & Paper (Pa)

Consolidated Signal (Mo)

Constable Hart (E)

Cornbrook (B)

Coventry Gauge & Tool (E)

Cropper (Pa)

Currys (Mo)

Derby Midland Mills (T)

Duttons Blackburn (B)

Easterns (D)

Electric Construction (E)

Enfield Rolling Mills (E)

English Velvets (T)

Foister Clay Ward (T)

Fore Street Warehouse (D)

Foster Clarke (F)

Gamage (D)

Gieves (D)

Glacier Metal (E)

Goodacre William (T)

Gorringe Fred (D)

Greeff Chemicals (D)

Greenwood & Batley (E)

Grout (T)

Groves (B)

Hampshire F. W. (F)

Hanson Samuel (F)

Hickson Lloyd & King (D)

Hide & Co. (D)

Hield Bros. (T)

Hinde (Fras) (T)

Holborn Frascati (D)

Hope Bros. (D)

Hovis (F)

Jaguar (Mo)

Jones & Higgins (D)

Jury Holloware (E)

Keystone Knitting Mills (T)

Kirklees (T)

Mandleberg (T)

Mann, Egerton (Mo)

Mann & Overton (D)

Maynards (D)

Mazawattee (F)

Metal Agencies (D)

Metal Closures (E)

Morgan (B)

Oakey (Pa)

Ohlssons (B)

Parnall Yate (Mo)

Peek Bros. (D)

Qualcast (E)

Reeves & Sons (Ch)

Revo Electric (E)

Rover (Mo)

Seagar Evans (B)

B	= Breweries	F	= Food
Ch	= Chemicals	Mo	= Motors and other vehicles
D	= Distribution Trades	Pa	= Paper
E	= Engineering	T	= Textiles
		X	= Miscellaneous

Slaters & Bodega (D)
Smith's Crisps (F)
Stone Lighting (E)
Tarry E. W. (D)
Taylor C. F. (T)
Telegraph Construction (E)
Telephone Mfg. (E)
Travers J. & Sons (D)
Tuck (Raphael) (Pa)

Usher Wiltshire (B)
Valor (E)
Vavasseur (D)
Wallis Thos. (D)
Wallis Tin Stamping (E)
Wardle & Davenport (T)
Williams & Williams (E)
Yates Castle (B)
Yeo, John (D)

B = Breweries
Ch = Chemicals
D = Distribution Trades
E = Engineering
F = Food
Mo = Motors and other vehicles
Pa = Paper
T = Textiles
X = Miscellaneous

APPENDIX B

DETAILS OF THE THIRTY VERY LARGE INDUSTRIAL AND COMMERCIAL COMPANIES PROBABLY OWNER-CONTROLLED OR MARGINALLY SO IN 1951 *

THIS appendix gives detailed information about the share capital and voting rights, the names and holdings of the twenty largest voteholders and the names and ordinary shareholdings of the directors who hold more than qualifying shares. The total number of shareholders can only be given approximately. If there is more than one category of shareholders the total number is not normally the sum of the number of the several categories since many shareholders may hold shares of several categories, for instance, ordinary and preference. The holdings given for the directors are those that appear in the Register under their names; some of the holdings may, of course, be included under " and another " or " and others " in joint holdings.

This appendix has been abbreviated as far as compatible with presenting all significant data. In consequence, slight disparities with Appendix A 1 may arise owing (1) to rounding off percentage voteholding to one place of decimals, (2) to the exclusion of directors owning no more than the qualifying shares. The number of directors named should equal the total number, when the number (given in Appendix A 1) holding no more than minimum qualifying shares is added. Thus for British Match Corporation this appendix names seven directors: five are given in Appendix A 1 as holding no more than the minimum share qualification and the total of directors is thus twelve.

---

* Chap. V § 6 and Table V E.

ALBRIGHT & WILSON LIMITED

SHARE CAPITAL

Authorised	£5,500,000
Issued	£4,112,888
Ordinary 5s. Shares (8,113,136) ..	£2,028,284
5% Preference Shares	£2,084,604

Voting: 1 vote per 5s. Ordinary Stock. Total vote: 8,113,136

SHAREHOLDERS: (approx.) 3,025

20 *Largest Voteholders*

* Indicates Director.

Type		% of votes held
P.	K. H. Wilson* and others	8·8
P.	John C. Wilson* and others	7·6
P.	K. J. Wilson and others..	5·2
P.	W. B. A. Albright *	4·0
P.	R. E. Threlfall* and others	3·6
P.	Miss R. A. Wilson	2·1
P.	Mrs. R. Giles	1·9
P.	B. Topley *	1·8
P.	Mrs. H. Wilson	1·8
P.	Mrs. Freyhan	1·7
P.	S. Barratt*	1·7
P.	Miss D. Albright	1·7
P.	John C. Christopherson *	1·6
P.	Mrs. A. Wilson	1·3
P.	R. I. Threlfall and others	1·2
P.	A. King	1·2
I.	Prudential Assurance	1·2
P.	Mrs. Lloyd	1·1
P.	Mrs. M. Albright	1·1
P.	Miss R. P. Albright	1·1

DIRECTORS

Qualifying shares: £1,000. Ordinary.

Total Number: 8.

Directors and holdings (*if above qualifying*).

	Amount (£)	
	Ordinary	Preference
Chairman: Kenneth H. Wilson	143,456 10s.	17,642
Kenneth H. Wilson and others	353	—
Kenneth H. Wilson plus Pension Fund	1,818	—
Kenneth H. Wilson and J. C. Wilson	34,800	—
Managing Director: W. B. Albright	89,018	1,824

						Amount (£) Ordinary	Preference
S. Barratt	..	..	..	..	..	35,687	—
J. G. Clarke	..	..	..	..	..	1,250	—
J. C. Christopherson	..	..	..	..	..	12,034	3,000
J. C. Christopherson and another		..	..	..	19,112·10	2,500
R. E. Threlfall	..	..	..	..	..	14,288	—
R. E. Threlfall and others	..	..	..	..	59,638	—
B. Topley	..	..	..	..	..	36,195·10	—
J. C. Wilson	..	..	..	..	..	82,090	288
J. C. Wilson and others ..	..	..	..	..	77,182	50,860

ASSOCIATED BRITISH PICTURES CORPORATION LTD.

SHARE CAPITAL

Authorised and Issued	£9,000,000
Preference	£5,000,000
1st Preference	£2,000,000
Ordinary (5s.) shares (8,000,000) ..	£2,000,000

Voting: 1 vote per 5s. Ordinary Stock. Total vote: 8,000,000.

SHAREHOLDERS: (approx.) 14,525.

20 *Largest Voteholders*
*Indicates Director

Type		% of votes held
N.	Branch Noms.	25·2
P.	Sir P. Warter* and others	12·5
P.	Mrs. C. S. Maxwell	7·7
I.	National Provincial Bank Fixed holdings	·9
I.	Midland Bank Ex. and Trustee (Manchester)	·8
N.	Commercial Bank of Scotland London Noms.	·6
I.	Midland Bank Ex. and Trustee Poultry	·6
I.	Clydesdale North of Scotland Bank	·6
N.	London Noms. Union Bank of Scotland	·6
N.	Consolidated Noms.	·5
N.	Glasgow Office Royal Bank of Scotland Noms.	·4
P.	Edward Maloney*	·4
N.	Bishopsgate Noms.	·3
N.	Lombard St. Noms.	·2
P.	O. M. Williams	·2
P.	J. W. Russell	·2
I.	Commercial Securities Ltd.	·2
N.	Barclays Noms. Lombard Street	·1
N.	C. O. Noms.	·1
N.	British Linen Bank, London Noms.	·1

DIRECTORS

Qualifying Shares: £100.

Total Number: 5.

Directors and holdings (*if above qualifying*)
(*None hold* 6% *Pref.*)

	Amount (£) in	
	4½% 1st Pref.	Ordinary
Chairman: Sir P. Warter	—	125
Sir P. Warter and others	—	250,000
Edward Maloney	—	7,601/5
Deputy Chairman: E. G. M. Fletcher	15,000	250
Managing Director: C. J. Latta (U.S.A.)	—	125
Robert Clark	—	125

ASSOCIATED ELECTRICAL INDUSTRIES

SHARE CAPITAL

Authorised	£8,696,050
Issued	£8,669,240
Ordinary Shares of £1 each	£6,000,000
Pref. 8% of £2 each	£2,669,240

Voting: 1 vote per £2 Preference Share or £1 Ordinary Share. Total votes: 7,334,620.

SHAREHOLDERS: (approx.) 12,000.

20 *Largest Voting Shareholders*
* Indicates Director

Type		% of votes held
C.	International G.E.C. Corporation	29·1
I.	Church Commissioners for England	1·0
I.	Wesleyan and Gen. Ass.	·6
I.	Custodian Holdings	·5
I.	Royal London Mutual Ass.	·5
N.	Guaranty Noms.	·5
I.	Co-op. Insurance Society	·4
I.	Refuge Assurance	·3
N.	Lloyds Bank City Office Noms.	·3
N.	London Office Royal Bank Scot. Noms.	·3
I.	Ocean Accident & Guarantee	·3
I.	London Assurance	·2
I.	Legal & General Assurance	·2
I.	Royal Exchange Ass.	·2
I.	Scottish Union & Nat. Ins.	·2
I.	Provident Mutual Life Ass.	·2
I.	N. British & Mercantile Ins.	·2
I.	London & Manchester Ass.	·2
N.	Barclays Noms. Lombard St.	·2
N.	C. O. Noms.	·1

DIRECTORS

Qualifying Shares: £1,000 either class.
Total Number: 13.

Directors and holdings (*if above qualifying*)

	Number of Ordinary	Preference
Chairman: Rt. Hon. Oliver Lyttleton	1,250	—
Deputy Chairman: Sir Geo. E. Bailey..	—	1,454
Lord Bicester	1,400	—
Sir A. J. Boyd	1,200	—
I. R. Cox	1,170	—
Sir Felix J. C. Pole	1,200	—

BOVRIL

SHARE CAPITAL

Authorised	£3,750,000
Issued	£3,700,000

Voting: 2 votes per Pre. Pref. Stock .. .. .. £500,000 Pre. Pref.
1 vote per £1 Pref. Stock .. .. .. £1,200,000 Pref.
1 vote per £2 Ordinary .. .. .. £1,000,000 Ordinary
1 vote for £2 Deferred .. .. .. £1,000,000 Deferred

Total vote: 3,200,000

SHAREHOLDERS: (approx.) 10,600

20 *Largest Voteholders*

Type	* Indicates Director	% of votes held
P.	Lord Luke* and another	7·1
I.	Southern Cross Trust Co. Ltd.	6·9
P.	Wm. E. Lawson Johnson and another	5·7
I.	London and Manchester Ass.	1·9
I.	Royal London Mutual Ins.	1·1
I.	Legal and General Assurance Soc. Ltd.	1·1
P.	H. de B. Lawson Johnson* and another	1·0
I.	Equity and Law Life Ass. Soc.	·9
P.	Countess of Lauderdale and others	·9
I.	Nat. Prov. Bank Fixed holdings	·5
I.	Standard Life Ass. Co.	·4
I.	Salvation Army Assoc. Soc. Ltd.	·4
I.	Refuge Ass. Co. Ltd.	·4
I.	White Cross Ins.	·3
I.	Friends Prov. and Century Life Office	·3
I.	Refuge Church Body	·3
N.	Brit. Linen Bank, London Noms.	·2
I.	Guardian Ass. Co. Ltd.	·2
I.	Pensions Funds Securities	·2
I.	Church Commissioners for England	·2

DIRECTORS

Qualifying Shares. £250 any class.
Total Number 6.

Directors and holdings (*if above qualifying*)	Amount (£) in			
	Pre. Pref.	Pref.	Ord.	Def.
Chairman and Managing Director: Lord Luke ..	1,550	4,350	10	69
Lord Luke and another	112,098	195	500	156
Hugh de B. Lawson Johnston	3,000	—	355	132
Hugh de B. Lawson Johnston and another	10,965	4,350	—	—
Managing Director: S. P. Dormer ..	1,000	—	200	—
F. P. Lubbock	—	—	—	1,000
I. J. Pitman	1,000	—	—	—
L. Powell	800	2	6	200

Appendix B

BRISTOL AEROPLANE COMPANY

SHARE CAPITAL

Authorised and Issued	£3,900,000
Ordinary (10s. shares) (6,000,000) ..	£3,300,000
5% Preference	£600,000

Voting: 1 vote per Ordinary 10s. Share.   Total vote: 6,600,000.

SHAREHOLDERS: (approx.) 8,240.

20 *Largest Voteholders*

Type	* Indicates Director	% of votes held
P.	Sir G. Stanley White*	8·7
P.	Geo. S. M. White* and others	7·7
P.	Miss G. Smith	6·7
P.	Sir Wm. G. Verdon Smith* and others	5·7
P.	Mrs. H. Thurstan	3·3
P.	Mrs. E. Smith	3·0
P.	W. R. Verdon Smith* and others	2·5
P.	Lloyds Bank Trustee and Mrs. H. Thurstan	2·1
P.	Mrs. Stevenson	1·1
N.	London Office Royal Bank Scot. Noms.	1·0
I.	Prudential Assurance	·9
N.	West Noms.	·7
C.	Cable and Wireless (Holding)	·6
P.	W. Thurstan	·6
P.	Mrs. Thomas	·5
N.	London Noms. Union Bank of Scotland	·5
P.	Mrs. Ling	·5
P.	Mrs. Baker	·5
I.	United Kingdom Temperance and Gen. Prov. Institution ..	·4
P.	Miss J. Thurstan	·4

DIRECTORS

Qualifying shares.   £200 in either class.
Total Number 8.

Directors and holdings (*if above qualifying*)

	Number of Ordinary	Preference
Chairman: Sir William G. Verdon Smith ..	379,000	400
Sir William G. Verdon Smith and W. R. Verdon Smith	—	3,000
Managing Director: Sir G. Stanley White	578,750	200
Geo. S. M. White	470,080	2,000
Geo. S. M. White and others	40,000	—
W. R. Verdon Smith	147,700	—
W. R. Verdon Smith and others	20,000	—
N. Rowbotham	1,100	—
K. J. G. Bartlett	1,400	—
C. F. Uwins	1,000	—
B. Davidson	4,000	—

BRITISH COCOA AND CHOCOLATE CO. LTD

SHARE CAPITAL

Authorised	£6,250,000
Issued	£6,245,452
Ordinary Shares	£5,423,758
Pref. Shares of £1	£821,694

Voting: 1 vote per Ordinary Share. Total vote: 5,423,758.

20 *Largest Voteholders*
* Indicates Director

Type		% of votes held
P.	Barrow Cadbury and others	12·7
P.	George Cadbury* and others	11·7
P.	John Cadbury* and others	5·3
I.	Cocoa Investment Ltd.	4·9
P.	Wm. A. Cadbury and others	2·6
P.	L. J. Cadbury* and others	2·6
P.	C. R. Fry and others	2·5
P.	Miss Dorothy Cadbury* and others	2·4
P.	Brandon Cadbury and others	2·2
P.	G. Breeze	2·1
P.	Sir G. Fry and others	2·0
P.	C. Taylor and others	2·0
P.	C. W. Gillett* and others	2·0
P.	Major Egbert Cadbury*	2·0
P.	S. Grace	1·9
P.	M. Tatham* and others	1·7
P.	J. C. Cadbury* and others	1·7
P.	G. N. Cadbury and others	1·3
P.	David Cadbury	1·3
P.	Peter Cadbury	1·2

DIRECTORS

Qualifying Shares. £100 Ordinary.

Total Number 11.

Directors and holdings (if above qualifying)

	Number of Preference	Ordinary
George Cadbury	25	51,374
George Cadbury and others	118,966	584,820
Chairman: Laurence Cadbury	—	87,600
Laurence Cadbury and others	29,226	50,980
Vice-Chairman: C. R. Fry	—	38,000
C. R. Fry and others	—	95,766
John Cadbury	—	88,090

Appendix B

					Number of	
					Preference	*Ordinary*
John Cadbury and others	..	..	..	..	28,500	200,000
Egbert Cadbury ..	..	..	..	..	—	106,160
C. W. Gillett	..	..	..	..	1,250	47,120
C. W. Gillett and others	..	..	..	..	—	59,325
Miss Dorothy Cadbury	..	..	..	..	—	44,150
Miss Dorothy Cadbury and others	..	..	..	9,329	86,572
Paul S. Cadbury	..	..	..	..	2,655	20,522
Paul S. Cadbury and others	..	..	..	..	8,634	—
M. Tatham	..	..	..	..	..	500	700
M. Tatham and others ..	..	..	..	..	—	94,188
Managing Director J. C. Cadbury	..	..	..	—	20,160
J. C. Cadbury and others	..	..	..	..	—	71,436
G. H. Boucher ..	..	..	..	..	..	—	700

BRITISH MATCH CORPORATION LIMITED

SHARE CAPITAL

Authorised	£8,500,000
Issued	£6,712,500
Ordinary Shares	£6,187,500
Preference Shares	£525,000

Voting: 1 vote per £1 Ordinary. Total vote: 6,187,000.

SHAREHOLDERS: (approx.) 5,440.

20 *Largest Voteholders*

Type	* Indicates Director	% of votes held
C.	Svenska Tandsticks Aktiebolaget	12·9
I.	Stockholms Enskild Bank Aktiebolag	8·0
I.	Skandinaviska Banken Aktiebolag	8·0
P.	J. H. G. Reed* and others	1·3
P.	E. D. Evans*	1·1
P.	Arthur Hacking*..	1·1
P.	Mrs. M. Hacking	1·0
N.	C. O. Noms.	1·0
P.	H. Moreland	·7
P.	Sir Clive Milnes Coates and another	·7
I.	Barclays Bank	·4
P.	Geo. Mathers	·4
N.	Royal Bank of Scotland Noms.	·3
I.	London Life Assoc. Ltd.	·3
I.	N. Brit. Mercantile Ins. Co. Ltd.	·3
I.	Scottish Amicable Ass. Soc.	·3
I.	Pearl Assoc. Co. Ltd.	·3
I.	Nat. Prov. Bank. Fixed Holdings	·3
L.	Embankment Trust	·2
P.	Mrs. C. Moreland	·2

DIRECTORS

Qualifying Shares. £500.

Total Number: 12.

Directors and holdings (if above qualifying)	Number of	
	Ordinary	Preference
E. G. D. Evans	72,500	—
Chairman: Arthur Hacking	65,400	—
Joint Managing		
Director: J. H. G. Reed	55,000	—
J. H. G. Reed and others	28,000	3,200
Lord Hacking	9,600	—
D. H. Hepburn	3,500	3,000
K. H. Wilson and another	—	1,650
Joint Managing Director: H. O. Agrell	1,000	—
Sir R. Glyn	280	550

BRITISH UNITED SHOE MACHINERY LIMITED

SHARE CAPITAL

Authorised	..	..	..	..	£3,159,961
Issued	..	..	..	..	£3,150,921
Ordinary Shares of £1	..	..	..		£2,759,961
6% Preference Shares of £1		..	..		£390,960

Voting: 1 vote per Ordinary Share. Total vote: 2,759,961.

SHAREHOLDERS: (approx.) 2,050.

20 *Largest Voteholders*
* Indicates Director

Type		% of votes held
C.	United Shoe Machinery Co.	79·2
P.	Claud Bennion* and others	1·0
P.	Rt. Hon. Sir Milne Barbour*	·7
P.	Chas. F. Bennion	·6
P.	Mrs. Wheeler	·6
M.	Royal Bank Scot. Noms. London Office	·4
P.	Chas. G. Bennion*	·4
P.	Ulster Bank for J. M. Barbour (deceased)	·4
B.	Westminster Bank ' A ' ..	·4
P.	Mrs. Westley	·3
P.	R. Frearson and another	·3
P.	Miss Westley	·3
M.	Com. Bank Scot. London Noms.	·3
I.	Britannic Assurance	·3
C.	Linen Thread Co.	·2
P.	Mrs. Margery Bennion	·2
P.	C. H. Bennion	·2
M.	Mid. Bank Princes Street, Noms.	·2
P.	Mrs. E. Harrison	·2
P.	S. Harrison and others ..	·2

DIRECTORS

Qualifying shares: £100.

Total Number: 17.

Directors and holdings (*if above qualifying*)

	Number of	
	Ordinary	Preference
Chairman and Managing Director: Claud Bennion ..	20,500	—
Claud Bennion and others	7,238	2,236
Deputy Managing Director: K. S. Gimson ..	3,627	—
Assistant Managing Director: C. G. Bennion	11,336	200
Sir J. Milne Barbour	20,000	9,810
A. R. Bullock	—	200
G. W. Holmes	—	120
G. P. Swales	1,500	750
Assistant Managing Director: L. P. Mellerio	256	50

BURTON (MONTAGUE) LIMITED

SHARE CAPITAL

Authorised	..	..	..	..	£5,500,000
Issued	..	..	..	..	£5,229,163
6% A Pref. Shares of £1		..	..	£1,000,000
7% Pref. Shares of £1	..	..	..	£2,000,000
Ordinary Shares of 10s. each		..	..	£2,229,163

Voting: 1 vote per Ordinary Share.   Total vote: 4,459,000.

SHAREHOLDERS: (approx.) 30,300.

20 *Largest Voteholders*

Type	* Indicates Director	% of votes held
P.	Sir M. Burton* and others	69·0
I.	Prudential Assurance	·6
I.	Norwich Union Life Ass.	·6
N.	Chase Noms.	·3
N.	Lloyds Bank City Office Noms.	·2
P.	Mrs. S. Clegg	·2
I.	Midland Bank Exec. and T. Co.	·2
I.	Eagle Star Ins. Co. " D "	·2
P.	A. J. Burton and others	·2
P.	John C. Lucas	·1
P.	Mrs. B. Karmal	·1
P.	P. Benjamin	·1
N.	Consolidated Noms.	·1
P.	Geo. F. Gray	·1
P.	R. G. Aldridge	·1
I.	London Maritime Inv. Co.	·1
N.	Lombard Street Noms.	·1
N.	Princes Street Noms.	·1
P.	Mrs. Leighton	·1
N.	Mid. Bank Princes Street Noms.	·1

DIRECTORS

Qualifying share: £100 in any class.

Total Number: 8.

Directors and holdings (if above qualifying)

	Number of	
	7% Pref.	Ordinary
Chairman and		
Managing Director: Sir Montague M. Burton ..	100	425,915
" H " and " S " Accounts	—	272,828
Sir Montague M. Burton and others	111,282	2,376,807
Stan. Howard Burton	100	2,216
Stan. Howard Burton and others	—	4,000

Appendix B

						Number of 7% Pref.	Ordinary
Bernard Burton	..	..	..	..	..	600	1,158
Ray M. Burton	..	..	..	..	..	—	750
Ray M. Burton and others	..	..	..	..	—	2,000
Arnold J. Burton	..	..	..	..	..	5	1,151
Arnold J. Burton and others	..	..	..	..	—	6,000
Ellis Hurwitz	..	..	..	..	..	400	7
Arch. Wm. Wansbrough	..	..	..	..	3,730	—

CARRERAS

SHARE CAPITAL

Authorised	£5,075,000
Issued	£5,020,300
Pref. (1,300,000, including A, B and C)	£1,300,000
Ord. (240,000 of £1)	£240,000
Ord. A (1,011,570 of £1)	£1,011,570
Ord. B (19,749,840 of 2s. 6d.)	£2,468,730

Voting: 1 vote per 1 Ordinary Share only (not for A and B Ordinary). Total vote: 240,000.

SHAREHOLDERS: (approx.) 34,080.

20 *Largest Voteholders*

* Indicates Director

Type		% of votes held
P.	Sir E. Baron* and others	26·7
P.	Mrs. E. Tritton	20·9
P.	Major Yapp	20·8
P.	Lady Baron	3·7
P.	Maurice Baron*	2·6
P.	Mrs. Hand	2·1
P.	Paul Baron* and others	2·1
P.	Theodore Baron* and others	1·1
P.	Roland Rendall and another	·8
I.	Westminster Bank	·6
I.	Continental and Industrial Trust Ltd.	·4
N.	Control Nominees	·4
P.	Harry Danbury*	·3
P.	Wm. Rhodes	·2
P.	A. Carden	·2
P.	Lady Humphreys	·2
I.	Pension Funds Securities Ltd.	·2
P.	John Self	·2
I.	Scottish Equitable Life Ass.	·2
P.	A. Adler	·2

DIRECTORS

Qualifying Shares: £250 any class except A and B.
Total Number: 9.

Appendix B

Directors and holdings (if above qualifying)

Amount of holding (£)

	6% Pref.	6%A	7%B	4%C	Ord.	Ord. A	Ord. B
Chairman and Managing Director: Sir E. Baron ..	—	—	—	—	38,372	—	2,650
Sir E. Baron and others	—	—	—	—	25,947	556	152,919
Maurice Baron	—	—	—	—	6,360	579	13,009
Maurice Baron and others	—	—	—	—	—	2,515	36,747
Managing Director: John A. Sinclair	—	—	—	—	250	62	16,395
John A. Sinclair and others ..	—	—	—	2,000	—	—	3,000
Paul Baron ..	—	—	—	—	4,161	—	—
Paul Baron and others ..	—	—	—	—	853	—	—
Theodore Baron	—	—	—	—	2,500	—	—
Theodore Baron and others	—	—	—	—	100	—	—
Henry Danbury	—	67	72	—	800	1,000	—
Alfred S. Arthur	100	—	—	150	10	—	588
Sir F. Humphreys ..	—	—	—	250	100	—	—
James Tucker	—	—	—	—	300	—	—

J. & J. COLMAN LIMITED

SHARE CAPITAL

Authorised and issued	£3,502,632
Ordinary Shares	£2,007,012
Preference Shares	£1,495,620

Voting: 1 vote per £1 Ordinary.   Total vote: 2,007,012.

SHAREHOLDERS: (approx.) 6,130.

20 *Largest Voteholders*
* Indicates Director

Type		% of votes held
P.	N. Colman*	7·4
P.	F. Colman*	7·2
P.	Sir J. Colman*	6·9
P.	Sir B. Mayhew* and others	5·7
I.	Prudential Assurance	3·4
P.	Execs. of R. J. Colman	3·4
P.	Publ. Tr. and Sir B. Mayhew A and B	2·5
P.	Capt. Belville	1·7
P.	Mrs. E. M. Colman	1·5
I.	United Kingdom Temperance and Gen. Prov. Institution ..	1·4
N.	London Office Royal Bank Scot. Noms.	1·3
P.	Westminster Bank and Wm. Rollo "A" and "B"	1·2
P.	Lady E. Colman	1·2
I.	Royal London Mutual Ass.	·8
P.	H. H. Foster	·7
P.	Mrs. E. Martyr and others	·6
P.	Mrs. Whetstone	·6
I.	Mid. Bank Exec. and Tr. "B"	·5
I.	Salvation Army	·5
I.	Mid. Bank. Exec. and Tr. "A"	·5

DIRECTORS

Qualifying Shares: £200.

Total Number: 7.

Directors and holdings (*if above qualifying*)

	Number of	
	Preference	Ordinary
Chairman: Sir Jeremiah Colman	110,000	140,000
Sir Jeremiah Colman and others	9,000	—
Col. F. G. D. Colman	90,253	145,124
N. C. D. Colman	100,000	150,000
Sir Basil E. Mayhew	—	14,115
Sir Basil E. Mayhew and others	1,125	101,707
H. A. G. Salter	1,500	1,200
Andrew Ryrie	—	1,100

Appendix B

CONSOLIDATED TIN SMELTERS LIMITED

SHARE CAPITAL

Authorised	£5,000,000
Issued	£3,257,931
Ordinary Shares	£1,998,470
Preference Shares	£1,259,461

Voting: 1 vote per £1 Ordinary Share.   Total vote: 1,998,470.

SHAREHOLDERS: (approx.) 1,000.

20 *Largest Shareholders*
* Indicates Director

Type		% of votes held
N.	Balsa Noms.	50·0
C.	N. V. Gemeenschappelijke	15·3
N.	Truclata Noms.	7·0
C.	M. Maatschappij	4·5
I.	Ban Hin Lee Bank	4·2
N.	Lloyds Bank City Office Noms.	2·5
I.	Hongkong and Shanghai Banking Corp.	2·2
N.	Raffles Noms.	·9
P.	Limcheny Tee and others	·6
N.	Mid. Bank Overseas Noms.	·6
P.	Yeap Chor Ee	·5
N.	Hambros Bank Noms.	·4
I.	Pearl Assurance	·3
I.	Gt. Eastern Life Ass. Co.	·3
P.	A. Baddeley	·2
P.	Mr. Lee Teow	·2
N.	Commercial Bank Scot. London Noms.	·1
I.	Lloyds Bank, 39 Threadneedle Street	·1
I.	Malayan Investors	·1
P.	Mrs. Tan Saw Gan	·1

DIRECTORS

Qualifying Shares: £100.

Total Number: 9.

Directors and holdings (*if above qualifying*)

	Number of	
	Ordinary	Preference
Managing Director: G. C. Pearce	—	875
J. C. Budd	—	1,000
Viscount Marchwood	—	500
Count Guy du Boisrouvay	500	—

CROMPTON PARKINSON LIMITED

SHARE CAPITAL

Authorised Capital	.. .. ..	£4,200,000
Issued		£3,748,522 10s.
8% 1st Pref.		£170,725
6% 2nd Pref.		£500,000
Ordinary Stock (200,000 at 15s.) ..		£150,000
A Ordinary (No Vote)		£2,927,797

Voting: 2 Votes per 15s. Ordinary Stock.   Total vote: 400,000.

SHAREHOLDERS: 10,000.

20 *Largest Voteholders*

Type	* Indicates Director	% of votes held
P.	Arthur Parkinson* and another	34·5
P.	L. Le Neve Foster	6·8
N.	Commercial Bank of Scot. Kingsway Noms...	3·1
I.	Union Pension Trust	1·4
I.	Whitehall Trust	·8
P.	F. Le Neve Foster and others	·6
P.	Bernard Moore*	·5
P.	W. Agate	·3
P.	L. S. Holroyde*	·2
P.	J. Williamson	·2
P.	C. D. Vernon	·2
P.	Wm. Perkins	·2
P.	R. Briebach*	·2
I.	R. Plate Trust Loan and Agency	·2
P.	Mrs. Powell	·2
P.	R. Rumball	·2
P.	Mrs. Fisher	·1
P.	Mrs. Walker and another	·1
P.	R. Bailey	·1
P.	Mrs. Lash	·1

DIRECTORS

Qualifying Shares: 500 Units of Stock of either class.
Total Number: 12.

Directors and holdings (*if above qualifying*)	Amount (£)	
	Ordinary (15s.)	A. Ord. (no vote)
Chairman: Albert Parkinson	—	25,000
Albert Parkinson and another	—	5,270
Arthur Parkinson	36,144	—
Arthur Parkinson and another	15,000	—
Ronald E. P. Briebach	265 5s.	272 15s.
Vice-Chairman: Eustace C. Holroyde	343 15s.	500
Bernard Moore	729 10s.	744 10s.

Appendix B

FORD MOTOR CO. LIMITED

SHARE CAPITAL

Authorised	.. ..	£12,000,000
Issued	.. ..	£11,943,140
Ordinary Shares of £1 each	.. ..	£4,000,000
Ordinary Stock	.. ..	£5,000,000
4½% Preference Shares of 16s.		
(3,678,925)	.. ..	£2,943,140

Voting: 1 vote per £1 Ordinary Capital.   Total Vote: 9,000,000.

SHAREHOLDERS: (approx.) 12,000.

20 *Largest Voteholders*

* Indicates Director

Type		% of votes held
C.	Ford Motor Co. U.S.A. (Stock) (Shares)	59·1
N.	Guaranty Noms.	10·0
I.	Ford Foundation	·5
N.	Commercial Bank Scot. London Noms.	·4
N.	London Office Royal Bank Scot. Noms.	·3
N.	Control Noms.	·2
N.	London Noms. Union Bank Scot	·2
I.	Lloyds Bank Trustees	·2
I.	Ocean Accident Guarantee Corp.	·2
P.	B. Dulanty	·1
I.	Pension Fund Securities	·1
I.	Norwich Union Life Assurance	·1
I.	N. British and Mercantile Ins.	·1
P.	P. Bilton	·1
N.	Lloyds Bank City Office Noms.	·1
N.	Barclays Noms. Lombard Street	·1
I.	Scottish Union and Nat. Ins. Co.	·1
C.	Sea Steamship Co.	·1
P.	F. Varney	·1
N.	Lloyds Bank Law Courts Branches Noms.	·1

DIRECTORS

Qualifying Shares: £1,000.
Total Number: 11.

Directors and holdings (if above qualifying)

	Number of	
	Ordinary	*Preference*
Lord Airedale	1,286	1,286
Vice-Chairman: Sir Stanford Cooper	1,400	—
Deputy Chairman Managing: Sir Patrick Hennessey ..	1,000	1,000
Henry Ford II (in America) and another	2,286	1,286
Lord Perry of Stock Harvard	2,000	2,000
Basil Sanderson	1,000	1,000
Viscount Portal of Hungerford	1,000	1,000
E. C. Woodall	1,000	1,000
Chairman: Sir A. Rowland Smith	1,000	1,000

Appendix B

ILLUSTRATED NEWSPAPERS

SHARE CAPITAL

Authorised and issued	£3,200,000
5,600,000 Ordinary Shares of 5s. ..	£1,400,000
1,800,000 5½% Preference Shares of £1	£1,800,000

Voting: 1 vote per 5s. Ordinary Share.   Total vote: 5,600,000.

SHAREHOLDERS: (approx.) 8,230.

20 *Largest Voteholders*

* Indicates Director

Type		% of votes held
P.	H. Davenport Price*	22·8
P.	A. C. S. Irwin*	12·2
P.	C. F. Pratt	5·6
P.	A. E. Bridges Webb*	4·7
N.	Barclays Bank D. C. and O. Noms.	·3
N.	Glasgow Office Royal Bank Scot. Noms.	·2
P.	R. Mitchell and another	·2
P.	J. Foster	·2
P.	Col. J. R. Warren	·2
N.	G. S. Noms.	·2
N.	Com. Bank Scot. Glasgow Noms.	·1
P.	J. Wheeldon	·1
P.	Mrs. Bradfield	·1
P.	A. Fulton	·1
P.	J. E. Morris (exec. and another)	·1
I.	Clydesdale N. Scot. Bank	·1
P.	W. C. Nisbett*	·1
P.	Lt. Col. G. Scott	·1
P.	E. Herron	·1
P.	Mrs. Blackler	·1

DIRECTORS

Qualifying Shares: £1,000 any class.

Total Number : 8

Directors and holdings (*if above qualifying*)

	Number of	
	Preference	Ordinary
Chairman: Major H. Davenport Price	—	1,273,349
Major H. Davenport Price and another	—	235
Vice-Chairman: Chas. Snelling	1,240	—
Managing: W. C. Nisbett	100	3,494
A. E. Bridges Webb	—	261,429
Angus C. S. Irwin	—	680,655
W. W. J. Studd	2,050	1,455

KEMSLEY NEWSPAPERS LIMITED
(Formerly Allied Newspapers)

SHARE CAPITAL

Authorised and issued	..	..	..	£9,250,000
Ordinary Shares ..	..	..	..	£2,500,000
1st Preference	..	..	..	£2,000,000
Preference	..	..	..	£4,750,000

Voting: 1 vote per £1 Ordinary Share.   Total vote: 2,500,000.

SHAREHOLDERS: (approx.) 20,950.

20 *Largest Voteholders*

* Indicates Director

Type		% of votes held
P.	Lord Kemsley* and others	9·6
P.	Hon. Lionel Kemsley* and others	8·4
N.	Control Noms. ..	7·9
I.	Kemsley Estates Ltd.	1·2
N.	London Noms. Union Bank of Scotland	1·0
1.	Banque Belge pour l'étranger overseas	·8
I.	Pearl Assurance ..	·4
C.	A. Ellis and Sons Ltd.	·4
N.	London Office Royal Bank Scotland Noms. ..	·3
N.	Bishopsgate Noms.	·3
N.	North of Scotland Bank London Noms.	·3
P.	V. E. Berry*	·2
N.	Glasgow Office Royal Bank Scotland Noms.	·2
N.	Lombard St. Noms. Ltd.	·2
I.	Norwich Union Life Assurance	·2
C.	Staveley Iron and Coal Co.	·2
N.	Glasgow Noms. Union Bank Scotland	·1
N.	Abchurch Noms.	·1
N.	National Bank Scotland, Glasgow Noms.	·1
N.	Brit. Linen Bank Glasgow Noms. Vincent Street	·1

DIRECTORS

Qualifying Shares: £500.

Total Number: 18.

Directors and holdings (if above qualifying)

	Number of		
	6½% *Pref.*	8% *Pref.*	*Ordinary*
Chairman: Viscount Kemsley	—	—	42,471
Viscount Kemsley and others	—	—	197,467
Deputy Chairman: Hon. G. Lionel Berry	—	500	—
Hon. G. Lionel Berry and others ..	—	—	210,000
V. E. Berry	—	—	6,325
N. H. Booth	—	600	250
H. N. Heywood	300	250	250
J. H. Oldham	—	—	750
H. J. Staines	500	—	500
Sir R. Webber	1,000	—	600

LEBUS (HARRIS) LIMITED

SHARE CAPITAL

Authorised	..	..	..	..	£4,000,000
Issued	..	..	..	..	£3,000,000
Ordinary	..	..	..	..	£2,000,000
4% Preference	..	..	..	..	£1,000,000

Voting: One vote per £1 Ordinary Stock.   Total vote: 2,000,000.

SHAREHOLDERS: (approx.) 2,250.

20 *Largest Voteholders*

* Indicates Director

Type								% of votes held
P.	Sir H. Lebus* and others	..	..	..	..	..	13·1
P.	Mrs. Elizabeth Lebus	..	..	..	..	..	8·3
P.	Louis H. Lebus	..	..	..	..	..	8·1
P.	Oliver Lebus*	..	..	..	..	..	6·1
P.	Simon Lebus	..	..	..	..	..	6·0
P.	Anthony Lebus*	..	..	..	..	..	5·5
P.	Lady E. Lebus	..	..	..	..	..	3·7
N.	Control Noms.	..	..	..	..	..	3·6
P.	Mrs. B. Richards	..	..	..	..	..	3·1
N.	Morgan Noms.	..	..	..	..	..	2·7
P.	Louis S. Lebus*	..	..	..	..	..	2·5
I.	Royal Exchange Assurance	..	..	..	..	..	2·5
P.	Mrs. E. Lebus	..	..	..	..	..	2·0
I.	Prudential Assurance Co.	..	..	..	..	..	1·2
I.	Royal London Mutual Ins. Soc.	..	..	..	..	1·0
N.	Midland Bank Princes St. Noms.	..	..	..	..	·7
I.	United Kingdom and Gen. Prov. Inst.	..	..	..	·5
P.	Peter A. Lebus	..	..	..	..	..	·5
P.	John E. L. Lebus	..	..	..	..	..	·5
I.	Debenture Corporation	..	..	..	..	..	·5

DIRECTORS

Qualifying Shares: £100 Capital of either class.

Total Number: 10.

Appendix B

Directors and holdings (if above qualifying)

	Number of Ordinary	Preference
Chairman and Managing Director: Sir Herman Lebus	172,972	—
Sir Herman Lebus and others	94,000	—
Joint Assistant Managing Director: Louis S. Lebus ..	50,001	—
Louis S. Lebus and others	50,001	34,000
Joint Assistant Managing Director and Secretary: Cuthbert Greig	8,000	—
Anthony H. H. Lebus	110,839	—
Oliver H. H. Lebus	122,089	4,333
Alex. D. Jessup	500	—
Special Directors:		
Bernard Humphrey	1,000	—
Desmond P. Stratton	200	100
Alex R. Lamb	500	—
Arthur E. Tunley	200	200

LEWIS (JOHN) & CO. LTD.

SHARE CAPITAL

Authorised and issued	£3,150,000
5% 1st Pref. Shares	£1,500,000
7% Preference Shares	£750,000
Ordinary Shares of £1 each	£900,000

The ordinary Shares are owned by John Lewis Partnership Ltd. and the Trustees of John Lewis Partnership.

Voting: 1 vote per Ordinary Share and £10 Preference (all classes); but one vote per £1 Pref. of either class on questions affecting the rights of the holders or in a winding up, reduction of capital, sale of undertaking or if dividend is 3 months in arrear. Total vote: 1,125,000.

SHAREHOLDERS: (approx.) 8,255.

Type			% of votes held
3 holding all the Ordinary Stock			
P.	John Spedan Lewis* ⎫		
	Sara Beatrice Lewis ⎬	600,000	53·33
	C. V. Robinson ⎭		
C.	John Lewis Partnership Ltd.	200,000	17·78
N.	Branch Noms.	100,000	8·90
17 Largest Pref. Voteholders			
I.	Nat. Prov. Ins.		·18
I.	U.K. Temp. and Gen. Prov. Ins.		·13
I.	Bankers Inv. Trust		·11
I.	Inv. Trust Corporation		·10
I.	Sterling Trust		·09
I.	Nat. Mutual Life Ass.		·06
N.	Com. Bank of Scot. London Noms.		·05
N.	North of Scot. Bank London Noms.		·05
P.	C. F. Sutro and others		·05
N.	West Noms.		·04
I.	U.S. and Gen. Trust Corp.		·04
I.	Royal Nat. Pension Fund for Nurses		·04
I.	Rhodesia Railways Trust		·04
I.	Yorkshire Ins. Co.		·04
I.	Sun Ins. Office		·04
P.	I. S. Emmanuel		·04
I.	Bournville Men's Pension Trust		·04

DIRECTORS

Qualifying Shares: £300 in capital of any class.

Total Number: 8.

Appendix B

Directors and holdings (if above qualifying)

				Number of		
				Preference		Ordinary
				5%	7%	
Chairman: J. Spedan Lewis	..	..	..	302	417	—
J. Spedan Lewis and others	..	..	..	—	—	600,000
Deputy Chairman: Oswald Lewis	..	..	—	2,800	—

MARKS AND SPENCER LIMITED

SHARE CAPITAL

Authorised	£3,950,000
Issued	£3,562,577
10% Preference Shares	£350,000
7% Preference Shares	£1,000,000
Ordinary Shares of 5s. each	£600,000
A Ordinary Shares of 5s. each ..	£1,612,577

Voting: 1 vote per 2 Ordinary Shares. (A Ordinary Shares carry no voting rights). Total vote: 1,200,000.

SHAREHOLDERS: (approx.) 25,900.

20 *Largest Voteholders*

* Indicates Director

Type		% of votes held
I.	Prudential Assurance	10·5
P.	Sir Simon Marks* and others	6·1
P.	Mrs. M. Sacher	4·2
P.	Michael D. Sieff* and others	4·2
P.	Mrs. R. Sieff and others	2·4
I.	Marks and Spencer Benevolent Fund ' A '	2·2
P.	Michael Marks	1·9
P.	Harry Sacher* and others	1·3
P.	Marcus J. Sieff and others	1·2
P.	Mrs. Lerner	1·0
P.	Mrs. Susman	1·0
P.	Lady M. Marks	1·0
P.	J. Edward Sieff*	1·0
P.	Mrs. Sara Sieff and others	·8
I.	Nat. Pro. Bank, fixed Holdings	·8
P.	Gabriel Sacher	·8
I.	Mid. Bank E. and T. Co. ' D '	·8
I.	Mid. Bank E. and T. Co. ' A '	·8
P.	A. Lerner	·8
P.	F. W. Moore	·6

DIRECTORS

Qualifying Shares: £500 in stock of any class.
Total Number: 8.

Appendix B

Directors and holdings (if above qualifying)

	A Ord. (no vote)	Number of 7%	Number of 10%	Ordinary
Chairman and Managing Director: Sir Simon Marks	1,650	—	—	28,223
Sir Simon Marks and others	2,017	—	—	118,595
Vice-Chairman and Joint Managing Director: Israel M. Sieff	—	500	—	10,000
Israel M. Sieff and others	392	—	790	600
Assistant Managing Director: J. Edward Sieff	—	—	—	24,000
Harry Sacher	3,399	—	—	15,336
Harry Sacher and others	588	—	—	15,200
Michael D. Sieff and others	75	—	—	100,875
W. F. Norris	1,865	—	—	5,618

MORGAN CRUCIBLE CO. LTD.

SHARE CAPITAL

Authorised	..	..	..	.. £4,587,000
Issued	..	..	..	.. £4,538,960
A Ordinary	..	..	..	.. £1,501,960
B Ordinary	..	..	..	.. £800,000 (privately held)
C Ordinary	..	..	..	.. £158,000 (privately held)
1st Preference	..	..	..	.. £1,000,000
2nd Preference	..	..	..	.. £1,079,000

Voting: 1 vote per £1 Ordinary. Total votes: 2,459,260.

SHAREHOLDERS: (approx.) 4,950.

20 *Largest Voteholders*
* Indicates Director

Type		% of votes held
P.	L. J. E. Hooper*	6·4
P.	G. W. Edward*	3·2
P.	A. R. F. Bosman*	2·9
P.	H. C. V. Adams ..	2·6
P.	Sir G. K. Peto ..	2·6
P.	C. W. Speirs	2·5
P.	P. Lindsay*	1·8
P.	H. C. Mills*	1·7
I.	Prudential Assurance	1·6
P.	L. S. Emms	1·6
P.	P. Hunter Brown	1·5
P.	G. C. Manson	1·4
P.	J. K. V. Morgan*	1·1
P.	R. C. Gregory*	1·1
P.	A. S. Perkins	1·0
I.	Midland Bank Exec. and Tr. Co.	1·0
I.	Coutts & Co.	·9
P.	A. L. Stock*	·9
P.	S. C. Ramsay	·8
P.	R. A. Peto	·8

DIRECTORS
Qualifying Shares: £2,500.
Total Number: 11.

Appendix B

Directors and holdings (*if above qualifying*)

	Ord. A	Ord. B	Number of Ord. C	1st Pref.	2nd Pref.
A. R. Bosman	41,705	30,335	—	—	—
A. R. Bosman and another ..	781	—	—	—	—
G. W. Edward	47,770	31,907	—	36	3,160
L. J. E. Hooper	—	—	158,000	—	—
H. C. Mills	15,005	26,110	—	—	—
F. P. D. Scott	4,120	11,000	—	—	—
A. L. Stock	9,852	12,818	—	—	—
R. C. Gregory	9,913	16,242	—	1,610	67
J. K. V. Morgan	15,908	11,008	—	—	—
J. Walker	2,427	6,560	—	—	—
Chairman: Peter Lindsay ..	1,440	42,024	—	—	—
Peter Lindsay and another ..	130	190	—	3,320	468

ODEON THEATRES LIMITED

SHARE CAPITAL

Authorised	£6,000,000
Issued	£3,696,991
Ordinary Shares of 5s. (3,787,964) ..	£946,991
6% Pref. Shares of £1	£2,750,000

Voting: 1 vote per Ordinary Share. Total vote: 3,787,964.

SHAREHOLDERS: (approx.) 6,200.

20 *Largest Voteholders*

Type	* Indicates Director	% of votes held
N.	Midland Bank Threadneedle Street Noms.	38·3
I.	Eagle Star Ins.	·6
N.	Midland Bank Pall Mall Noms.	·5
I.	Foy Investment	·2
P.	Mrs. E. Frangopula	·2
P.	Miss I. Deutsch and others	·2
P.	H. R. Turner	·1
P.	J. Arthur Rank*	·1
P.	K. Hargreaves*	·1
P.	K. Winckles*	·1
P.	J. A. Callum*	·1
P.	Col. A. Christie*	·1
P.	Sir Michael Balcon*	·1
P.	H. R. Moore*	·1
P.	G. I. Woodham Smith*	·1
P.	Earl Winterton*	·1
N.	West Noms.	·1
N.	Bishopsgate Noms.	·1
P.	Capt. Salvesden	·1
P.	E. Hyde	·1

DIRECTORS

Qualifying Shares: £1,000 in shares of either class.
Total Number: 12.

Directors and holdings (*if above qualifying*)

	Number of	
	Preference	Ordinary
Chairman: J. Arthur Rank	50	4,000
Joint Assistant Managing Director: K. N. Hargreaves	—	4,000
Joint Assistant Managing Director: K. Winckles ..	—	4,000
J. A. Callum	—	4,000
Col. A. Christie	—	4,000
Sir Michael Balcon	—	4,000
H. R. Moore	—	4,000
Rt. Hon. Earl Winterton	4,870	3,895
G. I. Woodham Smith	—	4,000

Appendix B

RANKS

SHARE CAPITAL

Authorised	..	..	..	..	£8,295,600
Issued	..	..	..	..	£7,668,198 15s.
6% 1st Pref. of £1	..	..	..	£2,000,000
6% A Pref. of £1	..	..	..	£2,206,500
Ordinary Stock £1	..	..	..	£2,503,561
Ordinary 5s. Shares (voting)	..	..	£958,137

Voting: 1 vote per 5s. share. Total vote: 3,832,550.

SHAREHOLDERS: (approx.) 13,000.

Largest Voteholders

* Indicates Director

Type		% of votes held
P.	James V. Rank* and others	36·4
P.	J. Arthur Rank* and others	26·1
P.	S. B. Askew*	10·3
P.	I. V. Askew	5·4
P.	A. B. Askew	5·3
P.	G. R. Askew	5·0
P.	Mrs. Eve	2·6
P.	Mrs. Packard	2·6
P.	Mrs. V. H. Rank	2·6
P.	Mrs. McAlpine	2·5
P.	Mrs. M. H. Askew	·8
P.	Mrs. Dorothy Askew	·4

Only 12 appear to hold voting shares.

DIRECTORS

Qualifying Shares: £100.

Total Number: 3.

Directors and holdings (if above qualifying)

	Amount of shares (in £)			
	1st Pref.	A Pref.	Ord.	Ord. (voting)
J. Arthur Rank and others ..	3,010	15,200	164,666	250,899
S. B. Askew and others ..	10	211	9,226	98,787 10s.
James V. Rank and others ..	320,329	1,600	284,076	350,668

ROBINSON (E. S. & A.) LTD.

SHARE CAPITAL

Authorised	£5,000,000
Issued	£4,557,976
6% Preference Shares	£948,190
4% Preference Shares	£1,000,000
10% Preference Shares	£172,150
8% Pref. (Workers)	£200,000
Ordinary Shares of £1	£2,237,636

Voting: 1 vote per Ordinary Share. Total vote: 2,237,636.

SHAREHOLDERS: (approx.) 7,700.

20 *Largest Voteholders*

* Indicates Director

Type		% of votes held
P.	Foster G. Robinson* and others	7·0
P.	John H. King*	2·7
P.	Laurence C. Robinson	2·6
P.	Harold G. Robinson	2·1
P.	Comdr. V. Robinson	2·0
P.	Estate of Percy Robinson	1·8
P.	Edward Robinson	1·5
P.	Miss Frances Robinson	1·5
P.	Mrs. P. R. Robinson	1·3
P.	Miss Katherine Robinson	1·2
P.	Ian Laird	1·2
P.	R. Golding	1·2
I.	London Assurance	1·1
N.	Clydesdale and North of Scotland Bank	1·0
P.	John F. Robinson* and another	·9
P.	Theodore Robinson	·9
N.	Glasgow Noms. Union Bank of Scotland	·9
P.	R. Laird	·8
P.	Major Heseltine	·8
I.	Friends Provident and Century Life Office	·8

DIRECTORS

Qualifying Shares: £1,000 Capital of any class.
Total Number: 9.

Directors and holdings (if above qualifying)

	Preference 8%	6%	Number of 10%	4%	Ordinary
Chairman: Foster G. Robinson..	—	—	—	—	39,475 ⎱
Foster G. Robinson and others ..	—	1,750	3,334	—	89,700 ⎰
Foster G. Robinson and Public Trustee	—	—	5,152	—	17,454
Managing Director: Kenneth W. Davies	—	—	—	—	10,974
Managing Director: John F. Robinson	—	—	—	—	19,146 ⎱
John F. Robinson and another ..	—	—	—	—	1,000 ⎰
Managing Director: Wm. W. H. Orr	—	—	—	—	4,000
John H. King	—	500	857	—	59,022 ⎱
John H. King and another ..	—	2,000	3,500	—	3,428 ⎰
Hector Godfrey	—	—	—	—	4,750
Philip N. Robinson	—	—	—	—	10,080
Harold W. Bodey	—	—	200	—	10,464
E. H. St. John Maclure ..	—	—	—	—	3,500

ROOTES MOTORS LIMITED

SHARE CAPITAL

Authorised	.. ..	£4,525,000
Issued	.. ..	£3,025,000
Ordinary Shares of 4s. (5,000,000)	..	£1,000,000
5% Redeemable Pref. Shares of £1	..	£2,025,000

Voting: 1 vote per Ordinary Share. Total vote: 5,000,000.

SHAREHOLDERS: (approx.) 5,000.

20 *Largest Voteholders*

Type	* Indicates Director	% *of votes held*
P.	Sir W. Rootes*	18·7
I.	Bank of N. T. Butterfield and Son (Bermuda)	12·3
P.	Sir R. Rootes*	10·9
N.	Lloyds Bank City Office Noms.	3·2
P.	O. Arton (Bermuda)	2·0
P.	Lily J. Baroness May of Weybridge	1·0
I.	Royal London Mutual Ins. Co.	1·0
I.	Cushion Trust	·8
P.	D. B. Wilkinson	·7
N.	R. F. Noms.	·7
N.	London Noms. Union Bank Scotland	·6
I.	Pearl Assurance	·5
N.	Lloyds Bank Branches Noms.	·4
I.	Union Assurance Society	·4
I.	London Life Assoc.	·4
P.	Lt. Col. J. A. Cole*	·3
P.	R. W. Hammond*	·3
I.	Inv. Trust Corp.	·3
P.	Sir S. Marks	·2
P.	The Marquess of Willingdon	·2

DIRECTORS

Qualifying Shares: £100 in shares of either class.
Total Number: 9.

Directors and holdings (if above qualifying)

	Number of	
	Preference	*Ordinary*
Chairman: Sir Wm. Rootes	24,393	936,232
Deputy Chairman: Sir R. Rootes	367	543,173
Lt. Col. J. A. Cole	—	15,921
R. W. Hammond	—	15,443
A. F. Murray	—	500
B. G. Rootes	—	6,743
T. D. Rootes	—	5,732
W. G. Rootes	—	5,732
B. B. Winter	600	600

Appendix B

ROWNTREE & CO.

SHARE CAPITAL

Authorised	..	..	..	..	£3,500,000
Issued	..	..	..	..	£3,015,000
6% 1st Pref.	..	..	..	..	£1,000,000
7% 2nd Pref.	..	..	..	..	£765,000
7½% 3rd Pref.	..	..	..	..	£750,000
Ordinary Shares of £1 each		..	..		£500,000

Voting: 3 votes per Ordinary Share plus 2 votes per 5 Ordinary Shares held. 1 vote per 5 1st and 2nd Pref. Shares (Pref. mostly in small amounts). Total vote: 2,000,000 (approx.).

SHAREHOLDERS: (approx.) 8,980.

20 *Largest Voting Shareholders*
* Indicates Director

Type								% of votes held
P.	B. S. Rowntree and others	..	..	..	..	..	..	43·8
I.	Rowntree Social Service Trust	..	..	..	..	..	..	10·4
P.	Theodore Rowntree and others		..	..	..	..	..	3·3
P.	B. Morrell	..	..	..	..	..	..	3·1
P.	Joseph Rowntree and others	..	..	..	..	..	..	2·5
P.	C. Morrell	..	..	..	..	..	..	1·7
P.	Mrs. Crossley	..	..	..	..	..	..	1·6
P.	Peter Rowntree	..	..	..	..	..	..	·9
P.	Miss J. Rowntree	..	..	..	..	..	..	·8
P.	Mrs. Baldwin	..	..	..	..	..	..	·8
I.	Yorkshire Insurance	..	..	..	..	..	..	·7
P.	Julian Rowntree	..	..	..	..	..	..	·7
P.	Mrs. Naish	..	..	..	..	..	..	·6
P.	P. Rowntree*	..	..	..	..	..	..	·6
I.	Ind. and Gen. Trust	..	..	..	..	..	..	·5
P.	Mrs. K. Rowntree	..	..	..	..	..	..	·4
T.	Rowntree Pension Trust	..	..	..	..	..	..	·2
I.	Royal London Mutual Ins. Soc.	..	..	..	..	..	..	·2
I.	Refuge Assurance	..	..	..	..	..	..	·1

DIRECTORS

Qualifying Shares: £100 in shares of any class.
Total Number: 9.

Directors and holdings (*if above qualifying*)

	Number of Ordinary	1st	Preference 2nd	3rd
Deputy Chairman: W. Wallace..	—	—	700	—
C. W. Gilderdale	300	100	—	—
P. Rowntree	3,634	—	—	—
O. Sheldon	250	—	—	—

SMITH (W. H.) & SON (HOLDINGS) LTD.

SHARE CAPITAL

Authorised and issued	£6,000,000
7% Preference Shares	£500,000
4½% Redeem. Pref.	£2,500,000
A Ordinary Shares of £1	£2,500,000
B Ordinary Shares of 4s. (2,500,000) ..	£500,000

Voting: 1 vote per Ordinary Share (A or B). Total vote: 5,000,000.

SHAREHOLDERS: (approx.) 24,400.

20 *Largest Voteholders*

* Indicates Director

Type		% of votes held
P.	Viscountess Hambledon and others	24·3
P.	R. B. Sears and others	9·1
I.	Prudential Assurance	2·4
P.	Michael Hornby* and others	1·5
I.	Pearl Assurance	1·1
I.	Midland Bank Ex. and Tr. Co.	1·0
N.	London Office Royal Bank of Scot. N.	·8
I.	Public Trustee	·8
P.	A. Power	·7
P.	Earl Cranford	·5
P.	J. Morrison* and another	·5
P.	A. D. Power	·4
P.	Sir Wm. H. D. Acland	·3
I.	Royal Exch. Ass. B.	·3
P.	E. Hornby	·3
N.	Lloyds Bank Branches Noms.	·3
N.	West Noms.	·3
P.	A. W. Acland*	·3
N.	Bank of Scotland London Noms.	·2
P.	Mrs. D. Hornby	·2

DIRECTORS
  Qualifying Shares: £100.
  Total Number: 7.

Appendix B

Directors and holdings (if above qualifying)

	Pref. 7%	4½%	Number of A Ord.	B Ord.
Chairman: Hon. David John Smith ..	—	—	—	500
Michael Chas. St. John Hornby ..	18,000	—	11,709	47,700
Michael Chas. St. John Hornby and another	14,000	—	6,000	6,000
Arthur Wm. Acland	—	—	—	15,000
Hon. James Fred A. Smith	2,800	—	4,200	4,200
John Granville Morrison	—	—	5,000	7,000
John Granville Morrison and another ..	—	—	—	13,000
Viscount Harcourt	—	—	1,000	2,000
C. H. Troughton	—	—	1,540	1,540
C. H. Troughton and others	—	7,840	3,080	5,800

TOBACCO SECURITIES TRUST CO.

SHARE CAPITAL

Authorised	£5,000,000
Issued	£4,875,000
Ordinary Shares	£1,000,000
Deferred Stock	£862,500
Ordinary Stock of £1	£3,000,000
Deferred Shares of 5s. (50,000) =	£12,500

Voting: 1 vote per £1, Ordinary or 5s. Deferred Shares, but holders of Ordinary Shares Nos. 1-500,000 and Deferred Shares Nos. 1-500,000 are also entitled collectively to 4 times as many votes as the holders of all the other capital of their respective classes. Total vote: 4,700,000.

SHAREHOLDERS: (approx.) 18,200.
Precise % of the total vote cannot be given for each voting shareholder owing to the complications of the voting rights, but the three voting shareholders that are clearly the largest are given below in the order of their vote. The single largest held three times the Ordinary Shares of the next largest and can be presumed to have over 20% of the vote. This company can be counted as of Grade II C. (See Chapter III).

C.	Imperial Tobacco Company	(1st)
C.	British American Tobacco Co.	(2nd)
N.	Guaranty Noms.	(3rd)

DIRECTORS
Qualifying shares: £1,000 in Ordinary.
Total number: 8.

Directors and holdings (*if above qualifying*)	Ordinary Shares	Ordinary Stock	Amounts (£) Deferred
Chairman: H. R. Gough	1,000	3,000	—
Duncan M. Oppenheim	—	2,000	400
Sir Robert John Sinclair	—	1,018	4.10s.

Appendix B

UNION INTERNATIONAL CO. LTD.

SHARE CAPITAL

Authorised Capital	£12,000,000
6% Preference Shares	£8,000,000
7% Preference Shares	£2,000,000
10% A Preference Shares	£1,000,000
Ordinary Shares	£1,000,000

Voting: 1 vote per £1 stock Ordinary and 10% Preference. Total vote: 2,000,000.

SHAREHOLDERS: (approx.) 975.

20 *Largest Voteholders*

Type	* Indicates Director	% of votes held
N.	Lloyds Bank Branches Noms.	17·5
P.	G. Brown and another	10·7
P.	J. G. Hannay* and others	10·7
P.	W. R. M. Gribble	4·7
P.	H. Robinson	4·5
P.	J. Wakeling	4·5
N.	Bank Scotland London Noms.	4·5
I.	Western United Ins. Co. Ltd.	4·5
P.	C. M. Bond	3·5
P.	G. C. Taylor	3·5
P.	T. White *	3·1
N.	Westcastle Noms.	2·5
P.	G. H. Barton	1·5
P.	W. Bentley	1·0
N.	British Linen Bank London Noms.	·8
P.	Miss L. Rose	·7
N.	Barclays Noms. Branches	·5
P.	G. D. Riches	·5
I.	Mid. Bank Exec. and Trustee Co.	·5
I.	Liverpool Council of Education	·3

DIRECTORS

Qualifying Shares: £500 either class.
Total Number: 6.

Directors and holdings (*if above qualifying*)

	Preference			Ordinary
	10%	6%	7%	
Chairman: Sir E. H. Vestey	10	—	500	—
Rt. Hon. Lord Vestey and others ..	1,210	3,010	1,500	—
R. A. Vestey	10	—	500	—
Thos. White	62,210	500	—	—
J. G. Hannay and others	215,129	500	—	—

WINTERBOTTOM BOOK CLOTH CO.

SHARE CAPITAL

Authorised Capital	.. .. ..	£3,340,000
Issued	.. ..	£3,325,281
6% 1st Pref. Shares	.. .. ..	£389,290
7½% 2nd Pref. Shares	.. .. ..	£300,000
10% Pref. Ord. Shares	.. .. ..	£499,050
Ordinary Shares ..	.. .. ..	£2,136,941

Voting: 1 vote per £10 stock of Preferred Ordinary and Ordinary up to £5,000, and 1 vote per £50 beyond. Total vote: Maximum 263,600.

SHAREHOLDERS: (approx.) 4,350.

20 *Largest Voteholders*

* Indicates Director

Type		% of votes held
P.	M. P. Magor	8·4
P.	Mrs. Winterbottom and 3 others	4·8
I.	Prudential Assurance	3·4
I.	District Bank Ltd.	1·8
P.	H. C. Bentley* and another	1·8
I.	Williams Deacon's Bank	1·6
P.	Mrs. N. Magor	1·0
I.	Royal London Mutual Insurance Society	·9
P.	O. Winterbottom*	·9
I.	Pearl Assurance	·8
I.	Church Commissioners for England	·7
P.	Bernard Mason* and others	·7
N.	London Office Royal Bank Scot. Noms.	·7
P.	O. Bentley	·6
P.	Mark Brickhill* and another	·5
I.	Equity and Law Life Ass.	·5
I.	Refuge Assurance	·5
P.	Mrs. A. Payne	·5
P.	Mrs. E. Longfield and others	·5
N.	Union Bank Scotland London Noms...	·5

DIRECTORS

Qualifying Shares: £1,000 cap. stock of any class.
Total Number: 9.

Appendix B

Directors and holdings (*if above qualifying*)

	Pref. 6%	Pref. 7%	Pref. Ord.	Ord.
		Number of		
Chairman: Mark Brickhill	650	10,000	6,000	7,000
Mark Brickhill and another	28,780	1,350	935	—
Deputy Chairman: Oscar D. Winter-bottom	800	—	5,500	19,385
Harold C. Bentley	—	800	—	10,385
Harold C. Bentley and another ..	2,900	8,400	6,900	48,975
Harold Brickhill	3,343	438	1,393	390
Fred. T. Carmichael	—	—	—	1,250
Fred. T. Carmichael and others ..	—	—	—	187
Bernard Mason	—	—	—	14,400
Bernard Mason and 2 others	—	—	—	4,042
Cyrus T. Pott	—	—	—	8,500
Elkanah Stott	—	—	—	7,866
Sir Harold Webbe	—	—	—	1,448

F. W. WOOLWORTH

SHARE CAPITAL

Authorised and issued	..	.. ..	£20,000,000
6% Cum. Pref. Shares	..	.. ..	£5,000,000
Ordinary Shares (5s.) (60,000,000)		..	£15,000,000

Voting: 1 vote per 5s. Ordinary Share. Total vote: 60,000,000.

SHAREHOLDERS: (approx.) 74,650. (8 Ordinary to 1 Preference).

20 *Largest Voteholders*

* Indicates Director

Type		% of votes held
C.	F. W. Woolworth Co. N.Y.	52·7
I.	N.B. Investment Corp. U.S.A.	3·3
P.	A. G. Mattey	1·9
P.	Norman Bailey Woolworth and another (N.Y.)	1·4
N.	Guaranty Noms.	1·1
N.	Chase Noms.	1·0
I.	Delas Inv. Corp. (Delaware)	1·0
N.	Branch Noms.	1·0
I.	Prudential Assurance	·7
P.	R. H. Parker	·5
P.	A. Hubbard	·2
N.	C. O. Noms.	·2
T.	Lloyds Bank Trustees	·2
I.	Pearl Assurance	·2
N.	West Noms.	·2
P.	Mrs. C. Hubbard	·2
I.	National Provincial Bank	·2
I.	Church Commissioners for England	·1
N.	London Office Royal Bank Scot. Noms.	·1
N.	Hambros Bk. Noms.	·1

DIRECTORS

Qualifying Shares: £1,000.

Total Number: 12.

Directors and holdings (if above qualifying)

	Number of Shares	
	Pref.	Ord of 5s.
Chairman: S. V. Swash	1,000	400
L. H. Read	1,000	500
C. S. Watt	1,680	8,100
I. W. Keffer	—	8,000
K. Erskine	1,000	5,700
W. J. Turner	1,000	3,000
J. L. Farmer	—	8,000
G. C. V. Rogers	—	1,300

APPENDIX C

STATISTICAL GLOSSARY

THE statistical measures that we have used in the text are (I) two types of average, the Arithmetic Mean and the Median; (II) three summary measures of the scatter or variation of item-values round the average, the Standard Deviation and the Interdecile Range (which are absolute values) and the Coefficient of Variation which is relative to the size of the average; and (III) three measures of the relationship between two characteristics of a series of items, the Coefficient of Association and two Coefficients of Correlation.

To explain these summary measures, the simplest possible arithmetical illustration will be used, namely a set of only fourteen small numbers: 3, 4, 4, 5, 5, 5, 5, 6, 6, 6, 7, 8, 12, 22.*

I. MEASURES OF THE AVERAGE

§ 1. The AVERAGE sums up in a single number the most representative, typical, value or position (along the scale) upon which the whole distribution of item-values centres. Among averages found in common use are the Arithmetic Mean, the Mode and the Median.

§ 2. The ARITHMETIC MEAN (A.M.) is the sum of the values of the items divided by the number of items (N). It is often spoken of as the average *par excellence*. Of fourteen items, 3,4,4,5,5,5,5,6,6,6,7,8,12,22 the sum is 98 and the arithmetic mean $\frac{98}{14} = 7$.

§ 3. The MEDIAN is the value on each side of which are half the items when the items are listed or ranked in order of the magnitude of their values. It is the value of the item in the middle of the list, or where the number of items is even, it is conventionally taken as the value half-way between that of the *two* middle items. Of the fourteen items, 3,4,4,5,5,5,5,6,6,6,7,8,12,22, half (*i.e.*, seven) have values at or below 5 and half have values at or above 6. The median is therefore half-way between 5 and 6=5½.

To find the median quickly, items are ranked in order of their values and the item picked which is the $(\frac{n}{2}+\frac{1}{2})$th where n is the total number of items. Of fourteen items, the median item is the $\frac{14}{2}+\frac{1}{2}=7\frac{1}{2}$th. When the fourteen

---

* This glossary is an abridgment of the glossary in Florence, *The Statistical Method in Economics and Political Science* (1929), pp. 495–508. It uses the same illustrations.

values are ranked, the value of the 7th is 5, of the 8th, 6 and the midmost or median value is thus $5\frac{1}{2}$.

In many calculations in this book involving a great number of items, the items are classed together as within certain ranges of values. Yet the median value must be given more accurately than by a range of values or just its mid-point. Suppose that in our illustrative series of numbers there was no 22 and that the remaining numbers represented ranges of value (*e.g.*, 4 means from $3\frac{1}{2}$ to $4\frac{1}{2}$). Then of the 13 remaining items the median item would be the 7th. Its value would fall among the four 5's, *i.e.*, in the range $4\frac{1}{2}$ to $5\frac{1}{2}$. The 5's rank, 4th, 5th, 6th and 7th so that the values of the 7th item should be at the top end of the range, nearer $5\frac{1}{2}$ than $4\frac{1}{2}$. Assuming values evenly spaced within the range, the 7th item would, to be exact, have a value three-quarters of the way up this range. An exact pinpointing of the median value of the 13 items would thus put it at $5\frac{1}{4}$. All textbooks of statistical method give formulae for this pinpointing and in the text we shall refer to such a median value as " pinpointed."

§ 4. Though both are measures of the average, the median often differs considerably from the arithmetic mean. In our simple illustration the median is $5\frac{1}{2}$, the arithmetic mean 7, and this possible divergence is the main reason for our using *both* measures in the text. In our illustration divergence occurs because there are a few comparatively high values such as 12 and 22, not balanced by correspondingly low values. These high values push up the arithmetic mean, but as they do not include the midmost value they do not affect the median. Lack of balance or symmetry in a distribution of values is known as a SKEW and subtraction of the median from the arithmetic mean yields some indication of skew. In our illustration the measure is $7-5\frac{1}{2}=+1\frac{1}{2}$ indicating a positive skew, the exceptional values being high. When the exceptional values are low, a negative measure of skew is involved. More precise measures are given in § 7.

II. MEASURES OF SCATTER

§ 5. The DISPERSION measure, or measure of VARIATION, sums up in a single number the degree of homogeneity or conformity of the distribution of item values to the average. It indicates how far the average is really typical, representative, or certain. Two such measures are used in the text, the Standard Deviation and the Interdecile Range.

§ 6. The STANDARD DEVIATION OF ROOT MEAN SQUARE DEVIATION (S.D. or σ) is the square root of the arithmetic mean of the squares of the item deviations. These item deviations are always the deviations of the item values from their arithmetic mean.

For the fourteen (N) items 3,4,4,5,5,5,5,6,6,6,7,8,12,22 this measure of dispersion may be obtained as follows:

Values of the (N) 14 *items*	d Deviation of item from mean	d² Square of deviation	
3	(−) 4	16	
4	(−) 3	9	
4	(−) 3	9	
5	(−) 2	4	Standard Deviation
5	(−) 2	4	
5	(−) 2	4	SD or $\sigma = \sqrt{\dfrac{\Sigma d^2}{N}}$
5	(−) 2	4	
6	(−) 1	1	
6	(−) 1	1	
6	(−) 1	1	$\sqrt{\dfrac{304}{14}} = 4{\cdot}66$
7	0	0	
8	(+) 1	1	
12	(+) 5	25	
22	(+) 15	225	
Totals (Σ)	42	304	

§ 7. It is possible to summarise a whole scatter of item-values by the method adopted to find the median average. If, again, items are ranked in order of their values, other items beside that in the middle of the rank can be picked, for instance, the items one-tenth, one-quarter, three-quarters or nine-tenths, down the ranks. The values of these items are known as the upper (or ninth) decile, the upper quartile (here 7, the value of the 11th item), the lower quartile (here 5, the value of the 4th item), the lower (or first) decile. Between the upper and lower quartiles Q3 and Q1 (*i.e.*, within the INTERQUARTILE RANGE) will fall half the item-values; but since this measure is rather similar to the standard deviation, we have used, as a supplement to the standard deviation, only the INTERDECILE RANGE within which will fall eight-tenths, *i.e.*, the " bulk " of the values. The formula for finding which are the items that form the upper and lower deciles follows the median-finding pattern already described. D1, the lower decile, is the $\frac{N}{10} + \frac{1}{2}$th item; D9, the upper decile, is the $\frac{9N}{10} + \frac{1}{2}$th item. Fourteen items are too few to illustrate deciles, but if there were 145 items the lower decile would be the value of the $14{\cdot}5 + \frac{1}{2}$th or 15th item, the upper decile would be the value of the $130{\cdot}5 + \frac{1}{2}$th, *i.e.*, the 131st item.

The quartiles and deciles are also useful in measuring the SKEW of a scatter of values—that is, the lack of symmetry of the deviations about an average. If Q3 or D9 are further from the median than Q1 or D1 (as is the case in our example) we speak of a positive skew, if nearer of a negative skew.

The formula for measuring the degree of skew based on the quartiles is $\dfrac{Q3+Q1-2 \text{ Median}}{Q3-Q1}$ in our example $\dfrac{7+5-11}{7-5}=+\frac{1}{2}$ or $+50\%$. The degree of skew can also be measured by using as numerator three times the difference between the two averages A.M. – Median, and, as denominator, the standard deviation. An illustration of the use of measures of skew occurs in Chapter VII § 2 (b).

§ 8. Experience of the scatter of a large number of items, say gains and losses of any type of investment over a past period, is particularly important in considering the future risk of any investment of similar type. But the more orthodox measures of scatter, such as the standard deviation or the inter-quartile range may not be of much interest to the investor. He may not really want to know the range of values within which there is an even chance of gain, but rather what are the values of which there is a relatively small, say 10%, chance of gain or loss. The upper decile gain tells him that, on the basis of past experience, there is a 1 in 10 chance of making such a gain, the lower decile gain or loss that there is a 1 in 10 chance of suffering such a low gain or positive loss. If the investor is a speculator he may seek even finer shades and statistical analysis can give him measures such as the upper and lower " vigin-tiles " and " percentiles," that is the 1 in 20 or 1 in 100 chances of gain or loss.

§ 9. Where it is desired to compare the measure of dispersion in one series of items with that of another series, allowance must be made for the fact that the size of the average value of each series affects the size of the dispersion measure. If we multiplied all the fourteen values in our series by ten, the dispersion measure would rise with the average tenfold, yet *relatively* to the average the dispersion is the same. To obtain the *relative* variation of a series of items many measures have been devised, of which the COEFFICIENT OF VARIA-TION is the most commonly used. This is quite simply, the Standard Deviation described in § 6 divided by the Arithmetic Mean described in § 2. For our fourteen numbers $\dfrac{\text{S.D.}}{\text{A.M.}}$ is $\dfrac{4\cdot66}{7}=0\cdot66$.

III. MEASURES OF RELATIONSHIP BETWEEN CHARACTERS

§ 10. Our illustration gives a number of items having various values of one particular character. But in real life items have more than one character and it is often required to measure the nature and degree of relationship, if any, between the values of one character and the values of another character, mani-fested by the same set of items.

Two or more characters conjointly manifested by any item may be related or unrelated and may be said to be dependent or independent. One character is *unrelated* to (or *independent* of) another if its value (quality or quantity) in any item tends in no degree to vary with variations in the values of the other character or characters conjointly manifested by the same item. Otherwise it is *related* (or *dependent*).

A relation between characters may be either positive (congruent) or negative (inverse). It is positive if a comparatively high value tends in some degree to occur in one character when the value of the other character is comparatively high and similarly of low values. The relation is negative if a comparatively high value tends to occur in some degree in one character when the other character has a comparatively low value.

§ 11. Let us suppose that the values assigned to our fourteen illustrative items were breadths and that the lengths of the items with the given breadths were as follows:—

Item	Breadth		Length	
(1)	3		9	(Short)
(2)	4		12	(Short)
(3)	4		13	(Short)
(4)	5		13	(Short)
(5)	5	(Narrow)	12	(Short)
(6)	5		11	(Short)
(7)	5		16	(Long)
(8)	6		16	(Long)
(9)	6		13	(Short)
(10)	6		15	(Short)
(11)	7		15	(Short)
(12)	8	(Wide)	18	(Long)
(13)	12		25	(Long)
(14)	22		36	(Long)

How can we measure how far lengths and breadths are independent of one another or are associated and correlated? " Association " is traditionally used in connection with only qualitative; " *correlation* " in connection with quantitative differences.

§ 12. To begin with, we may suppose differences in breadth and length to be stated only *qualitatively*. Any item 6 units or less broad may be considered " narrow," over 7 units, wide; any item 15 units or less long, short, 16 units or over, long. With such vague descriptions it might be thought that statistical methods were useless, since there are no numbers to be dealt with. But this neglects the fact of the variable number of frequencies of items manifesting the four possible combinations of qualities.

> 8 are narrow and short items,
> 2 are narrow and long items,
> 1 is a wide and short item,
> 3 are wide and long items.

If narrowness and shortness tended neither to be associated nor disassociated but quite *independent* characters, then a certain theoretical proportion of narrow items should also be short and a certain theoretical proportion also long, namely, exactly that proportion in which all (narrow *and* wide) items are distributed between short and long; in this case 9 and 5, or $\frac{9}{14}$ths of the total of items short and $\frac{5}{14}$ths. of the total items long. Of the 10 *narrow* items $\frac{9}{14}$ths or $6\frac{3}{7}$ items should be short, $\frac{5}{14}$ths, *i.e.*, $3\frac{4}{7}$ items should be long. Similarly, among the 4 wide items $\frac{9}{14}$ths or $2\frac{4}{7}$ items should be short, $\frac{5}{14}$ths or $1\frac{3}{7}$ items should be long.

MODEL ASSOCIATION TABLE

	Narrower than Average (*Values* 3 to 6)	Wider than Average (*Values* 7 to 22)	Total Items
Shorter than Average	Actual 8 Items Theoretical $6\frac{3}{7}$ Items (Difference $+1\frac{4}{7}$)	Actual 1 Item Theoretical $2\frac{4}{7}$ Items (Difference $-1\frac{4}{7}$)	9
Longer than Average	Actual 2 Items Theoretical $3\frac{4}{7}$ Items (Difference $-1\frac{4}{7}$)	Actual 3 Items Theoretical $1\frac{3}{7}$ Items (Difference $+1\frac{4}{7}$)	5
Total Items	10	4	14

Comparing actual to theoretical distribution a difference of $1\frac{4}{7}$ will be seen in all four boxes of the Table. Where the difference has a $+$ sign the qualities manifested are combined in more items than theoretically expected and can be considered more or less associated; where the difference is negative, qualities are more or less disassociated. This common *difference* between the actual distribution and that *theoretically* worked out on the basis of complete independence or non-relation, is used as a measure of the exact degree of positive or negative association of the qualities.

When there is complete independence the common difference is clearly 0, but if it is to serve as a coefficient this common difference must not vary beyond some well-defined limits such as $+1$ or -1 when there is complete positive or negative association, complete association or disassociation.

The usual formula for obtaining such a COEFFICIENT OF ASSOCIA-TION is to *multiply the common difference by the total number of items and divide this by the sum of the products of frequencies with a plus, and of frequencies with a minus common difference.*

In the table the coefficient of association between length and width, or shortness and narrowness is:

$$\frac{+\ 1\frac{4}{7} \times 14}{(8 \times 3) + (2 \times 1)} = +\ \frac{22}{26} = +\ \cdot846;$$

the qualities are markedly associated positively. Between length and narrowness, and width and shortness the coefficient is $-\cdot846$; the qualities are markedly disassociated or negatively associated. A formula for calculating the significance or reliability of this coefficient is illustrated in Chapter V § 5, p. 128.

§ 13. Now let us suppose the values for lengths and breadths to be exactly, *quantitatively*, known, as in the table already given. How can we set about finding the degree of *correlation* between length and breadth ?

In this brief glossary it is not possible to enter into the theoretical basis of the various measures that have been devised. They will be found in all text-books of statistical method. We can only give the formula for two measures used very frequently, as in this book, of the COEFFICIENT OF CORRELA-TION ranging from + to –1, stated in words as well as symbols and illustrated from our fourteen items.

§ 14. The simplest measure of the correlation of various quantities of two characters is to rank those quantities in order of their magnitude. In our illustration in § 11 this " ranking" of breadths and lengths would be as follows:

Item	Breadth (*Rank*)	Length Rank	*d* difference of rank	(*d*)²
(1)	3 (1st)	9 1st	0	0
(2)	4 (2½th)	12 3½th	1	1
(3)	4 (2½th)	13 6th	3½	12¼
(4)	5 (5½th)	13 6th	½	¼
(5)	5 (5½th)	12 3½th	2	4
(6)	5 (5½th)	11 2nd	3½	12¼
(7)	5 (5½th)	16 10½th	5	25
(8)	6 (9th)	16 10½th	1½	2¼
(9)	6 (9th)	13 6th	3	9
(10)	6 (9th)	15 8½th	½	¼
(11)	7 (11th)	15 8½th	2½	6¼
(12)	8 (12th)	18 12th	0	0
(13)	12 (13th)	25 13th	0	0
(14)	22 (14th)	36 14th	0	0
14 (=N)	—	—	—	72½ (=Σd²)

The *Coefficient of Rank Correlation,* associated with the name of Professor Spearman, is obtained by subtracting from unity six times the sum of the squares of the differences in rank, divided by the cube of the number of items minus that number.

In symbols $r = 1 - \dfrac{6\,\Sigma d^2}{N^3 - N}$; in our illustration.

The coefficient is $1 - \dfrac{6 \times 72\frac{1}{2}}{14^3 - 14} = 1 - \dfrac{435}{2730} = \cdot 841.$

§ 15. The *Coefficient of Correlation* (" R ") associated with the name of Professor Pearson can be expressed in words as the *arithmetic mean of the products of the deviations of the two characters of each item from their arithmetic mean, divided by the product of the standard deviations of the two characters.*

Since the arithmetic mean is the sum of values divided by the number of items, this may be written:

$$R = \frac{\text{Sum of the products of the deviations of each item}}{\text{Number of items} \times \text{Product of S.D. of the two characters.}}$$

A table for working out the coefficient of correlation in our illustrative case would run as follows:

MODEL CORRELATION TABLE

Items	Original Values Breadths	Original Values Lengths	Deviations from Average (Arithmetic Mean) Breadths Original x	Deviations from Average (Arithmetic Mean) Breadths Squared x^2	Deviations from Average (Arithmetic Mean) Lengths Original y	Deviations from Average (Arithmetic Mean) Lengths Squared y^2	Products of (Original) Deviations xy
(1)	3	9	-4	16	-7	49	28
(2)	4	12	-3	9	-4	16	12
(3)	4	13	-3	9	-3	9	9
(4)	5	13	-2	4	-3	9	6
(5)	5	12	-2	4	-4	16	8
(6)	5	11	-2	4	-5	25	10
(7)	5	16	-2	4	0	0	0
(8)	6	16	-1	1	0	0	0
(9)	6	13	-1	1	-3	9	3
(10)	6	15	-1	1	-1	1	1
(11)	7	15	0	0	-1	1	0
(12)	8	18	$+1$	1	$+2$	4	2
(13)	12	25	$+5$	25	$+9$	81	45
(14)	22	36	$+15$	225	$+20$	400	300
Total				304		620	424
Average (A.M.)	7	16					

The standard deviation of the breadths (symbol σx) is

$$\sqrt{\tfrac{304}{14}} = \sqrt{21 \cdot 7} = 4 \cdot 66$$

The standard deviation of the lengths (symbol σy) is

$$\sqrt{\tfrac{620}{14}} = \sqrt{44 \cdot 3} = 6 \cdot 65$$

The coefficient of correlation is (in symbols) $\dfrac{\Sigma\ xy}{N\ \sigma xy}$

$$= \frac{424}{14(4 \cdot 66 \times 6 \cdot 65)} = + 0 \cdot 97$$

APPENDIX D

ILLUSTRATIVE BALANCE-SHEET

**Simplified Standard Form of Balance Sheet
to Explain Net Tangible Assets, and its Relation to Capital and Reserves**

[1] SHARE CAPITAL   FIXED ASSETS (Depreciated)
                              Freehold and Leasehold Property
     Preference   Plant and Machinery
                              Vehicles
     Ordinary   Furniture and Fixtures
                              Trade Investments

[2] LOAN CAPITAL   Other
     Debentures

                            Total   (1)

[3] RESERVES   LESS DEFERRED
                            LIABILITIES AND
                            PROVISIONS[1]   (2)
     Capital   **NET FIXED ASSETS**   (3) = (1) − (2)
     Revenue   LIQUID ASSETS

[4] PROFIT AND LOSS   Stock and Work in Progress (Inventories)
     BALANCE or   Debtors (Accounts receivable)
     CARRY FORWARD   Investments
                            Cash
                            Other

                            Total   (4)
             LESS CURRENT LIABILITIES
                  AND PROVISIONS[2]   (5)
             NET LIQUID ASSETS   (6) = (4) − (5)

[1] + [2] + [3] + [4]   =   NET TANGIBLE ASSETS   = (3) + (6)

---

[1] Includes provision for future tax, minority interests.
[2] Includes creditors, bank overdraft, tax, dividends.

APPENDIX E

SELECT AND CLASSIFIED BIBLIOGRAPHY

A. General Background

Andrews, P. W. S: *Manufacturing Business.* MacMillan, 1954.

Evely and Little: *Concentration in British Industry.* Cambridge Press, 1960.

Florence, P. Sargant: *The Logic of British and American Industry.* Kegan Paul, 1953 (2nd ed., 1960).

Grant, A. T. K.: *A Study of the Capital Market in Post-War Britain.* Macmillan, 1937.

Gordon, R. A.: *Business Leadership in the Large Corporation.* Brookings Institution, 1945.

Henderson, R. F.: *The New Issues Market and the Finance of Industry.* Bowes and Bowes, 1951.

Hobson, J. A.: *Evolution of Modern Capitalism.* Contemporary Science Series, 1906.

Hunt, P. C.: *The Development of the Business Corporation in England 1800–1867.* Harvard, 1936.

Hurff, G. B.: *Social Aspects of Enterprise in the Large Corporation.* Pennsylvania University Press, 1950.

Lavington, F.: *The English Capital Market.* Methuen, 1921.

Mason, E. S., Editor: *The Corporation in Modern Society.* Oxford Press, 1960.

Marshall, A.: *Industry and Trade.* Macmillan, 1919.

Penrose, E.: *The Theory of the Growth of the Firm.* Blackwell, 1959.

Robinson, E. A. G.: *The Structure of Competitive Industry.* Cambridge Press, 1931.

Robertson, Sir Dennis: *Control of Industry.* Cambridge Press, 1927.

Veblen, T.: *Absentee Ownership.* Huebsch, English edition, 1924.

B. Analysis of the Company and Company Policy

Baker, J. C.: *Directors and their Function.* Harvard Press, 1945.

Berle and Means: *The Modern Corporation and Private Property.* Macmillan Co., New York, 1932.

Copeland, M. T. and Towl, A. R.: *The Board of Directors and Business Management.* Harvard Press, 1947.

Copeman, G. H.: *Leaders of British Industry.* Gee, 1955.

Dobrovolsky, S. P.: *Corporate Income Retention 1915–43.* National Bureau of Economic Research, 1951.

Graham and Dodd: *Security Analysis.* McGraw Hill, 1951.

Kimmel, L. H.: *Share Ownership in the United States.* Brookings Institution, 1952.

Levy, A. B.: *Private Corporations and their Control.* Routledge and Kegan Paul, 1950.

275

Miller, M. and Campbell, D.: *Financial Democracy.* 1933.

Milward, G. E. (Editor): *Large Scale Organisation.* McDonald and Evans, 1950.

Parkinson, H.: *Scientific Investment.* Pitman, 1932.

Parkinson, H.: *Ownership of Industry.* Eyre and Spottiswoode, 1951.

Tew, B. and Henderson, R. F.: *Studies in Company Finance.* Cambridge Press, 1959.

U.S. Temporary National Economic Committee: Monograph 29.

Wheelwright, E. L.: *Ownership and Control of Australian Companies.* Law Book Co. of Australia, 1957.

C. Recent Articles in Learned and Specialised Journals

Barritt, D. P.: " The Stated Qualifications of Directors of Large Public Companies." *Journal of Industrial Economics.* July 1957.

Florence, P. Sargant: " The Statistical Analysis of Joint Stock Company Control," *Statistical Journal*, 1947, Part I.

Florence, P. Sargant: " The Reward of Risk-bearing by Shareholders in Large Companies," *Journal of Industrial Economics*, March 1957.

Florence, P. Sargant: " Tests of the Validity of some Stock Exchange Folklore," *Three Banks Review*, March, 1958.

Florence, P. Sargant: " Size of Company and Other Factors in Dividend Policy," *Statistical Journal*, 1959, Part I.

Hart, P. E. and Prais, S. J.: " The Analysis of Business Concentrations. A Statistical Approach," *Statistical Journal*, 1956, Part 2.

Leak, H. and Maizels, A.: " The Structure of British Industries," *Statistical Journal*, 1945, Parts I/II.

Luboff, A.: " Some Aspects of Post-War Company Finance," *Accounting Research*, Vol. 7, No. 2.   April 1956.

Prais, S. J.: " The Financial Experience of Giant Companies," *Economic Journal*, June 1957.

Wilson, T.: " Equities and Growth," *Lloyds Bank Review*, October 1959.

D. Works of Reference

Cohen Committee: Report on Company Law Amendment 1945.

Central Statistical Office: National Income and Expenditure, H.M.S.O., published annually.

Directory of Directors.

Moody's Services: Memoranda on Individual Companies.

National Institute of Social and Economic Research: A Classified List of Large Companies Engaged in British Industry 1956.

National Institute of Social and Economic Research: Company Income and Finance 1949–53.

London Stock Exchange: Interest and Dividends upon Securities Quoted on the Stock Exchange.   Published annually.

Stock Exchange Official Year Book.

INDEX

Accounting Gain, 49–51, 161, 176–83, 186, 190, 192
America, 22, 52, 80, 106, 147–8, 152n., 155, 187
Assets,
  definition, 44
  liquid, 138, 154
  net tangible, 6, 42–4, 51, 54, 56, 59, 98, 145n., 148, 151, 154, 176–83
  See also Accounting Gain.
Automation, 24

Baker, J. C., 80
Baldamus, W., 87, 107
Balogh, T., 155
Banks, 5, 83, 85–6, 88, 185
  as nominees, 47, 118
Barnard, Chester, 80
Barritt, D. P., 107, 108
Beesley, M., 103n.
Birmingham, University of, 25, 87, 103n.
Board of Trade, 3, 6
Bonus Shares, 51, 81, 152–3, 153n., 177, 186
Breweries. *See* Industries, Particular.

Capital,
  formation of, 27, 29–31, 140–1, 154
  gain, 49–51, 140, 154, 156, 159–83, 186, 190, 192
  growth of, 178
  intensity of, 15, 23, 188, 190
  issued, 6, 42–5, 145n.
  structure. *See* Gearing.
  supply of. *See* Plough-back, New Issues.
Carr-Saunders, Sir A., 25
Carter and Williams, 23n., 175n.
Census of Production, 15
  of Population, 3
Chemicals. *See* Industries, Particular.
Clements, A. V., 108
Coal Board, 26
Cohen Committee, 118n.
Colwyn Committee on National Debt and Taxation, 52, 154
Companies Act, 1948...51, 53, 141
Company Registry Office, 35, 44, 48
Concentration of Control, 59–60, 67, 80, 190
  by companies within an industry. *See* Monopoly.
  by shareholders' votes within a company, 38, 44–8, 56–77, 98, 109–38, 185–6, 188

Consolidation of Accounts, 51, 53, 144n., 185
Consols, 31, 32
Co-operative Societies, 25
Co-option of Directors, 82n.
Copeland and Towl, 81
Copeman, G. H., 108
Crosland, A., 25

Debentures, 18, 32, 42–4, 56–9, 63–4, 81, 148, 177
  holders, 21
  interest, 180
Decision making, 19, 48, 78, 82, 137–8
Deferred Shares, 43
Dennison, S. R., 59
Depreciation, 31, 44, 147, 147n., 180, 187
Development Industries, 146, 172, 187.
  See also Growth of Companies, Science.
Directors,
  activities, 81–2
  amongst largest vote-holders, 48, 93–105, 126–8, 134, 185, 191–3
  control, 60, 78–81, 96–8, 129
  interlocking, 48, 80–3, 87–92, 101, 103, 106, 138, 191
  risk bearing, 48, 92
  shareholdings, 48, 60, 79, 92–100, 103–5, 124–9, 130–5, 185–93
  size of board, 78–9, 82–92, 97, 101, 185, 188, 191–3
  training, 108
  types, 49, 80, 105–8, 191–3
Directors in Common. *See* Directors, Interlocking.
Distributive Trades. *See* Industries, Particular.
Dividend,
  association with capital gain, 140, 159, 160, 186, 187, 192
  distribution, 43, 51–3, 138, 140–58, 177, 182, 185, 188, 190
  effect on price, 50, 156, 182
  gain, 49–51, 140, 159–83
  policy, 44, 139, 140–58
  rate of, 27, 31, 42, 56–7, 81, 98, 190
  stability, 147–53, 187
Dobrovolsky, S. P., 152n.
Duopoly, 28

Edwards, G. W., 3n.
Ellinger and Carter, 116n.

277